NEPA DESKBOOK

The book was purchased with funds provided under EPA Grant No. X995807-01 - Survey Evaluation and Acquisition of Materials to Support a Course in Wetland Evaluation and Management

An ELI Deskbook

Environmental Law Reporter
Environmental Law Institute
Washington, D.C.

Published With Support From the Andrew W. Mellon Foundation

Copyright © 1989 **Environmental Law Institute**
1616 P Street NW, Washington, DC 20036

Published 1989. Fifth printing September 1994.

Printed in the United States of America
ISBN 0-911937-30-7

Library of Congress Cataloging-in-Publication Data

NEPA deskbook.
      p.   cm. — (ELI deskbook series)
   ISBN 0-911937-30-7: $85.00
    1. Environmental law—United States. 2. Environmental impact
statements—Law and legislation—United States. I. Environmental Law
Institute. II. Series.
KF3775.N47   1989
344.73'046—dc20
[347.30446]   89-39768
                                            CIP

NEPA
DESKBOOK

The Environmental Law Reporter

Foreword

The Environmental Law Institute has a special interest in the National Environmental Policy Act dating back to our shared birth date 20 years ago in December 1969. Over the years, the staffs of the Environmental Law Institute and the Council on Environmental Quality, NEPA's federal agency, have cooperated in conferences and research projects. We've watched NEPA grow, and while the statute has not reached its potential, it is the most successful of our environmental laws. Because of NEPA, environmental considerations are factored into federal planning and decision-making. Today, with President Bush's avowal to breathe new life into the CEQ, NEPA appears to be on the threshold of a new surge in importance.

NEPA is a statute of constitutional dimensions because it adjusts the relationships of the body politic. It empowers citizens to participate directly in environmental planning and it forces coordination among federal, state, municipal, and private agencies that would not occur otherwise.

NEPA has been the single most useful development in opening up federal agency decisionmaking to environmental groups that do not have budgets or staff to investigate projects. Citizen groups find environmental impact statements particularly useful because they include key information about projects in one easily accessible document. EISs are also trustworthy because the law requires full disclosure about projects. An agency that withholds or falsifies information risks an injunction halting the project.

NEPA also works as a coordinating device to get federal and state agencies to work together. While the environmental field overall often is characterized by regulatory gridlock, NEPA has acted as a consensus-building tool to ease these impasses.

The spirit of NEPA calls for active citizen and interest group participation to forge consensus and wise environmental decisions. In this effort, there is much work for lawyers. The ELI *NEPA Deskbook* is designed to assist practitioners by assembling the necessary legal materials in one place.

The introductory chapter of the Deskbook presents a detailed analysis of the statute by the leading U.S. expert on NEPA. Nicholas C. Yost now leads a nationwide environmental and natural resources law practice with the firm of Dickstein, Shapiro & Morin in Washington, D.C. As General Counsel of the Council on Environmental Quality from 1977 until 1981, he led the successful effort to write regulations that put administrative flesh on the bare bones of the statute. He has also served as Deputy Attorney General in Charge, Environmental Unit, California Justice Department, from 1971 until 1977; as a lawyer specializing in administrative law in the California Attorney General's Office; and as counsel to the California State Environmental Quality Study Council. His coauthor is James W. Rubin, an environmental attorney at Dickstein, Shapiro & Morin.

This expert legal commentary is accompanied by the text of the statute, the regulations, key policy memos that give insight into the implementation of NEPA, and sample documents prepared under the statute. An especially useful feature of the Deskbook is its collection of summaries of U.S. Supreme Court cases prepared by *Environmental Law Reporter* staff. Almost all of the more than two thousand lawsuits filed under NEPA have arisen from §102's requirement that the lead agency file an EIS for each "major Federal action significantly affecting the quality of the human environment." It is ironic that NEPA's importance flows out of the mundane requirements of §102, which calls for reforms in administrative procedure, rather than the sonorous goals of §101, which declares a national policy on the environment. But the courts have chosen to make the procedural requirements of NEPA the workhorse of environmental litigation, and lawyers play a key role in assuring compliance with its requirements. Knowledge of case law is especially essential in this area.

The *NEPA Deskbook* builds on ELI's 20 years of NEPA work. The Institute's staff has worked with state and federal agencies on implementation efforts, designed and conducted training courses and workshops, and published extensively on the problems and promise of NEPA. The Deskbook is an outgrowth of research efforts led by the lawyers of the *Environmental Law Reporter*. The *Reporter*, issued since 1971, is a monthly looseleaf reference service on legal, regulatory, and judicial developments in environmental law. It is the only publication in the field edited by lawyers for lawyers. Comprising more than 2000 pages annually, the *Reporter* provides its subscribers with full texts and digests of recent federal and state trial and appeals court decisions and administrative decisions; summaries of pleadings in important environmental cases; analyses of current developments through a regular series of timely articles and comments; and status reports and updates on pending environmental legislation, environmental lawsuits before the U.S. Supreme Court, and actions by federal agencies. The ELR staff puts special emphasis on tracking NEPA developments and on publishing analyses aimed at better NEPA practice.

The Deskbook series is a spinoff of the *Reporter*'s work in tracking and analyzing legislative developments. Companion Deskbooks, the *Superfund Deskbook*, the *Clean Water Deskbook*, and the *Community Right-to-Know Deskbook*, have drawn an enthusiastic response from environmental law practitioners. The Deskbooks combine the expertise of active practitioners with encyclopedic coverage provided by the *Environmental Law Reporter* staff who monitor environmental law developments on an ongoing basis. Deskbooks are meant to be concise, compact enough to be easy to use and to carry along in a briefcase, but also complete enough to give comprehensive coverage of the important issues.

As a national environmental research and publishing organization dedicated to the development of more effective and more efficient environmental protection efforts, the Environmental Law Institute is pleased to present the *NEPA Deskbook*. We hope that it will assist environmental lawyers and managers in their efforts to make this central and most important statute work to protect the environment.

—J. William Futrell
President
Environmental Law Institute

The National Environmental Policy Act

by Nicholas C. Yost
James W. Rubin

Adapted from Yost, *Administrative Implementation of and Judicial Review Under the National Environmental Policy Act*, in LAW OF ENVIRONMENTAL PROTECTION (S. Novick ed. 1987). Reprinted with permission of the publisher, Clark Boardman Company, Ltd., 435 Hudson Street, New York, New York 10014.

Contents

Glossary

The following abbreviations are used throughout this article:

CEQ: Council on Environmental Quality
EA: Environmental assessment
EIS: Environmental impact statement
EOP: Executive Office of the President
EPA: Environmental Protection Agency
FONSI: Finding of no significant impact
NEPA: National Environmental Policy Act

I. OVERVIEW

Introduction

The National Environmental Policy Act (NEPA) is the most pervasive of America's panoply of environmental laws. Other statutes seek to conserve specific media (such as air, water, or land), to regulate specific endeavors (such as surface mining or introduction of new chemicals), or to protect specific places or flora or fauna (such as wilderness areas or endangered species). In contrast, NEPA involves all these areas, seeking to balance a broad range of environmental factors as well as "other essential considerations of national policy."[1] An understanding of NEPA and its processes is a necessary predicate to the practice of environmental law. This Deskbook is intended to provide that understanding.

The Deskbook is organized as a reference for practitioners working with NEPA as well as for others seeking an explanation of the law's requirements and operation. Section I of this article provides an overview of the legislation, examining Congress' intent in passing it, its stated purposes, and the institutional actors responsible for its implementation. Section II analyzes NEPA's administrative process, placing special emphasis on the stages leading to preparation of an environmental impact statement, NEPA's most conspicuous requirement. Finally, Section III examines the role of the courts in enforcing NEPA and reviewing agency decisions.

NEPA's Purposes

The National Environmental Policy Act is "our basic national charter for protection of the environment."[2] Its purposes and policy, as declared in sections 2 and 101,[3] are broadly worded, demonstrating the Act's wide reach and intent.[4] As noted above, the breadth of its stated goals sets NEPA apart from all other environmental statutes, which regulate specific aspects of our environment. NEPA encompasses all environmental values and forces the federal government and its permittees to bear those values in mind as they plan ahead. To accomplish this task, NEPA sets out two basic and related objectives: preventing environmental damage and ensuring that agency decisionmakers take environmental factors into account.

The First Objective: Preventing Environmental Damage

Section 2 of NEPA expressly declares a purpose of promoting efforts "which will prevent or eliminate damage to the environment" while encouraging productive and enjoyable harmony between people and their environment.[5] Section 101 pursues this objective, declaring it the national environmental policy that the federal government use all practicable means to "fulfill the responsibilities of each generation as trustee of the environment for succeeding generations."[6]

Federal agencies' slighting of these responsibilities and overall lack of concern for environmental protection occasioned NEPA's passage. Congress had seen accumulating "evidence of environmental mismanagement,"[7] and it viewed increasing citizen indignation and protest over federal agency action or inaction as indicative of the "public's growing concern" about this mismanagement. Congress responded by enacting what NEPA's Senate author, the late Henry Jackson, described as "the most important and far-reaching environmental and conservation measure ever enacted . . . ."[8] NEPA's House author was no less eloquent in his description of the Act's protective purpose. Congressman John Dingell spoke of man's exploitation and free use of the resources provided by his natural environment, "secure in his belief that nature's bounty would last forever, heedless of any consequences in his headlong push toward greater power and prosperity."[9] Dingell continued, "[w]e have not yet learned that we must consider the natural environment as a whole and assess its quality continuously if we really wish to make strides in improving and preserving it."[10] Congress determined that federal agencies would never again act without heed to the environment, declaring a "national policy to guide Federal activities which are involved with or related to the management of the environment or which have an impact on the quality of the environment."[11]

Nicholas C. Yost is a partner in Dickstein, Shapiro & Morin in Washington, D.C. James W. Rubin is an associate in the same firm. Mr. Yost was formerly General Counsel of the Council on Environmental Quality, where he was responsible for drafting the CEQ NEPA regulations. He has also served as Deputy Attorney General in charge of the Environmental Unit of the California Department of Justice and as a Visiting Scholar at the Environmental Law Institute.

1. NEPA §101(b), 42 U.S.C. §4331(b), *infra* at 28.

2. 40 C.F.R. §1500.1(a), *infra* at 51; *see generally* Yost, *The National Environmental Policy Act*, §9.01, in LAW OF ENVIRONMENTAL PROTECTION (S. Novick ed. 1987).

3. 42 U.S.C. §§4321, 4331, *infra* at 28, 28.

4. The Council on Environmental Quality's NEPA regulations describe the Act's purposes and organizational scheme:

   The National Environmental Policy Act (NEPA) is our basic national charter for protection of the environment. It establishes policy, sets goals (section 101), and provides means (section 102) for carrying out the policy. Section 102(2) contains "action-forcing" provisions to make sure that federal agencies act according to the letter and spirit of the Act. The regulations that follow implement section 102(2). Their purpose is to tell federal agencies what they must do to comply with the procedures and achieve the goals of the Act. The President, the federal agencies, and the courts share responsibility for enforcing the Act so as to achieve the substantive requirements of section 101.

   40 C.F.R. §1500.1(a), *infra* at 51.

5. 42 U.S.C. §4321, *infra* at 28.

6. *Id.* §4331, *infra* at 28.

7. *See* S. REP. No. 296, 91st Cong., 1st Sess. 8 (1969). The report listed numerous examples of mismanagement, including both federal activities and federally authorized private activities. *Id.*

8. 115 CONG. REC. 40416 (1969). Gordon Allott, ranking House minority member and later Senator, stressed that it was "significant [that NEPA] enjoys the sponsorship of every single member of the Senate Interior Committee." 115 CONG. REC. 40422 (1969). President Nixon dramatized NEPA's significance by signing it on January 1, 1970, as "my first official act of the decade. . . ." COUNCIL ON ENVIRONMENTAL QUALITY, ENVIRONMENTAL QUALITY 1970, at viii (1970); *see* Yost, *Streamlining NEPA—An Environmental Success Story*, 9 B.C. ENVTL. AFF. L. REV. 507 (1981-1982).

9. 115 CONG. REC. 26571 (1969).

10. *Id.*

11. S. REP. No. 296, 91st Cong., 1st Sess. 8 (1969). Senator Jackson explained the national policy to the Senate before its final passage of NEPA:

    A statement of environmental policy is more than a statement of what we believe as a people and as a Nation. It establishes

To ensure that federal agencies followed this policy, Congress created in NEPA a statute regulating those agencies.[12] Congress was aware that "if goals and principles are to be effective, they must be capable of being applied in action."[13] Hence, Congress incorporated "certain 'action-forcing' provisions and procedures . . . designed to assure that all Federal agencies plan and work toward meeting the challenge of a better environment."[14] The most important of these "action-forcing" devices is the environmental impact statement (EIS).[15]

The Second Objective: Ensuring That Agency Decisionmakers Take Environmental Factors Into Account

NEPA's "action-forcing" provisions, particularly those requiring EIS preparation, express Congress' second objective: ensuring that federal agency decisionmakers give environmental factors appropriate consideration and weight. Informed, environmentally responsible decision-making is an objective in itself as well as the means by which Congress sought to achieve its other NEPA objective, environmental protection.[16] As the District of Columbia Circuit has observed, uninformed decisionmaking is itself a harm that NEPA was meant to address and for which relief may be granted:

> The harm against which NEPA's impact statement requirement was directed was not solely or even primarily adverse consequences to the environment; such consequences may ensue despite the fullest compliance. Rather NEPA was intended to ensure that decisions about federal actions would be made only after responsible decisionmakers had fully adverted to the environmental consequences of the actions, and had decided that the public benefits flowing from the actions outweighed their environmental costs. Thus, the harm with which courts must be concerned in NEPA cases is not, strictly speaking, harm to the environment, but rather the failure of decision-makers to take environmental factors into account in the way that NEPA mandates. And, for purposes of deciding whether equitable relief is appropriate, we think that this harm matures simultaneously with NEPA's requirements, i.e., at the time the agency is, under NEPA, obliged to file the impact statement and fails to do so.[17]

The District of Columbia Circuit is not alone in emphasizing the importance of the NEPA procedures that agencies must follow. In the Supreme Court's words, "NEPA

---

priorities and gives expression to our national goals and aspirations. It provides a statutory foundation to which administrators may refer . . . for guidance in making decisions which find environmental values in conflict with other values. What is involved is a congressional declaration that we do not intend, as a government or as a people, to initiate actions which endanger the continued existence or the health of mankind: That we will not intentionally initiate actions which will do irreparable damage to the air, land, and water which support life on earth. An environmental policy is for people. Its primary concern is with man and his future. The basic principle of the policy is that we must strive in all that we do, to achieve a standard of excellence in man's relationships to his physical surroundings. If there are to be departures from this standard of excellence they should be exceptions to the rule and the policy. And as exceptions, they will have to be justified in the light of the public scrutiny as required by section 102.

115 CONG. REC. 40416 (1969).

12. In cases involving federal permitting, leasing, or funding, the law necessarily affects private or state or local government applicants to federal agencies as well as the agencies themselves.

13. S. REP. No. 296, 91st Cong., 1st Sess. 9 (1969).

14. *Id.* As the final bill came out of conference, Senator Jackson explained that "to insure that the policies and goals defined in this act are infused into the ongoing programs and actions of the Federal Government, the Act . . . establishes some important 'action-forcing' procedures." 115 CONG. REC. 40416 (1969). According to the CEQ NEPA regulations, "section 102(2) contains 'action-forcing' provisions to make sure that federal agencies act according to the letter and spirit of the Act." 40 C.F.R. §1500.1(a), *infra* at 51. The "action-forcing" provisions of NEPA, particularly the environmental impact statement (EIS) requirement, were part of the Senate bill, but not of the House bill; the legislative history of the EIS is found only in the Senate report. *See* S. REP. No. 296, 91st Cong., 1st Sess. (1969); *see also* H.R. REP. No. 765, 91st Cong., 1st Sess. (1969) (Conference Report), *reprinted in* 1969 U.S. CODE CONG. & AD. NEWS 2767. *See generally* Robertson v. Methow Valley Citizens Council, 57 U.S.L.W. 4497, 4501-02, 19 ELR 20743, 20746-48 (U.S. May 1, 1989); Andrus v. Sierra Club, 442 U.S. 347, 350, 9 ELR 20390, 20391 (1979); Kleppe v. Sierra Club, 427 U.S. 390, 409, 6 ELR 20532, 20536-37 (1976).

15. According to NEPA regulations, "the primary purpose of an environmental impact statement is to serve as an action-forcing device to insure that the policies and goals defined in the Act are infused into the ongoing programs and actions of the Federal Government." 40 C.F.R. §1502.1, *infra* at 54. The regulations also state that "ultimately, of course, it is not better documents but better decisions that count. NEPA's purpose is not to generate paperwork—even excellent paperwork—but to foster excellent action." *Id.* §1500.1(c), *infra* at 54.

16. As the Supreme Court has stated in Robertson v. Methow Valley Citizens Council, *supra* note 14, 57 U.S.L.W. at 4501, 19 ELR at 20746:

> [B]y focusing the agency's attention on the environmental consequences of a proposed project, NEPA ensures that important effects will not be overlooked or underestimated only to be discovered after resources have been committed or the die otherwise cast.

See also Marsh v. Oregon Natural Resources Council, 57 U.S.L.W. 4504, 4507, 19 ELR 20749 (U.S. May 1, 1989).

17. Jones v. District of Columbia Redev. Land Agency, 499 F.2d 502, 512, 4 ELR 20479, 20483 (D.C. Cir. 1974), *cert. denied*, 423 U.S. 937 (1975) (footnote omitted). Unlike the substantive policy of the Act, which is flexible and allows for responsible exercise of discretion, "the Act also contains very important 'procedural' provisions—provisions which are designed to see that all federal agencies do in fact exercise substantive discretion given them." Calvert Cliffs Coordinating Comm. Inc. v. AEC, 449 F.2d 1109, 1112, 1 ELR 20346, 20347 (D.C. Cir. 1971), *cert. denied*, 404 U.S. 942 (1972); *see* Sierra Club v. Sigler, 695 F.2d 957, 965-67, 13 ELR 20210, 20214 (5th Cir. 1983). These procedural provisions "are not highly flexible." *Calvert Cliffs*, 449 F.2d at 1112, 1 ELR at 20347. "Indeed, they establish a strict standard of compliance." *Id.* Specifically, the decision to prepare an EIS "is not committed to the agency's discretion." Foundation for N. Am. Wild Sheep v. Dep't of Agriculture, 681 F.2d 1172, 1177 n.24, 12 ELR 20968, 20969 n.24 (9th Cir. 1982). NEPA's importance lies not only in the aid it gives the agency's decisionmaking process, but also in the notice it gives the public of environmental issues, both those that the agency is aware of and those that it has missed. Illinois Commerce Comm'n v. I.C.C., 848 F.2d 1246, 1260 (D.C. Cir. 1988), *cert. denied*, ____U.S.____ (1989). In the Supreme Court's words, the EIS

> [E]nsures that the agency, in reaching its decision, will have available and will carefully consider detailed information concerning significant environmental impacts; it also guarantees that the relevant information will be made available to the larger audience that may also play a role in both the decision-making process and the implementation of that decision . . . . Publication of an EIS, both in draft and final form, also serves a larger informational role. It gives the public the assurance that the agency "has indeed considered environmental concerns in its decisionmaking process," and, perhaps more significantly, provides a springboard for public comment. . . .

Robertson. v. Methow Valley Citizens Council, *supra* note 14, 57 U.S.L.W. at 4501, 19 ELR at 20746 [citation omitted]; *see* Marsh v. Oregon Natural Resources Council, *supra* note 16, 57 U.S.L.W. at 4507, 19 ELR at 20752.

does set forth significant substantive goals for the Nation, but its mandate to the agencies is essentially procedural."[18]

In crafting these "action-forcing procedures," Congress envisioned a scheme of agency self-regulation; it did not create a regulatory body to enforce compliance.[19] This is why judicial enforcement of the Act is so important. The binding Council on Environmental Quality (CEQ) NEPA regulations clearly make all federal actors joint partners in implementing NEPA, stating that "[t]he President, the federal agencies, and the courts share responsibility for enforcing the Act. . . ."[20]

Agency Responsibilities under NEPA

NEPA and subsequent legislation establish different roles for different agencies. The Act creates one agency, the Council on Environmental Quality (CEQ).[21] However, since NEPA is directed at "all agencies of the Federal Government,"[22] every federal agency plays a role in its implementation. One such agency occupies a special dual position: the Environmental Protection Agency (EPA) is both an entity regulated under NEPA and a co-participant with the CEQ in the process of overseeing NEPA compliance by other federal agencies.

Council on Environmental Quality

NEPA's House sponsors considered creation of the CEQ the landmark achievement of the new legislation.[23] Congress modeled the new agency on the Council of Economic Advisers (CEA), an organization within the Executive Office of the President (EOP) that gives the President general advice on economic issues. Congress intended that the CEQ provide the same sort of pervasive advice concerning the environment.[24] The "only precedent and parallel to what

is proposed," said Senator Jackson, was the Full Employment Act of 1946 which declared the national economic policy and established the CEA.[25]

President Nixon originally charged the CEQ with various environmental oversight responsibilities, including adoption of "guidelines" for all agencies' implementation of NEPA's EIS requirement.[26] President Carter strengthened the CEQ's role and authority: The CEQ "guidelines" became mandatory regulations, and their scope was broadened beyond EISs to include all "the procedural provisions of the Act."[27] The regulations, which in large part codified existing case law, became effective in 1979.[28] The Supreme Court subsequently described the new measures as a "single set of uniform, mandatory regulations" adopted through a "detailed and comprehensive process, ordered by the President, of transforming advisory guidelines into mandatory regulations applicable to all Federal agencies."[29]

The CEQ is an organization of modest size within the EOP, and its limited resources preclude extensive involvement in individual NEPA problems. Thus, its participation in the NEPA process is largely generic. The CEQ adopts regulations applicable to all agencies and oversees

CONG. & AD. NEWS 2751, 2759. *See also* Pacific Legal Found. v. CEQ, 636 F.2d 1259, 1263-64, 10 ELR 20919, 20920 (D.C. Cir. 1980).

25. 115 CONG. REC. 40416 (1969) (remarks of Sen. Jackson).

26. Exec. Order No. 11514, §3(h), 3 C.F.R. §904 (1970), *infra* at 45.

27. Exec. Order No. 11991, §2(g) ¶3(h), 3 C.F.R. §§124-25 (1977), *infra* at 45.

28. 40 C.F.R. §§1500-1508, *infra* at 51-66. The regulatory history of the CEQ NEPA regulations appears largely in the preamble that accompanied their publication in the Federal Register. 43 Fed. Reg. 55978 (1978), *infra* at 248 [hereinafter cited as Preamble]. CEQ published its official explanations of the meaning of certain provisions in *Forty Most Asked Questions Concerning CEQ's NEPA Regulations*, 46 Fed. Reg. 18026 (1981), *infra* at 268 [hereinafter cited as *Forty Questions*]; *see* 51 Fed. Reg. 15618 (1986), *infra* at 261 (Question 20 withdrawn). CEQ has since issued further similar guidance. *See* 48 Fed. Reg. 34263 (1983), *infra* at 286. The most recent appendices to the regulations are Appendix I—List of Federal and Federal-State Agency National Environmental Policy Act (NEPA) Contacts; Appendix II—Federal and Federal-State Agencies with Jurisdiction By Law or Special Expertise On Environmental Quality Issues; and Appendix III—Federal and Federal-State Agency Offices for Receiving and Commenting on Other Agencies' Environmental Documents. 49 Fed. Reg. 49750-82 (1984), *infra* at 66-99. *See also Hearings on Implementation of the National Environmental Policy Act by the Council on Environmental Quality, Subcomm. on Toxic Substances and Envtl. Oversight, Senate Comm. on Env't and Pub. Works*, 97th Cong., 2d Sess. 77-83 (1983); *Hearings on Council on Environmental Quality Reauthorization and Oversight, Subcomm. on Fisheries and Wildlife Conservation and the Env't, Comm. on Merchant Marine and Fisheries*, 98th Cong., 2d Sess. 40-42 (1984) [hereinafter cited as *CEQ Reauthorization and Oversight Hearing*]; Yost, *supra* note 8.

29. Andrus v. Sierra Club, *supra* note 14, 442 U.S. at 357-58, 9 ELR at 20393; *see* Robertson v. Methow Valley Citizens Council, *supra* note 14, 57 U.S.L.W. at 4501-03, 19 ELR at 20744-45. The Supreme Court also said that "CEQ's interpretation of NEPA is entitled to substantial deference." Andrus v. Sierra Club, *supra* note 14, 442 U.S. at 358, 9 ELR at 20393; *see* Robertson v. Methow Valley Citizens Council, *supra* note 14, 57 U.S.L.W. at 4503, 19 ELR at 20746; Marsh v. Oregon Natural Resources Council, *supra* note 16, 19 ELR at 20750, 57 U.S.L.W. at 4507. It is important to emphasize that in interpreting NEPA it is to the CEQ that deference is due, not to the agency undertaking the action. It is the CEQ that is charged with overseeing the Act's implementation. The actions of other agencies are what is regulated by NEPA. Those agencies, whose conduct NEPA was enacted to redirect, are hardly those to whose interpretations of this Act (unlike statutes which they administer) deference is appropriate. Such agencies, in the context of litigation, universally attempt to justify noncompliance.

18. Vermont Yankee Nuclear Power Corp. v. Natural Resources Defense Council, Inc., 435 U.S. 519, 558, 8 ELR 20288, 20297 (1979). The Supreme Court continued that administrative decisions should be set aside "only for substantial procedural or substantive reasons as mandated by statute. . . ." *Id. See* Robertson v. Methow Valley Citizens Council, *supra* note 14, 57 U.S.L.W. at 4501-02, 19 ELR at 20743.

19. The CEQ does have NEPA oversight responsibilities, but, as a modestly sized agency within the Executive Office of the President (EOP), it does not have the resources to become involved in individual cases, except in the rare instance where, based on an EIS, an agency head believes that another agency's proposal is so environmentally harmful that EOP resolution of the issue is merited. The project is then referred to the CEQ, whose power depends largely on persuasion. 40 C.F.R. pt. 1504, *infra* at 58; *see* Clean Air Act §309, 42 U.S.C. §7609, *infra* at 41. *See infra* notes 229-35 and accompanying text.

20. 40 C.F.R. §1500.1(a), *infra* at 51; *see id.* §1500.6, *infra* at 52. Despite the mandate on all federal participants, "the substantive backbone of NEPA ultimately is dependent upon the courts' willingness to order agencies to change their plans or to abandon some pursuits." W. RODGERS, HANDBOOK ON ENVIRONMENTAL LAW 805 (1977).

21. NEPA §201, 42 U.S.C. §4341, *infra* at 30.

22. NEPA §102(2), 42 U.S.C. §4332(2), *infra* at 28.

23. Senate sponsors, on the other hand, viewed as the critical accomplishment of the new Act the linkage between the congressional statement of policy and the "action-forcing" procedures devised to achieve that policy. *Compare* 115 CONG. REC. 26571-91 (1969) (remarks of Rep. Dingell) *and* H.R. REP. No. 378, 91st Cong., 1st Sess. (1969) *with* 115 CONG. REC. 40416 (1969) (remarks of Sen. Jackson).

24. *See* S. REP. No. 296, 91st Cong., 1st Sess. 10 (1969); H.R. REP. No. 378, 91st Cong., 1st Sess. 8 (1969), *reprinted in* 1969 U.S. CODE

adoption of individual agency implementing procedures.[30] It gets directly involved with individual issues only on rare occasions, such as when it receives ''referrals'' from EPA under section 309 of the Clean Air Act or from other agencies under part 1504 of the CEQ regulations.[31] The CEQ will also involve itself in an occasional project or program visible enough to warrant a diversion of its limited resources.[32]

Environmental Protection Agency

EPA occupies a position somewhere between the CEQ and other federal agencies. Like the CEQ, EPA is a participant in the process of overseeing other agencies' preparation of EISs. Yet EPA is also a federal agency regulated under NEPA, so it must prepare EISs for certain of its own environmentally protective actions.[33] In fact, a 1986 CEQ report ranked EPA fifth among all agencies in number of EISs prepared.[34]

EPA came to play this unique role partly as a result of a later statutory attempt to bridge two approaches to environmental legislation. Under Senator Jackson's environmental charter approach, embodied in NEPA, Congress gave an all-embracing directive and left administrators to fill in the details. Under Senator Muskie's approach, embodied in the Clean Air Act, a wary Congress gave far more detailed directives and left considerably less scope for agency discretion. In the Clean Air Act, passed a year after NEPA, Congress expressly made EPA the environmental evaluator of all agencies' actions by requiring it to review and comment on the environmental impact of other agencies' projects subject to the EIS requirement.[35] Under this authority, EPA not only comments generally upon the impact of other agencies' proposals, but publicly rates the quality of their EISs.[36] EPA also coordinates EIS public notice and distribution procedures by publishing notices of all EISs when they are filed with it.[37] EPA must refer other agencies' actions to the CEQ if it finds them environmentally unsound.[38]

Other Federal Agencies

NEPA makes ''all agencies of the Federal Government'' participants in pursuing the goal of environmental protection.[39] Only Congress,[40] the judiciary, and the President are excluded from this broad mandate.[41] Section 102 of NEPA requires that agencies ''to the fullest extent possible'' administer their laws in accordance with the national environmental policy and implement the action forcing provisions of the Act.[42] According to the conference committee report on NEPA, this phrase means that agencies are expected to comply with the Act to the fullest extent possible under their statutory authorizations. They are not to interpret the words so as to avoid compliance, nor are they to construe their statutory authorizations excessively narrowly.[43] Indeed, the Act states that its policies and goals are supplementary to those in agencies' existing statutory authorizations.[44] NEPA thus makes environmental protection the mandate of every federal agency.[45]

---

30. 40 C.F.R. §1507.3, *infra* at 62.

31. 42 U.S.C. §7609, *infra* at 41; 40 C.F.R. pt. 1504, *infra* at 58; *see infra* notes 229-35 and accompanying text.

32. For example, the CEQ has been involved in the U.S. Army's decision process regarding disposal of chemical weapons stockpiles. *See* Council on Environmental Quality, Environmental Quality 1985, at 149-58. For a discussion of the range of the CEQ's responsibilities, see generally *CEQ Reauthorization and Oversight Hearing, supra* note 28, at 34-36. 33 *See infra* notes 34-35 & 127-207 and accompanying text.

33. *See infra* notes 34-35 & 127-207 and accompanying text.

34. Council on Environmental Quality, Environmental Quality 1984, at 719 (1986) (Table A-69). EPA again ranked fifth, along with the Department of Housing and Urban Development, in production of EISs in 1986. Council on Environmental Quality, Environmental Quality 1986, at 245-247 (1988) (Table B-6). Many EPA impact statements are occasioned by sewage treatment plant construction or issuance of national pollution discharge elimination system (NPDES) permits under the Federal Water Pollution Control Act (FWPCA). Other EPA actions have been either statutorily exempted from NEPA or found by courts to be exempt because they provide ''functional equivalents'' of NEPA procedures. *See infra* notes 298-300 and accompanying text.

35. Clean Air Act §309, 42 U.S.C. §7609, *infra* at 41. Section 309 provides:

    Policy Review. (a) The Administrator shall review and comment in writing on the environmental impact of any matter relating to duties and responsibilities granted pursuant to this chapter or other provisions of the authority of the Administrator, contained in any (1) legislation proposed by any federal department or agency, (2) newly authorized federal projects for construction and any major federal agency action (other than a project for construction) to which section 4332(2)(C) of this title applies, and (3) proposed regulations published by any department or agency of the Federal Government. Such written comment shall be made public at the conclusion of any such review.
    (b) In the event the Administrator determines that any such

legislation, action, or regulation is unsatisfactory from the standpoint of public health or welfare or environmental quality, he shall publish his determination and the matter shall be referred to the Council on Environmental Quality.

    For discussion of Senator Muskie's intentions regarding this important section, see F. Anderson, NEPA in the Courts 23031 (1973) [hereinafter cited as NEPA in the Courts]; F. Anderson, Federal Environmental Law 266-67 (1974) [hereinafter cited as Federal Environmental Law].

36. *See, e.g.*, 49 Fed. Reg. 41108 (1984).

37. 40 C.F.R. §§1506.9-.10, *infra* at 61.

38. Clean Air Act §309(b), 42 U.S.C. §7609(b), *infra* at 41; *see infra* notes 229-35 and accompanying text.

39. NEPA §102(2), 42 U.S.C. §4332(2), *infra* at 28.

40. In some situations, a proposal to Congress by the executive branch or an independent regulatory agency requires an EIS. NEPA §102(2)(C), 42 U.S.C. §4332(2)(C), *infra* at 28; 40 C.F.R. §§1506.8, 1508.17, *infra* at 61, 64.

41. Performance of staff functions for the President in the EOP is also excluded. 40 C.F.R. §1508.12, *infra* at 63. For NEPA purposes a ''federal agency'' may include a state or local government or an Indian Tribe that assumes NEPA responsibilities as a condition of receiving funds under §104(h) of the Housing and Community Development Act of 1974, 42 U.S.C. §5304(a). 40 C.F.R. §1508.12, *infra* at 63.

42. The Supreme Court has interpreted the term ''fullest extent possible'' as furthering NEPA's environmental mandate. *See* Flint Ridge Dev. Co. v. Scenic Rivers Ass'n, 426 U.S. 776, 6 ELR 20528 (1976).

43. H.R. Rep. No. 765, 91st Cong., 1st Sess. 3 (1969), *reprinted in* 1969 U.S. Code Cong. & Ad. News 2767, 2770.

44. NEPA §105, 42 U.S.C. §4335, *infra* at 29. A more ambiguous provision, *id.* §104, 42 U.S.C. §4334, *infra* at 29, was intended to harmonize NEPA and the pollution abatement legislation simultaneously being considered by Congress. The somewhat uneasy result is discussed *infra* at 17.

45. *Calvert Cliffs, supra* note 17, 449 F.2d at 112, 1 ELR at 20347. For examples of judicial approval of agencies, use of NEPA to expand their mandates, see, *e.g.*, Detroit Edison Co. v. NRC, 630 F.2d 540, 10 ELR 20879 (6th Cir. 1980); Gulf Oil Co. v. Morton, 493 F.2d 141 (9th Cir. 1973); Zabel v. Tabb, 430 F.2d 199, 1 ELR 20023 (5th Cir. 1970), *cert. denied*, 401 U.S. 910 (1971).

II. THE ADMINISTRATIVE PROCESS UNDER NEPA

NEPA's administrative process is most easily understood if it is examined chronologically. Because the EIS is the most conspicuous part of the process,[46] the following discussion is organized chronologically by reference to the EIS. The discussion first covers prestatement procedures—early planning, followed by the decision on whether and when an EIS is required. It then proceeds through preparation of the statement, and finally describes post-statement procedures. This approach parallels the bulk of the CEQ regulations, which trace the NEPA administrative process chronologically from agency planning[47] through EIS preparation[48] to commenting[49] and referrals of environmentally unsatisfactory projects to the CEQ,[50] and finally to agency decisions and their implementation.[51]

Other procedural requirements are also summarized throughout the discussion, for while litigation has concentrated largely on the EIS requirement and on the requirement of considering alternatives in less detail in environmental assessments (EAs),[52] the administrative process shaping all federal agency activity in light of environmental considerations is pervasive. CEQ's NEPA regulations encapsulate the various procedural requirements, in large part codifying case law and the administrative experience of NEPA's early years. Those regulations discuss NEPA's purposes,[53] provide uniform terminology,[54] make clear what agencies must do to enable themselves to comply with NEPA,[55] and summarize various other NEPA requirements.[56] Throughout the analysis of NEPA-'s administrative process, it is important to remember that all of NEPA's procedural requirements must be strictly observed.[57]

It is also useful to remember that those procedural requirements are to be interpreted in light of NEPA's purposes.[58] The procedures of §102 are, after all, merely means of carrying out the policies of §101.[59] Ultimately, the regulations caution that "it is not better documents but better decisions that count."[60] NEPA's purpose is "not to generate paperwork—even excellent paperwork—but to foster excellent action."[61]

Above all, it should be stressed that although the Act forces decisionmakers to pay heed to environmental factors, the NEPA regulations are also designed to reduce paperwork[62] and delay.[63] Implementation of NEPA's administrative procedures must be sensitive to these two goals.[64]

Prestatement Procedures

Procedures for Determining Whether an EIS Is Required

The NEPA process begins with agency planning[65] and requires that environmental considerations be integrated into that planning.[66] The CEQ regulations give agencies detailed guidance on how to accomplish this integration.[67] They also provide direction for situation in which an applicant, rather than a federal agency, is developing a proposal.[68]

Once an agency begins to plan an action, it must determine whether it must complete an EIS on the proposed action. This threshold determination is governed by NEPA, the CEQ regulations, and the agency's own procedures. Agency actions can be divided into three categories. First, agency procedures may provide for "categorical exclusions"[69] of categories of actions that individually or cumulatively do not have significant effects on the environment.[70] Since actions in these categories do not require EISs, the agency may simply proceed with them.[71] Second, agency procedures may specify cases that normally do require EISs; in such cases, the agency undertakes the process leading to EIS preparation.[72] Third, an agency may not have decided in advance whether a given type of action requires an EIS. In such a situation—the occasion for both disputes and litigation—the agency is to prepare an EA before proceeding.[73]

While the CEQ regulations set out the minimum requirements for considering environmental impacts, NEPA always permits agencies to do more if they choose. Thus, if a situation is categorically excluded, an agency could decide to prepare an EA or EIS anyway. Similarly, if an EA would initially suffice, the agency could nonetheless undertake an EIS directly without first preparing an EA. Agencies may do this when they want to avoid controversy, or when they genuinely desire the additional environmental analysis that more complete documentation would provide.

☐ *The Environmental Assessment.* The EA is a concise public document designed to provide sufficient evidence

46. NEPA §102(2)(C), 42 U.S.C. §4332(2)(C), *infra* at 28. While §102(2)(E) of NEPA, 42 U.S.C. §4332(2)(E), *infra* at 29, also requires agencies to consider alternatives, independent of the requirement that they prepare EISs, it is the EIS process that has occasioned the bulk of the litigation under NEPA.

47. 40 C.F.R. pt. 1501, *infra* at 52.

48. *Id.* pt. 1502, *infra* at 54.

49. *Id.* pt. 1503, *infra* at 57.

50. *Id.* pt. 1504, *infra* at 58.

51. *Id.* pt. 1505, *infra* at 59.

52. *Id.* §1508.9, *infra* at 59.

53. *Id.* pt. 1500, *infra* at 51.

54. *Id.* pt. 1508, *infra* at 63.

55. *Id.* pt. 1507, *infra* at 62.

56. *Id.* pt. 1506, *infra* at 59.

57. *Calvert Cliffs, supra* note 17, 449 F.2d at 1112, 1 ELR at 20347. The NEPA regulations do caution that "trivial violations" are not intended to give rise to independent causes of action. 40 C.F.R. §1500.3, *infra* at 51.

58. *See generally* 40 C.F.R. pt. 1500, *infra* at 51.

59. *Id.* §1500.1, *infra* at 51. The CEQ regulations stress that the President, federal agencies, and the courts share responsibility for enforcing the Act so as to achieve the substantive requirements of §101. *Id.* §1500.1(a), *infra* at 51.

60. *Id.* §1500.1(c), *infra* at 51.

61. *Id.*

62. *Id.* §1500.4, *infra* at 51.

63. *Id.* §1500.5, *infra* at 52.

64. *See* Exec. Order No. 11991, 3 C.F.R. 123 (1977), *infra* at 45.

65. 40 C.F.R. pt. 1501, *infra* at 52.

66. *Id.* §1501.1(a), *infra* at 52.

67. *Id.* §1501.2, *infra* at 52.

68. *Id.* §1501.2(d), *infra* at 52.

69. *Id.* §1507.3(b)(2)(ii), *infra* at 62.

70. *Id.* §1508.4, *infra* at 63.

71. *Id.* §1501.4(a)(2), *infra* at 52.

72. *Id.* §1507.3(b)(2)(i), *infra* at 62; *see* §§1501.3(a), 1501.4(a)(1), *infra* at 52, 52.

73. *Id.* §§1501.4(b), 1508.9, *infra* at 52, 63.

and analysis for an agency to determine whether to prepare an EIS or a finding of no significant impact (FONSI).[74] An EA may also help an agency comply with NEPA when no EIS is needed,[75] and may facilitate preparation of an EIS when one is needed.[76] An EA must include brief discussions of the need for the proposed action, of the alternatives required under NEPA §102(2)(E), and of the environmental impacts of both the proposed action and the alternatives. The EA must also list the agencies and persons consulted during its preparation.[77]

☐ *Finding of No Significant Impact.* Preparation of an EA can lead to one of two results. If the agency finds, based on the EA, that its proposal will have no significant impact on the environment, it prepares a FONSI, and no EIS is required.[78] A FONSI is a document briefly explaining why the proposal will have no such impact. A FONSI must include the EA or a summary of it and must note any other environmental documents related to the EA.[79]

If, on the other hand, the agency determines in its EA that there may or will be a significant environmental impact, it takes the first steps toward preparing an EIS.[80]

Definitions of Terms Regarding When an EIS is Required: Proposals for Major Federal Actions Significantly Affecting the Quality of the Human Environment

NEPA never actually uses the phrase "environmental impact statement." Rather, it requires a "detailed statement" that includes discussions of various environmental impacts.[81] This statement is to be included by all agencies in "every recommendation or report on proposals for legislation and other major Federal actions significantly affecting the quality of the human environment. . . ."[82] The CEQ regulations elaborate upon every word or phrase in this, the most litigated language in NEPA.

☐ *"Proposal."* The regulations define the term "proposal" largely in terms of timing. A "proposal" exists when an agency has a goal and is actively preparing to make a decision on one or more means of accomplishing it, and the effects of that decision can be meaningfully evaluated.[83] This definition essentially steers a line between two sets of concerns. First, the Supreme Court has expressed concern that EISs not be prepared until prospective proposals are more concrete than mere contemplation.[84] Second, administrators and applicants are concerned that EIS preparation not be put off so as to delay underlying actions. The regulations require that an EIS be timed so that it will be complete and ready to be included in the agency's report or recommendation on the proposal.[85]

Proposals for legislation differ from other agency proposals for action in that the agency has no control over the action that is the subject of the EIS—the legislation. Rather, that control lies with a congressional committee. The CEQ regulations reflect this difference by providing a modified set of administrative procedures for legislative proposals, integrating the NEPA process with the legislative process.[86] On a related matter, the Supreme Court has upheld the CEQ's determination that NEPA's legislative EIS requirement does not extend to requests for appropriations.[87]

☐ *"Other Major Federal Actions."* In contrast to the modified requirements for proposals for legislation, the NEPA procedures for proposals for "other major Federal actions"[88] are more commonly used, since these actions occasion the preparation of most EISs. "Other major Federal actions" are defined broadly to include "projects and programs entirely or partly financed, assisted, conducted, regulated, or approved by federal agencies; new or revised agency rules, regulations, plans, policies, or procedures; and legislative proposals. . . ."[89] Federal activities that may occasion EISs thus fall into four categories, sometimes known as the "four P's"—policies, plans, programs, and projects.[90]

The NEPA regulations further define the term to include actions potentially subject to federal control and responsibility.[91] The regulations also state that "major" reinforces but has no meaning independent of "significantly."[92] This CEQ determination follows a well-reasoned line of cases,[93] and was quoted with apparent approval by the Supreme Court in *Andrus v. Sierra Club.*[94] Finally, the regulations provide that in certain circumstances, a failure to act can also be an "action."[95]

74. *Id.* §1508.9(a)(1), *infra* at 63.

75. *Id.* §1508.9(a)(2), *infra* at 63.

76. *Id.* §1508.9(a)(3), *infra* at 63.

77. *Id.* §1508.9(b), *infra* at 63.

78. *Id.* §1501.4(e), *infra* at 53.

79. *Id.* §1508.13, *infra* at 63. A FONSI that includes an EA need not repeat the discussion in the EA but may incorporate it by reference. *Id.*

80. *Id.* §§1501.4(d), 1508.3, 1508.11, *infra* at 52, 63, 63.

81. NEPA §102(2)(C), 42 U.S.C. §4332(2)(C), *infra* at 28; *see* 40 C.F.R. §1508.11, *infra* at 63.

82. NEPA §102(2)(C), 42 U.S.C. §4332(2)(C), *infra* at 28; 40 C.F.R. §1502.3, *infra* at 54.

83. 40 C.F.R. §1508.23, *infra* at 64.

84. Kleppe v. Sierra Club, *supra* note 14, 427 U.S. at 390, 6 ELR at 20532 (1976).

85. 40 C.F.R. §1508.23, *infra* at 64.

86. *Id.* §§1506.8, 1508.17, 1508.18(a), *infra* at 61, 64, 64. Only a limited number of EISs are prepared on proposals for legislation. *See* Bear, *NEPA at 19: A Primer,* 19 ELR 10060, 10067-68 (1989) (discussing inattention to legislative EISs).

87. *See* Andrus v. Sierra Club, *supra* note 14, 442 U.S. at 347, 9 ELR at 20390 (1979); 40 C.F.R. §1508.17, *infra* at 64.

88. NEPA §102(2)(C), 42 U.S.C. §4332(2)(C), *infra* at 28; 40 C.F.R. §1508.18, *infra* at 64.

89. 40 C.F.R. §1508.18(a), *infra* at 64.

90. *Id.* §1508.18(b), *infra* at 64.

91. *Id.* §1508.18, *infra* at 64. For a discussion of what is "federal," see W. RODGERS, *supra* note 20, at 761; Ellis & Smith, *The Limits of Federal Environmental Responsibility and Control Under the National Environmental Policy Act,* 18 ELR 10055 (1988).

92. 40 C.F.R. §1508.18, *infra* at 64.

93. *See, e.g.,* Minnesota Pub. Interest Research Group v. Butz, 498 F.2d 1314, 4 ELR 20700 (8th Cir. 1974) (en banc), *permanent injunction issued,* 401 F. Supp. 1276, 6 ELR 20133 (D. Minn.), *injunction dissolved,* 541 F.2d 1292, 6 ELR 20736 (8th Cir. 1975). In following this line of cases, the CEQ rejected another. *See, e.g.,* NAACP v. Wilmington Medical Center, Inc., 584 F.2d 619, 8 ELR 20699 (3d Cir. 1978).

94. 442 U.S. at 361 n.20, 9 ELR at 20394. For the legislative history of the CEQ regulations, see Preamble, *supra* note 28, at 55999, *infra* at 248.

95. 40 C.F.R. §1508.18, *infra* at 64.

☐ *"Significantly."* The term "significantly" presents the threshold for the EIS requirement, and no other term in NEPA has been the subject of more attention. Although there has been much litigation on the meaning of the word, the cases have been very fact-specific.[96] As a result, rather than formulating a universal interpretation, the CEQ regulations distill generalized direction from case law, and present this direction as a non-exclusive checklist.[97]

The regulations define "significantly" in terms of both "context"[98] and "intensity."[99] The former term recognizes that significance varies with the setting of the proposed action and also indicates that an action should be viewed from several different perspectives (e.g., local, regional, and national).[100] The latter term refers to severity of impact and is to be evaluated according to various listed factors, including beneficial as well as adverse impacts;[101] effects on public health or safety;[102] unique characteristics of a geographic area;[103] whether the effects are highly controversial;[104] whether there are highly uncertain effects or unique or unknown risks;[105] whether the action may establish a precedent;[106] whether the action is related to other actions with individually insignificant but cumulatively significant effects;[107] whether historic, cultural, or scientific resources are affected;[108] whether endangered or threatened species are involved;[109] and whether the action threatens to violate federal, state, or local requirements protecting the environment.[110] In NEPA litigation, factual showings are likely to revolve around one or more of these factors.

☐ *"Affecting."* The regulations define "affecting" to mean "will or may have an effect on."[111] The rationale for this definition lies in the phraseology of NEPA itself, and is supported by case law.[112] If there will be no significant environmental impact, no EIS is required. An EIS is required, however, both when a significant impact is certain and when it is not known whether there will be such an impact.[113]

The regulations define "effects" to include both "direct effects," those that are caused by the action and occur at the same time and place,[114] and "indirect effects," those that are caused by the action and occur later or farther away but are still reasonably foreseeable.[115] Indirect effects may include growth-inducing effects and other effects of induced changes in land use patterns.[116] Environmental "effects" are generally synonymous with environmental "impacts" and encompass a broad range—ecological, aesthetic, historic, cultural, economic, social, and health effects.[117] Socio-economic impacts may only be considered, however, if they accompany physical impacts.[118] "Effects" include both the beneficial and the detrimental effects of an action, even if an agency considers the overall impact beneficial.[119]

☐ *"The Quality of the Human Environment."* The final term in §102(2)(C)'s description of when an EIS is required is "the quality of the human environment." The regulations interpret this term comprehensively "to include the natural and physical environment and the relationship of people with that environment."[120] Economic and social effects by themselves do not require preparation of an EIS, but then an EIS is prepared and economic or social and natural or physical environmental effects are interrelated, and the EIS must discuss all of them.[121]

Scoping

Once an agency determines through an EA or otherwise that a proposal may significantly affect the environment, it must prepare an EIS. The next step is "scoping," defined by the regulations as "an early and open process for determining the scope of issues to be addressed and for identifying the significant issues related to a proposed action."[122] One purpose of scoping is to notify and involve all agencies and individuals concerned about the proposed action. Another is to identify issues that should be analyzed in depth and eliminate from study those that are not significant.[123] To help achieve these purposes, the regulations en-

96. For summaries of some of these cases, see W. RODGERS, *supra* note 20, at 750-61.

97. 40 C.F.R. §1508.27, *infra* at 65.

98. *Id.* §1508.27(a), *infra* at 65.

99. *Id.* §1508.27(b), *infra* at 65.

100. *Id.* §1508.27(a), *infra* at 65.

101. *Id.* §1508.27(b)(1), *infra* at 65.

102. *Id.* §1508.27(b)(2), *infra* at 65.

103. *Id.* §1508.27(b)(3), *infra* at 65. These unique characteristics include proximity to historic or cultural resources, park lands, prime farmlands, wetlands, wild and scenic rivers, or ecologically critical areas. *Id.*

104. *Id.* §1508.27(b)(4), *infra* at 65.

105. *Id.* §1508.27(b)(5), *infra* at 65.

106. *Id.* §1508.27(b)(6), *infra* at 65.

107. *Id.* §1508.27(b)(7), *infra* at 65. Significance cannot be avoided by terming an action temporary or by breaking it down into small component parts. *Id. See also id.* §1508.7, *infra* at 63.

108. *Id.* §1508.27(b)(8), *infra* at 65.

109. *Id.* §1508.27(b)(9), *infra* at 65.

110. *Id.* §1508.27(b)(10), *infra* at 65.

111. *Id.* §1508.3, *infra* at 63.

112. *See, e.g.,* Save Our Ten Acres v. Kreger, 472 F.2d 463, 3 ELR 20041 (5th Cir. 1973).

113. *See* Louisiana v. Lee, 758 F.2d 1081, 1084-85, 15 ELR 20609, 20610-11 (5th Cir. 1985), *cert. denied sub nom.* Dravo Basic

Materials Co. v. Louisiana, 475 U.S. 1044 (1986); *see also* Sierra Club v. Marsh, 769 F.2d 868, 871, 15 ELR 20911, 20912 (1st Cir. 1985); *Foundation for N. Am. Wild Sheep, supra* note 17, 681 F.2d at 1178, 12 ELR at 20969; *Minnesota Pub. Interest Research Group, supra* note 93, 498 F.2d at 11320, 4 ELR at 20702-03; Hanly v. Kleindienst, 471 F.2d 823, 831, 2 ELR 20717, 20720-21 (2d Cir. 1972), *cert. denied,* 412 U.S. 908 (1973); *see also* W. RODGERS, *supra* note 20, at 754-55.

114. 40 C.F.R. §1508.8(a), *infra* at 63.

115. *Id.* §1508.8(b), *infra* at 63.

116. *Id.* These indirect effects were sometimes called "secondary impacts" prior to adoption of the CEQ NEPA regulations. The regulations opted for the direct-indirect distinction rather than the primary-secondary one because the latter sometimes led to the not necessarily accurate conclusion that secondary meant less important.

117. *Id.*

118. *Id.* §1508.14, *infra* at 64.

119. *Id.* §1508.8(b), *infra* at 63.

120. *Id.* §1508.14, *infra* at 64.

121. *Id.*

122. *Id.* §§1501.7, 1508.25, *infra* at 53, 64. *See generally* CEQ Memorandum for General Counsel, NEPA Liaisons and Participants in Scoping, Scoping Guidance (Apr. 30, 1981), *infra* at 279. No scoping is required for EISs on legislative proposals. 40 C.F.R. §1506.8, *infra* at 61.

123. *Id.* §1501.7, *infra* at 53. *See* Northwest Coalition for Alternatives

courage, but do not require, agencies to hold scoping meetings.[124] Finally, scoping is the appropriate occasion for an agency to set time limits for the entire NEPA process.[125] The agency may do this on its own, and "shall" do it if an applicant so requests.[126]

Preparation of the Statement

The next step in the NEPA process is preparation of the EIS itself.[127] At the outset, it is important to stress several aspects of the EIS. First and foremost, the EIS is not an end in itself, but rather a tool to promote environmentally sensitive decisionmaking.[128] Second, the document is to be analytic rather than encyclopedic.[129] It is to be concise—no longer than absolutely necessary to meet the law's requirements.[130] The regulations, in fact, impose a page limit of 150 pages, although they allow up to 300 pages for proposals of unusual scope or complexity.[131] Third, the statement should indicate how the proposal will achieve the policies of NEPA.[132] Above all, the EIS should be used to assess environmental impacts, not to justify decisions already made.[133]

With these considerations in mind, we now review the actual process of preparing an EIS, first determining who prepares the statement and then analyzing the chronological sequence of preparation.

Who Prepares the EIS

It is important to emphasize that NEPA requires federal agencies to be the entities preparing EISs, but, as will appear below, others may prepare supporting documents. When applicants are involved, two desirable goals conflict—eliminating duplication between the work done by the agency and that done by the applicants or their consultants, and ensuring that the agency exercises independent judgment by doing its own work either directly or through its consultant. The applicable regulation tracks case law on this issue[134] but gives deference to both considerations.[135]

The regulation provides different treatment for information, for EAs, and for EISs. An applicant may submit[136] information to an agency either on its own or at the agency's request.[137] If an agency requests information, however, it must evaluate that information independently and is responsible for its accuracy. It is the regulation's intent that agencies verify, but not redo, acceptable work.[138]

An agency may permit an applicant to prepare an EA. However, the agency must make its own evaluation of the environmental issues and take responsibility for the document's scope and content.[139]

Finally, an applicant cannot prepare an EIS; that document is solely the responsibility of the agency.[140] Thus, the EIS may only be prepared directly by the agency or by a contractor "solely" selected by an agency.[141] The process is designed to avoid the potential conflict of interest arising from an applicant's selection of a consultant whose analysis could serve the applicant's own interests. A contractor selected by an agency must execute a disclosure statement specifying that it has no financial or other interest in the outcome of the project.[142] Further, the agency must furnish guidance to the contractor and must independently evaluate and take responsibility for the document.[143]

It is important to discuss the roles agencies play when more than one is expected to be heavily involved in the EIS process. In this situation, the NEPA regulations provide for a "lead agency"[144] to take "primary responsibility"[145] for preparation of the EIS and to supervise the process.[146] This simplifies EIS preparation and avoids duplication.

The regulations further allow the lead agency to designate as "cooperating agencies" other agencies that have jurisdiction by law over a project.[147] The lead agency may also so designate other agencies with special expertise on any environmental issues that the EIS should discuss.[148] This mechanism is designed to promote agency cooperation early in the NEPA process, hopefully ensuring that all agencies' concerns are addressed and averting subsequent squabbles.

---

to Pesticides v. Lyng, 844 F.2d 588, 594-95, 18 ELR 20738, 20741-42 (9th Cir. 1988) (agency violated spirit and letter of CEQ scoping regulations by failing to invite environmental organizations that had previously enjoined agency's proposal).

124. 40 C.F.R. §1501.7(b)(4), *infra* at 54.

125. *Id.* §§1501.7(b)(2), 1501.8, *infra* at 54, 54.

126. *Id.* §1501.8(a), *infra* at 54.

127. *Id.* pt. 1502, *infra* at 54.

128. *Id.* §§1500.1, 1502.1, *infra* at 51, 54.

129. *Id.* §1502.2(a), *infra* at 54.

130. *Id.* §1502.2(c), *infra* at 54.

131. *Id.* §1502.7, *infra* at 55.

132. *Id.* §1502.2(d), *infra* at 54.

133. *Id.* §1502.2(g), *infra* at 54.

134. *See, e.g.,* Greene County Planning Bd. v. FPC, 455 F.2d 412, 2 ELR 20017 (2d Cir.), *cert. denied,* 490 U.S. 849 (1972), *stay granted,* 490 F.2d 256, 4 ELR 20080 (2d Cir. 1973).

135. 40 C.F.R. §1506.5, *infra* at 60.

136. *Id.* §1506.5(a), (c), *infra* at 60.

137. *Id.* §1506.5(a), *infra* at 60.

138. *Id. See* People ex rel. Van de Kamp v. Marsh, 687 F. Supp. 495, 499 (N.D. Cal. 1988).

139. 40 C.F.R. §1506.5(b), *infra* at 60.

140. *Id.* §1506.5(c), *infra* at 60.

141. *Id.*

142. *Id.*

143. *Id.* A provision does exist for an agency to select a contractor whom the applicant then pays. *Forty Questions, supra* note 28, at 18031, *infra* at 272. In some cases this procedure, known as a "third party contract," will expedite the processing of the application.

144. *Id.* §§1501.5, 1508.16, *infra* at 53, 64. When there is a dispute over which agency is to be the lead agency, the regulations provide criteria for resolution, *id.* §1501.5(c), *infra* at 53, and, if necessary, a mechanism for an independent and final determination by the CEQ. *Id.* §1501.5(d)-(f), *infra* at 53.

145. *Id.* §1508.16, *infra* at 64.

146. *Id.* §1501.5, *infra* at 53.

147. *Id.* §§1501.6, 1508.5, *infra* at 53, 63. Other agencies may opt out of the cooperating agency role based on other program commitments. *Id.* §1501.6(c), *infra* at 53. The provision empowering lead agencies to appoint cooperating agencies is designed, however, to stimulate agencies with jurisdiction to cooperate with the lead agency from the beginning, rather than holding their fire until they see a draft EIS and then taking pot shots at it.

148. *Id.* §1501.6, *infra* at 53. A state or local agency or Indian Tribe possessing jurisdiction by law or special expertise may also, by agreement with the lead agency, become a cooperating agency. *Id.* §1508.5, *infra* at 63.

The Environmental Impact Statement

The lead agency preparing the EIS must address the following issues:

☐ *Determining the Scope of the EIS.* Although the agency should already have considered the scope of the EIS during the scoping process,[149] the regulations require that it further define that scope as it prepares the EIS.[150] Questions of scope cannot be manipulated so as to avoid the EIS process; for example, an agency may not segment an environmentally significant project into less significant portions that do not require EISs.[151] On the other hand, proposals or parts of proposals that are so closely related as to be, in effect, a single course of action may be treated as such in a single EIS.[152] EISs may also be prepared for broad proposals. Such statements may, for example, evaluate similar actions generically, or consider all actions that occur within given geographic areas.[153]

☐ *Tiering.* In some instances, the regulations suggest that agencies employ "tiering" to help them focus on those issues ripe for decision.[154] Tiering is appropriate when different stages of development—such as a nationwide program and a specific project under that program—are the subjects of separate EISs. Tiering is a method of gearing each EIS to the appropriate stage of development, incorporating by reference what has gone before. Each EIS therefore avoids addressing issues that are premature or have been analyzed already.[155]

☐ *Timing, Interdisciplinary Approach, and Plain Language.* The NEPA regulations provide, as a general rule, that EISs are to be prepared earlier rather than later to eliminate subsequent delay and to integrate environmental considerations most effectively into the decisionmaking process.[156] The timing of a statement, while usually obvious, can present difficult issues. The regulations address these specifically, providing different rules for federally undertaken projects,[157] applications to agencies,[158] adjudication,[159] and rulemaking.[160]

EISs are to be prepared using an interdisciplinary approach, integrating where appropriate the natural and social sciences and the environmental design arts.[161] The statements are to be prepared in language that can be readily understood.[162]

☐ *Stages and Format of the EIS.* EISs are almost always prepared in two stages, draft and final.[163] The one exception to this rule is for EISs for legislative proposals, which need only be prepared as draft statements.[164] For a nonlegislative proposal, the lead agency, in conjunction with any cooperating agencies, prepares a draft EIS and circulates it for comment.[165] After receiving comments, the lead agency prepares a final EIS, indicating its responses to any issues raised by the comments and discussing any responsible opposing views that were not adequately discussed in the draft.[166] An EIS may be supplemented,[167] and must be if the agency makes "substantial changes in the proposed action" that are relevant to environmental concerns, or if there are "significant new circumstances or information relevant to environmental concerns and bearing on the proposed action or its impacts."[168]

The NEPA regulations recommend that statements follow a format[169] consisting of a cover sheet;[170] a summary not to exceed 15 pages;[171] a brief specification of the purpose of and need for the proposed action;[172] analyses of the alternatives,[173] the affected environment that exists before the action,[174] and the environmental consequences;[175] a list of preparers;[176] and an optional appendix.[177]

---

161. *Id.* §1502.6, *infra* at 55. NEPA specifically mentions these professional disciplines. §102(2)(A), 42 U.S.C. §4332(2)(A), *infra* at 28.

162. 40 C.F.R. §1502.8, *infra* at 55. *See* Oregon Envtl. Council v. Kunzman, 817 F.2d 484, 493-94, 17 ELR 20756, 20759-60 (9th Cir. 1987).

163. 40 C.F.R. §§1502.9, 1506.8, *infra* at 55, 61.

164. *Id.* §1502.9, *infra* at 55. This exception is itself subject to four exceptions requiring preparation of both draft and final statements. *Id.* §1506.8(b)(2), *infra* at 61.

165. *Id.* §1502.9(a), pt. 1503, *infra* at 55, 57.

166. *Id.* §1502.9(b), *infra* at 55.

167. *Id.* §1502.9(c), *infra* at 55.

168. *Id.* §1502.9(c)(1), *infra* at 55. Preparation of a supplemental statement "at times necessary to satisfy the Act's 'action-forcing' purpose." Marsh v. Oregon Natural Resources Council, *supra* note 16, 57 U.S.L.W. at 4507, 19 ELR at 20752. In the Supreme Court's words:

> It would be incongruous with [NEPA's] approach to environmental protection, and with the Act's manifest concern with preventing uninformed action, for the blinders to adverse environmental effects, once unequivocally removed, to be restored prior to the completion of agency action simply because the relevant proposal has received initial approval.

Id.; see id. at 4507-08, 19 ELR at 20752-53.

169. 40 C.F.R. §1502.10, *infra* at 55.

170. *Id.* §1502.11, *infra* at 55.

171. *Id.* §1502.12, *infra* at 56.

172. *Id.* §1502.13, *infra* at 56. The regulations as originally proposed limited this section to one page under normal circumstances, 43 Fed. Reg. 25237 (1978), but the final regulations removed this limitation, 43 Fed. Reg. 55996 (1978), on the ground that in "some cases" more than one page would be needed, 43 Fed. Reg. 55983 (1978), *infra* at 253.

173. 40 C.F.R. §1502.14, *infra* at 56.

174. *Id.* §1502.15, *infra* at 56.

175. *Id.* §1502.16, *infra* at 56. This section represents the principal analytic discussion. The regulations require the section to include discussions of eight factors. *Id.* §1502.16(a)-(h), *infra* at 56; *see infra* notes 179-86 and accompanying text.

176. *Id.* §1502.17, *infra* at 56.

177. *Id.* §1502.18, *infra* at 56.

---

149. 40 C.F.R. §§1502.4, 1508.25, *infra* at 54, 64.

150. *Id.*

151. Named Individual Members of the San Antonio Conservation Soc'y v. Texas Highway Dep't, 446 F.2d 1013, 1 ELR 20379 (5th Cir. 1971), *cert. denied,* 406 U.S. 933 (1972) (segmentation of major highway project into less significant portions does not allow agency to avoid EIS process); *see also* Taxpayers Watchdog, Inc. v. Stanley, 819 F.2d 294, 299, 17 ELR 20905, 20906-07 (D.C. Cir. 1987).

152. 40 C.F.R. §1502.4(a), *infra* at 54.

153. *Id.* §1502.4(b), (c), *infra* at 55. As examples of broad programs, the regulations cite adoption of new agency programs or regulations. *Id.; see id.* §1508.18, *infra* at 64.

154. *Id.* §§1502.4(d), 1502.20, 1508.28, *infra* at 55, 56, 65.

155. *Id.*

156. *Id.* §1502.5, *infra* at 55.

157. *Id.* §1502.5(a), *infra* at 55.

158. *Id.* §1502.5(b), *infra* at 55.

159. *Id.* §1502.5(c), *infra* at 55. By adjudication, the regulations primarily mean actions undertaken by independent regulatory agencies. *Id.*

160. *Id.* §1502.5(d), *infra* at 55.

☐ *Environmental Consequences and Alternatives.* The discussions of the environmental consequences of and the alternatives to a proposal are the most critical sections of the EIS.[178] The environmental consequences section is intended to form "the scientific and analytic basis for the comparisons" in the alternatives section,[179] and to incorporate the discussions required by various subparagraphs of NEPA §102(2)(C). Hence, the regulations require the environmental consequences section to discuss: the direct[180] and indirect effects[181] of the proposal and alternatives;[182] possible conflicts with land use plans;[183] energy requirements and conservation potential;[184] natural or depletable resources requirements and conservation potential;[185] effects on the urban, historic, and built environment and reuse and conservation potential;[186] and means of mitigating adverse environmental effects.[187]

The alternatives section is based on the information and analysis in the environmental consequences section, but should not duplicate that section.[188] Described as the "heart of the environmental impact statement," the alternatives section is to "present the environmental impacts of the proposal and the alternatives in comparative form, thus sharply defining the issues and providing a clear basis for choice among options by the decisionmakers and the public."[189] The discussion is to "[r]igorously explore and objectively evaluate all reasonable alternatives," giving "substantial treatment" to each alternative that is considered in detail.[190] The agency is to identify its "preferred alternative," if it has one, at the draft stage, and must iden-

tify that alternative when it prepares the final statement.[191] Mitigation must be discussed in this section if it has not been discussed elsewhere.[192]

☐ *Incomplete or Unavailable Information.* One provision of the regulations, while only occasionally applied, has excited considerable controversy—the section on "incomplete or unavailable information."[193] According to the CEQ, "incomplete information" is that which cannot be obtained because the overall costs of obtaining it are exorbitant.[194] "Unavailable information" is that which cannot be obtained because the means of obtaining it are not known.[195]

The CEQ regulations provide that when information on reasonably foreseeable adverse impacts evaluated in an EIS is essential to making a reasoned choice and the costs of obtaining it are not exorbitant, the agency must secure it.[196] However, if this information is incomplete or unavailable—that is, if the costs of obtaining it are exorbitant or the means of obtaining it are beyond the state of the art—the agency must "make clear that such information is lacking."[197] The agency must follow four prescribed steps.[198]

---

178. The description of the "affected environment" is consciously downgraded. The notorious "dandelion counts," overly descriptive discussions that accounted for much of the unneeded bulk of many early EISs, are discouraged. In the regulation's own words, "[v]erbose descriptions of the affected environment are themselves no measure of the adequacy of an environmental impact statement." *Id.* §1502.15, *infra* at 56. As a generality, if the affected environment description in an EIS is longer than the two analytic sections (§§1502.14, 1502.16, *infra* at 56, 56), one may justifiably look askance at undue padding of the former at the expense of the latter.

179. *Id.* §1502.16, *infra* at 56.

180. *Id.* §1502.16(a), *infra* at 56.

181. *Id.* §1502.16(b), *infra* at 56. Indirect effects include off-site impacts. Robertson v. Methow Valley Citizens Council, *supra* note 14, 57 U.S.L.W. at 4498, 4503, 19 ELR at 20744, 20747.

182. 40 C.F.R. §1502.16(d), *infra* at 56.

183. *Id.* §1502.16(c), *infra* at 56.

184. *Id.* §1502.16(e), *infra* at 56.

185. *Id.* §1502.16(f), *infra* at 56.

186. *Id.* §1502.16(g), *infra* at 56.

187. *Id.* §1502.16(h), *infra* at 56. NEPA §102(2)(C)(ii), 42 U.S.C. §4332(2)(C), *infra* at 28, specifically requires discussion of adverse impacts that "cannot be avoided should the proposal be implemented. . . ." In the Supreme Court's words, "one important ingredient of an EIS is the discussion of steps that can be taken to mitigate adverse environmental consequences." Robertson v. Methow Valley Citizens Council, *supra* note 14, 57 U.S.L.W. at 4502, 19 ELR at 20747. Indeed, "omission of a reasonably complete discussion of possible mitigation measures would undermine the 'action-forcing' function of NEPA." *Id.* While *Robertson* holds that a full mitigation plan need not be adopted, such a plan is enforceable once it is adopted by the agency in its Record of Decision. 40 C.F.R. §§1505.2(c), 1505.3, *infra* at 59, 59.

188. 40 C.F.R. §1502.14, *infra* at 56.

189. *Id.*

190. *Id.* §1502.14(d), *infra* at 56. "Substantial treatment," rather than equal treatment, is required, since the treatment must necessarily vary with the degree of impact.

191. *Id.* §1502.14(e), *infra* at 56. An exception is made for situations in which other laws may prohibit expression of such a preference at this stage. *Id.* This exception was designed to cover independent regulatory agencies, where staff may prepare a draft and final EIS, but only the commissioners may express an agency preference, and they may not do so until after the final EIS is prepared.

192. *Id.* §1502.14(f), *infra* at 56.

193. *Id.* §1502.22, *infra* at 57. *See generally* Robertson v. Methow v. Valley Citizens Council, *supra* note 14, 57 U.S.L.W. at 4502-03, 19 ELR at 20746-48; Masterman, *Worst Case Analysis: The Final Chapter?,* 19 ELR 10026 (1989); Yost, *Don't Gut Worst Case Analysis,* 13 ELR 10394 (1983); *see also* Friends of Endangered Species v. Jantzen, 760 F.2d 976, 15 ELR 20455 (9th Cir. 1985); Save Our Ecosystems v. Clark, 747 F.2d 1240, 15 ELR 20035 (9th Cir. 1984); Southern Oregon Citizens Against Toxic Sprays, Inc. v. Clark, 720 F.2d 1475, 14 ELR 20061 (9th Cir. 1983), *cert. denied,* 469 U.S. 1028 (1984); City of New York v. Dep't of Transp., 715 F.2d 732, 13 ELR 20823 (2d Cir. 1983), *appeal dismissed, cert. denied,* 465 U.S. 1055 (1984); Sierra Club v. Sigler, 695 F.2d 957, 13 ELR 20210 (5th Cir. 1983); Oregon Envtl. Council v. Kunzman, 614 F. Supp. 657, 15 ELR 20499 (D. Or. 1985), *injunction dissolved,* 636 F. Supp. 632, 16 ELR 20658 (D. Or. 1986), *aff'd,* 817 F.2d 484, 17 ELR 20756 (9th Cir. 1987).

194. 51 Fed. Reg. 15618, 15621 (1986), *infra* at 263.

195. *Id.*

196. 40 C.F.R. §1502.22(a), *infra* at 57.

197. *Id.* §1502.22, *infra* at 57. *See* Scientists' Inst. for Pub. Information v. AEC, 481 F.2d 1079, 1091-92, 3 ELR 20525, 20531-32 (D.C. Cir. 1973). In that case, the court stated:

> It must be remembered that the basic thrust of an agency's responsibilities under NEPA is to predict the environmental effects of a proposed action *before* the action is taken and those effects fully known. *Reasonable forecasting and speculation is thus implicit in NEPA* and we must reject any attempt by agencies to shirk their responsibilities under NEPA by labeling any and all discussion of future environmental effects a "crystal ball inquiry."

Id.. at 1092, 3 ELR at 20531-32 (emphasis added). *See also* Kleppe v. Sierra Club, *supra* note 14, 427 U.S. at 410 n.21, 6 ELR at 20537 n.21; Massachusetts v. Andrus, 594 F.2d 872, 892, 9 ELR 20162, 20173 (1st Cir. 1979); Alaska v. Andrus, 580 F.2d 465, 473-74, 8 ELR 20237, 20242 (D.C. Cir. 1978), *vacated on other grounds sub nom.* Western Oil & Gas Ass'n v. Alaska, 439 U.S. 922 (1978); Ethyl Corp. v. EPA, 541 F.2d 1, 18, 6 ELR 20267, 20279 (D.C. Cir.) (en banc), *cert. denied,* 426 U.S. 941 (1976); I-291 Why? Ass'n v. Burns, 517 F.2d 1077, 1081, 5 ELR 20430, 20432 (2d Cir. 1975) (per curiam).

198. 40 C.F.R. §1502.22, *infra* at 57. This the only regulation that the CEQ has amended since it promulgated the NEPA regulations. The

First, it must state that the information is incomplete or unavailable.[199] Second, it must state the relevance of the missing information.[200] Third, it must summarize the existing credible scientific evidence relevant to its evaluation of reasonably foreseeable impacts.[201] Fourth, it must analyze those impacts based upon theoretical approaches or scientific methods generally accepted in the scientific community.[202] The regulation clearly states that agencies must consider impacts with low probability but catastrophic consequences as long as the analysis "is supported by credible scientific evidence, is not based on pure conjecture, and is within the rule of reason."[203]

Risk analysis of improbable but highly significant impacts is not a new concept.[204] As articulated by the First Circuit in *Massachusetts v. Andrus*:

---

regulation as amended in 1986 shares certain goals with the prior regulation: disclosure that information is missing, acquisition of that information, and evaluation of impacts in the absence of all information. *See* 51 Fed. Reg. 15619, 15620-21 (1986), *infra* at 262-63.

The amendment does, however, make one significant change in the method by which agencies consider incomplete or unavailable information. The earlier regulation provided that when cost or lack of appropriate methodology precluded acquisition of relevant information, the agency had to weigh the need for the action against the risk and severity of possible adverse impacts were the action to proceed in the face of uncertainty. Before proceeding, an agency had to perform a "worst case analysis," indicating both the probability and the improbability of the occurrence of that worst case. Application of worst case analysis, particularly by the Ninth Circuit in Save our Ecosystems v. Clark, *supra* note 193, 747 F.2d at 140, 15 ELR at 20035, and *Southern Oregon Citizens Against Toxic Sprays, supra* note 193, 720 F.2d at 1475, 14 ELR at 20051, engendered a certain unhappiness among some government agencies that thought they had to go beyond reasonable limits to develop a "worst case scenario."

The CEQ amended the regulation to delete the worst case analysis requirement. The amendment was to apply to all EISs for which a notice of intent was published in the *Federal Register* on or after May 27, 1986. For EISs in progress before then, the agency may choose to comply with either the original or the amended regulation. 40 C.F.R. §1502.22(c), *infra* at 57. The Supreme Court has upheld the new regulation as within the deference to be accorded to the CEQ (while suggesting that the former regulation was also within that deference). Robertson v. Methow Valley Citizens Council, *supra* note 14, 57 U.S.L.W. at 4502-03, 19 ELR at 20746-48; *see* Marsh v. Oregon Natural Resources Council, *supra* note 16, 57 U.S.L.W. at 4506-07, 19 ELR at 20752-54.

199. 40 C.F.R. §1502.22(b)(1), *infra* at 57.
200. *Id.* §1502.22(b)(2), *infra* at 57.
201. *Id.* §1502.22(b)(3), *infra* at 57.
202. *Id.* §1502.22(b)(4), *infra* at 57. The CEQ intends for evaluations of reasonably foreseeable significant impacts to be carefully conducted and based upon credible scientific evidence. All scientific evidence must be disclosed, including responsible opposing views supported by generally accepted theoretical approaches or scientific methods. 51 Fed. Reg. 15618, 15621 (1986), *infra* at 263.
203. This portion of the amended regulation is specifically intended to substitute for worst case analysis.
204. Both the prior regulation and the amended regulation incorporate this concept. Moreover, a pre-amendment Supreme Court case recognized the difference between considering the impacts of improbable but possible occurrences should they actually occur and considering the more speculative impacts generated by apprehension of those occurrences. In Metropolitan Edison Co. v. People Against Nuclear Energy, 460 U.S. 766, 13 ELR 20515 (1983), the Court declined to apply NEPA to the psychological fears generated by the "risk" of a nuclear accident at Three Mile Island but acknowledged the need to consider improbable but possible accidents, stating:

We emphasize that in this case we are considering effects caused by the risk of an accident. The situation where an agency is asked to consider effects that will occur if a risk is realized, for example, if an accident occurs at TMI-1, is an entirely different case. The NRC considered, in the original

If it were 100% certain that particular precautions would obviate all danger, the task would be simple; but there is a large element of the unknown created by gaps in science, by possible human errors, and by freak weather conditions. Thus, the Secretary must engage in an uneasy calculus akin to that described by Judge Learned Hand, weighing "the possibility" of accident, "the gravity of the resulting injury" and "the burden of adequate precautions."[205]

The District of Columbia Circuit made the same point in *Ethyl Corp. v. EPA*:

Danger . . . is not set by a fixed probability of harm, but rather is composed of reciprocal elements of risk and harm, or probability and severity. . . . That is to say, the public health may properly be found endangered both by a lesser risk of a greater harm, and by a greater risk of a lesser harm.[206]

NEPA essentially requires analysis of both the lesser risks of greater harms and the greater risks of lesser harms before actions are taken to bring about the risks. As courts recognize, such "[r]easonable forecasting and speculation is thus implicit in NEPA. . . ."[207]

☐ *Streamlining.* As noted above, the NEPA regulations set out as goals the reduction of both paperwork[208] and delay in the NEPA process.[209] The procedures accordingly contain certain streamlining provisions designed to simplify NEPA's implementation and to mesh its application with that of other laws. For example, one section permits EISs to incorporate certain material by reference when this will cut down on their bulk.[210] However, the incorporated information must be cited, briefly described, and made publicly available so as not to impede review by other agencies and the public.[211] Another provision allows an agency to "adopt" in whole or in part another EIS prepared by the same or a different federal agency, thus eliminating unnecessary duplication of work.[212]

Similarly, the regulations seek to eliminate duplication with state environmental procedures,[213] specifically directing federal agencies to prepare joint statements in coopera-

---

EIS and in the most recent EIA for TMI-1, the possible adverse effects of a number of accidents that might occur at TMI-1.

Id. at 775 n.9, 13 ELR at 25021 n.9.

205. 594 F.2d 872, 892, 9 ELR 20162, 20173 (1st Cir. 1979). Evaluation of uncertainties has always been a part of the legal process. "Certainty," in Justice Holmes' famous phrase, "generally is illusion." O. HOLMES, COLLECTED LEGAL PAPERS 181 (1920). Nevertheless, in the absence of certainty we do the best we can. As lucidly put by Justice Cardozo: "The law is not an exact science, we are told, and there the matter ends, if we are willing to end it. . . . Exactness may be impossible, but that is not enough to cause the mind to acquiesce in a predestined incoherence." B. CARDOZO, THE PARADOXES OF LEGAL SCIENCE A 2-3 (1928).
206. 541 F.2d at 18, 6 ELR at 20279.
207. *Scientists' Inst. for Pub. Information, supra* note 197, 481 F.2d at 1092, 3 ELR at 20532. *See also* Kleppe v. Sierra Club, *supra* note 14, 427 U.S. at 410 n.21, 6 ELR at 20537 n.21 (1976); Alaska v. Andrus, *supra* note 197, 580 F.2d at 473-74, 8 at 20242; I-291 Why? Ass'n v. Burns, *supra*, 517 F.2d at 1081, 5 ELR at 20432.
208. 40 C.F.R. §1500.4, *infra* at 51.
209. *Id.* §1500.5, *infra* at 52.
210. *Id.* §1502.21, *infra* at 57.
211. *Id.* Material based on proprietary data that is itself not available for public review cannot be incorporated by reference. *Id.*
212. *Id.* §1506.3, *infra* at 60. This section requires that the adopted EIS meet the standards of an adequate EIS, and specifically describes the kind of circulation necessary for an adopted statement. *Id.*
213. *Id.* §1506.2(b), *infra* at 60.

tion with states that themselves have EIS requirements.[214] Indeed, the regulations allow an EIS to be combined with any other environmental document to reduce paperwork and duplication.[215] When streamlining is appropriate, agencies must nevertheless ensure the professional and scientific integrity of environmental analyses.[216]

Commenting

Once the draft EIS is prepared, it is to be circulated for comment to all relevant federal, state, and local agencies, to applicants, if any, and to members of the public who request it.[217] Both the Act[218] and the regulations[219] mandate that lead agencies "obtain" comments from federal agencies with jurisdiction by law over a project or with special expertise. Lead agencies generally need only "request" comments from other federal agencies, state and local agencies, affected Indian Tribes, applicants, and the public.[220] Agency comments are to be as specific as possible, and agencies making critical comments must specify what they believe should be done to address the problems they identify.[221] The usual comment period on a draft EIS is not less than 45 days,[222] although provisions exist for both reducing and extending that period.[223]

Response to Comments and the Final EIS

Consistent with NEPA's goal of public-private cooperation in environmental protection,[224] the regulations impose a requirement unique among environmental and, perhaps, all governmental obligations: in the final EIS, the lead agency must explain its position in writing to any member of the public who chooses to comment. When preparing its final EIS, the agency "shall respond" to comments by adding to or modifying its analyses, by making factual corrections, or by explaining why the comments do not warrant these actions, citing "the sources, authorities, or reasons" supporting its position.[225]

After responding to comments, the agency must circulate its final EIS in much the same manner as it did its draft EIS.[226] Although agencies do not usually request additional comments on final EISs, they may do so and anyone can still comment on a final statement before the agency makes its final decision.[227] The regulations require that the agency make no decision until 30 days after the final EIS if filed. This allows time for comment and ensures that the agency has adequate time to consider the statement.[228]

Post-statement Procedures

CEQ Referrals

After an EIS is complete but before a decision is made on the proposal, an infrequent but important procedure may intervene: referral to the CEQ of environmentally unsatisfactory federal actions.[229] Under section 309 of the Clean Air Act,[230] EPA may refer any proposed federal agency action to the CEQ if EPA determines that the action is environmentally unsatisfactory.[231] Under NEPA, other agencies may refer allegedly unsatisfactory proposed actions to the CEQ as well.[232] Only a small number of visible and significant agency proposals are referred to the CEQ.[233] As of 1987, the CEQ had received 23 referrals.[234]

A 1986 report concluded that the referral process causes agencies to consider the environmental impacts of their proposals more fully, and facilitates interagency communication and dispute resolution. The report concluded that the effectiveness of the process depends substantially on, and varies with, the CEQ's perceived competence, objectivity, and White House backing. Earlier CEQ involvement in potential disputes and increased monitoring of

214. *Id.* §1506.2(c), *infra* at 60. For a discussion of state mini-NEPAs, see McElfish, *State Environmental Law and Programs*, §6.03[1][c], in LAW OF ENVIRONMENTAL PROTECTION (S. Novick ed. 1987).

215. 40 C.F.R. §1506.4, *infra* at 60. Environmental statements are to be integrated to the fullest extent possible with other environmental analyses required by the Fish and Wildlife Coordination Act, the National Historic Preservation Act, and the Endangered Species Act, as well as other environmental review laws. *Id.* §1502.25(a), *infra* at 57. The draft EIS must also list all other federal permits that will be required. *Id.* §1502.25(b), *infra* at 57.

216. *Id.* §1502.24, *infra* at 57. The CEQ NEPA regulations do not require cost-benefit analyses, but give specific guidance as to the contents of such analyses if they are included. *Id.* §1502.23, *infra* at 57.

217. *Id.* §1502.19, *infra* at 56. Section 1506.6, *infra* at 60 is the provision governing public involvement throughout the NEPA process. This involvement is extensive.

218. NEPA §102(2)(C), 42 U.S.C. §4332(2)(C), *infra* at 28.

219. 40 C.F.R. §§1503.1(a)(1), 1503.2, *infra* at 57, 57.

220. *Id.* §1503.1(a)(2), *infra* at 57.

221. *Id.* §1503.3, *infra* at 58.

222. *Id.* §1506.10(c), *infra* at 61.

223. *Id.* §1506.10(d), *infra* at 62.

224. NEPA §101(a), 42 U.S.C. §4331(a), *infra* at 28.

225. 40 C.F.R. §1503.4, *infra* at 58.

226. *Id.* §1502.19, *infra* at 56.

227. *Id.* §1503.1(b), *infra* at 57. On the rare occasion when a draft EIS is "so inadequate as to preclude meaningful analysis," the agency is required to recirculate a revised draft. *Id.* §1502.9(a), *infra* at 55.

228. *Id.* §1506.10(b)(2), *infra* at 61. The decision must also be made at least 90 days after the draft EIS. *Id.* §1506.10(b)(1). All dates are measured from the date an EIS is filed with EPA in Washington, D.C. *Id.* §§1506.9, 1506.10, *infra* at 61, 61. That filing date is not the actual date of receipt, but the date of public notice by EPA in the *Federal Register* of the statements received during the preceding week. *Id.* §1506.10(a), *infra* at 61. The applicable regulation has specific provisions governing special timing situations, such as agency rulemaking and decisions subject to internal appeal, in which the normal time limits may be adjusted. *Id.* §1506.10(b), *infra* at 61. If the final EIS is filed within 90 days after the draft EIS is filed, the minimum 30-day and minimum 90-day periods may run concurrently, although agencies cannot allow less than 45 days for comments on the draft statement. *Id.* §1506.10(c), *infra* at 62. Lead agencies may also extend prescribed periods; EPA may, upon a showing of need by the lead agency, reduce them. *Id.* §1506.10(d), *infra* at 62.

229. *Id.* pt. 1504, *infra* at 58.

230. 42 U.S.C. §7609, *infra* at 41.

231. 40 C.F.R. §1504.1(b), *infra* at 58.

232. *Id.* §§1504.1-.2, *infra* at 58.

233. The CEQ referral process is not discussed in detail because it is used so infrequently. Any agency or person affected, however, should become closely familiar with the regulations. *See id.* §1504.2-.3, *infra* at 58.

234. ENVIRONMENTAL LAW INSTITUTE, ENVIRONMENTAL REFERRALS AND THE COUNCIL ON ENVIRONMENTAL QUALITY (1986), *reprinted in* COUNCIL ON ENVIRONMENTAL QUALITY, ENVIRONMENTAL QUALITY 1986, at 252. One reason for the paucity of referrals may be that lead agencies seek to avoid them by working more closely with other involved agencies at earlier stages. The very existence of the referral process may thus increase interagency cooperation, even if the process is not actually used much. *Id.* at 253.

CEQ recommendations on referrals, the report continued, could enhance that effectiveness further.[235]

Agency Decisionmaking and the Record of Decision

The NEPA process is to be thoroughly integrated into agency decisionmaking, and the CEQ regulations are designed to ensure this integration. For example, the regulations require each agency to adopt procedures ensuring that its decisions accord with the policies and processes of NEPA.[236] In addition, the regulations require agencies to prepare a document, second in importance only to the EIS, which is designed to ensure that agency decisionmakers respect the environment: the "record of decision"[237] (ROD). An agency must prepare a concise and public ROD whenever it makes a decision following preparation of a final EIS.[238] The ROD must state the decision[239] and identify all alternatives. It must specify the alternative or alternatives "considered to be environmentally preferable,"[240] and may specify alternatives considered to be preferable from the point of view of other "essential considerations of national policy."[241] The agency is to discuss these considerations in explaining how it reached its decision. The ROD must also state "whether all practicable means to avoid or minimize environmental harm from the alternative selected have been adopted and if not, why they were not."[242] Finally, a ROD must adopt and summarize a monitoring and enforcement program, if applicable, for any mitigation.[243]

Agency Actions During the Pendency of an EIS

As a general rule, agencies may not take any action concerning a proposal while an EIS is pending. The NEPA regulations address this important issue with specificity,[244] tracking both case law[245] and administrative practice. When, as is usually the case, a proposal is not part of an overall program, the applicable regulation prohibits taking any action on the proposal before issuance of a ROD, if the action would have an adverse environmental impact or limit the choice of reasonable alternatives.[246] An individual action that is part of a larger program[247] cannot proceed while the program's EIS is pending unless the action meets three criteria: (1) it is justified independently of the program; (2) it is itself accompanied by an adequate EIS; and (3) it will not prejudice the ultimate decision on the program.[248] The regulation also specifically addresses situations involving applications to agencies, both in general[249] and when applicants are developing plans or designs or are performing other work necessary to support their applications.[250]

III. JUDICIAL REVIEW

Introduction

The Importance of Courts in the NEPA Process

It is judicial review that has given NEPA its significance. The Act places regulatory obligations on agencies without apparent means of oversight. By the conscious choice of its drafters, NEPA internalizes each agency's environmental obligations and is thus essentially self-regulatory in nature. Rather than relying on an outside agency for environmental analysis, each agency is to consider the environmental impacts of its own actions. While NEPA supplies a pervasive impetus for environmentally responsible decisionmaking throughout the government, the absence of institutional enforcement invites administrative inattention and noncompliance.[251] The CEQ, as a White House agency, is too small to get involved in numerous individual projects. EPA's leverage under §309 of the Clean Air Act is murky at best, and the Agency is no disinterested party, given its conflicting role as a principal preparer of EISs on its own actions. Clearly, successful implementation of NEPA must depend on some other institution removed from the administrative process.

NEPA's enforcement ultimately depends on the courts. Fortunately, the action-forcing provisions of the Act neatly lend themselves to judicial enforcement. The importance of the role these provisions have played in fostering judicial acceptance of the Act cannot be overemphasized. Judges may, and usually should, reasonably question their competence to second-guess the scientific determinations of administrative agencies. Judges may also lack understanding of or sympathy for claimants' environmental goals. But all judges understand procedure. The requirement that an EIS must be filed as a condition precedent to an action is just the sort of requirement that taps familiar judicial strains. Implementation of the procedural provisions of NEPA is judicially comfortable. It has also ensured the success of the Act.

---

235. *Id.* The possibility that CEQ will publish findings that do not support an agency's position and that can be used in litigation also serves as an impetus to agencies to pay heed to environmental factors.

236. *Id.* §1505.1, *infra* at 59. *See, infra* pp. 100-02 (list of agency regulations adopted under NEPA).

237. *Id.* §1505.2, *infra* at 59.

238. *Id.*

239. *Id.* §1505.2(a), *infra* at 59.

240. *Id.* §1505.2(b), *infra* at 59.

241. NEPA §101(b), 42 U.S.C. §4331(b), *infra* at 28; 40 C.F.R. §1505.2(b), *infra* at 59.

242. 40 C.F.R. §1505.2(c), *infra* at 59.

243. *Id.* The regulations provide specific guidance for implementation of mitigation and post-decision monitoring. *Id.* §1505.3, *infra* at 59.

244. 40 C.F.R. §1506.1, *infra* at 59.

245. The most important case in this regard is Kleppe v. Sierra Club, *supra* note 14.

246. 40 C.F.R. §1506.1(a), *infra* at 59.

247. 40 C.F.R. §1506.1(c), *infra* at 60, refers to a program for which an EIS is "required" in order to ensure that individual actions are not held up when an agency voluntarily (without being required to do so, but in furtherance of good environmental practice) undertakes preparation of a program EIS.

248. *Id.* "Prejudice to the ultimate decision on the program" is defined as a tendency to determine subsequent development or to limit alternatives. *Id.*

249. *Id.* §1506.1(b), *infra* at 60. If an agency considering an application becomes aware that an applicant is about to take an action that may adversely impact the environment or limit the choice of reasonable alternatives, the agency must promptly notify the applicant that it will "take appropriate action to insure that the objectives and procedures of NEPA are achieved." *Id.*

250. *Id.* §1506.1(d), *infra* at 60. Such actions are not precluded.

251. Senator Muskie was somewhat leery of NEPA's self-scrutiny approach. As part of the negotiation between Senators Jackson and Muskie, the requirement of a "detailed statement"—the NEPA term for what has become popularly known as the EIS—was substituted for a requirement of "findings," because Senator Muskie believed that such findings would too strongly reflect self-serving agencies' mission-oriented priorities. 115 CONG. REC. 29053 (1969).

NEPA Litigation in the Courts

NEPA litigation, while not extensive, constitutes a significant proportion of the environmental litigation against the government. In 1980, for example, the United States was a party to 63,628 actions commenced in federal district court.[252] 26,835 of these actions were brought under statutes;[253] of these, the United States was plaintiff in 8,600 cases and defendant in 18,235.[254] 457 of the statutory cases involved environmental causes of action, and the United States was defendant in 201 of those cases.[255] In that same year, the CEQ reported that 140 cases were brought challenging federal actions under NEPA.[256] Therefore, litigation under NEPA is not statistically significant relative to litigation generally involving the government, but it does comprise a substantial portion (approximately 70 percent in 1980) of the environmental litigation against the United States.[257]

Overview of the Judicial Process in NEPA Cases

The Complaint

A typical NEPA case begins with a plaintiff filing a complaint in federal court seeking both declaratory and injunctive relief. The complaint will typically name as defendants the various federal agency officials in the chain of command responsible for the proposed action that is alleged to violate NEPA. A complaint should also name state officials if their agencies are involved in joint lead capacities.[258] Private applicants need not be named as defendants since an injunction barring issuance of a permit will necessarily prevent the private action. Should a plaintiff be concerned that a private party might proceed with a plan in spite of injunctive relief against the agency, the plaintiff can name the private party as a co-defendant; this does

not preclude the plaintiff from seeking an injunction against the private party in a separate proceeding.[259] In any event, as a practical matter, a private applicant will probably seek to intervene in an action against an agency.[260]

Venue

A limited measure of forum shopping is available under NEPA in that naming a particular official as a defendant may establish venue in a desirable locale. Venue in NEPA cases is determined under the general venue statute for suits against the federal government.[261] That statute is permissive and allows the plaintiff wide leeway in the initial choice of forum. As in other suits against the government, that choice is subject to a motion to change venue for the convenience of the parties and in the interest of justice.[262]

Discovery

Discovery is somewhat more limited in environmental litigation than in litigation generally because judicial review is ordinarily confined to the administrative record.[263] However, it is sometimes necessary to look outside the record in order to properly evaluate what information was not considered.[264] The limitations on what may be added to the record will determine what information the government will seek or divulge during discovery. In some cases, the government may also assert a deliberative process privilege. In any event, the plaintiff should still press its discovery program if it is critical or useful to the case. Defendants typically have less to gain from discovery, except that discovery may bolster defenses such as standing, and, if plaintiffs have succeeded in introducing further evidence, discovery may enable defendants to examine that evidence or its presenting witnesses.

The Course of Litigation

In a NEPA case, either the Department of Justice or the local U.S. Attorney represents the federal agency, although the agency itself may answer the complaint and proceed

---

252. ANNUAL REPORT OF THE DIRECTOR OF THE ADMINISTRATIVE OFFICE OF THE UNITED STATES COURTS, 1980 at 376 (1981) (Table C3).

253. The nonstatutory cases were overwhelmingly actions under contracts, while the balance primarily involved torts and real property. *Id.*

254. *Id.* at 374 (Table C2).

255. *Id.* Less than 1 percent (.716 percent) of the cases to which the United States was a party were environmental in nature. Of the statutory actions in which the United States was a defendant, 1.102 percent were environmental.

256. COUNCIL ON ENVIRONMENTAL QUALITY, ENVIRONMENTAL QUALITY 1981, at 183 (1982). The total includes lawsuits with causes of action in addition to those under NEPA. The CEQ maintains and annually reports statistics concerning all NEPA actions—the number of cases, the nature of the causes of action, the nature of relief, and the institutional identity (environmentalists, states, businesses, and so on) of the plaintiffs.

257. In 1985, according to the most recent CEQ data published, 77 NEPA suits were filed. COUNCIL ON ENVIRONMENTAL QUALITY, ENVIRONMENTAL QUALITY 1986, at 240 (1988). This number is the lowest recorded since the enactment of NEPA—a high of 189 cases were filed in 1974—and may reflect federal agencies' greater experience and expertise in carrying out their NEPA responsibilities. *Id.* The greatest number of cases—37—alleged that EISs should have been prepared. Less than half that many cases—18, comprising the next largest category—alleged that EISs that were prepared were inadequate. *Id.* at 242. Thus, the greatest portion of NEPA litigation occurs when EISs have not been prepared. This has been true in the majority of years since NEPA's enactment. *Id.* at 240. It is worth noting that injunctions were issued in only 8 cases in 1985, another all-time low number. *Id.*

258. State officials might also be involved in highway construction projects under NEPA §102(2)(D), 42 U.S.C. §4332(2)(D), *infra* at 29.

259. *See* FED. R. CIV. P. 65(d); *see also* Foundation on Economic Trends v. Heckler, 756 F.2d 143, 155, 15 ELR 20248, 20254 (D.C. Cir. 1985).

260. An applicant will usually find it important to intervene, since its interests and the agency's may not coincide. A plaintiff generally will not resist such intervention.

261. 28 U.S.C. §1391(e). This provision allows a plaintiff to bring suit: (1) where a defendant resides; (2) where the cause of action arose; (3) where the real property involved in the action is situated; or (4) where the plaintiff resides if real property is not involved. *Id.* Section 1391 also provides for nationwide service of process.

262. *Id.* §1404(a).

263. Citizens to Preserve Overton Park v. Volpe, 401 U.S. 402, 1 ELR 20110 (1971). Of course, the alert participant in the NEPA process places all he or she wishes into the administrative record when the structure of the proceeding so permits. When an EIS is prepared, the commenting process provides the usual occasion to place such information in the record. *See generally* McMillan & Peterson, *The Permissible Scope of Hearings, Discovery, and Additional Factfinding During Judicial Review of Informal Agency Action,* 1982 DUKE L.J. 333 (1982).

264. County of Suffolk v. Secretary of the Interior, 562 F.2d 1368, 1384, 7 ELR 20637, 20644 (2d Cir. 1977). *See* Animal Defense Council v. Hodel, 840 F.2d 1432, 1436-37, 18 ELR 20497, 20499-500 (9th Cir. 1988); Greenpeace v. Evans, 688 F. Supp. 579, 584-85, 17 ELR 21207, 21209 (W.D. Wash. 1987).

through discovery to trial.[265] As with discovery, the usual course of NEPA litigation is more abbreviated than that of general litigation because of the time pressures that typify projects reviewed under NEPA. A plaintiff may take several steps to expedite the litigation. For example, the plaintiff may move for a preliminary injunction. As a practical matter, the case may end if the plaintiff loses at this stage and the project proceeds in the interim between the ruling and trial. Alternatively, the plaintiff can seek to have the hearing on the preliminary injunction consolidated with an advanced trial on the merits.[266] Often the plaintiff will move for summary judgment based on the administrative record, since that record was generated by the agency and purportedly contains undisputed facts. The defendant agency or intervening applicant will probably file a motion or crossmotion for summary judgment or dismissal. At any rate, most NEPA actions are resolved on motion.

Remedies

"When a court has found that a party is in violation of NEPA," the Fifth Circuit has said, "the remedy should be shaped so as to fulfill the objectives of the statute as closely as possible, consistent with the broader public interest."[267] As stated at the outset of this article, those objectives are to prevent or eliminate damage to the environment and to ensure environmentally responsible decision-making by agencies. In order to achieve these objectives, plaintiffs may ask for, and courts may grant, preliminary or permanent injunctive relief.

Preliminary Relief

In order to receive preliminary injunctive relief, plaintiffs ordinarily must show: (1) a substantial likelihood of success on the merits; (2) a substantial threat of irreparable injury absent an injunction; (3) that this threatened injury outweighs the harm to defendants of granting the injunction; and (4) that an injunction would be in the public interest.[268] These standards impose a greater burden on a plaintiff than do those for permanent relief once a violation of NEPA is found. Of course, the general judicial policy of shaping injunctions to implement NEPA's objectives, rather than thwart them, will prevail.[269]

Permanent Relief

Once a violation of NEPA has been established, a plaintiff faces a somewhat lesser burden in seeking permanent injunctive relief, particularly since it need no longer show

a probability of success on the merits. Nevertheless, both preliminary and permanent injunctions are equitable in nature and the considerations for whether they should issue have much in common.[270]

When a NEPA violation has been found, the court typically shapes the injunction to remedy it. For example, if a court determines that an EIS should have been prepared, it will order the agency to prepare one.[271] Courts do differ, though, on when they consider permanent injunctive relief appropriate. Some courts hold that injunctive relief is appropriate to encourage rapid and thorough compliance with NEPA, but that principles of general equity may limit that relief.[272] Other courts appear more willing to grant injunctions. One court has held that a NEPA violation in itself constitutes irreparable harm, entitling a plaintiff "to blanket injunctive relief."[273] Some courts have created a rebuttable presumption that a NEPA violation causes irreparable injury warranting injunctive relief.[274] Still other courts presume irreparable harm and award injunctive relief if there has been either a failure to evaluate properly the environmental impact of a major federal action[275] or a continuing denial of plaintiffs' rights.[276]

Courts that have held that a NEPA violation raises a presumption of injunctive relief have done so in order to ensure the integrity of the NEPA process. In Judge Wilkey's words, "[o]rdinarily where an action is being undertaken in violation of NEPA, there is a presumption that injunctive relief should be granted until the agency brings itself into compliance."[277] Judge Wilkey explained that a NEPA analysis might reveal substantial environmental consequences critical to further consideration of the propriety of the action. Further, an injunction is justified on an ongoing project because the decisionmakers are entitled to all the information relevant to a determination whether to abandon or alter the project.[278] Injunctive relief also preserves the widest freedom of choice for the agency

---

265. Note that when United States officers are parties in a NEPA case, the government has 60 days to file its answer. Fed. R. Civ. P. 12(a).

266. Fed. R. Civ. P. 65(a)(2).

267. Environmental Defense Fund, Inc. v. Marsh, 651 F.2d 983, 1005, 11 ELR 21012, 21022 (5th Cir. 1981).

268. National Wildlife Fed'n v. Marsh, 721 F.2d 767, 770 n.3, 14 ELR 20172, 20173 n.3 (11th Cir. 1983); *see* Foundation on Economic Trends v. Heckler, *supra* note 259, 756 F.2d at 157, 15 ELR at 20255; Piedmont Heights Civic Club, Inc. v. Moreland, 637 F.2d 430, 435, 11 ELR 20257, 20259 (5th Cir. 1981); Canal Auth. of Fla. v. Callaway, 489 F.2d 567, 577-78, 4 ELR 20164, 20169 (5th Cir. 1974); Latham v. Volpe, 455 F.2d 1111, 1116-17, 1 ELR 20602, 20603 (9th Cir. 1971).

269. *See Foundation on Economic Trends, supra* note 259, 756 F.2d at 157, 15 ELR at 20255.

270. *See* C. Wright & A. Miller, Federal Practice and Procedure §2942 (1973).

271. *See, e.g.,* Environmental Defense Fund, Inc. v. Marsh, *supra* note 267, 651 F.2d at 1005-06, 11 ELR at 21022.

272. *See, e.g., id.; see also* Northern Cheyenne Tribe v. Hodel, 851 F.2d 1152, 1158, 18 ELR 20865, 20867 (9th Cir. 1988); Save the Yaak Comm. v. Block, 840 F.2d 714, 722, 18 ELR 20869, 20873 (9th Cir. 1988); Richland Park Homeowners Ass'n v. Pierce, 671 F.2d 935, 942, 12 ELR 20717, 20719 (5th Cir. 1982).

273. Environmental Defense Fund, Inc. v. Froehlke, 477 F.2d 1033, 1037, 3 ELR 20383, 20384 (8th Cir. 1973).

274. American Motorcyclist Ass'n v. Watt, 714 F.2d 962, 966, 15 ELR 20735 (9th Cir. 1983); Alpine Lakes Protection Soc'y v. Schlapfer, 518 F.2d 1089, 1090, 5 ELR 20322 (9th Cir. 1975).

275. Thomas v. Peterson, 753 F.2d 754, 764, 15 ELR 20225, 20230 (9th Cir. 1985); Save Our Ecosystem v. Clark, *supra* note 193, 747 F.2d at 1250, 15 ELR at 20040; *see also Foundation on Economic Trends, supra* note 259, 756 F.2d at 157, 15 ELR at 20255.

276. Environmental Defense Fund, Inc. v. Tennessee Valley Auth., 468 F.2d 1164, 1184, 2 ELR 20726, 20734-35 (6th Cir. 1972).
   It is worth noting that in some cases, judicial insistence upon NEPA compliance prior to issuance of a permit bars the activity sought to be permitted without the need for an injunction. *See, e.g.,* Sierra Club v. Sigler, 695 F.2d 957, 13 ELR 20210 (5th Cir. 1983) (no action on project was undertaken during pendency of litigation or after Corps of Engineers was ordered to correct deficiencies in EIS).

277. Realty Income Trust v. Eckerd, 564 F.2d 447, 456, 7 ELR 20541, 20545 (D.C. Cir. 1977) (footnote omitted).

278. *Id.*

when it reconsiders its action after preparing an EIS. "This rationale," continued Judge Wilkey, "often requires an injunction against all the activities of a project, even activities that themselves have no effect on the environment."[279] Accordingly, courts "*should not prejudge*" the outcome of reconsideration "once the full environmental consequences . . . have been determined."[280]

In sum, the "presumption is that an action proceeding in violation of NEPA should be enjoined."[281] Such an injunction has been appropriately termed "the vehicle through which the congressional policy behind NEPA can be effectuated."[282] Otherwise stated, the policies underlying NEPA "weigh the scales in favor of those seeking the suspension of all action until the Act's requirements are met."[283] Without injunctive relief, "application of a 'rule of reason' would convert an EIS into a mere rubber stamp for *post hoc* rationalization of decisions already made."[284] Injunctive relief in a NEPA case, of course, is designed to maintain the status quo until the appropriate EIS has been prepared.[285]

Two recent Supreme Court cases have given some indication that the Court prefers appellate courts to defer to trial courts' traditional balancing of equitable factors rather than to apply presumptions necessitating injunctive relief. Those cases, *Weinberger v. Romero-Barcelo*[286] and

Amoco Production Co. v. Village of Gambell,[287] held that violations of federal environmental statutes do not necessarily compel injunctions or raise presumptions of irreparable harm. While neither case explicitly addressed injunctive relief under NEPA, they have led some lower courts to question whether Congress intended NEPA to limit their traditional equitable discretion in enforcing the statute.[288]

Defenses

Before plaintiffs can obtain temporary or permanent injunctive relief, they may have to overcome defenses typically raised by defendants or intervenors in NEPA cases. These defenses are lack of standing, inapplicability of NEPA, and certain procedural defenses not specifically related to the Act.

Standing

Provided that the facts are suitable and the complaint is properly worded, a standing defense should not present a significant hurdle to the plaintiff.[289] The leading case on standing in environmental litigation, *Sierra Club v. Morton*,[290] made clear that environmental as well as economic interests allow a plaintiff to meet this threshold requirement as long as injury to those interests is particularized to the plaintiff. Thus, it is insufficient for a plaintiff to assert a general interest in protecting the environment. Rather, the complaint must state that the plaintiff in fact uses and enjoys the environmental amenity alleged to be threatened. If the plaintiff is an organization, it must allege that some of its members use and enjoy that amenity. In *Morton,* for example, it was not enough for the plaintiffs to allege that they were interested in protecting the Mineral King Valley in California. Instead, they had to allege that they used and enjoyed the valley.[291]

---

279. *Id.* The reason underlying this analysis is well explained in Jones v. District of Columbia Redev. Land Agency, *supra* note 17, 499 F.2d at 511-13, 4 ELR at 20483. In brief, the harm to be remedied by the EIS is of two kinds—the actual degradation of the environment, and the failure of federal agency officials to take the environment into account in the manner prescribed by NEPA.

280. *Realty Income Trust, supra* note 277, 564 F.2d at 456-57, 7 ELR at 20545 (emphasis in original).

281. *Id.* at 457, 7 ELR at 20546.

282. Environmental Defense Fund, Inc. v. Froehlke, *supra* note 273, 477 F.2d at 1037, 3 ELR at 20384.

283. *Save Our Ecosystem, supra* note 193, 747 F.2d at 1250, 15 ELR at 20040 (quoting Alpine Lakes Protection Soc'y v. Schlapfer, *supra* note 274, 518 F.2d at 1090, 5 ELR at 20322).

284. Natural Resources Defense Council, Inc. v. Callaway, 524 F.2d 79, 90, 5 ELR 20640, 20648 (2d Cir. 1975). Injunctive relief in a NEPA case runs both against the federal agency and, where private activity is permitted, against the company. See FED. R. CIV. P. 65(d); *Foundation on Economic Trends, supra* note 259, 756 F.2d at 155, 15 ELR at 20254; Biderman v. Morton, 497 F.2d 1141, 1147, 4 ELR 20487, 20490 (2d Cir. 1974); Silva v. Romney, 473 F.2d 287, 289-90, 3 ELR 20082, 20083-84 (1st Cir. 1973).

285. *See* Environmental Defense Fund, Inc. v. Marsh, *supra* note 267, 651 F.2d at 1005-06, 11 ELR at 21022; Natural Resources Defense Council, Inc. v. Callaway, *supra* note 284, 524 F.2d at 95, 5 ELR at 20648; Jones v. District of Columbia Redev. Land Agency, *supra* note 17, 499 F.2d at 512-13, 4 ELR at 20483. Relicensing is more akin to an irreversible and irretrievable commitment of resources than a mere continuation of the status quo. See Confederated Tribes & Bands of the Yakima Indian Nation v. FERC, 746 F.2d 466, 475-76, 14 ELR 20593, 20597-98 (9th Cir. 1984) *cert. denied,* 471 U.S. 1116 (1985). For examples of the numerous cases granting injunctive relief to bar or severely limit an action pending completion of an adequate EIS, *see Save Our Ecosystem, supra* note 193, 747 F.2d at 1250, 15 ELR at 20040; Sierra Club v. United States Army Corps of Eng'rs, 701 F.2d 1011, 1034, 13 ELR 20326, 20337-38 (2d Cir. 1983); Environmental Defense Fund, Inc. v. Marsh, *supra* note 267, 651 F.2d at 1005-06, 11 ELR at 21022; Natural Resources Defense Council, Inc. v. Callaway, *supra* note 284, 524 F.2d at 94-95, 5 ELR at 20647-48; Manatee County v. Gorsuch, 554 F. Supp. 778, 794, 13 ELR 20180, 20187-88 (M.D. Fla. 1982); Montgomery v. Ellis, 364 F. Supp. 517, 535, 3 ELR 20845, 20852-53 (N.D. Ala. 1973).

286. 456 U.S. 305, 12 ELR 20538 (1982). In *Romero-Barcelo,* the Court held that federal courts are not compelled to issue injunctions against violators of §402 of the FWPCA, since the Act provided for alternative means of enforcement.

287. 480 U.S. 531, 17 ELR 20574 (1987). In *Gambell,* the Court held that the Ninth Circuit erroneously applied a presumption of irreparable injury to the question of whether injunctive relief was appropriate for a violation of §810 of the Alaska National Interest Lands Conservation Act (ANILCA). Section 810(a) of ANILCA requires an evaluation of any decision relating to the use or disposition of public lands before that decision is made of the impact on Alaskan native subsistence uses and needs. If the evaluation indicates that the proposed use would significantly restrict subsistence uses, the proposal may not be implemented until certain notice and mitigation requirements are met. 16 U.S.C. §3120(a) (1985). Concluding that the environment can be protected without a presumption of irreparable harm, the Court questioned the Ninth Circuit's adherence to the principle that "[i]rreparable damage is presumed when an agency fails to evaluate thoroughly the environmental impact of a proposed action." *Gambell, supra,* 480 U.S. at 544-45, 17 ELR at 20577.

288. *See* Northern Cheyenne Tribe v. Hodel, *supra* note 272, 851 F.2d at 1158, 18 ELR at 20867; Save the Yaak Comm. v. Block, *supra* note 272, 840 F.2d at 722, 18 ELR at 20873; *see also* Sierra Club v. United States Forest Service, 843 F.2d 1190, 1195, 18 ELR 20749, 20752 (9th Cir. 1988).

289. *See generally* F. ANDERSON, *supra* note 35, at 283; W. RODGERS, *supra* note 20, at 23-30.

290. 405 U.S. 727, 2 ELR 20192 (1972). *See* Defenders of Wildlife, Friends of Animals and Their Environment v. Hodel, 851 F.2d 1035, 1039-40, 18 ELR 21343, 21345-46 (8th Cir. 1988). The injury may be threatened or contingent. *Id.*

291. The Supreme Court held that the Sierra Club's allegation of interest in environmental protection was insufficient for standing, but noted in a footnote that actual use would suffice. Sierra Club v. Morton, *supra* note 290, 405 U.S. at 735 n.8, 2 ELR at 20194 n.8. On re-

As another early NEPA case, *United States v. Students Challenging Regulatory Agency Procedures (SCRAP)*,[292] made clear, the Supreme Court's broad view of standing is not diminished by pervasiveness of the alleged environmental injury. In *SCRAP*, the Court found that plaintiffs had standing to challenge nationwide freight rates for recycled goods. The environmental injury alleged—damage to plaintiffs' recreational use and enjoyment of forests, streams, mountains, and other resources in the Washington, D.C., metropolitan region—was widely shared, but still gave plaintiffs standing to sue.

Given these and subsequent cases, plaintiffs who are individuals affected by a proposed action, organizations whose members include such individuals, or state or local governments[293] whose citizens are so affected should not have difficulty establishing standing if the required injury in fact exists and it is set out with sufficient particularity. Some business plaintiffs, however, may have difficulty establishing that their interests are within the zone of interests protected by NEPA, a prerequisite to standing under the Act.[294] Business plaintiffs are a significant proportion of the parties filing NEPA cases,[295] though, and in some of these cases environmental and business interests coincide, so that the two types of organizations join as plaintiffs.[296]

Inapplicability of NEPA

Defendants and intervenors have attempted to escape judicial enforcement of NEPA by arguing that their proposals lie outside the coverage of the Act. Again, such arguments may be easily overcome and have met with little success. This is due largely to NEPA's broad mandate as affirmed by the Supreme Court; the Act applies to all agency actions, absent clear conflicts of statutory authority.[297] Only one significant exception has been carved into NEPA's reach, partly by Congress[298] and partly by the courts:[299] certain limited regulatory activities conducted for purposes of environmental protection are said to constitute the "functional equivalents" of EISs.

One important question regarding NEPA's applicability is the extent to which the statute covers toxic waste cleanups under the Comprehensive Environmental Response, Compensation, and Liability Act (CERCLA), also known as Superfund. This promises to be a major issue in coming years.[300]

Procedural Defenses

NEPA defendants and intervenors may raise general procedural defenses not directly related to NEPA, such as ripeness, exhaustion, laches, and mootness. These defenses, like those discussed above, have rarely been successful. Ripeness is covered by CEQ regulations; the other procedural defenses have been addressed by the courts.

Two NEPA regulations bear directly on the procedural aspects of judicial relief. Both were adopted to assuage apprehensions that the new regulations—designed in part to relieve delay in the NEPA process—could, paradoxically, have the opposite effect. Fears were expressed that because the regulations had a greater number of explicit commands, there would be more provisions to violate, and would therefore be earlier and more frequent litigation that could undermine the delay-reducing purpose of the regulations. The CEQ responded by adding the two provisions on judicial relief. The first directly addresses the issue of ripeness and provides that it is the

Council's intention that judicial review of agency compliance with these regulations not occur before any agency

mand, the appropriate allegations of use were made and standing was achieved. Sierra Club v. Morton, 348 F. Supp. 219, 2 ELR 20576 (N.D. Cal. 1972). *See also* Sierra Club v. SCM Corp., 747 F.2d 99, 14 ELR 20890 (2d Cir. 1984).

292. 412 U.S. 669, 3 ELR 20536 (1973). *See also* Oregon Envtl. Council v. Kunzman, *supra* note 162, 817 F.2d at 491-92, 17 ELR at 20758 (9th Cir. 1987) (plaintiffs have standing to challenge nationwide spraying program because they live in state that is part of program, and thus have "geographical nexus").

293. A significant proportion of NEPA litigation typically includes state or local governmental plaintiffs. The proportion has ranged from 28 percent of the cases filed in 1978, COUNCIL ON ENVIRONMENTAL QUALITY, ENVIRONMENTAL QUALITY 1979, at 589 (1979), to 14 percent of those filed in 1982, COUNCIL ON ENVIRONMENTAL QUALITY, ENVIRONMENTAL QUALITY 1983, at 266 (1984) (Table 7-2), to 30 percent of those filed in 1985, COUNCIL ON ENVIRONMENTAL QUALITY, ENVIRONMENTAL QUALITY 1986, at 243 (1988) (Table B-4). These percentages were computed by comparing the number of plaintiffs by category to the total number of suits filed. *See* City of Davis v. Coleman, 521 F.2d 661, 5 ELR 20633 (9th Cir. 1975); *see also* Louisiana v. Lee, *supra* note 113, 596 F. Supp. at 649-50, 15 ELR at 20142.

294. *See, e.g.,* Lone Pine Steering Comm. v. EPA, 600 F. Supp. 1487, 1499 n.2, 15 ELR 20109, 20116 n.2 (D.N.J.), *aff'd,* 777 F.2d 882, 888 n.4, 16 ELR 20009, 20012 n.4 (3d Cir. 1985); *cert. denied,* 476 U.S. 1115 (1986). It is worth observing, however, that both the district court and the court of appeals noted plaintiffs' failure to plead or demonstrate their interest in general environmental concerns. *Id.*

295. Business and industry plaintiffs were involved in 19 percent of the NEPA cases filed in 1978, COUNCIL ON ENVIRONMENTAL QUALITY, ENVIRONMENTAL QUALITY 1979, at 589 (1979); in 12 percent in 1983, COUNCIL ON ENVIRONMENTAL QUALITY, ENVIRONMENTAL QUALITY 1984, at 523 (1986) (Table 12-2); and in 7.4 percent in 1985, COUNCIL ON ENVIRONMENTAL QUALITY, ENVIRONMENTAL QUALITY 1986, at 243 (1988) (Table B-4).

296. For example, NEPA litigation challenging construction of locks and dams that facilitate barge traffic on rivers may be brought both by environmental groups and by railroads, whose interests can be assumed to be at least partly competitive. *See* Environmental Defense Fund, Inc. v. Marsh, *supra* note 267, 651 F.2d at 983, 11 ELR at 21012 (5th Cir. 1981) (EDF joined with Louisville & Nashville R.R. Co. in litigation over Tennessee-Tombigbee Waterway); Izaak Walton League v. Marsh, 655 F.2d 346, 11 ELR 20707 (D.C. Cir.) (environmental organization joined with Atcheson, Topeka & Santa Fe Ry. in suit concerning locks on Mississippi River), *cert. denied,* 454 U.S. 1092 (1981).

297. Flint Ridge Dev. Co. v. Scenic Rivers Ass'n, *supra* note 42, 426 U.S. at 777-78, 6 ELR at 20529. *See also* Concerned About Trident v. Rumsfeld, 555 F.2d 817, 823, 6 ELR 20787, 20789-90 (D.C. Cir. 1977); *cf.* Ellis & Smith, *supra* note 91 (analyzing scope of "federal action" subject to NEPA).

298. All of EPA's actions under the Clean Air Act, and some of those under the FWPCA, are exempted. 15 U.S.C. §793(c)(1) (no action taken under Clean Air Act is "major Federal action" within meaning of NEPA); FWPCA §511, 33 U.S.C. §1371(c)(1), ELR STAT. FWPCA 061 (only construction of publicly owned treatment works under 33 U.S.C. §1281 and issuance of new pollution source permits under *id.* §§1316, 1342 not exempted).

299. *See* Portland Cement Ass'n v. Ruckelshaus, 486 F.2d 375, 3 ELR 20642 (D.C. Cir. 1973), *cert. denied,* 417 U.S. 921 (1974); *see also* W. RODGERS, *supra* note 20, at 764.

300. The issue was raised but not decided in *Lone Pine Steering Comm., supra* note 294, 600 F. Supp. at 1488, 15 ELR at 20110. A state court in California has applied the state's NEPA equivalent to a Superfund cleanup. *See* County of Kern v. State Dep't of Health Servs., No. 190784 (Cal. Super. Ct., County of Kern, 1985). The legislative history of Superfund makes clear the intent that NEPA apply in some, but not all, situations. *See generally* S. REP. No. 948, 96th Cong., 2d Sess. 61 (1980).

has filed the final environmental impact statement or has made a final finding of no significant impact (when such a finding will result in action affecting the environment), or takes action that will result in irreparable injury.[301]

The second provision asserts the CEQ's intention that a "trivial violation" of the regulation "not give rise to any independent cause of action."[302] Litigation prior to an agency's final decision and litigation on minor technical flaws in the agency's procedure under NEPA are thus discouraged.

The doctrine of exhaustion of administrative remedies raises the question of the degree to which objectors must make their environmental reservations known to an agency as a condition of later asserting them in court. There is a certain tension between an agency's NEPA obligations and this more traditional doctrine of administrative law. NEPA obligates an agency to gather information itself to protect the public rather than to act as an umpire between opposing parties, but a basic tenet of administrative law demands that one who has information bring it to the agency's attention before seeking judicial review.[303] Given NEPA's mandate that agencies consider all pertinent environmental impacts, courts have favored demanding more from agencies than from plaintiffs and have quite properly been reluctant to penalize plaintiffs for tardily bringing to an agency's attention what the agency itself should have known from its own studies.[304]

Standards of Review of NEPA Cases

As noted above, the majority of NEPA cases filed allege that an EIS should have been prepared but was not, or that an EIS that was prepared was inadequate.[305] Hence,

most substantive review of NEPA cases involves these issues. A considerably smaller number of cases allege inadequate EAs or other violations of the Act.[306] The following discussion briefly analyzes the standards of review employed by courts examining these various claims.

Failure to Prepare an EIS

Courts have applied various standards in reviewing complaints alleging that EISs should have been prepared. The majority have employed a "reasonableness" standard, applying searching scrutiny to an agency's determination that no EIS was required.[307] A minority have employed the "arbitrary and capricious" standard, a standard typically applied in the field of administrative law.[308] Finally, a few courts have taken middle positions.[309]

The Supreme Court, while stating that it was only deciding the "narrow question" of what standard of review governed failure to supplement an EIS, appears to have come down on the side of the arbitrary and capricious standard.[310] In doing so, however, the Court stressed that a "searching and careful" inquiry must be made[311] and observed that the difference between the two standards "is not of great pragmatic consequence."[312] "Accordingly," the Court continued, "our decision today will not require a substantial reworking of long-established NEPA law."[313]

The rationale for a searching and careful review of an agency's threshold decision on whether to prepare an EIS therefore remains valid. That rationale was clearly articulated by the Fifth Circuit in *Save Our Ten Acres v. Kreger:*[314]

> NEPA was intended not only to insure that the appropriate responsible official considered the environmental effects of the project, but also provided Congress (and others receiving such recommendation or proposal) with a sound basis for evaluating the environmental aspects of the particular project or proposal. The spirit of the Act would die aborning if a facile, *ex parte* decision that the project was

301. 40 C.F.R. §1500.3, *infra* at 51.

302. *Id.* See Preamble, *supra* note 28, at 55981, *infra* at 251. Of course the converse is also the case—significant violations of the regulations do provide grounds for judicial relief. This is precisely how NEPA and its regulations are enforced.

   The question of ripeness overlaps with that of when a "proposal" exists that may require an EIS. This issue is discussed *supra* notes 83-87 and accompanying text. *See also* NEPA IN THE COURTS, *supra* note 35, at 46-47.

303. *See* Greene County v. FPC, *supra* note 134, 455 F.2d at 419, 2 ELR at 20019-20; NEPA IN THE COURTS, *supra* note 35, at 45-46. In adopting its "scoping" regulation, *see supra* notes 122-26 and accompanying text, the CEQ clearly intended to make sure that interested persons or groups are alerted to pending federal proposals before NEPA studies are undertaken. In this way, the concerns of these parties can be known and addressed. However, other implications also follow. The opportunity to comment makes it more difficult for a person or group who is given notice but does not participate to come to court later and complain.

304. *See* Park Count Resource Council v. United States Dep't of Agriculture, 817 F.2d 609, 619, 17 ELR 20851, 20854 (10th Cir. 1987). Anderson quite appropriately suggests a greater obligation to exhaust remedies where "extensive administrative proceedings" precede the agency's action. NEPA IN THE COURTS, *supra* note 35, at 46.

   Courts have been as reluctant to apply the doctrine of laches to preclude NEPA claims as they have been to dismiss for failure to exhaust administrative remedies. *See, e.g.,* Park County Resource Council, *supra*, 817 F.2d at 617-19, 17 ELR at 20854; Headwaters, Inc. v. BLM, Medford Dist., 665 F. Supp. 873, 876, 18 ELR 21370, 21371 (D. Or. 1987); *but see* National Parks & Conservation Ass'n v. Hodel, 679 F. Supp. 49, 54 (D.D.C. 1987) (laches bars action).

   Courts may also be reluctant to declare a NEPA complaint moot when an agency has produced an inadequate EIS, but indicates it will not implement the decision it made based on that statement, if the agency's NEPA violation is capable of repetition but evading review. *See* Oregon Envtl. Council v. Kunzman, *supra* note 162, 817 F.2d at 492, 17 ELR at 20758.

305. *See supra* note 257 and accompanying text.

306. COUNCIL ON ENVIRONMENTAL QUALITY, ENVIRONMENTAL QUALITY 1986, at 243 (1988) (Table B-4).

307. *See* Hoskins, *Judicial Review of an Agency's Decision Not to Prepare an Environmental Impact Statement*, 18 ELR 10331, 10339-45 (1988) (analyzing cases applying reasonableness standard).

308. *Id.* at 10336-39 (analyzing cases applying arbitrary and capricious standard).

309. Several courts have questioned whether there is any difference between the standards. *See* Sierra Club v. Marsh, 769 F.2d 868, 871, 15 ELR 20911, 20912 (1st Cir. 1985); River Road Alliance v. Corps of Eng'rs, 764 F.2d 445, 449, 15 ELR 20518, 20519; Quinonez-Lopez v. Coco Lagoon Dev. Corp., 733 F.2d 1, 3, 14 ELR 20445, 20446 (1st Cir. 1984); Lower Alloways Creek Twp. v. Public Serv. Elec. & Gas Co., 687 F.2d 732, 742, 12 ELR 21029, 21033-34 (3d Cir. 1982); Boles v. Onton Dock Inc., 659 F.2d 74, 75, 11 ELR 20986, 20987 (6th Cir. 1981); *see also* Marsh v. Oregon Natural Resources Council, *supra* note 16, 57 U.S.L.W. at 4509 n.23, 19 ELR at 20753 n.23; City of Alexandria v. Federal Highway Admin., 756 F.2d 1014, 1017 (4th Cir. 1985); Committee for Auto Responsibility v. Solomon, 603 F.2d 992, 9 ELR 20575 (D.C. Cir. 1973); Peshlakai v. Duncan, 476 F. Supp. 1247, 1252, 9 ELR 20690, 20692 (D.D.C. 1979); *cert. denied,* 445 U.S. 915 (1980).

310. Marsh v. Oregon Natural Resources Council, *supra* note 16, 57 U.S.L.W. at 4508, 19 ELR at 20754-55; *see id.* at 4508-09, 19 ELR at 20754-55.

311. *Id.* at 4509, 19 ELR at 20754-55. The Court also emphasized that the ultimate standard of review was a narrow one.

312. *Id.* at 4509 n.23, 19 ELR at 20753 n.23.

313. *Id.*

314. *Supra* note 112, 472 F.2d 463, 3 ELR 20041 (5th Cir. 1973).

minor or did not significantly affect the environment were too well shielded from impartial review. Every such decision pretermits all consideration of that which Congress has directed be considered "to the fullest extent possible." The primary decision to give or bypass the consideration required by the Act must be subject to inspection under a more searching standard.[315]

This guidance retains its wisdom. The threshold determination of whether to prepare an EIS is not the informed exercise of agency discretion, which should properly receive considerable deference. Rather, that determination is the agency's decision whether or not to inform its discretion by preparing an EIS that will provide the information it needs to evaluate the environmental consequences of a project. Judicial solicitude for agency discretion is proper when, based on whatever record the law requires, the agency exercises *informed* discretion. An agency's decision not to prepare an EIS, however, is a decision not to inform its discretion and therefore invites more exacting judicial scrutiny. An agency should not be enabled to bypass the entire EIS requirement with a cursory assessment to which a court gives an equally cursory review.

Inadequacy of an EIS or EA

Cases challenging the adequacy of EISs or EAs are reviewed under a less disputed standard than decisions on whether to prepare EISs.[316] This is primarily due to the fact that such cases present factual rather than legal issues, and courts traditionally afford substantial deference to agency determinations of fact. While NEPA does not specifically provide for judicial review of EISs, these documents are usually reviewed under the Administrative Procedure Act[317] standard for review of agency actions: an agency action is to be set aside if found to be "arbitrary, capricious, an abuse of discretion, or otherwise not in accordance with law,"[318] or "without observance of procedure as required by law."[319] EAs are also judicially reviewable under this standard,[320] and allegations of EA inadequacy form a significant portion of NEPA litigation.[321]

Other Nontrivial Violations of NEPA

While the CEQ does not intend for trivial violations of its

regulations to give rise to independent actions,[322] nontrivial violations of the law or regulations may do so. These violations constitute the third most frequent group of allegations made in NEPA suits.[323] Where agency decisionmaking is alleged to violate NEPA regulations, the same standard applies as in cases alleging inadequate EISs—the arbitrary and capricious standard.[324]

Substantive Review of NEPA Actions

One final issue concerning judicial review merits attention—the degree to which a court can reverse an agency decision made in compliance with NEPA procedures. NEPA and its procedures seek to ensure environmentally responsible decisionmaking, but an agency may quite possibly comply with the Act and still fail to choose the action most consistent with the national environmental policy stated in §§101 and 102(1) of the Act. Early in NEPA's development there were considerable indications that the judiciary would go beyond procedure and show a greater willingness to conduct substantive review of final agency decisions.[325] The Supreme Court has limited, but has not completely foreclosed, such developments. In *Vermont Yankee Nuclear Power Corp. v. Natural Resources Defense Council, Inc.*,[326] the Court said that NEPA sets forth "significant substantive goals" for the nation, but that its mandate to the agencies is "essentially procedural."[327] That remains an accurate statement.[328] Even acknowledging the deference properly due to agencies in their decisionmaking, CEQ has certainly taken the view that their actions can be so violative of NEPA's "substantive requirements"[329] as to merit review under the arbitrary and capricious standard.[330]

---

315. *Id.* at 466, 3 ELR at 20042.

316. Indeed, the standard of judicial review in this area has been accurately described as "relatively stable." D. MANDELKER, NEPA LAW & LITIGATION §10.13, at 30 (1984); *see* FEDERAL ENVIRONMENTAL LAW, *supra* note 35, at 375.

317. 5 U.S.C. §706.

318. *Id.* §706(2)(A). *See* Oregon Envtl. Council v. Kunzman, *supra* note 162, 817 F.2d at 492, 17 ELR at 20759; Sierra Club v. United States Army Corps of Eng'rs, 772 F.2d 1043, 1050, 15 ELR 20998, 21001 (2d Cir. 1985).

319. 5 U.S.C. §706(2)(D). *See* Oregon Envtl. Council v. Kunzman, *supra* note 162, 817 F.2d at 492, 17 ELR at 20759; Natural Resources Defense Council, Inc. v. SEC, 606 F.2d 1031, 9 ELR 20367 (D.C. Cir. 1979). *See also* 5 U.S.C. §706(2)(C) ("in excess of statutory jurisdiction, authority, or limitation. . . .").

320. Hanly v. Kleindienst, 471 F.2d 823, 2 ELR 20717 (2d Cir. 1972), *cert. denied*, 412 U.S. 908 (1973).

321. Seven of 77 NEPA suits filed in 1985 alleged this ground while three others alleged that an EA should have been prepared but was not. COUNCIL ON ENVIRONMENTAL QUALITY, ENVIRONMENTAL QUALITY 1986, at 242 (1988) (Table B-3).

322. 40 C.F.R. §1500.3, *infra* at 51.

323. In 1985, 12 of 77 suits brought under NEPA were filed on bases other than those mentioned above. An additional five concerned the filing or the adequacy of supplemental EISs. COUNCIL ON ENVIRONMENTAL QUALITY, ENVIRONMENTAL QUALITY 1986, at 242 (1988) (Table B-3).

324. *See supra* notes 316-21 and accompanying text.

325. *See* W. RODGERS, *supra* note 20, at 738-50; *see also* COUNCIL ON ENVIRONMENTAL QUALITY, ENVIRONMENTAL QUALITY 1978, at 403-05 (1979) (summarizing cases).

326. 435 U.S. 519, 8 ELR 20288 (1978).

327. *Id.* at 558, 8 ELR at 20297. *See* Baltimore Gas & Elec. Co. v. Natural Resources Defense Council, Inc., 462 U.S. 87, 13 ELR 20544 (1983); Strycker's Bay Neighborhood Council v. Karlen, 444 U.S. 223, 10 ELR 20079 (1980); Weinstein, *Substantive Review Under NEPA after Vermont Yankee IV*, 36 SYRACUSE L. REV. 837 (1985). The Court has defined the judicial role as that of ensuring that agencies take a "hard look" at environmental consequences in their actions under NEPA. Kleppe v. Sierra Club, *supra* note 14, 427 U.S. at 390, 6 ELR at 20532. This means that a reviewing court must make a pragmatic judgment as to whether the form, content, and preparation of the EIS foster "both informed decisionmaking and informed public participation." Northwest Coalition for Alternatives to Pesticides v. Lyng, *supra* note 123, 844 F.2d at 590-91, 18 ELR at 20739.

328. Robertson v. Methow Valley Citizens Council, *supra* note 14, 57 U.S.L.W. at 4501-02, 19 ELR at 20746-48.

329. 40 C.F.R. §1500.1(a), *infra* at 51; *see supra* note 328.

330. *See* FEDERAL ENVIRONMENTAL LAW, *supra* note 35; W. RODGERS, *supra* note 20, at §7.5; Weinstein, *supra* note 327. *See also* 40 C.F.R. §§1500.1, 1502.2(d), 1505.1(a), 1505.2(b), *infra* at 51, 54, 59, 59. The most recent Supreme Court discussion of this issue, however, further narrows the opportunity for review beyond the essentially procedural. Robertson v. Methow Valley Citizens Council, *supra* note 14.

IV. CONCLUSION

The congressional framers of NEPA sought to change the way the federal government operates. After two decades of experience, it may fairly be concluded that they succeeded. Federal officials know that they must consider the environment in all that they do. Those who care about the environment are armed with NEPA's action-forcing provisions. Those less environmentally inclined are brought into line by this congressional enactment, butressed by the ever-present prospect of litigation. In short, NEPA works.

Statutes

National Environmental Policy Act
42 U.S.C §§4321-4370d

National Environmental Policy Act
42 U.S.C. §§4321-4370d

§ 4321.　[NEPA §2]
Congressional declaration of purpose

The purposes of this chapter are: To declare a national policy which will encourage productive and enjoyable harmony between man and his environment; to promote efforts which will prevent or eliminate damage to the environment and biosphere and stimulate the health and welfare of man; to enrich the understanding of the ecological systems and natural resources important to the Nation; and to establish a Council on Environmental Quality.

(Pub. L. 91-190, §2, Jan. 1, 1970, 83 Stat. 852.)

Short Title

Section 1 of Pub. L. 91-190 provided: "That this Act (enacting this chapter) may be cited as the 'National Environmental Policy Act of 1969'."

Pollution Prosecution

Pub. L. 101-593, title II, Nov. 16, 1990, 104 Stat. 2962, provided that:

"SEC. 201. SHORT TITLE.

"This title may be cited as the 'Pollution Prosecution Act of 1990'.

"SEC. 202. EPA OFFICE OF CRIMINAL INVESTIGATION.

"(a) The Administrator of the Environmental Protection Agency (hereinafter referred to as the 'Administrator') shall increase the number of criminal investigators assigned to the Office of Criminal Investigations by such numbers as may be necessary to assure that the number of criminal investigators assigned to the office—

"(1) for the period October 1, 1991, through September 30, 1992, is not less than 72;

"(2) for the period October 1, 1992, through September 30, 1993, is not less than 110;

"(3) for the period October 1, 1993, through September 30, 1994, is not less than 123;

"(4) for the period October 1, 1994, through September 30, 1995, is not less than 160;

"(5) beginning October 1, 1995, is not less than 200.

"(b) For fiscal year 1991 and in each of the following 4 fiscal years, the Administrator shall, during each such fiscal year, provide increasing numbers of additional support staff to the Office of Criminal Investigations.

"(c) The head of the Office of Criminal Investigations shall be a position in the competitive service as defined in 2102 of title 5 U.S.C. or a career reserve position as defined in 3132(A) of title 5 U.S.C. and the head of such office shall report directly, without intervening review or approval, to the Assistant Administrator for Enforcement.

"SEC. 203. CIVIL INVESTIGATORS.

"The Administrator, as soon as practicable following the date of the enactment of this Act [Nov. 16, 1990], but no later than September 30, 1991, shall increase by fifty the number of civil investigators assigned to assist the Office of Enforcement in developing and prosecuting civil and administrative actions and carrying out its other functions.

"SEC. 204. NATIONAL TRAINING INSTITUTE.

"The Administrator shall, as soon as practicable but no later than September 30, 1991 establish within the Office of Enforcement the National Enforcement Training Institute. It shall be the function of the Institute, among others, to train Federal, State, and local lawyers, inspectors, civil and criminal investigators, and technical experts in the enforcement of the Nation's environmental laws.

"SEC. 205. AUTHORIZATION.

"For the purposes of carrying out the provisions of this Act [probably should be 'this title'], there is authorized to be appropriated to the Environmental Protection Agency $13,000,000 for fiscal year 1991, $18,000,000 for fiscal year 1992, $20,000,000 for fiscal year 1993, $26,000,000 for fiscal year 1994, and $33,000,000 for fiscal year 1995."

Subchapter I—Policies and Goals

§ 4331.   [NEPA §101]

Congressional declaration of national environmental policy

(a) The Congress, recognizing the profound impact of man's activity on the interrelations of all components of the natural environment, particularly the profound influences of population growth, high-density urbanization, industrial expansion, resource exploitation, and new and expanding technological advances and recognizing further the critical importance of restoring and maintaining environmental quality to the overall welfare and development of man, declares that it is the continuing policy of the Federal Government, in cooperation with State and local governments, and other concerned public and private organizations, to use all practicable means and measures, including financial and technical assistance, in a manner calculated to foster and promote the general welfare, to create and maintain conditions under which man and nature can exist in productive harmony, and fulfill the social, economic, and other requirements of present and future generations of Americans.

(b) In order to carry out the policy set forth in this chapter, it is the continuing responsibility of the Federal Government to use all practicable means, consistent with other essential considerations of national policy, to improve and coordinate Federal plans, functions, programs, and resources to the end that the Nation may—

(1) fulfill the responsibilities of each generation as trustee of the environment for succeeding generations;

(2) assure for all Americans safe, healthful, productive, and esthetically and culturally pleasing surroundings;

(3) attain the widest range of beneficial uses of the environment without degradation, risk to health or safety, or other undesirable and unintended consequences;

(4) preserve important historic, cultural, and natural aspects of our national heritage, and maintain, wherever possible, an environment which supports diversity and variety of individual choice;

(5) achieve a balance between population and resource use which will permit high standards of living and a wide sharing of life's amenities; and

(6) enhance the quality of renewable resources and approach the maximum attainable recycling of depletable resources.

(c) The Congress recognizes that each person should enjoy a healthful environment and that each person has a responsibility to contribute to the preservation and enhancement of the environment.

(Pub. L. 91-190, title I, §101, Jan. 1, 1970, 83 Stat. 852.)

Commission On Population Growth And The American Future

Pub. L. 91-213, Sec. 1-9, Mar. 16, 1970, 84 Stat. 67-69, established the Commission on Population Growth and the American Future to conduct and sponsor such studies and research and make such recommendations as might be necessary to provide information and education to all levels of government in the United States, and to our people regarding a broad range of problems associated with population growth and their implications for America's future; prescribed the composition of the Commission; provided for the appointment of its members, and the designation of a Chairman and Vice Chairman; required a majority of the members of the Commission to constitute a quorum, but allowed a lesser number to conduct hearings; prescribed the compensation of members of the Commission; required the Commission to conduct an inquiry into certain prescribed aspects of population growth in the United States and its foreseeable social consequences; provided for the appointment of an Executive Director and other personnel and prescribed their compensation; authorized the Commission to enter into contracts with public agencies, private firms, institutions, and individuals for the conduct of research and surveys, the preparation of reports, and other activities necessary to the discharge of its duties, and to request from any Federal department or agency any information and assistance it deems necessary to carry out its functions; required the General Services Administration to provide administrative services for the Commission on a reimbursable basis; required the Commission to submit an interim report to the President and the Congress one year after it was established and to submit its final report two years after Mar. 16, 1970; terminated the Commission sixty days after the date of the submission of its final report; and authorized to be appropriated, out of any money in the Treasury not otherwise appropriated, such amounts as might be necessary to carry out the provisions of Pub. L. 91-213.

§ 4332.   [NEPA §102]

Cooperation of agencies; reports; availability of information; recommendations; international and national coordination of efforts

The Congress authorizes and directs that, to the fullest extent possible: (1) the policies, regulations, and public laws of the United States shall be interpreted and administered in accordance with the policies set forth in this chapter, and (2) all agencies of the Federal Government shall—

(A) utilize a systematic, interdisciplinary approach which will insure the integrated use of the natural and social sciences and the environmental design arts in planning and in decisonmaking which may have an impact on man's environment;

(B) identify and develop methods and procedures, in consultation with the Council on Environmental Quality established by subchapter II of this chapter, which will insure that presently unquantified environmental amenities and values may be given appropriate consideration in decisionmaking along with economic and technical considerations;

(C) include in every recommendation or report on proposals for legislation and other major Federal actions significantly affecting the quality of the human environment, a detailed statement by the responsible official on—

(i) the environmental impact of the proposed action,

(ii) any adverse environmental effects which cannot be avoided should the proposal be implemented,

(iii) alternatives to the proposed action,

(iv) the relationship between local short-term uses of man's environment and the maintenance and enhancement of long-term productivity, and

(v) any irreversible and irretrievable commitments of resources which would be involved in the proposed action should it be implemented.

Prior to making any detailed statement, the responsible Federal official shall consult with and obtain the comments of any Federal agency which has jurisdiction by law or special expertise with respect to any environmental impact involved. Copies of such statement and the comments and views of the appropriate Federal, State, and local agencies, which are authorized to develop and enforce environmental standards, shall be made available to the President, the Council on Environmental Quality and to the public as provided by section 552 of title 5, and shall accompany the proposal through the existing agency review processes;

(D) Any detailed statement required under subparagraph (C) after January 1, 1970, for any major Federal action funded under a program of grants to States shall not be deemed to be legally insufficient solely by reason of having been prepared by a State agency or official, if:

(i) the State agency or official has statewide jurisdiction and has the responsibility for such action,

(ii) the responsible Federal official furnishes guidance and participates in such preparation,

(iii) the responsible Federal official independently evaluates such statement prior to its approval and adoption, and

(iv) after January 1, 1976, the responsible Federal official provides early notification to, and solicits the views of, any other State or any Federal land management entity of any action or any alternative thereto which may have significant impacts upon such State or affected Federal land management entity and, if there is any disagreement on such impacts, prepares a written assessment of such impacts and views for incorporation into such detailed statement.

The procedures in this subparagraph shall not relieve the Federal official of his responsibilities for the scope, objectivity, and content of the entire statement or of any other responsibility under this chapter; and further, this subparagraph does not affect the legal sufficiency of statements prepared by State agencies with less than statewide jurisdiction.[1]

(E) study, develop, and describe appropriate alternatives to recommended courses of action in any proposal which involves unresolved conflicts concerning alternative uses of available resources;

(F) recognize the worldwide and long-range character of environmental problems and, where consistent with the foreign policy of the United States, lend appropriate support to initiatives, resolutions, and programs designed to maximize international cooperation in anticipating and preventing a decline in the quality of mankind's world environment;

(G) make available to States, counties, municipalities, institutions, and individuals, advice and information useful in restoring, maintaining, and enhancing the quality of the environment;

(H) initiate and utilize ecological information in the planning and development of resource-oriented projects; and

(I) assist the Council on Environmental Quality established by subchapter II of this chapter.

(Pub. L. 91-190, title I, §102, Jan. 1, 1970, 83 Stat. 853; Pub. L. 94-83, Aug. 9, 1975, 89 Stat. 424.)

§ 4333.   [NEPA §103]

Conformity of administrative procedures to national environmental policy

All agencies of the Federal Government shall review their present statutory authority, administrative regulations, and current policies and procedures for the purpose of determining whether there are any deficiencies or inconsistencies therein which prohibit full compliance with the purposes and provisions of this chapter and shall propose to the President not later than July 1, 1971, such measures as may be necessary to bring their authority and policies into conformity with the intent, purposes, and procedures set forth in this chapter.

(Pub. L. 91-190, title I, §103, Jan. 1, 1970, 83 Stat. 854.)

§ 4334.   [NEPA §104]

Other statutory obligations of agencies

Nothing in section 4332 or 4333 of this title shall in any way affect the specific statutory obligations of any Federal agency (1) to comply with criteria or standards of environmental quality, (2) to coordinate or consult with any other Federal or State agency, or (3) to act, or refrain from acting contingent upon the recommendations or certification of any other Federal or State agency.

(Pub. L. 91-190, title I, §104, Jan. 1, 1970, 83 Stat. 854.)

§ 4335.   [NEPA §105]

Efforts supplemental to existing authorizations

The policies and goals set forth in this chapter are supplementary to those set forth in existing authorizations of Federal agencies.

(Pub. L. 91-190, title I, §105, Jan. 1, 1970, 83 Stat. 854.)

---

1.   So in original. The period probably should be a semicolon.

Subchapter II—Council on Environmental Quality

§ 4341.   [NEPA §201]

Reports to Congress; recommendations for legislation

The President shall transmit to the Congress annually beginning July 1, 1970, an Environmental Quality Report (hereinafter referred to as the "report") which shall set forth (1) the status and condition of the major natural, manmade, or altered environmental classes of the Nation, including, but not limited to, the air, the aquatic, including marine, estuarine, and fresh water, and the terrestrial environment, including, but not limited to, the forest, dryland, wetland, range, urban, suburban, and rural environment; (2) current and foreseeable trends in the quality, management and utilization of such environments and the effects of those trends on the social, economic, and other requirements of the Nation; (3) the adequacy of available natural resources for fulfilling human and economic requirements of the Nation in the light of expected population pressures; (4) a review of the programs and activities (including regulatory activities) of the Federal Government, the State and local governments, and nongovernmental entities or individuals, with particular reference to their effect on the environment and on the conservation, development and utilization of natural resources; and (5) a program for remedying the deficiencies of existing programs and activities, together with recommendations for legislation.

(Pub. L. 91-190, title II, §201, Jan. 1, 1970, 83 Stat. 854.)

§ 4342.   [NEPA §202]

Establishment; membership; Chairman; appointments

There is created in the Executive Office of the President a Council on Environmental Quality (hereinafter referred to as the "Council"). The Council shall be composed of three members who shall be appointed by the President to serve at his pleasure, by and with the advice and consent of the Senate. The President shall designate one of the members of the Council to serve as Chairman. Each member shall be a person who, as a result of his training, experience, and attainments, is exceptionally well qualified to analyze and interpret environmental trends and information of all kinds; to appraise programs and activities of the Federal Government in the light of the policy set forth in subchapter I of this chapter; to be conscious of and responsive to the scientific, economic, social, esthetic, and cultural needs and interests of the Nation; and to formulate and recommend national policies to promote the improvement of the quality of the environment.

(Pub. L. 91-190, title II, §202, Jan. 1, 1970, 83 Stat. 854.)

§ 4343.   [NEPA §203]

Employment of personnel, experts and consultants

(a) The Council may employ such officers and employees as may be necessary to carry out its functions under this chapter. In addition, the Council may employ and fix the compensation of such experts and consultants as may be necessary for the carrying out of its functions under this chapter, in accordance with section 3109 of title 5 (but without regard to the last sentence thereof).

(b) Notwithstanding section 1342 of title 31, the Council may accept and employ voluntary and uncompensated services in furtherance of the purposes of the Council.

(Pub. L. 91-190, title II, §203, Jan. 1, 1970, 83 Stat. 855; Pub. L. 94-52, §2, July 3, 1975, 89 Stat. 258.)

Codification

In subsec. (b), "section 1342 of title 31" substituted for "section 3679(b) of the Revised Statutes (31 U.S.C. 665(b))" on authority of Pub. L. 97-258, Sec. 4(b), Sept. 13, 1982, 96 Stat. 1067, the first section of which enacted Title 31, Money and Finance.

§ 4344.   [NEPA §204]

Duties and functions

It shall be the duty and function of the Council—

(1) to assist and advise the President in the preparation of the Environmental Quality Report required by section 4341 of this title;

(2) to gather timely and authoritative information concerning the conditions and trends in the quality of the environment both current

and prospective, to analyze and interpret such information for the purpose of determining whether such conditions and trends are interfering, or are likely to interfere, with the achievement of the policy set forth in subchapter I of this chapter, and to compile and submit to the President studies relating to such conditions and trends;

(3) to review and appraise the various programs and activities of the Federal Government in the light of the policy set forth in subchapter I of this chapter for the purpose of determining the extent to which such programs and activities are contributing to the achievement of such policy, and to make recommendations to the President with respect thereto;

(4) to develop and recommend to the President national policies to foster and promote the improvement of environmental quality to meet the conservation, social, economic, health, and other requirements and goals of the Nation;

(5) to conduct investigations, studies, surveys, research, and analyses relating to ecological systems and environmental quality;

(6) to document and define changes in the natural environment, including the plant and animal systems, and to accumulate necessary data and other information for a continuing analysis of these changes or trends and an interpretation of their underlying causes;

(7) to report at least once each year to the President on the state and condition of the environment; and

(8) to make and furnish such studies, reports thereon, and recommendations with respect to matters of policy and legislation as the President may request.

(Pub. L. 91-190, title II, §204, Jan. 1, 1970, 83 Stat. 855.)

§ 4345.   [NEPA §205]

Consultation with Citizens' Advisory Committee on Environmental Quality and other representatives

In exercising its powers, functions, and duties under this chapter, the Council shall—

(1) consult with the Citizens' Advisory Committee on Environmental Quality established by Executive Order numbered 11472, dated May 29, 1969, and with such representatives of science, industry, agriculture, labor, conservation organizations, State and local governments and other groups, as it deems advisable; and

(2) utilize, to the fullest extent possible, the services, facilities, and information (including statistical information) of public and private agencies and organizations, and individuals, in order that duplication of effort and expense may be avoided, thus assuring that the Council's activities will not unnecessarily overlap or conflict with similar activities authorized by law and performed by established agencies.

(Pub. L. 91-190, title II, §205, Jan. 1, 1970, 83 Stat. 855.)

§ 4346.   [NEPA §206]

Tenure and compensation of members

Members of the Council shall serve full time and the Chairman of the Council shall be compensated at the rate provided for Level II of the Executive Schedule Pay Rates (5 U.S.C. 5313). The other members of the Council shall be compensated at the rate provided for Level IV or[2] the Executive Schedule Pay Rates (5 U.S.C. 5315).

(Pub. L. 91-190, title II, §206, Jan. 1, 1970, 83 Stat. 856.)

§ 4346a.   [NEPA §207]

Travel reimbursement by private organizations and Federal, State, and local governments

The Council may accept reimbursements from any private nonprofit organization or from any department, agency, or instrumentality of the Federal Government, any State, or local government, for the reasonable travel expenses incurred by an officer or employee of the Council in connection with his attendance at any conference, seminar, or similar meeting conducted for the benefit of the Council.

(Pub. L. 91-190, title II, §207, as added Pub. L. 94-52, §3, July 3, 1975, 89 Stat. 258.)

---

2.   So in original. Probably should be "of".

§ 4346b.   [NEPA §208]
Expenditures in support of international activities

The Council may make expenditures in support of its international activities, including expenditures for: (1) international travel; (2) activities in implementation of international agreements; and (3) the support of international exchange programs in the United States and in foreign countries.

(Pub. L. 91-190, title II, §208, as added Pub. L. 94-52, §3, July 3, 1975, 89 Stat. 258.)

§ 4347.   [NEPA §209]
Authorization of appropriations

There are authorized to be appropriated to carry out the provisions of this chapter not to exceed $300,000 for fiscal year 1970, $700,000 for fiscal year 1971, and $1,000,000 for each fiscal year thereafter.

(Pub. L. 91-190, title II, §209, formerly §207, Jan. 1, 1970, 83 Stat. 856, renumbered §209, Pub. L. 94-52, §3, July 3, 1975, 89 Stat. 258.)

Subchapter III—Miscellaneous Provisions

§ 4361.

Plan for research, development, and demonstration

The Administrator of the Environmental Protection Agency shall transmit to the Congress, within 6 months after October 11, 1976, a comprehensive 5-year plan for environmental research, development, and demonstration. This plan shall be appropriately revised annually, and such revisions shall be transmitted to the Congress no later than two weeks after the President submits his annual budget to the Congress in such year.

(Pub. L. 94-475, §5, Oct. 11, 1976, 90 Stat. 2071.)

Codification

Section was enacted as part of the Environmental Research, Development, and Demonstration Authorization Act of 1976, and not as part of the National Environmental Policy Act of 1969 which comprises this chapter.

§ 4361a.

Budget projections in annual revisions of plan for research, development, and demonstration

The Administrator of the Environmental Protection Agency, in each annual revision of the five-year plan transmitted to the Congress under section 4361 of this title, shall include budget projections for a "no-growth" budget, for a "moderate-growth" budget, and for a "high-growth" budget. In addition, each such annual revision shall include a detailed explanation of the relationship of each budget projection to the existing laws which authorize the Administration's environmental research, development, and demonstration programs.

(Pub. L. 95-155, §4, Nov. 8, 1977, 91 Stat. 1258.)

Codification

Section was enacted as part of the Environmental Research, Development, and Demonstration Authorization Act of 1978, and not as part of the National Environmental Policy Act of 1969 which comprises this chapter.

§ 4361b.

Implementation by Administrator of Environmental Protection Agency of recommendations of "CHESS" Investigative Report; waiver; inclusion of status of implementation requirements in annual revisions of plan for research, development, and demonstration

The Administrator of the Environmental Protection Agency shall implement the recommendations of the report prepared for the House Committee on Science and Technology entitled "The Environmental Protection Agency Research Program with primary emphasis on the Community Health and Environmental Surveillance System (CHESS): An Investigative Report", unless for any specific recommendation he determines (1) that such recommendation has been implemented, (2) that implementation of such recommendation would not enhance the quality of the research, or (3) that implementation of such recommendation will require funding which is not available. Where such funding is not available, the Administrator shall request the required authorization or appropriation for such implementation. The Administrator shall report the status of such implementation in each annual revision of the five-year plan transmitted to the Congress under section 4361 of this title.

(Pub. L. 95-155, §10, Nov. 8, 1977, 91 Stat. 1262.)

Codification

Section was enacted as part of the Environmental Research, Development, and Demonstration Authorization Act of 1978, and not as part of the National Environmental Policy Act of 1969 which comprises this chapter.

§ 4361c.

Staff management

(a) Appointments for educational programs

(1) The Administrator is authorized to select and appoint up to 75 full-time permanent staff members in the Office of Research and Development to pursue full-time educational programs for the purpose of (A) securing an advanced degree or (B) securing academic training, for the purpose of making a career change in order to better carry out the Agency's research mission.

(2) The Administrator shall select and appoint staff members for these assignments according to rules and criteria promulgated by him. The Agency may continue to pay the salary and benefits of the appointees as well as reasonable and appropriate relocation expenses and tuition.

(3) The term of each appointment shall be for up to one year, with a single renewal of up to one year in appropriate cases at the discretion of the Administrator.

(4) Staff members appointed to this program shall not count against any Agency personnel ceiling during the term of their appointment.

(b) Post-doctoral research fellows

(1) The Administrator is authorized to appoint up to 25 Post-doctoral Research Fellows in accordance with the provisions of section 213.3102(aa) of title 5 of the Code of Federal Regulations.

(2) Persons holding these appointments shall not count against any personnel ceiling of the Agency.

(c) Non-Government research associates

(1) The Administrator is authorized and encouraged to utilize research associates from outside the Federal Government in conducting the research, development, and demonstration programs of the Agency.

(2) These persons shall be selected and shall serve according to rules and criteria promulgated by the Administrator.

(d) Women and minority groups

For all programs in this section, the Administrator shall place special emphasis on providing opportunities for education and training of women and minority groups.

(Pub. L. 95-477, §6, Oct. 18, 1978, 92 Stat. 1510.)

Codification

Section was enacted as part of the Environmental Research, Development, and Demonstration Authorization Act of 1979, and not as part of the National Environmental Policy Act of 1969 which comprises this chapter.

§ 4362.

Interagency cooperation on prevention of environmental cancer and heart and lung disease

(a) Not later than three months after August 7, 1977, there shall be established a Task Force on Environmental Cancer and Heart and Lung Disease (hereinafter referred to as the "Task Force"). The Task Force shall include representatives of the Environmental Protection Agency, the National Cancer Institute, the National Heart, Lung, and Blood Institute, the National Institute of Occupational Safety and Health, and the National Institute on Environmental Health Sciences, and shall be chaired by the Administrator (or his delegate).

(b) The Task Force shall—

(1) recommend a comprehensive research program to determine and quantify the relationship between environmental pollution and human cancer and heart and lung disease;

(2) recommend comprehensive strategies to reduce or eliminate the risks of cancer or such other diseases associated with environmental pollution;

(3) recommend research and such other measures as may be appropriate to prevent or reduce the incidence of environmentally related cancer and heart and lung diseases;

(4) coordinate research by, and stimulate cooperation between, the Environmental Protection Agency, the Department of Health and Human Services, and such other agencies as may be appropriate to prevent environmentally related cancer and heart and lung diseases; and

(5) report to Congress, not later than one year after August 7, 1977, and annually thereafter, on the problems and progress in carrying out this section.

(Pub. L. 95-95, title IV, §402, Aug. 7, 1977, 91 Stat. 791; Pub. L. 96-88, title V, §509(b), Oct. 17, 1979, 93 Stat. 695.)

Codification

Section was enacted as part of the Clean Air Act Amendments of 1977, and not as part of the National Environmental Policy Act of 1969 which comprises this chapter.

Effective Date

Section effective Aug. 7, 1977, except as otherwise expressly provided, see section

406(d) of Pub. L. 95-95, set out as an Effective Date of 1977 Amendment note under section 7401 of this title.

§ 4362a.

Task Force on Environmental Cancer and Heart and Lung Disease; membership of Director of National Center for Health Statistics and of head of Center for Disease Control

The Director of the National Center for Health Statistics and the head of the Center for Disease Control (or the successor to such entity) shall each serve as members of the Task Force on Environmental Cancer and Heart and Lung Disease established under section 4362 of this title.

(Pub. L. 95-623, §9, Nov. 9, 1978, 92 Stat. 3455.)

Codification

Section was enacted as part of the Health Services Research, Health Statistics, and Health Care Technology Act of 1978, and not as part of the National Environmental Policy Act of 1969 which comprises this chapter.

§ 4363.

Continuing and long-term environmental research and development

The Administrator of the Environmental Protection Agency shall establish a separately identified program of continuing, long-term environmental research and development for each activity listed in section 2(a) of this Act. Unless otherwise specified by law, at least 15 per centum of funds appropriated to the Administrator for environmental research and development for each activity listed in section 2(a) of this Act shall be obligated and expended for such long-term environmental research and development under this section.

(Pub. L. 96-569, §2(f), Dec. 22, 1980, 94 Stat. 3337.)

References In Text

Section 2(a) of this Act, referred to in text, is section 2(a) of Pub. L. 96-569, Dec. 22, 1980, 94 Stat. 3335, which is not classified to the Code.

Codification

Section was enacted as part of the Environmental Research, Development, and Demonstration Authorization Act of 1981, and not as part of the National Environmental Policy Act of 1969 which comprises this chapter.

Similar Provisions

Provisions similar to those comprising this section were contained in the following prior authorization acts:

1980—Pub. L. 96-229, Sec. 2(e), Apr. 7, 1980, 94 Stat. 327.
1977—Pub. L. 95-155, Sec. 6, Nov. 8, 1977, 91 Stat. 1259.

§ 4363a.

Pollution control technologies demonstrations

(1) The Administrator shall continue to be responsible for conducting and shall continue to conduct full-scale demonstrations of energy-related pollution control technologies as necessary in his judgment to fulfill the provisions of the Clean Air Act as amended [42 U.S.C. 7401 et seq.], the Federal Water Pollution Control Act as amended [33 U.S.C. 1251 et seq.], and other pertinent pollution control statutes.

(2) Energy-related environmental protection projects authorized to be administered by the Environmental Protection Agency under this Act shall not be transferred administratively to the Department of Energy or reduced through budget amendment. No action shall be taken through administrative or budgetary means to diminish the ability of the Environmental Protection Agency to initiate such projects.

(Pub. L. 96-229, §2(d), Apr. 7, 1980, 94 Stat. 327.)

References In Text

This Act, referred to in par. (2), is Pub. L. 96-229, Apr. 7, 1980, 94 Stat. 325, known as the Environmental, Research, Development, and Demonstration Authorization Act of 1980, which enacted sections 4363, 4363a, 4369a, and 4370 of this title. For complete classification of this Act to the Code, see Tables.

Codification

Section was enacted as part of the Environmental Research, Development, and Demonstration Authorization Act of 1980, and not as part of the National Environmental Policy Act of 1969 which comprises this chapter.

Similar Provisions

Provisions similar to those comprising this section were contained in the following prior authorization act:

1979—Pub. L. 95-477, Sec. 2(d), Oct. 18, 1978, 92 Stat. 1508.

§ 4364.

Expenditure of funds for research and development related to regulatory program activities

(a) Coordination, etc., with research needs and priorities of program offices and Environmental Protection Agency

The Administrator of the Environmental Protection Agency shall assure that the expenditure of any funds appropriated pursuant to this Act or any other provision of law for environmental research and development related to regulatory program activities shall be coordinated with and reflect the research needs and priorities of the program offices, as well as the overall research needs and priorities of the Agency, including those defined in the five-year research plan.

(b) Program offices subject to coverage

For purposes of subsection (a) of this section, the appropriate program offices are—

(1) the Office of Air and Waste Management, for air quality activities;

(2) the Office of Water and Hazardous Materials, for water quality activities and water supply activities;

(3) the Office of Pesticides, for environmental effects of pesticides;

(4) the Office of Solid Waste, for solid waste activities;

(5) the Office of Toxic Substances, for toxic substance activities;

(6) the Office of Radiation Programs, for radiation activities; and

(7) the Office of Noise Abatement and Control, for noise activities.

(c) Report to Congress; contents

The Administrator shall submit to the President and the Congress a report concerning the most appropriate means of assuring, on a continuing basis, that the research efforts of the Agency reflect the needs and priorities of the regulatory program offices, while maintaining a high level of scientific quality. Such report shall be submitted on or before March 31, 1978.

(Pub. L. 95-155, §7, Nov. 8, 1977, 91 Stat. 1259.)

References In Text

This Act, referred to in subsec. (a), is Pub. L. 95-155, Nov. 8, 1977, 91 Stat. 1257, as amended, known as the Environmental Research, Development, and Demonstration Authorization Act of 1978, which to the extent classified to the Code enacted sections 300j-3a, 4361a, 4361b, and 4363 to 4367 of this title. For complete classification of this Act to the Code, see Tables.

Codification

Section was enacted as part of the Environmental Research, Development, and Demonstration Authorization Act of 1978, and not as part of the National Environmental Policy Act of 1969 which comprises this chapter.

§ 4365.

Science Advisory Board

(a) Establishment; requests for advice by Administrator of Environmental Protection Agency and Congressional committees

The Administrator of the Environmental Protection Agency shall establish a Science Advisory Board which shall provide such scientific advice as may be requested by the Administrator, the Committee on Environment and Public Works of the United States Senate, or the Committees on Science and Technology, Energy and Commerce, or Public Works and Transportation of the House of Representatives.

(b) Membership; Chairman; meetings; qualifications of members

Such Board shall be composed of at least nine members, one of whom shall be designated Chairman, and shall meet at such times and places as may be designated by the Chairman of the Board in consultation with the Administrator. Each member of the Board shall be qualified by education, training, and experience to evaluate scientific and technical information on matters referred to the Board under this section.

(c) Review and comment on plan for research, development, and demonstration and annual revisions; transmission to Congress

In addition to providing scientific advice when requested by the Administrator under subsection (a) of this section, the Board shall review and comment on the Administration's five-year plan for environmental research, development, and demonstration provided for by section 4361 of this title and on each annual revision thereof. Such review and comment shall be transmitted to the Congress by the Administrator, together with his comments thereon, at the time of the transmission to the Congress of the annual revision involved.

(d) Review and report to Administrator, President, and Congress concerning authorized health effects research, etc.

The Board shall conduct a review of and submit a report to the Administrator, the President, and the Congress, not later than October 1, 1978, concerning—

(1) the health effects research authorized by this Act and other laws;

(2) the procedures generally used in the conduct of such research;

(3) the internal and external reporting of the results of such research;

(4) the review procedures for such research and results;

(5) the procedures by which such results are used in internal and external recommendations on policy, regulations, and legislation; and

(6) the findings and recommendations of the report to the House Committee on Science and Technology entitled "The Environmental Protection Agency's Research Program with primary emphasis on the Community Health and Environmental Surveillance System (CHESS): An Investigative Report".

The review shall focus special attention on the procedural safeguards required to preserve the scientific integrity of such research and to insure reporting and use of the results of such research in subsequent recommendations. The report shall include specific recommendations on the results of the review to ensure scientific integrity throughout the Agency's health effects research, review, reporting, and recommendation process.

(e) Proposed environmental criteria document, standard, limitation, or regulation; functions respecting in conjunction with Administrator

(1) The Administrator, at the time any proposed criteria document, standard, limitation, or regulation under the Clean Air Act [42 U.S.C. 7401 et seq.], the Federal Water Pollution Control Act [33 U.S.C. 1251 et seq.], the Resource Conservation and Recovery Act of 1976 [42 U.S.C. 6901 et seq.], the Noise Control Act [42 U.S.C. 4901 et seq.], the Toxic Substances Control Act [15 U.S.C. 2601 et seq.], or the Safe Drinking Water Act [42 U.S.C. 300f et seq.], or under any other authority of the Administrator, is provided to any other Federal agency for formal review and comment, shall make available to the Board such proposed criteria document, standard, limitation, or regulation, together with relevant scientific and technical information in the possession of the Environmental Protection Agency on which the proposed action is based.

(2) The Board may make available to the Administrator, within the time specified by the Administrator, its advice and comments on the adequacy of the scientific and technical basis of the proposed criteria document, standard, limitation, or regulation, together with any pertinent information in the Board's possession.

(f) Utilization of technical and scientific capabilities of Federal agencies and national environmental laboratories for determining adequacy of scientific and technical basis of proposed criteria document, etc.

In preparing such advice and comments, the Board shall avail itself of the technical and scientific capabilities of any Federal agency, including the Environmental Protection Agency and any national environmental laboratories.

(g) Member committees and investigative panels; establishment; chairmenship

The Board is authorized to constitute such member committees and investigative panels as the Administrator and the Board find necessary to carry out this section. Each such member committee or investigative panel shall be chaired by a member of the Board.

(h) Appointment and compensation of secretary and other personnel; compensation of members

(1) Upon the recommendation of the Board, the Administrator shall appoint a secretary, and such other employees as deemed necessary to exercise and fulfill the Board's powers and responsibilities. The compensation of all employees appointed under this

paragraph shall be fixed in accordance with chapter 51 and subchapter III of chapter 53 of title 5.

(2) Members of the Board may be compensated at a rate to be fixed by the President but not in excess of the maximum rate of pay for grade GS-18, as provided in the General Schedule under section 5332 of title 5.

(i) Consultation and coordination with Scientific Advisory Panel

In carrying out the functions assigned by this section, the Board shall consult and coordinate its activities with the Scientific Advisory Panel established by the Administrator pursuant to section 136w(d) of title 7.

(Pub. L. 95-155, §8, Nov. 8, 1977, 91 Stat. 1260; H. Res. 549, Mar. 25, 1980; Pub. L. 96-569, §3, Dec. 22, 1980, 94 Stat. 3337.)

References In Text

The Noise Control Act, referred to in subsec. (e)(1), probably means the Noise Control Act of 1972, Pub. L. 92-574, Oct. 27, 1972, 86 Stat. 1234, as amended, which is classified principally to chapter 65 (Sec. 4901 et seq.) of this title. For complete classification of this Act to the Code, see Short Title note set out under section 4901 of this title and Tables.

Codification

Section was enacted as part of the Environmental Research, Development, and Demonstration Authorization Act of 1978, and not as part of the National Environmental Policy Act of 1969 which comprises this chapter.

§ 4366.

Identification and coordination of research, development, and demonstration activities

(a) Consultation and cooperation of Administrator of Environmental Protection Agency with heads of Federal agencies; inclusion of activities in annual revisions of plan for research, etc.

The Administrator of the Environmental Protection Agency, in consultation and cooperation with the heads of other Federal agencies, shall take such actions on a continuing basis as may be necessary or appropriate—

(1) to identify environmental research, development, and demonstration activities, within and outside the Federal Government, which may need to be more effectively coordinated in order to minimize unnecessary duplication of programs, projects, and research facilities;

(2) to determine the steps which might be taken under existing law, by him and by the heads of such other agencies, to accomplish or promote such coordination, and to provide for or encourage the taking of such steps; and

(3) to determine the additional legislative actions which would be needed to assure such coordination to the maximum extent possible.

The Administrator shall include in each annual revision of the five-year plan provided for by section 4361 of this title a full and complete report on the actions taken and determinations made during the preceding year under this subsection, and may submit interim reports on such actions and determinations at such other times as he deems appropriate.

(b) Coordination of programs by Administrator

The Administrator of the Environmental Protection Agency shall coordinate environmental research, development, and demonstration programs of such Agency with the heads of other Federal agencies in order to minimize unnecessary duplication of programs, projects, and research facilities.

(c) Joint study by Council on Environmental Quality in consultation with Office of Science and Technology Policy for coordination of activities; report to President and Congress; report by President to Congress on implementation of joint study and report

(1) In order to promote the coordination of environmental research and development activities, and to assure that the action taken and methods used (under subsection (a) of this section and otherwise) to bring about such coordination will be as effective as possible for that purpose, the Council on Environmental Quality in consultation with the Office of Science and Technology Policy shall promptly undertake and carry out a joint study of all aspects of the coordination of environmental research and development. The Chairman of the Council shall prepare a report on the results of such study, together with such recommendations (including legislative recommendations) as he deems appropriate, and shall submit such report to the President and the Congress not later than May 31, 1978.

(2) Not later than September 30, 1978, the President shall report to the Congress on steps he has taken to implement the recommendations included in the report under paragraph (1), including any recommendations he may have for legislation.

(Pub. L. 95-155, §9, Nov. 8, 1977, 91 Stat. 1261.)

Codification

Section was enacted as part of the Environmental Research, Development, and Demonstration Authorization Act of 1978, and not as part of the National Environmental Policy Act of 1969 which comprises this chapter.

Coordination Of Environmental Research, Development, And Demonstration Efforts; Study And Report

Pub. L. 95-477, Sec. 3(c), Oct. 18, 1978, 92 Stat. 1509, authorized to be appropriated to the Environmental Protection Agency for the fiscal year 1979, $1,000,000, and for the fiscal year 1980, $1,000,000, for a study and report, under a contract let by the Administrator, to be conducted outside the Federal Government, on coordination of the Federal Government's efforts in environmental research, development, and demonstration, and the application of the results of such efforts to environmental problems, with the report on the study submitted to the President, the Administrator, and the Congress within two years after Oct. 18, 1978, accompanied by recommendations for action by the President, the Administrator, other agencies, or the Congress, as may be appropriate.

§ 4366a.

Development of data base of environmental research articles indexed by geographic location

(a) Research journals

Within 6 months following November 16, 1990, and from time to time thereafter, the Environmental Protection Agency shall identify not less than 35 important environmental research journals, conference proceedings or other reference sources in which scientific research or engineering studies related to air, water, or soil quality or pollution or other environmental issues are routinely published. In carrying out the requirements of this subsection, at least 50 journals or proceedings shall be reviewed.

(b) Index

(1) Within 12 months following November 16, 1990, and annually thereafter, the Environmental Protection Agency shall review the journals and other materials identified in subsection (a) of this section and compile, maintain and publish an index of the articles contained therein during the preceding calendar year by geographic location. A copy of such index shall be made available to the Service for distribution to the public, and a copy shall be submitted to the Congress not less than 30 days prior to the date on which it is made available to the Service.

(2) Beginning 12 months after November 16, 1990, the Agency shall identify not less than 20 materials identified in subsection (a) of this section which were published during the time period from 1970 to the year preceding November 16, 1990, and shall compile and publish a series of indices of articles contained therein by geographic location. The time frame which each index contains should not exceed 5 years.

(c) Purchase of information

The Environmental Protection Agency is authorized to enter into contracts or other arrangements for the acquisition of data and other information necessary for purposes of this Act.

(d) Revising list

The Environmental Protection Agency shall review the list of references developed under this section at least biennially and shall revise the list of sources as appropriate.

(e) Specific location of research projects

Unless exempted by the Administrator of the Environmental Protection Agency, all reports resulting from research projects sponsored by the Environmental Protection Agency and initiated after the expiration of the 36-month period following November 16, 1990, shall indicate the specific location to which the research pertains.

(Pub. L. 101-617, §4, Nov. 16, 1990, 104 Stat. 3287.)

Termination Of Section

For termination of section by section 6 of Pub. L. 101-617, see Termination Date note below.

References In Text

This Act, referred to in subsec. (c), is Pub. L. 101-617, Nov. 16, 1990, 104 Stat. 3287, known as the Environmental Research Geographic Location Information Act, which enacted this section and provisions set out below. For complete classification of this Act to the Code, see Short Title note below and Tables.

Codification

Section was enacted as part of the Environmental Research Geographic Location Information Act, and not as part of the National Environmental Policy Act of 1969 which comprises this chapter.

Termination Date

Section 6 of Pub. L. 101-617 provided that: "This Act [enacting this section and provisions set out below] shall expire 10 years after the date of its enactment [Nov. 16, 1990]."

Short Title; Findings; Purpose; Authorization

Sections 1 to 3 and 5 of Pub. L. 101-617 provided that:

"SECTION 1. SHORT TITLE.

"This Act (enacting this section and provisions set out above) may be cited as the 'Environmental Research Geographic Location Information Act'.

"SEC. 2. FINDINGS.

"The Congress finds that—

"(1) at present, there is no reliable method of locating private or Government research on environmental issues by geographic location; and

"(2) a means of identifying environmental research conducted at specific geographic locations is needed for purposes such as detecting trends in environmental quality, assisting the public in learning about the quality and issues of their local environment, and providing a data base for identifying areas of critical environmental concern.

"SEC. 3. PURPOSE.

"The purpose of this Act is to develop a data base of environmental research articles indexed by geographic location.

"SEC. 5. AUTHORIZATIONS.

"There are authorized to be appropriated such sums as may be necessary to carry out this Act."

§ 4367.

Reporting requirements of financial interests of officers and employees of Environmental Protection Agency

(a) Covered officers and employees

Each officer or employee of the Environmental Protection Agency who—

(1) performs any function or duty under this Act; and

(2) has any known financial interest in any person who applies for or receives grants, contracts, or other forms of financial assistance under this Act,

shall, beginning on February 1, 1978, annually file with the Administrator a written statement concerning all such interests held by such officer or employee during the preceding calendar year. Such statement shall be available to the public.

(b) Implementation of requirements by Administrator

The Administrator shall—

(1) act within ninety days after November 8, 1977—

(A) to define the term "known financial interest" for purposes of subsection (a) of this section; and

(B) to establish the methods by which the requirement to file written statements specified in subsection (a) of this section will be monitored and enforced, including appropriate provision for the filing by such officers and employees of such statements and the review by the Administrator of such statements; and

(2) report to the Congress on June 1 of each calendar year with respect to such disclosures and the actions taken in regard thereto during the preceding calendar year.

(c) Exemption of positions by Administrator

In the rules prescribed under subsection (b) of this section, the Administrator may identify specific positions of a nonpolicymaking nature within the Administration and provide that officers or employees occupying such positions shall be exempt from the requirements of this section.

(d) Violations; penalties

Any officer or employee who is subject to, and knowingly violates, this section, shall be fined not more than $2,500 or imprisoned not more than one year, or both.

(Pub. L. 95-155, §12, Nov. 8, 1977, 91 Stat. 1263.)

References In Text

This Act, referred to in subsec. (a)(1), (2), is Pub. L. 95-155, Nov. 8, 1977, 91 Stat. 1257, as amended, known as the Environmental Research, Development, and Demonstration Authorization Act of 1978, which to the extent classified to the Code enacted sections 300j-3a, 4361a, 4361b, and 4363 to 4367 of this title. For complete classification of this Act to the Code, see Tables.

Codification

Section was enacted as part of the Environmental Research, Development, and Demonstration Authorization Act of 1978, and not as part of the National Environmental Policy Act of 1969 which comprises this chapter.

§ 4368.

Grants to qualified citizens groups

(1) There is authorized to be appropriated to the Environmental Protection Agency, for grants to qualified citizens groups in States and regions, $3,000,000.

(2) Grants under this section may be made for the purpose of supporting and encouraging participation by qualified citizens groups in determining how scientific, technological, and social trends and changes affect the future environment and quality of life of an area, and for setting goals and identifying measures for improvement.

(3) The term "qualified citizens group" shall mean a nonprofit organization of citizens having an area based focus, which is not single-issue oriented and which can demonstrate a prior record of interest and involvement in goal-setting and research concerned with improving the quality of life, including plans to identify, protect and enhance significant natural and cultural resources and the environment.

(4) A citizens group shall be eligible for assistance only if certified by the Governor in consultation with the State legislature as a bonafide organization entitled to receive Federal assistance to pursue the aims of this program. The group shall further demonstrate its capacity to employ usefully the funds for the purposes of this program and its broad-based representative nature.

(5) After an initial application for assistance under this section has been approved, the Administrator may make grants on an annual basis, on condition that the Governor recertify the group and that the applicant submits to the Administrator annually—

(A) an evaluation of the progress made during the previous year in meeting the objectives for which the grant was made;

(B) a description of any changes in the objectives of the activities; and

(C) a description of the proposed activities for the succeeding one year period.

(6) A grant made under this program shall not exceed 75 per centum of the estimated cost of the project or program for which the grant is made, and no group shall receive more than $50,000 in any one year.

(7) No financial assistance provided under this section shall be used to support lobbying or litigation by any recipient group.

(Pub. L. 95-477, §3(d), Oct. 18, 1978, 92 Stat. 1509.)

References In Text

This section, referred to in par. (5), means section 3 of Pub. L. 95-477, in its entirety, subsec. (d) of which enacted this section, subsecs. (a) and (b) of which were not classified to the Code, and subsec. (c) of which is set out as a note under section 4366 of this title.

Codification

Section was enacted as part of the Environmental Research, Development, and Demonstration Authorization Act of 1979, and not as part of the National Environmental Policy Act of 1969 which comprises this chapter.

§ 4368a.

Utilization of talents of older Americans in projects of pollution prevention, abatement, and control

(a) Technical assistance to environmental agencies

Notwithstanding any other provision of law relating to Federal grants and cooperative agreements, the Administrator of the Environmental Protection Agency is authorized to make grants to, or enter into cooperative agreements with, private nonprofit organizations designated by the Secretary of Labor under title V of the Older Americans Act of 1965 [42 U.S.C. 3056 et seq.] to utilize the talents of older Americans in programs authorized by other provisions of law administered by the Administrator (and consistent with such provisions of law) in providing technical assistance to Federal, State, and local environmental agencies for projects of pollution prevention, abatement, and control. Funding for such grants or agreements may be made available from such programs or through title V of the Older Americans Act of 1965 and title IV of the Job Training Partnership Act [29 U.S.C. 1671 et seq.].

(b) Pre-award certifications

Prior to awarding any grant or agreement under subsection (a) of this section, the applicable Federal, State, or local environmental agency shall certify to the Administrator that such grants or agreements will not—

(1) result in the displacement of individuals currently employed by the environmental agency concerned (including partial displacement through reduction of nonovertime hours, wages, or employment benefits);

(2) result in the employment of any individual when any other person is in a layoff status from the same or substantially equivalent job within the jurisdiction of the environmental agency concerned; or

(3) affect existing contracts for services.

(c) Prior appropriation Acts

Grants or agreements awarded under this section shall be subject to prior appropriation Acts.

(Pub. L. 98-313, §2, June 12, 1984, 98 Stat. 235.)

Codification

Section was enacted as part of the Environmental Programs Assistance Act of 1984, and not as part of the National Environmental Policy Act of 1969 which comprises this chapter.

Short Title

Section 1 of Pub. L. 98-313 provided that: "This Act [enacting this section] may be cited as the 'Environmental Programs Assistance Act of 1984'."

§ 4368b.

General Assistance Program

(a) Short title

This section may be cited as the "Indian Environmental General Assistance Program Act of 1992".

(b) Purposes

The purposes of this section are to—

(1) provide general assistance grants to Indian tribal governments and intertribal consortia to build capacity to administer environmental regulatory programs that may be delegated by the Environmental Protection Agency on Indian lands; and

(2) provide technical assistance from the Environmental Protection Agency to Indian tribal governments and intertribal consortia in the development of multimedia programs to address environmental issues on Indian lands.

(c) Definitions

For purposes of this section:

(1) The term "Indian tribal government" means any Indian tribe, band, nation, or other organized group or community, including any Alaska Native village or regional or village corporation (as defined in, or established pursuant to, the Alaska Native Claims Settlement Act (43 U.S.C.A. 1601, et seq.)), which is recognized as eligible for the special services provided by the United States to Indians because of their status as Indians.

(2) The term "intertribal consortia" or "intertribal consortium" means a partnership between two or more Indian tribal governments authorized by the governing bodies of those tribes to apply for and receive assistance pursuant to this section.

(3) The term "Administrator" means the Administrator of the Environmental Protection Agency.

(d) General assistance program

(1) The Administrator of the Environmental Protection Agency shall establish an Indian Environmental General Assistance Program that provides grants to eligible Indian tribal governments or intertribal consortia to cover the costs of planning, developing, and establishing environmental protection programs consistent with other applicable provisions of law providing for enforcement of such laws by Indian tribes on Indian lands.

(2) Each grant awarded for general assistance under this subsection for a fiscal year shall be no less than $75,000, and no single grant may be awarded to an Indian tribal government or intertribal consortium for more than 10 percent of the funds appropriated under subsection (h) of this section.

(3) The term of any general assistance award made under this subsection may exceed one year. Any awards made pursuant to this section shall remain available until expended. An Indian tribal government or intertribal consortium may receive a general assistance grant for a period of up to four years in each specific media area.

(e) No reduction in amounts

In no case shall the award of a general assistance grant to an Indian tribal government or intertribal consortium under this section result in a reduction of Environmental Protection Agency grants for environmental programs to that tribal government or consortium. Nothing in this section shall preclude an Indian tribal government or intertribal consortium from receiving individual media grants or cooperative agreements. Funds provided by the Environmental Protection Agency through the general assistance program shall be used by an Indian tribal government or intertribal consortium to supplement other funds provided by the Environmental Protection Agency through individual media grants or cooperative agreements.

(f) Expenditure of general assistance

Any general assistance under this section shall be expended for the purpose of planning, developing, and establishing the capability to implement programs administered by the Environmental Protection Agency and specified in the assistance agreement. Purposes and programs authorized under this section shall include the development and implementation of solid and hazardous waste programs for Indian lands. An Indian tribal government or intertribal consortium receiving general assistance pursuant to this section shall utilize such funds for programs and purposes to be carried out in accordance with the terms of the assistance agreement. Such programs and general assistance shall be carried out in accordance with the purposes and requirements of applicable provisions of law, including the Solid Waste Disposal Act (42 U.S.C. 6901, et seq.).

(g) Procedures

(1) Within 12 months following the date of the enactment of this section, the Administrator shall promulgate regulations establishing procedures under which an Indian tribal government or intertribal consortium may apply for general assistance grants under this section.

(2) The Administrator shall publish regulations issued pursuant to this section in the Federal Register.

(3) The Administrator shall establish procedures for accounting, auditing, evaluating, and reviewing any programs or activities funded in whole or in part for a general assistance grant under this section.

(h) Authorization

There are authorized to be appropriated to carry out the provisions of this section, $15,000,000 for each of the fiscal years 1993, 1994, 1995, 1996, 1997, and 1998.

(i) Report to Congress

The Administrator shall transmit an annual report to the appropriate Committees of the Congress with jurisdiction over the applicable environmental laws and Indian tribes describing which Indian tribes or intertribal consortia have been granted approval by the Administrator pursuant to law to enforce certain environmental laws and the effectiveness of any such enforcement.

(Pub. L. 102-497, §11, Oct. 24, 1992, 106 Stat. 3258, 3259, 3260; Pub. L. 103-155, Nov. 24, 1993, 107 Stat. 1523-24.)

Codification

Section was enacted as part of the Act entitled "An Act to make technical amendments to certain Federal Indian statutes, " and not as part of the National Environmental Policy Act of 1969 which comprises this chapter.

§ 4369.

Miscellaneous reports

(a) Availability to Congressional committees

All reports to or by the Administrator relevant to the Agency's program of research, development, and demonstration shall promptly be made available to the Committee on Science and Technology of the House of Representatives and the Committee on Environment and Public Works of the Senate, unless otherwise prohibited by law.

(b) Transmittal of jurisdictional information

The Administrator shall keep the Committee on Science and Technology of the House of Representatives and the Committee on Environment and Public Works of the Senate fully and currently informed with respect to matters falling within or related to the jurisdiction of the committees.

(c) Comment by Government agencies and the public

The reports provided for in section 5910 of this title shall be made available to the public for comment, and to the heads of affected agencies for comment and, in the case of recommendations for action, for response.

(d) Transmittal of research information to the Department of Energy

For the purpose of assisting the Department of Energy in planning and assigning priorities in research development and demonstration activities related to environmental control technologies, the Administrator shall actively make available to the Department all information on research activities and results of research programs of the Environmental Protection Agency.

(Pub. L. 95-477, §5, Oct. 18, 1978, 92 Stat. 1510.)

Codification

Section was enacted as part of the Environmental Research, Development, and Demonstration Authorization Act of 1979, and not as part of the National Environmental Policy Act of 1969 which comprises this chapter.

§ 4369a.

Reports on environmental research and development activities of Agency

(a) Reports to keep Congressional committees fully and currently informed

The Administrator shall keep the appropriate committees of the House and the Senate fully and currently informed about all aspects of the environmental research and development activities of the Environmental Protection Agency.

(b) Annual reports relating requested funds to activities to be carried out with those funds

Each year, at the time of the submission of the President's annual budget request, the Administrator shall make available to the appropriate committees of Congress sufficient copies of a report fully describing funds requested and the environmental research and development activities to be carried out with these funds.

(Pub. L. 96-229, §4, Apr. 7, 1980, 94 Stat. 328.)

Codification

Section was enacted as part of the Environmental Research, Development, and Demonstration Authorization Act of 1980, and not as part of the National Environmental Policy Act of 1969 which comprises this chapter.

§ 4370.

Reimbursement for use of facilities

(a) Authority to allow outside groups or individuals to use research and test facilities; reimbursement

The Administrator is authorized to allow appropriate use of special Environmental Protection Agency research and test facilities by outside groups or individuals and to receive reimbursement or fees for costs incurred thereby when he finds this to be in the public interest. Such reimbursement or fees are to be used by the Agency to defray the costs of use by outside groups or individuals.

(b) Rules and regulations

The Administrator may promulgate regulations to cover such use of Agency facilities in accordance with generally accepted accounting, safety, and laboratory practices.

(c) Waiver of reimbursement by Administrator

When he finds it is in the public interest the Administrator may waive reimbursement or fees for outside use of Agency facilities by nonprofit private or public entities.

(Pub. L. 96-229, §5, Apr. 7, 1980, 94 Stat. 328.)

Codification

Section was enacted as part of the Environmental Research, Development, and Demonstration Authorization Act of 1980, and not as part of the National Environmental Policy Act of 1969 which comprises this chapter.

§ 4370a.

Assistant Administrators of Environmental Protection Agency; appointment; duties

(a) The President, by and with the advice and consent of the Senate, may appoint three Assistant Administrators of the Environmental Protection Agency in addition to—

(1) the five Assistant Administrators provided for in section 1(d) of Reorganization Plan Numbered 3 of 1970 (5 U.S.C. Appendix);

(2) the Assistant Administrator provided by section 2625(g) of title 15; and

(3) the Assistant Administrator provided by section 6911a of this title.

(b) Each Assistant Administrator appointed under subsection (a) of this section shall perform such duties as the Administrator of the Environmental Protection Agency may prescribe.

(Pub. L. 98-80, §1, Aug. 23, 1983, 97 Stat. 485.)

Codification

Section was not enacted as part of the National Environmental Policy Act of 1969 which comprises this chapter.

§ 4370b.

Availability of fees and charges to carry out Agency programs

Notwithstanding any other provision of law, after September 30, 1990, amounts deposited in the Licensing and Other Services Fund from fees and charges assessed and collected by the Administrator for services and activities carried out pursuant to the statutes administered by the Environmental Protection Agency shall thereafter be available to carry out the Agency's activities in the programs for which the fees or charges are made.

(Pub. L. 101-144, title III, Nov. 9, 1989, 103 Stat. 858.)

Codification

Section was enacted as part of the Departments of Veterans Affairs and Housing and Urban Development, and Independent Agencies Appropriations Act, 1990, and not as part of the National Environmental Policy Act of 1969 which comprises this chapter.

§ 4370c.

Environmental Protection Agency fees

(a) Assessment and collection

The Administrator of the Environmental Protection Agency shall, by regulation, assess and collect fees and charges for services and activities carried out pursuant to laws administered by the Environmental Protection Agency.

(b) Amount of fees and charges

Fees and charges assessed pursuant to this section shall be in such amounts as may be necessary to ensure that the aggregate amount of fees and charges collected pursuant to this section, in excess of the amount of fees and charges collected under current law—

(1) in fiscal year 1991, is not less than $28,000,000; and

(2) in each of fiscal years 1992, 1993, 1994, and 1995, is not less than $38,000,000.

(c) Limitation on fees and charges

(1) The maximum aggregate amount of fees and charges in excess of the amounts being collected under current law which may be assessed and collected pursuant to this section in a fiscal year—

(A) for services and activities carried out pursuant ot[3] the Federal Water Pollution Control Act [33 U.S.C. 1251 et seq.] is $10,000,000; and

(B) for services and activities in programs within the jurisdiction of the House Committee on Energy and Commerce and administered by the Environmental Protection Agency through the Administrator, shall be limited to such sums collected as of November 5, 1990, pursuant to sections 2625(b) and 2665(e)(2) of title 15, and such sums specifically authorized by the Clean Air Act Amendments of 1990.

(2) Any remaining amounts required to be collected under this section shall be collected from services and programs administered by the Environmental Protection Agency other than those specified in subparagraphs (A) and (B) of paragraph (1).

(d) Rule of construction

Nothing in this section increases or diminishes the authority of the Administrator to promulgate regulations pursuant to section 9701 of title 31.

(e) Uses of fees

Fees and charges collected pursuant to this section shall be deposited into a special account for environmental services in the Treasury of the United States. Subject to appropriation Acts, such funds shall be available to the Environmental Protection Agency to carry out the activities for which such fees and charges are collected. Such funds shall remain available until expended.

(Pub. L. 101-508, title VI, §6501, Nov. 5, 1990, 104 Stat. 1388-320.)

References In Text

The Clean Air Act Amendments of 1990, referred to in subsec. (c)(1)(B), means Pub. L. 101-549, Nov. 15, 1990, 104 Stat. 2399. For complete classification of this Act to the Code, see Short Title of 1990 Amendment note set out under section 7401 of this title and Tables.

Codification

In subsec. (d), "section 9701 of title 31" was in the original "the Independent Office Appropriations Act (31 U.S.C. 9701)" and substitution was made as if it read for "title V of the Independent Offices Appropriation Act of 1952" on authority of Pub. L. 97-258, Sec. 4(b), Sept. 13, 1982, 96 Stat. 1067, the first section of which enacted Title 31, Money and Finance.

Section was enacted as part of the Omnibus Budget Reconciliation Act of 1990, and not as part of the National Environmental Policy Act of 1969 which comprises this chapter.

§ 4370d.

Business and industry, women, disadvantaged, contracts

The Administrator of the Environmental Protection Agency shall, hereafter, to the fullest extent possible, ensure that at least 8 per centum of Federal funding for prime and subcontracts awarded in support of authorized programs, including grants, loans, and contracts for waste-water treatment and leaking underground storage tanks grants, be made available to business concerns or other organizations owned or controlled by socially and economically disadvantaged individuals (within the meaning of section 8(a) (5) and (6) of the Small Business Act (15 U.S.C. 637(a)(5) and (6))), including historically black colleges and universities. For purposes of this section, economically and socially disadvantaged individuals shall be deemed to include women.

During fiscal year 1993, notwithstanding any other provision of law, average employment in the headquarter's offices of the Environmental Protection Agency shall not exceed: (1) 56 workyears for the Immediate Office of the Administrator; (2) 45 workyears for the Office of Congressional and Legislative Affairs; (3) 78 workyears for the Office of Communications, Education, and Public Affairs; (4) 192 workyears for the Office of General Counsel; and (5) 1,477 workyears for the Office of Administration and Resources Management, of which 120 workyears shall be for contract management activities.

(Pub. L. 102-389, title III, Oct. 6, 1992, 106 Stat. 1602.)

Codification

Section was enacted as part of the Act entitled "An Act making appropriations for the Department of Veterans Affairs and Housing and Urban Development, and for sundry independent agencies, boards, commissions, corporations, and offices for the fiscal year ending September 30, 1993, and for other purposes," and not as part of the National Environmental Policy Act of 1969 which comprises this chapter.

---

3.   So in original. Probably should be "to".

Environmental Quality Improvement Act
42 U.S.C. §§4371-4375

Environmental Quality Improvement Act
42 U.S.C. §§4371-4375

§ 4371.   [EQIA §202]

Congressional findings, declarations, and purposes

(a) The Congress finds—

  (1) that man has caused changes in the environment;

  (2) that many of these changes may affect the relationship between man and his environment; and

  (3) that population increases and urban concentration contribute directly to pollution and the degradation of our environment.

(b)(1) The Congress declares that there is a national policy for the environment which provides for the enhancement of environmental quality. This policy is evidenced by statutes heretofore enacted relating to the prevention, abatement, and control of environmental pollution, water and land resources, transportation, and economic and regional development.

  (2) The primary responsibility for implementing this policy rests with State and local government.

  (3) The Federal Government encourages and supports implementation of this policy through appropriate regional organizations established under existing law.

(c) The purposes of this chapter are—

  (1) to assure that each Federal department and agency conducting or supporting public works activities which affect the environment shall implement the policies established under existing law; and

  (2) to authorize an Office of Environmental Quality, which, notwithstanding any other provision of law, shall provide the professional and administrative staff for the Council on Environmental Quality established by Public Law 91-190.

(Pub. L. 91-224, title II, §202, Apr. 3, 1970, 84 Stat. 114.)

References In Text

Public Law 91-190, referred to in subsec. (c)(2), is Pub. L. 91-190, Jan. 1, 1970, 83 Stat. 852, as amended, known as the National Environmental Policy Act of 1969, which is classified generally to chapter 55 (Sec. 4321 et seq.) of this title. For complete classification of this Act to the Code, see Short Title note set out under section 4321 of this title and Tables.

Short Title

Section 201 of Pub. L. 91-224 provided that: "This title [enacting this chapter] may be cited as the 'Environmental Quality Improvement Act of 1970'."

§ 4372.   [EQIA §203]

Office of Environmental Quality

(a) Establishment; Director; Deputy Director

There is established in the Executive Office of the President an office to be known as the Office of Environmental Quality (hereafter in this chapter referred to as the "Office"). The Chairman of the Council on Environmental Quality established by Public Law 91-190 shall be the Director of the Office. There shall be in the Office a Deputy Director who shall be appointed by the President, by and with the advice and consent of the Senate.

(b) Compensation of Deputy Director

The compensation of the Deputy Director shall be fixed by the President at a rate not in excess of the annual rate of compensation payable to the Deputy Director of the Office of Management and Budget.

(c) Employment of personnel, experts, and consultants; compensation

The Director is authorized to employ such officers and employees (including experts and consultants) as may be necessary to enable the Office to carry out its functions under this chapter and Public Law 91-190, except that he may employ no more than ten specialists and other experts without regard to the provisions of title 5, governing appointments in the competitive service, and pay such specialists and experts without regard to the provisions of chapter 51 and subchapter III of chapter 53 of such title relating to classification and General Schedule pay rates, but no such specialist or expert shall be paid at a rate in excess of the maximum rate for GS-18 of the General Schedule under section 5332 of title 5.

(d) Duties and functions of Director

In carrying out his functions the Director shall assist and advise the President on policies and programs of the Federal Government affecting environmental quality by—

  (1) providing the professional and administrative staff and support for the Council on Environmental Quality established by Public Law 91-190.

  (2) assisting the Federal agencies and departments in appraising the effectiveness of existing and proposed facilities, programs, policies, and activities of the Federal Government, and those specific major projects designated by the President which do not require individual project authorization by Congress, which affect environmental quality;

  (3) reviewing the adequacy of existing systems for monitoring and predicting environmental changes in order to achieve effective coverage and efficient use of research facilities and other resources;

  (4) promoting the advancement of scientific knowledge of the effects of actions and technology on the environment and encourage the development of the means to prevent or reduce adverse effects that endanger the health and well-being of man;

  (5) assisting in coordinating among the Federal departments and agencies those programs and activities which affect, protect, and improve environmental quality;

  (6) assisting the Federal departments and agencies in the development and interrelationship of environmental quality criteria and standards established through the Federal Government;

  (7) collecting, collating, analyzing, and interpreting data and information on environmental quality, ecological research, and evaluation.

(e) Authority of Director to contract

The Director is authorized to contract with public or private agencies, institutions, and organizations and with individuals without regard to section 3324(a) and (b) of title 31 and section 5 of title 41 in carrying out his functions.

(Pub. L. 91-224, title II, §203, Apr. 3, 1970, 84 Stat. 114; 1970 Reorg. Plan No. 2, §102, eff. July 1, 1970, 35 F.R. 7959, 84 Stat. 2085.)

References In Text

Public Law 91-190, referred to in subsecs. (a), (c), and (d), is Pub. L. 91-190, Jan. 1, 1970, 83 Stat. 852, as amended, known as the National Environmental Policy Act of 1969, which is classified generally to chapter 55 (Sec. 4321 et seq.) of this title. For complete classification of this Act to the Code, see Short Title note set out under section 4321 of this title and Tables.

The provisions of title 5, governing appointments in the competitive service, referred to in subsec. (c), are classified to section 3301 et seq. of Title 5, Government Organization and Employees.

The General Schedule, referred to in subsec. (c), is set out under section 5332 of Title 5.

Codification

In subsec. (e), "section 3324(a) and (b) of title 31" substituted for reference to section 3648 of the Revised Statutes (31 U.S.C. 529) on authority of Pub. L. 97-258, Sec. 4(b), Sept. 13, 1982, 96 Stat. 1067, the first section of which enacted Title 31, Money and Finance.

§ 4373.   [EQIA §204]

Referral of Environmental Quality Reports to standing committees having jurisdiction

Each Environmental Quality Report required by Public Law 91-190 shall, upon transmittal to Congress, be referred to each standing committee having jurisdiction over any part of the subject matter of the Report.

(Pub. L. 91-224, title II, §204, Apr. 3, 1970, 84 Stat. 115.)

References In Text

Public Law 91-190, referred to in text, is Pub. L. 91-190, Jan. 1, 1970, 83 Stat. 852, as amended, known as the National Environmental Policy Act of 1969, which is classified generally to chapter 55 (Sec. 4321 et seq.) of this title. For complete classification of this Act to the Code, see Short Title note set out under section 4321 of this title and Tables.

§ 4374.   [EQIA §205]

Authorization of appropriations

There are hereby authorized to be appropriated for the operations of the Office of Environmental Quality and the Council on Environmental Quality not to exceed the following sums for the following fiscal years which sums are in addition to those contained in Public Law 91-190:

(a) $2,126,000 for the fiscal year ending September 30, 1979.

(b) $3,000,000 for each of the fiscal years ending September 30, 1980, and September 30, 1981.

(c) $44,000 for the fiscal years ending September 30, 1982, 1983, and 1984.

(d) $480,000 for each of the fiscal years ending September 30, 1985 and September 30, 1986.

(Pub. L. 91-224, title II, §205, Apr. 3, 1970, 84 Stat. 115; Pub. L. 93-36, May 18, 1973, 87 Stat. 72; Pub. L. 94-52, §1, July 3, 1975, 89 Stat. 258; Pub. L. 94-298, May 29, 1976, 90 Stat. 587; Pub. L. 95-300, June 26, 1978, 92 Stat. 342; Pub. L. 97-350, §1, Oct. 18, 1982, 96 Stat. 1661; Pub. L. 98-581, §1, Oct. 30, 1984, 98 Stat. 3093.)

References In Text

Public Law 91-190, referred to in text, is Pub. L. 91-190, Jan. 1, 1970, 83 Stat. 852, as amended, known as the National Environmental Policy Act of 1969, which is classified generally to chapter 55 (Sec. 4321 et seq.) of this title. For complete classification of this Act to the Code, see Short Title note set out under section 4321 of this title and Tables.

§ 4375. [EQIA §206]

Office of Environmental Quality Management Fund

(a) Establishment; financing of study contracts and Federal interagency environmental projects

There is established an Office of Environmental Quality Management Fund (hereinafter referred to as the "Fund") to receive advance payments from other agencies or accounts that may be used solely to finance—

(1) study contracts that are jointly sponsored by the Office and one or more other Federal agencies; and

(2) Federal interagency environmental projects (including task forces) in which the Office participates.

(b) Study contract or project initiative

Any study contract or project that is to be financed under subsection (a) of this section may be initiated only with the approval of the Director.

(c) Regulations

The Director shall promulgate regulations setting forth policies and procedures for operation of the Fund.

(Pub. L. 91-224, title II, §206, as added Pub. L. 98-581, §2, Oct. 30, 1984, 98 Stat. 3093.)

Clean Air Act §309

42 U.S.C. §7609. [CAA §309]
Policy review

(a) The Administrator shall review and comment in writing on the environmental impact of any matter relating to duties and responsibilities granted pursuant to this Act or other provisions of the authority of the Administrator, contained in any (1) legislation proposed by any Federal department or agency, (2) newly authorized Federal projects for construction and any major Federal agency action (other than a project for construction) to which section 102(2)(C) of Public Law 91-190 applies, and (3) proposed regulations published by any department or agency of the Federal Government. Such written comment shall be made public at the conclusion of any such review.

(b) In the event the Administrator determines that any such legislation, action, or regulation is unsatisfactory from the standpoint of public health or welfare or environmental quality, he shall publish his determination and the matter shall be referred to the Council on Environmental Quality.

(July 14, 1955, ch. 360, tit. III, §309, as added Dec. 31, 1970, Pub.L. 91-604, §12(a), 84 Stat. 1709.)

State "Mini-NEPAs"

Note: This list includes the 16 statutes that require states to review the environmental impacts of their proposed actions. In addition, Michigan, New Jersey, Texas, and Utah have adopted environmental review requirements by executive order, and other states have adopted such requirements in the context of specific programs.

Cal. Pub. Res. Code §§21000-21176
Conn. Gen. Stat. Ann. §§22a-1 to -7
Hawaii Rev. Stat. §§343-1 to -8
Ind. Code Ann. §§13-1-10-1 to 13-1-10-8
Md. Nat. Res. Code Ann. §§1-301 to -305
Mass. Gen. Laws Ann. ch. 30, §61 *et seq.*
Minn. Stat. Ann. §§116D.01-.07
Mont. Code Ann. §§75-1-101 to -324
N.Y. Envtl. Conserv. Law §8-0101 to -0117
N.C. Gen. Stat. §§113-A-1 to -10
P.R. Laws Ann. tit. 12, §1121 *et seq.*
S.D. Codified Laws Ann. §§34A-9-1 to -13
Va. Code §§10-107 *et seq.*, 10-177 *et seq.*
Wash. Rev. Code Ann. §43.21C.010 *et seq.*
Wis. Stat. Ann. §1.11

Executive Orders

Executive Order 11514
Protection and Enhancement of Environmental Quality
3 C.F.R. 902 (1966-70); as amended by Executive Order 11991, 3 C.F.R. 123 (1978)

By virtue of the authority vested in me as President of the United States and in furtherance of the purpose and policy of the National Environmental Policy Act of 1969 (Public Law No. 91-190, approved January 1, 1970), it is ordered as follows:

SECTION 1. *Policy.* The Federal Government shall provide leadership in protecting and enhancing the quality of the Nation's environment to sustain and enrich human life. Federal agencies shall initiate measures needed to direct their policies, plans and programs so as to meet national environmental goals. The Council on Environmental Quality, through the Chairman, shall advise and assist the President in leading this national effort.

SEC. 2. *Responsibilities of Federal agencies.* Consonant with Title I of the National Environmental Policy Act of 1969, hereinafter referred to as the "Act", the heads of Federal agencies shall:

(a) Monitor, evaluate, and control on a continuing basis their agencies' activities so as to protect and enhance the quality of the environment. Such activities shall include those directed to controlling pollution and enhancing the environment and those designed to accomplish other program objectives which may affect the quality of the environment. Agencies shall develop programs and measures to protect and enhance environmental quality and shall assess progress in meeting the specific objectives of such activities. Heads of agencies shall consult with appropriate Federal, State and local agencies in carrying out their activities as they affect the quality of the environment.

(b) Develop procedures to ensure the fullest practicable provision of timely public information and understanding of Federal plans and programs with environmental impact in order to obtain the views of interested parties. These procedures shall include, whenever appropriate, provision for public hearings, and shall provide the public with relevant information, including information on alternative courses of action. Federal agencies shall also encourage State and local agencies to adopt similar procedures for informing the public concerning their activities affecting the quality of the environment.

(c) Insure that information regarding existing or potential environmental problems and control methods developed as part of research, development, demonstration, test, or evaluation activities is made available to Federal agencies, States, counties, municipalities, institutions, and other entities, as appropriate.

(d) Review their agencies' statutory authority, administrative regulations, policies, and procedures, including those relating to loans, grants, contracts, leases, licenses, or permits, in order to identify any deficiencies or inconsistencies therein which prohibit or limit full compliance with the purposes and provisions of the Act. A report on this review and the corrective actions taken or planned, including such measures to be proposed to the President as may be necessary to bring their authority and policies into conformance with the intent, purposes and procedures of the Act, shall be provided to the Council on Environmental Quality not later than September 1, 1970.

(e) Engage in exchange of data and research results, and

cooperate with agencies of other governments to foster the purposes of the Act.

(f) Proceed, in coordination with other agencies, with actions required by section 102 of the Act.

(g) In carrying out their responsibilities under the Act and this Order, comply with the regulations issued by the Council except where such compliance would be inconsistent with statutory requirements.

[SEC. 2(g) added by Executive Order 11991.]

SEC. 3. *Responsibilities of Council on Environmental Quality.* The Council on Environmental Quality shall:

(a) Evaluate existing and proposed policies and activities of the Federal Government directed to the control of pollution and the enhancement of the environment and to the accomplishment of other objectives which affect the quality of the environment. This shall include continuing review of procedures employed in the development and enforcement of Federal standards affecting environmental quality. Based upon such evaluations the Council shall, where appropriate, recommend to the President policies of environmental quality and shall, where appropriate, seek resolution of significant environmental issues.

(b) Recommend to the President and to the agencies priorities among programs designed for the control of pollution and for enhancement of the environment.

(c) Determine the need for new policies and programs for dealing with environmental problems not being adequately addressed.

(d) Conduct, as it determines to be appropriate, public hearings or conferences on issues of environmental significance.

(e) Promote the development and use of indices and monitoring systems (1) to assess environmental conditions and trends, (2) to predict the environmental impact of proposed public and private actions, and (3) to determine the effectiveness of programs of protecting and enhancing environmental quality.

(f) Coordinate Federal programs related to environmental quality.

(g) Advise and assist the President and the agencies in achieving international cooperation for dealing with environmental problems, under the foreign policy guidance of the Secretary of State.

(h) Issue regulations to Federal agencies for the implementation of the procedural provisions of the Act (42 U.S.C. 4332(2)). Such regulations shall be developed after consultation with affected agencies and after such public hearings as may be appropriate. They will be designed to make the environmental impact statement process more useful to decisionmakers and the public; and to reduce paperwork and the accumulation of extraneous background data, in order to emphasize the need to focus on real environmental issues and alternatives. They will require impact statements to be concise, clear, and to the point, and supported by evidence that agencies have made the necessary environmental analyses. The Council shall include in its regulations procedures (1) for the early preparation of environmental impact statements, and (2) for the referral to the Council of conflicts between agencies concerning the implementation of the National Environmental Policy Act of 1969, as amended, and Section 309 of the Clean Air Act, as amended, for the Council's recommendation as to their prompt resolution.

[SEC. 3(h) revised by Executive Order 11991.]

(i) Issue such other instructions to agencies, and request such reports and other information from them, as may be required to carry out the Council's responsibilities under the Act.

(j) Assist the President in preparing the annual Environmental Quality Report provided for in section 201 of the Act.

(k) Foster investigations, studies, surveys, research, and analyses relating to (i) ecological systems and environmental quality, (ii) the impact of new and changing technologies thereon, and (iii) means of preventing or reducing adverse effects from such technologies.

SEC. 4. *Amendments of E.O. 11472. [Omitted—Ed.].*

RICHARD NIXON

The White House
March 5, 1970

Executive Order 12114
Environmental Effects Abroad of Major Federal Actions
3 C.F.R. 356 (1980)

By virtue of the authority vested in me by the Constitution and the laws of the United States, and as President of the United States, in order to further environmental objectives consistent with the foreign policy and national security policy of the United States, it is ordered as follows:

SECTION 1.

1-1. *Purpose and Scope.* The purpose of this Executive Order is to enable responsible officials of Federal agencies having ultimate responsibility for authorizing and approving actions encompassed by this Order to be informed of pertinent environmental considerations and to take such considerations into account, with other pertinent considerations of national policy, in making decisions regarding such actions. While based on independent authority, this Order furthers the purpose of the National Environmental Policy Act and the Marine Protection Research and Sanctuaries Act and the Deepwater Port Act consistent with the foreign policy and national security policy of the United States, and represents the United States government's exclusive and complete determination of the procedural and other actions to be taken by Federal agencies to further the purpose of the National Environmental Policy Act, with respect to the environment outside the United States, its territories and possessions.

SEC. 2.

2-1. *Agency Procedures.* Every Federal agency taking major Federal actions encompassed hereby and not exempted herefrom having significant effects on the environment outside the geographical borders of the United States and its territories and possessions shall within eight months after the effective date of this Order have in effect procedures to implement this Order. Agencies shall consult with the Department of State and the Council on Environmental Quality concerning such procedures prior to placing them in effect.

2-2. *Information Exchange.* To assist in effectuating the foregoing purpose, the Department of State and the Council on Environmental Quality in collaboration with other interested Federal agencies and other nations shall conduct a program for exchange on a continuing basis of information concerning the environment. The objectives of this program shall be to provide information for use by decisionmakers, to heighten awareness of and interest in environmental concerns and, as appropriate, to facilitate environmental cooperation with foreign nations.

2-3. *Actions Included.* Agencies in their procedures under Section 2-1 shall establish procedures by which their officers having ultimate responsibility for authorizing and approving actions in one of the following categories encompassed by this Order, take into consideration in making decisions concerning such actions, a document described in Section 2-4(a):

(a) major Federal actions significantly affecting the environment of the global commons outside the jurisdiction of any nation (e.g., the oceans or Antarctica);

(b) major Federal actions significantly affecting the environment of a foreign nation not participating with the United States and not otherwise involved in the action;

(c) major Federal actions significantly affecting the environment of a foreign nation which provide to that nation:

(1) a product, or physical project producing a principal product or an emission or effluent, which is prohibited or strictly regulated by Federal law in the United States because its toxic effects on the environment create a serious public health risk; or

(2) a physical project which in the United States is prohibited or strictly regulated by Federal law to protect the environment against radioactive substances.

(d) major Federal actions outside the United States, its territories and possessions which significantly affect natural or ecological resources of global importance designated for protection under this subsection by the President, or, in the case of such a resource protected by international agreement binding on the United States, by the Secretary of State. Recommendations to the President under this subsection shall be accompanied by the views of the Council on Environmental Quality and the Secretary of State.

2-4. *Applicable Procedures.* (a) There are the following types of documents to be used in connection with actions described in Section 2-3:

(i) environmental impact statements (including generic, program and specific statements);

(ii) bilateral or multilateral environmental studies, relevant or related to the proposed action, by the United States and one or more foreign nations, or by an international body or organization in which the United States is a member or participant; or

(iii) concise reviews of the environmental issues involved, including environmental assessments, summary environmental analyses or other appropriate documents.

(b) Agencies shall in their procedures provide for preparation of documents described in Section 2-4(a), with respect to actions described in Section 2-3, as follows:

(i) for effects described in Section 2-3(a), an environmental impact statement described in Section 2-4(a)(i);

(ii) for effects described in Section 2-3(b), a document described in Section 2-4(a)(ii) or (iii), as determined by the agency;

(iii) for effects described in Section 2-3(c), a document described in Section 2-4(a)(ii) or (iii), as determined by the agency;

(iv) for effects described in Section 2-3(d), a document described in Section 2-4(a)(i), (ii) or (iii), as determined by the agency.

Such procedures may provide that an agency need not prepare a new document when a document described in Section 2-4(a) already exists.

(c) Nothing in this Order shall serve to invalidate any existing regulations of any agency which have been adopted pursuant to court order or pursuant to judicial settlement of any case or to prevent any agency from providing in its procedures for measures in addition to those provided for herein to further the purpose of the National Environmental Policy Act and other environmental laws, including the Marine Protection Research and Sanctuaries Act and the Deepwater Port Act, consistent with the foreign and national security policies of the United States.

(d) Except as provided in Section 2-5(b), agencies taking action encompassed by this Order shall, as soon as feasible, inform other Federal agencies with relevant expertise of the availability of environmental documents prepared under this Order.

Agencies in their procedures under Section 2-1 shall make appropriate provision for determining when an affected nation shall be informed in accordance with Section 3-2 of this Order of the availability of environmental documents prepared pursuant to those procedures.

In order to avoid duplication of resources, agencies in their procedures shall provide for appropriate utilization of the resources of other Federal agencies with relevant environmental jurisdiction or expertise.

2-5. *Exemptions and Considerations.*

(a) Notwithstanding Section 2-3, the following actions are exempt from this Order:

(i) actions not having a significant effect on the environment outside the United States as determined by the agency;

(ii) actions taken by the President;

(iii) actions taken by or pursuant to the direction of the President or Cabinet officer when the national security or interest is involved or when the action occurs in the course of an armed conflict;

(iv) intelligence activities and arms transfers;

(v) export licenses or permits or export approvals, and actions relating to nuclear activities except actions providing to a foreign nation a nuclear production or utilization facility as defined in the Atomic Energy Act of 1954, as amended, or a nuclear waste management facility;

(vi) votes and other actions in international conferences and organizations;

(vii) disaster and emergency relief action.

(b) Agency procedures under Section 2-1 implementing Section 2-4 may provide for appropriate modifications in the contents, timing and availability of documents to other affected Federal agencies and affected nations, where necessary to:

(i) enable the agency to decide and act promptly as and when required;

(ii) avoid adverse impacts on foreign relations or infringement in fact or appearance of other nations' sovereign responsibilities; or

(iii) ensure appropriate reflection of:

(1) diplomatic factors;

(2) international commercial, competitive and export promotion factors;

(3) needs for governmental or commercial confidentiality;

(4) national security considerations;

(5) difficulties of obtaining information and agency ability to analyze meaningfully environmental effects of a proposed action; and

(6) the degree to which the agency is involved in or able to affect a decision to be made.

(c) Agency procedures under Section 2-1 may provide for categorical exclusions and for such exemptions in addition to those specified in subsection (a) of this Section as may be necessary to meet emergency circumstances, situations involving exceptional foreign policy and national security sensitivities and other such special circumstances. In utilizing such additional exemptions agencies shall, as soon as feasible, consult with the Department of State and the Council on Environmental Quality.

(d) The provisions of Section 2-5 do not apply to actions described in Section 2-3(a) unless permitted by law.

Sec. 3.

3-1. *Rights of Action.* This Order is solely for the purpose of establishing internal procedures for Federal agencies to consider the significant effects of their actions on the environment outside the United States, its territories and possessions, and nothing in this Order shall be construed to create a cause of action.

3-2. *Foreign Relations.* The Department of State shall coordinate all communications by agencies with foreign governments concerning environmental agreements and other arrangements in implementation of this Order.

3-3. *Multi-Agency Actions.* Where more than one Federal agency is involved in an action or program, a lead agency, as determined by the agencies involved, shall have responsibility for implementation of this Order.

3-4. *Certain Terms.* For purposes of this Order, "environment" means the natural and physical environment and excludes social, economic and other environments; and an action significantly affects the environment if it does significant harm to the environment even though on balance the agency believes the action to be beneficial to the environment. The term "export approvals" in Section 2-5(a)(v) does not mean or include direct loans to finance exports.

3-5. *Multiple Impacts.* If a major Federal action having effects on the environment of the United States or the global commons requires preparation of an environmental impact statement, and if the action also has effects on the environment of a foreign nation, an environmental impact statement need not be prepared with respect to the effects on the environment of the foreign nation.

JIMMY CARTER

The White House,
January 4, 1979.

[Filed with the Office of the Federal Register, 3:38 p.m., January 5, 1979]

Regulations

Note: Each federal department or agency issues its own NEPA regulations or procedures. This Deskbook includes those issued by the departments and agencies that normally prepare the most EISs and face the most NEPA lawsuits. In dealing with any federal bureau or office, it is necessary to look to the NEPA regulations and procedures issued by the department as well as to those issued by the particular bureau or office. A complete list of NEPA regulations and procedures is found in the Outline of Agency NEPA Regulations and Procedures.

Council on Environmental Quality
NEPA Regulations
40 C.F.R. Pts. 1500-1508

PART 1500—PURPOSE, POLICY, AND MANDATE

Sec.
1500.1 Purpose.
1500.2 Policy.
1500.3 Mandate.
1500.4 Reducing paperwork.
1500.5 Reducing delay.
1500.6 Agency authority.

AUTHORITY: NEPA, the Environmental Quality Improvement Act of 1970, as amended (42 U.S.C. 4371 et seq.), sec. 309 of the Clean Air Act, as amended (42 U.S.C. 7609) and E.O. 11514, Mar. 5, 1970, as amended by E.O. 11991, May 24, 1977).

SOURCE: 43 FR 55990, Nov. 28, 1978, unless otherwise noted.

§ 1500.1 Purpose.

(a) The National Environmental Policy Act (NEPA) is our basic national charter for protection of the environment. It establishes policy, sets goals (section 101), and provides means (section 102) for carrying out the policy. Section 102(2) contains "action-forcing" provisions to make sure that federal agencies act according to the letter and spirit of the Act. The regulations that follow implement section 102(2). Their purpose is to tell federal agencies what they must do to comply with the procedures and achieve the goals of the Act. The President, the federal agencies, and the courts share responsibility for enforcing the Act so as to achieve the substantive requirements of section 101.

(b) NEPA procedures must insure that environmental information is available to public officials and citizens before decisions are made and before actions are taken. The information must be of high quality. Accurate scientific analysis, expert agency comments, and public scrutiny are essential to implementing NEPA. Most important, NEPA documents must concentrate on the issues that are truly significant to the action in question, rather than amassing needless detail.

(c) Ultimately, of course, it is not better documents but better decisions that count. NEPA's purpose is not to generate paperwork—even excellent paperwork—but to foster excellent action. The NEPA process is intended to help public officials make decisions that are based on understanding of environmental consequences, and take actions that protect, restore, and enhance the environment. These regulations provide the direction to achieve this purpose.

§ 1500.2 Policy.

Federal agencies shall to the fullest extent possible:

(a) Interpret and administer the policies, regulations, and public laws of the United States in accordance with the policies set forth in the Act and in these regulations.

(b) Implement procedures to make the NEPA process more useful to decisionmakers and the public; to reduce paperwork and the accumulation of extraneous background data; and to emphasize real environmental issues and alternatives. Environmental impact statements shall be concise, clear, and to the point, and shall be supported by evidence that agencies have made the necessary environmental analyses.

(c) Integrate the requirements of NEPA with other planning and environmental review procedures required by law or by agency practice so that all such procedures run concurrently rather than consecutively.

(d) Encourage and facilitate public involvement in decisions which affect the quality of the human environment.

(e) Use the NEPA process to identify and assess the reasonable alternatives to proposed actions that will avoid or minimize adverse effects of these actions upon the quality of the human environment.

(f) Use all practicable means, consistent with the requirements of the Act and other essential considerations of national policy, to restore and enhance the quality of the human environment and avoid or minimize any possible adverse effects of their actions upon the quality of the human environment.

§ 1500.3 Mandate.

Parts 1500 through 1508 of this title provide regulations applicable to and binding on all Federal agencies for implementing the procedural provisions of the National Environmental Policy Act of 1969, as amended (Pub. L. 91-190, 42 U.S.C. 4321 et seq.) (NEPA or the Act) except where compliance would be inconsistent with other statutory requirements. These regulations are issued pursuant to NEPA, the Environmental Quality Improvement Act of 1970, as amended (42 U.S.C. 4371 et seq.) section 309 of the Clean Air Act, as amended (42 U.S.C. 7609) and Executive Order 11514, Protection and Enhancement of Environmental Quality (March 5, 1970, as amended by Executive Order 11991, May 24, 1977). These regulations, unlike the predecessor guidelines, are not confined to sec. 102(2)(C) (environmental impact statements). The regulations apply to the whole of section 102(2). The provisions of the Act and of these regulations must be read together as a whole in order to comply with the spirit and letter of the law. It is the Council's intention that judicial review of agency compliance with these regulations not occur before an agency has filed the final environmental impact statement, or has made a final finding of no significant impact (when such a finding will result in action affecting the environment), or takes action that will result in irreparable injury. Furthermore, it is the Council's intention that any trivial violation of these regulations not give rise to any independent cause of action.

§ 1500.4 Reducing paperwork.

Agencies shall reduce excessive paperwork by:

(a) Reducing the length of environmental impact statements (§ 1502.2(c)), by means such as setting appropriate page limits (§§ 1501.7(b)(1) and 1502.7).

(b) Preparing analytic rather than encyclopedic environmental impact statements (§ 1502.2(a)).

(c) Discussing only briefly issues other than significant ones (§ 1502.2(b)).

(d) Writing environmental impact statements in plain language (§ 1502.8).

(e) Following a clear format for environmental impact statements (§ 1502.10).

(f) Emphasizing the portions of the environmental impact statement that are useful to decisionmakers and the public (§§ 1502.14 and 1502.15) and reducing emphasis on background material (§ 1502.16).

(g) Using the scoping process, not only to identify significant environmental issues deserving of study, but also to deemphasize insignificant issues, narrowing the scope of the environmental impact statement process accordingly (§ 1501.7).

(h) Summarizing the environmental impact statement (§ 1502.12) and circulating the summary instead of the entire environmental impact statement if the latter is unusually long (§ 1502.19).

(i) Using program, policy, or plan environmental impact statements and tiering from statements of broad scope to those of narrower scope, to eliminate repetitive discussions of the same issues (§§ 1502.4 and 1502.20).

(j) Incorporating by reference (§ 1502.21).

(k) Integrating NEPA requirements with other environmental review and consultation requirements (§ 1502.25).

(l) Requiring comments to be as specific as possible (§ 1503.3).

(m) Attaching and circulating only changes to the draft environmental impact statement, rather than rewriting and circulating the entire statement when changes are minor (§ 1503.4(c)).

(n) Eliminating duplication with State and local procedures, by providing for joint preparation (§ 1506.2), and with other Federal procedures, by providing that an agency may adopt appropriate environmental documents prepared by another agency (§ 1506.3).

(o) Combining environmental documents with other documents (§ 1506.4).

(p) Using categorical exclusions to define categories of actions which do not individually or cumulatively have a significant effect on the human environment and which are therefore exempt from requirements to prepare an environmental impact statement (§ 1508.4).

(q) Using a finding of no significant impact when an action not otherwise excluded will not have a significant effect on the human environment and is therefore exempt from requirements to prepare an environmental impact statement (§ 1508.13).

[43 FR 55990, Nov. 29, 1978; 44 FR 873, Jan. 3, 1979]

§ 1500.5 Reducing delay.

Agencies shall reduce delay by:

(a) Integrating the NEPA process into early planning (§ 1501.2).

(b) Emphasizing interagency cooperation before the environmental impact statement is prepared, rather than submission of adversary comments on a completed document (§ 1501.6).

(c) Insuring the swift and fair resolution of lead agency disputes (§ 1501.5).

(d) Using the scoping process for an early identification of what are and what are not the real issues (§ 1501.7).

(e) Establishing appropriate time limits for the environmental impact statement process (§§ 1501.7(b)(2) and 1501.8).

(f) Preparing environmental impact statements early in the process (§ 1502.5).

(g) Integrating NEPA requirements with other environmental review and consultation requirements (§ 1502.25).

(h) Eliminating duplication with State and local procedures by providing for joint preparation (§ 1506.2) and with other Federal procedures by providing that an agency may adopt appropriate environmental documents prepared by another agency (§ 1506.3).

(i) Combining environmental documents with other documents (§ 1506.4).

(j) Using accelerated procedures for proposals for legislation (§ 1506.8).

(k) Using categorical exclusions to define categories of actions which do not individually or cumulatively have a significant effect on the human environment (§ 1508.4) and which are therefore exempt from requirements to prepare an environmental impact statement.

(l) Using a finding of no significant impact when an action not otherwise excluded will not have a significant effect on the human environment (§ 1508.13) and is therefore exempt from requirements to prepare an environmental impact statement.

§ 1500.6 Agency authority.

Each agency shall interpret the provisions of the Act as a supplement to its existing authority and as a mandate to view traditional policies and missions in the light of the Act's national environmental objectives. Agencies shall review their policies, procedures, and regulations accordingly and revise them as necessary to insure full compliance with the purposes and provisions of the Act. The phrase "to the fullest extent possible" in section 102 means that each agency of the Federal Government shall comply with that section unless existing law applicable to the agency's operations expressly prohibits or makes compliance impossible.

PART 1501—NEPA AND AGENCY PLANNING

Sec.
1501.1 Purpose.
1501.2 Apply NEPA early in the process.
1501.3 When to prepare an environmental assessment.
1501.4 Whether to prepare an environmental impact statement.
1501.5 Lead agencies.
1501.6 Cooperating agencies.
1501.7 Scoping.
1501.8 Time limits.

AUTHORITY: NEPA, the Environmental Quality Improvement Act of 1970, as amended (42 U.S.C. 4371 *et seq.*), sec. 309 of the Clean Air Act, as amended (42 U.S.C. 7609, and E.O. 11514 (Mar. 5, 1970, as amended by E.O. 11991, May 24, 1977).

SOURCE: 43 FR 55992, Nov. 29, 1978, unless otherwise noted.

§ 1501.1 Purpose.

The purposes of this part include:

(a) Integrating the NEPA process into early planning to insure appropriate consideration of NEPA's policies and to eliminate delay.

(b) Emphasizing cooperative consultation among agencies before the environmental impact statement is prepared rather than submission of adversary comments on a completed document.

(c) Providing for the swift and fair resolution of lead agency disputes.

(d) Identifying at an early stage the significant environmental issues deserving of study and deemphasizing insignificant issues, narrowing the scope of the environmental impact statement accordingly.

(e) Providing a mechanism for putting appropriate time limits on the environmental impact statement process.

§ 1501.2 Apply NEPA early in the process.

Agencies shall integrate the NEPA process with other planning at the earliest possible time to insure that planning and decisions reflect environmental values, to avoid delays later in the process, and to head off potential conflicts. Each agency shall:

(a) Comply with the mandate of section 102(2)(A) to "utilize a systematic, interdisciplinary approach which will insure the integrated use of the natural and social sciences and the environmental design arts in planning and in decisionmaking which may have an impact on man's environment," as specified by § 1507.2.

(b) Identify environmental effects and values in adequate detail so they can be compared to economic and technical analyses. Environmental documents and appropriate analyses shall be circulated and reviewed at the same time as other planning documents.

(c) Study, develop, and describe appropriate alternatives to recommended courses of action in any proposal which involves unresolved conflicts concerning alternative uses of available resources as provided by section 102(2)(E) of the Act.

(d) Provide for cases where actions are planned by private applicants or other non-Federal entities before Federal involvement so that:

(1) Policies or designated staff are available to advise potential applicants of studies or other information foreseeably required for later Federal action.

(2) The Federal agency consults early with appropriate State and local agencies and Indian tribes and with interested private persons and organizations when its own involvement is reasonably foreseeable.

(3) The Federal agency commences its NEPA process at the earliest possible time.

§ 1501.3 When to prepare an environmental assessment.

(a) Agencies shall prepare an environmental assessment (§ 1508.9) when necessary under the procedures adopted by individual agencies to supplement these regulations as described in § 1507.3. An assessment is not necessary if the agency has decided to prepare an environmental impact statement.

(b) Agencies may prepare an environmental assessment on any action at any time in order to assist agency planning and decisionmaking.

§ 1501.4 Whether to prepare an environmental impact statement.

In determining whether to prepare an environmental impact statement the Federal agency shall:

(a) Determine under its procedures supplementing these regulations (described in § 1507.3) whether the proposal is one which:

(1) Normally requires an environmental impact statement, or

(2) Normally does not require either an environmental impact statement or an environmental assessment (categorical exclusion).

(b) If the proposed action is not covered by paragraph (a) of this section, prepare an environmental assessment (§ 1508.9). The agency shall involve environmental agencies, applicants, and the public, to the extent practicable, in preparing assessments required by § 1508.9(a)(1).

(c) Based on the environmental assessment make its determination whether to prepare an environmental impact statement.

(d) Commence the scoping process (§ 1501.7), if the agency will prepare an environmental impact statement.

(e) Prepare a finding of no significant impact (§ 1508.13), if the agency determines on the basis of the environmental assessment not to prepare a statement.

(1) The agency shall make the finding of no significant impact available to the affected public as specified in § 1506.6.

(2) In certain limited circumstances, which the agency may cover in its procedures under § 1507.3, the agency shall make the finding of no significant impact available for public review (including State and areawide clearinghouses) for 30 days before the agency makes its final determination whether to prepare an environmental impact statement and before the action may begin. The circumstances are:

(i) The proposed action is, or is closely similar to, one which normally requires the preparation of an environmental impact statement under the procedures adopted by the agency pursuant to § 1507.3, or

(ii) The nature of the proposed action is one without precedent.

§ 1501.5 Lead agencies.

(a) A lead agency shall supervise the preparation of an environmental impact statement if more than one Federal agency either:

(1) Proposes or is involved in the same action; or

(2) Is involved in a group of actions directly related to each other because of their functional interdependence or geographical proximity.

(b) Federal, State, or local agencies, including at least one Federal agency, may act as joint lead agencies to prepare an environmental impact statement (§ 1506.2).

(c) If an action falls within the provisions of paragraph (a) of this section the potential lead agencies shall determine by letter or memorandum which agency shall be the lead agency and which shall be cooperating agencies. The agencies shall resolve the lead agency question so as not to cause delay. If there is disagreement among the agencies, the following factors (which are listed in order of descending importance) shall determine lead agency designation:

(1) Magnitude of agency's involvement.

(2) Project approval/disapproval authority.

(3) Expertise concerning the action's environmental effects.

(4) Duration of agency's involvement.

(5) Sequence of agency's involvement.

(d) Any Federal agency, or any State or local agency or private person substantially affected by the absence of lead agency designation, may make a written request to the potential lead agencies that a lead agency be designated.

(e) If Federal agencies are unable to agree on which agency will be the lead agency or if the procedure described in paragraph (c) of this section has not resulted within 45 days in a lead agency designation, any of the agencies or persons concerned may file a request with the Council asking it to determine which Federal agency shall be the lead agency.

A copy of the request shall be transmitted to each potential lead agency. The request shall consist of:

(1) A precise description of the nature and extent of the proposed action.

(2) A detailed statement of why each potential lead agency should or should not be the lead agency under the criteria specified in paragraph (c) of this section.

(f) A response may be filed by any potential lead agency concerned within 20 days after a request is filed with the Council. The Council shall determine as soon as possible but not later than 20 days after receiving the request and all responses to it which Federal agency shall be the lead agency and which other Federal agencies shall be cooperating agencies.

[43 FR 55992, Nov. 29, 1978; 44 FR 873, Jan. 3, 1979]

§ 1501.6 Cooperating agencies.

The purpose of this section is to emphasize agency cooperation early in the NEPA process. Upon request of the lead agency, any other Federal agency which has jurisdiction by law shall be a cooperating agency. In addition any other Federal agency which has special expertise with respect to any environmental issue, which should be addressed in the statement may be a cooperating agency upon request of the lead agency. An agency may request the lead agency to designate it a cooperating agency.

(a) The lead agency shall:

(1) Request the participation of each cooperating agency in the NEPA process at the earliest possible time.

(2) Use the environmental analysis and proposals of cooperating agencies with jurisdiction by law or special expertise, to the maximum extent possible consistent with its responsibility as lead agency.

(3) Meet with a cooperating agency at the latter's request.

(b) Each cooperating agency shall:

(1) Participate in the NEPA process at the earliest possible time.

(2) Participate in the scoping process (described below in § 1501.7).

(3) Assume on request of the lead agency responsibility for developing information and preparing environmental analyses including portions of the environmental impact statement concerning which the cooperating agency has special expertise.

(4) Make available staff support at the lead agency's request to enhance the latter's interdisciplinary capability.

(5) Normally use its own funds. The lead agency shall, to the extent available funds permit, fund those major activities or analyses it requests from cooperating agencies. Potential lead agencies shall include such funding requirements in their budget requests.

(c) A cooperating agency may in response to a lead agency's request for assistance in preparing the environmental impact statement (described in paragraph (b)(3), (4), or (5) of this section) reply that other program commitments preclude any involvement or the degree of involvement requested in the action that is the subject of the environmental impact statement. A copy of this reply shall be submitted to the Council.

§ 1501.7 Scoping.

There shall be an early and open process for determining the scope of issues to be addressed and for identifying the significant issues related to a proposed action. This process shall be termed scoping. As soon as practicable after its decision to prepare an environmental impact statement and before the scoping process the lead agency shall publish a notice of intent (§ 1508.22) in the FEDERAL REGISTER except as provided in § 1507.3(e).

(a) As part of the scoping process the lead agency shall:

(1) Invite the participation of affected Federal, State, and local agencies, any affected Indian tribe, the proponent of the action, and other interested persons (including those who might not be in accord with the action on environmental grounds), unless there is a limited exception under § 1507.3(c). An agency may give notice in accordance with § 1506.6.

(2) Determine the scope (§ 1508.25) and the significant issues to be analyzed in depth in the environmental impact statement.

(3) Identify and eliminate from detailed study the issues which are not significant or which have been covered by prior environmental review (§ 1506.3), narrowing the discussion of these issues in the statement to a brief presentation of why they will not have a significant effect on the human environment or providing a reference to their coverage elsewhere.

(4) Allocate assignments for preparation of the environmental impact statement among the lead and cooperating agencies, with the lead agency retaining responsibility for the statement.

(5) Indicate any public environmental assessments and other environmental impact statements which are being or will be prepared that are related to but are not part of the scope of the impact statement under consideration.

(6) Identify other environmental review and consultation requirements so the lead and cooperating agencies may prepare other required analyses and studies concurrently with, and integrated with, the environmental impact statement as provided in § 1502.25.

(7) Indicate the relationship between the timing of the preparation of environmental analyses and the agency's tentative planning and decisionmaking schedule.

(b) As part of the scoping process the lead agency may:

(1) Set page limits on environmental documents (§ 1502.7).

(2) Set time limits (§ 1501.8).

(3) Adopt procedures under § 1507.3 to combine its environmental assessment process with its scoping process.

(4) Hold an early scoping meeting or meetings which may be integrated with any other early planning meeting the agency has. Such a scoping meeting will often be appropriate when the impacts of a particular action are confined to specific sites.

(c) An agency shall revise the determinations made under paragraphs (a) and (b) of this section if substantial changes are made later in the proposed action, or if significant new circumstances or information arise which bear on the proposal or its impacts.

§ 1501.8 Time limits.

Although the Council has decided that prescribed universal time limits for the entire NEPA process are too inflexible, Federal agencies are encouraged to set time limits appropriate to individual actions (consistent with the time intervals required by § 1506.10). When multiple agencies are involved the reference to agency below means lead agency.

(a) The agency shall set time limits if an applicant for the proposed action requests them: *Provided,* That the limits are consistent with the purposes of NEPA and other essential considerations of national policy.

(b) The agency may:

(1) Consider the following factors in determining time limits:

(i) Potential for environmental harm.

(ii) Size of the proposed action.

(iii) State of the art of analytic techniques.

(iv) Degree of public need for the proposed action, including the consequences of delay.

(v) Number of persons and agencies affected.

(vi) Degree to which relevant information is known and if not known the time required for obtaining it.

(vii) Degree to which the action is controversial.

(viii) Other time limits imposed on the agency by law, regulations, or executive order.

(2) Set overall time limits or limits for each constituent part of the NEPA process, which may include:

(i) Decision on whether to prepare an environmental impact statement (if not already decided).

(ii) Determination of the scope of the environmental impact statement.

(iii) Preparation of the draft environmental impact statement.

(iv) Review of any comments on the draft environmental impact statement from the public and agencies.

(v) Preparation of the final environmental impact statement.

(vi) Review of any comments on the final environmental impact statement.

(vii) Decision on the action based in part on the environmental impact statement.

(3) Designate a person (such as the project manager or a person in the agency's office with NEPA responsibilities) to expedite the NEPA process.

(c) State or local agencies or members of the public may request a Federal Agency to set time limits.

PART 1502—ENVIRONMENTAL IMPACT STATEMENT

Sec.
1502.1　Purpose.
1502.2　Implementation.
1502.3　Statutory requirements for statements.
1502.4　Major Federal actions requiring the preparation of environmental impact statements.
1502.5　Timing.
1502.6　Interdisciplinary preparation.
1502.7　Page limits.
1502.8　Writing.
1502.9　Draft, final, and supplemental statements.
1502.10　Recommended format.
1502.11　Cover sheet.
1502.12　Summary.
1502.13　Purpose and need.
1502.14　Alternatives including the proposed action.
1502.15　Affected environment.
1502.16　Environmental consequences.
1502.17　List of preparers.
1502.18　Appendix.
1502.19　Circulation of the environmental impact statement.
1502.20　Tiering.
1502.21　Incorporation by reference.
1502.22　Incomplete or unavailable information.
1502.23　Cost-benefit analysis.
1502.24　Methodology and scientific accuracy.
1502.25　Environmental review and consultation requirements.

AUTHORITY: NEPA, the Environmental Quality Improvement Act of 1970, as amended (42 U.S.C. 4371 *et seq.*), sec. 309 of the Clean Air Act, as amended (42 U.S.C. 7609), and E.O. 11514 (Mar. 5, 1970, as amended by E.O. 11991, May 24, 1977).

SOURCE: 43 FR 55994, Nov. 29, 1978, unless otherwise noted.

§ 1502.1 Purpose.

The primary purpose of an environmental impact statement is to serve as an action-forcing device to insure that the policies and goals defined in the Act are infused into the ongoing programs and actions of the Federal Government. It shall provide full and fair discussion of significant environmental impacts and shall inform decisionmakers and the public of the reasonable alternatives which would avoid or minimize adverse impacts or enhance the quality of the human environment. Agencies shall focus on significant environmental issues and alternatives and shall reduce paperwork and the accumulation of extraneous background data. Statements shall be concise, clear, and to the point, and shall be supported by evidence that the agency has made the necessary environmental analyses. An environmental impact statement is more than a disclosure document. It shall be used by Federal officials in conjunction with other relevant material to plan actions and make decisions.

§ 1502.2 Implementation.

To achieve the purposes set forth in § 1502.1 agencies shall prepare environmental impact statements in the following manner:

(a) Environmental impact statements shall be analytic rather than encyclopedic.

(b) Impacts shall be discussed in proportion to their significance. There shall be only brief discussion of other than significant issues. As in a finding of no significant impact, there should be only enough discussion to show why more study is not warranted.

(c) Environmental impact statements shall be kept concise and shall be no longer than absolutely necessary to comply with NEPA and with these regulations. Length should vary first with potential environmental problems and then with project size.

(d) Environmental impact statements shall state how alternatives considered in it and decisions based on it will or will not achieve the requirements of sections 101 and 102(1) of the Act and other environmental laws and policies.

(e) The range of alternatives discussed in environmental impact statements shall encompass those to be considered by the ultimate agency decisionmaker.

(f) Agencies shall not commit resources prejudicing selection of alternatives before making a final decision (§ 1506.1).

(g) Environmental impact statements shall serve as the means of assessing the environmental impact of proposed agency actions, rather than justifying decisions already made.

§ 1502.3 Statutory requirements for statements.

As required by sec. 102(2)(C) of NEPA environmental impact statements (§ 1508.11) are to be included in every recommendation or report.

On proposals (§ 1508.23).

For legislation and (§ 1508.17).

Other major Federal actions (§ 1508.18).

Significantly (§ 1508.27).

Affecting (§§ 1508.3, 1508.8).

The quality of the human environment (§ 1508.14).

§ 1502.4 Major Federal actions requiring the preparation of environmental impact statements.

(a) Agencies shall make sure the proposal which is the subject of an environmental impact statement is properly defined. Agencies shall use the criteria for scope (§ 1508.25) to determine which proposal(s) shall be the subject of a particular statement. Proposals or parts of proposals which are related to each other closely enough to be, in effect, a single course of action shall be evaluated in a single impact statement.

(b) Environmental impact statements may be prepared, and are sometimes required, for broad Federal actions such as the adoption of new agency programs or regulations (§ 1508.18). Agencies shall prepare statements on broad actions so that they are relevant to policy and are timed to coincide with meaningful points in agency planning and decisionmaking.

(c) When preparing statements on broad actions (including proposals by more than one agency), agencies may find it useful to evaluate the proposal(s) in one of the following ways:

(1) Geographically, including actions occurring in the same general location, such as body of water, region, or metropolitan area.

(2) Generically, including actions which have relevant similarities, such as common timing, impacts, alternatives, methods of implementation, media, or subject matter.

(3) By stage of technological development including federal or federally assisted research, development or demonstration programs for new technologies which, if applied, could significantly affect the quality of the human environment. Statements shall be prepared on such programs and shall be available before the program has reached a stage of investment or commitment to implementation likely to determine subsequent development or restrict later alternatives.

(d) Agencies shall as appropriate employ scoping (§ 1501.7), tiering (§ 1502.20), and other methods listed in §§ 1500.4 and 1500.5 to relate broad and narrow actions and to avoid duplication and delay.

§ 1502.5 Timing.

An agency shall commence preparation of an environmental impact statement as close as possible to the time the agency is developing or is presented with a proposal (§ 1508.23) so that preparation can be completed in time for the final statement to be included in any recommendation or report on the proposal. The statement shall be prepared early enough so that it can serve practically as an important contribution to the decisionmaking process and will not be used to rationalize or justify decisions already made (§§ 1500.2(c), 1501.2, and 1502.2). For instance:

(a) For projects directly undertaken by Federal agencies the environmental impact statement shall be prepared at the feasibility analysis (go-no go) stage and may be supplemented at a later stage if necessary.

(b) For applications to the agency appropriate environmental assessments or statements shall be commenced no later than immediately after the application is received. Federal agencies are encouraged to begin preparation of such assessments or statements earlier, preferably jointly with applicable State or local agencies.

(c) For adjudication, the final environmental impact statement shall nor-

mally precede the final staff recommendation and that portion of the public hearing related to the impact study. In appropriate circumstances the statement may follow preliminary hearings designed to gather information for use in the statements.

(d) For informal rulemaking the draft environmental impact statement shall normally accompany the proposed rule.

§ 1502.6 Interdisciplinary preparation.

Environmental impact statements shall be prepared using an inter-disciplinary approach which will insure the integrated use of the natural and social sciences and the environmental design arts (section 102(2)(A) of the Act). The disciplines of the preparers shall be appropriate to the scope and issues identified in the scoping process (§ 1501.7).

§ 1502.7 Page limits.

The text of final environmental impact statements (e.g., paragraphs (d) through (g) of § 1502.10) shall normally be less than 150 pages and for proposals of unusual scope or complexity shall normally be less than 300 pages.

§ 1502.8 Writing.

Environmental impact statements shall be written in plain language and may use appropriate graphics so that decisionmakers and the public can readily understand them. Agencies should employ writers of clear prose or editors to write, review, or edit statements, which will be based upon the analysis and supporting data from the natural and social sciences and the environmental design arts.

§ 1502.9 Draft, final, and supplemental statements.

Except for proposals for legislation as provided in § 1506.8 environmental impact statements shall be prepared in two stages and may be supplemented.

(a) Draft environmental impact statements shall be prepared in accordance with the scope decided upon in the scoping process. The lead agency shall work with the cooperating agencies and shall obtain comments as required in Part 1503 of this chapter. The draft statement must fulfill and satisfy to the fullest extent possible the requirements established for final statements in section 102(2)(C) of the Act. If a draft statement is so inadequate as to preclude meaningful analysis, the agency shall prepare and circulate a revised draft of the appropriate portion. The agency shall make every effort to disclose and discuss at appropriate points in the draft statement all major points of view on the environmental impacts of the alternatives including the proposed action.

(b) Final environmental impact statements shall respond to comments as required in Part 1503 of this chapter. The agency shall discuss at appropriate points in the final statement

any responsible opposing view which was not adequately discussed in the draft statement and shall indicate the agency's response to the issues raised.

(c) Agencies:

(1) Shall prepare supplements to either draft or final environmental impact statements if:

(i) The agency makes substantial changes in the proposed action that are relevant to environmental concerns; or

(ii) There are significant new circumstances or information relevant to environmental concerns and bearing on the proposed action or its impacts.

(2) May also prepare supplements when the agency determines that the purposes of the Act will be furthered by doing so.

(3) Shall adopt procedures for introducing a supplement into its formal administrative record, if such a record exists.

(4) Shall prepare, circulate, and file a supplement to a statement in the same fashion (exclusive of scoping) as a draft and final statement unless alternative procedures are approved by the Council.

§ 1502.10 Recommended format.

Agencies shall use a format for environmental impact statements which will encourage good analysis and clear presentation of the alternatives including the proposed action. The following standard format for environmental impact statements should be followed unless the agency determines that there is a compelling reason to do otherwise:

(a) Cover sheet.

(b) Summary.

(c) Table of contents.

(d) Purpose of and need for action.

(e) Alternatives including proposed action (sections 102(2)(C)(iii) and 102(2)(E) of the Act).

(f) Affected environment.

(g) Environmental consequences (especially sections 102(2)(C)(i), (ii), (iv), and (v) of the Act).

(h) List of preparers.

(i) List of Agencies, Organizations, and persons to whom copies of the statement are sent.

(j) Index.

(k) Appendices (if any).

If a different format is used, it shall include paragraphs (a), (b), (c), (h), (i), and (j), of this section and shall include the substance of paragraphs (d), (e), (f), (g), and (k) of this section, as further described in §§ 1502.11 through 1502.18, in any appropriate format.

§ 1502.11 Cover sheet.

The cover sheet shall not exceed one page. It shall include:

(a) A list of the responsible agencies including the lead agency and any cooperating agencies.

(b) The title of the proposed action that is the subject of the statement (and if appropriate the titles of related cooperating agency actions), together with the State(s) and county(ies) (or other jurisdiction if applicable) where the action is located.

(c) The name, address, and telephone number of the person at the agency who can supply further information.

(d) A designation of the statement as a draft, final, or draft or final supplement.

(e) A one paragraph abstract of the statement.

(f) The date by which comments must be received (computed in cooperation with EPA under § 1506.10).

The information required by this section may be entered on Standard Form 424 (in items 4, 6, 7, 10, and 18).

§ 1502.12 Summary.

Each environmental impact statement shall contain a summary which adequately and accurately summarizes the statement. The summary shall stress the major conclusions, areas of controversy (including issues raised by agencies and the public), and the issues to be resolved (including the choice among alternatives). The summary will normally not exceed 15 pages.

§ 1502.13 Purpose and need.

The statement shall briefly specify the underlying purpose and need to which the agency is responding in proposing the alternatives including the proposed action.

§ 1502.14 Alternatives including the proposed action.

This section is the heart of the environmental impact statement. Based on the information and analysis presented in the sections on the Affected Environment (§ 1502.15) and the Environmental Consequences (§ 1502.16), it should present the environmental impacts of the proposal and the alternatives in comparative form, thus sharply defining the issues and providing a clear basis for choice among options by the decisionmaker and the public. In this section agencies shall:

(a) Rigorously explore and objectively evaluate all reasonable alternatives, and for alternatives which were eliminated from detailed study, briefly discuss the reasons for their having been eliminated.

(b) Devote substantial treatment to each alternative considered in detail including the proposed action so that reviewers may evaluate their comparative merits.

(c) Include reasonable alternatives not within the jurisdiction of the lead agency.

(d) Include the alternative of no action.

(e) Identify the agency's preferred alternative or alternatives, if one or more exists, in the draft statement and identify such alternative in the final statement unless another law prohibits the expression of such a preference.

(f) Include appropriate mitigation measures not already included in the proposed action or alternatives.

§ 1502.15 Affected environment.

The environmental impact statement shall succinctly describe the environment of the area(s) to be affected or created by the alternatives under consideration. The descriptions shall be no longer than is necessary to understand the effects of the alternatives. Data and analyses in a statement shall be commensurate with the importance of the impact, with less important material summarized, consolidated, or simply referenced. Agencies shall avoid useless bulk in statements and shall concentrate effort and attention on important issues. Verbose descriptions of the affected environment are themselves no measure of the adequacy of an environmental impact statement.

§ 1502.16 Environmental consequences.

This section forms the scientific and analytic basis for the comparisons under § 1502.14. It shall consolidate the discussions of those elements required by sections 102(2)(C)(i), (ii), (iv), and (v) of NEPA which are within the scope of the statement and as much of section 102(2)(C)(iii) as is necessary to support the comparisons. The discussion will include the environmental impacts of the alternatives including the proposed action, any adverse environmental effects which cannot be avoided should the proposal be implemented, the relationship between short-term uses of man's environment and the maintenance and enhancement of long-term productivity, and any irreversible or irretrievable commitments of resources which would be involved in the proposal should it be implemented. This section should not duplicate discussions in § 1502.14. It shall include discussions of:

(a) Direct effects and their significance (§ 1508.8).

(b) Indirect effects and their significance (§ 1508.8).

(c) Possible conflicts between the proposed action and the objectives of Federal, regional, State, and local (and in the case of a reservation, Indian tribe) land use plans, policies and controls for the area concerned. (See § 1506.2(d).)

(d) The environmental effects of alternatives including the proposed action. The comparisons under § 1502.14 will be based on this discussion.

(e) Energy requirements and conservation potential of various alternatives and mitigation measures.

(f) Natural or depletable resource requirements and conservation potential of various alternatives and mitigation measures.

(g) Urban quality, historic and cultural resources, and the design of the built environment, including the reuse and conservation potential of various alternatives and mitigation measures.

(h) Means to mitigate adverse environmental impacts (if not fully covered under § 1502.14(f)).

[43 FR 55994, Nov. 29, 1978; 44 FR 873, Jan. 3, 1979]

§ 1502.17 List of preparers.

The environmental impact statement shall list the names, together with their qualifications (expertise, experience, professional disciplines), of the persons who were primarily responsible for preparing the environmental impact statement or significant background papers, including basic components of the statement (§§ 1502.6 and 1502.8). Where possible the persons who are responsible for a particular analysis, including analyses in background papers, shall be identified. Normally the list will not exceed two pages.

§ 1502.18 Appendix.

If an agency prepares an appendix to an environmental impact statement the appendix shall:

(a) Consist of material prepared in connection with an environmental impact statement (as distinct from material which is not so prepared and which is incorporated by reference (§ 1502.21)).

(b) Normally consist of material which substantiates any analysis fundamental to the impact statement.

(c) Normally be analytic and relevant to the decision to be made.

(d) Be circulated with the environmental impact statement or be readily available on request.

§ 1502.19 Circulation of the environmental impact statement.

Agencies shall circulate the entire draft and final environmental impact statements except for certain appendices as provided in § 1502.18(d) and unchanged statements as provided in § 1503.4(c). However, if the statement is unusually long, the agency may circulate the summary instead, except that the entire statement shall be furnished to:

(a) Any Federal agency which has jurisdiction by law or special expertise with respect to any environmental impact involved and any appropriate Federal, State or local agency authorized to develop and enforce environmental standards.

(b) The applicant, if any.

(c) Any person, organization, or agency requesting the entire environmental impact statement.

(d) In the case of a final environmental impact statement any person, organization, or agency which submitted substantive comments on the draft.

If the agency circulates the summary and thereafter receives a timely request for the entire statement and for additional time to comment, the time for that requestor only shall be extended by at least 15 days beyond the minimum period.

§ 1502.20 Tiering.

Agencies are encouraged to tier their environmental impact statements to eliminate repetitive discussions of the same issues and to focus on the actual issues ripe for decision at each level of environmental review (§ 1508.28). Whenever a broad environmental impact statement has been prepared (such as a program or policy statement) and a subsequent statement or environmental assessment is then prepared on an action included within the entire program or policy (such as a site specific action) the subsequent statement or environmental assessment need only summarize the issues discussed in the broader statement and incorporate discussions from the broader statement by reference and shall concentrate on the issues specific to the subsequent action. The subsequent document shall state where the earlier document is available. Tiering may also be appropriate for different stages of actions. (Section 1508.28).

§ 1502.21 Incorporation by reference.

Agencies shall incorporate material into an environmental impact statement by reference when the effect will be to cut down on bulk without impeding agency and public review of the action. The incorporated material shall be cited in the statement and its content briefly described. No material may be incorporated by reference unless it is reasonably available for inspection by potentially interested persons within the time allowed for comment. Material based on proprietary data which is itself not available for review and comment shall not be incorporated by reference.

§ 1502.22 Incomplete or unavailable information.

When an agency is evaluating reasonably foreseeable significant adverse effects on the human environment in an environmental impact statement and there is incomplete or unavailable information, the agency shall always make clear that such information is lacking.

(a) If the incomplete information relevant to reasonably foreseeable significant adverse impacts is essential to a reasoned choice among alternatives and the overall costs of obtaining it are not exorbitant, the agency shall include the information in the environmental impact statement.

(b) If the information relevant to reasonably foreseeable significant adverse impacts cannot be obtained because the overall costs of obtaining it are exorbitant or the means to obtain it are not known, the agency shall include within the environmental impact statement:

(1) A statement that such information is incomplete or unavailable; (2) a statement of the relevance of the incomplete or unavailable information to evaluating reasonably foreseeable significant adverse impacts on the human environment; (3) a summary of existing credible scientific evidence which is relevant to evaluating the reasonably foreseeable significant adverse impacts on the human environ-

ment, and (4) the agency's evaluation of such impacts based upon theoretical approaches or research methods generally accepted in the scientific community. For the purposes of this section, "reasonably foreseeable" includes impacts which have catastrophic consequences, even if their probability of occurrence is low, provided that the analysis of the impacts is supported by credible scientific evidence, is not based on pure conjecture, and is within the rule of reason.

(c) The amended regulation will be applicable to all environmental impact statements for which a Notice of Intent (40 CFR 1508.22) is published in the FEDERAL REGISTER on or after May 27, 1986. For environmental impact statements in progress, agencies may choose to comply with the requirements of either the original or amended regulation.

[51 FR 15625, Apr. 25, 1986]

§ 1502.23 Cost-benefit analysis.

If a cost-benefit analysis relevant to the choice among environmentally different alternatives is being considered for the proposed action, it shall be incorporated by reference or appended to the statement as an aid in evaluating the environmental consequences. To assess the adequacy of compliance with section 102(2)(B) of the Act the statement shall, when a cost-benefit analysis is prepared, discuss the relationship between that analysis and any analyses of unquantified environmental impacts, values, and amenities. For purposes of complying with the Act, the weighing of the merits and drawbacks of the various alternatives need not be displayed in a monetary cost-benefit analysis and should not be when there are important qualitative considerations. In any event, an environmental impact statement should at least indicate those considerations, including factors not related to environmental quality, which are likely to be relevant and important to a decision.

§ 1502.24 Methodology and scientific accuracy.

Agencies shall insure the professional integrity, including scientific integrity, of the discussions and analyses in environmental impact statements. They shall identify any methodologies used and shall make explicit reference by footnote to the scientific and other sources relied upon for conclusions in the statement. An agency may place discussion of methodology in an appendix.

§ 1502.25 Environmental review and consultation requirements.

(a) To the fullest extent possible, agencies shall prepare draft environmental impact statements concurrently with and integrated with environmental impact analyses and related surveys and studies required by the Fish and Wildlife Coordination Act (16 U.S.C. 661 et seq.), the National Historic Preservation Act of 1966 (16 U.S.C. 470 et seq.), the Endangered

Species Act of 1973 (16 U.S.C. 1531 et seq.), and other environmental review laws and executive orders.

(b) The draft environmental impact statement shall list all Federal permits, licenses, and other entitlements which must be obtained in implementing the proposal. If it is uncertain whether a Federal permit, license, or other entitlement is necessary, the draft environmental impact statement shall so indicate.

PART 1503—COMMENTING

Sec.
1503.1 Inviting comments.
1503.2 Duty to comment.
1503.3 Specificity of comments.
1503.4 Response to comments.

AUTHORITY: NEPA, the Environmental Quality Improvement Act of 1970, as amended (42 U.S.C. 4371 et seq.), sec. 309 of the Clean Air Act, as amended (42 U.S.C. 7609), and E.O. 11514 (Mar. 5, 1970, as amended by E.O. 11991, May 24, 1977).

SOURCE: 43 FR 55997, Nov. 29, 1978, unless otherwise noted.

§ 1503.1 Inviting comments.

(a) After preparing a draft environmental impact statement and before preparing a final environmental impact statement the agency shall:

(1) Obtain the comments of any Federal agency which has jurisdiction by law or special expertise with respect to any environmental impact involved or which is authorized to develop and enforce environmental standards.

(2) Request the comments of:

(i) Appropriate State and local agencies which are authorized to develop and enforce environmental standards;

(ii) Indian tribes, when the effects may be on a reservation; and

(iii) Any agency which has requested that it receive statements on actions of the kind proposed.

Office of Management and Budget Circular A-95 (Revised), through its system of clearinghouses, provides a means of securing the views of State and local environmental agencies. The clearinghouses may be used, by mutual agreement of the lead agency and the clearinghouse, for securing State and local reviews of the draft environmental impact statements.

(3) Request comments from the applicant, if any.

(4) Request comments from the public, affirmatively soliciting comments from those persons or organizations who may be interested or affected.

(b) An agency may request comments on a final environmental impact statement before the decision is finally made. In any case other agencies or persons may make comments before the final decision unless a different time is provided under § 1506.10.

§ 1503.2 Duty to comment.

Federal agencies with jurisdiction by law or special expertise with respect to any environmental impact involved and agencies which are authorized to develop and enforce environmental standards shall comment on statements within their jurisdiction, expertise, or authority. Agencies shall comment within the time period specified for comment in § 1506.10. A Federal agency may reply that it has no comment. If a cooperating agency is satisfied that its views are adequately reflected in the environmental impact statement, it should reply that it has no comment.

§ 1503.3 Specificity of comments.

(a) Comments on an environmental impact statement or on a proposed action shall be as specific as possible and may address either the adequacy of the statement or the merits of the alternatives discussed or both.

(b) When a commenting agency criticizes a lead agency's predictive methodology, the commenting agency should describe the alternative methodology which it prefers and why.

(c) A cooperating agency shall specify in its comments whether it needs additional information to fulfill other applicable environmental reviews or consultation requirements and what information it needs. In particular, it shall specify any additional information it needs to comment adequately on the draft statement's analysis of significant site-specific effects associated with the granting or approving by that cooperating agency of necessary Federal permits, licenses, or entitlements.

(d) When a cooperating agency with jurisdiction by law objects to or expresses reservations about the proposal on grounds of environmental impacts, the agency expressing the objection or reservation shall specify the mitigation measures it considers necessary to allow the agency to grant or approve applicable permit, license, or related requirements or concurrences.

§ 1503.4 Response to comments.

(a) An agency preparing a final environmental impact statement shall assess and consider comments both individually and collectively, and shall respond by one or more of the means listed below, stating its response in the final statement. Possible responses are to:

(1) Modify alternatives including the proposed action.

(2) Develop and evaluate alternatives not previously given serious consideration by the agency.

(3) Supplement, improve, or modify its analyses.

(4) Make factual corrections.

(5) Explain why the comments do not warrant further agency response, citing the sources, authorities, or reasons which support the agency's position and, if appropriate, indicate those circumstances which would trigger agency reappraisal or further response.

(b) All substantive comments received on the draft statement (or summaries thereof where the response has been exceptionally voluminous), should be attached to the final statement whether or not the comment is thought to merit individual discussion by the agency in the text of the statement.

(c) If changes in response to comments are minor and are confined to the responses described in paragraphs (a)(4) and (5) of this section, agencies may write them on errata sheets and attach them to the statement instead of rewriting the draft statement. In such cases only the comments, the responses, and the changes and not the final statement need be circulated (§ 1502.19). The entire document with a new cover sheet shall be filed as the final statement (§ 1506.9).

PART 1504—PREDECISION REFERRALS TO THE COUNCIL OF PROPOSED FEDERAL ACTIONS DETERMINED TO BE ENVIRONMENTALLY UNSATISFACTORY

Sec.
1504.1 Purpose.
1504.2 Criteria for referral.
1504.3 Procedure for referrals and response.

AUTHORITY: NEPA, the Environmental Quality Improvement Act of 1970, as amended (42 U.S.C. 4371 et seq.), sec. 309 of the Clean Air Act, as amended (42 U.S.C. 7609), and E.O. 11514 (Mar. 5, 1970, as amended by E.O. 11991, May 24, 1977).

SOURCE: 43 FR 55998, Nov. 29, 1978, unless otherwise noted.

§ 1504.1 Purpose.

(a) This part establishes procedures for referring to the Council Federal interagency disagreements concerning proposed major Federal actions that might cause unsatisfactory environmental effects. It provides means for early resolution of such disagreements.

(b) Under section 309 of the Clean Air Act (42 U.S.C. 7609), the Administrator of the Environmental Protection Agency is directed to review and comment publicly on the environmental impacts of Federal activities, including actions for which environmental impact statements are prepared. If after this review the Administrator determines that the matter is "unsatisfactory from the standpoint of public health or welfare or environmental quality," section 309 directs that the matter be referred to the Council (hereafter "environmental referrals").

(c) Under section 102(2)(C) of the Act other Federal agencies may make similar reviews of environmental impact statements, including judgments on the acceptability of anticipated environmental impacts. These reviews must be made available to the President, the Council and the public.

§ 1504.2 Criteria for referral.

Environmental referrals should be made to the Council only after concerted, timely (as early as possible in the process), but unsuccessful attempts to resolve differences with the lead agency. In determining what environmental objections to the matter are appropriate to refer to the Council, an agency should weigh potential adverse environmental impacts, considering:

(a) Possible violation of national environmental standards or policies.

(b) Severity.

(c) Geographical scope.

(d) Duration.

(e) Importance as precedents.

(f) Availability of environmentally preferable alternatives.

§ 1504.3 Procedure for referrals and response.

(a) A Federal agency making the referral to the Council shall:

(1) Advise the lead agency at the earliest possible time that it intends to refer a matter to the Council unless a satisfactory agreement is reached.

(2) Include such advice in the referring agency's comments on the draft environmental impact statement, except when the statement does not contain adequate information to permit an assessment of the matter's environmental acceptability.

(3) Identify any essential information that is lacking and request that it be made available at the earliest possible time.

(4) Send copies of such advice to the Council.

(b) The referring agency shall deliver its referral to the Council not later than twenty-five (25) days after the final environmental impact statement has been made available to the Environmental Protection Agency, commenting agencies, and the public. Except when an extension of this period has been granted by the lead agency, the Council will not accept a referral after that date.

(c) The referral shall consist of:

(1) A copy of the letter signed by the head of the referring agency and delivered to the lead agency informing the lead agency of the referral and the reasons for it, and requesting that no action be taken to implement the matter until the Council acts upon the referral. The letter shall include a copy of the statement referred to in (c)(2) of this section.

(2) A statement supported by factual evidence leading to the conclusion that the matter is unsatisfactory from the standpoint of public health or welfare or environmental quality. The statement shall:

(i) Identify any material facts in controversy and incorporate (by reference if appropriate) agreed upon facts,

(ii) Identify any existing environmental requirements or policies which would be violated by the matter,

(iii) Present the reasons why the referring agency believes the matter is environmentally unsatisfactory,

(iv) Contain a finding by the agency whether the issue raised is of national importance because of the threat to national environmental resources or policies or for some other reason,

(v) Review the steps taken by the referring agency to bring its concerns to the attention of the lead agency at the earliest possible time, and

(vi) Give the referring agency's recommendations as to what mitigation alternative, further study, or other course of action (including abandonment of the matter) are necessary to remedy the situation.

(d) Not later than twenty-five (25) days after the referral to the Council the lead agency may deliver a response to the Council, and the referring agency. If the lead agency requests more time and gives assurance that the matter will not go forward in the interim, the Council may grant an extension. The response shall:

(1) Address fully the issues raised in the referral.

(2) Be supported by evidence.

(3) Give the lead agency's response to the referring agency's recommendations.

(e) Interested persons (including the applicant) may deliver their views in writing to the Council. Views in support of the referral should be delivered not later than the referral. Views in support of the response shall be delivered not later than the response.

(f) Not later than twenty-five (25) days after receipt of both the referral and any response or upon being informed that there will be no response (unless the lead agency agrees to a longer time), the Council may take one or more of the following actions:

(1) Conclude that the process of referral and response has successfully resolved the problem.

(2) Initiate discussions with the agencies with the objective of mediation with referring and lead agencies.

(3) Hold public meetings or hearings to obtain additional views and information.

(4) Determine that the issue is not one of national importance and request the referring and lead agencies to pursue their decision process.

(5) Determine that the issue should be further negotiated by the referring and lead agencies and is not appropriate for Council consideration until one or more heads of agencies report to the Council that the agencies' disagreements are irreconcilable.

(6) Publish its findings and recommendations (including where appropriate a finding that the submitted evidence does not support the position of an agency).

(7) When appropriate, submit the referral and the response together with the Council's recommendation to the President for action.

(g) The Council shall take no longer than 60 days to complete the actions specified in paragraph (f)(2), (3), or (5) of this section.

(h) When the referral involves an action required by statute to be determined on the record after opportunity for agency hearing, the referral shall be conducted in a manner consistent with 5 U.S.C. 557(d) (Administrative Procedure Act).

[43 FR 55998, Nov. 29, 1978; 44 FR 873, Jan. 3, 1979]

PART 1505—NEPA AND AGENCY DECISIONMAKING

Sec.
1505.1 Agency decisionmaking procedures.
1505.2 Record of decision in cases requiring environmental impact statements.
1505.3 Implementing the decision.

AUTHORITY: NEPA, the Environmental Quality Improvement Act of 1970, as amended (42 U.S.C. 4371 *et seq.*), sec. 309 of the Clean Air Act, as amended (42 U.S.C. 7609), and E.O. 11514 (Mar. 5, 1970, as amended by E.O. 11991, May 24, 1977).

SOURCE: 43 FR 55999, Nov. 29, 1978, unless otherwise noted.

§ 1505.1 Agency decisionmaking procedures.

Agencies shall adopt procedures (§ 1507.3) to ensure that decisions are made in accordance with the policies and purposes of the Act. Such procedures shall include but not be limited to:

(a) Implementing procedures under section 102(2) to achieve the requirements of sections 101 and 102(1).

(b) Designating the major decision points for the agency's principal programs likely to have a significant effect on the human environment and assuring that the NEPA process corresponds with them.

(c) Requiring that relevant environmental documents, comments, and responses be part of the record in formal rulemaking or adjudicatory proceedings.

(d) Requiring that relevant environmental documents, comments, and responses accompany the proposal through existing agency review processes so that agency officials use the statement in making decisions.

(e) Requiring that the alternatives considered by the decisionmaker are encompassed by the range of alternatives discussed in the relevant environmental documents and that the decisionmaker consider the alternatives described in the environmental impact statement. If another decision document accompanies the relevant environmental documents to the decisionmaker, agencies are encouraged to make available to the public before the decision is made any part of that document that relates to the comparison of alternatives.

§ 1505.2 Record of decision in cases requiring environmental impact statements.

At the time of its decision (§ 1506.10) or, if appropriate, its recommendation to Congress, each agency shall prepare a concise public record of decision. The record, which may be integrated into any other record prepared by the agency, including that required by OMB Circular A-95 (Revised), part I, sections 6(c) and (d), and Part II, section 5(b)(4), shall:

(a) State what the decision was.

(b) Identify all alternatives considered by the agency in reaching its decision, specifying the alternative or alternatives which were considered to be environmentally preferable. An agency may discuss preferences among alternatives based on relevant factors including economic and technical considerations and agency statutory missions. An agency shall identify and discuss all such factors including any essential considerations of national policy which were balanced by the agency in making its decision and state how those considerations entered into its decision.

(c) State whether all practicable means to avoid or minimize environmental harm from the alternative selected have been adopted, and if not, why they were not. A monitoring and enforcement program shall be adopted and summarized where applicable for any mitigation.

§ 1505.3 Implementing the decision.

Agencies may provide for monitoring to assure that their decisions are carried out and should do so in important cases. Mitigation (§ 1505.2(c)) and other conditions established in the environmental impact statement or during its review and committed as part of the decision shall be implemented by the lead agency or other appropriate consenting agency. The lead agency shall:

(a) Include appropriate conditions in grants, permits or other approvals.

(b) Condition funding of actions on mitigation.

(c) Upon request, inform cooperating or commenting agencies on progress in carrying out mitigation measures which they have proposed and which were adopted by the agency making the decision.

(d) Upon request, make available to the public the results of relevant monitoring.

PART 1506—OTHER REQUIREMENTS OF NEPA

Sec.
1506.1 Limitations on actions during NEPA process.
1506.2 Elimination of duplication with State and local procedures.
1506.3 Adoption.
1506.4 Combining documents.
1506.5 Agency responsibility.
1506.6 Public involvement.
1506.7 Further guidance.
1506.8 Proposals for legislation.
1506.9 Filing requirements.
1506.10 Timing of agency action.
1506.11 Emergencies.
1506.12 Effective date.

AUTHORITY: NEPA, the Environmental Quality Improvement Act of 1970, as amended (42 U.S.C. 4371 *et seq.*), sec. 309 of the Clean Air Act, as amended (42 U.S.C. 7609), and E.O. 11514 (Mar. 5, 1970, as amended by E.O. 11991, May 24, 1977).

SOURCE: 43 FR 56000, Nov. 29, 1978, unless otherwise noted.

§ 1506.1 Limitations on actions during NEPA process.

(a) Until an agency issues a record of decision as provided in § 1505.2 (except as provided in paragraph (c) of this section), no action concerning the proposal shall be taken which would:

(1) Have an adverse environmental impact; or

(2) Limit the choice of reasonable alternatives.

(b) If any agency is considering an application from a non-Federal entity, and is aware that the applicant is about to take an action within the agency's jurisdiction that would meet either of the criteria in paragraph (a) of this section, then the agency shall promptly notify the applicant that the agency will take appropriate action to insure that the objectives and procedures of NEPA are achieved.

(c) While work on a required program environmental impact statement is in progress and the action is not covered by an existing program statement, agencies shall not undertake in the interim any major Federal action covered by the program which may significantly affect the quality of the human environment unless such action:

(1) Is justified independently of the program;

(2) Is itself accompanied by an adequate environmental impact statement; and

(3) Will not prejudice the ultimate decision on the program. Interim action prejudices the ultimate decision on the program when it tends to determine subsequent development or limit alternatives.

(d) This section does not preclude development by applicants of plans or designs or performance of other work necessary to support an application for Federal, State or local permits or assistance. Nothing in this section shall preclude Rural Electrification Administration approval of minimal expenditures not affecting the environment (*e.g.* long leadtime equipment and purchase options) made by nongovernmental entities seeking loan guarantees from the Administration.

§ 1506.2 Elimination of duplication with State and local procedures.

(a) Agencies authorized by law to cooperate with State agencies of statewide jurisdiction pursuant to section 102(2)(D) of the Act may do so.

(b) Agencies shall cooperate with State and local agencies to the fullest extent possible to reduce duplication between NEPA and State and local requirements, unless the agencies are specifically barred from doing so by some other law. Except for cases covered by paragraph (a) of this section, such cooperation shall to the fullest extent possible include:

(1) Joint planning processes.

(2) Joint environmental research and studies.

(3) Joint public hearings (except where otherwise provided by statute).

(4) Joint environmental assessments.

(c) Agencies shall cooperate with State and local agencies to the fullest extent possible to reduce duplication between NEPA and comparable State and local requirements, unless the agencies are specifically barred from

doing so by some other law. Except for cases covered by paragraph (a) of this section, such cooperation shall to the fullest extent possible include joint environmental impact statements. In such cases one or more Federal agencies and one or more State or local agencies shall be joint lead agencies. Where State laws or local ordinances have environmental impact statement requirements in addition to but not in conflict with those in NEPA, Federal agencies shall cooperate in fulfilling these requirements as well as those of Federal laws so that one document will comply with all applicable laws.

(d) To better integrate environmental impact statements into State or local planning processes, statements shall discuss any inconsistency of a proposed action with any approved State or local plan and laws (whether or not federally sanctioned). Where an inconsistency exists, the statement should describe the extent to which the agency would reconcile its proposed action with the plan or law.

§ 1506.3 Adoption.

(a) An agency may adopt a Federal draft or final environmental impact statement or portion thereof provided that the statement or portion thereof meets the standards for an adequate statement under these regulations.

(b) If the actions covered by the original environmental impact statement and the proposed action are substantially the same, the agency adopting another agency's statement is not required to recirculate it except as a final statement. Otherwise the adopting agency shall treat the statement as a draft and recirculate it (except as provided in paragraph (c) of this section).

(c) A cooperating agency may adopt without recirculating the environmental impact statement of a lead agency when, after an independent review of the statement, the cooperating agency concludes that its comments and suggestions have been satisfied.

(d) When an agency adopts a statement which is not final within the agency that prepared it, or when the action it assesses is the subject of a referral under Part 1504, or when the statement's adequacy is the subject of a judicial action which is not final, the agency shall so specify.

§ 1506.4 Combining documents.

Any environmental document in compliance with NEPA may be combined with any other agency document to reduce duplication and paperwork.

§ 1506.5 Agency responsibility.

(a) *Information.* If an agency requires an applicant to submit environmental information for possible use by the agency in preparing an environmental impact statement, then the agency should assist the applicant by outlining the types of information required. The agency shall independent-

ly evaluate the information submitted and shall be responsible for its accuracy. If the agency chooses to use the information submitted by the applicant in the environmental impact statement, either directly or by reference, then the names of the persons responsible for the independent evaluation shall be included in the list of preparers (§ 1502.17). It is the intent of this paragraph that acceptable work not be redone, but that it be verified by the agency.

(b) *Environmental assessments.* If an agency permits an applicant to prepare an environmental assessment, the agency, besides fulfilling the requirements of paragraph (a) of this section, shall make its own evaluation of the environmental issues and take responsibility for the scope and content of the environmental assessment.

(c) *Environmental impact statements.* Except as provided in §§ 1506.2 and 1506.3 any environmental impact statement prepared pursuant to the requirements of NEPA shall be prepared directly by or by a contractor selected by the lead agency or where appropriate under § 1501.6(b), a cooperating agency. It is the intent of these regulations that the contractor be chosen solely by the lead agency, or by the lead agency in cooperation with cooperating agencies, or where appropriate by a cooperating agency to avoid any conflict of interest. Contractors shall execute a disclosure statement prepared by the lead agency, or where appropriate the cooperating agency, specifying that they have no financial or other interest in the outcome of the project. If the document is prepared by contract, the responsible Federal official shall furnish guidance and participate in the preparation and shall independently evaluate the statement prior to its approval and take responsibility for its scope and contents. Nothing in this section is intended to prohibit any agency from requesting any person to submit information to it or to prohibit any person from submitting information to any agency.

§ 1506.6 Public involvement.

Agencies shall:

(a) Make diligent efforts to involve the public in preparing and implementing their NEPA procedures.

(b) Provide public notice of NEPA-related hearings, public meetings, and the availability of environmental documents so as to inform those persons and agencies who may be interested or affected.

(1) In all cases the agency shall mail notice to those who have requested it on an individual action.

(2) In the case of an action with effects of national concern notice shall include publication in the FEDERAL REGISTER and notice by mail to national organizations reasonably expected to be interested in the matter and may include listing in the *102 Monitor.* An agency engaged in rulemaking may provide notice by mail to national or-

ganizations who have requested that notice regularly be provided. Agencies shall maintain a list of such organizations.

(3) In the case of an action with effects primarily of local concern the notice may include:

(i) Notice to State and areawide clearinghouses pursuant to OMB Circular A-95 (Revised).

(ii) Notice to Indian tribes when effects may occur on reservations.

(iii) Following the affected State's public notice procedures for comparable actions.

(iv) Publication in local newspapers (in papers of general circulation rather than legal papers).

(v) Notice through other local media.

(vi) Notice to potentially interested community organizations including small business associations.

(vii) Publication in newsletters that may be expected to reach potentially interested persons.

(viii) Direct mailing to owners and occupants of nearby or affected property.

(ix) Posting of notice on and off site in the area where the action is to be located.

(c) Hold or sponsor public hearings or public meetings whenever appropriate or in accordance with statutory requirements applicable to the agency. Criteria shall include whether there is:

(1) Substantial environmental controversy concerning the proposed action or substantial interest in holding the hearing.

(2) A request for a hearing by another agency with jurisdiction over the action supported by reasons why a hearing will be helpful. If a draft environmental impact statement is to be considered at a public hearing, the agency should make the statement available to the public at least 15 days in advance (unless the purpose of the hearing is to provide information for the draft environmental impact statement).

(d) Solicit appropriate information from the public.

(e) Explain in its procedures where interested persons can get information or status reports on environmental impact statements and other elements of the NEPA process.

(f) Make environmental impact statements, the comments received, and any underlying documents available to the public pursuant to the provisions of the Freedom of Information Act (5 U.S.C. 552), without regard to the exclusion for interagency memoranda where such memoranda transmit comments of Federal agencies on the environmental impact of the proposed action. Materials to be made available to the public shall be provided to the public without charge to the extent practicable, or at a fee which is not more than the actual costs of reproducing copies required to be sent to other Federal agencies, including the Council.

§ 1506.7 Further guidance.

The Council may provide further guidance concerning NEPA and its procedures including:

(a) A handbook which the Council may supplement from time to time, which shall in plain language provide guidance and instructions concerning the application of NEPA and these regulations.

(b) Publication of the Council's Memoranda to Heads of Agencies.

(c) In conjunction with the Environmental Protection Agency and the publication of the 102 Monitor, notice of:

(1) Research activities;

(2) Meetings and conferences related to NEPA; and

(3) Successful and innovative procedures used by agencies to implement NEPA.

§ 1506.8 Proposals for legislation.

(a) The NEPA process for proposals for legislation (§ 1508.17) significantly affecting the quality of the human environment shall be integrated with the legislative process of the Congress. A legislative environmental impact statement is the detailed statement required by law to be included in a recommendation or report on a legislative proposal to Congress. A legislative environmental impact statement shall be considered part of the formal transmittal of a legislative proposal to Congress; however, it may be transmitted to Congress up to 30 days later in order to allow time for completion of an accurate statement which can serve as the basis for public and Congressional debate. The statement must be available in time for Congressional hearings and deliberations.

(b) Preparation of a legislative environmental impact statement shall conform to the requirements of these regulations except as follows:

(1) There need not be a scoping process.

(2) The legislative statement shall be prepared in the same manner as a draft statement, but shall be considered the "detailed statement" required by statute; *Provided,* That when any of the following conditions exist both the draft and final environmental impact statement on the legislative proposal shall be prepared and circulated as provided by §§ 1503.1 and 1506.10.

(i) A Congressional Committee with jurisdiction over the proposal has a rule requiring both draft and final environmental impact statements.

(ii) The proposal results from a study process required by statute (such as those required by the Wild and Scenic Rivers Act (16 U.S.C. 1271 *et seq.*) and the Wilderness Act (16 U.S.C. 1131 *et seq.*)).

(iii) Legislative approval is sought for Federal or federally assisted construction or other projects which the agency recommends be located at specific geographic locations. For proposals requiring an environmental impact statement for the acquisition of space

by the General Services Administration, a draft statement shall accompany the Prospectus or the 11(b) Report of Building Project Surveys to the Congress, and a final statement shall be completed before site acquisition.

(iv) The agency decides to prepare draft and final statements.

(c) Comments on the legislative statement shall be given to the lead agency which shall forward them along with its own responses to the Congressional committees with jurisdiction.

§ 1506.9 Filing requirements.

Environmental impact statements together with comments and responses shall be filed with the Environmental Protection Agency, attention Office of Federal Activities (A-104), 401 M Street SW., Washington, DC 20460. Statements shall be filed with EPA no earlier than they are also transmitted to commenting agencies and made available to the public. EPA shall deliver one copy of each statement to the Council, which shall satisfy the requirement of availability to the President. EPA may issue guidelines to agencies to implement its responsibilities under this section and § 1506.10.

§ 1506.10 Timing of agency action.

(a) The Environmental Protection Agency shall publish a notice in the FEDERAL REGISTER each week of the environmental impact statements filed during the preceding week. The minimum time periods set forth in this section shall be calculated from the date of publication of this notice.

(b) No decision on the proposed action shall be made or recorded under § 1505.2 by a Federal agency until the later of the following dates:

(1) Ninety (90) days after publication of the notice described above in paragraph (a) of this section for a draft environmental impact statement.

(2) Thirty (30) days after publication of the notice described above in paragraph (a) of this section for a final environmental impact statement.

An exception to the rules on timing may be made in the case of an agency decision which is subject to a formal internal appeal. Some agencies have a formally established appeal process which allows other agencies or the public to take appeals on a decision and make their views known, after publication of the final environmental impact statement. In such cases, where a real opportunity exists to alter the decision, the decision may be made and recorded at the same time the environmental impact statement is published. This means that the period for appeal of the decision and the 30-day period prescribed in paragraph (b)(2) of this section may run concurrently. In such cases the environmental impact statement shall explain the timing and the public's right of appeal. An agency engaged in rulemaking under the Administrative Procedure Act or other statute for the purpose of protecting the public health or safety, may waive the time period in paragraph (b)(2) of this section and publish a decision on the final rule simultaneously with publication of the notice of the availability of the final environmental impact statement as described in paragraph (a) of this section.

(c) If the final environmental impact statement is filed within ninety (90) days after a draft environmental impact statement is filed with the Environmental Protection Agency, the minimum thirty (30) day period and the minimum ninety (90) day period may run concurrently. However, subject to paragraph (d) of this section agencies shall allow not less than 45 days for comments on draft statements.

(d) The lead agency may extend prescribed periods. The Environmental Protection Agency may upon a showing by the lead agency of compelling reasons of national policy reduce the prescribed periods and may upon a showing by any other Federal agency of compelling reasons of national policy also extend prescribed periods, but only after consultation with the lead agency. (Also see § 1507.3(d).) Failure to file timely comments shall not be a sufficient reason for extending a period. If the lead agency does not concur with the extension of time, EPA may not extend it for more than 30 days. When the Environmental Protection Agency reduces or extends any period of time it shall notify the Council.

[43 FR 56000, Nov. 29, 1978; 44 FR 874, Jan. 3, 1979]

§ 1506.11 Emergencies.

Where emergency circumstances make it necessary to take an action with significant environmental impact without observing the provisions of these regulations, the Federal agency taking the action should consult with the Council about alternative arrangements. Agencies and the Council will limit such arrangements to actions necessary to control the immediate impacts of the emergency. Other actions remain subject to NEPA review.

§ 1506.12 Effective date.

The effective date of these regulations is July 30, 1979, except that for agencies that administer programs that qualify under section 102(2)(D) of the Act or under section 104(h) of the Housing and Community Development Act of 1974 an additional four months shall be allowed for the State or local agencies to adopt their implementing procedures.

(a) These regulations shall apply to the fullest extent practicable to ongoing activities and environmental documents begun before the effective date. These regulations do not apply to an environmental impact statement or supplement if the draft statement was filed before the effective date of these regulations. No completed environmental documents need be redone by reasons of these regulations. Until these regulations are applicable, the

Council's guidelines published in the FEDERAL REGISTER of August 1, 1973, shall continue to be applicable. In cases where these regulations are applicable the guidelines are superseded. However, nothing shall prevent an agency from proceeding under these regulations at an earlier time.

(b) NEPA shall continue to be applicable to actions begun before January 1, 1970, to the fullest extent possible.

PART 1507—AGENCY COMPLIANCE

Sec.
1507.1 Compliance.
1507.2 Agency capability to comply.
1507.3 Agency procedures.

AUTHORITY: NEPA, the Environmental Quality Improvement Act of 1970, as amended (42 U.S.C. 4371 *et seq.*), sec. 309 of the Clean Air Act, as amended (42 U.S.C. 7609), and E.O. 11514 (Mar. 5, 1970, as amended by E.O. 11991, May 24, 1977).

SOURCE: 43 FR 56002, Nov. 29, 1978, unless otherwise noted.

§ 1507.1 Compliance.

All agencies of the Federal Government shall comply with these regulations. It is the intent of these regulations to allow each agency flexibility in adapting its implementing procedures authorized by § 1507.3 to the requirements of other applicable laws.

§ 1507.2 Agency capability to comply.

Each agency shall be capable (in terms of personnel and other resources) of complying with the requirements enumerated below. Such compliance may include use of other's resources, but the using agency shall itself have sufficient capability to evaluate what others do for it. Agencies shall:

(a) Fulfill the requirements of section 102(2)(A) of the Act to utilize a systematic, interdisciplinary approach which will insure the integrated use of the natural and social sciences and the environmental design arts in planning and in decisionmaking which may have an impact on the human environment. Agencies shall designate a person to be responsible for overall review of agency NEPA compliance.

(b) Identify methods and procedures required by section 102(2)(B) to insure that presently unquantified environmental amenities and values may be given appropriate consideration.

(c) Prepare adequate environmental impact statements pursuant to section 102(2)(C) and comment on statements in the areas where the agency has jurisdiction by law or special expertise or is authorized to develop and enforce environmental standards.

(d) Study, develop, and describe alternatives to recommended courses of action in any proposal which involves unresolved conflicts concerning alternative uses of available resources. This requirement of section 102(2)(E) extends to all such proposals, not just the more limited scope of section 102(2)(C)(iii) where the discussion of alternatives is confined to impact statements.

(e) Comply with the requirements of section 102(2)(H) that the agency initiate and utilize ecological information in the planning and development of resource-oriented projects.

(f) Fulfill the requirements of sections 102(2)(F), 102(2)(G), and 102(2)(I), of the Act and of Executive Order 11514, Protection and Enhancement of Environmental Quality, Sec. 2.

§ 1507.3 Agency procedures.

(a) Not later than eight months after publication of these regulations as finally adopted in the FEDERAL REGISTER, or five months after the establishment of an agency, whichever shall come later, each agency shall as necessary adopt procedures to supplement these regulations. When the agency is a department, major subunits are encouraged (with the consent of the department) to adopt their own procedures. Such procedures shall not paraphrase these regulations. They shall confine themselves to implementing procedures. Each agency shall consult with the Council while developing its procedures and before publishing them in the FEDERAL REGISTER for comment. Agencies with similar programs should consult with each other and the Council to coordinate their procedures, especially for programs requesting similar information from applicants. The procedures shall be adopted only after an opportunity for public review and after review by the Council for conformity with the Act and these regulations. The Council shall complete its review within 30 days. Once in effect they shall be filed with the Council and made readily available to the public. Agencies are encouraged to publish explanatory guidance for these regulations and their own procedures. Agencies shall continue to review their policies and procedures and in consultation with the Council to revise them as necessary to ensure full compliance with the purposes and provisions of the Act.

(b) Agency procedures shall comply with these regulations except where compliance would be inconsistent with statutory requirements and shall include:

(1) Those procedures required by §§ 1501.2(d), 1502.9(c)(3), 1505.1, 1506.6(e), and 1508.4.

(2) Specific criteria for and identification of those typical classes of action:

(i) Which normally do require environmental impact statements.

(ii) Which normally do not require either an environmental impact statement or an environmental assessment (categorical exclusions (§ 1508.4)).

(iii) Which normally require environmental assessments but not necessarily environmental impact statements.

(c) Agency procedures may include specific criteria for providing limited exceptions to the provisions of these regulations for classified proposals. They are proposed actions which are specifically authorized under criteria established by an Executive Order or statute to be kept secret in the interest of national defense or foreign policy and are in fact properly classified pursuant to such Executive Order or statute. Environmental assessments and environmental impact statements which address classified proposals may be safeguarded and restricted from public dissemination in accordance with agencies' own regulations applicable to classified information. These documents may be organized so that classified portions can be included as annexes, in order that the unclassified portions can be made available to the public.

(d) Agency procedures may provide for periods of time other than those presented in § 1506.10 when necessary to comply with other specific statutory requirements.

(e) Agency procedures may provide that where there is a lengthy period between the agency's decision to prepare an environmental impact statement and the time of actual preparation, the notice of intent required by § 1501.7 may be published at a reasonable time in advance of preparation of the draft statement.

PART 1508—TERMINOLOGY AND INDEX

Authority: NEPA, the Environmental Quality Improvement Act of 1970, as amended (42 U.S.C. 4371 et seq.), sec. 309 of the Clean Air Act, as amended (42 U.S.C. 7609), and E.O. 11514 (Mar. 5, 1970, as amended by E.O. 11991, May 24, 1977).

Source: 43 FR 56003, Nov. 29, 1978, unless otherwise noted.

§ 1508.1   Terminology.

The terminology of this part shall be uniform throughout the Federal Government.

§ 1508.2   Act.

"Act" means the National Environmental Policy Act, as amended (42 U.S.C. 4321, et seq.) which is also referred to as "NEPA."

§ 1508.3   Affecting.

"Affecting" means will or may have an effect on.

§ 1508.4   Categorical exclusion.

"Categorical exclusion" means a category of actions which do not individually or cumulatively have a significant effect on the human environment and which have been found to have no such effect in procedures adopted by a Federal agency in implementation of these regulations (§ 1507.3) and for which, therefore, neither an environmental assessment nor an environmental impact statement is required. An agency may decide in its procedures or otherwise, to prepare environmental assessments for the reasons stated in § 1508.9 even though it is not required to do so. Any procedures under this section shall provide for extraordinary circumstances in which a normally excluded action may have a significant environmental effect.

§ 1508.5   Cooperating agency.

"Cooperating agency" means any Federal agency other than a lead agency which has jurisdiction by law or special expertise with respect to any environmental impact involved in a proposal (or a reasonable alternative) for legislation or other major Federal action significantly affecting the quality of the human environment. The selection and responsibilities of a cooperating agency are described in § 1501.6. A State or local agency of similar qualifications or, when the effects are on a reservation, an Indian Tribe, may by agreement with the lead agency become a cooperating agency.

§ 1508.6   Council.

"Council" means the Council on Environmental Quality established by Title II of the Act.

§ 1508.7   Cumulative impact.

"Cumulative impact" is the impact on the environment which results from the incremental impact of the action when added to other past, present, and reasonably foreseeable future actions regardless of what agency (Federal or non-Federal) or person undertakes such other actions. Cumulative impacts can result from individually minor but collectively significant actions taking place over a period of time.

§ 1508.8   Effects.

"Effects" include:

(a) Direct effects, which are caused by the action and occur at the same time and place.

(b) Indirect effects, which are caused by the action and are later in time or farther removed in distance, but are still reasonably foreseeable. Indirect effects may include growth inducing effects and other effects related to induced changes in the pattern of land use, population density or growth rate, and related effects on air and water and other natural systems, including ecosystems.

Effects and impacts as used in these regulations are synonymous. Effects includes ecological (such as the effects on natural resources and on the components, structures, and functioning of affected ecosystems), aesthetic, historic, cultural, economic, social, or health, whether direct, indirect, or cumulative. Effects may also include those resulting from actions which may have both beneficial and detrimental effects, even if on balance the agency believes that the effect will be beneficial.

§ 1508.9   Environmental assessment.

"Environmental assessment":

(a) Means a concise public document for which a Federal agency is responsible that serves to:

(1) Briefly provide sufficient evidence and analysis for determining whether to prepare an environmental impact statement or a finding of no significant impact.

(2) Aid an agency's compliance with the Act when no environmental impact statement is necessary.

(3) Facilitate preparation of a statement when one is necessary.

(b) Shall include brief discussions of the need for the proposal, of alternatives as required by section 102(2)(E), of the environmental impacts of the proposed action and alternatives, and a listing of agencies and persons consulted.

§ 1508.10   Environmental document.

"Environmental document" includes the documents specified in § 1508.9 (environmental assessment), § 1508.11 (environmental impact statement), § 1508.13 (finding of no significant impact), and § 1508.22 (notice of intent).

§ 1508.11   Environmental impact statement.

"Environmental impact statement" means a detailed written statement as required by section 102(2)(C) of the Act.

§ 1508.12   Federal agency.

"Federal agency" means all agencies of the Federal Government. It does not mean the Congress, the Judiciary, or the President, including the performance of staff functions for the President in his Executive Office. It also includes for purposes of these regulations States and units of general local government and Indian tribes assuming NEPA responsibilities under section 104(h) of the Housing and Community Development Act of 1974.

§ 1508.13   Finding of no significant impact.

"Finding of no significant impact" means a document by a Federal agency briefly presenting the reasons why an action, not otherwise excluded (§ 1508.4), will not have a significant effect on the human environment and for which an environmental impact statement therefore will not be prepared. It shall include the environmental assessment or a summary of it and shall note any other environmental documents related to it (§ 1501.7(a)(5)). If the assessment is included, the finding need not repeat any of the discussion in the assessment but may incorporate it by reference.

§ 1508.14   Human environment.

"Human environment" shall be interpreted comprehensively to include the natural and physical environment and the relationship of people with that environment. (See the definition of "effects" (§ 1508.8).) This means that economic or social effects are not intended by themselves to require preparation of an environmental impact statement. When an environmental impact statement is prepared and economic or social and natural or physical environmental effects are interrelated, then the environmental impact statement will discuss all of these effects on the human environment.

§ 1508.15   Jurisdiction by law.

"Jurisdiction by law" means agency authority to approve, veto, or finance all or part of the proposal.

§ 1508.16   Lead agency.

"Lead agency" means the agency or agencies preparing or having taken primary responsibility for preparing the environmental impact statement.

§ 1508.17   Legislation.

"Legislation" includes a bill or legislative proposal to Congress developed by or with the significant cooperation and support of a Federal agency, but does not include requests for appropriations. The test for significant cooperation is whether the proposal is in fact predominantly that of the agency rather than another source. Drafting does not by itself constitute significant cooperation. Proposals for legislation include requests for ratification of treaties. Only the agency which has primary responsibility for the subject matter involved will prepare a legislative environmental impact statement.

§ 1508.18   Major Federal action.

"Major Federal action" includes actions with effects that may be major and which are potentially subject to Federal control and responsibility. Major reinforces but does not have a meaning independent of significantly (§ 1508.27). Actions include the circumstance where the responsible officials fail to act and that failure to act is reviewable by courts or administrative tribunals under the Administrative Procedure Act or other applicable law as agency action.

(a) Actions include new and continuing activities, including projects and programs entirely or partly financed, assisted, conducted, regulated, or approved by federal agencies; new or re-vised agency rules, regulations, plans, policies, or procedures; and legislative proposals (§§ 1506.8, 1508.17). Actions do not include funding assistance solely in the form of general revenue sharing funds, distributed under the State and Local Fiscal Assistance Act of 1972, 31 U.S.C. 1221 et seq., with no Federal agency control over the subsequent use of such funds. Actions do not include bringing judicial or administrative civil or criminal enforcement actions.

(b) Federal actions tend to fall within one of the following categories:

(1) Adoption of official policy, such as rules, regulations, and interpretations adopted pursuant to the Administrative Procedure Act, 5 U.S.C. 551 et seq.; treaties and international conventions or agreements; formal documents establishing an agency's policies which will result in or substantially alter agency programs.

(2) Adoption of formal plans, such as official documents prepared or approved by federal agencies which guide or prescribe alternative uses of Federal resources, upon which future agency actions will be based.

(3) Adoption of programs, such as a group of concerted actions to implement a specific policy or plan; systematic and connected agency decisions allocating agency resources to implement a specific statutory program or executive directive.

(4) Approval of specific projects, such as construction or management activities located in a defined geographic area. Projects include actions approved by permit or other regulatory decision as well as federal and federally assisted activities.

§ 1508.19   Matter.

"Matter" includes for purposes of Part 1504:

(a) With respect to the Environmental Protection Agency, any proposed legislation, project, action or regulation as those terms are used in section 309(a) of the Clean Air Act (42 U.S.C. 7609).

(b) With respect to all other agencies, any proposed major federal action to which section 102(2)(C) of NEPA applies.

§ 1508.20   Mitigation.

"Mitigation" includes:

(a) Avoiding the impact altogether by not taking a certain action or parts of an action.

(b) Minimizing impacts by limiting the degree or magnitude of the action and its implementation.

(c) Rectifying the impact by repairing, rehabilitating, or restoring the affected environment.

(d) Reducing or eliminating the impact over time by preservation and maintenance operations during the life of the action.

(e) Compensating for the impact by replacing or providing substitute resources or environments.

§ 1508.21   NEPA process.

"NEPA process" means all measures necessary for compliance with the requirements of section 2 and Title I of NEPA.

§ 1508.22   Notice of intent.

"Notice of intent" means a notice that an environmental impact statement will be prepared and considered. The notice shall briefly:

(a) Describe the proposed action and possible alternatives.

(b) Describe the agency's proposed scoping process including whether, when, and where any scoping meeting will be held.

(c) State the name and address of a person within the agency who can answer questions about the proposed action and the environmental impact statement.

§ 1508.23   Proposal.

"Proposal" exists at that stage in the development of an action when an agency subject to the Act has a goal and is actively preparing to make a decision on one or more alternative means of accomplishing that goal and the effects can be meaningfully evaluated. Preparation of an environmental impact statement on a proposal should be timed (§ 1502.5) so that the final statement may be completed in time for the statement to be included in any recommendation or report on the proposal. A proposal may exist in fact as well as by agency declaration that one exists.

§ 1508.24   Referring agency.

"Referring agency" means the federal agency which has referred any matter to the Council after a determination that the matter is unsatisfactory from the standpoint of public health or welfare or environmental quality.

§ 1508.25   Scope.

Scope consists of the range of actions, alternatives, and impacts to be considered in an environmental impact statement. The scope of an individual statement may depend on its relationships to other statements (§§1502.20 and 1508.28). To determine the scope of environmental impact statements, agencies shall consider 3 types of actions, 3 types of alternatives, and 3 types of impacts. They include:

(a) Actions (other than unconnected single actions) which may be:

(1) Connected actions, which means that they are closely related and therefore should be discussed in the same impact statement. Actions are connected if they:

(i) Automatically trigger other actions which may require environmental impact statements.

(ii) Cannot or will not proceed unless other actions are taken previously or simultaneously.

(iii) Are interdependent parts of a larger action and depend on the larger action for their justification.

(2) Cumulative actions, which when viewed with other proposed actions have cumulatively significant impacts and should therefore be discussed in the same impact statement.

(3) Similar actions, which when viewed with other reasonably foreseeable or proposed agency actions, have similarities that provide a basis for evaluating their environmental consequences together, such as common timing or geography. An agency may wish to analyze these actions in the same impact statement. It should do so when the best way to assess adequately the combined impacts of similar actions or reasonable alternatives to such actions is to treat them in a single impact statement.

(b) Alternatives, which include: (1) No action alternative.

(2) Other reasonable courses of actions.

(3) Mitigation measures (not in the proposed action).

(c) Impacts, which may be: (1) Direct; (2) indirect; (3) cumulative.

§ 1508.26 Special expertise.

"Special expertise" means statutory responsibility, agency mission, or related program experience.

§ 1508.27 Significantly.

"Significantly" as used in NEPA requires considerations of both context and intensity:

(a) *Context.* This means that the significance of an action must be analyzed in several contexts such as society as a whole (human, national), the affected region, the affected interests, and the locality. Significance varies with the setting of the proposed action. For instance, in the case of a site-specific action, significance would usually depend upon the effects in the locale rather than in the world as a whole. Both short- and long-term effects are relevant.

(b) *Intensity.* This refers to the severity of impact. Responsible officials must bear in mind that more than one agency may make decisions about partial aspects of a major action. The following should be considered in evaluating intensity:

(1) Impacts that may be both beneficial and adverse. A significant effect may exist even if the Federal agency believes that on balance the effect will be beneficial.

(2) The degree to which the proposed action affects public health or safety.

(3) Unique characteristics of the geographic area such as proximity to historic or cultural resources, park lands, prime farmlands, wetlands, wild and scenic rivers, or ecologically critical areas.

(4) The degree to which the effects on the quality of the human environment are likely to be highly controversial.

(5) The degree to which the possible effects on the human environment are highly uncertain or involve unique or unknown risks.

(6) The degree to which the action may establish a precedent for future actions with significant effects or represents a decision in principle about a future consideration.

(7) Whether the action is related to other actions with individually insignificant but cumulatively significant impacts. Significance exists if it is reasonable to anticipate a cumulatively significant impact on the environment. Significance cannot be avoided by terming an action temporary or by breaking it down into small component parts.

(8) The degree to which the action may adversely affect districts, sites, highways, structures, or objects listed in or eligible for listing in the National Register of Historic Places or may cause loss or destruction of significant scientific, cultural, or historical resources.

(9) The degree to which the action may adversely affect an endangered or threatened species or its habitat that has been determined to be critical under the Endangered Species Act of 1973.

(10) Whether the action threatens a violation of Federal, State, or local law or requirements imposed for the protection of the environment.

[43 FR 56003, Nov. 29, 1978; 44 FR 874, Jan. 3, 1979]

§ 1508.28 Tiering.

"Tiering" refers to the coverage of general matters in broader environmental impact statements (such as national program or policy statements) with subsequent narrower statements or environmental analyses (such as regional or basinwide program statements or ultimately site-specific statements) incorporating by reference the general discussions and concentrating solely on the issues specific to the statement subsequently prepared. Tiering is appropriate when the sequence of statements or analyses is:

(a) From a program, plan, or policy environmental impact statement to a program, plan, or policy statement or analysis of lesser scope or to a site-specific statement or analysis.

(b) From an environmental impact statement on a specific action at an early stage (such as need and site selection) to a supplement (which is preferred) or a subsequent statement or analysis at a later stage (such as environmental mitigation). Tiering in such cases is appropriate when it helps the lead agency to focus on the issues which are ripe for decision and exclude from consideration issues already decided or not yet ripe.

Index to Parts 1500 Through 1508

Council on Environmental Quality
National Environmental Policy Act (NEPA) Implementation Procedures; Appendixes I, II, and III
49 Fed. Reg. 49750 (Dec. 21, 1984)

SUMMARY: These appendices are intended to improve public participation and facilitate agency compliance with the National Environmental Policy Act (NEPA) and the Council on Environmental Quality's NEPA Regulations.

Appendix I updates and replaces the Federal and Federal-State Agency NEPA Contacts that appeared in Appendix I in the **Federal Register** of Thursday, August 28, 1980 (45 FR 57488).

Appendix II updates and replaces the compilation of Federal and Federal-State Agencies With Jurisdiction by Law or Special Expertise on Environmental Quality Issues that appeared in Appendix II in the **Federal Register** of Thursday, August 28, 1980 (45 FR 57491).

Appendix III is reinstated as, and is an update of, the listing of Federal and Federal-State Agency Offices for Receiving and Commenting on Other Agencies' Environmental Documents. Appendix III last appeared in the **Federal Register** of August 1, 1973 (38 FR 20559).

EFFECTIVE DATE: December 21, 1984.

ADDRESSES: Comments should be addressed to General Counsel, Council on Environmental Quality, 722 Jackson Place, NW., Washington, DC 20006–4978.

FOR INFORMATION CONTACT: Dinah Bear, General Counsel, Council on Environmental Quality, 722 Jackson Place, NW, Washington, DC 20006–4978 (202) 395–5754.

SUPPLEMENTARY INFORMATION:

Appendix I—Federal and Federal-State Agency National Environmental Policy Act (NEPA) Contacts

Section 1507.2 of the Council's regulations for implementing the procedural provisions of the National Environmental Policy Act requires agencies to have an individual responsible for overall NEPA compliance. This appendix identifies the individual within each agency that is responsible for coordinating with the Council on behalf of that agency and for exercising NEPA oversight within that agency. This person can provide basic information about the agency's NEPA activities and about the procedures which the agency has adopted to supplement the Council regulations (40 CFR 1507.3).

To ascertain the proper office in an agency for receiving and commenting on other agencies' environmental documents, refer to Appendix III of this issuance.

Appendix II—Federal and Federal-State Agencies With Jurisdiction by Law or Special Expertise on Environmental Quality Issues

This appendix is a compilation of Federal and Federal-State agencies with jurisdiction by law, a statutorily mandated consultative role, or special expertise on environmental quality issues. Both the public and private sectors and governmental agencies can use this list as a reference guide to facilitate their participation in and compliance with NEPA process.

The appendix is organized into four broad categories: pollution control, energy, land use, and natural resource management. Because most actions involve environmental issues falling into more than one of these categories, users should consult all pertinent entries.

The areas of special expertise are listed in parentheses *following* the agency name. They are intended to provide examples rather than define the limits of an agency's total expertise in that area.

The areas of jurisdiction by law and statutorily mandated consultations are listed *below* each appropriate agency or component. Entries dealing with jurisdiction by law relate to that agency's authority to approve, deny, or finance all or part of a proposal and include permits and licenses. Because experience in implementing NEPA has proven that identification of an agency's statutorily mandated consultative role is of equal significance to users of this list, those responsibilities are now specifically cited and include such authorities as the National Historic Preservation Act of 1966 (16 U.S.C. Sec. 470 *et seq.*), the Fish and Wildlife Coordination Act (16 U.S.C. Sec. 661 *et seq.*), and the Endangered Species Act of 1973 (16 U.S.C. Sec. 1531 *et seq.*). Because laws are amended and new laws enacted, the responsibilities identified in this appendix may change or new ones may be added. Hence, the definitive responsibility of an agency depends on the then current law and not on this index.

The Council on Environmental Quality has prepared this list to supplement its NEPA regulations and believes that it will be helpful in the following ways:

First, the Council's NEPA regulations require the Federal agency having primary responsibility for preparing an environmental impact statement (EIS) under NEPA (the lead agency) to determine whether any other Federal agencies have jurisdiction by law or special expertise with respect to any environmental effects involved in a proposal for legislation or other major Federal action significantly affecting the human environment. 40 CFR 1501.5(a), 1501.6(a), 1501.7(a). The Federal lead agency must, early in the NEPA process, request the participation of Federal cooperating agencies with jurisdiction by law or special expertise concerning the proposal. 40 CFR 1501.6(a), 1501.7(a). The lead agency and those involved in the "scoping process" (see 40 CFR 1501.7) may use this list to help determine which other Federal agencies should be requested to participate as cooperating agencies in the NEPA process. The list will also be helpful to the lead agency in determining which agencies should receive copies of the draft environmental impact statement for review and comment. 40 CFR 1503.1.

Second, this compilation will prove useful to those whose activities or proposed actions require Federal regulatory approvals by facilitating the identification of:

a. Those Federal agencies with the authority to issue applicable permits, licenses or other Federal regulatory approvals, and

b. Those Federal agencies that have a statutorily mandated consultative role that must be carried out before a decision is made.

Third, a major goal of NEPA and the CEQ regulations is to encourage public participation in agency decisionmaking. 40 CFR 1500.2(d). Individuals, citizen groups and State and local governments who are interested in an environmental issue may use the list to help identify those agencies that have jurisdiction by law over or special expertise in the subject matter of a proposal. Those interested may then contact the potentially involved agencies to obtain information on the issues and to participate in the NEPA process.

Appendix III—Federal and Federal-State Agency Offices for Receiving and Commenting on Other Agencies' Environmental Documents

Section 1503.1 of the Council's regulations for implementing the procedural provisions of the National Environmental Policy Act requires the agency that has prepared a draft environmental impact statement to "obtain the comments of any Federal agency which has jurisdiction by law or special expertise with respect to any environmental impact involved or which is authorized to develop and enforce environmental standards." Section 1503.2 discusses the "Duty to Comment" by those Federal agencies. This appendix identifies the location of the Federal and Federal-State agency offices for receiving and commenting on other agencies' environmental documents. The agency distributing the environmental document should give special attention to the instruction immediately following the agency name to ensure that the comment request and document(s) are sent to the correct office, e.g., some agencies ask that documents concerning legislation, regulations, national program proposals and other major policy issues be sent only to its headquarters office with all other documents to be sent to a regional office. If a transmitting agency has questions about where to send a document, consult the Federal agency NEPA contact listed in Appendix I.

Other Information

Since agency responsibilities, legal authorities, programs, and other data appearing in these Appendices change regularly, the Council will update the Appendices periodically. Agencies and the public are strongly encouraged to send comments noting changes or corrections that should be made to any Appendix.

Dated: December 14, 1984.

Dinah Bear,
General Counsel.

Editorial Note: The following appendices will not appear in the CFR.

Appendix I—Federal and Federal-State Agency National Environmental Policy Act (NEPA) Contacts

DEPARTMENTS

Department of Agriculture

Assistant Secretary for Natural Resources and Environment, Department of Agriculture; Attn: Executive Secretary, Natural Resources and Environment Committee; Room 242 W, Administration Bldg., 14th St. and Independence Ave., SW, Wash., D.C. 20250–0001. (202) 447–5166.

Department of Agriculture Components

Agricultural Research Service: Deputy Administrator, National Program Staff, Agricultural Research Service, Department of Agriculture; Room 125, Bldg. 005, Agricultural Research Center-West, Beltsville, MD 20705–2350. (301) 344–3084.

Agricultural Stabilization and Conservation Service: Chief, Planning and Evaluation Branch, Conservation and Environmental Protection Division; Agricultural Stabilization and Conservation Service, Department of Agriculture, Room

4714, South Agriculture Bldg., 14th St. and Independence Ave., SW, P.O. Box 2415, Wash., D.C. 20013–2415. (202) 447–3264.

Animal and Plant Health Inspection Service: Environmental Coordinator, Animal and Plant Health Inspection Service, Department of Agriculture; Room 600, Federal Bldg., 6505 Belcrest Road, Hyattsville, MD 20782–2058. (301) 436–8896.

Economic Research Service: Director, Natural Resource Economics Division, Economic Research Service, Department of Agriculture, Room 412, GHI Bldg., 500 12th St. SW, Wash., D.C. 20250–0001. (202) 447–8239.

Extension Service: Deputy Administrator, Natural Resources and Rural Development, Extension Service, Department of Agriculture, Room 3909, South Agriculture Bldg., 14th St. and Independence Ave., SW, Wash., D.C. 20250–0001. (202) 447–7947.

Farmers Home Administration: Environmental Protection Specialist, Program Support Staff; Farmers Home Administration, Department of Agriculture, Room 6309, South Agriculture Bldg., 14th St. and Independence Ave., SW, Wash., D.C. 20250–0001. (202) 382–9619.

Food Safety and Inspection Service: Director, Regulations Office, Food Safety and Inspection Service, Department of Agriculture, Room 2940, South Agriculture Bldg., 14th St. and Independence Ave., SW, Wash., D.C. 20250–0001. (202) 447–3317.

Forest Service: Director, Environmental Coordination Staff, Forest Service, Department of Agriculture; Room 4204, South Agriculture Bldg., 14th St. and Independence Ave., SW, P.O. Box 2417, Wash., D.C. 20013–2417. (202) 447–4708.

Rural Electrification Administration: Environmental Policy Specialist, Engineering Standards Division, Rural Electrification Administration, Department of Agriculture, Room 1257, South Agriculture Bldg., 14th St. and Independence Ave., SW, Wash., D.C. 20250–0001. (202) 382–0097.

Soil Conservation Service: National Environmental Coordinator, Environmental Activities Branch, Ecological Sciences Division, Soil Conservation Service, Department of Agriculture, Room 6155, South Agriculture Bldg., 14th St. and Independence Ave., SW, P.O. Box 2890, Wash., D.C. 20013–2890. (202) 447–4912.

Department of Commerce

Chief, Ecology and Conservation Division, Office of Policy and Planning, National Oceanic and Atmospheric Administration, Department of Commerce, Room H–6111, Herbert Hoover Bldg., 14th St. and Constitution Ave., NW, Wash., D.C. 20230–0001. (202) 377–5181.

Department of Commerce Components

Economic Development Administration: Associate Director for Environment, Economic Development Adminstration, Department of Commerce, Room 7319, Herbert Hoover Bldg., 14th St. and Constitution Ave., NW, Wash., D.C. 20230–0001. (202) 377–4208.

National Oceanic and Atmospheric Administration: Chief, Ecology and Conservation Division, Office of Policy and Planning, National Oceanic and Atmospheric

Administration, Department of Commerce, Room H–6111, Herbert Hoover Bldg., 14th St. and Constitution Ave., NW, Wash., D.C. 20230–0001. (202) 377–5181.

Department of Defense

Director, Environmental Policy, Office of the Assistant Secretary of Defense (Manpower, Installations and Logistics), Department of Defense, Room 3D833, The Pentagon, Wash., D.C. 20301–0001. (202) 695–7820.

Department of Defense Components

Defense Logistics Agency: Staff Director, Office of Installation Services and Environmental Protection, Defense Logistics Agency, Department of Defense, Cameron Station, Room 4D446, Alexandria, VA 22304–6100. (202) 274–6124.

Department of the Air Force: Deputy for Environment and Safety, Office of the Deputy Assistant Secretary for Installations, Environment and Safety, Department of the Air Force, Room 4C916, The Pentagon, Wash., D.C. 20330–0001. (202) 697–9297.

Department of the Army: Chief, Army Environmental Office, Attn: HQDA (DAEN–ZCE); Department of the Army, Room 1E676, The Pentagon, Wash., D.C. 20310–2600. (202) 694–3434.

Corps of Engineers: Assistant Director of Civil Works, Environmental Programs (DAEN–CWZ–P), Office of the Chief of Engineers, Room 7233, Pulaski Bldg., 20 Massachusetts Avenue, NW., Wash., D.C. 20314–1000. (202) 272–0103.

Department of the Navy: Director, Environmental Protection and Occupational Safety and Health Division (OP–453), Office of the Chief of Naval Operations, Department of the Navy, Bldg. 200, Room S–3, Washington Navy Yard, Wash., D.C. 20374–0001. (202) 433–2426.

U.S. Marine Corps: Head, Land Resources and Environmental Branch, Code: LFL, U.S. Marine Corps, Commonwealth Bldg., Room 614, 1300 Wilson Blvd., Arlington, VA. (202) 694–9237/38. MAILING ADDRESS: Commandant, U.S. Marine Corps, ATTN: Land Resources and Environmental Branch, Code: LFL, Wash., D.C. 20380–0001.

Department of Energy

Director, Office of Environmental Compliance (PE–25), Department of Energy, Room 4G–085, Forrestal Building, 1000 Independence Ave., SW, Wash., D.C. 20585–0001. (202) 252–4600.

Department of Health and Human Services

Departmental Environmental Officer, Office of the Assistant Secretary for Management Analysis and Systems, Department of Health and Human Services, Room 542 E, Hubert H. Humphrey Bldg., 200 Independence Ave., SW, Wash., D.C. 20201–0001. (202) 245–7354.

Department of Health and Human Services Components

Center for Disease Control: Chief, Environmental Affairs Group, Center for Environmental Health, Center for Disease Control, Room 1015, Bldg.: Chamblee–9,

Atlanta, GA 30329–4018. (404) 452–4257; (FTS) 236–4257.

Food and Drug Administration: Chief, Environmental Impact Staff (HFV–310) Food and Drug Administration, Parklawn Bldg., Room 7–89, 5600 Fishers Lane, Rockville, MD 20857–0001. (301) 443–1880.

Health Resources and Services Administration: Chief Environmental Health Branch, Division of Clinical and Environmental Services, Indian Health Service, Health Resources and Services Administration, Parklawn Building, Room 6A–54, 5600 Fishers Lane, Rockville, MD 20857–0001. (301) 443–1043.

National Institutes of Health: Chief, Environmental Protection Branch, National Institutes of Health, Bldg. 13, Room 2E55, 9100 Rockville Pike, Bethesda, MD 20205–0001. (301) 496–3537.

Office of Community Services: Director, Office of State Project Assistance, Office of Community Services, Room 500, Brown Bldg., 1200 19th St., NW., Wash., D.C. 20506–0007. (202) 653–5675.

Department of Housing and Urban Development

Director, Office of Environment and Energy, Department of Housing and Urban Development, Room 7154, HUD Building, 451 Seventh St., SW., Wash., D.C. 20410–0001. (202) 755–7894.

Department of the Interior

Director, Office of Environmental Project Review, Department of the Interior, Room 4260, Interior Bldg., 18th and C Sts., NW., Wash., D.C. 20240–0001. (202) 343–3891.

Department of the Interior Components

Fish and Wildlife Services: Chief, Division of Environmental Coordination, Fish and Wildlife Service, Department of the Interior, Room 402, Hamilton Bldg., 1375 K St., NW., Wash., D.C. (202) 343–5685. MAILING ADDRESS: 18th & C Sts., NW., Wash., D.C. 20240–0001.

Geological Survey: Chief, Review Unit, Environmental Affairs Program (MS–423), U.S. Geological Survey, Department of the Interior, Room 2D318, 12201 Sunrise Valley Drive, Reston, VA 22092–9998. (703) 860–7556.

Bureau of Indian Affairs: Chief, Environmental Services Staff, Office of Trust Responsibilities, Bureau of Indian Affairs, Department of the Interior, Room 4560, Interior Bldg., 18th and C Sts., NW., Wash., D.C. 20245–0001. (202) 343–6574.

Bureau of Land Management: Chief, Office of Planning and Environmental Coordination, Bureau of Land Management, Department of the Interior, Room 906, Premier Bldg., 1725 I St., NW., Wash., D.C. 20240–0001. (202) 653–8830.

Minerals Management Service: Chief, Offshore Environmental Assessment Division, Mineral Management Service, Department of the Interior, Room 2044, Interior Bldg., 18th and C Sts., NW., D.C. 20240–0001 (202) 343–2097.

Bureau of Mines: Special Assistant for Environmental Assessment, Bureau of Mines, Department of the Interior, Room 1004, Columbia Plaza Bldg., 2401 E St., NW., Wash., D.C. 20241–0001. (202) 634–1310.

National Park Service: Chief, Environmental Compliance Division (762), National Park Service, Department of the Interior, Room 1210, Interior Bldg., 18th and C Sts., NW., Wash., D.C. 20240–0001. (202) 343–2163.

Bureau of Reclamation: Director, Office of Environmental Affairs, Bureau of Reclamation, Department of the Interior, Room 7622, Interior Bldg., 18th and C Sts., NW., Wash., D.C. 20240–0001. (202) 343–4991.

Office of Surface Mining: Chief, Division of Permits and Environmental Analysis, Office of Surface Mining Reclamation and Enforcement, Department of the Interior, Room 134, Interior-South Bldg., 1951 Constitution Ave., NW., Wash., D.C. 20240–0001. (202) 343–5261.

Department of Justice

Assistant Chief, General Litigation Section, Land and Natural Resources Division, Department of Justice, Room 2133, Justice Bldg., 9th St. and Pennsylvania Ave., NW, Wash., D.C. 20530–0001. (202) 633–2704.

Department of Justice Components

Bureau of Prisons: Chief, Office of Facilities Development and Operations, Bureau of Prisons, Department of Justice, 320 First St., NW, Wash., D.C. 20534–0001. (202) 724–3232.

Drug Enforcement Administration: Deputy Assistant Administrator, Office of Science and Technology, Drug Enforcement Administration, Department of Justice, 1405 Eye St., NW, Wash., D.C. 20537–0001. (202) 633–1211.

Immigration and Naturalization Service: Chief, Facilities and Engineering Branch, Immigration and Naturalization Service, Department of Justice, 425 Eye St., NW, Wash., D.C. 20536–0001. (202) 633–4448.

Office of Justice Assistance, Research and Statistics: Director, Office of Justice Assistance, Research and Statistics; Department of Justice, Room 1300, 633 Indiana Ave., NW, Wash., D.C. 20531–0001. (202) 724–5933.

Office of Legal Counsel: Assistant Attorney General, Office of Legal Counsel, Department of Justice, Room 5214, Justice Bldg., 9th St. and Pennsylvania Ave., NW, Wash., D.C. 20530–0001. (202) 633–2041.

Department of Labor

Director, Office of Regulatory Economics, Assistant Secretary for Policy, Department of Labor, Room S–2312, Frances Perkins Bldg., 200 Constitution Ave., NW, Wash., D.C. 20210–0001. (202) 523–6197.

Department of Labor Components

Mine Safety and Health Administration: Chief, Office of Standards, Regulations and Variances, Mine Safety and Health Administration, Department of Labor, Room 627, Ballston Tower #3, 4015 Wilson Blvd., Arlington, VA 22203–1923. (703) 235–1910.

Occupational Safety and Health Administration: Director, Office of Regulatory Analysis, Occupational Safety and Health Administration, Department of Labor, Room N–3635, Frances Perkins Bldg., 200 Constitution Ave., NW, Wash., D.C. 20210–0001. (202) 523–8017.

Department of State

Director, Office of Environment and Health, Department of State, Room 4325, State Department Bldg., 21st and C Sts., NW, Wash., D.C. 20520–0001.(202) 632–9266.

Department of Transportation

Deputy Director for Environment and Policy Review, Office of Economics, Department of Transportation, Room 10309 Nassif Bldg., 400 Seventh St., SW, Wash., D.C. 20590–0001. (202) 426–4357.

Department of Transportation Components

Federal Aviation Administration: Director, Office of Environment and Energy (AEE–1), Federal Aviation Administration, Room 432, FOB–10A, 800 Independence Ave., SW, Wash., D.C. 20591–0001. (202) 426–8406.

Federal Highway Administration: Director, Office of Environmental Policy (HEV–1), Federal Highway Administration, Room 3222, Nassif Bldg., 400 Seventh St., SW, Wash., D.C. 20590–0001. (202) 426–0351.

Federal Railroad Administration: Director, Office of Economic Analysis (RRP–30), Federal Railroad Administration, Room 8300, Nassif Bldg., 400 Seventh St., SW, Wash., D.C. 20590–0001. (202) 426–7391.

Maritime Administration: Head, Environmental Activities Group (MAR–700.4), Maritime Administration, Room 2120, Nassif Bldg., 400 Seventh St., SW, Wash., D.C. 20590–0001. (202) 426–5739.

National Highway Traffic Safety Administration: Assistant Chief Counsel for General Law, Office of Chief Counsel (NOA–33), National Highway Traffic Safety Administration, Room 5219, Nassif Bldg., 400 Seventh St., SW, Wash., D.C. 20590–0001. (202) 426–1834.

Research and Special Programs Administration (includes Materials Transportation Bureau): Chief, Environmental Technology Division (DTS–48), Research and Special Programs Administration, US–DOT, Transportation Systems Center, Room 3–55, Kendall Square, Cambridge, MA 02142–1001. (617) 494–2018; (FTS) 837–2018.

St. Lawrence Seaway Development Corporation: Deputy Chief Engineer, St. Lawrence Seaway Development Corporation, Seaway Administration Bldg., 180 Andrews St., P.O. Box 520, Massena, NY 13662–1760. (315) 764–3256; (FTS) 953–0256.

United States Coast Guard: Chief, Environmental Compliance and Review Branch (G–WP–3), Office of Marine Environment and Systems, U.S. Coast Guard, 2100 2nd St., SW, Wash., D.C. 20593–0001. (202) 426–3300.

Urban Mass Transportation Administration: Director, Office of Planning Assistance (UGM–20), Urban Mass Transportation Administration, Room 9311, Nassif Bldg., 400 Seventh St., SW, Wash., D.C. 20590–0001. (202) 426–2360.

Department of Treasury

Manager, Environmental Quality, Physical Security and Safety Division, Department of the Treasury, Room 800, Treasury Bldg., 1331 G St., NW, Wash., D.C. 20220–0001. (202) 376–0289.

INDEPENDENT AGENCIES

ACTION

Assistant Director, Office of Policy and Planning, ACTION, Room M–606, 806 Connecticut Ave., NW, Wash., D.C. 20525–0001. (202) 634–9304; WATS #800–424–8580, ext. 81.

Advisory Council on Historic Preservation

Director, Office of Cultural Resource Preservation, Advisory Council on Historic Preservation, Old Post Office Building, Suite 803, 1100 Pennsylvania Ave., NW, Wash., D.C. 20004–2590. (202) 786–0505.

Appalachian Regional Commission

Director, Division of Housing and Community Development, Appalachian Regional Commission, 1666 Connecticut Ave., NW, Wash., D.C. 20235–0001. (202) 673–7845.

Arms Control and Disarmament Agency

General Counsel, Arms Control and Disarmament Agency, Room 5534, 320 21st St., NW, Wash., D.C. 20451–0001. (202) 632–3582.

Central Intelligence Agency

Chief, Real Estate and Construction Division, Office of Logistics, Central Intelligence Agency, Room 2F09, Page Bldg., 803 Follin Lane, Vienna, VA. (703) 281–8111. MAILING ADDRESS: Washington, D.C. 20505–0001.

Civil Aeronautics Board

Chief, Environmental and Energy Programs (B–60C), Civil Aeronautics Board, Room 909, Universal Bldg., 1825 Connecticut Ave., NW, Wash., D.C. 20428–0001. (202) 426–9622.

Consumer Product Safety Commission

Assistant General Counsel, Office of the General Counsel, Consumer Product Safety Commission, Room 200, 5401 Westbard Ave., Bethesda, MD. (301) 492–6550. MAILING ADDRESS: Washington, D.C. 20207–0001.

Delaware River Basin Commission

Executive Director, Delaware River Basin Commission, 25 State Police Drive, P.O. Box 7360, West Trenton, NJ 08628–0360. (609) 883–9500; (FTS) 483–2077.

Environmental Protection Agency

Director, Office of Federal Activities (A–104), Environmental Protection Agency, Room 2119–I, 401 M St., SW, Wash., D.C. 20460–0001. (202) 382–5053.

Export-Import Bank of the United States

General Counsel, Export-Import Bank of the United States, Room 947, Lafayette Bldg., Room 947, 811 Vermont Ave., NW, Wash., D.C. 20571–0001. (202) 566–8334.

Farm Credit Administration

Deputy Governor—Region I, Office of Examination and Supervision, Farm Credit Administration, 1501 Farm Credit Drive, McLean, VA 22102–5090. (703) 883–4161.

Federal Communications Commission

Staff Attorney, Legal Counsel Division, Office of General Counsel, Federal Communications Commission, Room 621, 1919 M St., NW, Wash., D.C. 20554–0001. (202) 632–6990.

Federal Deposit Insurance Corporation

Director, Division of Accounting and Corporate Services, Federal Deposit Insurance Corporation, Room 6120, 550 Seventeenth St., NW, Wash., D.C. 20429–0001. (202) 389–4691.

Federal Emergency Management Agency

Associate General Counsel, Federal Emergency Management Agency, Room 840, 500 C St., SW, Wash., D.C. 20472–0001. (202) 287–0387.

Federal Energy Regulatory Commission

(1) Legal Matters: Deputy Assistant General Counsel, Division of Rulemaking and Policy Coordination, Office of General Counsel, Federal Energy Regulatory Commission, Room 8600A, 825 N. Capitol St., NE, Wash., D.C. 20426–0001. (202) 357–8033.

(2) Natural Gas Matters: Chief, Environmental Evaluation Branch, Office of Pipeline and Producer Regulation, Federal Energy Regulatory Commission, Room 7102A, 825 N. Capitol St., NE, Wash., D.C. 20426–0001. (202) 357–8098.

(3) Electric and Hydroelectric Matters: Director, Division of Environmental Analysis, Office of Hydropower Licensing, Federal Energy Regulatory Commission, Room 308, Railway Labor Building, 400 First St., NW, Wash., D.C. 20426–0001. (202) 376–1768.

Federal Home Loan Bank Board

Deputy Director for Corporate, Corporate and Securities Division, Office of General Counsel, Federal Home Loan Bank Board, Third Floor, East Wing, 1700 G St., NW, Wash., D.C. 20552–0001. (202) 377–6411.

Federal Maritime Commission

Director, Office of Energy and Environmental Impact, Federal Maritime Commission, 1100 L St., NW, Wash., D.C. 20573–0001. (202) 523–5835.

Federal Reserve Board

Senior Attorney, Office of General Counsel, Federal Reserve Board, Room B–1016E, 20th St. and Constitution Ave., NW, Wash., D.C. 20551–0001. (202) 452–3236.

Federal Trade Commission

Deputy Assistant General Counsel, Federal Trade Commission, Room 582, 6th St. and Pennsylvania Ave., NW, Wash., D.C. 20580–0001. (202) 523–1928.

General Services Administration

Director, Environmental Affairs Staff (PRE), Office of Space Management, Public Buildings Service, General Services Administration, Room 2323, 18th and F Sts., NW, Wash., D.C. 20405–0001. (202) 566–0654.

International Boundary and Water Commission, United States Section

Principal Engineer, Investigations and Planning Division, International Boundary and Water Commission, United States Section, IBWC Bldg., 4110 Rio Bravo, El Paso, TX 79902–1091. (915) 541–7304; (FTS) 572–7304.

Interstate Commerce Commission

Chief, Section of Energy and Environment, Office of Transportation Analysis, Interstate Commerce Commission, Room 4143, 12th St. and Constitution Ave., NW, Wash., D.C. 20423–0001. (202) 275–0800.

Lowell Historic Preservation Commission

Planning Director, Lowell Historic Preservation Commission, 204 Middle Street, Lowell, MA 01852–1815. (617) 458–7653; (FTS) 829–0766.

Marine Mammal Commission

General Counsel, Marine Mammal Commission, Room 307, 1625 Eye St., NW, Wash., D.C. 20006–3054. (202) 653–6237.

National Academy of Sciences

Staff Director, Environmental Studies Board, National Academy of Sciences, Room JH–804, 2101 Constitution Ave., NW, Wash., D.C. 20418–0001. (202) 334–3060.

National Aeronautics and Space Administration

Environmental Compliance Officer, Facilities Engineering Division (NXG), National Aeronautics and Space Administration, Room 5031, 400 Maryland Ave., SW, Wash., D.C. 20546–0001. (202) 453–1958.

National Capital Planning Commission

Environmental/Energy Officer, Division of Planning Services, National Capital Planning Commission, Room 1024, 1325 G St., NW, Wash., D.C. 20576–0001. (202) 724–0179.

National Credit Union Administration

Director, Department of Legal Services, National Credit Union Administration, Room 6261, 1776 G St., NW, Wash., D.C. 20456–0001. (202) 357–1030.

National Science Foundation

Chairman and Staff Associate, Committee on Environmental Matters; Office of Astronomical, Atmospheric, Earth and Ocean Sciences; National Science Foundation, Room 641, 1800 G St., NW, Wash., D.C. 20550–0001. (202) 357–7615.

Nuclear Regulatory Commission

(1) Director, Division of Engineering, Office of Nuclear Reactor Regulation, Nuclear Regulatory Commission, Room P–202, Phillips Bldg., 7920 Norfolk Ave., Bethesda, MD 20814–2587. (301) 492–7207.

(2) Director, Division of Fuel Cycle and Materials Safety, Office of Nuclear Material Safety and Safeguards, Nuclear Regulatory Commission, Room 562, Willste Building, 7915 Eastern Ave., Silver Spring, MD 20910–4896. (301) 427–4485.

Pennsylvania Avenue Development Corporation

Director of Development, Pennsylvania Avenue Development Corporation, Suite 1248, 425 13th St., NW, Wash., D.C. 20004–1856. (202) 523–5477.

Securities and Exchange Commission

Special Counsel, Office of Public Utility Regulation, Securities and Exchange

Commission, Room 7012, 450 Fifth St., NW, Wash., D.C. 20549–0001. (202) 272–7648.

Small Business Administration

Director, Office of Business Loans, Small Business Administration, Room 804–C, 1441 L St., NW, Wash., D.C. 20416–0001. (202) 653–6696.

Susquehanna River Basin Commission

Executive Director, Susquehanna River Basin Commission, 1721 N. Front St., Harrisburg, PA. 17102–2391. (717) 238–0422.

Tennessee Valley Authority

Director, Environmental Quality Staff, Tennessee Valley Authority, 201 Summer Place Building, 309 Walnut St., Knoxville, TN 37902–1411. (615) 632–6578; (FTS) 856–6578.

United States Information Agency

Assistant General Counsel, United States Information Agency, 301 Fourth St., SW, Wash., D.C. 20547–0001. (202) 485–7976.

United States International Development Cooperation Agency

(1) Environmental Affairs Coordinator, Office of External Affairs, U.S. Agency for International Development, Department of State Bldg., 320 21st St., NW, Wash., D.C. 20523–0001. (202) 632–8268.

(2) International Economist/Environmental Officer, Office of Development, Overseas Private Investment Corporation, 1129 20th St., NW, Wash., D.C. 20527–0001. (202) 653–2904.

United States Postal Service

Director, Office of Program Planning, Real Estate and Buildings Department, United States Postal Service, Room 4014, 475 L'Enfant Plaza West, SW, Wash., D.C. 20260–6420. (202) 245–4304.

Veterans Administration

Director, Environmental Affairs, Veterans Administration, Code 005, 810 Vermont Ave. NW, Wash., D.C. 20420–0001. (202) 389–2192.

Appendix II—Federal and Federal-State Agencies With Jurisdiction by Law or Special Expertise on Environmental Quality Issues

Index

I. Pollution Control
  A. Air Quality
  B. Water Quality
  C. Waste Disposal on Land
  D. Noise
  E. Radiation
  F. Hazardous Substances
    (1) Toxic, Explosive, and Flammable Materials
    (2) Food Additives and Contamination
    (3) Pesticides
II. Energy
  A. Electric Power
  B. Oil and Gas
  C. Coal
  D. Uranium
  E. Geothermal Resources
  F. Other Energy Sources—Solar, Wind, Biomass, etc.
  G. Energy Conservation
III. Land Use
  A. Land Use Planning, Regulation, and Development
  B. Federal Land Management
  C. Coastal Areas
  D. Environmentally Sensitive Areas
  E. Outdoor Recreation
  F. Community Development
  G. Historic, Architectural, and Archeological Resources
IV. Natural Resources Management
  A. Weather Modification
  B. Marine Resources
  C. Water Resources Development and Regulation
  D. Watershed Protection and Soil Conservation
  E. Forest, Range, and Vegetative Resources
  F. Fish and Wildlife Resources
  G. Non-energy Mineral Resources
  H. Natural Resources Conservation

I. POLLUTION CONTROL

A. Air Quality

Department of Agriculture

• Agricultural Research Service (effects of air pollution on vegetative growth).

• Farmers Home Administration (effects of air pollution on housing, community, and business loan programs, and farmer loan programs).

• Forest Service (effects of air pollution on vegetation and visibility; fire smoke management on National Forest and Grasslands).

• Rural Electrification Administration (electric power plant emissions).

• Soil Conservation Service (effects of air pollution on vegetation; wind erosion).

Department of Commerce

• National Bureau of Standards (air quality measurements, standards, data and methods).

• National Oceanic and Atmospheric Administration (meteorological and climatological research and monitoring in relation to urban air pollution; incorporation of national air quality standards in Coastal Zone Management Plans for management and protection of coastal and marine resources).

Department of Defense

• Department of the Air Force (air pollution from military aircraft).

• Department of the Army (emissions from military vehicles).

Department of Energy

• Economic Regulatory Administration (emissions from power plants and other major fuel-burning installations):

—Exemptions from prohibitions against burning of natural gas and oil in power plants and major fuel-burning installations. 42 U.S.C 7101 and 8301 (10 CFR Part 500, *et seq.*).

• Office of Policy, Safety, and Environment (air quality in relation to general energy policies, programs, and projects; emissions from energy sources).

Department of Health and Human Services

• Public Health Service: Center for Disease Control (effects of air pollution on health); National Institutes of Health (effects of air pollution on health).

Department of Housing and Urban Development

• Office of Community Planning and Development (effects of air pollution on the built environment; air pollution abatement; energy costs and State Implementation Plans).

• Office of Housing (effect of air pollution on housing values and marketability; economic impacts).

Department of the Interior

• Fish and Wildlife Service (effects of air pollution, including acid rain, on endangered species and critical habitats; National Wildlife Refuge System areas; and other fish and wildlife resources).

• Geological Survey (effects of acid rain on surface and ground waters).

• Bureau of Indian Affairs (effects of air pollution on Indian lands).

• Bureau of Land Management (effects of air pollution, including smoke from forest fires and prescribed burning, on public lands, vegetation and visibility).

• Minerals Management Service (emissions from outer continental shelf lease operations):

—Oil, gas, and sulphur operations on the outer continental shelf—air quality. 43 U.S.C. 1331, *et seq.*, and 42 U.S.C. 7411 (30 CFR Part 250.57).

• Bureau of Mines (air pollution from mining and minerals processing).

• National Park Service (visibility and other effects of air pollution on National Park System areas; effects of air pollution on recreation areas and historic, archeological and architectural sites).

• Office of Surface Mining Reclamation and Enforcement (air pollution from surface coal mining and reclamation operations; control of wind erosion at surface coal mines; control of coal waste fires).

Department of Labor

• Mine Safety and Health Administration (airborne hazards in mining operations).

• Occupational Safety and Health Administration (airborne hazards in the workplace):

—Air contaminants, toxic and hazardous substances. 29 U.S.C. 655, *et seq.* (29 CFR Part 1910, Subpart Z).

Department of State (international aspects of air pollution).

Department of Transportation

• Coast Guard (cargo tank venting and vapor recovery systems).

• Federal Aviation Administration (aircraft emissions):

—Fuel venting and exhaust emission requirements for turbine engine powered airplanes. Special Federal Aviation Regulation 27 (SFAR). 42 U.S.C. 1857, *et seq.*, 7571 and 7601; 49 U.S.C. 1345, 1348, 1421, 1423 and 1655 (14 CFR Part 11; 40 CFR Part 87).

• Federal Highway Administration (highway related air quality impacts; vehicle emissions):

—Air quality conformity of highway projects. 23 U.S.C. 109; 42 U.S.C. 7401, *et seq.*, and 7506 (23 CFR Part 770).

• Federal Railroad Administration (locomotive emissions).

• Urban Mass Transportation Administration (air quality effects of urban transportation systems):

—Air quality conformity of transit projects. 42 U.S.C. 7401, *et seq.*, and 7506 (49 CFR Part 623).

Advisory Council on Historic Preservation (effects of air pollution on historic districts, buildings and monuments).

Consumer Product Safety Commission (toxic emissions from consumer products and household substances):

—Consumer products and household substances regulations. 15 U.S.C. 1261, *et seq.*, and 2051, *et seq.* (16 CFR Part 1000, *et seq.*).

Environmental Protection Agency (effect of air pollution on public health and welfare; air quality criteria and standards; air pollution control and abatement technologies; transportation emissions and air quality impacts; stationary source emissions; monitoring technology):

—Air quality programs in general. 42 U.S.C. 1857, *et seq.*; 7401, *et seq.*; 7501, *et seq.*; and 7601, *et seq.* (40 CFR Parts 50–87).

—Prevention of significant air quality deterioration. 42 U.S.C. 7470, *et seq.* (40 CFR Parts 51, 52 and 124).

—Approval of State Implementation Plans (SIPs) for National primary and secondary ambient air quality standards. 42 U.S.C. 7410 (40 CFR Parts 51 and 52).

—Approval of State plans for standards of performance for new stationary emission sources (NSPS). 42 U.S.C. 7411 (40 CFR Part 60).

—Applications for primary non-ferrous smelter orders. 42 U.S.C. 7419 (40 CFR Part 57).

—Assuring that Federal projects conform with State Implementation Plans. 42 U.S.C. 7616 (40 CFR Part 20).

—Certification of new emission sources for conformance with National Emission Standards for Hazardous Air Pollutants including radioactive materials. 42 U.S.C. 7412(c) (40 CFR Part 61).

Interstate Commerce Commission (air pollution from trucks and railroads).

National Aeronautics and Space Administration (advanced technology for remote sensing of air quality parameters and for reduction of aircraft engine emissions).

Nuclear Regulatory Commission (radioactive substances in air pollution):

—For jurisdictional responsibilities see Part I.E—Radiation.

Tennessee Valley Authority (air quality in the Tennessee Valley region; measurement and control of air pollution from fossil-fueled steamplants; effects on vegetation).

B. Water Quality

Department of Agriculture

• Agricultural Research Service (research on erosion and sediment control, pesticide degradation and runoff, and salinity).

• Agricultural Stabilization and Conservation Service (water quality on agricultural lands; Water Bank Program).

• Farmers Home Administration (water quality in relation to housing, community, and business loan programs, and farmer loan programs).

• Forest Service (effects of water pollution on National Forests and Grasslands, and on forest and range land in general):

—Consultation regarding effects of pollution on rivers established as units of the National Wild and Scenic Rivers System and on those rivers designated for study as potential additions to that System. 16 U.S.C. 1278, *et seq.*

—Management of municipal watersheds on National Forest lands. (36 CFR Parts 251.9 and 251.35).

• Soil Conservation Service (water quality in relation to agricultural waste management, erosion and sediment control and stabilization of rural abandoned mines; salinity control; peticides in conservation systems):

—Reclamation of rural abandoned mined land. 30 U.S.C. 1201 *et seq.* (7 CFR Part 632).

—Program for land conservation and utilization, and aquaculture. 7 U.S.C. 1011(e).

Department of Commerce

• National Bureau of Standards (water quality measurements, standards, data, and methods).

• National Oceanic and Atmospheric Administration (water quality in the management and protection of coastal and marine resources, marine pollution research and monitoring for ocean mining):

—National Ocean Pollution Planning Act. 33 U.S.C. 1701, *et seq.*

—Marine Protection, Research, and Sanctuaries Act. 16 U.S.C. 1431, *et seq.* 15 CFR Part 922, *et seq.*).

Department of Defense

• Army Corps of Engineers (water pollution from activities in navigable waters):

—Rules governing work or structure in or affecting navigable waters of the United States. 33 U.S.C. 401 and 403 (33 CFR Parts 321 and 322).

—Authority to enjoin dumping of, or force removal of, refuse placed in or on the banks of a navigable water or tributary of a navigable water. 33 U.S.C. 407 (33 CFR Part 320.2(d)).

—Permits for discharges of dredged or fill materials into waters of the United States. 33 U.S.C. 1344 (33 CFR Part 323).

—Guidelines controlling discharge of dredged or fill material in waters of the U.S. including wetlands. 33 U.S.C. 1344(b) and 1361(a) (40 CFR Part 230).

—Permits for transportation of dredged materials for dumping into ocean waters. 33 U.S.C. 1413 (33 CFR Part 324).

—Regulation of artificial islands, installations and devices on the outer continental shelf. 43 U.S.C. 1333(e). (33 CFR Part 320.2(b)).

• Department of Navy (water pollution control for ships and naval installations; oceanography).

Department of Energy

• Office of Policy, Safety, and Environment (water quality and marine pollution in relation to general energy policies, programs and projects).

Department of Health and Human Services

• Center for desease Control (effects of water quality on health).

• Food and Drug Administration (shellfish sanitation; contamination of fish and shellfish with toxics).

Department of Housing and Urban Development

• Office of Community Planning and Development (effects of water pollution community planning and on sole source aquifers, floodplains, wetlands, and urban coastal zones).

Department of the Interior

• Fish and Wildlife Service (effects of water pollution on National Wildlife Refuge and National Fish Hatchery System areas, endangered species and their critical habitats, migratory waterfowl, floodplains, wetlands, estuarine areas, marine sanctuaries, barrier islands, and sport fisheries and wildlife resources).

• Geological Survey (general hydrology and water quality; National Water Summary; National Stream Quality Accounting Network [NASQAN]).

• Bureau of Indian Affairs (water quality on Indian lands).

• Bureau of Land Management (water quality on public lands):

—Permits and leases for facilities to control/ reduce water pollution. 43 U.S.C. 1732(b) and 1761(a)(1) (43 CFR Part 2800).

• Minerals Management Service (effects of marine pollution on the outer continental shelf and coastal waters):

—Control of pollution from mineral mining, including oil and gas development, on the outer continental shelf. 43 U.S.C. 1331–1343. (30 CFR Parts 250, 251, 252 and 256).

• Bureau of Mines (water pollution from mining and mineral processing; acid mine drainage).

• National Park Service (effects of water pollution on National Park System areas including National Seashores and Lakeshores, on outdoor recreational values, and on historic, archeological, and architectural resources):

—Consultations regarding effects of pollution on rivers established as units of the National Wild and Scenic Rivers System and on those rivers designated for study as potential additions to that System. 16 U.S.C. 1278, *et seq.*

• Bureau of Reclamation (effects of public works, salinity control, sedimentation, and irrigation on water quality; effects of water developments on estuarine areas; research in weather modification, water quality and quantity, and desalinization).

• Office of Surface Mining Reclamation and Enforcement (effects of surface coal mining and reclamation operations on water quality and hydrologic balance).

Department of State (international aspects of water pollution):

—Facilities for export/import of water and sewage. Executive Order 11423.

Department of Transportation

• Coast Guard (effects of oil spills and ship sanitation on water quality; ocean dumping enforcement; marine resource protection):

—Tanker construction, equipment, manning, operation. 46 U.S.C. 391(a) (33 CFR Part 157).

—Control of pollution by oil and hazardous substance discharges in ports, waterways, and offshore facilities. 33 U.S.C. 1008-1011, 1221, and 1321; 50 U.S.C. 191 (33 CFR Parts 151 and 154-156).

—Certification of marine sanitation devices. 33 U.S.C. 1322 (33 CFR Part 159).

• Federal Highway Administration (effects of highways, traffic and use of salt on water quality).

• Maritime Administration (water pollution from ships; destruction/treatment of wastes at sea):

—Merchant vessels, polluting discharges and dumping. 46 U.S.C. 1101, *et seq.*

—Port operations, polluting discharges and dumping. 46 U.S.C. 867.

• Research and Special Programs Administration: Materials Transportation Bureau (effects of hazardous substances transportation on water quality).

Advisory Council on Historic Preservation (effects of water pollution on historic districts, buildings and monuments).

Environmental Protection Agency (waste water treatment works; effluent limitations; oil and hazardous substance discharges; protection of drinking water supplies; thermal discharges; ocean dumping; monitoring technology):

—Water quality programs in general. 33 U.S.C. 1160, *et seq.* and 1251, *et seq.*; 42 U.S.C. 300f, *et seq.*, and 6901, *et seq.* (40 CFR Parts 100-149).

—Effluent guidelines and standards. 33 U.S.C. 1251, *et seq.* (40 CFR Part 401, *et seq.*).

—Ocean dumping in general. 33 U.S.C. 1344, 1361 and 1412-1418 (40 CFR Parts 220-231).

—Permits for discharge of specific pollutants from aquaculture projects. 33 U.S.C. 1328 (40 CFR Parts 122-124).

—Review of permits for transportation of dredged material for ocean dumping. 33 U.S.C. 1413 (40 CFR Parts 220-229).

—Permits for transportation of materials (other than dredged material) for ocean dumping. 33 U.S.C. 1412 and 1414 (40 CFR Parts 220-229).

—Permits for disposal of sewage sludge. 33 U.S.C. 1345 (40 CFR Parts 122-125).

—Permits for ocean discharges. 33 U.S.C. 1343 (40 CFR Parts 125.120-125.124).

—Regulation of discharges of oil and hazardous substances in waters of the United States. 33 U.S.C. 1321 and 1361 (40 CFR Part 112).

—Permits for treatment, storage or disposal of hazardous wastes. 2 U.S.C. 6925 (40 CFR Parts 124, 270, and 271).

—Review of permits for discharges of dredged or fill materials into navigable waters. 33 U.S.C. 1344(c) (40 CFR Part 230).

—Guidelines controlling the discharge of dredged or fill material in waters of the U.S. including wetlands. 33 U.S.C. 1344(b) and 1361(a) (40 CFR Part 230).

—Assistance for construction of publicly-owned waste water treatment works. 33 U.S.C. 1281 (40 CFR Parts 30 and 35).

—Underground injection control permits. 42 U.S.C. 300f, *et seq.* (40 CFR Parts 122-124 and 144-146).

—National Pollutant Discharge Elimination System (NPDES) wastewater permits. 33 U.S.C. 1342 (40 CFR Parts 122-125, 129, 133, and 136).

—Designation of Sole Source Aquifers. 42 U.S.C. 300f and h-3(e) (40 CFR Part 148).

Federal Emergency Management Agency (water quality in floodplain management).

Federal Maritime Commission (vessel certification with respect to liability for water pollution):

—Certificates of financial responsibility for water pollution. 33 U.S.C. 1321 (46 CFR Part 542); 42 U.S.C. 1643 (46 CFR Part 543); 43 U.S.C. 1815 (46 CFR Part 544).

International Boundary and Water Commission, United States Section (U.S.-Mexico border water quality, salinity, and sanitation problems).

National Aeronautics and Space Administration (advanced technology for remote sensing of water quality and marine pollution).

Nuclear Regulatory Commission (radioactive substances in water pollution):

—For jurisdictional responsibilities, see PART I. E—Radiation.

Tennessee Valley Authority (water quality in the Tennessee Valley; effects of chemical and thermal effluents).

C. Waste Disposal on Land

Department of Agriculture

• Agricultural Research Service (effects of agricultural wastes and sludge on cropland).

• Agriculture Stabilization and Conservation Service (effects of solid waste, especially sludge disposal, on cropland).

• Forest Service (effects of solid and liquid wastes on National Forests and Grasslands):

—Permits for disposal sites on National Forest System lands. 16 U.S.C. 495, 497, 532-538 and 580 (36 CFR Part 251).

• Rural Electrification Administration (solid waste disposal from electric power plants).

• Soil Conservation Service (agriculture waste management; siting of disposal areas; sludge application on cropland for beneficial purposes).

Department of Commerce

• National Bureau of Standards (measurements, standards, data, and methods relating to solid and liquid wastes).

• National Oceanic and Atmospheric Administration (disposal of solid wastes in the management and protection of coastal and marine resources).

Department of Health and Human Services

• Center for Disease Control (effects of wastes on health).

• Food and Drug Administration (contamination of food resulting from disposal of municipal and industrial waste treatment sludge).

Department of the Interior

• Fish and Wildlife Service (effects of solid wastes on National Wildlife Refuge and National Fish Hatchery System areas,

endangered species and their critical habitats, and other fish and wildlife resources).

• Geological Survey (geologic and hydrologic effects of solid and liquid wastes).

• Bureau of Indian Affairs (effects of solid wastes on Indian lands).

• Bureau of Land Management (effects of solid wastes on public lands):

—Sale or lease of land for solid waste disposal sites. 43 U.S.C. 869, *et seq.* (for sale—43 CFR Part 2740; for lease—43 CFR Part 2912).

• Bureau of Mines (mine wastes; mineral processing wastes; tailings stabilization; impoundment structures; municipal solid wastes; recycling).

• National Park Service (effects of solid wastes on National Park System areas).

• Office of Surface Mining Reclamation and Enforcement (surface coal mining and reclamation operation wastes).

Department of Labor

• Mine Safety and Health Administration (mine waste control).

Department of Transportation

• Maritime Administration (destruction/treatment of wastes at sea).

• Research and Special Programs Administration: Materials Transportation Bureau (transport of hazardous wastes):

—Hazardous materials regulations. (49 CFR Part 171, *et seq.*).

Environmental Protection Agency (solid wastes; hazardous waste; resource conservation and recovery; removal and remedial actions; environmental effects):

Solid wastes in general. 42 U.S.C. 3251, *et seq.*, and 6901, *et seq.* (40 CFR Parts 240-271); 42 U.S.C. 9601 *et seq.* (40 CFR Part 300, *et seq.*).

—Permits for disposal of sewage sludge. 33 U.S.C. 1345 (40 CFR Parts 122-125).

—Solid Waste Disposal Act permits. 42 U.S.C. 3251, *et seq.*, and 6901, *et seq.* (40 CFR Parts 124, 257, 270, 271 and 350).

—Criteria for classification of solid waste disposal facilities and practices. 42 U.S.C. 6907(a)(3) and 6944(a); 33 U.S.C. 1345 (40 CFR Part 257).

—Identification and listing of hazardous wastes. 42 U.S.C. 6921 (40 CFR Part 261).

—Standards applicable to generators and transporters of hazardous waste, and for owners and operators of hazardous waste treatment, storage, and disposal facilities. 42 U.S.C. 6922-6924 (40 CFR Parts 260-267).

—Permits for hazardous waste treatment, storage, and disposal facilities. 42 U.S.C. 6925 (40 CFR Parts 123, 124, 270 and 271).

—Preliminary notification of hazardous waste activities. 42 U.S.C. 6930 (40 CFR Parts 261.5, 262.12, and 263.11).

—Removal and remedial actions taken in response to the release or threatened release of hazardous substances. 42 U.S.C. 9601 (23) and (24) 40 CFR Part 300).

—National Contingency plan for the release of oil and hazardous substances into the environment. 42 U.S.C. 9605 (40 CFR Part 300).

—Notification requirements for the release of hazardous substances into the environment. 42 U.S.C. 9605 (40 CFR Part 302).
—Assistance for construction of solid waste disposal facilities. 42 U.S.C. 6981, et seq. (40 CFR Parts 30 and 35).
Federal Emergency Management Agency (hazardous materials emergency management and disaster relief assistance).
General Services Administration (wastes in public buildings).
Nuclear Regulatory Commission (radioactive waste disposal):
—For jurisdictional responsibilities, see PART I. E—Radiation.
Tennessee Valley Authority (coal combustion products).

D. Noise

Department of Agriculture

• Farmers Home Administration (noise in relation to housing, community, and business loan programs, and farmer loan programs).
• Forest Service (noise effects on National Forests and Grasslands).
• Rural Electrification Administration (electric generating facility, powerline, and substation noise).

Department of Commerce

• National Oceanic and Atmospheric Administration (effects of noise on marine mammals).

Department of Defense

• Department of the Air Force (military aircraft noise).
• Department of the Army (noise from rotary wing aircraft and other military vehicles).

Department of Health and Human Services

• Public Health Service (effects of noise on health).

Department of Housing and Urban Development

• Office of Community Planning and Development (aircraft and vehicular noise and land use compatibility):
—Noise abatement and control. (24 CFR Part 51, Subpart B).
—Siting of HUD assisted projects in runway clear zones (civil airports) and clear zones and accident potential zones (military airfields). (24 CFR Part 51, Subpart D).
• Office of Housing (noise standards for housing; noise abatement and control).

Department of Interior

• Fish and Wildlife Service (effects of noise on endangered species and their critical habitats, National Wildlife Refuge System areas, and other fish and wildlife resources).
• Bureau of Indian Affairs (noise effects on Indian lands).
• Bureau of Land Management (noise effects on public lands; noise abatement and control).
• Minerals Management Service (effects of noise on marine mammals).
• Bureau of Mines (mine noise, blasting and vibration).
• National Park Service (effects of noise on National Parks system areas, including off-

road vehicular noise; effects of noise and vibration on historic, archeological, and architectural sites, and recreational resources).
• Bureau of Reclamation (effects of noise on reclamation project lands).
• Office of Surface Mining Reclamation and Enforcement (noise from surface coal mining and reclamation operations, and from the use of explosives).

Department of Labor

• Mining Safety and Health Administration (noise in mining operations).
• Occupational Safety and Health Administration (noise in the workplace):
—Occupational noise exposure. 29 U.S.C. 655, et seq. (29 CFR Part 1910.95).

Department of Transportation

• Federal Aviation Administration (aircraft noise and land use compatibility):
—Airport noise compatibility planning. 49 U.S.C. 1341, 1348, 1354, 1421, 1431, 1655 and 2101–2104 (14 CFR Part 150).
—Noise standards: Aircraft type and airworthiness certification. 49 U.S.C. 1354, 1421, 1423, 1431 and 1655 (14 CFR Part 36).
—Operating noise limits. 49 U.S.C. 1344, et seq.; 1421, et seq., and 1655 (14 CFR Part 91, Subpart E).
—Civil aircraft sonic boom. (14 CFR Part 91.55).
• Federal Highway Administration (traffic and motor vehicle noise):
—Procedures for abatement of highway traffic and construction noise. 23 U.S.C. 109 (23 CFR Part 772).
• Federal Railroad Administration (railroad noise):
—Railroad noise emission compliance regulation. 42 U.S.C. 4901, et seq. (49 CFR Part 210).
—Noise standards for railroad employees. (49 CFR Parts 228–229).
• Urban Mass Transportation Administration (urban transportation system noise).
Advisory Council on Historic Preservation (effects of noise and vibration on historic districts, buildings and monuments).
Consumer Products Safety Commission (hazardous noise from consumer products):
—Consumer products regulations. 15 U.S.C. 1261, et seq., and 2051, et seq. (16 CFR Part 1000, et seq.).
Environmental Protection Agency (noise exposure standards; noise abatement and control techniques; noise impact assessment techniques; environmental effects):
—Noise abatement programs. 42 U.S.C. 4901, et seq. (40 CFR Part 201, et seq.).
Interstate Commerce Commission (noise effects from trucks and railroads).
National Aeronautics and Space Administration (advanced technology for reduction of aircraft noise).

E. Radiation

Department of Agriculture

• Agricultural Research Service (effects of irradiation on insects and microorganisms in food).

• Forest Service (disposal of radioactive materials in National forests and Grasslands; electromagnetic radiation from powerlines and radio transmission systems).
• Rural Electrification Administration (electromagnetic radiation from high voltage sources).

Department of Commerce

• National Bureau of Standards (radiation measurements, standards, methods and data).
• National Oceanic and Atmospheric Administration (electromagnetic radiation from radar systems and telecommunications).

Department of Energy

• Office of Civilian Radioactive Waste Management (storage and disposal of commercial high-level radioactive waste and spent nuclear fuel).
• Office of Defense Programs (storage and disposal of Defense nuclear waste).
• Office of Energy Research (health effects of radiation and nuclear energy).
• Office of Policy, Safety, and Environment (nuclear energy and radioactive waste disposal; radiation effects).

Department of Health and Human Services

• Food and Drug Administration (effects of radiation on health and safety; contamination of food with radioactive materials).
• National Institutes of Health (effects of radiation on health).

Department of Housing and Urban Development

• Office of Community Planning and Development (radiation health and safety factors; siting and distance criteria):
—Policy guidance on problems posed by toxic chemicals and radioactive materials. (HUD Notice 79–33 of Sept. 10, 1979).
• Office of Housing (radiation location factors affecting value and marketability).

Department of the Interior

• Fish and Wildlife Service (effects of radiation on National Wildlife Refuges, endangered species and their critical habitats, and other fish and wildlife resources).
• Geological Survey (effects of radioactive waste disposal).
• Bureau of Indian Affairs (effects of radiation on Indian lands).
• Bureau of Land Management (effects of radiation on public lands):
—Withdrawal of public lands for deep-burial depositories for radioactive waste. 43 U.S.C. 1714 (43 CFR Part 2300, et seq.).
• Bureau of Mines (radiation from uranium mines).
• National Park Service (effects of radiation on National Park System areas).

Department of Labor

• Mining Safety and Health Administration (worker protection from radiation exposure in mining).
• Occupational Safety and Health Administration (worker protection from exposure to sources of radiation not covered by other Federal agencies):

—Ionizing and nonionizing radiation. 29 U.S.C. 655, *et seq.* (29 CFR Parts 1910.96 and 1910.97).

Department of Transportation

• Federal Aviation Administration (radiation effects on air traffic; transport of radioactive materials).

• Federal Highway Administration: Bureau of Motor Carrier Safety (radioactive material transportation in interstate commerce):

—Hazardous materials tables and communications regulations. (49 CFR Part 172).

• Research and Special Programs Administration: Materials Transportation Bureau (transportation of radioactive materials):

—Hazardous materials regulations. 49 U.S.C. 1801, *et seq.* (49 CFR Part 171, *et seq.*).

Consumer Product Safety Commission (radiation from consumer products and household substances):

—Consumer products and household substances regulations. 15 U.S.C. 1261, *et seq.*; 2051, *et seq.*, and 2080 (16 CFR Part 1000, *et seq.*).

Environmental Protection Agency (radiation protection standards and guidance; radioactive air emissions; ocean disposal of radioactive waste; radiation limits for drinking water; radiation monitoring):

—Radiation protection programs. 42 U.S.C. 2011, *et seq.* (40 CFR Part 190, *et seq.*).

—Standards for the uranium fuel cycle. 42 U.S.C. 2011, *et seq.* (40 CFR Part 190).

—Standards for uranium mill tailings. 42 U.S.C. 2022. (40 CFR Part 192).

—Radiation standards for drinking water. 42 U.S.C. 300f, *et seq.* (40 CFR Part 141).

—Guidance to other Federal agencies for environmental radiation standards. 42 U.S.C. 2021(h).

Federal Emergency Management Agency (review and approval of state and local nuclear incident emergency response plans; Federal contingency plans; radiation hazards emergency management).

Nuclear Regulatory Commission (radioactive wastes, radiation effects in general):

—Standards for protection against radiation. 42 U.S.C. 2073, *et seq.*, and 5841, *et seq.* (10 CFR Part 20).

—Licensing of byproduct material. 42 U.S.C. 2014, *et seq.*, and 5841, *et seq.* (10 CFR Parts 30–33 and 35).

—Licensing and radiation safety requirements for radiography. 42 U.S.C. 2111, *et seq.*, and 5841, *et seq.* (10 CFR Part 34).

—Licensing of source material. 42 U.S.C. 2014 *et seq.*, and 5841, *et seq.* (10 CFR Part 40).

—Licensing of production and utilization facilities. 42 U.S.C. 2073, *et seq.* and 5841, *et seq.* (10 CFR Parts 50, 51 and 55).

—Disposal of high level radioactive waste. 42 U.S.C. 2021, *et seq.*, and 5842, *et seq.* (10 CFR Parts 60 and 61).

—Licensing of special nuclear material. 42 U.S.C. 2014, *et seq.*, and 5841, *et seq.* (10 CFR Part 70).

—Packaging and transportation of radioactive material. 42 U.S.C. 2073, *et seq.*, and 5841 *et seq.* (10 CFR Part 71).

—Licensing for storage of spent fuel. 42 U.S.C. 2021, *et seq.*, and 5872 *et seq.* (10 CFR Part 72).

—Reactor site criteria. 42 U.S.C. 2133, *et seq.*, and 5841, *et seq.* (10 CFR Part 100).

—Export and import of nuclear material. 42 U.S.C. 2073, *et seq.*, and 5841 (10 CFR Part 110).

—Licenses for Department of Energy demonstration reactors. 42 U.S.C. 5842 (1) and (2).

—Licenses for receipt and long-term storage of high-level radioactive wastes at Department of Energy facilities. 42 U.S.C. 5842 (3) and (4).

Tennessee Valley Authority (nuclear power plant planning; radiation monitoring).

F. Hazardous Substances

(1) Toxic, Explosive, and Flammable Materials

Department of Agriculture

• Agricultural Marketing Services (toxic materials and consumer protection).

• Animal and Plant Health Inspection Service (toxic materials in the control of plant pests, noxious weeds, animal diseases, and vectors).

• Food Safety and Inspection Service (toxic materials and consumer protection).

• Forest Service (effects of toxic materials on National Forests and Grasslands).

• Soil Conservation Service (toxic materials in the control of insects and other plant pests).

Department of Commerce

• National Bureau of Standards (toxic material measurements, standards, methods and data).

• National Oceanic and Atmospheric Administration (toxic materials in coastal and marine resources management and protection; ocean pollution research and monitoring).

Department of Defense (toxic materials in military operations).

Department of Health and Human Services

• Center for Disease Control (toxic materials and health issues).

• Food and Drug Administration (toxic materials and contamination of food).

• National Institutes of Health (toxic materials and health issues).

Department of Housing and Urban Development

• Office of Community Planning and Development (hazardous waste disposal, treatment, and compatible land use):

—Assurances that HUD assisted projects are located in a safe and healthful environment. 42 U.S.C. 1441, *et seq.*

—Policy guidance on problems posed by toxic chemicals and radioactive materials. (HUD Notice 79–33 of Sept. 10, 1979).

—Siting of HUD assisted projects near hazardous operations handling explosive or flammable materials. (24 CFR Part 51, Subpart C).

• Office of Housing (lead-based paint poisoning prevention; hazardous material storage and effects on property values).

Department of the Interior

• Fish and Wildlife Service (effects of toxic materials, including lead shot, on endangered species and critical habitats, National Wildlife Refuge and National Fish Hatchery System areas, and other fish and wildlife resources).

• Geological Survey (effects of the disposal of toxic wastes).

• Bureau of Indian Affairs (toxic materials on Indian lands).

• Bureau of Land Management (toxic materials on public lands).

• Minerals Management Service (toxic materials from outer continental shelf mineral, including oil and gas, operations):

—Discharges from outer continental shelf mineral, including oil and gas, operations. 43 U.S.C. 1331, *et seq.* (30 CFR Part 250).

• Bureau of Mines (disposal methods for selected milling and mine wastes).

• National Park Service (effects of toxic materials on National Park System areas).

• Bureau of Reclamation (effects of toxic materials on water storage and delivery projects).

• Office of Surface Mining Reclamation and Enforcement (toxic materials from surface coal mining and reclamation wastes).

Department of Labor

• Mining Safety and Health Administration (toxic materials in mining).

• Occupational Safety and Health Administration (toxic materials in the workplace):

—Hazardous and toxic materials and substances. 29 U.S.C. 655, *et seq.* (29 CFR Part 1910, Subparts H and Z).

Department of Transportation

• Coast Guard (transportation of toxic materials by vessel; discharges to navigable waters):

—Transportation of hazardous materials by vessel. 46 U.S.C. 170, 375, 391(a) and 416(j); 49 U.S.C. 1655, 1803, 1804 and 1808(j); 50 U.S.C. 191 (33 CFR Parts 151, *et seq.*, and 160, *et seq.* (46 CFR Chapter I).

—Hazardous substance discharge in navigable waters. 33 U.S.C. 1321 (33 CFR Parts 25 and 151, *et seq.*; 46 CFR Part 542, *et seq.*).

• Federal Aviation Administration (hazardous aircraft cargo).

• Federal Highway Administration: Bureau of Motor Carrier Safety (hazardous material transportation in interstate commerce):

—Hazardous materials tables and communications regulations. (49 CFR Part 172).

—Transportation of hazardous materials—driving and parking rules. (49 CFR Part 397).

• Federal Railroad Administration (railroad transport of hazardous materials).

• Maritime Administration (port, coastal and ocean pollution from hazardous materials):

—Merchant vessels, polluting discharges, dumping, and destruction/treatment of wastes at sea. 46 U.S.C. 1101, *et seq.*

• Research and Special Programs Administration: Materials Transportation Bureau (hazardous cargo; hazardous materials in pipelines):

—Transportation of hazardous materials. 49 U.S.C. 1801, *et seq*. (49 CFR Part 171, *et seq.*, and 190, *et seq.*).

—Approval for shipments of Class A explosives. 49 U.S.C. 1707 (7).

—Permits for facilities to handle hazardous materials. 49 U.S.C. 1801, *et seq*.

Consumer Product Safety Commission (toxic consumer products and hazardous household substances):

—Consumer product and household substances regulations. 15 U.S.C. 1261, *et seq.*; 1471, *et seq.*; and 2051, *et seq*. (16 CFR Part 1000, *et seq.*).

Environmental Protection Agency (hazardous material pollution control and environmental effects):

—Permits for the treatment, storage and disposal of hazardous wastes. 42 U.S.C. 6901, *et seq*. (40 CFR Parts 122–124, 257, 270, and 271).

—Criteria for classification of hazardous waste disposal facilities and practices. 42 U.S.C. 6907(a)(3) and 6944(a); 33 U.S.C. 1345 (40 CFR Part 257).

—Identification and listing of hazardous waste. 42 U.S.C. 6921 (40 CFR Part 261).

—Standards applicable to generators and transporters of hazardous wastes and for owners and operators of hazardous waste treatment, storage and disposal facilities. 42 U.S.C. 6901, *et seq*. (40 CFR Parts 260–267).

—Preliminary notification of hazardous waste activities. 42 U.S.C. 6930 (40 CFR Parts 261.5, 262.12 and 263.11).

—National emission standards for hazardous air pollutants (NESHAP). 42 U.S.C. 1857, *et seq*. General provisions: (40 CFR Part 61).

—Hazardous substances in water. 33 U.S.C. 1251, *et seq*. (40 CFR Parts 116 and 117).

—Toxic effluent standards. 33 U.S.C. 1251, *et seq*. (40 CFR Part 129).

—Control of toxic substances in general. 15 U.S.C. 2601, *et seq*. (40 CFR Part 702, *et seq.*).

—Regulation of hazardous chemical substances and mixtures. 15 U.S.C. 2605 (40 CFR Part 750).

—Reporting of toxic substances inventory and retention of information. 15 U.S.C. 2607 (40 CFR Parts 710, 716, 761 and 763).

—Testing of chemical substances and mixtures. 15 U.S.C. 2603.

Federal Emergency Management Agency (evacuations and relocations resulting from hazardous materials released into the environment):

—Temporary evacuation and housing and permanent relocation due to hazardous substances pollution. 42 U.S.C. 9604(a)(1) and 9607 (23) and (24).

(2) Food Additives and Contamination of Food

Department of Agriculture

• Agricultural Research Service (detection of additives and contaminants in food).

• Agricultural Marketing Service (food quality standards).

• Food Safety and Inspection Service (contamination of meat and poultry products).

Department of Commerce

• National Oceanic and Atmospheric Administration (seafood quality).

Department of Health and Human Services

• Food and Drug Administration (effects of food additives and contamination on health).

Department of the Interior

• Fish and Wildlife Service (effects of contaminated food on endangered and threatened species and other Federally protected fish and wildlife).

Environmental Protection Agency (contamination of the environment and food from pesticide use and other toxic materials).

(3) Pesticides

Department of Agriculture

• Agricultural Research Service (biological controls; pesticides in food and fiber production).

• Animal Plant Health and Inspection Service (pesticides in the control of animal and plant pests and exotic noxious weeds).

• Food Safety and Inspection Service (pesticide residues and consumer protection).

• Forest Service (pesticides in the control of animal and plant pests; pesticide use on National Forests and Grasslands).

• Soil Conservation Service (pesticides in conservation systems; watershed resource protection).

Department of Commerce

• National Oceanic and Atmospheric Administration (effects of pesticides on marine life, the coastal zone, and seafood quality; ocean pollution research and monitoring).

Department of Defense

• Armed Forces Pest Management Board (pesticide use on military lands, facilities and equipment; control of disease vectors).

Department of Health and Human Services

• Center for Disease Control (effects of pesticides on health).

• Food and Drug Administration (pesticide contamination of food).

Department of the Interior

• Fish and Wildlife Service (pesticide use on National Wildlife Refuge and National Fish Hatchery System lands; effects of pesticides on endangered species and their critical habitats, and other fish and wildlife resources).

• Geological Survey (effects of pesticides on water quality).

• Bureau of Indian Affairs (pesticide use on Indian lands).

• Bureau of Land Management (pesticide use on public lands).

• Bureau of Reclamation (pesticide use on irrigated lands and other project lands, facilities and rights-of-way).

• National Park Service (pesticide use in National Park System areas).

Department of Labor

• Occupational Safety and Health Administration (worker exposures during manufacture of pesticides):

—Hazardous and toxic materials and substances. 29 U.S.C. 655, *et seq*. (29 CFR Part 1910, Subparts H and Z).

Department of Transportation

• Coast Guard (transportation of pesticides by vessel):

—Permits for transportation of hazardous substances by vessel. 46 U.S.C. 170, and 391a (33 CFR Parts 151, *et seq.*, and 160, *et seq.*; 46 CFR Chapter I).

• Federal Aviation Administration (transport and use of pesticides by aircraft).

• Federal Highway Administistion: Bureau of Motor Carrier Safety (pesticide transport in interstate commerce):

—Hazardous materials tables and communications regulations. (49 CFR Part 172).

• Federal Railroad Administration (transport of pesticides by railroads).

• Research and Special Programs Administration: Materials Transportation Bureau (transport of pesticides):

—Transportation of hazardous materials. 49 U.S.C. 1801, *et seq*. (49 CFR Part 171, *et seq.*).

Environmental Protection Agency (pollution control and environmental effects of pesticides):

—Pesticide programs in general. 7 U.S.C. 136, *et seq.*; 21 U.S.C. 346a (40 CFR Part 162, *et seq.*).

—Certification of pesticide applicators. 7 U.S.C. 136b (40 CFR Part 171).

—Registration of pesticides. 7 U.S.C. 136a (40 CFR Part 162).

—Experimental pesticide use permits. 7 U.S.C. 136c (40 CFR Part 172).

—Establishment of pesticide tolerances. 21 U.S.C. 346a (40 CFR Part 180 and 21 CFR Part 193).

—Pesticide disposal and transportation. 7 U.S.C. 136q (40 CFR Part 165).

—Worker protection standards for agricultural pesticides. 7 U.S.C. 136 (40 CFR Part 170).

—Emergency exemptions for pesticides use. 7 U.S.C. 136p (40 CFR Part 166).

Tennessee Valley Authority (pesticide use on public lands and waters in Tennessee Valley region).

II. ENERGY

A. Electric Power (Development, Generation, Transmission, and Use)

Department of Agriculture

• Farmers Home Administration (small hydro, solar, and wind projects):

—Approval of plans and specifications for FMHA funded projects. 7 U.S.C. 1942 (7 CFR Parts 1924, 1942 and 1944).

• Forest Service (power development in National Forests and Grasslands):

—Permits, easements, and leases for power transmission, road, and hydro

developments. 16 U.S.C. 522, *et seq.;* 43 U.S.C. 1761 (36 CFR Part 251.50, *et seq.*).
—Permits for commercial use of existing roads. 16 U.S.C. 537 (37 CFR Part 212).
—Consultations regarding power developments on rivers established as units of the National Wild and Scenic Rivers System and on those rivers designated for study as potential additions to that System. 16 U.S.C. 1278, *et seq.*
• Rural Electrification Administration (power development in and for rural areas):
—Electrical generation and transmission projects. 7 U.S.C. 901 *et seq.* (7 CFR Part 1700, *et seq.*

Department of Commerce
• National Oceanic and Atmospheric Administration (coastal energy facility planning and siting):
—Approval of licenses for siting, design, and operation of ocean-thermal energy facilities. 42 U.S.C. 9101, *et seq.* (15 CFR Part 981).

Department of Defense
• Army Corps of Engineers (hydroelectric projects; effects of power development on navigable waters):
—For jurisdictional responsibilities, see PART I. B.—Water Quality.

Department of Energy
• Economic Regulatory Administration (regulation of power plants and other major fuel-burning installations):
—Exemptions from prohibitions against the burning of natural gas and petroleum in power plants and major fuel burning installations. 42 U.S.C. 7101 and 8301 (10 CFR Part 500, *et seq.*).
—Transmission of electric energy to a foreign country. 16 U.S.C. 824a(e); E.O. 10485 and E.O. 12038 (18 CFR Parts 32.30–32.38 and 10 CFR Parts 205.300–205.309).
• Office of Policy, Safety, and Environment (general energy policies, programs and projects).
• Alaska Power Administration (hydroelectric generation and transmission systems in Alaska).
• Bonneville Power Administration (electric transmission systems in the Pacific northwest).
• Southeastern Power Administration (electric transmission systems in the southeastern States).
• Southwestern Power Administration (electric transmission systems in the southwestern States).
• Western Area Power Administration (electric transmission systems in the western States).

Department of Housing and Urban Development
• Office of Community Planning and Development (energy policy; demonstration programs; research; assistance for community and economic development; assistance for energy efficiency):
—Housing and Community Development Act of 1974. 42 U.S.C. 5301, *et seq.* (24 CFR Part 570).
• Office of Housing (energy factors in rehabilitation and retrofitting).

• Office of Policy Development and Research (building energy technology; urban energy studies).
• Office of Solar Energy and Conservation (new technologies and research).

Department of the Interior
• Fish and Wildlife Service (effects of power development, including transmission line and tower construction, on endangered species and their critical habitats, National Wildlife Refuge and National Fish Hatchery System areas, and other fish and wildlife resources):
—Easements/permits for transmission line rights-of-way across National Wildlife Refuge and National Fish Hatchery System land. For refuges—16 U.S.C. 668dd; for hatcheries—43 U.S.C. 931 c and d (50 CFR Part 29.21).
—Permits for rights-of-way on National Wildlife Monuments (Alaska only). 16 U.S.C. 432, 460(k)-3 and 742(f) (50 CFR Part 96).
—For additional jurisdictional responsibilities, see PART IV. C— Water Resources Development.
• Geological Survey (geologic and hydrologic siting constraints for power developments; National Water Summary).
• Bureau of Indian Affairs (power development on Indian lands):
—Approval of leases and permits for Indian lands. 25 U.S.C. 380, 393–395, 397, 402–403, 413, 415, 477 and 635 (25 CFR Part 162).
—Rights-of-way over Indian lands. 25 U.S.C. 311–321 and 323–328 (25 CFR Part 169).
—Specific power systems. (25 CFR Parts 175–177).
• Bureau of Land Management (power development on public lands):
—Easements/permits for rights-of-way. 30 U.S.C. 185 and 43 U.S.C. 1701, *et seq.* (43 CFR Parts 2800–2887).
—Exchange of Federal lands to facilitate energy development. 43 U.S.C. 1716 (43 CFR Parts 2200–2270).
• National Park Service (effects of power development on National Park System lands; on historic archeologic and architectural sites; and on recreational values):
—Easements for rights-of-way across National Park system land. 16 U.S.C. 5 (36 CFR Parts 7 and 14) .
—Consultations about extent to which proposed recreational developments at hydroelectric projects conform to and are in accord with the Statewide Comprehensive Outdoor Recreation Plans. 16 U.S.C. 460.
—Consultations regarding power developments on rivers established as units of the National Wild and Scenic Rivers System and on those rivers designated for study as potential additions to that System. 16 U.S.C. 1278, *et seq.*
• Bureau of Reclamation (hydroelectric power development in the 17 contiguous western states, impact of power development on State water laws; analysis of cost sharing).
—Easements/permits for powerline rights-of-way. 43 U.S.C. 3871.

Department of Labor
• Occupational Safety and Health Administration (workers safety and health issues):
—Construction, transmission and distribution facilities. 29 U.S.C. 655, *et seq.* (29 CFR Part 1926, Subpart V).

Department of Transportation
• Federal Highway Administration (highways and electric utility facilities):
—Relocation and accommodation of utility facilities on highway rights-of-way. 23 U.S.C. 109(1), 116 and 123 (23 CFR Part 645).

Advisory Council on Historic Preservation (effects of power developments on historic properties).

Environmental Protection Agency (pollution control and environmental effects of power development):
—For jurisdictional responsibilities see PART I.A.—Air Quality, PART I.B.—Water Quality, and PART I.C.—Waste Disposal on Land.

Federal Emergency Management Agency (review and approval of state and local nuclear incident emergency response plans).

Federal Energy Regulatory Commission (hydroelectric power projects; electric transmission; electric supply; facility siting):
—Regulation of interconnection of electric transmission facilities and regulation of enlargement of electric transmission facilities. 16 U.S.C. 824–825K (18 CFR Part 32).
—Regulation of the development of water power including the licensing of non-Federal hydroelectric power projects. 16 U.S.C. 791–825r (18 CFR Parts 4–25, 36, 131 and 141).
—Application for order directing the establishment of physical connection facilities. 16 U.S.C. 834(b).
—Withdrawal of Federal lands for power and powersite development purposes. 16 U.S.C. 818 (43 CFR Part 2344, *et seq.).*

International Boundary and Water Commission, United States Section (hydroelectric power installations on the Rio Grande).

Nuclear Regulatory Commission (nuclear power development in general):
—Licensing of production and utilization facilities. 42 U.S.C. 2073, *et seq.*, and 5841, *et seq.* (10 CFR Parts 50 and 51).
—Nuclear power reactor operators' licenses. 42 U.S.C. 2137, *et seq.*, and 5841, *et seq.* (10 CFR Part 55).
—Reactor site criteria. 42 U.S.C. 2133, *et seq.*, and 5841, *et seq.* (10 CFR Part 100).
—For other jurisdictional responsibilities, see PART I.E.—Radiation.

Tennessee Valley Authority (power development in the Tennessee Valley Region).

B. Oil and Gas (Development, Extraction, Refining, Transport and Use)

Department of Agriculture
• Forest Service (effects of oil and gas development on National Forests and Grasslands):

—Permits and rights-of-way on National Forest System lands. 16 U.S.C. 471–472, 478, 495, 497–498, 528, 531–538, 551, 572 and 580 (36 CFR Parts 212, 251 and 261).

Department of Commerce

• National Oceanic and Atmospheric Administration (effects of oil and gas development and coastal and marine resources, management, and protection).

Department of Defense

• Army Corps of Engineers (effects of oil and gas development on navigable waters):
—For jurisdictional responsibilities, see PART I.B—Water Quality.

Department of Energy

• Economic Regulatory Administration (regulation of power plants and other major fuel-burning installations):
—Exemptions from prohibitions against the burning of petroleum in power plants and major fuel-burning installations. 42 U.S.C. 7101 and 8301 (10 CFR Part 500, *et seq.*).
• Office of Policy, Safety, and Environment (general energy policies, programs, and projects).

Department of Housing and Urban Development

• Office of Community Planning and Development (health and safety standards; distance factors for pipeline, storage, and production facilities including sour gas wells; assistance for community and economic development; assistance to conserve petroleum and natural gas energy efficiency):
—Assurances that HUD assisted projects are located in a safe and healthful environment. 42 U.S.C. 1441, *et seq.*
—Siting of HUD assisted projects near hazardous operations handling petroleum products or chemicals of an explosive or flammable nature. (24 CFR Part 51, Subpart C).
—Housing and Community Development Act of 1974. 42 U.S.C. 5301, *et seq.* (24 CFR Part 570).
• Office of Housing (siting standards and effects on housing values and marketability).

Department of the Interior

• Fish and Wildlife Service (effects of oil and gas development on endangered species and their critical habitats, National Wildlife Refuge and National Fish Hatchery System areas, and other fish and wildlife resources):
—Permits for oil and gas pipeline rights-of-way across National Wildlife Refuge and National Fish Hatchery Systems lands. For refuges—16 U.S.C. 668dd; for hatcheries—43 U.S.C. 931c and d (50 CFR Part 29.21).
—Permits for rights-of-way across National Wildlife Monuments (Alaska only). 16 U.S.C. 432. 460(k)-3 and 742(f) (50 CFR Part 96).
• Geological Survey (oil and gas resources in general).
• Bureau of Indian Affairs (oil and gas development on Indian lands):
—Leases and permits on Indian lands. 25 U.S.C. 380, 393–395, 397, 402–403, 413, 415. 477 and 635 (25 CFR Part 162).
—Rights-of-way over Indian lands. 25 U.S.C. 311–321 and 323–328 (25 CFR Part 169).

—Mining leases (including oil and gas) on Indian lands. 25 U.S.C. 376, 396, 476–477 and 509 (25 CFR Parts 211–215 and 226–227).
• Bureau of Land Management (oil and gas development on public lands):
—Leases for oil and gas deposits:
(a) Public domain lands. 30 U.S.C. 181, *et seq.;* 43 CFR Parts 3100, *et seq.*, and 3160.
(b) Acquired lands. 30 U.S.C. 351–359 (43 CFR Parts 3100, *et seq.*, and 3160).
(c) In and under railroad and other rights-of-way acquired under laws of the United States. 30 U.S.C. 301–306 (43 CFR Part 3100).
(d) Indian lands. 25 U.S.C. 396a, *et seq.* (25 CFR Parts 211, 213, 226 and 227).
—Leases and land exchanges for oil shale, native asphalt, solid and semisolid bitumen and bituminous rock. For leases—30 U.S.C. 241 (43 CFR Part 3500); for exchanges—43 U.S.C. 1716 (43 CFR Parts 2200–2270).
—Easements/permits for oil and gas pipeline rights-of-way. 30 U.S.C. 185 and 43 U.S.C. 1701, *et seq.* (43 CFR Parts 2800–2887).
—Easements/leases/permits for use, occupancy and development of public lands. 43 U.S.C. 1732 (43 CFR Subchapters 2000 and 3000).
—Disposal of government royalty oil (non-OCS oil). 30 U.S.C. 189, 192 and 359 (30 CFR Part 208).
—Exchange of non-OCS Federal lands with oil and gas deposits. 43 U.S.C. 1716 (43 CFR Parts 2200–2207).
• Minerals Management Service (oil and gas development on the outer continental shelf):
—Leases for minerals on the outer continental shelf. 43 U.S.C. 1331–1343 (30 CFR Parts 250, 251, 252 and 256).
—Permits/easements for rights-of-way for "common carrier" oil gas pipelines on the outer continental shelf. 43 U.S.C. 1331 (30 CFR Part 256, Subpart N).
—Permits for exploration and development activities on Federal leases on the outer continental shelf. 43 U.S.C. 1331, *et seq.* (30 CFR Parts 250 and 251).
—Easements/rights-of-way for gathering pipelines, artificial islands, platforms, and other fixed structures on any Federal or State outer continental shelf oil and gas lease. 43 U.S.C. 1334–1335 (30 CFR Parts 250.18–250.19).
—Applications for purchase of government royalty oil from the outer continental shelf. 43 U.S.C. 1334 (30 CFR Part 225a).
—Permits for geological and geophysical exploration on the outer continental shelf. 43 U.S.C. 1334 and 1340 (30 CFR Part 251).
—Drilling permits. 43 U.S.C. 1351.
• Bureau of Mines (environmental, health, and safety aspects of mining oil, tar sands, and oil shale; coalbed methane control and recovery; helium conservation).
• National Park Service (effects of oil and gas development on National Park System areas on historic, archeological, and architectural sites, and on recreational values):
—Permits for oil and gas operations on National Park system areas. 16 U.S.C. 1 (36 CFR Part 9).
—Determination of significance of effects for combined hydrocarbon lease conversions

in Glen Canyon NRA. (43 CFR Parts 3140.7 and 3141.2).
• Bureau of Reclamation (effects of oil and gas development on water storage and delivery systems):
—Easements/permits for pipeline rights-of-way. 43 U.S.C. 3871.

Department of Labor

• Occupational Safety and Health Administration (general worker safety and health issues):
—Oil and gas well drilling. 29 U.S.C. 655, *et seq.* (29 CFR Part 1910.270).

Department of State (international aspects of oil and gas development):
—Facilities for export/import of petroleum and petroleum products. E.O. 11423.

Department of Transportation

• Coast Guard (oil and gas transport by vessel):
—Tank vessel regulation. 46 U.S.C. 391(a) (33 CFR Part 157).
—Ports and waterways safety. 33 U.S.C. 1221 (33 CFR Part 160, *et seq.*).
—Construction and alteration of bridges for pipelines over navigable waters. 33 U.S.C. 491, *et seq.*; 511, *et seq.*; 525, *et seq.*. and 535 (33 CFR Part 114, *et seq.*).
—Outer continental shelf structures. 43 U.S.C. 1331 (33 CFR Part 140, *et seq.*).
• Maritime Administration (effects of oil and gas development on port, coastal and ocean pollution):
—Merchant vessels, including liquefied natural gas vessels. 42 U.S.C. 1101, *et seq.* (46 CFR Part 250, *et seq.*).
—Port operations, including loading/unloading of liquefied natural gas vessels. 42 U.S.C. 867 (46 CFR Part 346, *et seq.*).
• Federal Highway Administration (pipelines and highway rights-of-way):
—Relocation and accommodation of pipelines on highway rights-of-way. 23 U.S.C. 109(1), 116 and 123 (23 CFR Part 645).
• Federal Railroad Administration (railroad transport of oil and gas).
• Research and Special Programs Administration: Materials Transportation Bureau (pipeline safety; oil and gas shipments; natural gas marine terminals):
—Pipeline safety. 49 U.S.C. 1671, *et seq.*. and 2001, *et seq.* (49 CFR Part 190, *et seq.*).

Advisory Council on Historic Preservation (effects of oil and gas development on historic properties):

Environmental Protection Agency (pollution control and environmental effects of oil and gas development):
—For jurisdictional responsibilities, see PART I.A.—Air Quality, PART I.B.—Water Quality, and PART I.C.—Waste Disposal on Land.

Federal Energy Regulatory Commission (charges/rates for transportation of oil and gas by pipeline; transportation, storage, and sale of natural gas):
—Certificates for natural gas facilities (underground storage fields, LNG facilities. and transmission pipeline facilities); sale. exchange and transportation of gas:

abandonment of facilities and curtailment of natural gas service; authorization to import and export natural gas. 15 U.S.C. 717–717(w); E.O. 10485 and E.O. 12038 (18 CFR Part 152, et seq.).
—Authorization compelling the expansion, improvement or connection of natural gas facilities. 15 U.S.C. 717f(a) (18 CFR Part 156).

Interstate Commerce Commission (regulation of petroleum and natural gas carriers).

C. Coal (Development, Mining, Conversion, Processing, Transport and Use)

Department of Agriculture

• Forest Service (effects of coal development on National Forests and Grasslands):
—Permits and rights-of-way on National Forest System lands. 16 U.S.C. 471–472, 478, 495, 497–498, 525, 528, 531–538, 551, 572 and 580 (36 CFR Parts 212, 251 and 261).
—Coal leasing. 30 U.S.C. 201–352.
—Surface coal mining operations. 30 U.S.C. 1272.

• Rural Electrification Administration (coal development in relation to rural electrification):
—Financial assistance for purchase of coal mines and mining facilities. 7 U.S.C. 901, et seq. (7 CFR Part 1700, et seq.).

• Soil Conservation Service (abandoned rural mined land, mine reclamation, and transportation):
—Reclamation of rural abandoned mined land. 30 U.S.C. 1201, et seq. (7 CFR Part 632).

Department of Commerce

• National Oceanic and Atmospheric Administration (atmospheric dispersion of effluents; acid rain; management and protection of coastal and marine resources; air and water pollution from mining; offshore and coastal mining; port planning).

Department of Defense

• Army Corps of Engineers (effects of coal development on navigable waters):
—For jurisdictional responsibilities, see PART I. B.—Water Quality.

Department of Energy

• Economic Regulatory Administration (regulation of powerplants and other major fuel-burning installations):
—Exemption from prohibitions against burning of natural gas and oil in powerplants and major fuel-burning installations. 42 U.S.C. 7101 and 8301 (10 CFR Part 500, et seq.).

• Office of Policy, Safety, and Environment (general energy policies, programs, and projects).

• Office of Fossil Energy (coal research, coal liquification projects, and emerging coal technologies).

Department of Housing and Urban Development

• Office of Community Planning and Development (assistance for community impacts due to rapid development):

—Housing and Community Development Act of 1974. 42 U.S.C. 5301, et seq. (24 CFR Part 570).

• Office of Housing (subsidence from mining operations and soil factors related to housing).

Department of the Interior

• Fish and Wildlife Service (effects of coal development on endangered species and their critical habitats, National Wildlife Refuge and National Fish Hatchery System areas, and other fish and wildlife resources):
—Permits for use of National Wildlife Refuge and National Fish Hatchery System lands. For refuges—16 U.S.C. 668 dd and ee; for hatcheries—43 U.S.C. 931 c and d (50 CFR Parts 25.41 and 29.21).
—Permits for rights-of-way across National Wildlife Monuments (Alaska only). 16 U.S.C. 432, 460(k–3) and 742(f) (50 CFR Part 96).

• Geological Survey (coal resources in general; hydrologic effects of coal mining and reclamation).

• Bureau of Indian Affairs (coal development on Indian lands):
—Leases and permits on Indian lands. 25 U.S.C. 380, 393–395, 397, 402–403, 413, 415, 477 and 635 (25 CFR Part 162).
—Rights-of-way over Indian lands. 25 U.S.C. 311–321 and 328 (25 CFR Part 169).
—Mining leases on Indian lands. U.S.C. 356, 396, 476–477 and 509 (25 CFR Parts 211–215 and 226–227).
—Surface exploration and reclamation. 25 U.S.C. 355, 396, 473 and 501–502 (25 CFR Part 216).

• Bureau of Land Management (coal development on public lands):
—Exploration licenses for coal deposits on unleased lands. 30 U.S.C. 181 and 201(b) (43 CFR Part 3400).
—Leases/permits for recovery of coal deposits. 30 U.S.C. 181, et seq., 201b and 202a; 43 U.S.C. 1701, et seq. (43 CFR Parts 3400 and 3480).
—Easements/lease/permits for use, occupancy and development of public lands. 43 U.S.C. 1732 (43 CFR Subchapters 2000 and 3000).
—Permits to mine coal for domestic needs. 30 U.S.C. 208 (43 CFR Part 3440).
—Easements/permits for rights-of-way. 30 U.S.C. 185 and 43 U.S.C. 1701, et seq. (43 CFR Parts 2800–2887).
—Exchange of Federal lands with coal or uranium deposits. 43 U.S.C. 1716 (43 CFR Parts 2200–2270).

• Bureau of Mines (mining technology, health and safety, subsidence prediction and control, and land reclamation).

• National Park Service (effects of coal development on National Park System areas and on historic and recreational values):
—Leases, permits and licenses for mining on National Park System lands involved in Wild and Scenic River Systems. 16 U.S.C. 1280.
—Access permits for mining activity within the National Park System. 16 U.S.C. 1902 and 1908 (36 CFR Part 9).
—Easements for rights-of-way across National Park System land. 16 U.S.C. 1, et seq. (36 CFR Part 9, et seq.).

• Bureau of Reclamation (effects of coal development on water storage and delivery projects):
—Easement/permits for access rights-of-way. 43 U.S.C. 3871.

• Office of Surface Mining Reclamation and Enforcement (surface coal mining and reclamation; general effects of surface coal mining operations):
—Identification of certain lands considered unsuitable for surface coal mining operations. 30 U.S.C. 1272 (30 CFR Chapter 7, Subchapter F).
—Permits for coal exploration operations on Federal lands within an approved mining permit area, and, if there is no approved State Coal Mining Regulatory Program, on non-Federal and non-Indian lands. 30 U.S.C. 1262 (30 CFR Chapter VII and 43 CFR Part 3400).
—Permits for surface coal mining and reclamation operations (includes underground mines with surface effects) on Federal lands except the States may do this when there is both an approved State Coal Mining Regulatory Program and a Cooperative Agreement between the State and the Secretary of the Interior. 30 U.S.C. 1256, 1267, 1266, 1271 and 1273 (30 CFR Chapter VII).
—Permits for surface coal mining and reclamation operations (includes underground mines with surface effects) on non-Federal lands in those States where there is no approved State Coal Mining Regulatory Program. 30 U.S.C. 1256–1262 (30 CFR Chapter VII).
—Permits for surface coal mining and reclamation operations (includes underground mines with surface effects) on Indian lands. 30 U.S.C. 1300 (30 CFR Chapter VII and 25 CFR Part 216).
—Grants for reclamation of abandoned mined lands. 30 U.S.C. 1231–1235 and 1237–1243 (30 CFR Chapter VII).

Department of Labor

• Mining Safety and Health Administration (safety and health issues in mining operations).

• Occupational Safety and Health Administration (worker safety and health issues):
—Coal tar pitch volatiles. 29 U.S.C. 655, et seq. (29 CFR Part 1910.1002).

Department of State (international aspects of coal development):
—Facilities for export/import of coal. E.O. 11423.

Department of Transportation

• Coast Guard (vessel transport of coal):
—Construction and alterations of bridges and causeways over navigable waters. 33 U.S.C. 491, et seq.; 511, et seq.; 525, et seq., and 535 (33 CFR Part 114, et seq.).
—Ports and waterways safety. 33 U.S.C. 1221 (33 CFR Part 160, et seq.).

• Federal Highway Administration (coal haul roads; effects of railroad coal transport on roads and streets).

• Federal Railroad Administration (railroad transport of coal).

• Maritime Administration (bulk shipping of coal and other minerals in the inland waterways, domestic oceans, Great Lakes, and U.S. foreign trade).

Advisory Council on Historic Preservation (effects of coal development on historic properties).

Environmental Protection Agency (pollution control and environmental effects of coal development):

—For jurisdictional responsibilities see PART I. A.—Air Quality, PART I. B.—Water Quality, and PART I. C.—Waste Disposal on Land.

Interstate Commerce Commission (regulation of coal rail-carriers and rates; impacts from railroad construction for moving coal, including downline impacts).

Tennessee Valley Authority (coal development in the Tennessee Valley region).

D. Uranium (Exploration, Mining, Transport and Use)

Department of Agriculture

• Forest Service (uranium in National Forests and Grasslands):

—Permits and rights-of-way on National Forest System lands. 16 U.S.C. 471–472, 478, 495, 497–498, 525, 528, 531–538, 551, 572 and 580 (36 CFR Parts 212, 251 and 261).

—Surface use of public domain lands under U.S. mining laws. 16 U.S.C. 478 and 551 (36 CFR Part 228).

—Mineral development on acquired lands. For solid (hardrock) minerals—16 U.S.C. 520 (43 CFR Part 3500); for phosphate, sodium, potassium and sulphur—30 U.S.C. 351, *et seq.*

• Soil Conservation Service (abandoned mine land, mine reclamation, and transportation).

Department of Commerce

• National Oceanic and Atmospheric Administration (air and water pollution from mining; offshore and coastal mining; port planning; management and protection of coastal and marine resources):

—Approval of licenses for deep seabed hard mineral exploration and development. 30 U.S.C. 1401, *et seq.* (15 CFR Part 970).

Department of Defense

• Army Corps of Engineers (effects of uranium mining on navigable waters):

—For jurisdictional responsibilities, see PART I.B.—Water Quality.

Department of Energy

• Office of Policy, Safety, and Environment (general energy policies, programs and projects).

• Office of Civilian Radioactive Waste Management (management of commercial radioactive wastes).

• Office of Defense Programs (management of Defense radioactive wastes).

• Office of Nuclear Energy (nuclear energy in general).

Department of Housing and Urban Development

• Office of Housing (subsidence from mining operations and soil factors related to housing).

Department of the Interior

• Fish and Wildlife Service (effects of uranium mining on endangered species and their critical habitats, National Wildlife Refuge and National Fish Hatchery System areas, and other fish and wildlife resources):

—Easements/permits on National Wildlife Refuge and National Fish Hatchery System land. 16 U.S.C. 668 dd, *et seq.*; 43 U.S.C. 931 c and d (50 CFR Parts 25.41 and 29.21).

—Permits for rights-of-way across National Wildlife Monuments (Alaska only). 16 U.S.C. 432, 460(k–3) and 742(f) (50 CFR Part 96).

• Geological Survey (uranium resources in general).

• Bureau of Indian Affairs (uranium on Indian lands):

—Leases and permits on Indian lands. 25 U.S.C. 380, 393–395, 397, 402–403, 413, 415, 477 and 635 (25 CFR Part 162).

—Rights-of-way over Indian lands. 25 U.S.C. 311–321 and 323–328 (25 CFR Part 169).

—Mining leases on Indian lands. 25 U.S.C. 356, 396, 476–477 and 509 (25 CFR Parts 211–215 and 226–227).

—Surface exploration and reclamation. 25 U.S.C. 355, 396, 473 and 501–502 (25 CFR Part 216).

• Bureau of Land Management (uranium on public lands):

—Exchange of Federal lands with coal or uranium deposits. 43 U.S.C. 1716 (43 CFR Parts 2200–2270).

—Leases for uranium exploration and mining. 30 U.S.C. 181, 351–359 and 1201, *et seq.* (43 CFR Parts 3500–3800).

—Approval of plan of operations in connection with uranium leases. 30 U.S.C. 22, *et seq.*; 30 U.S.C. 181, *et seq.*; and 43 U.S.C. 1701, *et seq.* (43 CFR Parts 3570 and 3802).

—Easements/leases/permits for use, occupancy and development of public lands. 43 U.S.C. 1732 (43 CFR Subchapter 2000 and 3000).

—Exploration licenses to explore for uranium and other leasable minerals on unleased lands. 30 U.S.C. 181, *et seq.*, and 201(b) (43 CFR Parts 3400 and 3480).

—Leases, permits and licenses for mining in Wild and Scenic River System areas. 16 U.S.C. 1280 (each area has special Federal Regulations).

—Concurrence for mining use of public lands withdrawn or reserved for power development or for a power site. 30 U.S.C. 621 (43 CFR Part 3730).

—Easements/permits for rights-of-way. 30 U.S.C. 185 and 43 U.S.C. 1701, *et seq.* (43 CFR Parts 2800–2900).

• Bureau of Mines (uranium mining in general).

• National Park Service (effects of uranium mining on public park and recreation values; on historic, archeological and architectural sites; and on National Park System areas):

—Permits, leases, and easements for rights-of-way. 16 U.S.C. 1, *et seq.* (36 CFR Part 9, *et seq.*).

—Leases, permits and license for mining on National Park System lands involved in Wild and Scenic River Systems. 16 U.S.C. 1280.

—Access permits for mining activity within the National Park System. 16 U.S.C. 1902 and 1908; 30 U.S.C. 21, *et seq.* (36 CFR Part 9).

• Bureau of Reclamation (effects of uranium mining on water storage and delivery projects):

—Easements/permits for access, pipeline, and other rights-of-way. 43 U.S.C. 3871.

Department of Labor

• Mining Safety and Health Administration (safety and health issues in mining operations).

• Occupational Safety and Health Administration (general worker safety and health issues):

—General industrial, and construction standards. 29 U.S.C. 655, *et seq.* (29 CFR Parts 1910 and 1926).

Department of State (international aspects of uranium mining):

—Facilities for export/import of minerals. E.O. 11423.

Department of Transportation

• Coast Guard (vessel transport of m   als):

—   nstruction and alterations of bridges and causeways over navigable waters. 33 U.S.C. 491, *et seq.*; 511, *et seq.*; 525, *et seq.*, and 535 (33 CFR Part 114, *et seq.*).

—Ports and waterways safety. 33 U.S.C 1221 (33 CFR Part 160, *et seq.*).

Advisory Council on Historic Preservation (effects of uranium mining on historic properties).

Environmental Protection Agency (pollution control and environmental effects of uranium mining):

—For jurisdictional responsibilities, see Part I.A.—Air Quality, PART I. B.—Water Quality, PART I. C.—Waste Disposal on Land, and PART I. E.—Radiation.

Nuclear Regulatory Commission (nuclear power development in general):

—Licensing uranium milling operations. 42 U.S.C. 2091 *et seq.* (10 CFR Part 40).

Tennessee Valley Authority (uranium mining and milling).

E. Geothermal Resources (Development, Transmission, and Use)

Department of Agriculture

• Forest Service (effects of geothermal resource development on National Forests and Grasslands):

—Leases for geothermal resource developments. 30 U.S.C. 1014.

—Permits and rights-of-way on National Forest System lands. 16 U.S.C. 471–472, 478, 495, 497–498, 525, 538, 531–538, 551, 572 and 580 (36 CFR Parts 212, 251 and 261).

Department of Commerce

• National Oceanic and Atmospheric Administration (air and water pollution from geothermal development).

Department of Defense

• Army Corps of Engineers (effects of geothermal development on navigable waters):

—For jurisdictional responsibilities, see PART I. B.—Water Quality.

Department of Energy

• Office of Policy, Safety, and Environment (general energy policies, programs and projects).

• Office of Conservation and Renewable Energy (research and development on geothermal energy sources).

Department of the Interior

• Fish and Wildlife Service (effects of geothermal development on endangered species and their critical habitats, National Wildlife Refuge and National Fish Hatchery System areas, and other fish and wildlife resources):

—Easements/permits on National Wildlife Refuge and National Fish Hatchery System land. For refuges—16 U.S.C. 668 dd, *et seq.*, for hatcheries—43 U.S.C. 931 c and d (50 CFR Parts 25.41 and 29.21).

—Permits for rights-of-way across National Wildlife Monuments (Alaska only). 16 U.S.C. 432, 460(k–3) and 742(f) (50 CFR Part 96).

• Geological Survey (geothermal resources in general).

• Bureau of Indian Affairs (geothermal development on Indian lands):

—Leases and permits on Indian lands. 25 U.S.C. 380, 393–395, 397, 402–403, 413, 415, 477 and 635 (25 CFR Part 162).

—Rights-of-way over Indian lands, 25 U.S.C. 311–321 and 323–328 (25 CFR Part 169).

• Bureau of Land Management (geothermal development on public lands):

—Permits for geothermal resources exploration. 30 U.S.C. 1023 (43 CFR Part 3260).

—Leases for geothermal resources recovery. 30 U.S.C. 1001–1025 (43 CFR Parts 3200–3250, 3260 and 3280).

—Licenses for geothermal powerplants. 30 U.S.C. 1001–1025 (43 CFR Part 3250).

—Easements/leases/permits for use, occupancy and development of public lands. 43 U.S.C 1732 (43 CFR Subchapter 2000 and 3000).

Easements/permits for rights-of-way. 30 U.S.C. 185 and 43 U.S.C 1701, *et seq.* (43 CFR Parts 2800–2900).

• Bureau of Mines (recovery of mineral values in geothermal operations; materials for construction of geothermal facilities).

• National Park Service (effects of geothermal development on public park and recreation values, on historic, archeological and architectural sites, and on National Park System areas).

• Bureau of Reclamation (alternative energy studies; coordination of geothermal operations with hydroelectric generation):

—Easements/permits for access, pipeline, and other rights-of-way. 43 U.S.C. 3871.

Department of Labor

• Occupational Safety and Health Administration (worker safety and health issues):

—General industrial and construction standards. 29 U.S.C. 655, *et seq.* (29 CFR Parts 1910 and 1926).

Advisory Council on Historic Preservation (effects of geothermal development on historic properties).

Environmental Protection Agency (pollution control and environmental effects of geothermal development):

—For jurisdictional responsibilities, see PART I. A.—Air Quality, PART I. B.—Water Quality, and PART I. C.—Waste Disposal on Land.

F. Other Energy Sources—Solar, Wind, Biomass, etc. (Development and Use)

Department of Agriculture

• Agricultural Research Service (utilization of biomass, wastes, solar, and wind energy sources in agricultural production).

• Farmers Home Administration (small hydro, solar, and wind projects):

—Approval of plans and specifications for FMHA-funded projects. 7 U.S.C. 1942 (7 CFR Parts 1924, 1942 and 1944).

• Forest Service (uses and rights-of-way on National Forests and Grasslands):

—Permits and rights-of-way on National Forest System lands. 16 U.S.C. 471–472, 478, 495, 497–498, 525, 528, 531–538, 551, 572 and 580 (36 CFR Parts 212, 251 and 261).

• Office of Energy (general energy policies related to agriculture):

—Solar and wind energy facility siting, 16 U.S.C. 470 (36 CFR Part 200).

Department of Commerce

• National Oceanic and Atmospheric Administration (coastal energy facility planning and siting; basic weather data and research):

—Approval of licenses for siting, design, and operation of ocean-thermal energy facilities, 42 U.S.C. 9101, *et seq.* (15 CFR Part 981).

Department of Energy

• Office of Policy, Safety, and Environment (general energy policies, programs and projects).

• Office of Conservation and Renewable Energy (research and development programs on alternative energy sources).

Department of Housing and Urban Development

• Office of Community Planning and Development (alternative energy policy, including district heating and cogeneration; demonstration programs; research; technical assistance and feasibility studies; building rehabilitation and retrofit; assistance for community and economic development):

—Housing and Community Development Act of 1974. 42 U.S.C. 5301. *et seq.* (24 CFR Part 570).

—Urban Development Action Grant Handbook. HUD 6050.1 of Oct. 1982.

• Solar Energy and Energy Conservation Bank (assistance for energy conservation improvements to residential, commercial, and agricultural buildings, including solar energy systems):

—Energy Security Act of 1980. 12 U.S.C. 3601, *et seq.* (24 CFR Part 1800, *et seq.*).

Department of the Interior

• Fish and Wildlife Service (effects of alternative energy development on endangered species and their critical habitats, National Wildlife Refuge and National Fish Hatchery System areas, and other fish and wildlife resources).

• Geological Survey (geology and hydrologic siting constraints for alternative energy development).

• Bureau of Indian Affairs (alternative energy development on Indian lands).

• Bureau of Land Management (alternative energy development on public lands):

—Licenses for synthetic liquid fuel facilities. 30 U.S.C. 323.

—Solar energy facility siting. 43 U.S.C. 1761.

• National Park Service (effects of alternative energy development on park and recreation values on historic, archeological and architectural sites, and on National Park System areas).

• Bureau of Reclamation (alternative energy studies; coordination of operations with hydroelectric generation).

Department of Labor

• Occupational Health and Safety Administration (worker safety and health issues):

—General industrial and construction standards. 29 U.S.C. 655, *et seq.* (29 CFR Parts 1910 and 1926).

Advisory Council on Historic Preservation (effects of alternative energy development on historic properties).

Environmental Protection Agency (pollution control and environmental effects of alternative energy development):

—For jurisdictional responsibilities, see PART I.—POLLUTION CONTROL.

G. Energy Conservation

Department of Agriculture

• Extension Service (rural family energy conservation).

• Farmers Home Administration (energy conservation in relation to agency funded projects).

• Forest Service (energy conservation in National Forests and Grasslands).

• Office of Energy (general agricultural energy policies).

• Rural Electrification Administration (energy conservation in relation to power development in rural areas).

Department of Commerce

• National Bureau of Standards (energy efficiency objectives and standards).

• National Oceanic and Atmospheric Administration (heating fuel usage forecasting; weather forecasting in relation to energy conservation).

Department of Energy

• Office of Policy, Safety, and Environment (general energy policies, programs and projects).

• Office of Conservation and Renewable Energy (energy efficiency of transportation, building, and industrial systems; assistance programs for energy planning and conservation):

—Energy conservation standards for new buildings. 42 U.S.C. 6834 (10 CFR Part 450, *et seq.*).
• Bonneville Power Administration (energy conservation studies in the Pacific Northwest):
—Regional planning and conservation. 16 U.S.C. 839, *et seq.*

Department of Housing and Urban Development
• Office of Community Planning and Development (energy conservation policy; demonstration and research programs; technical assistance; assistance for community and neighborhood development, economic development, public facilities, residential and commercial rehabilitation and retrofit for energy efficiency; comprehensive energy use strategies):
—Housing and Community Development Act of 1974. 42 U.S.C. 5301, *et seq.* (24 CFR Part 570).
—Urban Development Action Grant Handbook. HUD 6050.1 of Oct. 1982.
—Housing Act of 1937. 42 U.S.C. 1401, *et seq.*
• Solar Energy and Energy Conservation Bank (assistance for energy conservation improvements to residential, commercial, and agricultural buildings, including solar energy systems):
—Energy Security Act of 1980. 12 U.S.C. 3601, *et seq.* (24 CFR Part 1800, *et seq.*).
• Office of Manufactured Housing and Construction Standards (building materials; new materials standards and performance criteria).
• Office of Policy Development and Research (building energy technology).
• Office of Public Housing (energy factors in rehabilitation and retrofitting; urban energy studies).

Department of the Interior
• Fish and Wildlife Service (energy conservation in National Wildlife Refuge and National Fish Hatchery System areas, and effects of energy conservation projects on endangered species and critical habitats).
• Bureau of Indian Affairs (energy conservation on Indian lands).
• Bureau of Land Management (energy conservation on public lands).
• National Park Service (energy conservation in National Park System areas; effects of energy conservation on historic, archeological, and architectural sites, and on park and recreation values).
• Bureau of Reclamation (energy conservation in relation to hydroelectric power development, and water storage and delivery systems).

Department of Transportation
• Federal Aviation Administration (aviation energy conservation and energy-use assessments).
• Federal Highway Administration (energy conservation in relation to highway systems).
• National Highway Traffic Safety Administration (fuel economy standards for motor vehicles):
—Fuel economy standards. 15 U.S.C. 2001, *et seq.* (49 CFR Parts 525–527, 531, 533 and 537.

• Research and Special Programs Administration: Transportation Systems Center (energy conservation and transportation systems in general).
• Urban Mass Transportation Administration (energy conservation in relation to urban transportation systems).
Advisory Council on Historic Preservation (effects of energy conservation on historic properties).
Interstate Commerce Commission (assessment of differences in energy efficiencies between transport modes).
Tennessee Valley Authority (energy conservation in general).

III. LAND USE

A. Land Use Planning, Regulation, and Development

Department of Agriculture
• Agricultural Research Service (effects of agricultural practices on resource quality and off-farm pollution).
• Agricultural Stabilization and Conservation Service (Federally subsidized agricultural conservation and land use programs).
• Economic, Research Service and Statistical Reporting Service (data on natural resources; analysis of the economic impacts of agriculturally related pollution and resource degradation; interactions of environmental programs with other Federal farm policy objectives).
• Extension Service (rural and community development).
• Farmers Home Administration (farmland protection; rural and community development):
—Farmland Protection Policy Act. Secretary's Memorandum 9500–2, *Statement on Land Use Policy* (7 CFR Part 1940).
• Forest Service (effects of adjacent land uses on National Forests and Grasslands):
—Coordination with other public planning efforts. (36 CFR Part 219.7).
• Soil Conservation Service (land use data; soil and water resource condition data and related natural resources data; resource management technology and technical planning assistance for watershed protection):
—Soil, water, and related resource data. 7 U.S.C. 1010a.
—Program for land conservation and utilization. 7 U.S.C. 1011(e).

Department of Commerce
• National Oceanic and Atmospheric Administration (management and protection of coastal and marine resources).

Department of Defense
• Army Corps of Engineers (land use in flood plains and wetlands):
—For jurisdictional responsibilities see PART I.B.—Water Quality.
• Department of the Air Force (land use around military airfields).

Department of Energy
• Office of Policy, Safety, and Environment (effects of energy policies, programs, and projects on adjacent land uses).

Department of Housing and Urban Development
• Office of Community Planning and Development (land use planning; environmental criteria and compatible uses near hazards; noise abatement and mitigation measures):
—Assurances that HUD assisted projects are located in a safe and healthful environment. 42 U.S.C. 1441, *et seq.*
—Siting of HUD assisted projects near hazardous operations handling explosive or flammable materials. (24 CFR Part 51, Subpart C).
—Siting of HUD assisted projects in runway clear zones (civil airports) and clear zones and accident potential zones (military airfields). (24 CFR Part 51, Subpart D).
• Office of Interstate Land Sales (subdivided land sales):
—Subdivided land sales, registration, and disclosure statements. 15 U.S.C. 1701 (24 CFR Part 1700, *et seq.*).

Department of the Interior
• Fish and Wildlife Service (effects of land use on endangered species and their critical habitats, other fish and wildlife resources, and components of the National Wildlife Refuge and National Fish Hatchery Systems):
—Approval of conversion of use for State lands acquired, developed or improved with grants under the: (1) Pittman-Robertson Act, (2) Dingell-Johnson Act, (3) Endangered Species Act and/or (4) Anadromous Fish Conservation Act. For (1)–16 U.S.C. 669 (50 CFR Parts 80.4 and 80.14); for (2)–16 U.S.C. 777 (50 CFR Parts 80.4 and 80.14); for (3)–16 U.S.C. 1535; and for (4)–16 U.S.C. 757(a) and (b).
—Consultation regarding any Federal actions that may directly or indirectly affect a designated coastal barrier. 16 U.S.C. 3501 (for advisory guidelines, see 48 FR 45664 of Oct. 6, 1983).
—Consultation concerning the protection of fish and wildlife refuges, which may be impacted by transportation projects. 49 U.S.C. 303.
—For jurisdictional responsibilities of the Fish and Wildlife Service on Federal lands see PART III. B.—Federal Land Management.
• Geological Survey (land use planning; geologic and hydrologic hazards; flood studies; geologic, topographic, land use, and photographic mapping).
• Bureau of Indian Affairs (effects of land uses on Indian lands):
—Approval of leases and permits on Indian lands. 25 U.S.C. 380, 393–395, 397, 402–403, 413, 415, 477 and 635 (25 CFR Part 162).
—Sale of Indian land. 25 U.S.C. 293–294, 355, 372–73, 378–79, 385–386, 404–405, 463–464, 483 and 608 (25 CFR Parts 152 and 159–160).
—Rights-of-way over Indian lands. 25 U.S.C. 311–321 and 323–328 (25 CFR Part 169).
—Permits concessions and leases on lands withdrawn or acquired in connection with Indian irrigation projects. 25 U.S.C. 390 (25 CFR Part 173).
—For jurisdictional responsibilities on Federal lands administered by Bureau of

Indian Affairs, see PART III. B.—Federal
Land Management.

•Bureau of Land Management (effects of
land uses on public lands):

—For jurisdiction responsibilities on Federal
lands administered by the Bureau of Land
Management, see PART III. B.—Federal
Land Management.

• Bureau of Mines (mineral resources and
land use).

• National Park Service (effects of land
uses on National Park System areas; National
Trails System; Wild and Scenic River System;
park and recreation areas and values; and
historic, archeological and architectural
sites):

—Approval of a conversion to a non-
designated use for State and local lands
acquired or developed, in whole or in part,
with a Land and Water Conservation Fund
Act grant. 16 U.S.C. 4601.

—Assistance to State and local agencies,
through an Urban Park and Recreation
Recovery Act grant, for the development
and/or improvement of park and recreation
areas. 16 U.S.C. 2504 (36 CFR Part 69).

—Approval of a conversion to other than
public recreation uses for State and local
areas developed or improved with an
Urban Park and Recreation Recovery Act
grant. 16 U.S.C. 2504 (36 CFR Part 69).

—Consultations regarding land uses and
effects on rivers established as units of the
National Wild and Scenic Rivers System
and on those rivers designated for study as
potential additions to that System. 16
U.S.C. 1278, et seq.

—Permits for use of National Historic and
National Scenic Trails administered by the
National Park Service. 16 U.S.C. 1246.

—Approval of a conversion to a non-
designated use for lands deeded by the
Federal government to State and local
entities as park demonstration areas, as
recreation areas, as wildlife conservation
preserves and refuges and as historic
monuments and properties under: (1)
Recreation Demonstration Act of 1942 and
(2) Federal Property and Administrative
Services Act of 1949. For (1)–16 U.S.C. 459
(r-t); for (2)–40 U.S.C. 484(k)(2) (41 CFR Part
101–47).

—Approval of a conversion to a non-
designated use of abandoned railroad
rights-of-way acquired by State and local
governments under Section 809(b) of the
Railroad Revitalization and Regulatory
Reform Act of 1976. 49 U.S.C. 1(a) (36 CFR
Part 64).

—Consultation concerning the protection of
park, recreation, and cultural resources
which may be impacted by transportation
projects, 49 U.S.C. 303.

—For other jurisdictional responsibilities of
the National Park Service, see PART III.
B.—Federal Land Management.

• Bureau of Reclamation (effects of land
use on Federal water storage and distribution
projects; planning for water development
projects; basin-wide water studies and land
use aspects of the National Water Summary):

—Sale of farm units on Federal irrigation
projects. (Statutory authority appears in
individual project authorizations.)

—Administration of excess lands and
residency requirements. 43 U.S.C. 371.

• Office of Surface Mining Reclamation
and Enforcement (land use and surface coal
mining and reclamation operations):

—For jurisdictional responsibilities of the
Office of Surface Mining, see PART II. C.—
Coal.

Department of Transportation

Office of the Secretary (general effects of
transportation projects on land use):

—Approval of transportation programs or
projects that require the use of or have
significant impacts on park and recreation
areas, fish and wildlife refuges, and
historic sites. 49 U.S.C. 303.

• Coast Guard (effects of bridges on land
use):

—Permits for bridges and causeways over
navigable waters. 33 U.S.C. 491, et seq.; 511,
et seq.; 525, et seq.; and 535 (33 CFR Part
114 et seq.).

• Federal Aviation Administration (airport
land use compatibility):

—Airport aid program. 49 U.S.C. 1711–1727
(14 CFR Part 152).

—Acquisition of U.S. land for public airports.
49 U.S.C. 1723 (14 CFR Part 154).

—Notice of construction, alteration,
activiation, and deactivation of airports 49
U.S.C. 1350, 1354 and 1355 (14 CFR Part
157).

—Objects affecting navigable airspace. 49
U.S.C. 1655 (14 CFR Part 77).

—Release of airport property from surplus
property disposal restrictions. 49 U.S.C.
1101–1119 (14 CFR Part 155).

• Federal Highway Administration (effects
of highways on land use):

—Approval of highway projects and
programs. 23 U.S.C. 101–156, generally, and
23 U.S.C. 201–219.

—Consultations, in cooperation with the
Urban Mass Transportation
Administration, with State and local
officials concerning urban transportation
related systems. 23 U.S.C. 105(d) and
134(a); 49 U.S.C. 1604(g) (23 CFR Part 450).

—Regulation of highway-related land use. For
highway beautification—23 U.S.C. 131 (23
CFR Part 750); for junkyard control and
acquisition—23 U.S.C. 136 (23 CFR Part
751); for landscape and roadside
development—23 U.S.C. 131 and 319 (23
CFR Part 752); for protection of parklands,
recreation areas, wildlife refuges, and
historic sites—23 U.S.C. 138 (23 CFR Part
771).

• Urban Mass Transportation
Administration (effects of urban
transportation systems on land use):

—Consultation, in cooperation with the
Federal Highway Administration, with
State and local officials concerning urban
transportation related systems. 23 U.S.C.
105(d) and 134(a); 49 U.S.C. 1604(g) (49 CFR
Part 613).

—Approval for substituting mass transit or
other transit projects in lieu of an interstate
highway project. 23 U.S.C. 103(e)(4).

Advisory Council on Historic Preservation
(effects of land use planning on historic
properties):

Environmental Protection Agency (effects
of land use on pollution control and
environmental quality):

—For jurisdictional responsibilities see PART
I. A.—Air Quality, PART I. B.—Water
Quality, and PART I. C.—Waste Disposal
on Land.

Federal Emergency Management Agency
(national flood insurance program; disaster
relief assistance; mitigation of natural
hazards).

Federal Energy Regulatory Commission
(effects of power projects on land use):

—Regulation of development of water
resources. 16 U.S.C. 791–825(r) (18 CFR
Parts 4–25, 36, 131 and 141).

*International Boundary and Water
Commission, United States Section* (land use
along international boundary with Mexico).

Interstate Commerce Commission (land
use and interstate commerce):

—Approval of Public Convenience and
Necessity Certificate for new railroad lines.
49 U.S.C. 10901.

*National Aeronautics and Space
Administration* (remote sensing of land use
and land cover).

National Capital Planning Commission
(land use in the National Capital Region):

—Approval of land-use plans and
construction in National Capital Region. 40
U.S.C. 74a (DC Code 9–404, DC Code 8–
102); 40 U.S.C. 122 (DC Code 8–111, DC
Code 5–432).

Tennessee Valley Authority (land use
planning on public lands in Tennessee Valley
region; assistance to local planning
organizations).

B. Federal Land Management

Department of Agriculture

• Forest Service (National Forests and
Grasslands management, including fire
management):

—National Forest System Management
Planning. 16 U.S.C. 1604 and 1613 (36 CFR
Part 219).

—Special use permits, archeological permits,
leases and easements. 16 U.S.C. 497 and
580(d); 43 U.S.C. 1761 and 48 U.S.C. 341 (36
CFR Parts 251 and 261).

—Easement and road rights-of-way on
National Forests and other lands. 16 U.S.C.
533 (36 CFR Part 212.10).

—Permits for commercial use of existing
roads. 16 U.S.C. 537 (36 CFR Part 212).

—Bankhead-Jones Farm Tenant Act, Title III
permits on National Grasslands. 7 U.S.C.
1010–12 (36 CFR Part 213.3).

Department of Commerce

• National Oceanic and Atmospheric
Administration (consistency of Federal land
uses with coastal zone management
programs).

Department of Defense (overall
management of Department of Defense
lands).

• Department of the Army (management of
Army lands):

—Permits and leases for use of Army
reservations.

—Permits and leases for use and occupancy
of lands at water development projects of
the Corps of Engineers.

- Department of the Air Force
(management of Air Force lands):
—Permits and leases for use of Air Force reservations.
- Department of the Navy (management of Navy and Marine Corps lands):
—Permits and leases for uses of naval reservations.

Department of the Interior

- Fish and Wildlife Service (effects of Federal land management on endangered species and their critical habitats and other fish and wildlife resources, management of National Wildlife Refuge and National Fish Hatchery System areas):
—Easements/permits for right-of-way across National Wildlife Refuge and National Fish Hatchery System land. For refuges—16 U.S.C. 668dd, *et seq.;* for hatcheries—43 U.S.C. 931 c and d (50 CFR Parts 25.41 and 29.21).
—Permits for rights-of-way across National Wildlife Monuments (Alaska only). 16 U.S.C. 432, 460k–3 and 742(f) (50 CFR Part 96).
—Permits for off-road vehicular use on National Wildlife Refuge System areas. E.O. 11644 (50 CFR Part 26.34).
—Consultation concerning the protection of fish and wildlife refuges which may be impacted by transportation projects. 49 U.S.C. 303.
- Geological Survey (Federal land mineral resource potential; wilderness reviews, land-use planning; geologic and hydrologic hazards; flood studies; geologic, topographic, land use, and photographic mapping).
- Bureau of Indian Affairs (effects of Federal land management on Indian lands; management of Bureau of Indian Affairs lands):
—Sale of Federal land purchased for Indian administrative uses. 25 U.S.C. 293.
—Rights-of-way over Federal lands under BIA jurisdiction. 25 U.S.C. 323–328 (25 CFR Part 160).
—Leases for mining, oil and gas, coal, farming and other uses on Federal lands under BIA jurisdiction. 5 U.S.C. 301 and 25 U.S.C. 393, *et seq.* (25 CFR Part 162).
—For the trust responsibilities of the Bureau of Indian Affairs for Indian lands, see PART III. A.—Land Use Planning, etc.
- Bureau of Land Management (management of Federal lands):
—Easements/permits for rights-of-way. 43 U.S.C. 9 and 1701, *et seq.* (43 CFR Parts 2800–2900).
—Special land-use permits for habitation, occupation and other purposes. 43 U.S.C. 1732(b) (43 CFR Part 2920).
—Conditions and standards for off-road vehicle use on BLM lands. 43 U.S.C. 1201; E.O. 11644 (43 CFR Part 8340).
—Permits for off-road vehicular use special events, i.e., tours and competitions. 43 U.S.C. 1701, *et seq.*, and 16 U.S.C. 460(1–6a) (43 CFR Part 8372).
—Exchange of Federal lands for other property. 43 U.S.C. 1716 (43 CFR Parts 2200–2270).
—Leases/transfers of public lands for a public airport. 43 U.S.C. 1201 and 49 U.S.C. 1115 (43 CFR Part 2640).

—Sales/leases of Federal land to State and local agencies and non-profit groups for recreational and public purposes. 43 U.S.C. 869, *et seq.* for sales—43 CFR Part 2740; for leases—43 CFR Part 2912).
—Permits for commercial recreational use of public lands. 43 U.S.C. 1701, *et seq.* (43 CFR Part 8370).
- Bureau of Mines (mineral land assessment).
- National Park Service (management of National Park System areas; units of the National Wild and Scenic Rivers System; National Trails System):
—Permits, leases, and easements of rights-of-way and other uses of National Park System areas. 16 U.S.C. 1, *et seq.* (36 CFR Parts 9 and 14).
—Permits for commercial operations on National Park System areas. 16 U.S.C. 1, *et seq.* (36 CFR Parts 7, 14, 50 and 51).
—Permits for off-road vehicular use in National Park System areas. E.O. 11644 (36 CFR Part 7).
—Consultations regarding use of and effect on rivers established as units of the National Wild and Scenic Rivers System and on those rivers designated for study as potential additions to that System. 16 U.S.C. 1278, *et seq.*
—Permits for use of National Historic and National Scenic Trails administered by the National Park Service. 16 U.S.C. 1246.
—Consultation concerning the protection of park, recreation, and cultural resources which may be impacted by transportation projects. 49 U.S.C. 303.
- Bureau of Reclamation (management of public water storage and delivery projects and recreational developments; irrigation; and impacts of Federal land management of State water planning):
—Sale or lease of project lands to a governmental entity or a non-profit group for recreational or other public purposes. 43 U.S.C. 869.
—Lease of project lands for commercial recreational developments. 43 U.S.C. 391, *et seq.*

Department of Transportation

- Office of the Secretary (effects of transportation projects on Federal land):
—Approval of transportation programs and projects which use a publicly owned park and recreation area, wildlife or waterfowl refuge, or any historic site. 49 U.S.C. 303.
- Federal Highway Administration (construction and management of Federal Lands Highways, including forest highways and National Park Service roads and parkways):
—Federal Lands Highways Program. 23 U.S.C. 204 (23 CFR Parts 660 and 667).

Advisory Council on Historic Preservation (effects of Federal land management on historic properties).

Environmental Protection Agency (effects of Federal land management on pollution control and environmental quality; pesticide use and integrated pest management on public lands):
—Underground injection control permits on Indian lands. 42 U.S.C. 300(f), *et seq.*

—Air emissions from Federal facilities. 42 U.S.C. 7418.
—Wastewater discharges from Federal facilities. 33 U.S.C. 1323.
—Solid wastes and hazardous wastes from Federal facilities. 42 U.S.C. 6961.
—Pesticide use of public lands. 7 U.S.C. 136.
—For other jurisdictional responsibilities, see PART I.—POLLUTION CONTROL.

Federal Emergency Management Agency (effects of the National Flood Insurance Program and disaster relief assistance on Federal land management).

General Services Administration

- Public Buildings Service (management of public buildings and property).
- Federal Property Resources Service (public land disposal).

National Aeronautics and Space Administration (advanced technology for remote sensing of land use and land cover).

Tennessee Valley Authority (TVA reservoir property, secondary use of reservoir property, and reservation planning).

C. Coastal Areas

Department of Agriculture

- Farmers Home Administration (housing, community, and business loan programs; and farmer loan programs in coastal areas).
- Forest Service (National Forests in coastal areas).
—Consultations regarding uses and effects on rivers established as units of the National Wild and Scenic Rivers System and on those rivers designated for study as potential additions to that System. 16 U.S.C. 1278, *et seq.*
- Soil Conservation Service (coastal soil stabilization).

Department of Commerce

- National Oceanic and Atmospheric Administration (coastal and marine resources and protection):
—Permits for activities in designated marine sanctuaries. 16 U.S.C. 143, *et seq.* (15 CFR Part 922).
—Approval and funding of State coastal management programs. 16 U.S.C. 1451, *et seq.* (15 CFR Parts 923 and 930).
—Establishment of estuarine sanctuaries. 16 U.S.C. 1461 (15 CFR Part 921).
—Determinations to insure Federal development projects and federally permitted or funded projects are consistent with an approved State coastal zone management plan. 16 U.S.C. 1451 (15 CFR Part 930).
—Grants and loans under Coastal Energy Impact Program. 16 U.S.C. 1456(a) (15 CFR Part 931).

Department of Defense

- Army Corps of Engineers (beach erosion and stabilization; dredge and fill permits; ocean dumping; Refuse Act permits):
—For jurisdictional responsibilities, see PART I. B.—Water Quality.

Department of Energy

• Office of Policy, Safety, and Environment (effects of energy policies, programs and projects on coastal areas).

Department of Housing and Urban Development

• Office of Housing and Office of Community Planning and Development (development in coastal areas; consistency with coastal zone management plans; consistency with Coastal Barrier Resources Act).

Department of the Interior

• Fish and Wildlife Service (effects of coastal land uses on endangered species and their critical habitats, National Wildlife Refuge and National Fish Hatchery System areas, and other fish and wildlife resources):
—Consultation regarding any Federal actions that may directly or indirectly affect a designated coastal barrier. 16 U.S.C. 3501. (For advisory guidelines, see 48 FR 45664 of Oct. 6, 1983).
—Consultation regarding Federal projects that may affect an estuarine area 15 U.S.C. 1224.
—Consultation regarding Federal or Federally permitted projects that affect fish and wildlife resources under the Fish and Wildlife Coordination Act. 16 U.S.C. 661, *et seq.*
—U.S. Fish and Wildlife Service Mitigation Policy. 16 U.S.C. 661, *et seq.*; 742(a)–754 and 1001–1009 (46 FR 7644 of Jan. 23, 1981).

• Geological Survey (land use planning; geologic and hydrologic hazards; geologic, topographic, land use, and photographic mapping, including areas of the outer continental shelf and Exclusive Economic Zone).

• Bureau of Indian Affairs (Indian lands in coastal areas).

• Bureau of Land Management (public land management in coastal areas).

• Minerals Management Service (coastal zone planning and management; outer continental shelf lands):
—Oil, gas, and sulphur exploration, development, and production on the outer continental shelf. (30 CFR Part 250.34).

• National Park Service (effects of coastal land use on National Park System areas, park and recreation areas, and historical, archeological and architectural sites; barrier island ecology and coastal processes):
—Identification and listing on the National Registry of Natural Landmarks of nationally significant natural areas in the United States. 16 U.S.C. 461 (36 CFR Part 62).
—Consultations regarding use of and effects on rivers established as units of the National Wild and Scenic Rivers System and on those rivers designated for study as potential additions to that System. 16 U.S.C. 1278, *et seq.*

• Bureau of Reclamation (water development projects in coastal areas, effects of water developments and irrigation on estuarine areas).

Department of Transportation

• Coast Guard (bridges, pipelines and transmission lines crossing navigable waters; navigation and deep water ports):
—Permits for bridges and causeways over navigable waters. 33 U.S.C. 491, *et seq.*; 511, *et seq.*; 525, *et seq.*, and 535 (33 CFR Part 114, *et seq.*).
—Permits for waterfront facilities. 33 U.S.C. 1221, *et seq.* (33 CFR Parts 125 and 126).
—Deepwater port regulation and licensing. 33 U.S.C. 1503–1524 (33 CFR Parts 148–150).

• Maritime Administration (coastal land use in relation to ports).

Advisory Council on Historic Preservation (effects of coastal land uses on historic properties).

Environmental Protection Agency (effects of coastal land uses on pollution control and environmental quality):
—For jurisdictional responsibilities see PART I.B.—Water Quality.

Federal Emergency Management Agency (National Flood Insurance Program; floodplain management; uses on sand dunes, mangrove forests and barrier islands; disaster relief assistance).

Federal Energy Regulatory Commission (effects of natural gas transportation, storage, and sale on coastal areas).

Marine Mammal Commission (conservation and protection of marine mammals and their habitat in coastal areas):
—Conservation and oversight responsibility for activities affecting marine mammals. 16 U.S.C. 1402.

National Aeronautics and Space Administration (advanced technology for remote sensing of land use and land cover).

D. Environmentally Sensitive Areas (Wilderness Areas, Wild and Scenic Rivers, Floodplains [see Executive Order 11988], Wetlands [see Executive Order 11990], Barrier Islands, Beaches and Dunes, Unstable Soils, Steep Slopes, Aquifer Recharge Areas, Tundra, etc.)

Department of Agriculture

• Agricultural Research Service (research activities to conserve and assist environmentally sensitive areas).

• Agricultural Stabilization and Conservation Service (commodity and land use programs; Water Bank).

• Farmers Home Administration (housing, community, and business loan programs; farmer loan programs in environmentally sensitive areas).

• Forest Service (management of environmentally sensitive areas on National Forest and Grassland System lands, including fire management):
—Permits for use of wilderness areas. 16 U.S.C. 472 and 551 (36 CFR Part 293).
—Consultations regarding use of and effects on rivers established as units of the National Wild and Scenic Rivers System and on those rivers designated for study as potential additions to that System. 16 U.S.C. 1278, *et seq.*

• Soil Conservation Service (conservation and protection of environmentally sensitive areas in rural regions).

Department of Commerce

• National Oceanic and Atmospheric Administration (management and protection of environmentally sensitive coastal and marine areas):
—Consultations concerning the protection of threatened and endangered marine species and their critical habitats. 16 U.S.C. 1531, *et seq.* (50 CFR Part 222).
—Permits for activities in designated marine sanctuaries. 16 U.S.C. 1431, *et seq.* (15 CFR Part 922).
—Establishment of estuarine sanctuaries. 16 U.S.C. 1461 (15 CFR Part 921).
—Habitat Conservation Policy (48 FR 53142 of Nov. 25, 1983).

Department of Defense

• Army Corps of Engineers (protection of beaches, wetlands, floodplains, barrier islands):
—For jurisdictional responsibilities, see PART I. B.—Water Quality.

Department of Health and Human Services

• Public Health Service: Center for Disease Control (environmentally sensitive areas in relation to human health issues).

Department of Housing and Urban Development

• Office of Community Planning and Development (locational criteria for floodplain and wetland development; sole source aquifer and critical habitat; development affecting endangered species and their critical habitats).

• Office of Housing (developable slope and soils criteria).

Department of Interior

• Fish and Wildlife Service (protection of endangered species and their critical habitats; conservation of environmentally sensitive areas in National Wildlife Refuges and National Fish Hatcheries):
—Consultations regarding any Federal actions that may directly or indirectly affect a designated coastal barrier. 16 U.S.C. 3501 (for advisory guidelines, see 48 FR 45664 of Oct. 6, 1983).
—Consultations concerning the protection of endangered species and their critical habitats. 16 U.S.C. 1531–1543 (50 CFR Part 402).
—Determination of critical habitats for endangered and threatened species of fish and wildlife and plants. 16 U.S.C. 1533 (50 CFR Parts 17, 402 and 424).

• Geological Survey (geologic and hydrologic assessments of sensitive areas, including energy and mineral resources in wilderness areas; earthquake, volcanic and other natural hazards).

• Bureau of Indian Affairs (environmentally sensitive areas on Indian lands).

• Bureau of Land Management (environmentally sensitive areas on public lands; management of special areas):
—Leases, permits and licenses for mining in Wild and Scenic Rivers System areas. 16 U.S.C. 1280 (each area has special Federal Regulations).

—Approval of plan of operations for a mining lease in a wilderness study area. 43 U.S.C. 1701, *et seq.*, and 1782; 12 U.S.C. 1201, *et seq.* (43 CFR Part 3802).

—Permits for use of a designated "special area" as defined in 43 CFR Part 8372.0–5(g). 43 U.S.C. 1701, *et seq.*; 16 U.S.C. 460 (1–6a) and 670 (g–n) (43 CFR Part 8370 *et seq.*).

—Restrictions on use of "outstanding natural areas" and "primitive areas." 43 U.S.C. 1701, *et seq.* (43 CFR Subpart 8352).

• National Park Service (historical and recreational values; Wild and Scenic Rivers System; National Trails System; National Park System areas):

—Identification and listing on the National Registry of Natural Landmarks of nationally significant natural areas in the United States. 16 U.S.C. 461 (36 CFR Part 62).

—Leases, permits, and licenses for mining on National Park System lands involved in Wild and Scenic Rivers System. 16 U.S.C. 1280.

—Consultations regarding use of and effect on rivers established as units of the National Wild and Scenic Rivers System and on those rivers designated for study as potential additions to that System. 16 U.S.C. 1278, *et seq.*

—Permits for use of National Historic and National Scenic Trails administered by the National Park Service. 16 U.S.C. 1246.

• Bureau of Reclamation (water resource planning and water storage and delivery projects in environmentally sensitive areas; National Water Summary).

• Office of Surface Mining Reclamation and Enforcement (surface coal mining and reclamation operations in environmentally sensitive areas):

—Identification of lands considered unsuitable for all or certain stipulated methods of coal mining involving surface coal mining operations. 30 U.S.C. 1272(e) (30 CFR Chapter 7, Subchapter F).

—Protection of prime farmlands during surface coal mining and reclamation operations. 30 U.S.C. 1265 (30 CFR Parts 785.17 and 823).

Department of Transportation

• Office of Secretary (effects of all types of transportation projects on environmentally sensitive areas).

• Coast Guard (port facilities and bridges in environmentally sensitive areas):

—Establishment of port access routes in environmentally sensitive areas. 33 U.S.C. 1221.

• Federal Highway Administration (highways in environmentally sensitive areas):

—Mitigation of impacts to privately owned wetlands. 23 U.S.C. 109; Executive Order 11990 (23 CFR Part 777).

Advisory Council on Historic Preservation (effects of activities in sensitive areas on historic properties).

Environmental Protection Agency (pollution control and environmental effects on wetlands, floodplains, prime agricultural lands, and other environmentally sensitive areas):

—For jurisdictional responsibilities, see PART I. A.—Air Quality, PART I. B.—Water Quality, and PART I. C.—Waste disposal on Land.

Federal Emergency Management Agency (National Flood Insurance Program; floodplain management; uses on sand dunes, mangrove forests, and barrier islands; disaster relief assistance).

National Science Foundation (conservation of Antarctic animals, plants, and ecosystems):

—Permits for the taking or collecting of Antarctic animals and plants, and for entry into certain designated areas. 16 U.S.C. 2401, *et seq.* (45 CFR Part 670).

Tennessee Valley Authority (Protection and management of environmentally sensitive areas in the Tennessee Valley region).

E. Outdoor Recreation

Department of Agriculture

• Forest Service (recreation in National Forests and Grasslands):

—Use of recreation areas. (36 CFR Parts 291, 292 and 294).

—Permits for use of wilderness areas. 16 U.S.C. 472 and 551 (36 CFR Part 293).

—Conditions and requirements for use of National Forest road and trail system. 16 U.S.C. 537 (36 CFR Part 212).

—Permits for use of National Scenic Trails administered by Forest Service. 16 U.S.C. 1246.

—Permits for hunting and fishing in fish and wildlife refuge lands. 16 U.S.C. 551 and 683.

—Conditions and standards for off-road vehicle use on National Forest System lands. 16 U.S.C. 551; E.O. 11644 (36 CFR Part 295).

—Consultations regarding use of and effects on rivers established as units of the National Wild and Scenic Rivers System and on those rivers designated for study as potential additions to that System. 16 U.S.C. 1278, *et seq.*

• Soil Conservation Service (recreation and watershed protection; planning assistance to private landowners):

—Assistance to State and local sponsors, through a Small Watershed Program grant, for reservoir and stream modification projects including development of basic public recreation facilities. 16 U.S.C. 1001, *et seq.* and 33 U.S.C. 701–1.

Department of Commerce

• National Oceanic and Atmospheric Administration (marine recreational fishing; coastal access planning in State coastal zone management programs).

Department of Defense

• Army Corps of Engineers (recreational areas on Corps project lands):

—Permits for activities and developments on water resources development projects. 16 U.S.C. 460(d) (36 CFR Parts 313 and 327).

Department of Health and Human Services

• Public Health Service: Center for Disease Control (outdoor recreation and health).

Department of Housing and Urban Development

• Office of Community Planning and Development (outdoor recreation in urban areas):

—Approval of a conversion to a non-designated use for State and local lands acquired or developed, in whole or in part, with an Open Space Land Program grant. 42 U.S.C. 1500–1500e.

Department of the Interior

• Fish and Wildlife Service (effects of recreation on endangered species and their critical habitats, and other fish and wildlife resources; recreation on National Wildlife Refuge and National Fish Hatchery System lands):

—Permits for special uses including concessions and other recreational facilities on National Wildlife Refuge System lands. 16 U.S.C. 668dd, *et seq.* (50 CFR Part 25.41, *et seq.*).

—Permits for off-road vehicular use on National Wildlife Refuge System lands. E.O. 11644 (50 CFR Part 26.34).

—Consultation concerning the protection of fish and wildlife refuges which may be impacted by transportation projects. 49 U.S.C. 303.

• Geological Survey (effects of water quality and erosion on recreation).

• Bureau of Indian Affairs (outdoor recreation on Indian lands).

• Bureau of Land Management (outdoor recreation on public lands generally, including ORV use and river management):

—Leases and sale of Federal land to State and local agencies and non-profit groups for recreational and public purposes. 43 U.S.C. 869, *et seq.* (For sales—43 CFR Part 2740; for leases—43 CFR Part 2912).

—Conditions and standards for off-road vehicle use on BLM lands. 43 U.S.C. 1201; E.O. 11644 (43 CFR Part 8340).

—Permits for off-road vehicular use special events, i.e., tours and competitions. 43 U.S.C. 1701, *et seq.*, and 16 U.S.C. 460 (1–6a) (43 CFR Part 8372).

—Permits for use of a national trail, developed facility and a designated "special area" as defined in 43 CFR Part 8372.0–5(g). 43 U.S.C. 1701, *et seq.*; 16 U.S.C. 460 (1–6a) and 670 (g–n) (43 CFR Part 8370).

—Permits for commercial recreation use of public lands. 43 U.S.C. 1701, *et seq.* (43 CFR Part 8370).

• National Park Service (outdoor recreation, urban parks, Wild and Scenic Rivers System, National Trails System; recreation in National Park System areas):

—Assistance to State and local agencies, through Land and Water Conservation Fund Act grants, for the acquisition and/or development of park and recreation areas and/or facilities. 16 U.S.C. 4601.

—Approval of a conversion to a non-designated use for State and local lands acquired or developed, in whole or in part, with a Land and Water Conservation Fund Act grant. 16 U.S.C. 4601.

—Assistance to State and local agencies, through Urban Park and Recreation Recovery Act grants, for the development and/or improvement of park and recreation areas. 16 U.S.C. 2504 (36 CFR Part 1228).

—Approval of a conversion to other than public recreation uses for State and local areas developed or improved with an Urban Park and Recreation Recovery Act grant. 16 U.S.C. 2504 (36 CFR Part 69).

—Consultations regarding use of and effects on rivers established as units of the National Wild and Scenic Rivers System and on those rivers designated for study as potential additions to that System. 16 U.S.C. 1278, et seq.

—Permits for use of National Historic and National Scenic Trails administered by the National Park Service. 16 U.S.C. 1246.

—Approval of a conversion to a non-designated use for lands deeded by the Federal government to State and local entities as park demonstration areas, recreation areas, wildlife conservation preserves and refuges and as historic monuments and properties under the (1) Recreation Demonstration Act of 1942 and (2) Federal Property and Administrative Services Act of 1949. For (1)—16 U.S.C. 459 r–t; for (2)—40 U.S.C. 484(k)(2) (41 CFR Part 101–47).

—Approval of a conversion to a non-designated use of abandoned railroad rights-of-way acquired by State and local governments under Section 809(b) of the Railroad Revitalization and Regulatory Reform Act of 1976. 49 U.S.C. 1a (36 CFR Part 64).

—Consultation concerning the protection of park, recreation, and cultural resources which may be impacted by transportation projects. 49 U.S.C. 303.

—Consultations about extent to which proposed recreational developments at hydroelectric projects conform to and are in accord with the Statewide Comprehensive Outdoor Recreation Plans. 16 U.S.C. 460.

—Permits for off-road vehicle use on National Park System lands. 16 U.S.C. 1, et seq.; E.O. 11644 (36 CFR Part 7).

• Bureau of Reclamation (recreation on water storage and delivery projects):

—Sale or lease of project lands to a governmental entity or a non-profit group for recreational purposes. 43 U.S.C. 869.

—Lease of project lands for commercial recreational developments. 43 U.S.C. 391, et seq.

—Permits for organized off-road vehicular events. (43 CFR Part 420.24).

• Office of Surface Mining Reclamation and Enforcement (use of abandoned mined lands for recreational purposes):

—Identification of park and recreation lands considered unsuitable for surface coal mining operations. 30 U.S.C. 1272(e) (30 CFR Chapter 7, Subchapter F).

Department of Transportation

• Office of the Secretary (general effects of transportation projects on parks and recreation areas):

—Approval of transportation programs or projects that require the use of or have significant impact on park and recreation areas. 49 U.S.C. 303.

• Coast Guard (recreational boating):

—Recreational boating regulations and permits. 46 U.S.C. 1451 (33 CFR Part 173, et seq.).

• Federal Highway Administration (effects of highways on parks and recreation areas):

—Special protection considerations for public park and recreation areas. 23 U.S.C. 138 and 49 U.S.C. 303 (23 CFR Part 771).

—Access highways to public recreation areas on lakes. 23 U.S.C. 155.

Advisory Council on Historic Preservation (effects of recreational activities and development on historic properties).

Environmental Protection Agency (pollution control and environmental quality in relation to outdoor recreation):

—For jurisdictional responsibilities, see PART I—POLLUTION CONTROL.

National Capital Planning Commission (recreation in the Washington, D.C. area):

—Approval of land use plans and construction in the National Capital Region. 40 U.S.C. 74a (D.C. Code 9–404, D.C. Code 8–102); 40 U.S.C. 122 (D.C. Code 8–11, D.C. Code 5–432).

Tennessee Valley Authority (recreation on public lands and waters in Tennessee Valley Region).

F. Community Development

Department of Agriculture

• Agricultural Stabilization and Conservation Service (rural development and farm programs).

• Extension Service (rural and community development programs).

• Farmers Home Administration (rural and community development programs).

• Forest Service (programs to assist in coordinating development of communities in and adjacent to National Forest System areas; urban forestry).

• Soil Conservation Service (soil and related resource surveys; land conservation and utilization):

—Soil, water, and related resource data. 7 U.S.C. 1010a.

—Program for land conservation and utilization. 7 U.S.C. 1011(e).

Department of Commerce

• Economic Development Administration (community development programs in designated areas).

• National Oceanic and Atmospheric Administration (energy development impacts on communities):

—Approval and funding of State coastal zone management programs. 16 U.S.C. 1451, et seq. (15 CFR Parts 130 and 923).

Department of Health and Human Services

• Center for Disease Control (community health issues).

• Office of Human Development Services (problems of handicapped, aged, children and Native Americans).

Department of Housing and Urban Development

• Office of Community Planning and Development (community development; effects on low income populations; economic revitalization in distressed areas; density and congestion mitigation; rehabilitation and urban homesteading):

—Assurances that HUD assisted projects are located in a safe and healthful environment. 42 U.S.C. 1441, et seq.

—Housing and Community Development Act of 1974. 42 U.S.C. 5301, et seq. (24 CFR Part 570).

—Approval of a conversion to a non-designated use for State and local lands acquired or developed, in whole or in part, with an Open Space Land Program grant. 42 U.S.C. 1500–1500e.

Department of the Interior

• Fish and Wildlife Service (effects of community developments on endangered species and their critical habitats, other fish and wildlife resources, and National Wildlife Refuge and National Fish Hatchery System areas).

• Geological Survey (effects of development on water resources and erosion; geologic and hydrologic hazards, including floods, subsidence, sink holes, landslides, and earthquakes).

• Bureau of Indian Affairs (community development for Indian peoples and on Indian lands).

• Bureau of Land Management (community developments on public lands):

—Leases and sale of Federal land to State and local agencies and non-profit groups for recreational and public purposes. 43 U.S.C. 869, et seq. (For sales—43 CFR Part 2740, for leases—43 CFR Part 2912).

—Leases/transfers of public lands for a public airport. 49 U.S.C. 1115 (43 CFR Part 2640).

—Exchange of Federal lands for other property. 43 U.S.C. 1716 (43 CFR Part 2200–2270).

• National Park Service (effects of community developments on natural and historic landmarks, archeological remains, outdoor recreation, urban parks, historic preservation, and National Park System areas):

—Approval of a conversion to a non-designated use for State and local lands acquired or developed, in whole or in part, with a Land and Water Conservation Fund Act grant. 16 U.S.C. 4601.

—Approval of a conversion to other than a public recreation use for State and local areas developed or improved with an Urban Park and Recreation Recovery Act grant. 16 U.S.C. 2504 (36 CFR Part 69).

—Approval of a conversion to a non-designated use for lands deeded by the Federal government to State and local entities as park demonstration areas, recreation areas, wildlife conservation preserves and refuges and as historic monuments and properties under the (1) Recreation Demonstration Act of 1942 and (2) Federal Property and Administrative Services Act of 1949. For (1)—16 U.S.C. 459 r–t; for (2)—40 U.S.C. 484(k)(2) (41 CFR Part 101–47).

—Approval of a conversion to a non-designated use of abandoned railroad right-of-way acquired by State and local governments under Section 809(b) of the

Railroad Revitalization and Regulatory Reform Act of 1976. 49 U.S.C. 1a (36 CFR Part 64).

—Assistance for the acquisition, rehabilitation, restoration and reconstruction of historic properties. 16 U.S.C. 470, *et seq.* (36 CFR Parts 60.3 and 68).

• Bureau of Reclamation (water storage, delivery, and irrigation systems for community development purposes):

—Sales of farm units on Federal irrigation projects (Statutory jurisdiction appears in individual project authorizations).

—Sale or lease of project lands to a governmental entity or nonprofit group for recreational or other public purposes. 43 U.S.C. 869.

• Office of Surface Mining Reclamation and Enforcement (effects of surface mining and reclamation operations on community development).

Department of Transportation

• Federal Aviation Administration (effects of airport development and use on communities):

—Approval of an airport noise compatibility program. 49 U.S.C. 2101, *et seq.* (14 CFR Part 150).

• Federal Highway Administration (effects of highways on communities):

—Relocation assistance in connection with highway projects. 42 U.S.C. 4601 *et seq.* (23 CFR Part 740 and 49 CFR Part 25).

—Grants for economic growth center development highways. 23 U.S.C. 143.

• Urban Mass Transportation Administration (effects of urban transportation systems on communities):

—Grants for Urban Mass Transportation Act projects. 49 U.S.C. 1610, *et seq.*

ACTION (effects of community development on low income populations).

Advisory Council on Historic Preservation (effects of community development on historic properties).

Environmental Protection Agency (air, noise, and water pollution control relating to community development):

—For jurisdictional responsibilities, see PART I.—POLLUTION CONTROL.

Federal Emergency Management Agency (National Flood Insurance Program; disaster relief assistance; mitigation of natural hazards).

General Services Administration

• Public Building Service (building design, construction, and use).

Interstate Commerce Commission (effects of rail line construction and abandonment on community development).

National Capital Planning Commission (community developments in the Washington, D.C. area):

—Approval of land use plans and construction in the National Capital Region. 40 U.S.C. 74a (DC Code 9–404, DC Code 8–102); 40 U.S.C. 122 (D.C. Code 8–111. DC Code 5–432).

National Endowment for the Arts (effects of development on artistic values).

G. Historic, Architectual, and Archeological Resources

Department of Agriculture

• Office of the Secretary (protection of archeological resources):

—Permits and procedures for the recovery and preservation of archeological resources on Department of Agriculture lands. 16 U.S.C. 470 aa–ll (36 CFR Part 296).

• Agricultural Stabilization and Conservation Service (effects on historic and archeological resources from agriculture).

• Farmers Home Administration (effects of housing, community, and business programs, and farmer programs on cultural resources).

• Forest Service (protection of historic and archeological resources in National Forests and Grasslands):

—Special-use permits, archeological permits, leases and easements. 16 U.S.C. 497 and 580(d); 43 U.S.C. 1761; 48 U.S.C. 341 (36 CFR Parts 251 and 261).

• Soil Conservation Service (effects of agriculture on cultural resources).

Department of Commerce

• National Oceanic and Atmospheric Administration (areas for preservation and restoration under State coastal zone management programs):

—National Marine Sanctuaries. 16 U.S.C. 1431 (15 CFR Part 922).

—National Estuarine Sanctuaries. 16 U.S.C. 1461 (15 CFR Part 921).

Department of Defense

• Office of the Secretary (protection of archeological resources):

—Permits/procedures for recovery and preservation of archeological resources on Department of Defense lands. 16 U.S.C. 470 aa–ll (32 CFR Part 229).

Department of Housing and Urban Development

• Office of Community Planning and Development (protection of historic and architectural resources in developed areas):

—Housing and Community Development Act of 1974. 42 U.S.C. 5304(f) (24 CFR Part 58).

Department of the Interior

• Fish and Wildlife Service (cultural resource management on National Wildlife Refuge and National Fish Hatchery System lands, and effects of cultural resource management on endangered species and critical habitats):

—Special use permit for antiquities search and collection activities—in addition to an antiquity permit. 16 U.S.C. 668(dd), *et seq.* (50 CFR Part 25.41); also see 16 U.S.C. 470 aa–ll (43 CFR Part 7).

• Geological Survey (paleontological resources in general).

• Bureau of Indian Affairs (protection of historic and archeological resources on Indian and Native American lands):

—Concurrence for issuance and supervision of antiquity permits on Indian lands. 16 U.S.C. 432 (25 CFR Part 261); also see 16 U.S.C. 470 aa–ll (43 CFR Part 7).

—Protection of access to sacred sites, use and possession of sacred objects and other rights of the American Indian, Eskimo, Aleut, and Native Hawaiian. 42 U.S.C. 1996.

• Bureau of Land Management (cultural resource management on public lands):

—Concurrence for issuance and supervision of antiquity permits. 16 U.S.C. 432 (43 CFR Part 3); also see 16 U.S.C. 470 aa–ll (43 CFR Part 7.)

• Minerals Management Service (protection of cultural resources on outer continental shelf lands):

—Outer Continental Shelf Lands Act. 43 U.S.C. 1331 (30 CFR Parts 250 and 251).

• National Park Service (protection of historic, archeological, architectual and paleontological properties; cultural resource management on National Park System lands):

—Nominations to and determinations of eligibility of properties for inclusion in the National Register of Historic Places. 16 U.S.C. 470, *et seq.* (36 CFR Part 60 and 63).

—Approval of procedures in State and local government historic preservation programs. 16 U.S.C. 470, *et seq.* (36 CFR Part 61).

—National Historic Landmarks Program—nominations and designations. 16 U.S.C. 461, *et seq.* (36 CFR Part 65).

—Historic Preservation Certifications pursuant to the Tax Reform Act of 1976, the Revenue Act of 1978, the Tax Treatment Extension Act of 1980, and the Economic Recovery Tax Act of 1981. 16 U.S.C. 470, *et seq.*; 90 Stat. 1519; 92 Stat. 2828; 94 Stat. 3204; 95 Stat. 172 (36 CFR Part 67).

—The Secretary of the Interior's Standards and Guidelines for Historic Preservation Projects. 16 U.S.C. 470, *et seq.*; Executive Order 11593 (36 CFR Part 68).

—The Secretary of the Interior's Standards and Guidelines for Archeology and Historic Preservation pursuant to Sections 101 and 110 of the National Historic Preservation Act. 16 U.S.C. 470, *et seq.* (48 FR 44716 of Sept. 29, 1983).

—Waiver of Federal Agency Responsibilities under Section 110 of the National Historic Preservation Act. 16 U.S.C. 470, *et seq.* (36 CFR Part 78).

—Protection of the world's cultural and natural heritage: the World Heritage Convention. 16 U.S.C. 470a–1 and 2–2d (36 CFR Part 73).

—Permits and procedures for the recovery and preservation of archeological resource on Department of the Interior lands. 16 U.S.C. 470 aa–ll (43 CFR Part 7).

—Permits to examine ruins, excavate archeological sites and gather objects of antiquity on Federal and Indian lands (Antiquity permits issued by the Departmental Consulting Archeologist). 16 U.S.C. 432 (43 CFR Part 3; 36 CFR Parts 2.20 and 2.25); also see 16 U.S.C. 470 aa–ll (43 CFR Part 7).

—Approval of a conversion to a non-designated use for lands deeded by the Federal government to State and local entities as park demonstration areas, recreation areas, wildlife conservation preserves and refuges and as historic monuments and properties under the (1) Recreation Demonstration Act of 1942 and (2) Federal Property and Administrative

Services Act of 1949. For (1)—16 U.S.C. 459 r–t; for (2)—40 U.S.C. 484(k)(2) (41 CFR Part 101–47).

—Consultation concerning the protection of any historic site which may be impacted by a transportation project. 49 U.S.C. 303.

• Bureau of Reclamation (protection of cultural resources on water storage and delivery project lands):

—Procedures for the administration and protection of cultural resources. E.O. 11593 (43 CFR Part 422).

—Concurrence for issuance and supervision of antiquity permits. 16 U.S.C. 432 (43 CFR Part 3); also see 16 U.S.C. 470 aa–ll (43 CFR Part 7).

• Office of Surface Mining Reclamation and Enforcement (protection of important historic, cultural, scientific, and aesthetic resources in surface coal mining and reclamation operations):

—Concurrence for issuance and the supervision of antiquity permits. 16 U.S.C. 432 (43 CFR Part 3); also see 16 U.S.C. 470 aa–ll (43 CFR Part 7).

Department of Transportation

• Office of the Secretary (general effects of transportation projects on cultural resources):

—Approval of transportation programs or projects that require the use of or have significant impacts on historic sites. 49 U.S.C. 303.

• Coast Guard (effects of bridges on cultural resources):

—Construction and alterations on bridges and causeways over navigable waters that are or require the use of or have significant impacts on historic sites. 33 U.S.C. 491, *et seq.*; 511, *et seq.*; 525, *et seq.*, and 535 (33 CFR Part 114, *et seq.*).

• Federal Aviation Administration (effects of airport developments and air traffic on cultural resources; sonic boom impacts).

• Federal Highway Administration (effects of highway projects on cultural resources):

—Approval of transportation programs or projects that require the use of or have significant impacts on historic sites. 23 U.S.C. 138 and 49 U.S.C. 303 (23 CFR Part 771).

—Archeological and paleontological salvage on Federal and Federal-aid highway projects. 23 U.S.C. 305.

• Federal Railroad Administration (effects of railroad projects on cultural resources).

• Urban Mass Transportation Administration (effects of urban transportation projects on architectural and historic resources).

Advisory Council on Historic Preservation (effects of development or other actions on historic properties):

—Consultation concerning the effects of any Federal, federally assisted, or federally regulated activity on historic properties. 16 U.S.C. 470, *et seq.* (36 CFR Part 800).

General Services Administration

• Public Buildings Service (effects of development and pollution on architectural and historic resources in urban areas).

Interstate Commerce Commission (effects of rail line construction and abandonment on cultural resources).

National Capital Planning Commission (effects of development and pollution on architectural, historic and archeological resources in the Washington, D.C. area):

—Approval of land use plans and construction in the National Capital Region. 40 U.S.C. 74a (D.C. Code 9–404, D.C. Code 8–102); 40 U.S.C. 122 (D.C. Code 8–111, D.C. Code 5–432).

Tennessee Valley Authority (effects of development and other actions on historic and archeological resources in the Tennessee Valley region):

—Permits and procedures for the recovery and preservation of archeological resources on TVA lands. 16 U.S.C. 470 aa–ll (18 CFR Part 1312).

IV. NATURAL RESOURCES MANAGEMENT

A. Weather Modification

Department of Agriculture

• Forest Service (effects of weather modification on National Forests and Grasslands).

• Soil Conservation Service (snow surveys and soil moisture monitoring).

• World Agricultural Outlook Board (data relating to weather and agricultural commodities).

Department of Commerce

• National Oceanic and Atmospheric Administration (weather research and development):

—Records and reports or weather modification activities. 85 Stat. 735 (15 CFR Part 908).

Department of Defense

• Department of the Air Force (fog dissipation).

Department of the Interior

• Bureau of Indian Affairs (effects of weather modification on Indian Lands).

• Bureau of Land Management (effects of weather modification on public lands).

• Fish and Wildlife Service (effects of weather modification on endangered species and their critical habitats, other fish and wildlife resources, and National Wildlife Refuge and National Fish Hatchery System areas).

• Geological Survey (effects of weather modification on water resources; paleoclimatic studies).

• National Park Service (effects of weather modification on National Park System areas).

• Bureau of Reclamation (effects of weather modification on water storage and delivery projects; research in relation to water resources):

—Precipitation augmentation through cloud seeding. 43 U.S.C. 377.

Environmental Protection Agency (effects of weather modification on pollution control and environmental quality).

B. Marine Resources

Department of Commerce

• National Oceanic and Atmospheric Administration (meteorological and oceanographic research and monitoring;

management and protection of coastal and marine resources; marine pollution research and monitoring; ocean pollution; ocean mining; ocean dumping; seafood quality; regulation of marine fisheries):

—Establishment of estuarine sanctuaries. 16 U.S.C. 1461 (15 CFR Part 921).

—Permits for activities in designated marine sanctuaries. 16 U.S.C. 1431, *et seq.* (15 CFR Part 922).

—Consultations regarding Federal or federally permitted projects affecting fish and wildlife habitat in coastal and offshore areas under the Fish and Wildlife Coordination Act. 16 U.S.C. 661, *et seq.*

—Consultations regarding projects which may affect any threatened or endangered marine species or its critical habitat. 16 U.S.C. 1531, *et seq.* (50 CFR Parts 222 and 402).

—Permits for scientific research and display of marine mammals. 16 U.S.C. 1374 (50 CFR Parts 216.31, 220 and 618)..

—Permits to enhance the propagation or survival of endangered or threatened marine species. 16 U.S.C. 1531 (50 CFR Part 222.21).

—Control of fishing by foreign and domestic vessels in the 3–200 mile Fishery Conservation Zone. 16 U.S.C. 1801, *et seq.* (50 CFR Chapter VI).

—Permits for importing marine mammals or products thereof. 16 U.S.C. 1361 and 1371–74 (50 CFR Parts 18 and 216).

—Licenses for siting, design, and operation of ocean-thermal energy facilities. 42 U.S.C. 9101, *et seq.* (15 CFR Part 981).

—Licenses and permits for deep seabed hard mineral resource exploration or recovery. 30 U.S.C. 1401, *et seq.* (15 CFR Part 970).

—Approval of fishery management plans. 16 U.S.C. 1801, *et seq.* (50 CFR Part 601).

—Permits for scientific research, propagation and survival of marine reptiles. 16 U.S.C. 1538 (50 CFR Part 223.23).

—Permits for whaling for scientific and subsistence purposes. 16 U.S.C. 916 (50 CFR Part 216).

Department of Defense

• Army Corps of Engineers (effects of activities in navigable waters on marine resources):

—Regulation of artificial islands, installations and devices on the outer continental shelf. 43 U.S.C. 1333(e) (33 CFR Part 320.2(b)).

—For other jurisdictional responsibilities, see PART I. B.—Water Quality.

• Department of the Navy (oceanography and hydrographic mapping; ship pollution).

Department of Energy

• Office of Policy, Safety, and Environment (effects of energy programs on marine resources).

Department of Health and Human Services

• Public Health Service (effects of marine pollution on health).

• Food and Drug Administration (shellfish sanitation; contamination of fish and shellfish with toxics).

Department of the Interior

• Fish and Wildlife Service (effects of marine pollution on endangered species and their critical habitats, estuarine areas, marine sanctuaries, sport fisheries, migratory waterfowl, barrier islands, and coastal National Wildlife Refuges):

—Consultation regarding Federal projects that may affect an estuarine area. 15 U.S.C. 1224.

—Habitat acquisition and improvement for designated marine mammals. 16 U.S.C. 136, *et seq.*

• Geological Survey (marine geophysical surveys, including assessment of marine energy and mineral deposits; offshore geologic studies).

• Minerals Management Service (emissions from outer continental shelf lease operations; effects of pollution from outer continental shelf mineral lease operations; protection of marine biological resources on outer continental shelf leases; management of outer continental shelf lands):

—For jurisdictional responsibilities see PART II. B.—Oil and Gas and PART IV. G—Non-energy Mineral Resources.

• Bureau of Mines (pollution from ocean mining).

• National Park Service (marine pollution affecting National Park System areas, especially National Seashores; marine recreational resources; historic and archeological sites in coastal areas and on the continental shelf).

• *Department of State* (international aspects of water pollution and marine resources, including migratory birds and marine mammals).

Department of Transportation

• Coast Guard (ocean dumping enforcement and marine resource protection; discharges of toxic materials in navigable waters; recreational boating):

—Transportation of hazardous materials by vessel. 46 U.S.C. 170, 375, 391(a) and 416(j); 49 U.S.C. 1655, 1803, 1804 and 1808(j); 50 U.S.C. 191 (33 CFR Parts 151, *et seq.;* and 160, *et seq.;* 46 CFR Chapter I).

—Hazardous substance discharge to navigable waters. 33 U.S.C. 1321 (33 CFR Parts 25 and 151, *et seq.;* 46 CFR Part 542, *et seq.*).

—Navigation and waterfront facility regulation. 33 U.S.C. 1221, *et seq.* (33 CFR Parts 125 and 126).

—Outer continental shelf structures. 43 U.S.C. 1331 (33 CFR Part 140, *et seq.*).

—Ports and waterways safety. 33 U.S.C. 1221 (33 CFR Part 160, *et seq.*).

—Deepwater port regulation and licensing. 33 U.S.C. 1503–1524 (33 CFR Parts 148–150).

—Recreational boating regulation. 46 U.S.C. 1451 (33 CFR Part 173, *et seq.*).

• Maritime Administration (port, coastal, and ocean pollution; marine pollution from ships; destruction/treatment of wastes at sea):

—Merchant vessels: polluting, discharging and dumping. 46 U.S.C. 1101, *et seq.*

—Port operations: polluting, discharging and dumping. 46 U.S.C. 867.

Advisory Council on Historic Preservation (effects of activities in coastal and marine areas on historic properties).

Environmental Protection Agency (marine discharges, oil spills, ocean dumping; environmental effects; ocean disposal of radioactive waste and hazardous materials):

—For jurisdictional responsibilities, see PART I. B.—Water Quality.

Federal Maritime Commission (vessel certification with respect to liability for water pollution):

—Certificates of financial responsibility for water pollution. 33 U.S.C. 1321 (46 CFR Part 542); 42 U.S.C. 1643 (46 CFR Part 543); 43 U.S.C. 1815 (46 CFR Part 544).

Marine Mammal Commission (conservation and protection of marine mammals and their habitat):

—Consultation and oversight responsibility for activities affecting marine mammals. 16 U.S.C. 1402.

—Review of permit applications for taking and importation of marine mammals and marine mammal products. 16 U.S.C. 1371(a).

National Aeronautics and Space Administration (advanced technology for remote sensing in oceanography and marine resource conservation).

Nuclear Regulatory Commission (radioactive substances in the marine environment).

C. Water Resources Development and Regulation

Department of Agriculture

• Agricultural Stabilization and Conservation Service (water resource conservation; Water Bank program).

• Animal and Plant Health Inspection Service (control of exotic noxious weeds in waterways and streams).

• Forest Service (effects of water resource developments on National Forests and Grasslands):

—Water resource development in wilderness areas. (36 CFR Part 293.15).

—Consultations regarding water resource development and effects on rivers established as units of the National Wild and Scenic Rivers System and on those rivers designated for study as potential additions to that System. 16 U.S.C. 1278, *et seq.*

• Agricultural Research Service (research on soil and water conservation).

• Soil Conservation Service (watershed protection; river basin studies, flood prevention, and habitat analysis):

—Assistance to State and local sponsors, through a Small Watershed Program grant, for watershed, reservoir, flood-control and drainage projects. 16 U.S.C. 1001, *et seq.;* 33 U.S.C. 701-1 and 42 U.S.C. 1962, *et seq.* (7 CFR Parts 620, *et seq.;* and 660).

Department of Commerce

• National Oceanic and Atmospheric Administration (estuarine and anadromous fish habitat; review of Federal permits affecting water resources and management; protection of coastal and marine resources; river and flood forecasting).

Department of Defense

• Army Corps of Engineers (water resource development and regulation activities in water of the United States):

—Rules governing work or structures in or affecting navigable waters of the United States. 33 U.S.C. 401, 403, and 419 (33 CFR Part 322).

—Permits for discharges of dredged or fill materials into waters of the United States. 33 U.S.C. 1344 (33 CFR Part 323).

—Guidelines controlling the discharge of dredged or fill material in waters of the United States including wetlands. (40 CFR Part 230).

—Permits for uses at Corps reservoirs managed by a lakeshore management plan. 33 U.S.C. 1251.

—Permits for use of river or harbor improvements built by United States. 33 U.S.C. 408 (33 CFR Part 320.2(e).

—For other jurisdictional responsibilities, see PART I. B.—Water Quality.

Department of Energy

• Office of Policy, Safety, and Environment (effect of energy policies, programs, and projects).

Department of the Interior

• Fish and Wildlife Service (effects of water resource developments on endangered species and their critical habitats, other fish and wildlife resources, and National Wildlife Refuge and National Fish Hatchery System areas):

—Consultation regarding Federal or Federally permitted projects which affect streams and water bodies. 16 U.S.C. 661, *et seq.*

—U. S. Fish and Wildlife Service Mitigation Policy. 16 U.S.C. 661–667(e), 742(a)–754 and 1001–1009 (46 FR 7644 of Jan. 23, 1981).

—Consultation regarding Federal projects that may affect an estuarine area under the Estuarine Protection Act. 15 U.S.C. 1224.

• Geological Survey (hydrologic research; collection, analysis, and dissemination of data on quantity and quality of surface and ground water; National Water Summary).

• Bureau of Indian Affairs (effects of water resources developments on Indian lands):

—Permits, concessions, and leases on lands withdrawn or acquired in connection with Indian irrigation projects. 25 U.S.C. 390 (25 CFR Part 173).

• Bureau of Land Management (effects of water resource developments on public lands):

—Permits, leases, and easements for water control projects. 43 U.S.C. 1732(b) and 1761(a)(1) (43 CFR Part 2800).

• Bureau of Mines (effects of water resource developments and regulation on mineral resources, production and transportation).

• National Park Service (effects of water resource developments on Wild and Scenic River System, outdoor recreation areas, and National Park System areas):

—Consultations regarding water resource developments and effects on rivers established as units of the National Wild

and Scenic Rivers System and on those rivers designated for study as potential additions to that System. 16 U.S.C. 1278, *et seq.*
—Consultations about extent to which proposed recreational developments at hydroelectric projects conform to and are in accord with the State Comprehensive Outdoor Recreation Plan. 16 U.S.C. 470.
• Bureau of Reclamation (water storage and delivery projects and their effects; water policy analysis; impacts on State water management):
—Construction and operation of works and structures for storage, diversion and development of waters, including flood control, navigation and river-flow regulation and control in the 17 contiguous western States. 43 U.S.C. 391 *et seq.*
• Office of Surface Mining Reclamation and Enforcement (effects of water resource developments on surface coal mining and reclamation operations).

Department of Transportation
• Coast Guard (vessel, bridge, port, and waterway regulation and safety; navigational aids):
—Ports and waterways safety. 33 U.S.C. 1221 (33 CFR Part 160, *et seq.*).
—Construction and alterations of bridges and causeways over navigable waters. 33 U.S.C. 491, *et seq.*; 511, *et seq.*; 525, *et seq.*, and 535 (33 CFR Part 114, *et seq.*).
• Federal Highway Administration (effects of water resource developments on highways):
—Approval of Federal-aid highway and bridge projects involving navigable waters and channel changes. 23 U.S.C. 144 (23 CFR Part 650).
—Approval of toll bridge and ferry projects. 23 U.S.C. 129.
• Saint Lawrence Seaway Development Corporation (Seaway regulation):
—Construction, development, operation, and maintenance of the United States part of the Seaway. 33 U.S.C. 981–990 (33 CFR Parts 401–403).

Advisory Council on Historic Preservation (effects of water resource developments on historic properties).
Delaware River Basin Commission (management of water resources in the Delaware River basin):
—Review and approval of water resource projects. 75 Stat. 708 (18 CFR Parts 401–430).
Environmental Protection Agency (effects of water resource developments on pollution control):
—Review of permits for discharge of dredged or fill materials into waters of the United States. 33 U.S.C. 1344 (40 CFR Part 230).
—Guidelines controlling the discharge of dredged or fill material in waters of the U.S. including wetlands. (40 CFR Part 230).
—For other jurisdictional responsibilities, see PART I. B.—Water Quality.
Federal Emergency Management Agency (floodplain mapping and floodplain management; dam and levee safety; mitigation of natural hazards).

Federal Energy Regulatory Commission (effects of power projects):
—Regulation of development of water resources. 16 U.S.C. 791–825(r) (18 CFR Parts 4–25, 36, 131 and 141).
International Boundary and Water Commission, United States Section (maintenance, restoration and protection of banks of Rio Grande and Colorado River where they form the international boundary with Mexico; construction and operation of works and structures for storage and diversion of waters, including flood control on the Rio Grande and Colorado Rivers).
National Capital Planning Commission (water resource developments in Washington, D.C. area):
—Approval of taking lines and general development plans for parks in stream valleys in Maryland and Virginia tributaries to the Potomac and Anacostia Rivers. Act of May 29, 1930; 46 Stat. 432 as amended.
Susquehanna River Basin Commission (management of water resources in the Susquehanna River basin):
—Review and approval of water resource projects. 84 Stat. 1509 *et seq.* (18 CFR Parts 801–803).
Tennessee Valley Authority (water resource developments and regulation in the Tennessee Valley region):
—Construction of dams, appurtenant works, or other waterway improvement activities affecting navigation, flood control, public lands or reservations on the Tennessee River System. 16 U.S.C. 831(y–1).

D. Watershed Protection and Soil Conservation

Department of Agriculture
• Agricultural Research Service (technical aspects of water and soil conservation).
• Agricultural Stabilization and Conservation Service (soil conservation; cost-sharing farm and forest conservation programs).
• Extension Service (extension programs in agricultural conservation).
• Farmers Home Administration (effects of housing, community, and business programs, and farmer programs on soil and water conservation; conservation loan programs).
• Forest Service (soil and water conservation, and their effects on National Forests and Grasslands; forest and range soil rehabilitation):
—Emergency soil and water conservation programs. 16 U.S.C. 2202, *et seq.*
• Soil Conservation Service (soil surveys; technical assistance in areas of soil, water, and related resource conservation for landowners and landusers through several multi-functional programs):
—Grants for Watershed Protection and Flood Prevention Act activities. 16 U.S.C. 1001, *et seq.* (7 CFR Part 620, *et seq.*, and 660).
—Land conservation and land utilization program. 7 U.S.C. 1010, *et seq.*

Department of Commerce
• National Oceanic and Atmospheric Administration (weather research, river and flood forecasting).

Department of Defense
• Army Corps of Engineers (dredging, flood control, control of aquatic plants, shoreline stabilization):
—For jurisdictional responsibilities, see PART I. B.—Water Quality.

Department of Energy
• Office of Policy, Safety, and Environment (effects of energy policies, programs and projects on watersheds).

Department of the Interior
• Fish and Wildlife Service (effects of soil erosion and watershed protection on endangered species and critical habitats, and on fish and wildlife resources in general):
—Consultation regarding small watershed projects of the Soil Conservation Service under the Watershed Protection and Flood Protection and Flood Prevention Act. 16 U.S.C. 1008.
• Geological Survey (geology and hydrology in general; National Water Summary; erosion and sedimentation; engineering geology).
• Bureau of Indian Affairs (soil conservation and watershed protection on Indian lands).
• Bureau of Land Management (watershed protection and soil conservation on public lands).
• Bureau of Mines (hydraulic impacts of mining; revegetation and reclamation after mining).
• National Park Service (watershed protection and soil conservation on National Park System lands):
—Special use permits, grazing permits, permits to collect soil, rock, water, and plant specimens. 16 U.S.C. 1, *et seq.* (36 CFR Parts 1, 2 and 7).
• Bureau of Reclamation (soil and moisture conservation; hydrology; erosion control on public lands; water storage and delivery project; water resources research; analysis of Federal role in groundwater management).
• Office of Surface Mining Reclamation and Enforcement (effects of surface coal mining and reclamation operations on erosion, aquifers and alluvial valley floors).

Department of Transportation
• Federal Highway Administration (erosion control on highway projects; vegetation management on highway rights-of-way; highway drainage problems on watersheds).
Advisory Council on Historic Preservation (effects of watershed protection activities on historic properties).
Environmental Protection Agency (watershed protection and soil conservation in relation to pollution control).
Federal Emergency Management Agency (floodplain mapping and management, mitigation of natural hazards).
Federal Energy Regulatory Commission (effects of power projects):
—Regulation of development of water resources. 16 U.S.C. 791–825(r) (18 CFR Parts 4–25, 36, 131 and 141).

National Aeronautics and Space Administration (advanced technology for remote sensing of watersheds and soils).

Tennessee Valley Authority (watershed protection and soil conservation in the Tennessee Valley region).

E. Forest, Range, and Vegetative Resources (Includes Development, Production, Harvest and Transport of These Renewable Resources)

Department of Agriculture

• Agricultural Research Service (forest and range management).

• Agricultural Stabilization and Conservation Service (renewable resource conservation programs; Forestry Incentives Program; Water Bank Program).

• Economic Research Service and Statistical Reporting Service (economic and statistical data on renewable resources).

• Extension Service (rural extension programs in renewable resource conservation and management).

• Farmers Home Administration (resource conservation and development loan programs).

• Forest Service (forest and grassland productivity in general; fire management; timber sale, free use of timber and other renewable resources, timber management activities and grazing habitat management in National Forests and Grasslands):

—Timber management. 16 U.S.C. 472, 528–531 and 1600–1614 (36 CFR Part 222).

—Grazing permits. 43 U.S.C. 1901 (36 CFR Part 222).

—Management and disposal of wild free-roaming horses and burros. 16 U.S.C. 1331–1340 (36 CFR Part 222, Subpart B).

• Soil Conservation Service (watershed resources protection; soil conservation technology).

Department of Commerce

• National Oceanic and Atmospheric Administration (coastal and marine resources management and development).

Department of Defense

• Army Corps of Engineers (effects of activities in the waters of the U.S. on renewable resources):

—For jurisdictional responsibilities, see PART I. B.—Water Quality.

Department of Energy

• Bonneville Power Administration (renewable resource development in the Pacific Northwest):

—Regional planning and conservation. 16 U.S.C. 839, *et seq.*

Department of the Interior

• Fish and Wildlife Service (effects of agriculture, forestry, and other renewable resource activities on endangered species and their critical habitats, National Wildlife Refuges and National Fish Hatchery systems, and other fish and wildlife resources).

• Geological Survey (effects of renewable resource activities on water resources and erosion; remote sensing of vegetation).

• Bureau of Indian Affairs (forest, range, and vegetative resources on Indian lands):

—Permits for grazing on Indian lands and on Federal lands under BIA jurisdiction. 5 U.S.C. 301; 25 U.S.C. 179, 345, 380, 393–394, 397, 402–403 and 413 (25 CFR Parts 166–168).

—Sale of timber from tribal and allotted lands. 25 U.S.C. 406–407, 413 and 466 (25 CFR Part 163).

—Permits, concessions, and leases on lands withdrawn or acquired in connection with Indian irrigation projects. 25 U.S.C. 390 (25 CFR Part 173).

—Leases for farming and other uses on Federal lands under BIA jurisdiction. 5 U.S.C. 301; 25 U.S.C. 380, 393–395, 397, 402–403, 413, 415, 477 and 635 (25 CFR Part 162).

• Bureau of Land Management (forest, range and vegetative resources on public lands):

—Permits for use of rangelands. 43 U.S.C. 315 (43 CFR Group 4100).

—Sale by contract of timber and other forest products. 30 U.S.C. 601, *et seq.;* 43 U.S.C. 315, 423, and 118(a) (43 CFR Group 5400).

—Permits for free use of timber. 16 U.S.C. 604, *et seq.;* 30 U.S.C. 189; 48 U.S.C. 423 (43 CFR Part 5510).

—Management and control of wild free-roaming horses and burros and agreements for their adoption. 16 U.S.C. 1331–1340 (43 CFR Group 4700).

• National Park Service (effects of forest, range, and other vegetative resource activities on historical and recreational values and on National Park System areas):

—Permits for farming and grazing. 16 U.S.C. Chapter 1, *et seq.* (36 CFR Parts 1, 2 and 7).

• Bureau of Reclamation (water storage and delivery projects and irrigation projects in relation to forest, range, and other vegetative resource activities; evaluation of water policy alternatives):

—Sale of farm units on Federal irrigation projects (statutory authority appears in individual project authorizations).

• Office of Surface Mining Reclamation and Enforcement (effects of surface coal mining and reclamation operations on renewable resources):

—Protection of prime farmlands during surface coal mining and reclamation operations. 30 U.S.C. 1265 (30 CFR Parts 785.17 and 823).

Department of Transportation

• Federal Highway Administration (development of forest haul and access roads, effects of highway projects on forest, range, and other vegetative resources).

Advisory Council on Historic Preservation (effects of renewable resource activities on historic properties).

Environmental Protection Agency (effects of pollution, pesticide, and other environmental quality controls on forest, range, and other vegetative resources).

Interstate Commerce Commission (freight rates for renewable resources).

Tennessee Valley Authority (effects of hydro-electric and other power developments on forest, range, and other vegetative resources; biomass production and use).

F. Fish and Wildlife

Department of Agriculture

• Agricultural Research Service (basic and applied research in animal and plant protection).

• Agricultural Stabilization and Conservation Service (fish and wildlife in relation to agricultural conservation and the Water Bank Program).

• Animal and Plant Health Inspection Service (animal and plant health in general; control of pests and diseases):

—Prevention of importation or exportation of diseased livestock or poultry. 21 U.S.C. 102–105, 111 and 132(a)–134(f).

• Farmers Home Administration (effects of farm housing, community, and business programs on fish and wildlife; conservation loan programs).

• Forest Service (fish and wildlife habitat management in National Forests and Grasslands; use of fire in habitat management):

—Fish and wildlife management (36 CFR Part 219.19).

—Management and disposal of wild free-roaming horses and burros. 16 U.S.C. 1331–1340 (36 CFR Part 222, Subpart B).

—Permits for hunting and fishing in refuge areas. 16 U.S.C. 551 and 683.

• Soil Conservation Service (fish and wildlife habitat, fish ponds, and raceways):

—Assistance to State and local sponsors, through a Small Watershed Program grant, for reservoir developments and stream modification projects including specific fish and wildlife habitat improvements. 16 U.S.C. 1001, *et seq.,* and 33 U.S.C. 701–1.

Department of Commerce

• National Oceanic and Atmospheric Administration (endangered species and critical habitats; coastal fish and wildlife management and protection):

—Approval and funding of State coastal zone management programs. 16 U.S.C. 1451, *et seq.* (15 CFR Parts 923 and 930).

—For other jurisdictional responsibilities, see PART IV. B.—Marine Resources.

Department of Defense

• Army Corps of Engineers (fish and wildlife mitigation measures at public works and navigable waterway projects, dredge and fill permits):

—For jurisdictional responsibilities, see PART I. B.—Water Quality.

• Department of the Air Force (bird/aircraft strike hazard reduction).

Department of Energy

• Bonneville Power Administration (fish and wildlife management and enhancement on power projects in the Pacific Northwest):

—Regional planning and conservation. 16 U.S.C. 839, *et seq.*

Department of the Interior

• Fish and Wildlife Service (endangered species and their critical habitats; management of effects on fish and wildlife in general):

—Permits to take bald and golden eagles for scientific, religious and other purposes. 16 U.S.C. 668(a) (50 CFR Part 22).

—Permits for the taking and importation of marine mammals. 16 U.S.C. 1361, et seq. (50 CFR Part 18).

—Permits to export/import and to take for scientific and other purposes endangered or threatened wildlife and plants. 16 U.S.C. 1531, et seq. (50 CFR Part 17).

—Permits for the importation of injurious mammals, birds, fish and other wildlife. 18 U.S.C. 42–44 (40 CFR Part 16.22).

—Permits for export/import and interstate transportation of wildlife. 18 U.S.C. 42, et seq. (50 CFR Part 14).

—Permits for the banding and marking of migratory birds. 16 U.S.C. 703–711 (50 CFR Part 21.22).

—Consultations regarding Federal projects that may affect an estuarine area. 15 U.S.C. 1224.

—Permits to perform taxidermy services on migratory birds, nests and eggs for commercial uses. 16 U.S.C. 704 (50 CFR Part 21.24).

—Permits for special purpose uses of migratory birds. 16 U.S.C. 701, et seq. (50 CFR Part 21.27).

—Certificates or permits of exception to Convention on International Trade in Endangered Species. 16 U.S.C. 1531–1543 (50 CFR Part 23).

—Consultations regarding projects which may effect any threatened or endangered species or its critical habitats. 16 U.S.C. 1531, et seq. (50 CFR Part 402).

—Determination of critical habitats for endangered and threatened species of fish, wildlife, and plants. 16 U.S.C. 1531, et seq. (50 CFR Parts 17, 402 and 424).

—Endangered species exemption process. 16 U.S.C. 1531, et seq. (50 CFR Parts 450–453).

—Consultation regarding Federal or federally permitted projects which affect fish and wildlife resources under the Fish and Wildlife Coordination Act. 16 U.S.C. 661, et seq.

—U.S. Fish and Wildlife Service Mitigation Policy. 16 U.S.C. 661–667(e), 742(a)–754 and 1001–1009 (see 46 FR 7644 of Jan. 23, 1981).

—Restoration and enhancement of anadromous fishery resources through grants for fish ladders, new anadromous fish hatcheries, new fishways, etc. 16 U.S.C. 742(a)–742(j) (50 CFR Part 401).

—Improvement of sport fishery resources through grants to States under the Dingell-Johnson (D–J) Program. 16 U.S.C. 777–777(k) (50 CFR Part 80).

—Restoration and enhancement of wildlife populations and resources through grants to States under the Pittman-Robertson (P–R) Program. 16 U.S.C. 669, et seq. (50 CFR Part 80).

—Approval of conversion of use for State lands acquired, developed or improved with grants under the (1) Pittman-Robertson Act, (2) Dingell-Johnson Act, (3) Endangered Species Act and/or (4) Anadromous Fish Conservation Act. For (1)—16 U.S.C. 669 (50 CFR Parts 80.4 and 80.14); for (2)—16 U.S.C. 777 (50 CFR Parts 80.4 and 80.14); (3)—16 U.S.C. 1535; and for (4)—16 U.S.C. 757 (a) and (b).

—Land acquisition, management, and other activities for endangered and threatened species through grants to States. 16 U.S.C. 1531–1543 (50 CFR Part 81).

—Consultation concerning the protection of fish and wildlife refuges which may be impacted by transportation projects. 49 U.S.C. 303.

• Geological Survey (water quality and quantity in relation to fish and wildlife resources).

• Bureau of Indian Affairs (fish and wildlife resource management on Indian lands; off-reservation treaty fishing).

• Bureau of Land Management (fish and wildlife management on public lands; wild horses and burros; endangered species and raptors; effects on fish and wildlife of power lines and other major projects crossing public lands):

—Management and disposal of wild free-roaming horses and burros. 16 U.S.C. 1331–1340 (43 CFR Part 4700).

• National Park Service (fishing, hunting and other outdoor recreational pursuits, fish and wildlife management in National Park System areas):

—Permits for collecting animal specimens from National Park System areas. 16 U.S.C. 1, et seq. (36 CFR Part 2).

—Licenses and permits for sport or commercial fishing in certain National Park System areas. (36 CFR Part 2).

—Disposition of surplus animals from National Park System areas. (36 CFR Part 10).

• Bureau of Reclamation (fish and wildlife management on water storage and delivery projects; hunting and fishing on project lands; mitigation measures; limnology).

• Office of Surface Mining Reclamation and Enforcement (effects of surface mining and reclamation operations on fish and wildlife).

Department of Health and Human Services

• Public Health Service: Centers for Disease Control (fish and wildlife in relation to human health); Food and Drug Administration (contamination of fish and shellfish with toxics).

Department of State (international issues concerning fish and wildlife, including migratory birds and marine mammals).

Department of Transportation

• Office of the Secretary (general effects of transportation projects on fish and wildlife refuges):

—Approval of transportation programs or projects that require the use of or have a significant impact on wildlife and waterfowl refuges. 49 U.S.C. 303.

• Federal Highway Administration (effects of highway projects on fish and wildlife habitat, and wildlife and waterfowl refuges):

—Preservation of park and recreation areas, and wildlife and waterfowl refuges. 23 U.S.C. 138 (23 CFR Part 771).

• Federal Aviation Administration (bird-aircraft strike hazard reduction).

• Coast Guard (enforcement of laws affecting Fishery Management Zones).

Environmental Protection Agency (effects of pollution control and water quality on fish and wildlife).

Marine Mammal Commission (conservation and protection of marine mammals and their habitat):

—Consultation and oversight responsibility for activities affecting marine mammals. 16 U.S.C. 1402.

—Review of permit applications for taking and importation of marine mammals and marine mammal products. 16 U.S.C. 1371(a).

National Science Foundation (conservation of antarctic animals, plants, and ecosystems):

—Permits for the taking or collecting of Antarctic animals and plants, and for entry into certain designated areas. 16 U.S.C. 2401, et seq. (45 CFR Part 670).

Tennessee Valley Authority (fish and wildlife management and conservation in the Tennessee Valley).

G. Non-Energy Mineral Resources

Department of Agriculture

• Forest Service (mineral resources development in National Forests and Grasslands; reclamation of disturbed lands):

—Permits and rights-of-way on National Forest System lands. 16 U.S.C. 471–472, 478, 495, 497–498, 525, 528, 531–538, 551, 572 and 580 (36 CFR Parts 212, 251 and 261).

—Surface use of public domain lands under U.S. mining laws. 16 U.S.C. 478 and 551 (36 CFR Part 228).

—Mineral development on acquired lands. For solid (hardrock) minerals—16 U.S.C. 520 (43 CFR Part 3500); for phosphate, sodium, potassium and sulphur—30 U.S.C. 351, et seq.

• Soil Conservation Service (abandoned mine land and mine reclamation).

Department of Commerce

• National Oceanic and Atmospheric Administration (air and water pollution from mining; offshore and coastal mining; port planning; management and protection of coastal and marine resources):

—Approval of licenses for deep seabed hard mineral exploration and development. 30 U.S.C. 1401, et seq. (15 CFR Part 970).

Department of Defense

• Army Corps of Engineers (effects of mineral development on navigable waters):

—For jurisdictional responsibilities, see PART I. B.—Water Quality.

Department of Housing and Urban Development

• Office of Housing (subsidence from mining operations and soil factors related to housing).

Department of the Interior

• Fish and Wildlife Service (effects of mineral development on endangered species and their critical habitats, National Wildlife Refuge and National Fish Hatchery Systems, and other fish and wildlife resources):

—Easements/permits for transmission line, pipelines and other rights-of-way across National Wildlife Refuge and National Fish Hatchery System land. For refuges—16 U.S.C. 668 dd, et seq.; for hatcheries—43

U.S.C. 931 c and (50 CFR Parts 25.41 and 29.21).

—Permits for rights-of-way across National Wildlife Monuments (Alaska only). 16 U.S.C. 432, 460(k–3) and 742(f) (50 CFR Part 96).

• Geological Survey (mineral resources in general, with emphasis on strategic and critical minerals; mineral resources assessment on public lands).

• Bureau of Indian Affairs (effects on Indian lands of mineral operations):

—Leases and permits on Indian lands. 25 U.S.C. 380, 393–395, 397, 402–403, 413, 415, 477 and 635 (25 CFR Part 162).

—Rights-of-way over Indian lands. 25 U.S.C. 311–321 and 323–328 (25 CFR Part 169).

—Mining leases on Indian lands. 25 U.S.C. 356, 396, 476–477 and 509 (25 CFR Parts 211–215 and 226–227).

—Permits for surface exploration and reclamation. 25 U.S.C. 355, 396, 473 and 501–502 (25 CFR Part 216).

• Bureau of Land Management (mineral development on public lands):

—Easements/leases/permits for use, occupancy and development of public lands. 43 U.S.C. 1732 (43 CFR Subchapters 2000 and 3000).

—Exploration licenses for leasable minerals on unleased land. 30 U.S.C. 181, et seq. and 201(b) (43 CFR Parts 3400 and 3480).

—Leases for phosphate, sodium, potassium, etc., exploration and mining. 30 U.S.C. 181, et seq. (43 CFR Group 3500 and Part 3570).

—Permits for sand, stone and gravel. 30 U.S.C. 601 and 602.

—Leases, permits and licenses for mining in Wild and Scenic River System areas. 16 U.S.C. 1280 (each area has special Federal Regulations).

—Concurrence for placer mining use of the surface of public lands withdrawn or reserved for power development or for a power site. 30 U.S.C. 621 (43 CFR Part 3730).

—Leases and permits for sulfur in Louisiana and New Mexico. 30 U.S.C. 271, et seq. (43 CFR Group 3500).

—Easements/permits for rights-of-way. 30 U.S.C. 185 and 43 U.S.C. 1701, et seq. (43 CFR Parts 2800–2887).

• Minerals Management Service (mineral development on the outer continental shelf):

—Leases for minerals on the outer continental shelf. 43 U.S.C. 1331–1343 (30 CFR Parts 250, 251, 252 and 256).

—Permits for exploration and development activities on Federal leases on the outer continental shelf. 43 U.S.C. 1331, et seq. (30 CFR Parts 250 and 251).

—Permits for geological and geophysical exploration on the outer continental shelf. 43 U.S.C. 1334 (30 CFR Part 251).

—Approval of geological geophysical exploration plans. 43 U.S.C. 1340 (30 CFR Part 251).

—Permits for artificial islands, platforms, and other fixed structures on any Federal or State outer continental shelf lease. 43 U.S.C. 1334–1335 (30 CFR 250.18 and 250.19).

• Bureau of Mines (mining, milling, and mineral land assessments):

—Agreements to dispose of helium of the United States. 43 U.S.C. 1201 and 30 U.S.C. 180, et seq. (43 CFR Part 16).

• National Park Service (effects of mineral development on public park, recreation and cultural/historical resources and values, and on National Park System areas):

—Permits, leases and easements for rights-of-way, grazing and other uses on National Park System areas. 16 U.S.C. 1, et seq. (36 CFR Parts 9 and 14).

—Leases, permits and licenses for mining on National Park System lands involved in National Wild and Scenic Rivers System. 16 U.S.C. 1280.

—Access permits for mining activity within the National Park System. 16 U.S.C. 1902 and 1908; 30 U.S.C. 21, et seq. (36 CFR Part 9).

• Bureau of Reclamation (effects of mineral development on water storage and delivery projects):

—Easements/permits for access, pipeline, and other rights-of-way. 43 U.S.C. 3871.

Department of Labor

• Mining Safety and Health Administration (safety and health issues in mining operations).

• Occupational Safety and Health Administration (general worker safety and health issues).

Department of State (international aspects of mineral development):

—Facilities for export/import of minerals. Executive Order 11423.

Department of Transportation

• Coast Guard (vessel transport of minerals):

—Ports and waterways safety. 33 U.S.C. 1221 (33 CFR Part 160, et seq.).

• Maritime Administration (dry bulk shipping of coal and other minerals in the inland waterways, domestic ocean, Great Lakes, and U.S. foreign trades).

Advisory Council on Historic Preservation (effects of mineral development activities on historic properties).

Environmental Protection Agency (pollution control and other environmental effects of minerals development):

—For jurisdictional responsibilities, see PART I—POLLUTION CONTROL.

H. Natural Resource Conservation

Department of Agriculture

• Agricultural Stabilization and Conservation Service (natural resource conservation programs; Forestry Incentives Program; Water Bank Program).

• Agricultural Research Service (research in technical aspects of soil and water conservation and forest and range management).

• Extension Service (rural area extension programs in conservation).

• Farmers Home Administration (farmer loan programs related to natural resource conservations).

• Forest Service (conservation of forest and rangeland resources; use of fire as a management tool).

• Soil Conservation Service (soil, water, and related resources conservation technology):

—Land conservation and utilization program. 7 U.S.C. 1010, et seq.

—Watershed protection, conservation and utilization of land and water resources. 16 U.S.C. 1001, et seq.

—Soil and water resources conservation. 16 U.S.C. 2001, et seq.

Department of Commerce

• National Oceanic and Atmospheric Administration (coastal and marine resources management and protection; national estuarine and marine sanctuaries; coastal energy facility planning and siting in State coastal zone management programs).

Department of Energy

• Bonneville Power Administration (resource conservation in the Pacific Northwest):

—Regional planning and conservation. 16 U.S.C. 839, et seq.

• Office of Policy, Safety, and Environment (general energy policies, programs and projects in relation to conservation).

Department of the Interior

• Fish and Wildlife Service (conservation of, and effects of conservation on, endangered species and their critical habitats, and other fish and wildlife resources; conservation in National Wildlife Refuge and National Fish Hatchery System areas).

• Geological Survey (conservation of water and mineral resources).

• Bureau of Indian Affairs (conservation of Indian lands).

• Bureau of Land Management (conservation on public lands).

• Minerals Management Service (conservation in relation to minerals management activities on the outer continental shelf).

• Bureau of Mines (conservation of mineral resources and land, air, and water resources associated with mineral deposits).

• National Park Service (conservation in relation to urban parks, outdoor recreation, historical and cultural resources, National Trails Systems, Wild and Scenic Rivers System, and the National Park System).

• Bureau of Reclamation (conservation in relation to water storage and delivery projects, water resources, and desalinization; Soil and Moisture Conservation Program; development of water policy options; National Water Summary).

• Office of Surface Mining Reclamation and Enforcement (conservation in relation to surface coal mining and reclamation operations).

Environmental Protection Agency (resource recovery from wastes; pollution and other environmental controls):

—Solid Waste Disposal Act permits. 42 U.S.C. 3251 et seq., and 6901, et seq. (40 CFR Parts 122, 123 and 124).

—Guidelines on solid waste collection and storage for Federal assistance. 42 U.S.C. 6907 (40 CFR Part 243).

—Resource recovery facilities. 42 U.S.C. 6907 (40 CFR Part 245).

—Materials recovery and solid waste management guidelines for source separation. 42 U.S.C. 6907 (40 CFR Part 246).

—Solid waste management guidelines for beverage containers. 42 U.S.C. 6907 (40 CFR Part 244).

Federal Energy Regulatory Commission (relation of conservation to hydroelectric power development and natural gas facilities).

National Science Foundation (conservation of antarctic animals, plants, and ecosystems):

—Permits for the taking or collecting of antarctic animals and plants, and for entry into certain designated areas. 16 U.S.C. 2401, *et seq.* (45 CFR Part 670).

Tennessee Valley Authority (soil and other natural resource conservation in the Tennessee Valley region).

Appendix III—Federal and Federal-State Agency Offices for Receiving and Commenting on Other Agencies' Environmental Documents

DEPARTMENTS

Department of Agriculture

Send request to the Departmental office for comments on environmental documents about legislation, regulations, national program proposals or other major policy issues. For other comment requests, send to the listed office of the departmental components.

Assistant Secretary for Natural Resources and Environment, Department of Agriculture; Attn: Executive Secretary, Natural Resources and Environment Committee; Room 242-W, Administration Bldg., 14th St. and Independence Ave., SW, Wash., D.C. 20250-0001. (202) 447-5166.

Department of Agriculture Components

Agricultural Research Service: Deputy Administrator, National Program Staff, Agricultural Research Service, Department of Agriculture, Room 125, Bldg. 005, Agricultural Research Center-West, Beltsville, MD 20705-2350. (301) 344-3084.

Agricultural Stabilization and Conservation Service: Chief, Planning and Evaluation Branch, Conservation and Environmental Protection Division, Agricultural Stabilization and Conservation Service, Department of Agriculture, Room 4714, South Agriculture Bldg., P.O. Box 2415; Wash., D.C. 20013-2415. (202) 447-3264.

Animal and Plant Health Inspection Service: Environmental Coordinator, Animal and Plant Health Inspection Service, Department of Agriculture, Room 600, Federal Bldg., 6505 Belcrest Road, Hyattsville, MD 20782-2058. (301) 436-8896.

Economic Research Service: Director, Natural Resource Economics Division, Economic Research Service, Department of Agriculture, Room 412, GHI Bldg., 500 12th St., SW, Wash., D.C. 20250-0001. (202) 447-8239.

Extension Service: Deputy Administrator, Natural Resources and Rural Development, Extension Service, Department of Agriculture,

Room 3909, South Agriculture Bldg., 14th St. and Independence Ave., SW, Wash., D.C. 20250-0001. (202) 447-7947.

Farmers Home Administration: Environmental Protection Specialist, Program Support Staff, Farmers Home Administration, Department of Agriculture, Room 6309, South Agriculture Bldg., 14th St. and Independence Ave., SW, Wash., D.C. 20250-0001. (202) 382-9619.

Food Safety and Inspection Service: Director, Regulations Office, Food Safety and Inspection Service, Department of Agriculture, Room 2940, South Agriculture Bldg., 14th St. and Independence Ave., SW, Wash., D.C. 20250-0001. (202) 447-3317.

Rural Electrification Administration: Environmental Policy Specialist, Engineering Standards Division, Rural Electrification Administration, Department of Agriculture, Room 1257, South Agriculture Bldg., 14th St. and Independence Ave., SW, Wash., D.C. 20250-0001. (202) 382-0097.

Soil Conservation Service: National Environmental Coordinator, Environmental Activities Branch, Ecological Sciences Division, Soil Conservation Service, Department of Agriculture, Room 6155, South Agriculture Bldg., P.O. Box 2890, Wash., D.C. 20013-2890. (202) 447-4912.

U.S. Forest Service

For actions of national or inter-regional scope, send comment request and documents to Wash., D.C. For actions of a regional, State or local scope, send comment request and documents to the Regional Forester and Area Director in whose area the proposed action (e.g., highway or water resource construction project) will take place.

Director, Environmental Coordination Staff, Forest Service, Department of Agriculture, Room 4204, South Agriculture Bldg., P.O. Box 2417, Wash., D.C. 20013-2417. (202) 447-4708.

Region 1, Northern Region (northern ID, MT, ND, and northwest SD): Regional Forester, Northern Region, Forest Service, USDA, Federal Bldg., P.O. Box 7669, Missoula, MT 59807-7669. (406) 329-3011; (FTS) 585-3316.

Region 2, Rocky Mountain Region (CO, KS, NE, SD, and eastern WY): Regional Forester, Rocky Mountain Region, Forest Service, USDA, 11177 W. 8th Ave., Box 25127, Lakewood, CO 80225-0127. (303) 234-3711.

Region 3, Southwestern Region (AZ, and NM): Regional Forester, Southwestern Region, Forest Service, USDA, Federal Bldg., 517 Gold Ave., SW, Albuquerque, NM 87102-3156. (505) 476-3300.

Region 4, Intermountain Region (southern ID, NV, UT, and western WY): Regional Forester, Intermountain Region, Forest Service, USDA, Federal Bldg., 324 25th St., Ogden, UT 84401-2310. (801) 625-5605; (FTS) 586-5605.

Region 5, Pacific Southwest Region (CA and HI): Regional Forester, Pacific Southwest Region, Forest Service, USDA, 630 Sansome St., San Francisco, CA 94111-2206. (415) 556-4310.

Region 6, Pacific Northwest Region (OR and WA): Regional Forester, Pacific Northwest Region, Forest Service, USDA, 319 SW Pine St., P.O. Box 3623, Portland, OR 97208-3623. (503) 211-3625; (FTS) 423-3625.

Region 8, Southern Region (AL, AR, FL, GA, KY, LA, MS, NC, OK, SC, TN, TX, VA, PR, and VI): Regional Forester, Southern Region, Forest Service, USDA, 1720 Peachtree Road, NW, Atlanta, GA 30367-9101. (404) 881-4177; (FTS) 257-4177.

Region 9, Eastern Region (CT, DE, IA, IL, IN, MA, MD, ME, MI, MN, MO, NH, NJ, NY, OH, PA, RI, VT, WI, and WV): Regional Forester, Eastern Region, Forest Service, USDA, Henry S. Reuss Federal Plaza, Suite 500, 310 W. Wisconsin Ave., Milwaukee, WI 53203-2211. (414) 291-3693; (FTS) 362-3600.

Region 10, Alaska Region (AK): Regional Forester, Alaska Region, Forest Service, USDA, Federal Office Building, Box 1628, Juneau, AK 99802-1628. (907) 586-7263.

Northeastern State and Private Forestry Area (Same as Region 9, above): Director, Northeastern State and Private Forestry Area, Forest Service, USDA, 370 Reed Road, Broomall, PA 19008-4086. (215) 461-3125; (FTS) 489-3125.

(In Regions 1 through 6, 8 and 10, State and private activities of the Forest Service are handled at regional offices.)

Department of Commerce

Chief, Ecology and Conservation Division, Office of Policy and Planning, National Oceanic and Atmospheric Administration, Department of Commerce, Room H6111, Herbert Hoover Bldg., 14th St. and Constitution Ave., NW, Wash., D.C. 20230-0001. (202) 377-5181.

Department of Defense

Send comment request and documents about legislation, regulations, national program proposals or other major policy issues to Department of Defense, except for the Corps of Engineers. For other comment requests, send to the listed office of the departmental components.

Director, Environmental Policy, Office of the Assistant Secretary of Defense (Manpower, Installations and Statistics), Department of Defense, Room 3D833, The Pentagon, Wash., D.C. 20301-0001. (202) 695-7820.

Department of Defense Components

Defense Logistics Agency: Staff Director, Office of Installation Services and Environmental Protection, Defense Logistics Agency, Department of Defense, Cameron Station, Room 4D446, Alexandria, VA 22304-6100. (202) 274-6124.

Department of the Air Force: Deputy for Environment and Safety; Office of the Deputy Assistant Secretary for Installations, Environment and Safety; Department of the Air Force, Room 4C916, The Pentagon, Wash., D.C. 20330-0001. (202) 697-9297.

Department of the Army: Chief, Army Environmental Office; Attn: HQDA (DAEN-ZCE); Department of the Army, Room 1E676, The Pentagon, Wash., D.C. 20310-2600. (202) 694-3434.

Department of the Navy: Director, Environmental Protection and Occupational Safety and Health Division (OP-453), Office of the Chief of Naval Operations, Department of the Navy, Bldg. 200, Room S-3, Washington Navy Yard, Wash., D.C. 20374-0001. (202) 433-2426.

U.S. Marine Corps: Head, Land Resources and Environmental Branch, Code: LFL, U.S. Marine Corps, Commonwealth Bldg., Room 614, 1300 Wilson Blvd., Arlington, VA. (202) 694–9237/38. MAILING ADDRESS: Commandant, U.S. Marine Corps; ATTN: Land Resources and Environmental Branch, Code: LFL; Wash., D.C. 20380–0001.

Corps of Engineers

Send comment request and documents about legislation, regulations, national program proposals or other major policy issues to:

Assistant Director of Civil Works, Environmental Programs (DAEN–CWZ–P), Office of the Chief of Engineers, Room 7233, Pulaski Bldg., 20 Massachusetts Ave., NW, Wash., D.C. 20314–1000. (202) 272–0103.

Send comment request and documents for other Federal actions to the Corps' District Engineer or the Division Engineer, in the case of Pacific Ocean and New England Division, in whose area the action will take place. If the action involves more than one Corps District, increase number of copies accordingly but send all to District Engineer primarily involved. For a map showing the Corps' Division and District Boundaries, contact the Director of Civil Works cited above.

• Division Engineer, U.S. Army Corps of Engineers, New England Division, 424 Trapelo Rd., Waltham, MA 02254–9194. (617) 647–8220; (FTS) 839–7220.
• District Engineer, U.S. Army Corps of Engineers, New York District, 26 Federal Plaza, New York, NY 10278–0022. (212) 264–0100.
• District Engineer, U.S. Army Corps of Engineers, Philadephia District, U.S. Custom House, 2nd and Chestnut Sts., Philadelphia, PA 19106–2912. (215) 597–4848.
• District Engineer, U.S. Army Corps of Engineers, Baltimore District, P.O. Box 1715, Baltimore MD 21203–1715. (301) 962–4545; (FTS) 922–4545.
• District Engineer, U.S. Army Corps of Engineers, Norfolk District, 803 Front St., Norfolk, VA 23510–1096. (804) 441–3601; (FTS) 827–3601.
• District Engineer, U.S. Army Corps of Engineers, Wilmington District, P.O. Box 1890, Wilmington, NC 28402–1890. (919) 343–4501; (FTS) 671–4501.
• District Engineer, U.S. Army Corps of Engineers, Charleston District, P.O. Box 919, Charleston, SC 29402–0919. (803) 724–4229; (FTS) 677–4229.
• District Engineer, U.S. Army Corps of Engineers, Savannah District, P.O. Box 889, Savannah, GA 31402–0889. (912) 944–5224; (FTS) 248–5224.
• District Engineer, U.S. Army Corps of Engineers, Jacksonville District, P.O. Box 4970, Jacksonville, FL 32201–4970. (904). 791–2241; (FTS) 946–2241.
• District Engineer, U.S. Army Corps of Engineers, Mobile District, P.O. Box 2288, Mobile, AL 26628–0001. (205) 690–2511; (FTS) 537–2511.
• District Engineer, U.S. Army Corps of Engineers, Vicksburg District, P.O. Box 60, Vicksburg, MS 39180–0060. (601) 634–5010; (FTS) 542–5010.
• District Engineer, U.S. Army Corps of Engineers, New Orleans District, P.O. Box 60267, New Orleans, LA 70160–0267. (504) 838–2204.
• District Engineer, U.S. Army Corps of Engineers, Memphis District, B–314 Clifford Davis Federal Bldg., Memphis, TN 38103–1816. (901) 521–3221; (FTS) 222–3221.
• District Engineer, U.S. Army Corps of Engineers, St. Louis District, 210 Tucker Blvd. North, St. Louis, MO 63101–1947. (314) 263–5660; (FTS) 273–5660.
• District Engineer, U.S. Army Corps of Engineers, Nashville District, P.O. Box 1070, Nashville, TN 37202–1070. (615) 251–5626; (FTS) 852–5626.
• District Engineer, U.S. Army Corps of Engineers, Louisville District, P.O. Box 59, Louisville, KY 40201–0059. (502) 582–5601; (FTS) 352–5601.
• District Engineer, U.S. Army Corps of Engineers, Huntington District, 502 8th St., Huntington, WV 25701–2070. (304) 529–5395; (FTS) 942–5395.
• District Engineer, U.S. Army Corps of Engineers, Pittsburgh District, William S. Moorehead Federal Bldg., 1000 Liberty Ave., Pittsburgh, PA 15222–4004. (412) 644–6800; (FTS) 722–6800.
• District Engineer, U.S. Army Corps of Engineers, Buffalo District, 1776 Niagara St. Buffalo, NY 14207–3199. (716) 876–5454, x2200; (FTS) 473–2200.
• District Engineer, U.S. Army Corps of Engineers, Chicago District, 219 S. Dearborn St., Chicago, IL 60604–1702. (312) 353–6400.
• District Engineer, U.S. Army Corps of Engineers, Rock Island District, Clock Tower Bldg., P.O. Box 2004, Rock Island, IL 61204–2004. (309) 788–6361, x6224; (FTS) 386–6011.
• District Engineer, U.S. Army Corps of Engineers, Detroit District, P.O. Box 1027, Detroit, MI 48231–1027. (313) 226–6762.
• District Engineer, U.S. Army Corps of Engineers, St. Paul District, 1135 USPO & Custom House, St. Paul, MN 55101–1479. (612) 725–7501.
• District Engineer, U.S. Army Corps of Engineers, Kansas City District, 700 Federal Bldg., 601 E. 12th St., Kansas City, MO 64106–2826. (816) 374–3201; (FTS) 758–3201.
• District Engineer, U.S. Army Corps of Engineers, Omaha District. 6014 USPO and Courthouse, Omaha, NE 68102–4910. (402) 221–3900; (FTS) 864–3900.
• District Engineer, U.S. Army Corps of Engineers, Little Rock District, P.O. Box 867, Little Rock, AR 72203–0867. (501) 378–5531; (FTS) 740–5531.
• District Engineer, U.S. Army Corps of Engineers, Tulsa District, P.O. Box 61, Tulsa, OK 74121–0061. (918) 581–7311; (FTS) 745–7311.
• District Engineer, U.S. Army Corps of Engineers, Galveston District, P.O. Box 1229, Galveston, TX 77553–1229. (409) 766–3006; (FTS) 527–6006.
• District Engineer, U.S. Army Corps of Engineers, Fort Worth District, P.O. Box 17300, Fort Worth, TX 76102–0300. (817) 334–2300.
• District Engineer, U.S. Army Corps of Engineers, Albuquerque District, P.O. Box 1580, Albuquerque, NM 87103–1580. (505) 766–2732; (FTS) 474–2732.
• District Engineer, U.S. Army Corps of Engineers, Los Angeles District, P.O. Box 2711, Los Angeles, CA 90053–2325. (213) 688–5300; (FTS) 798–5300.

• District Engineer, U.S. Army Corps of Engineers, San Francisco District, 211 Main Street, San Francisco, CA 94105–1905. (415) 974–0358; (FTS) 454–0358.
• District Engineer, U.S. Army Corps of Engineers, Sacramento District, 650 Capitol Mall, Sacramento, CA 95814–4708. (916) 440–2232; (FTS) 448–2232.
• District Engineer, U.S. Army Corps of Engineers, Portland District, P.O. Box 2946, Portland, OR 97208–2946. (503) 221–6000; (FTS) 423–6000.
• District Engineer, U.S. Army Corps of Engineers, Walla Walla District, Bldg. 602, City-County Airport, Walla Walla, WA 99362–9265. (509) 525–6509, ext. 100; (FTS) 434–6509.
• District Engineer, U.S. Army Corps of Engineers, Seattle District, P.O. Box C–3755, Seattle, WA 98124–2255. (206) 764–3690; (FTS) 399–3690.
• District Engineer, U.S. Army Corps of Engineers, Alaska District, Pouch 898, Anchorage, AK 99506–0001. (907) 279–1132.
• Division Engineer, U.S. Army Corps of Engineers, Pacific Ocean Division, Building 230, Ft. Shafter, HA. 96858–4910. (808) 438–1500.

Department of Energy

Director, Office of Environmental Compliance (PE–25), Department of Energy, Room 4G–085, Forrestal Building, 1000 Independence Ave., SW, Wash., D.C. 20585–0001. (202) 252–4600.

Department of Health and Human Services

Departmental Environmental Officer, Office of Management Analysis and Systems, Department of Health and Human Services, Room 542 E, Hubert H. Humphrey Bldg., 200 Independence Ave., SW, Wash., D.C. 20201–0001. (202) 245–7354.

Department of Housing and Urban Development

Send comment request and documents about legislation, regulations, national program proposals and other major policy issues to Wash., D.C. Send comment request and documents about other Federal actions to the Regional Environmental Officer in whose area the action will take place.

Director, Office of Environment and Energy, Department of Housing and Urban Development, Room 7154, HUD Bldg., 451 Seventh St., SW, Wash., D.C. 20410–0001. (202) 755–7894.

Federal Region I: Regional Environmental Officer, U.S. Department of Housing and Urban Development, Bulfinch Bldg., 15 New Chardon St., Boston, MA 02114–2598. (617) 223–1620.

Federal Region II: Regional Environmental Officer, U.S. Department of Housing and Urban Development, 26 Federal Plaza, New York, NY 10278–0022. (212) 264–5806.

Federal Region III: Regional Environmental Officer, U.S. Department of Housing and Urban Development, Curtis Building, 148 S. 6th St., Philadelphia, PA 19106–3313. (215) 597–3903.

Federal Region IV: Regional Environmental Officer, U.S. Department of Housing and Urban Development, Richard B. Russell

Federal Bldg., 75 Spring St., SW, Atlanta, GA 30303–3309. (404) 221–5197; (FTS) 242–5197.

Federal Region V: Regional Environmental Officer, U.S. Department of Housing and Urban Development, 300 S. Wacker Dr., Chicago, IL 60606–6606. (312) 353–1696.

Federal Region VI: Regional Environmental Officer, U.S. Department of Housing and Urban Development, 221 W. Lancaster Ave., P.O. Box 2905, Ft. Worth, TX 76113–2905. (817) 870–5482; (FTS) 728–5482.

Federal Region VII: Regional Environmental Officer, U.S. Department of Housing and Urban Development, Professional Bldg., 1103 Grand Ave., Kansas City, MO 64106–2496. (816) 374–3192; (FTS) 758–3192.

Federal Region VIII: Regional Environmental Officer, U.S. Department of Housing and Urban Development, Executive Tower Bldg., 1405 Curtis St., Denver, CO 80202–2394. (303) 837–3102; (FTS) 327–3102.

Federal Region IX: Regional Environmental Officer, U.S. Department of Housing and Urban Development, 450 Golden Gate Ave., P.O. Box 36003, San Francisco, CA 94102–3448. (415) 556–6642.

Federal Region X: Regional Environmental Officer, U.S. Department of Housing and Urban Development, 3051 Arcade Plaza Building, 1321 Second Ave., Seattle, WA 98101–2058. (206) 442–4521; (FTS) 399–4521.

Department of the Interior

Director, Office of Environmental Project Review, Department of the Interior, Room 4241, Interior Bldg., 18th and C Sts., NW, Wash., D.C. 20240–0001. (202) 343–3891.

Department of Labor

Director, Office of Regulatory Economics, Assistant Secretary for Policy, Department of Labor, Room S–2312, Frances Perkins Bldg., 200 Constitution Ave., NW, Wash., D.C. 20210–0001. (202) 523–6197.

Department of State

Director, Office of Environment and Health, Department of State, Room 4325, State Department Bldg., 21st and C Sts., NW, Wash., D.C. 20520–0001. (202) 632–9266.

Department of Transportation

For documents about legislation, regulations, national program proposals and any action with national policy implications, send comment request and documents to DOT's Office of Economics shown below. For an action which may involve more than one modal administration within DOT, send comment request and documents to the DOT Regional Secretarial Representative in whose area the action will take place. If the action involves more than one region, send request to each Regional Secretarial Representative (DOT will coordinate to provide a consolidated response). For an action which may involve only one modal administration, send comment request and documents to the regional office of the modal administration in whose area the action will take place but, if in doubt, send material to DOT's Regional Secretarial Representative.

Deputy Director for Environment and Policy Review, Office of Economics, Department of Transportation, Room 10309,

Nassif Bldg., 400 Seventh St., SW, Wash., D.C. 20590–0001. (202) 426–4357.

DOT Regional Secretarial Representatives

Federal Regions I, II and III: Secretarial Representative, U.S. Department of Transportation, Independence Bldg., Suite 1000, 430 Walnut St., Philadelphia, PA 19106–3714. (215) 597–9430.

Federal Region IV: Secretarial Representative, U.S. Department of Transportation, Suite 515, 1720 Peachtree Rd., NW, Atlanta, GA 30309–2405. (404) 881–3738; (FTS) 257–3738.

Federal Region V: Secretarial Representative, U.S. Department of Transportation, Room 700, 300 S. Wacker Dr., Chicago, IL 60606–6607. (312) 353–4000.

Federal Region VI: Secretarial Representative, U.S. Department of Transportation, Room 7A29, 819 Taylor St., Fort Worth, TX 76102–6114. (817) 334–2725.

Federal Regions VII and VIII: Secretarial Representative, U.S. Department of Transportation, Room 634, 601 E. 12th St., Room 634, Kansas City, MO 64106–2879. (816) 374–5801; (FTS) 758–5801.

Federal Regions IX and X: Secretarial Representative, U.S. Department of Transportation, Room 1005, 211 Main St., San Francisco, CA 94105–1924. (415) 974–8464; (FTS) 454–8464.

Federal Aviation Administration

New England Region (CT, ME, MA, NH, RI, and VT): Regional Director, Federal Aviation Administration, 12 New England Executive Park, P.O. Box 510, Burlington, MA 01803–0933. (617) 273–7244; (FTS) 836–1244.

Eastern Region (DE, DC, MD, NJ, NY, PA, VA, and WV): Regional Director, Federal Aviation Administration, Fitzgerald Building, JFK International Airport, Jamaica, NY 11430–2181. (212) 917–1005; (FTS) 667–1005.

Southern Region (AL, FL, GA, KY, MS, NC, PR, Republic of Panama, SC, and TN): Regional Director, Federal Aviation Administration, P.O. Box 20636, Atlanta, GA 30320–0636. (404) 763–7222; (FTS) 246–7222.

Great Lakes Region (IL, IN, MI, MN, ND, OH, SD, and WI): Regional Director, Federal Aviation Administration, 2300 East Devon Ave., Des Plaines, IL 60018–4686. (312) 694–7294; (FTS) 384–7294.

Southwest Region (AR, LA, NM, OK, and TX): Regional Director, Federal Aviation Administration, P.O. Box 1689, Fort Worth, TX 76101–1689. (817) 877–2100; (FTS) 734–2100.

Central Region (IA, KS, MO, and NE): Regional Director, Federal Aviation Administration, 601 E. 12th St., Kansas City, MO 64106–2894. (816) 374–5626; (FTS) 758–5626.

Western-Pacific Region (AZ, CA, HI, and NV): Regional Director, Federal Aviation Administration, P.O. Box 92007, World Way Postal Center, Los Angeles, CA 90009–2007. (213) 536–6427; (FTS) 966–6427.

Northwest Mountain Region (CO, ID, MT, OR, UT, WA, and WY): Regional Director, Federal Aviation Administration, 17900 Pacific Highway South, Seattle, WA 98168–0966. (206) 431–2001; (FTS) 446–2001.

Alaskan Region (AK): Regional Director, Federal Aviation Administration, P.O. Box 14,

701 C St., Anchorage, AK 99513–0001. (907) 271–5645.

Federal Highway Administration

Federal Regions I and II: Regional Administrator, Federal Highway Administration, 729 Leo W. O'Brien Federal Bldg., Clinton Ave. and N. Pearl St., Albany, NY. 12207–2396. (518) 472–6476; (FTS) 562–6476.

Federal Region III: Regional Administrator, Federal Highway Administration, Room 1633, George H. Fallon Federal Office Building, 31 Hopkins Plaza, Baltimore, MD 21201–2825. (301) 962–0093; (FTS) 922–2773.

Federal Region IV: Regional Administrator, Federal Highway Administration, Suite 200, 1720 Peachtree Road, NW, Atlanta, GA 30309–2405. (404) 881–4078; (FTS) 257–4078.

Federal Region V: Regional Administrator, Federal Highway Administration, 18209 Dixie Highway, Homewood, IL 60430–2205. (312) 799–6300; (FTS) 370–9102.

Federal Region VI: Regional Administrator, Federal Highway Administration, 819 Taylor St., Fort Worth, TX 76102–6187 (817) 334–3908; (FTS) 334–3232.

Federal Region VII: Regional Administrator, Federal Highway Administration, 6301 Rockhill Rd., Kansas City, MO 64131–1117. (816) 926–7563; (FTS) 926–7490.

Federal Region VIII: Regional Administrator, Federal Highway Administration, 555 Zang St., P.O. Box 25246, Denver, CO 80225–0246. (303) 234–4051.

Federal Region IX: Regional Administrator, Federal Highway Administration, 211 Main St., Room 1100, San Francisco, CA 94105–1905. (415) 974–8450; (FTS) 454–8450.

Federal Region X: Regional Administrator, Federal Highway Administration, Room 412, Mohawk Building, 708 S.W. Third St., Portland, OR 97204–2489. (503) 221–2053; (FTS) 423–2065.

Federal Railroad Administration: Director, Office of Economic Analysis (RRP–30), Federal Railroad Administration, Room 8300, Nassif Bldg., 400 Seventh St., SW, Wash., D.C. 20590–0001. (202) 426–7391.

Maritime Administration: Head, Environmental Activities Group (MAR–700.4), Maritime Administration, Room 2120, Nassif Bldg., 400 Seventh St., SW, Wash., D.C. 20590–0001. (202) 426–5739.

National Highway Traffic Safety Administration: Assistant Chief Counsel for General Law, Office of Chief Counsel (NOA–33), National Highway Traffic Safety Administration, Room 5219, Nassif Bldg., 400 Seventh St., SW, Wash., D.C. 20590–0001. (202) 426–1834.

Research and Special Programs Administration (includes Materials Transportation Bureau): Chief, Environmental Technology Division (DTS–48), Research and Special Programs Administration, US-DOT, Transportation Systems Center, Room 3–55, Kendall Square, Cambridge, MA 02142–1001. (617) 494–2018; (FTS) 837–2018.

St. Lawrence Seaway Development Corporation: Deputy Chief Engineer, St. Lawrence Seaway Development Corporation, Seaway Administration Bldg., 180 Andrews

St., P.O. Box 520, Massena, NY 13662–1760. (315) 764–3256; (FTS) 953–0256.

United States Coast Guard: Chief, Environmental Compliance and Review Branch (G–WP–3), Office of Marine Environment and Systems, U.S. Coast Guard, 2100 2nd St., SW, Wash., D.C. 20593–0001. (202) 426–3300.

District I (MA, ME, NH, RI, and eastern VT): Commander, First Coast Guard District, 150 Causeway St., Boston, MA 02114–1391. (617) 223–3603; (FTS) 223–3644.

District II (Northern AL, AR, CO, IL, IN, KY, KS, MN, MO, northern MS, ND, NE, OH, OK, western PA, SD, TN, WI, WV, and WY (except Great Lakes Area): Commander, Second Coast Guard District, 1430 Olive St., St. Louis, MO 63103–2398. (314) 425–4601; (FTS) 279–4601.

District III (CT, DE, NJ, eastern NY, eastern PA, and western VT): Commander, Third Coast Guard District, Governors Island, New York, NY 10004–5000. (212) 668–7196; (FTS) 664–7196.

District V (DC, MD, NC, and VA): Commander, Fifth Coast Guard District, Federal Bldg., 431 Crawford St., Portsmouth, VA 23704–5000. (804) 398–6000; (FTS) 827–9000.

District VII (Eastern FL, eastern GA, PR, SC, and VI): Commander, Seventh Coast Guard District, Room 1018, Federal Bldg., 51 SW 1st Ave., Miami, FL 33130–1608. (305) 350–5654.

District VIII (Southern AL, western FL, western GA, LA, southern MS, NM, and TX): Commander, Eighth Coast Guard District, Hale Boggs Federal Bldg., 500 Camp St., New Orleans, LA 70130–3313. (504) 589–6298; (FTS) 682–6298.

District IX (Great Lakes Area): Commander, Ninth Coast Guard District, 1240 E. 9th St., Cleveland, OH 44199–2060. (216) 522–3910; (FTS) 293–3910.

District XI (AZ, southern CA, southern NV, and southern UT): Commander, Eleventh Coast Guard District, Union Bank Bldg., 400 Oceangate Blvd., Long Beach, CA 90822–5399. (213) 590–2311; (FTS) 984–9311.

District XII (northern CA, northern NV, and northern UT): Commander, Twelfth Coast Guard District, Government Island, Alameda, CA 94501–9991. (415) 437–3196; (FTS) 536–3196.

District XIII (ID, MT, OR, and WA): Commander, Thirteenth Coast Guard District, Federal Bldg., 915 2nd Ave., Seattle, WA 98174–1001. (206) 442–5078; (FTS) 399–5078.

District XIV (AS, GU, HI, and TP): Commander, Fourteenth Coast Guard District, 9th Floor Prince Kalanianaole Federal Bldg., 300 Ala Moana Blvd., Honolulu, HI 96813–4982. (808) 546–5531.

District XVII (AK): Commander, Seventeenth Coast Guard District, P.O. Box 3–5000, Juneau, AK 99802–1217. (907) 586–2680.

Urban Mass Transportation Administration

Federal Region I: Regional Administrator, Urban Mass Transportation Administration, Transportation Systems Center, Room 921 55 Broadway, Cambridge, MA 02142–1001. (617) 494–2055; (FTS) 837–2055.

Federal Region II: Regional Administrator, Urban Mass Transportation Administration, 26 Federal Plaza, Suite 14–110, New York, NY 10278–0022. (212) 264–8162.

Federal Region III: Regional Administrator, Urban Mass Transportation Administration, Suite 1010, 434 Walnut St., Philadelphia, PA 19106–3790. (215) 597–8098.

Federal Region IV: Regional Administrator, Urban Mass Transportation Administration, Suite 400, 1720 Peachtree Road, NW, Atlanta, GA 30309–2472. (404) 881–3948; (FTS) 257–3948.

Federal Region V: Regional Administrator, Urban Mass Transportation Administration, Suite 1720, 300 S. Wacker Dr., Chicago, IL 60606–6755. (312) 353–2789.

Federal Region VI: Regional Administrator, Urban Mass Transportation Administration, Suite 9A32, 819 Taylor St., Dallas, TX 76102–6160. (817) 334–3787.

Federal Region VII: Regional Administrator, Urban Mass Transportation Administration, Suite 100, 6301 Rockhill, Rd., Kansas City, MO 64131–1117. (816) 926–5053.

Federal Region VIII: Regional Administrator, Urban Mass Transportation Administration, Prudential Plaza, Suite 1822, 1050 17th Street, Denver, CO 80265–1896. (303) 837–3242; (FTS) 327–3242.

Federal Region IX: Regional Administrator, Urban Mass Transportation, Room 1160, 211 Main St., San Francisco, CA 94105–1971. (415) 974–7313; (FTS) 454–7313.

Federal Region X: Regional Administrator, Urban Mass Transportation Administration, Suite 3142, 915 Second Avenue, Seattle, WA 98174–1001. (206) 442–4210; (FTS) 399–4210.

Department of Treasury

Manager, Environmental Quality, Physical Security and Safety Division, Department of the Treasury, Room 800, Treasury Bldg., 1331 G St., NW, Wash., D.C. 20220–0001. (202) 376–0289.

INDEPENDENT AGENCIES

ACTION

Assistant Director, Office of Policy and Planning, ACTION, Room M–606, 806 Connecticut Ave., NW, Wash., D.C. 20525–0001. (202) 634–9304; WATS #800–424–8580, ext. 81.

Advisory Council on Historic Preservation

Director, Office of Cultural Resource Preservation, Advisory Council on Historic Preservation, Old Post Office Building, Suite 803, 1100 Pennsylvania Ave., NW, Wash., D.C. 20004–2590. (202) 786–0505.

Appalachian Regional Commission

Director, Division of Housing and Community Development, Appalachian Regional Commission, 1666 Connecticut Ave., NW, Wash., D.C. 20235–0001. (202) 673–7845.

Civil Aeronautics Board

Chief, Environmental and Energy Programs (B–60C), Civil Aeronautics Board, Room 909, Universal Bldg., 1825 Connecticut Ave., NW, Wash., D.C. 20428–0001. (202) 426–9622.

Consumer Product Safety Commission

Assistant General Counsel, Office of the General Counsel, Consumer Product Safety Commission, Room 200, 5401 Westbard Ave., Bethesda, MD. (301) 492–6980. MAILING ADDRESS: Washington, D.C. 20207–0001.

Delaware River Basin Commission

Executive Director, Delaware River Basin Commission, 25 State Police Drive, P.O. Box 7360, West Trenton, NJ 08628–0360. (609) 883–9500; (FTS) 483–2077.

Environmental Protection Agency

Send comment request and documents about legislation, regulations, national program proposals and other major policy issues to Wash., D.C. Send comment request and documents about other Federal actions to the Federal Regional Administrator in whose area the action will take place. If the action involves more than one region, increase number of copies accordingly but send to the region primarily involved.

Director, Office of Federal Activities, Environmental Protection Agency, Room 2119–I, 401 M St., SW, Wash., D.C. 20460–0001. (202) 382–5053.

Federal Region I: Regional Administrator, U.S. Environmental Protection Agency, Room 2203, John F. Kennedy Federal Bldg., Boston, MA 02203–0001. (617) 223–7210.

Federal Region II: Regional Administrator, U.S. Environmental Protection Agency, Room 900, 26 Federal Plaza, New York, NY. 10278–0014. (212) 264–2525.

Federal Region III: Regional Administrator, U.S. Environmental Protection Agency, Curtis Bldg., 6th and Walnut Sts., Philadelphia, PA 19106–3310. (215) 597–9800.

Federal Region IV: Regional Administrator, U.S. Environmental Protection Agency, 345 Courtland Street, NE, Atlanta, GA 30365–2401. (404) 257–4727.

Federal Region V: Regional Administrator, U.S. Environmental Protection Agency, 230 S. Dearborn St., Chicago, IL 60604–1590. (312) 353–2000.

Federal Region VI: Regional Administrator, U.S. Environmental Protection Agency, 1201 Elm St., Dallas, TX 75270–2180. (214) 767–2600; (FTS) 729–2600.

Federal Region VII: Regional Administrator, U.S. Environmental Protection Agency, 324 E. 11th St., Kansas City. MO 64106–2467. (816) 374–5493; (FTS) 758–5493.

Federal Region VIII: Regional Administrator, U.S. Environmental Protection Agency, Suite 900, Lincoln Tower, 1860 Lincoln Street, Denver, CO 80295–0699. (303) 837–3895; (FTS) 327–3895.

Federal Region IX: Regional Administrator, U.S. Environmental Protection Agency, 215 Freemont St., San Francisco, CA 94105–2399. (415) 974–8153; (FTS) 454–8153.

Federal Region X: Regional Administrator, U.S. Environmental Protection Agency, 1200 Sixth Ave., Seattle, WA 98101–3188. (206) 442–5810; (FTS) 399–5810.

Federal Emergency Management Agency

Associate General Counsel, Federal Emergency Management Agency, Room 840, 500 C St., SW, Wash., D.C. 20472–0001. (202) 287–0387.

Federal Energy Regulatory Commission

Send comment requests and documents about legislation, regulations, national program proposals, major policy issues and Federal actions to:

For electric and hydroelectric matters—Director, Division of Environmental Analysis, Office of Hydropower Licensing, Federal Energy Regulatory Commission, Room 308, Railway Labor Building, 400 First St., NW, Wash., D.C. 20426–0001. (202) 376–1768.

For natural gas matters—Chief, Environmental Evaluation Branch, Office of Pipeline and Producer Regulation, Federal Energy Regulatory Commission, Room 7102A, 825 N. Capitol St., NE, Wash., D.C. 20426–0001. (202) 357–8098.

Federal Maritime Commission

Director, Office of Energy and Environmental Impact, Federal Maritime Commission, 1100 L St., NW, Wash., D.C. 20573–0001. (202) 523–5835.

Federal Trade Commission

Deputy Assistant General Counsel, Federal Trade Commission, Room 582, 6th St. and Pennsylvania Ave., NW, Wash., D.C. 20580–0001. (202) 523–1928.

General Services Administration

Send comment requests and documents about legislation, regulations, national program proposals and other major policy issues to Washington, D.C. Send comment requests and documents about other Federal actions to the regional office having responsibility for the area in which the action will take place.

Director, Environmental Affairs Staff (PRE), Office of Space Management, Public Buildings Service, General Services Administration, Room 2323, 18th and F Sts., NW, Wash., D.C. 20405–0001. (202) 566–0654.

Federal Region I: Chief, Planning Staff (1PEP) Public Buidings and Real Property, General Services Administration, John W. McCormack Post Office and Courthouse, Boston, MA 02109–4559. (617) 223–2707.

Federal Region II: Chief, Planning Staff (2PEP) Public Buildings and Real Property, General Services Administration, 26 Federal Plaza, New York, NY 10278–0022. (212) 264–3544.

Federal Region III: Chief, Planning Staff (3PEP) Public Buildings and Real Property, General Services Administration, 9th and Market Sts., Philadelphia, PA 19107–4269. (215) 597–0268.

Federal Region IV: Chief, Planning Staff (4PEP) Public Buildings and Real Property, General Services Administration, 75 Spring St., SW, Atlanta, GA 30303–3309. (404) 221–3080; (FTS) 242–3080.

Federal Region V: Chief, Planning Staff (5PEP) Public Buildings and Real Property, General Services Administration, 230 S. Dearborn St., Chicago, IL 60604–1602. (312) 353–5610.

Federal Region VI: Chief, Planning Staff (6PEP) Public Buildings and Real Property, General Services Administration, 1500 E.

Bannister Rd., Kansas City, MO 64131–3087. (816) 926–7240.

Federal Region VII: Chief, Planning Staff (7PEP) Public Buildings and Real Property, General Services Administration, 819 Taylor St., Fort Worth, TX 76102–6114. (817) 334–2531.

Federal Region VIII: Chief, Planning Staff (8PEP) Public Buildings and Real Property, General Services Administration, Building 41, Denver Federal Center Lakewood, CO 80225–0001. (303) 776–7244.

Federal Region IX: Chief, Planning Staff (9PEP) Public Buildings and Real Property, General Services Administration, 525 Market St., San Francisco, CA 94105–2708. (415) 974–7623; (FTS) 454–7623.

Federal Region X: Chief, Planning Staff (10PEP) Public Buildings and Real Property, General Services Administration, GSA Center, 1501 G St., SW, Auburn, WA 98001–6599. (206) 931–7265; (FTS) 396–7265.

Federal National Capital Region: Chief, Planning Staff (WPJ) Public Buildings and Real Property, General Services Administration, 7th & D Sts., SW, Wash., D.C. 20407–0001. (202) 472–1479.

International Boundary and Water Commission, United States Section

Principal Engineer, Investigations and Planning Division, International Boundary and Water Commission, United States Section, IBWC Bldg., 4110 Rio Bravo, El Paso, TX 79902–1091. (915) 541–7304; (FTS) 572–7304.

Interstate Commerce Commission

Chief, Section of Energy and Environment, Office of Transportation Analysis, Interstate Commerce Commission, Room 4143, 12th St. and Constitution Ave., NW, Wash., D.C. 20423–0001. (202) 275–0800.

Marine Mammal Commission

General Counsel, Marine Mammal Commission, Room 307, 1625 Eye St., NW, Wash., D.C. 20006–3054. (202) 653–6237.

National Aeronautics and Space Administration

Environmental Compliance Officer, Facilities Engineering Division, National Aeronautics and Space Administration, Code NXG, Room 5031, 400 Maryland Ave., SW, Wash., D.C. 20546–0001. (202) 453–1958.

National Capital Planning Commission

Environmental/Energy Officer, Division of Planning Services, National Capital Planning Commission, Room 1024, 1325 G St., NW, Wash., D.C. 20576–0001. (202) 724–0179.

National Science Foundation

Chairman and Staff Associate, Committee on Environmental Matters; Office of Astronomical, Atmospheric, Earth and Ocean Sciences; National Science Foundation, Room

641, 1800 G St., NW, Wash., D.C. 20550–0001. (202) 357–7615.

Nuclear Regulatory Commission:

Chief, Environmental and Hydrologic Engineering Branch, Division of Engineering, Office of Nuclear Reactor Regulation, Nuclear Regulatory Commission, Room P–312, Phillips Bldg., 7920 Norfolk Ave., Bethesda, MD 20814–2587. (301) 492–7972.

Pennsylvania Avenue Development Corporation

Director of Development, Pennsylvania Avenue Development Corporation, Suite 1248, 425 13th St., NW, Wash., D.C. 20004–1856. (202) 523–5477.

Small Business Administration

Chief, Loan Processing Branch, Office of Business Loans, Small Business Administration, Room 804–B, 1441 L St., NW, Wash., D.C. 20416–0001. (202) 653–6470.

Susquehanna River Basin Commission

Executive Director, Susquehanna River Basin Commission, 1721 N. Front St., Harrisburg, PA. 17102–2391. (717) 238–0422.

Tennessee Valley Authority

Director, Environmental Quality Staff, Tennessee Valley Authority, 201 Summer Place Building, 309 Walnut St., Knoxville, TN 37902–1411. (615) 632–6578; (FTS) 856–6578.

United States Information Agency

Assistant General Counsel, United States Information Agency, 301 Fourth St., SW, Wash., D.C. 20547–0001. (202) 485–7976.

United States International Development Cooperation Agency:

For USAID matters, send to—Environmental Affairs Coordinator, Office of External Affairs, U.S. Agency for International Development, Department of State Bldg., 320 Twenty-First St., NW, Wash., D.C. 20523–0001. (202) 632–8268.

For OPIC matters, send to—International Economist/Environmental Officer, Office of Development, Overseas Private Investment Corporation, 1129 Twentieth St., NW, Wash., D.C. 20527–0001. (202) 653–2904.

United States Postal Service

Director, Office of Program Planning, Real Estate and Building Department, United States Postal Service, Room 4014, 475 L'Enfant Plaza West, SW, Wash., D.C. 20260–6420. (202) 245–4304.

Veterans Administration

Director, Office of Environmental Affairs, Veterans Administration, Code 088C, 810 Vermont Ave., NW, Wash., D.C. 20420–0001. (202) 389–3316.

[FR Doc. 84–32983 Filed 12–20–84; 8:45 am]
BILLING CODE 3125–01–M

Outline of Regulations and Procedures Implementing the National Environmental Policy Act

Council on Environmental Quality: National Environmental Policy Act—Implementation of Procedural Provisions (40 CFR 1500-1508)

    Purpose, Policy and Mandate (40 CFR 1500)
    NEPA and Agency Planning (40 CFR 1501)
    Environmental Impact Statement (40 CFR 1502)
    Commenting (40 CFR 1503)
    Predecision Referrals to the Council of Proposed Federal Actions Determined to be Environmentally Unsatisfactory (40 CFR 1504)
    NEPA and Agency Decisionmaking (40 CFR 1505)
    Other Requirements of NEPA (40 CFR 1506)
    Agency Compliance (40 CFR 1507)
    Terminology (40 CFR 1508)

Current regulations found at: 40 CFR 1500-1508 (1987)

Federal Agency Regulations Implementing NEPA

    Advisory Council on Historic Preservation
    36 CFR 805 (1988)

    Agency for International Development
    22 CFR 216 (1988)

    Department of Agriculture

        Departmental
        7 CFR 1b, 3100 (1988)

        Agricultural Stabilization and Conservation Service
        7 CFR 799 (1988)

        Animal and Plant Health Inspection Service
        44 FR 50381 (8/28/79)

        Forest Service
        Forest Service Manual Chapter 1950
        50 FR 26078 (6/24/85), as amended by:
        52 FR 30935 (8/18/87) (17 ELR 10407; Oct. 1987)
        54 FR 9073 (3/3/89) (19 ELR 10273; May 1989)

        Soil Conservation Service
        7 CFR 650 (1988)

        Rural Electrification Administration
        7 CFR 1794 (1988)

    Arms Control Disarmament Agency
    45 FR 69510 (10/21/80)

    Central Intelligence Agency
    44 FR 45431 (8/2/79)

    Department of Commerce

        Economic Development Administration
        45 FR 63310 (9/24/80), as amended by:
        45 FR 74902 (11/13/80) (10 ELR 10204; Nov. 1980)

        National Oceanic and Atmospheric Administration
        48 FR 14734 (4/5/83)

Consumer Product Safety Commission
16 CFR 1021 (1988)

Department of Defense

    Departmental
    32 CFR 214 (1988)

    Department of the Air Force
    32 CFR 989 (1988)

    Department of the Army
    32 CFR 650, 651 (1988), as amended by:
    53 FR 46322 (11/16/88) (19 ELR 10037; Jan. 1988)

    Army Corps of Engineers
    33 CFR 230 (1988)

    Department of the Navy
    32 CFR 775 (1988)

Delaware River Basin Commission
18 CFR 401, Subpart D (1988)

Department of Energy

    Departmental
    45 FR 20694 (3/28/80), as amended by:
    47 FR 7976 (2/23/82)
    48 FR 685 (1/6/83)
    52 FR 659 (1/7/87)
    52 FR 47662 (12/15/87) (reprinted in entirety)

    Federal Energy Regulatory Commission
    18 CFR 2.80, 380 (1988)

Environmental Protection Agency
40 CFR 6 (1988)

Export-Import Bank
12 CFR 408 (1988)

Federal Communications Commission
47 CFR 1, Subpart I (1988)

Federal Emergency Management Agency
44 CFR 10 (1987)

Federal Maritime Commission
46 CFR 504 (1988)

Federal Trade Commission
16 CFR 1, Subpart I (1988)

General Services Administration
50 FR 7648 (2/25/85)

Department of Health and Human Services

    Departmental
    45 FR 76519 (11/19/80), as amended by:
    47 FR 2414 (1/15/82) (12 ELR 05021; Feb. 1982)

Food and Drug Administration
21 CFR 25 (1988)

Department of Housing and Urban Development

Departmental
24 CFR 50, 51 (1988), as amended by:
53 FR 11224 (4/5/88)

Community Development Block Grant Program
24 CFR 58 (1988), as amended by:
53 FR 30186 (8/10/88)

Department of the Interior

Departmental
Department Manual Part 516
45 FR 27541 (4/23/80), as amended by:
49 FR 21437 (5/21/84) (14 ELR 10286; July 1984)

Bureau of Indian Affairs
46 FR 7490 (1/23/81)

Bureau of Land Management
46 FR 7492 (1/23/81), as amended by:
48 FR 43731 (9/26/83) (13 ELR 10385; Nov. 1983)

Bureau of Mines
45 FR 85528 (12/29/80)

Bureau of Reclamation
45 FR 47944 (7/17/80), as amended by:
48 FR 17151 (4/21/83)

Fish and Wildlife Service
45 FR 47941 (7/17/80), as amended by:
47 FR 28841 (7/1/82) (12 ELR 05095; Aug. 1982)
49 FR 7881 (3/2/84) (14 ELR 10182; Apr. 1984)

Geological Survey
46 FR 7485 (1/23/81)

Minerals Management Service
51 FR 1855 (1/15/86)

National Park Service
46 FR 1042 (1/5/81)

International Boundary and Water Commission
46 FR 44083 (9/2/81)

International Communication Agency
44 FR 45489 (8/2/79)

Interstate Commerce Commission
49 CFR 1105 (1987), as amended by:
54 FR 9822 (3/8/89) (19 ELR 10241; May 1989)

Department of Justice

Departmental
28 CFR 61 (1988)

Bureau of Prisons
28 CFR 61, Appendix A (1988)

Drug Enforcement Administration
28 CFR 61, Appendix B (1988)

Immigration and Naturalization Service
28 CFR 61, Appendix C (1988)

Office of Justice Assistance, Research, and
Statistics
28 CFR 61, Appendix D (1988)

Department of Labor
29 CFR 11 (1988)

Marine Mammal Commission
50 CFR 530 (1988)

National Aeronautics and Space Administration
14 CFR 1216 (1988), as amended by:
53 FR 9759 (3/25/88)

National Capital Planning Commission
44 FR 64923 (11/8/79), as amended by:
46 FR 51327 (10/19/81) (11 ELR 10231; Dec. 1981)
47 FR 51481 (11/15/82) (13 ELR 10028; Jan. 1983)

National Science Foundation
45 CFR 640 (1987)

Nuclear Regulatory Commission
10 CFR 51 (1988), as amended by:
53 FR 13399 (4/25/88)
53 FR 24018 (6/27/88) (18 ELR 10321; Aug. 1988)
53 FR 31651 (8/19/88) (18 ELR 10454; Oct. 1988)
54 FR 15372 (4/18/89) (19 ELR 10276; June 1989)

Overseas Private Investment Corporation
44 FR 51385 (8/31/79)

Pennsylvania Avenue Development Corporation
36 CFR 907 (1988)

Postal Service
39 CFR 775 (1988)

Saint Lawrence Seaway Development Corporation
46 FR 28795 (5/28/81)

Securities and Exchange Commission
17 CFR 200, Subpart K (1988)

Small Business Administration
45 FR 7358 (2/1/80)

Department of State
22 CFR 161 (1988)

Tennessee Valley Authority
45 FR 54511 (8/15/80), as amended by:
47 FR 54586 (12/2/82) (13 ELR 10029; Jan. 1983)
48 FR 19264 (4/28/83) (13 ELR 10193; June 1983)

Department of Transportation

Departmental
44 FR 56420 (10/1/79)

Coast Guard
45 FR 32816 (5/19/80), as amended by:
50 FR 32944 (8/15/85) (15 ELR 10307; Sept. 1985)

Federal Aviation Administration
45 FR 2244 (1/10/80), as amended by:
49 FR 28501 (7/12/84) (14 ELR 10325; Aug. 1984)

Federal Highway Administration
23 CFR 771 (1988)

Federal Railroad Administration
45 FR 40854 (6/16/80)

National Highway Traffic Safety Administration
49 CFR 520 (1987)

Urban Mass Transportation Administration
23 CFR 771 (1988)

Department of the Treasury
45 FR 1828 (1/8/80)

Veterans Administration
38 CFR 26 (1988)

Water Resources Council
18 CFR 707 (1988)

Department of Agriculture
NEPA Regulations
7 C.F.R. Pts. 1b, 3100

PART 1b—NATIONAL ENVIRONMENTAL POLICY ACT

Sec.
1b.1 Purpose.
1b.2 Policy.
1b.3 Categorical exclusions.
1b.4 Exclusion of agencies.

AUTHORITY. National Environmental Policy Act (NEPA), as amended, 42 U.S.C. 4321 et seq.; E.O. 11514, 34 FR 4247, as amended by E.O. 11991, 42 FR 26927; E.O. 12114, 44 FR 1957; 5 U.S.C. 301; 40 CFR 1507.3.

SOURCE: 48 FR 11403, Mar. 18, 1983, unless otherwise noted.

§ 1b.1 Purpose.

(a) This subpart supplements the regulations for implementation of the National Environmental Policy Act (NEPA), for which regulations were published by the Council of Environmental Quality (CEQ) in 40 CFR Parts 1500 through 1508. The subpart incorporates and adopts those regulations.

(b) This subpart sets forth Departmental policy concerning NEPA, establishes categorical exclusions of actions carried out by the Department and its agencies, and sets forth those USDA agencies which are excluded from the requirement to prepare procedures implementing NEPA.

§ 1b.2 Policy.

(a) USDA agencies carry out programs for the purpose of encouraging sufficient and efficient production of food, fiber, and forest products; proper management and conservation of the Nation's natural resources; and the protection of consumers through inspection services. Programs to meet this mission are carried out through research; education; technical and financial assistance to landowners and operators, producers, and consumers; and management of the National Forest System.

(b) All policies and programs of the various USDA agencies shall be planned, developed, and implemented so as to achieve the goals and to follow the procedures declared by NEPA in order to assure responsible stewardship of the environment for present and future generations.

(c) Each USDA agency is responsible for compliance with the provisions of this subpart, the regulations of CEQ, and the provisions of NEPA. Compliance will include the preparation and implementation of specific procedures and processes relating to the programs and activities of the individual agency, as necessary.

(d) The Assistant Secretary, Natural Resources and Environment (NR&E), is responsible for ensuring that agency implementing procedures are consistent with CEQ's NEPA regulations and for coordinating NEPA compliance for the Department (7 CFR 2.19(b)). The Assistant Secretary, through the USDA Natural Resources and Environment Committee, will develop the necessary processes to be used by the Office of the Secretary in reviewing, implementing, and planning its NEPA activities, determinations, and policies.

(e) In connection with the policies and requirements set forth in this subpart, all USDA agencies are responsible for compliance with Executive Order 12114, "Environmental Effects Abroad of Major Federal Actions." Compliance will include the preparation and implementation of specific procedures and processes relative to the programs and activities of the individual agencies, as necessary. Agencies shall consult with the Department of State; the Council on Environmental Quality; and the Assistant Secretary, NR&E, prior to placing procedures and processes in effect.

§ 1b.3 Categorical exclusions.

(a) The following are categories of activities which have been determined not to have a significant individual or cumulative effect on the human environment and are excluded from the preparation of environmental assessment (EA's) or environmental impact statement (EIS's), unless individual agency procedures prescribed otherwise.

(1) Policy development, planning and implementation which relate to routine activities, such as personnel, organizational changes, or similar administrative functions;

(2) Activities which deal solely with the funding of programs, such as program budget proposals, disbursements, and transfer or reprogramming of funds;

(3) Inventories, research activities, and studies, such as resource inventories and routine data collection when such actions are clearly limited in context and intensity;

(4) Educational and informational programs and activities;

(5) Civil and criminal law enforcement and investigative activities;

(6) Activities which are advisory and consultative to other agencies and public and private entities, such as legal counselling and representation;

(7) Activities related to trade representation and market development activities abroad.

(b) Agencies will identify in their own procedures the activities which normally would not require an environmental assessment or environmental impact statement.

(c) Notwithstanding the exclusions listed above and in § 1b.4, or identified in agency procedures, agency heads may determine that circumstances dictate the need for preparation of an EA or EIS for a particular action. Agencies shall continue to scrutinize their activities to determine continued eligibility for categorical exclusion.

§ 1b.4 Exclusion of agencies.

(a) The USDA agencies listed below carry out programs and activities which have been found to have no individual or cumulative effect on the human environment. These agencies are excluded from the requirements to prepare implementing procedures. Actions of these agencies are categorically excluded from the preparation of an EA or EIS unless the agency head determines that an action may have a significant environmental effect.

(1) Agricultural Cooperative Service,
(2) Agricultural Marketing Service,
(3) Extension Service,
(4) Economic Research Service,
(5) Federal Crop Insurance Corporation,
(6) Federal Grain Inspection Service,
(7) Food and Nutrition Service,
(8) Food Safety and Inspection Service,
(9) Foreign Agricultural Service,
(10) Office of Transportation,
(11) Packers and Stockyards Administration,
(12) Statistical Reporting Service,
(13) Office of General Counsel,
(14) Office of Inspector General,
(15) National Agricultural Library.

PART 3100—CULTURAL AND ENVIRONMENTAL QUALITY

Subparts A-B [Reserved]

Subpart C—Enhancement, Protection, and Management of the Cultural Environment

Sec.
3100.40 Purpose.
3100.41 Authorities.
3100.42 Definitions.
3100.43 Policy.
3100.44 Implementation.
3100.45 Direction to agencies.
3100.46 Responsibilities of the Department of Agriculture.

Subparts A-B [Reserved]

Subpart C—Enhancement, Protection and Management of the Cultural Environment

AUTHORITY: Sec. 106, National Historic Preservation Act, as amended (16 U.S.C. 470f); National Environmental Policy Act, as amended (42 U.S.C. 4321 et seq); E.O. 11593, 36 FR 8921, May 13, 1971.

SOURCE: 44 FR 66181, Nov. 19, 1979, unless otherwise noted.

§ 3100.40 Purpose.

(a) This subpart establishes USDA policy regarding the enhancement, protection, and management of the cultural environment.

(b) This subpart establishes procedures for implementing Executive Order 11593, and regulations promulgated by the Advisory Council on Historic Preservation (ACHP) "Protection of Historical and Cultural Properties" in 36 CFR Part 800 as required by § 800.10 of those regulations.

(c) Direction is provided to the agencies of USDA for protection of the cultural environment.

§ 3100.41 Authorities.

These regulations are based upon and implement the following laws, regulations, and Presidential directives:

(a) *Antiquities Act of 1906* (Pub. L. 59-209; 34 Stat. 225; 16 U.S.C. 431 et seq.) which provides for the protection of historic or prehistoric remains or any object of antiquity on Federal lands; establishes criminal sanctions for unauthorized destruction or appropriation of antiquities; and authorizes scientific investigation of antiquities on Federal lands, subject to permit and regulations. Paleontological resources also are considered to fall within the authority of this Act.

(b) *Historic Sites Act of 1935* (Pub. L. 74-292; 49 Stat. 666; 16 U.S.C. 461 et seq.) which authorizes the establishment of National Historic Sites and otherwise authorizes the preservation of properties of national historical or archeological significance; authorizes the designation of National Historic Landmarks; establishes criminal sanctions for violation of regulations pursuant to the Act; authorizes interagency, intergovernmental, and interdisciplinary efforts for the preservation of cultural resources; and other provisions.

(c) *Reservoir Salvage Act of 1960* (Pub. L. 86-521; 74 Stat. 220; 16 U.S.C. 469-469c.) which provides for the recovery and preservation of historical and archeological data, including relics and specimens, that might be lost or destroyed as a result of the construction of dams, reservoirs, and attendant facilities and activities.

(d) *The National Historic Preservation Act of 1966* as amended (16 U.S.C. 470), which establishes positive national policy for the preservation of the cultural environment, and sets forth a mandate for protection in section 106. The purpose of section 106 is to protect properties on or eligible for the National Register of Historic Places through review and comment by the ACHP of Federal undertakings that affect such properties. Properties are listed on the National Register or declared eligible for listing by the Secretary of the Interior. As developed through the ACHP's regulations, section 106 establishes a public interest process in which the Federal agency proposing an undertaking, the State Historic Preservation Officer, the ACHP, interested organizations and individuals participate. The process is designed to insure that properties, impacts on them, and effects to them are identified, and that alternatives to avoid or mitigate an adverse effect on property eligible for the National Register are adequately considered in the planning process.

(e) *The National Environmental Policy Act of 1969* (NEPA) (Pub. L. 91-190; 83 Stat. 852; 42 U.S.C. 4321 et seq.) which declares that it is the policy of the Federal Government to preserve important historic, cultural, and natural aspects of our national heritage. Compliance with NEPA requires consideration of all environmental concerns during project planning and execution.

(f) *Executive Order 11593, "Protection and Enhancement of the Cultural Environment"*, which gives the Federal Government the responsibility for stewardship of our nation's heritage resources and charges Federal agencies with the task of inventorying historic and prehistoric sites on their lands. E.O. 11593 also charges agencies with the task of identifying and nominating all historic properties under their jurisdiction, and exercising caution to insure that they are not transferred, sold, demolished, or substantially altered.

(g) *Historical and Archeological Data Preservation Act of 1974.* (Pub. L. 93-291; 88 Stat. 174.) which amends the Reservoir Salvage Act of 1960 to extend its provisions beyond the construction of dams to any alteration of the terrain caused as a result of any Federal construction project or federally licensed activity or program. In addition, the Act provides a mechanism for funding the protection of historical and archeological data.

(h) *Presidential memorandum of July 12, 1978, "Environmental Quality and Water Resource Management"* which directs the ACHP to publish final regulations, implementing section 106 of the National Historic Preservation Act (NHPA), and further directs each agency with water and related land resources responsibilities to publish procedures implementing those regulations.

(i) *36 CFR Part 800, "Protection of Historic and Cultural Properties"* which establishes procedures for the implementation of section 106 of the NHPA, and directs publication of agency implementing procedures.

(j) *Land use policy of the USDA (Secretary's Memorandum No. 1827 Revised, with Supplement)* which establishes a commitment by the Department to the preservation of farms, rural communities, and rural landscapes.

(k) *Public Buildings Cooperative Use Act of 1976 (40 U.S.C. 611) and Executive Order 12072 (Federal Space Management).* The Act encourages adaptive use of historic buildings as administrative facilities for Federal agencies and activities; the Executive Order directs Federal agencies to locate administrative and other facilities in central business districts.

(l) *American Indian Religious Freedom Act of 1978 (42 U.S.C. 1996)* which declares it to be the policy of the United States to protect and preserve for American Indians their inherent right of freedom to believe, express, and exercise the traditional religions of the American Indian, Eskimo, Aleut, and Native Hawaiians.

§ 3100.42 Definitions.

All definitions are those which appear in 36 CFR Part 800. In addition, the following apply in this rule:

Cultural resources (heritage resources) are the remains or records of districts, sites, structures, buildings, networks, neighborhoods, objects, and events from the past. They may be historic, prehistoric, archeological, or architectural in nature. Cultural resources are an irreplaceable and nonrenewable aspect of our national heritage.

Cultural environment is that portion of the environment which includes reminders of the rich historic and prehistoric past of our nation.

§ 3100.43 Policy.

(a) The nonrenewable cultural environment of our country constitutes a valuable and treasured portion of the national heritage of the American people. The Department of Agriculture is committed to the management—identification, protection, preservation, interpretation, evaluation and nomination—of our prehistoric and historic cultural resources for the benefit of all people of this and future generations.

(b) The Department supports the cultural resource goals expressed in Federal legislation. Executive orders, and regulations.

(c) The Department supports the preservation and protection of farms, rural landscapes, and rural communities.

(d) The Department is committed to consideration of the needs of American Indians, Eskimo, Aleut, and Native Hawaiians in the practice of their traditional religions.

(e) The Department will aggressively implement these policies to meet goals for the positive management of the cultural environment.

§ 3100.44 Implementation.

(a) It is the intent of the Department to carry out its program of management of the cultural environment in the most effective and efficient manner possible. Implementation must consider natural resource utilization, must exemplify good government, and must constitute a noninflationary approach which makes the best use of tax dollars.

(b) The commitment to cultural resource protection is vital. That commitment will be balanced with the multiple-departmental goals of food and fiber production, environmental protection, natural resource and energy conservation, and rural development. It is essential that all of these be managed to reduce conflicts between programs. Positive management of the cultural environment can contribute to achieving better land use, protection of rural communities and farm lands, conservation of energy, and more efficient use of resources.

(c) In reaching decisions, the long-term needs of society and the irreversible nature of an action must be considered. The Department must act to preserve future options; loss of important cultural resources must be avoided except in the face of overriding national interest where there are no reasonable alternatives.

(d) To assure the protection of Native American religious practices, traditional religious leaders and other native leaders (or their representatives) should be consulted about potential conflict areas in the management of the cultural environment and the means to reduce or eliminate such conflicts.

§ 3100.45 Direction to agencies.

(a) Each agency of the Department shall consult with OEQ to determine whether its programs and activities may affect the cultural environment. Then, if needed, the agency, in consultation with the OEQ, shall develop its own specific procedures for implementing section 106 of the National Historic Preservation Act, Executive Order 11593, the regulations of the ACHP (36 CFR Part 800), the American Indian Religious Freedom Act of 1978 and other relevant legislation and regulations in accordance with the agency's programs, mission and authorities. Such implementing procedures shall be published as proposed and final procedures in the FEDERAL REGISTER, and must be consistent with the requirements of 36 CFR Part 800 and this subpart. Where applicable, each agency's procedures must contain mechanisms to insure:

(1) Compliance with section 106 of NHPA and mitigation of adverse effects to cultural properties on or eligible for the National Register of Historic Places;

(2) Clear definition of the kind and variety of sites and properties which should be managed;

(3) Development of a long-term program of management of the cultural environment on lands administered by USDA as well as direction for project-specific protection;

(4) Identification of all properties listed on or eligible for listing in the National Register that may be affected directly or indirectly by a proposed activity;

(5) Location, identification and nomination to the Register of all sites, buildings, objects, districts, neighborhoods, and networks under its management which appear to qualify (in compliance with E.O. 11593);

(6) The exercise of caution to assure that properties managed by USDA which may qualify for nomination are not transferred, sold, demolished, or substantially altered;

(7) Early consultation with, and involvement of, the State Historic Preservation Officer(s), the ACHP, Native American traditional religious leaders and appropriate tribal leaders, and others with appropriate interests or expertise;

(8) Early notification to insure substantive and meaningful involvement by the public in the agency's decision-making process as it relates to the cultural environment;

(9) Identification and consideration of alternatives to a proposed undertaking that would mitigate or minimize adverse effects to a property identified under paragraph (a)(4) of this section;

(10) Funding of mitigation measures where required to minimize the potential for adverse effects on the cultural environment. Funds for mitigation shall be available and shall be spent when needed during the life of the project to mitigate the expected loss; and

(11) Development of plans to provide for the management, protection, maintenance and/or restoration of Register sites under its management.

(b) Each agency of the Department which conducts programs or activities that may have an effect on the cultural environment shall recruit, place, develop, or otherwise have available, professional expertise in anthropology, archeology, history, historic preservation, historic architecture, and/or cultural resource management (depending upon specific need). Such arrangements may include internal hiring, Intergovernmental Personnel Act assignments, memoranda of agreement with other agencies or Departments, or other mechanisms which insure a professionally directed program. Agencies should use Department of the Interior professional standards (36 CFR 61.5) as guidelines to insure Departmentwide competence and consistency.

(c) Compliance with cultural resource legislation is the responsibility of each individual agency. Consideration of cultural resource values must begin during the earliest planning stages of any undertaking.

(d) Agency heads shall insure that cultural resource management activities meet professional standards as promulgated by the Department of the Interior (e.g., 36 CFR Parts 60, 63, 66, 1208).

(e) Cultural resource review requirements and compliance with section 106 of NHPA and Executive Order 11593 shall be integrated and run concurrently, rather than consecutively, with the other environmental considerations under NEPA regulations. As such, direct and indirect impacts on cultural resources must be addressed in the environmental assessment for every agency undertaking. In meeting these requirements, agencies shall be guided by regulations implementing the procedural provisions of NEPA (40 CFR Parts 1500-1508) and Department of Agriculture regulations (7 CFR Part 3100, Subpart B).

(f) Each agency shall work closely with the appropriate State Historic Preservation Officer(s) in their preparation of State plans, determination of inventory needs, and collection of data relevant to general plans or specific undertakings in carrying out mutual cultural resource responsibilities.

(g) Each agency shall, to the maximum extent possible, use existing historic structures for administrative purposes in compliance with Public Buildings Cooperative Use Act of 1976 and Executive Order 12072, "Federal Space Management".

(h) Each agency should consult with Native American traditional religious leaders or their representatives and other native leaders in the development and implementation of cultural resource programs which may affect their religious customs and practices.

§ 3100.46 Responsibilities of the Department of Agriculture.

(a) Within the Department, the responsibility for the protection of the cultural environment is assigned to the Office of Environmental Quality (OEQ). The Office is responsible for reviewing the development and implementation of agency procedures and insuring Departmental commitment to cultural resource goals.

(b) The Director of the OEQ is the Secretary's Designee to the ACHP.

(c) In order to carry out cultural resource responsibilities, there will be professional expertise within the OEQ to advise agencies, aid the Department in meeting its cultural resource management goals, and to insure that all Departmental and agency undertakings comply with applicable cultural resource protection legislation and regulations.

(d) The OEQ will be involved in individual compliance cases only where resolution cannot be reached at the agency level. Prior to the decision to refer a matter to the full Council of the ACHP, the OEQ will review the case and make recommendations to the Secretary regarding the position of the Department. The agency also will consult with the OEQ before reaching a final decision in response to the Council's comments. Copies of correspondence relevant to compliance with Section 106 shall be made available to OEQ.

Army Corps of Engineers
NEPA Regulations
53 Fed. Reg. 3127 (Feb. 3, 1988)

PART 230—PROCEDURES FOR IMPLEMENTING NEPA

Authority: National Environmental Policy Act (NEPA) (42 U.S.C. 4321 et seq.); E.O. 1514, Protection and Enhancement of Environmental Quality, March 5, 1970, as amended by E.O. 11991, May 24, 1977; and CEQ Regulations Implementing the Procedural Provisions of NEPA (40 CFR 1507.3).

§ 230.1   Purpose.

This regulation provides guidance for implementation of the procedural provisions of the National Environmental Policy Act (NEPA) for the Civil Works Program of the U.S. Army Corps of Engineers. It supplements Council on Environmental Quality (CEQ) regulations 40 CFR Parts 1500 through 1508, November 29, 1978, in accordance with 40 CFR 1507.3, and is intended to be used only in conjunction with the CEQ regulations. Whenever the guidance in this regulation is unclear or not specific the reader is referred to the CEQ regulations. Appendix A provides guidance on processing NEPA documents except for those concerning regulatory actions. Appendix C (formally ER 200–2–1) has been added to provide guidance on preparing and processing a notice of intent to prepare an EIS for publication in the **Federal Register** for all types of Corps actions. 33 CFR Part 325, Appendix B provides procedural guidance for preparing and processing NEPA documents for regulatory actions.

§ 230.2   Applicability.

This regulation is applicable to all HQUSACE elements and all Field Operating Activities (FOAs) having responsibility for preparing and processing environmental documents in support of Civil Works functions.

§ 230.3   References.

(a) Executive Order 12291, Federal Regulation, February 17, 1981 (46 FR 13193, February 19, 1981).

(b) Executive Order 12114, Environmental Effects Abroad of Major Federal Actions, January 4, 1979 (44 FR 1957, January 9, 1979).

(c) Clean Water Act (formerly known as the Federal Water Pollution Control Act) 33 U.S.C. 1344 (hereinafter referred to as section 404).

(d) Endangered Species Act of 1973, as amended, 16 U.S.C. 1531 et seq.

(e) Environmental Effects Abroad of Major Department of Defense Actions; Policies and Procedures 32 CFR Part 197 (44 FR 21786–92, April 12, 1979).

(f) Fish and Wildlife Coordination Act, 16 U.S.C. 661 et seq.

(g) National Environmental Policy Act of 1969, as amended, 42 U.S.C. 4321 et seq.

(h) National Historic Preservation Act of 1966, as amended, 16 U.S.C. 470 et seq.

(i) "Regulations for Implementing the Procedural Provisions of the National Environmental Policy Act of 1969," (40 CFR Parts 1500 through 1508, November 29, 1978), Council on Environmental Quality.

(j) Economic and Environmental Principles and Guidelines for Water and Related Land Resource Implementation Studies (48 CFR Parts 10249 through 10258, March 10, 1983).

(k) Regulatory Programs of the Corps of Engineers 33 CFR Parts 320 through 330, and 334.

(l) CEQ Information Memorandum to Agencies Containing Answers to 40 Most Asked Questions on NEPA Regulations (46 FR 34263–68, July 28, 1983).

(m) ER 310–1–5. Federal Register Act Requisitioning.

(n) ER 1105–2–10 thru 60. Planning Regulations.

§ 230.4   Definitions.

Refer to 40 CFR Part 1508; other definitions may be found in the references given above.

§ 230.5   Responsible officials.

The district commander is the Corps NEPA official responsible for compliance with NEPA for actions within district boundaries. The district commander also provides agency views on other agencies' environmental impact statements (EIS). The Office of Environmental Policy HQUSACE (CECW–RE) WASH DC 20314–1000 (phone number 202–272–0166) is the point of contact for information on Corps NEPA documents, NEPA oversight activities, review of other agencies' EISs and NEPA documents about legislation, regulations, national program proposals or other major policy issues. The Assistant Chief Counsel for Environmental Law and Regulatory Programs, HQUSACE (CECC–E) WASH DC 20314–1000, is the point of contact for legal questions involving environmental matters. Requests for information on regulatory permit actions should be directed to HQUSACE (CECW–OR) WASH DC 20314–1000.

§ 230.6   Actions normally requiring an EIS.

Actions normally requiring an EIS are:

(a) Feasibility reports for authorization and construction of major projects;

(b) Proposed changes in projects which increase size substantially or add additional purposes; and

(c) Proposed major changes in the operation and/or maintenance of completed projects.

District commanders may consider the use of an environmental assessment (EA) on these types of actions if early studies and coordination show that a particular action is not likely to have a significant impact on the quality of the human environment.

§ 230.7   Actions normally requiring an Environmental Assessment (EA) but not necessarily an EIS.

Actions normally requiring an EA, but not an EIS, are listed below:

(a) *Regulatory Actions.* Most permits will normally require only an EA.

(b) *Authorized Projects and Projects Under Construction.* Changes which may be approved under the discretionary authority of the Secretary of the Army.

(c) *Continuing Authorities Program.*

Projects recommended for approval of the Chief of Engineers under the following authorities:

(1) Section 205, Small Flood Control Authority;

(2) Section 208, Snagging and Clearing for Flood Control Authority;

(3) Section 107, Small Navigation Project Authority;

(4) Section 103, Small Beach Erosion Control Project Authority; and

(5) Section 111, Mitigation of Shore Damages Attributable to Navigation Projects.

(d) *Construction and Operations and Maintenance.* Changes in environmental impacts which were not considered in the project EIS or EA. Examples are changes in pool level operations, use of new disposal areas, location of bank protection works, etc.

(e) *Real Estate Management and Disposal Actions.* (1) Disposal of a Civil Works project or portions of project properties not reported as excess to the General Services Administration.

(2) Disposal of real property for public port and industrial purposes.

(3) Grants of leases or easements for other than minor oil and gas transmission lines, electric power transmission lines, road and highway rights-of-way, and sewage or water treatment facilities and land fills.

§ 230.8 Emergency Actions.

In responding to emergency situations to prevent or reduce imminent risk of life, health, property, or severe economic losses, district commanders may proceed without the specific documentation and procedural requirements of other sections of this regulation. District commanders shall consider the probable environmental consequences in determining appropriate emergency actions and when requesting approval to proceed on emergency actions, will describe proposed NEPA documentation or reasons for exclusion from documentation. NEPA documentation should be accomplished prior to initiation of emergency work if time constraints render this practicable. Such documentation may also be accomplished after the completion of emergency work, if appropriate. Emergency actions include Flood Control and Coastal Emergencies Activities pursuant to Pub. L. 84–99, as amended, and projects constructed under sections 3 of the River and Harbor Act of 1945 or 14 of the Flood Control Act of 1946 of the Continuing Authorities Program. When possible, emergency actions considered major in scope with potentially significant environmental impacts shall be referred through the division commanders to HQUSACE (CECW–RE) for consultation with CEQ about NEPA arrangements.

§ 230.9 Categorical exclusions.

Actions listed below when considered individually and cumulatively do not have significant effects on the quality of the human environment and are categorically excluded from NEPA documentation. However, district commanders should be alert for extraordinary circumstances which may dictate the need to prepare an EA or an EIS. Even though an EA or EIS is not indicated for a Federal action because of a "categorical exclusion", that fact does not exempt the action from compliance with any other Federal law. For example, compliance with the Endangered Species Act, the Fish and Wildlife Coordination Act, the National Historic Preservation Act, the Clean Water Act, etc., is always mandatory, even for actions not requiring an EA or EIS.

(a) For a period of one year from the effective date of these regulations, district commanders should maintain an information list on the type and number of categorical exclusion actions which due to extraordinary circumstances triggered the need for an EA and finding of no significant impact (FONSI) or an EIS. If a district commander determines that a categorical exclusion should be modified, the information will be furnished to the division commander, who will review and analyze the actions and circumstances to determine if there is a basis for recommending a modification to the list of categorical exclusions. HQUSACE (CECW–RE) will review recommended changes for Corps-wide consistency and revise the list accordingly. See 33 CFR Part 325, Appendix B for categorical exclusions for regulatory actions.

(b) Activities at completed Corps projects which carry out the authorized project purposes. Examples include routine operation and maintenance actions, general administration, equipment purchases, custodial actions, erosion control, painting, repair, rehabilitation, replacement of existing structures and facilities such as buildings, roads, levees, groins and utilities, and installation of new buildings utilities, or roadways in developed areas.

(c) Minor maintenance dredging using existing disposal sites.

(d) Planning and technical studies which do not contain recommendations for authorization or funding for construction, but may recommend further study. This does not exclude consideration of environmental matters in the studies.

(e) All Operations and Maintenance grants, general plans, agreements, etc., necessary to carry out land use, development and other measures proposed in project authorization documents, project design memoranda,

master plans, or reflected in the project NEPA documents.

(f) Real estate grants for use of excess or surplus real property.

(g) Real estate grants for Government-owned housing.

(h) Exchanges of excess real property and interests therein for property required for project purposes.

(i) Real estate grants for rights-of-way which involve only minor disturbances to earth, air, or water:

(1) Minor access roads, streets and boat ramps.

(2) Minor utility distribution and collection lines, including irrigation.

(3) Removal of sand, gravel, rock, and other material from existing borrow areas.

(4) Oil and gas seismic and gravity meter survey for exploration purposes.

(j) Real estate grants of consent to use Government-owned easement areas.

(k) Real estate grants for archeological and historical investigations compatible with the Corps Historic Preservation Act responsibilities.

(l) Renewal and minor amendments of existing real estate grants evidencing authority to use Government-owned real property.

(m) Reporting excess real property to the General Services Administration for disposal.

(n) Boundary line agreements and disposal of lands or release of deed restrictions to cure encroachments.

(o) Disposal of excess easement interest to the underlying fee owner.

(p) Disposal of existing buildings and improvements for off-site removal.

(q) Sale of existing cottage site areas.

(r) Return of public domain lands to the Department of the Interior.

(s) Transfer and grants of lands to other Federal agencies.

§ 230.10 Environmental Assessments (EA).

(a) *Purpose.* An EA is a brief document which provides sufficient information to the district commander on potential environmental effects of the proposed action and, if appropriate, its alternatives, for determining whether to prepare an EIS or a FONSI (40 CFR 1508.9). The district commander is responsible for making this determination and for keeping the public informed of the availability of the EA and FONSI.

(b) *Format.* While no special format is required, the EA should include a brief discussion of the need for the proposed action, or appropriate alternatives if there are unresolved conflicts concerning alternative uses of available resources, of the environmental impacts of the proposed action and alternatives and a list of the agencies, interested groups and the public consulted. The document is to be concise for meaningful review and decision.

(c) *Integration with Corps Reports.* In the case of planning and/or engineering reports not requiring an EIS, the EA may be combined with or integrated into the report. The same guidance on combining or integrating an EIS within the report shall apply equally to an EA. Where the EA is combined with a Corps report or prepared as a separate document in the case of construction, operating projects and real estate actions requiring an EA, the EA normally should not exceed 15 pages.

§ 230.11 Finding of No Significant Impact (FONSI).

A FONSI shall be prepared for a proposed action, not categorically excluded, for which an EIS will not be prepared. The FONSI will be a brief summary document as noted in 40 CFR 1508.13. In the case of feasibility, continuing authority, or special planning reports and certain planning/ engineering reports, the draft FONSI and EA should be included within the draft report and circulated for a minimum 30-day review to concerned agencies, organizations and the interested public (40 CFR 1501.4(e)(2)). In the case of operation and maintenance activities involving the discharge of dredged or fill material requiring a public notice, the notice will indicate the availability of the EA/FONSI. For all other Corps project actions a notice of availability of the FONSI will be sent to concerned agencies, organizations and the interested public (40 CFR 1501.4(e)(1)).

§ 230.12 Notice of intent and scoping.

As soon as practicable after a decision is made to prepare an EIS or supplement, the scoping process for the draft EIS or supplement will be announced in a notice of intent. Guidance on preparing a notice of intent to prepare an EIS for publication in the Federal Register is discussed in Appendix C. Also, a public notice will be widely distributed inviting public participation in the scoping process. As described in 40 CFR 1501.7 and reference 3(m), this process is the key to preparing a concise EIS and clarifying the significant issues to be analyzed in depth. Public concerns on issues, studies needed, alternatives to be examined, procedures and other related matters will be addressed during scoping.

§ 230.13 Environmental Impact Statement (EIS).

An EIS for feasibility or continuing authority reports and certain planning/ engineering reports may be combined with or integrated into the report in accordance with 40 CFR 1500.4(o) and

1506.4. An EIS combined with the report shall follow the format in 40 CFR 1502.10, follow the main report, use colored paper and not be an attachment or appendix. An EIS integrated within the report may follow the instructions in the last paragraph of 40 CFR 1502.10. Additional guidance on combining and integrating EISs is located in ER 1105-2-60. Where the EIS is not combined with or integrated into the project document, the EIS shall be a separate document and follow the format in 40 CFR 1502.10. CEQ regulations suggest maximum lengths for the text of an EIS at 40 CFR 1502.07. An effort should be exerted to cover the substantive topics simply and concisely to the extent practicable, and consistent with producing a legally and technically adequate EIS. Normally, the CEQ page limits should be met.

(a) *Draft and Final EISs.* Guidance on EISs prepared for planning and certain planning/engineering studies is contained in ER 1105-2-10 thru 60. 33 CFR Part 325, Appendix B contains guidance for regulatory actions. For final EISs which are not combined with or integrated into the report, the final EIS may take the form of an "abbreviated" document described in 40 CFR 1503.4(c). An abbreviated final EIS should consist of a new title page, summary, errata or correction sheet(s) and comments and responses. In filing the abbreviated final EIS with EPA (Washington Office), five copies of the draft EIS shall be included in the transmittal. District commanders shall be responsible for determining the type of final EIS to prepare.

(b) *Supplements.* A supplement to the draft or final EIS should be prepared whenever required as discussed in 40 CFR 1502.09(c). A supplement to a draft EIS should be prepared and filed in the same manner as a draft EIS and should be titled "Supplement I", "Supplement II", etc. The final EIS should address the changes noted in the supplement and substantive comments received as a result of circulation of the document. A supplement to a final EIS should be prepared and filed first as a *draft* supplement and then as a final supplement. Supplements will be filed and circulated in the same manner as a draft and final EIS (including the abbreviated procedure discussed in 13a. above). Supplements to a draft or final EIS filed before 30 July 1979 may follow the format of the previously filed EIS. Supplements to a draft EIS filed after this date will follow the format outlined in 40 CFR 1502.10. References to the draft or final EIS being supplemented should be used to eliminate repetitive discussions in order to focus on the important issues and impacts. The transmittal letter to EPA as well as the cover sheet should clearly identify the title and purpose of the document as well as the title and filing date of the

previous EIS being supplemented and how copies can be obtained. The decision may be made on the proposed action by the appropriate Corps official no sooner than 30 days after the final supplement has been on file. A record of decision will be signed when the decision is made.

(c) *Tiering.* Tiering is discussed in 40 CFR 1502.20 and 1508.28 and should be used in appropriate cases. The initial broad or programmatic EIS must present sufficient information regarding overall impacts of the proposed action so that the decision-makers can make a reasoned judgment on the merits of the action at the present stage of planning or development and exclude from consideration issues already decided or not ready for decision. The initial broad EIS should also identify data gaps and discuss future plans to supplement the data and prepare and circulate site specific EISs or EAs as appropriate.

(d) *Other Reports.* District commanders may also publish periodic fact sheets and/or other supplemental information documents on long-term or complex EISs to keep the public informed on the status of the proposed action. These documents will not be filed officially with EPA.

§ 230.14 Record of decision and implementation.

A record of decision shall be prepared by the district commander, in accordance with 40 CFR 1505.2, for the signature of the final decisionmaker as prescribed by applicable Corps regulations. Procedures implementing the decision are discussed in 40 CFR 1505.3. Incoming letters of comment on the final EIS will be furnished for review by the decisionmaker who signs the record of decision. For example, the record of decision for feasibility reports will be signed by the ASA(CW) at the time the report is transmitted to Congress for authorization.

§ 230.15 Mitigation and monitoring.

See 40 CFR 1505.2(c) and 1505.3. District commanders shall, upon request from interested agencies or the public, provide reports on the progress and status of required mitigation and other provisions of their decisions on Corps projects. The term monitoring will be interpreted as that oversight activity necessary to ensure that the decision, including required mitigation measures, is implemented.

§ 230.16 Lead and cooperating agencies.

Lead agency, joint lead agency, and cooperating agency designation and responsibilities are covered in 40 CFR 1501.5 and 1501.6. The district commander is authorized to enter into agreements with regional offices of other agencies as required by 40 CFR 1501.5(c). District or division commanders will consult with HQUSACE (CECW–RE), WASH DC 20314–1000 prior to requesting resolution by CEQ as outlined by 40 CFR 1501.5 (e) and (f).

(a) *Lead Agency.* The Corps will normally be lead agency for Corps civil works projects and will normally avoid joint agency lead agency arrangements. Lead agency status for regulatory actions will be determined on the basis of 40 CFR 1501.5(c).

(b) *Corps as a Cooperating Agency.* For cooperating agency designation the Corps area of expertise or jurisdiction by law is generally flood control, navigation, hydropower and Corps regulatory responsibilities. See Appendix II of CEQ regulations (49 FR 49750, December 21, 1984).

§ 230.17 Filing requirements.

Five copies of draft, final and supplement EISs should be sent to: Director, Office of Federal Activities (A-104), Environmental Protection Agency, 401 M Street SW., Washington, DC 20460. District commanders should file draft EISs and draft supplements directly with EPA. Final EISs and final supplements should be filed by appropriate elements within HQUSACE for feasibility and reevaluation reports requiring Congressional authorization. Division commanders should file final EISs and final supplements for all other Corps actions except for final EISs or final supplements for permit actions which should be filed by the district commander after appropriate reviews by division and the incorporation of division's comments in the EIS. HQUSACE and/or division will notify field office counterparts when to circulate the final EIS or final supplement and will file the final document with EPA after notified that distribution of the document has been accomplished.

(a) *Timing Requirements.* Specific timing requirements regarding the filing of EISs with EPA are discussed in 40 CFR 1506.10. District commanders will forward any expedited filing requests with appropriate supporting information through channels to CECW–RE. Once a decision is reached to prepare an EIS or supplement, district commanders will establish a time schedule for each step of the process based upon considerations listed in 40 CFR 1501.8 and upon other management considerations. The time required from the decision to prepare an EIS to filing the final EIS normally should not exceed one year (46 FR 18037, March 23, 1981). For feasibility, continuing authority, or reevaluation studies, where the project's study time is expected to exceed 12 months, the timing of the EIS should be commensurate with the study time. In appropriate circumstances where the

costs of completing studies or acquiring information for an EIS (i.e., cost in terms of money, time, or other resources) would be exorbitant, the district commander should consider using the mechanism described in 40 CFR 1502.22, as amended. In all cases, however, it is the district commander's responsibility to assure that the time-limit established for the preparation of an EIS or supplement is consistent with the purposes of NEPA.

(b) *Timing Requirements on Supplements.* Minimum review periods will be observed for draft and final supplements covering actions not having a bearing on the overall project for which a final EIS has been filed. Such supplements should not curtail other ongoing or scheduled actions on the overall project which have already complied with the procedural requirements of NEPA.

§ 230.18 Availability.

Draft and final EISs and supplements will be available to the public as provided in 40 CFR 1502.19 and 1506.6. A summary may be circulated in lieu of the EIS, as provided in 40 CFR 1502.19, if the statement is unusually long. These documents will normally be made available without charge except that, in unusual circumstances, reproduction costs may be recovered in accordance with 40 CFR 1506.6(f) from recipients other than those required by CEQ to receive the complete EIS.

§ 230.19 Comments.

District commanders shall request comments as set forth in 40 CFR 1503 and 1506.6. A lack of response may be presumed to indicate that the party has no comment to make.

(a) *Time Extensions.* District commanders will consider and act on requests for time extensions to review and comment on an EIS based on timeliness of distribution of the document, prior agency involvement in the proposed action, and the action's scope and complexity.

(b) *Public Meetings and Hearings.* See 40 CFR 1506.6(c). Refer to paragraph 12, 33 CFR Part 325, Appendix B for regulatory actions.

(c) *Comments Received on the Draft EIS.* See 40 CFR 1503.4. District commanders will pay particular attention to the display in the final EIS of comments received on the draft EIS. In the case of abbreviated final EISs, follow 40 CFR 1503.4(c). For all other final EISs, comments and agency responses thereto will be placed in an appendix in a format most efficient for users of the final EIS to understand the nature of public input and the district commander's consideration thereof. District commanders will avoid lengthy or repetitive verbatim reporting of

comments and will keep responses clear and concise.

(d) *Comments Received on the Final EIS.* Responses to comments received on the final EIS are required only when substantive issues are raised which have not been addressed in the EIS. In the case of feasibility reports where the final report and EIS, Board of Engineers for Rivers and Harbors (CEBRH) or Mississippi River Commission (CEMRC) report, and the proposed Chief's report are circulated for review, incoming comment letters will normally be answered, if appropriate, by CECW–P. After the review period is over, CECW–P will provide copies of all incoming comments received in HQUSACE to the district commander for use in preparing the draft record of decision. For all other Corps actions except regulatory actions (See 33 CFR Part 325, Appendix B), two copies of all incoming comment letters (even if the letters do not require an agency response) together with the district commander's responses (if appropriate) and the draft record of decision will be submitted through channels to the appropriate decision authority. In the case of a letter recommending a referral under 40 FR Part 1504, reporting officers will notify CECW–RE and request further guidance. The record of decision will not be signed nor any action taken on the proposal until the referral case is resolved.

(e) *Commenting on Other Agencies' EISs.* See 40 CFR 1503.2 and 1503.3. District commanders will provide comments directly to the requesting agency. CECW–RE will provide comments about legislation, national program proposals, regulations or other major policy issues to the requesting agency. See Appendix III of CEQ regulations. When the Corps is a cooperating agency, the Corps will provide comments on another Federal agency's draft EIS even if the response is no comment. Comments should be specific and restricted to areas of Corps jurisdiction by law and special expertise as defined in 40 CFR 1508.15 and 1508.26, generally including flood control, navigation, hydropower, and regulatory responsibilities. See Appendix II of CEQ regulations.

§ 230.20 Integration with State and local procedures.

See 40 CFR 1506.2.

§ 230.21 Adoption.

See 40 CFR 1506.3. A district commander will normally adopt another Federal agency's EIS and consider it to be adequate unless the district commander finds substantial doubt as to technical or procedural adequacy or omission of factors important to the Corps decision. In such cases, the district commander will prepare a draft and final supplement noting in the draft supplement why the EIS was considered inadequate. In all cases, except where the document is not recirculated as provided in 40 CFR 1506.3 (b) or (c), the adopted EIS with the supplement, if any, will be processed in accordance with this regulation. A district commander may also adopt another agency's EA/FONSI.

§ 230.22 Limitations on actions during the NEPA process.

See 40 CFR 1506.1.

§ 230.23 Predecision referrals.

See 40 CFR Part 1504. If the district commander determines that a predecision referral is appropriate, the case will be sent through division to reach CECW–RE not later than 15 days after the final EIS was filed with EPA. Corps actions referred to CEQ by another Federal agency shall be transmitted to CECW–RE for further guidance. See paragraph 19, 33 CFR Part 325, Appendix B, for guidance on predecision referrals affecting regulatory permit actions.

§ 230.24 Agency decision points.

The timing and processing of NEPA documents in relation to major decision points are addressed in paragraphs 11 and 14 and Appendix A for studies and projects and 33 CFR Part 320 through 330 for regulatory actions.

§ 230.25 Environmental review and consultation requirements.

See 40 CFR 1502.25.

(a) For Federal projects, NEPA documents shall be prepared concurrently with and utilize data from analyses required by other environmental laws and executive orders. A listing of environmental laws and orders is contained in table 3.4.3 of Economic and Environmental Principles and Guidelines for Water and Related Land Resources Implementation Studies. Reviews and consultation requirements, analyses, and status of coordination associated with applicable laws, executive orders and memoranda will be summarized in the draft document. The results of the coordination completed or underway pursuant to these authorities will be summarized in the final document. Where the results of the ongoing studies are not expected to materially affect the decision on the proposed action, the filing of the final EIS need not be delayed.

(b) *Executive Order 12114, Environmental Effects Abroad of Major Federal Actions, 4 January 1979.* For general policy guidance, see **Federal Register** of April 12, 1979, 32 CFR Part 197. Procedural requirements for Civil Works studies and projects are discussed below.

(1) The district commander through the division commander will notify CECW–PE, PN, PS or PW as appropriate, of an impending action which may impact on another country and for which environmental studies may be necessary to determine the extent and significance of the impact. The district commander will inform CECW–P whether entry into the country is necessary to study the base condition.

(2) CECW–P will notify the State Department, Office of Environment and Health (OES/ENH) of the district commander's concern, and whether a need exists at this point to notify officially the foreign nation of our intent to study potential impacts. Depending on expected extent and severity of impacts, or if entry is deemed necessary, the matter will be referred to the appropriate foreign desk for action.

(3) As soon as it becomes evident that the impacts of the proposed actions are considered significant, CECW–P will notify the State Department. The State Department will determine whether the foreign embassy needs to be notified, and will do so if deemed appropriate, requesting formal discussions on the matter. When the International Joint Commission (IJC) or the International Boundary and Water Commission, United States and Mexico (IBWC) is involved in a study, the State Department should be consulted to determine the foreign policy implications of any action and the proper course of action for formal consultations.

(4) Prior to public dissemination, press releases or reports dealing with impact assessments in foreign nations should be made available to the appropriate foreign desk at the State Department for clearance and coordination with the foreign embassy.

§ 230.26 General considerations in preparing corps EISs.

(a) *Interdisciplinary Preparation.* See (40 CFR 1502.6).

(b) *Incorporation by Reference.* To the maximum extent practicable, the EIS should incorporate material by reference in accordance with 40 CFR 1502.21. Footnotes should be used only where their use greatly aids the reader's understanding of the point discussed. Citation in the EIS of material incorporated by reference should be made by indicating an author's last name and date of the reference in parentheses at the appropriate location in the EIS. The list of references will be placed at the end of the EIS. Only information sources actually cited in the text should appear in the reference list. The reference list should include the author's name, the date and title of the publication, personal communications and type of communication (e.g., letter, telephone, interview, etc.).

Appendix A—Processing Corps NEPA Documents

NEPA documents for Civil Works activities other than permits will be processed in accordance with the instructions contained in this appendix and applicable paragraphs in the regulation.

Table of Contents

Title

1. Feasibility Studies

a. *Preparation and Draft Review.* During the reconnaissance phase, the district commander should undertake environmental studies along with engineering, economic and other technical studies to determine the probable environmental effects of alternatives and the appropriate NEPA document to accompany the feasibility report. This environmental evaluation should be continued in the feasibility phase, and if the need for an EIS develops the district commander will issue a notice of intent as early in the feasibility phase as possible. Following the guidance in ER 1105–2–10 through 60, the district commander will prepare a draft feasibility report combining or integrating the draft EIS or EA and draft FONSI (as appropriate), or a separate NEPA document and circulate it to agencies, organizations and members of the public known to have an interest in the study. Five copies of the draft EIS and report will be mailed to Director, Office of Federal Activities (A–104), Environmental Protection Agency, 401 M Street SW., Washington, DC 20460 for filing after distribution has been accomplished. After receipt and evaluation of comments received, the district commander will prepare the final report and EIS or EA and FONSI and submit it to the division commander for review.

b. *Division Review.* After review, the division commander will issue a public notice of report issuance and transmit the report to the CEBRH. On Mississippi River and Tributaries projects, the district commander will issue a public notice and submit the report to the CEMRC. For the purpose of this regulation, only the acronym CEBRH will be used since the review functions of CEMRC and CEBRH are similar. The notice will provide a 30-day period for comments to be submitted to CEBRH on the report and EIS. Although the EIS in the report is identified as "final" at this stage of processing, it should be made clear to all those requesting a copy that it is an "Interim Document under Agency Review—Subject to Revision" and will become the agency's final EIS when it is filed after CEBRH review.

c. *CEBRH Review.* CEBRH will review the EIS at the same time it reviews the final feasibility report. The report and EIS should be compatible. If the CEBRH review requires minor revisions (with insignificant impacts) to the plan as recommended by the division and district commanders, these changes and impacts shall be noted in the CEBRH report. If the CEBRH action results in major revisions to the recommended plan and revisions are variants of the plan or are within the range of alternatives considered and discussed in the draft EIS, an addendum to the final EIS will be prepared by CEBRH (with assistance from the district commander, as required). This addendum "package" will be identified as an "Addendum to the Final EIS—Environmental Consequences of the Modifications Recommended by the Board of Engineers for Rivers and Harbors—project name." The format shall include an abstract on the cover page; recommended changes to the division/district commander's proposed plan; rationale for the recommended changes; environmental consequences of the recommended changes; and the name, expertise/discipline, experience, and role of the principal preparer(s) of the addendum. Letters received during CEBRH review which provide new pertinent information having a bearing on the modifications recommended by CEBRH will be attached to the addendum. If CEBRH proposes to recommend a major revision or a new alternative to the plan recommended by the division and district commanders with significant impacts which were not discussed in the draft EIS, a supplement to the draft EIS will be required. After consultation with CEBRH and the division commander, the district commander will prepare and circulate the supplement to the draft EIS in accordance with paragraph 13(b). The supplement together with incoming letters of comment and Corps responses to substantive issues shall be incorporated into the existing final report and EIS with a minimum of page changes or revisions to reflect the modified or new proposed plan. CEBRH will review its proposed action in light of the comments received prior to taking final action on the report and EIS.

d. *Departmental Review.* The report and final EIS, together with the proposed report of the Chief of Engineers and the CEBRH report, will be filed with EPA at about the same time as it is circulated for the 90-day departmental review by Federal agencies at the Washington level and the concerned state(s). District commanders will circulate the proposed Chief's report, CEBRH report, and the report and final EIS to parties on the project mailing list not contacted by HQUSACE (groups and individuals known to have an interest in the study or who provided comments on the draft EIS) allowing the normal 30-day period of review. HQUSACE will provide a standard letter for the district to use to transmit these documents which explains the current status of the report and EIS and directs all comments to be sent to HQUSACE (CECW-P). Copies of the report appendices circulated with the draft need not be circulated with the report and final EIS. All letters of comment received on the report and final EIS together with HQUSACE responses and the draft record of decision (to be provided by the district commander) will be included with other papers furnished at the time the final Chief's report is transmitted to ASA(CW) for further review and processing.

e. *Executive Reviews.* After completion of review, the Chief of Engineers will sign his final report and transmit the report and accompanying documents to ASA(CW). After review ASA(CW) will transmit the report to OMB requesting its views in relation to the

programs of the President. After OMB provides its views, ASA(CW) will sign the record of decision (ROD) and transmit the report to Congress. In situations where Congress has acted to authorize construction of a project prior to receiving ASA(CW) recommendations, the Director of Civil Works is the designated official to sign the ROD. In this case the ROD should only address the project as authorized by the Congress and not attempt to provide any additional justification of the Congressional action.

2. Continuing Authorities Program Studies

a. *Preparation and Draft Review.* During the reconnaissance phase, the district commander should undertake environmental studies along with engineering, economic and other technical studies to determine the probable environmental effects of alternatives and the appropriate NEPA document to accompany the detailed project report (DPR). If the results of the reconnaissance phase warrant preparation of an EIS, the district commander will issue a notice of intent early in the ensuing feasibility study. Following the guidance in ER 1105-2-10 through 60 the district commander will prepare the draft DPR incorporating the EA and draft FONSI or draft EIS (as appropriate), and circulate it to agencies, organizations and members of the public known to have an interest in the study. If an EIS is prepared, five copies of the draft EIS and report will be mailed to Director, Office of Federal Activities (A-104), Environmental Protection Agency, 401 M Street SW, Washington, DC 20460 for filing after distribution has been accomplished.

b. *Agency Review.* After receipt and evaluation of comments the district commander will prepare the final DPR and EA/FONSI or final EIS and submit eight (8) copies to the division commander for review and approval. After review, the division commander will file five (5) copies of the final DPR and EIS with the Washington office of EPA. The division commander will not file the final EIS until notified by the district commander that distribution has been accomplished.

c. *Final Review.* Letters of comment on the final DPR including the final EIS will be answered by the district commander on an individual basis if appropriate. Two (2) copies of all incoming letters and the district commander's reply together with five copies of the final DPR and EIS and a draft of the record of decision will be submitted through division to the appropriate element within CECW-P. After review of the DPR and NEPA documents, the Director of Civil Works or Chief, Planning Division will approve the project and sign the record of decision if an EIS was prepared for the DPR.

3. Projects in Preconstruction Engineering and Design, Construction, and Completed Projects in an Operations and Maintenance Category

a. *General.* District commanders will review the existing NEPA document(s) to determine if there are new circumstances or significant impacts which warrant the preparation of a draft and final supplement to the EIS. If the proposed changes and new

impacts are not significant an EA and FONSI may be used.

b. *Preparation and Draft Review.* As soon as practicable after the district commander makes a determination to prepare an EIS or supplement for the proposed project, a notice of intent will be issued. The district commander will, in accordance with 40 CFR 1506.6, prepare and circulate the draft EIS or supplement for review and comment to agencies, groups and individuals known who may be interested or affected. Five (5) copies will be sent to Director, Office of Federal activities (A-104), Environmental Protection Agency, 401 M Street SW., Washington, DC 20460 for filing after distribution has been accomplished.

c. *Agency Review.* The district commander will prepare the final EIS or supplement after receipt and evaluation of comments. Eight (8) copies will be transmitted to the division commander for review. After review the division commander will file five (5) copies with the Washington office of EPA. A copy of the final EIS or supplement and transmittal letter to EPA will be provided to the appropriate counterpart office within HQUSACE. The division commander will file the final EIS when the district commander has made distribution.

d. *Final Review.* Letters of comment on the final EIS or supplement will be answered by the district commander on an individual basis as appropriate. Two (2) copies of the incoming letters and the district commander's reply together with two copies of the final EIS or supplement and a draft of the record of decision will be submitted to the appropriate Corps official having approval authority. After review of the NEPA documents and letters, the appropriate approving official will sign the record of decision.

4. Other Corps Projects. Draft and final EISs for other Civil Works projects or activities having significant environmental impacts which may be authorized by Congress without an EIS having been previously filed and for certain real estate management and disposal actions which may require an EIS should be processed in a manner similar to that discussed in paragraph 3 of this appendix except that CERE-MC will be the coordinating office within HQUSACE for real estate actions.

Appendix B—[Reserved]

Appendix C—Notice of Intent to Prepare a Draft EIS

1. *Purpose.* This appendix provides guidance on the preparation and processing of a notice of intent to prepare a draft EIS for publication in the Federal Register. A notice of intent to prepare a draft EIS or a draft supplement is discussed in 40 CFR 1508.22.

2. *Procedure.* District commanders shall publish a notice of intent in the Federal Register as soon as practicable after a decision is made to prepare a draft EIS or draft supplement. See 40 CFR 1507.3(e) for timing of notice of intent for Corps feasibility studies. Guidance on the format and content of the notice in the form of a sample notice of intent is contained in paragraph 4 of this appendix. District commanders shall also follow this guidance when publishing a notice

of intent to withdraw a notice of intent when a decision has been made to terminate the EIS process.

3. *Publishing Documents in the Federal Register.* The following information is furnished for preparation and publication of notices of intent in the **Federal Register**:

a. A brief transmittal letter inclosing three (3) signed copies of the notice of intent should be processed through local Chief, Information Management channels to: HQDA, SFIS–APP, ATTN: Department of the Army Liaison Officer with the Office of the Federal Register, Alexandria, VA 22331–0302. This office will review and correct (if needed) all documents prior to publication in the **Federal Register**.

b. The notice must be signed by the official issuing the document along with the signer's typed name, rank and position title for military officials or name and position title for civilian officials. A signer cannot sign "as acting" or "for" if another name is shown in the signature block. All three copies sent forward must be signed in ink. A xerox copy of the signature is not allowed.

c. A six-digit billing code number must be typed or handwritten in ink at the top of the first page on all three copies of a notice. This billing code number can be found on GPO bills, GPO Form 400, in the upper left corner opposite the address. The billing code number will be indicated as 3710–XX. FOAs must submit an open-end printing and binding requisition, Standard Form 1, each fiscal year to cover **Federal Register** printing costs (reference 3(n)). Completed requisitions (SF–1) must be forwarded to reach HQUSACE (CEIM–SP) WASH DC 20314–1000 by 1 June of each year. Consult the local chief, Information Management for Assistance.

4. *Sample Notice of Intent.* The following is a sample notice of intent to be used by district commanders:

Department of Defense
Corps of Engineer, Department of the Army, 3710–XX (Use Local Billing Code Number)
Intent To Prepare A Draft Environment Impact Statement (DEIS) For a Proposed (*Name and location of project, permit or activity*).
Agency: U.S. Army Corps of Engineers, DoD.
Action: Notice of Intent.
Summary: The summary should briefly state in simple language what action is being taken, why the action is necessary, and the intended effect of the action. Extensive discussion belongs under the Supplementary Information caption.

For Further Information Contact: Questions about the proposed action and DEIS can be answered by: (Provide name, telephone number, and address of the person in the district or division who can answer questions about the proposed action and the DEIS).

Supplementary Information: The Supplementary Information should contain the remainder of the necessary information of the document. It should contain any authority citation, **Federal Register** citation to a previously published document, or CFR citation when appropriate and include a discussion of the following topics:

1. Briefly describe the proposed action.
2. Briefly describe reasonable alternatives.
3. Briefly describe the Corps' scoping process which is reasonably foreseeable for the DEIS under consideration. The description:
  a. Shall discuss the proposed public involvement program and invite the participation of affected Federal, state and local agencies, affected Indian tribes, and other interested private organizations and parties.
  b. Shall identify significant issues to be analyzed in depth in the DEIS.
  c. May discuss possible assignments for input into the EIS under consideration among the lead and cooperating agencies.
  d. Shall identify other environmental review and consultation requirements.
4. Indicate whether or not a scoping meeting will be held. Indicate time, date and location if a meeting is scheduled.
5. Provide an estimated date when the DEIS will be made available to the public.
(Provide date)

_____
(Signature)
_____
See par. 3.b. for instructions on signature

Note

• Text to be double-spaced. Use block format.
• Place local billing code number at the top of the first page on all three copies.
• Margins—one inch on top, bottom and right side; and one and one-half inches on the left side.
• Pages must be numbered consecutively.
• Text should be typed on one side only.
• Use 8½ by 11 inch bond paper or photocopy paper.

PART 325—PROCESSING OF DEPARTMENT OF THE ARMY PERMITS

3. The authority citation for Part 325 continues to read as follows:

Authority: 33 U.S.C. 401 et seq.; 33 U.S.C. 1344; 33 U.S.C. 1413.

4. Part 325, Appendix B is added to read as follows:

*   *   *   *   *

Appendix B—NEPA Implementation Procedures for the Regulatory Program

1. Introduction
2. General
3. Development of Information and Data
4. Elimination of Duplication with State and Local Procedures
5. Public Involvement
6. Categorical Exclusions
7. EA/FONSI Document
8. Environmental Impact Statement—General
9. Organization and Content of Draft EISs
10. Notice of Intent
11. Public Hearing
12. Organization and Content of Final EIS
13. Comments Received on the Final EIS
14. EIS Supplement
15. Filing Requirement
16. Timing
17. Expedited Filing
18. Record of Decision
19. Predecision Referrals by Other Agencies
20. Review of Other Agencies' EISs
21. Monitoring

1. *Introduction.* In keeping with Executive Order 12291 and 40 CFR 1500.2, where interpretive problems arise in implementing this regulation, and consideration of all other factors do not give a clear indication of a reasonable interpretation (consistent with the spirit and intent of NEPA) which results in the least paperwork and delay will be used. Specific examples of ways to reduce paperwork in the NEPA process are found at 40 CFR 1500.4. Maximum advantage of these recommendations should be taken.

2. *General.* This Appendix sets forth implementing procedures for the Corps regulatory program. For additional guidance, see the Corps NEPA regulation 33 CFR Part 230 and for general policy guidance, see the CEQ regulations 40 CFR 1500–1508.

3. *Development of Information and Data.* See 40 CFR 1506.5. The district engineer may require the applicant to furnish appropriate information that the district engineer considers necessary for the preparation of an Environmental Assessment (EA) or Environmental Impact Statement (EIS). See also 40 CFR 1502.22 regarding incomplete or unavailable information.

4. *Elimination of Duplication with State and Local Procedures.* See 40 CFR 1506.2.

5. *Public Involvement.* Several paragraphs of this appendix (paragraphs 7, 8, 11, 13, and 19) provide information on the requirements for district engineers to make available to the public certain environmental documents in accordance with 40 CFR 1506.6.

6. Categorical Exclusions—a. *General.* Even though an EA or EIS is not legally mandated for any Federal action falling within one of the "categorical exclusions," that fact does not exempt any Federal action from procedural or substantive compliance with any other Federal law. For example, compliance with the Endangered Species Act, the Clean Water Act, etc., is always mandatory, even for actions not requiring an EA or EIS. The following activities are not considered to be major Federal actions significantly affecting the quality of the human environment and are therefore categorically excluded from NEPA documentation:
  (1) Fixed or floating small private piers, small docks, boat hoists and boathouses.
  (2) Minor utility distribution and collection lines including irrigation;
  (3) Minor maintenance dredging using existing disposal sites;
  (4) Boat launching ramps;
  (5) All applications which qualify as letters of permission (as described at 33 CFR 325.5(b)(2)).

  b. *Extraordinary Circumstances.* District engineers should be alert for extraordinary circumstances where normally excluded actions could have substantial environmental effects and thus require an EA or EIS. For a period of one year from the effective data of these regulations, district engineers should maintain an information list on the type and number of categorical exclusion actions which, due to extraordinary circumstances, triggered the need for an EA/FONSI or EIS. If a district engineer determines that a categorical exclusion should be modified, the information will be furnished to the division engineer who will review and analyze the actions and circumstances to determine if there is a basis for recommending a modification to the list of categorical exclusions. HQUSACE (CECW–OR) will review recommended changes for Corps-wide consistency and revise the list accordingly.

7. *EA/FONSI Document.* (See 40 CFR 1508.9 and 1508.13 for definitions)—a. *Environmental Assessment (EA) and Findings of No Significant Impact (FONSI).* The EA should normally be combined with other required documents (EA/404(b)(1)/ SOF/FONSI). "EA" as used throughout this Appendix normally refers to this combined document. The district engineer should complete an EA as soon as practicable after all relevant information is available (i.e., after the comment period for the public notice of the permit application has expired) and when the EA is a separate document it must be completed prior to completion of the statement of finding (SOF). When the EA confirms that the impact of the applicant's proposal is not significant and there are no "unresolved conflicts concerning alternative uses of available resources * * *" (section 102(2)(E) of NEPA), and the proposed activity is a "water dependent" activity as defined in 40 CFR 230.10(a)(3), the EA need not include a discussion on alternatives. In all other cases where the district engineer determines that there are unresolved conflicts concerning alternative uses of available resources, the EA shall include a discussion of the reasonable alternatives which are to be considered by the ultimate decision-maker. The decision options available to the Corps, which embrace all of the applicant's alternatives, are issue the permit, issue with modifications or deny the permit. Modifications are limited to those project modifications within the scope of established permit conditioning policy (See 33 CFR 325.4). The decision option to deny the permit results in the "no action" alternative (i.e. no activity requiring a Corps permit). The combined document normally should not exceed 15 pages and shall conclude with a FONSI (See 40 CFR 1508.13) or a determination that an EIS is required. The district engineer may delegate the signing of the NEPA document. Should the EA demonstrate that an EIS is necessary, the district engineer shall follow the procedures outlined in paragraph 8 of this Appendix. In those cases where it is obvious an EIS is required, an EA is not required. However, the district engineer should document his reasons for requiring an EIS.

b. *Scope of Analysis.* (1) In some situations, a permit applicant may propose to conduct a specific activity requiring a Department of the Army (DA) permit (e.g., construction of a pier in a navigable water of the United States) which is merely one component of a larger project (e.g., construction of an oil refinery on an upland area). The district engineer should establish the scope of the NEPA document (e.g., the EA or EIS) to address the impacts of the specific activity requiring a DA permit and those portions of the entire project over which the district engineer has sufficient control and responsibility to warrant Federal review.

(2) The district engineer is considered to have control and responsibility for portions of the project beyond the limits of Corps jurisdiction where the Federal involvement is sufficient to turn an essentially private action into a Federal action. These are cases where the environmental consequences of the larger project are essentially products of the Corps permit action.

Typical factors to be considered in determining whether sufficient "control and responsibility" exists include:

(i) Whether or not the regulated activity comprises "merely a link" in a corridor type project (e.g., a transportation or utility transmission project).

(ii) Whether there are aspects of the upland facility in the immediate vicinity of the regulated activity which affect the location and configuration of the regulated activity.

(iii) The extent to which the entire project will be within Corps jurisdiction.

(iv) The extent of cumulative Federal control and responsibility.

A. Federal control and responsibility will include the portions of the project beyond the limits of Corps jurisdiction where the cumulative Federal involvement of the Corps and other Federal agencies is sufficient to grant legal control over such additional portions of the project. These are cases where the environmental consequences of the additional portions of the projects are essentially products of Federal financing, assistance, direction, regulation, or approval (not including funding assistance solely in the form of general revenue sharing funds, with no Federal agency control over the subsequent use of such funds, and not including judicial or administrative civil or criminal enforcement actions).

B. In determining whether sufficient cumulative Federal involvement exists to expand the scope of Federal action the district engineer should consider whether other Federal agencies are required to take Federal action under the Fish and Wildlife Coordination Act (16 U.S.C. 661 *et seq.*), the National Historic Preservation Act of 1966 (16 U.S.C. 470 *et seq.*), the Endangered Species Act of 1973 (16 U.S.C. 1531 *et seq.*), Executive Order 11990, Protection of Wetlands, (42 U.S.C. 4321 91977), and other environmental review laws and executive orders.

C. The district engineer should also refer to paragraphs 8(b) and 8(c) of this appendix for guidance on determining whether it should be the lead or a cooperating agency in these situations.

These factors will be added to or modified through guidance as additional field experience develops.

(3) *Examples:* If a non-Federal oil refinery, electric generating plant, or industrial facility is proposed to be built on an upland site and the only DA permit requirement relates to a connecting pipeline, supply loading terminal or fill road, that pipeline, terminal or fill road permit, in and of itself, normally would not constitute sufficient overall Federal involvement with the project to justify expanding the scope of a Corps NEPA document to cover upland portions of the facility beyond the structures in the immediate vicinity of the regulated activity that would effect the location and configuration of the regulated activity.

Similarly, if an applicant seeks a DA permit to fill waters or wetlands on which other construction or work is proposed, the control and responsibility of the Corps, as well as its overall Federal involvement would extend to the portions of the project to be located on the permitted fill. However, the NEPA review would be extended to the entire project, including portions outside waters of the United States, only if sufficient Federal control and responsibility over the entire project is determined to exist; that is, if the regulated activities, and those activities involving regulation, funding, etc. by other Federal agencies, comprise a substantial portion of the overall project. In any case, once the scope of analysis has been defined, the NEPA analysis for that action should include direct, indirect and cumulative impacts on all Federal interests within the purview of the NEPA statute. The district engineer should, whenever practicable, incorporate by reference and rely upon the reviews of other Federal and State agencies.

For those regulated activities that comprise merely a link in a transportation or utility transmission project, the scope of analysis should address the Federal action, i.e., the specific activity requiring a DA permit and any other portion of the project that is within the control or responsibility of the Corps of Engineers (or other Federal agencies).

For example, a 50-mile electrical transmission cable crossing a 1 1/4 mile wide river that is a navigable water of the United States requires a DA permit. Neither the origin and destination of the cable nor its route to and from the navigable water, except as the route applies to the location and configuration of the crossing, are within the control or responsibility of the Corps of Engineers. Those matters would not be included in the scope of analysis which, in this case, would address the impacts of the specific cable crossing.

Conversely, for those activities that require a DA permit for a major portion of a transportation or utility transmission project, so that the Corps permit bears upon the origin and destination as well as the route of the project outside the Corps regulatory boundaries, the scope of analysis should include those portions of the project outside the boundaries of the Corps section 10/404 regulatory jurisdiction. To use the same example, if 30 miles of the 50-mile transmission line crossed wetlands or other "waters of the United States," the scope of analysis should reflect impacts of the whole 50-mile transmission line.

For those activities that require a DA permit for a major portion of a shoreside facility, the scope of analysis should extend to upland portions of the facility. For example, a shipping terminal normally requires dredging, wharves, bulkheads, berthing areas and disposal of dredged material in order to function. Permits for such activities are normally considered sufficient Federal control and responsibility to warrant extending the scope of analysis to include the upland portions of the facility.

In all cases, the scope of analysis used for analyzing both impacts and alternatives should be the same scope of analysis used for analyzing the benefits of a proposal.

8. *Environmental Impact Statement— General*—a. *Determination of Lead and Cooperating Agencies.* When the district engineer determines that an EIS is required, he will contact all appropriate Federal agencies to determine their respective role(s), i.e., that of lead agency or cooperating agency.

b. *Corps as Lead Agency.* When the Corps is lead agency, it will be responsible for managing the EIS process, including those portions which come under the jurisdiction of other Federal agencies. The district engineer is authorized to require the applicant to furnish appropriate information as discussed in paragraph 3 of this appendix. It is permissable for the Corps to reimburse, under agreement, staff support from other Federal agencies beyond the immediate jurisdiction of those agencies.

c. *Corps as Cooperating Agency.* If another agency is the lead agency as set forth by the CEQ regulations (40 CFR 1501.5 and 1501.6(a) and 1508.16), the district engineer will coordinate with that agency as a cooperating agency under 40 CFR 1501.6(b) and 1508.5 to insure that agency's resulting EIS may be adopted by the Corps for purposes of exercising its regulatory authority. As a cooperating agency the Corps will be responsible to the lead agency for providing environmental information which is directly related to the regulatory matter involved and which is required for the preparation of an EIS. This in no way shall be construed as lessening the district engineer's ability to request the applicant to furnish appropriate information as discussed in paragraph 3 of this appendix.

When the Corps is a cooperating agency because of a regulatory responsibility, the district engineer should, in accordance with 40 CFR 1501.6(b)(4), "make available staff support at the lead agency's request" to enhance the latter's interdisciplinary capability provided the request pertains to the Corps regulatory action covered by the EIS, to the extent this is practicable. Beyond this, Corps staff support will generally be made available to the lead agency to the extent practicable within its own responsibility and available resources. Any assistance to a lead agency beyond this will normally be by written agreement with the lead agency providing for the Corps expenses on a cost reimbursable basis. If the district engineer believes a public hearing should be held and another agency is lead agency, the district engineer should request such a hearing and provide his reasoning for the request. The district engineer should suggest a joint hearing and offer to take an active

part in the hearing and ensure coverage of the Corps concerns.

d. *Scope of Analysis.* See paragraph 7b.

e. *Scoping Process.* Refer to 40 CFR 1501.7 and 33 CFR 230.12.

f. *Contracting.* See 40 CFR 1506.5.

(1) The district engineer may prepare an EIS, or may obtain information needed to prepare an EIS, either with his own staff or by contract. In choosing a contractor who reports directly to the district engineer, the procedures of 40 CFR 1506.5(c) will be followed.

(2) Information required for an EIS also may be furnished by the applicant or a consultant employed by the applicant. Where this approach is followed, the district engineer will (i) advise the applicant and/or his consultant of the Corps information requirements, and (ii) meet with the applicant and/or his consultant from time to time and provide him with the district engineer's views regarding adequacy of the data that are being developed (including how the district engineer will view such data in light of any possible conflicts of interest).

The applicant and/or his consultant may accept or reject the district engineer's guidance. The district engineer, however, may after specifying the information in contention, require the applicant to resubmit any previously submitted data which the district engineer considers inadequate or inaccurate. In all cases, the district engineer should document in the record the Corps independent evaluation of the information and its accuracy, as required by 40 CFR 1506.5(a).

g. *Change in EIS Determination.* If it is determined that an EIS is not required after a notice of intent has been published, the district engineer shall terminate the EIS preparation and withdraw the notice of intent. The district engineer shall notify in writing the appropriate division engineer; HQUSACE (CECW–OR); the appropriate EPA regional administrator, the Director, Office of Federal Activities (A–104), EPA, 401 M Street SW., Washington, DC 20460 and the public of the determination.

h. *Time Limits.* For regulatory actions, the district engineer will follow 33 CFR 230.17(a) unless unusual delays caused by applicant inaction or compliance with other statutes require longer time frames for EIS preparation. At the outset of the EIS effort, schedule milestones will be developed and made available to the applicant and the public. If the milestone dates are not met the district engineer will notify the applicant and explain the reason for delay.

9. *Organization and Content of Draft EISs*—a. *General.* This section gives detailed information for preparing draft EISs. When the Corps is the lead agency, this draft EIS format and these procedures will be followed. When the Corps is one of the joint lead agencies, the joint lead agencies will mutually decide which agency's format and procedures will be followed.

b. *Format*—(1) *Cover Sheet.* (a) Ref. 40 CFR 1502.11.

(b) The "person at the agency who can supply further information" (40 CFR

1502.11(c) is the project manager handling that permit application.

(c) The cover sheet should identify the EIS as a Corps permit action and state the authorities (sections 9, 10, 404, 103, etc.) under which the Corps is exerting its jurisdiction.

(2) *Summary.* In addition to the requirements of 40 CFR 1502.12, this section should identify the proposed action as a Corps permit action stating the authorities (sections 9, 10, 404, 103, etc.) under which the Corps is exerting its jurisdiction. It shall also summarize the purpose and need for the proposed action and shall briefly state the beneficial/adverse impacts of the proposed action.

(3) *Table of Contents.*

(4) *Purpose and Need.* See 40 CFR 1502.13. If the scope of analysis for the NEPA document (see paragraph 7b) covers only the proposed specific activity requiring a Department of the Army permit, then the underlying purpose and need for that specific activity should be stated. (For example, "The purpose and need for the pipe is to obtain cooling water from the river for the electric generating plant.") If the scope of analysis covers a more extensive project, only part of which may require a DA permit, then the underlying purpose and need for the entire project should be stated. (For example, "The purpose and need for the electric generating plant is to provide increased supplies of electricity to the (named) geographic area.") Normally, the applicant should be encouraged to provide a statement of his proposed activity's purpose and need from his perspective (for example, "to construct an electric generating plant"). However, whenever the NEPA document's scope of analysis renders it appropriate, the Corps also should consider and express that activity's underlying purpose and need from a public interest perspective (to use that same example, "to meet the public's need for electric energy"). Also, while generally focusing on the applicant's statement, the Corps, will in all cases, exercise independent judgment in defining the purpose and need for the project from both the applicant's and the public's perspective.

(5) *Alternatives.* See 40 CFR 1502.14. The Corps is neither an opponent nor a proponent of the applicant's proposal; therefore, the applicant's final proposal will be identified as the "applicant's preferred alternative" in the final EIS. Decision options available to the district engineer, which embrace all of the applicant's alternatives, are issue the permit, issue with modifications or conditions or deny the permit.

(a) Only reasonable alternatives need be considered in detail, as specified in 40 CFR 1502.14(a). Reasonable alternatives must be those that are feasible and such feasibility must focus on the accomplishment of the underlying purpose and need (of the applicant or the public) that would be satisfied by the proposed Federal action (permit issuance). The alternatives analysis should be thorough enough to use for both the public interest review and the 404(b)(1) guidelines (40 CFR Part 230) where applicable. Those alternatives that are unavailable to the applicant, whether or not they require Federal action (permits), should normally be included in the analysis of the no-Federal-action (denial) alternative. Such alternatives should be evaluated only to the extent necessary to allow a complete and objective evaluation of the public interest and a fully informed decision regarding the permit application.

(b) The "no-action" alternative is one which results in no construction requiring a Corps permit. It may be brought by (1) the applicant electing to modify his proposal to eliminate work under the jurisdiction of the Corps or (2) by the denial of the permit. District engineers, when evaluating this alternative, should discuss, when appropriate, the consequences of other likely uses of a project site, should the permit be denied.

(c) The EIS should discuss geographic alternatives, e.g., changes in location and other site specific variables, and functional alternatives, e.g., project substitutes and design modifications.

(d) The Corps shall not prepare a cost-benefit analysis for projects requiring a Corps permit. 40 CFR 1502.23 states that the weighing of the various alternatives need not be displayed in a cost-benefit analysis and "* * * should not be when there are important qualitative considerations." The EIS should, however, indicate any cost considerations that are likely to be relevant to a decision.

(e) Mitigation is defined in 40 CFR 1508.20, and Federal action agencies are directed in 40 CFR 1502.14 to include appropriate mitigation measures. Guidance on the conditioning of permits to require mitigation is in 33 CFR 320.4(r) and 325.4. The nature and extent of mitigation conditions are dependent on the results of the public interest review in 33 CFR 320.4.

(6) *Affected Environment.* See Ref. 40 CFR 1502.15.

(7) *Environmental Consequences.* See Ref. 40 CFR 1502.16.

(8) *List of Preparers.* See Ref. 40 CFR 1502.17.

(9) *Public Involvement.* This section should list the dates and nature of all public notices, scoping meetings and public hearings and include a list of all parties notified.

(10) *Appendices.* See 40 CFR 1502.18. Appendices should be used to the maximum extent practicable to minimize the length of the main text of the EIS. Appendices normally should not be circulated with every copy of the EIS, but appropriate appendices should be provided routinely to parties with special interest and expertise in the particular subject.

(11) *Index.* The Index of an EIS, at the end of the document, should be designed to provide for easy reference to items discussed in the main text of the EIS.

10. *Notice of Intent.* The district engineer shall follow the guidance in 33 CFR Part 230, Appendix C in preparing a notice of intent to prepare a draft EIS for publication in the **Federal Register.**

11. *Public Hearing.* If a public hearing is to be held pursuant to 33 CFR Part 327 for a permit application requiring an EIS, the actions analyzed by the draft EIS should be considered at the public hearing. The district engineer should make the draft EIS available to the public at least 15 days in advance of the hearing. If a hearing request is received from another agency having jurisdiction as provided in 40 CFR 1506.6(c)(2), the district engineer should coordinate a joint hearing with that agency whenever appropriate.

12. *Organization and Content of Final EIS.* The organization and content of the final EIS including the abbreviated final EIS procedures shall follow the guidance in 33 CFR 230.14(a).

13. *Comments Received on the Final EIS.* For permit cases to be decided at the district level, the district engineer should consider all incoming comments and provide responses when substantive issues are raised which have not been addressed in the final EIS. For permit cases decided at higher authority, the district engineer shall forward the final EIS comment letters together with appropriate responses to higher authority along with the case. In the case of a letter recommending a referral under 40 CFR Part 1504, the district engineer will follow the guidance in paragraph 19 of this appendix.

14. *EIS Supplement.* See 33 CFR 230.13(b).

15. *Filing Requirements.* See 40 CFR 1506.9. Five (5) copies of EISs shall be sent to Director, Office of Federal Activities (A–104), Environmental Protection Agency, 401 M Street SW., Washington, DC 20460. The official review periods commence with EPA's publication of a notice of availability of the draft or final EISs in the **Federal Register.** Generally, this notice appears on Friday of each week. At the same time they are mailed to EPA for filing, one copy of each draft or final EIS, or EIS supplement should be mailed to HQUSACE (CECW–OR) WASH DC 20314–1000.

16. *Timing.* 40 CFR 1506.10 describes the timing of an agency action when an EIS is involved.

17. *Expedited Filing.* 40 CFR 1506.10 provides information on allowable time reductions and time extensions associated with the EIS process. The district engineer will provide the necessary information and facts to HQUSACE (CECW–RE) WASH DC 20314–1000 (with copy to CECW–OR) for consultation with EPA for a reduction in the prescribed review periods.

18. *Record of Decision.* In those cases involving an EIS, the statement of findings will be called the record of decision and shall incorporate the requirements of 40 CFR 1505.2. The record of decision is not to be included when filing a final EIS and may not be signed until 30 days after the notice of availability of the final EIS is published in the **Federal Register.** To avoid duplication, the record of decision may reference the EIS.

19. *Predecision Referrals by Other Agencies.* See 40 CFR Part 1504. The decisionmaker should notify any potential referring Federal agency and CEQ of a final decision if it is contrary to the announced position of a potential referring agency. (This pertains to a NEPA referral, not a 404(q) referral under the Clean Water Act. The procedures for a 404(q) referral are outlined in the 404(q) Memoranda of Agreement. The potential referring agency will then have 25 calendar days to refer the case to CEQ under 40 CFR Part 1504. Referrals will be transmitted through division to CECW–RE for further guidance with an information copy to CECW–OR.

20. *Review of Other Agencies' EISs.* District engineers should provide comments directly to the requesting agency specifically related to the Corps jurisdiction by law or special expertise as defined in 40 CFR 1508.15 and 1508.26 and identified in Appendix II of CEQ regulations (49 FR 49750, December 21, 1984). If the district engineer determines that another agency's draft EIS which involves a Corps permit action is inadequate with respect to the Corps permit action, the district engineer should attempt to resolve the differences concerning the Corps permit action prior to the filing of the final EIS by the other agency. If the district engineer finds that the final EIS is inadequate with respect to the Corps permit action, the district engineer should incorporate the other agency's final EIS or a portion thereof and prepare an appropriate and adequate NEPA document to address the Corps involvement with the proposed action. See 33 CFR 230.21 for guidance. The agency which prepared the original EIS should be given the opportunity to provide additional information to that contained in the EIS in order for the Corps to have all relevant information available for a sound decision on the permit.

21. *Monitoring.* Monitoring compliance with permit requirements should be carried out in accordance with 33 CFR 230.15 and with 33 CFR Part 325.

Environmental Protection Agency
NEPA Regulations
40 C.F.R. Pt. 6

AUTHORITY: Secs. 101, 102, and 103 of the National Environmental Policy Act of 1969 (42 U.S.C. 4321 *et seq.*); also, the Council on Environmental Quality Regulations dated Nov. 29, 1978 (40 CFR Part 1500).

SOURCE: 44 FR 64177, Nov. 6, 1979, unless otherwise noted.

EDITORIAL NOTE: Nomenclature changes affecting Part 6 appear at 50 FR 26315, June 25, 1985.

Subpart A—General

§ 6.100 Purpose and policy.

(a) The National Environmental Policy Act of 1969 (NEPA), 42 U.S.C. 4321 *et seq.*, as implemented by Executive Orders 11514 and 11991 and the Council on Environmental Quality (CEQ) Regulations of November 29, 1978 (43 FR 55978) requires that Federal agencies include in their decision-making processes appropriate and careful consideration of all environmental effects of proposed actions, analyze potential environmental effects of proposed actions and their alternatives for public understanding and scrutiny, avoid or minimize adverse effects of proposed actions, and restore and enhance environmental quality as much as possible. The Environmental Protection Agency (EPA) shall integrate these NEPA factors as early in the Agency planning processes as possible. The environmental review process shall be the focal point to assure NEPA considerations are taken into account. To the extent applicable, EPA shall prepare environmental impact statements (EISs) on those major actions determined to have significant impact on the quality of the human environment. This part takes into account the EIS exemptions set forth under section 511(c)(1) of the Clean Water Act (Pub. L. 92–500) and section 7(c)(1) of the Energy Supply and Environmental Coordination Act of 1974 (Pub. L. 93–319).

(b) This part establishes EPA policy and procedures for the identification and analysis of the environmental impacts of EPA-related activities and the preparation and processing of EISs.

§ 6.101 Definitions.

(a) *Terminology.* All terminology used in this part will be consistent with the terms as defined in 40 CFR Part 1508 (the CEQ Regulations). Any qualifications will be provided in the definitions set forth in each subpart of this regulation.

(b) The term "CEQ Regulations" means the regulations issued by the Council on Environmental Quality on November 29, 1978 (see 43 FR 55978), which implement Executive Order 11991. The CEQ Regulations will often be referred to throughout this regulation by reference to 40 CFR Part 1500 *et al.*

(c) The term "environmental review" means the process whereby an evaluation is undertaken by EPA to determine whether a proposed Agency action may have a significant impact on the environment and therefore require the preparation of the EIS.

(d) The term "environmental information document" means any written analysis prepared by an applicant, grantee or contractor describing the environmental impacts of a proposed action. This document will be of sufficient scope to enable the responsible official to prepare an environmental assessment as described in the remaining subparts of this regulation.

(e) The term "grant" as used in this part means an award of funds or other assistance by a written grant agreement or cooperative agreement under 40 CFR Chapter I, Subpart B.

§ 6.102 Applicability.

(a) *Administrative actions covered.* This part applies to the activities of EPA in accordance with the outline of the subparts set forth below. Each subpart describes the detailed environmental review procedures required for each action.

(1) Subpart A sets forth an overview of the regulation. Section 6.102(b) describes the requirements for EPA legislative proposals.

(2) Subpart B describes the requirements for the content of an EIS prepared pursuant to Subparts E, F, G, H, and I.

(3) Subpart C describes the requirements for coordination of all environmental laws during the environmental review undertaken pursuant to Subparts E, F, G, H, and I.

(4) Subpart D describes the public information requirements which must be undertaken in conjunction with the environmental review requirements under Subparts E, F, G, H, and I.

(5) Subpart E describes the environmental review requirements for the wastewater treatment construction grants program under Title II of the Clean Water Act.

(6) Subpart F describes the environmental review requirements for new source National Pollutant Discharge Elimination System (NPDES) permits under section 402 of the Clean Water Act.

(7) Subpart G describes the environmental review requirements for research and development programs undertaken by the Agency.

(8) Subpart H describes the environmental review requirements for solid waste demonstration projects undertaken by the Agency.

(9) Subpart I describes the environmental review requirements for construction of special purpose facilities and facility renovations by the Agency.

(b) *Legislative proposals.* As required by the CEQ Regulations, legislative EISs are required for any legislative proposal developed by EPA which significantly affects the quality of the human environment. A preliminary draft EIS shall be prepared by the responsible EPA office concurrently with the development of the legislative proposal and contain information required under Subpart B. The EIS shall be processed in accordance with the requirements set forth under 40 CFR 1506.8.

(c) *Application to ongoing activities*—(1) *General.* The effective date for these regulations is December 5, 1979. These regulations do not apply to an EIS or supplement to that EIS if the draft EIS was filed with the Office of External Affairs, (OEA) before July 30, 1979. No completed environmental documents need be redone by reason of these regulations.

(2) With regard to activities under Subpart E, these regulations shall apply to all EPA environmental review procedures effective December 15, 1979. However, for facility plans begun before December 15, 1979, the responsible official shall impose no new requirements on the grantee. Such grantees shall comply with requirements applicable before the effective date of this regulation. Notwithstanding the above, this regulation shall apply to any facility plan submitted to EPA after September 30, 1980.

[44 FR 64177, Nov. 6, 1979, as amended at 47 FR 9829, Mar. 8, 1982]

§ 6.103 Responsibilities.

(a) *General responsibilities.* (1) The responsible official's duties include:

(i) Requiring applicants, contractors, and grantees to submit environmental information documents and related documents and assuring that environmental reviews are conducted on proposed EPA projects at the earliest possible point in EPA's decision-making process. In this regard, the responsible official shall assure the early involvement and availability of information for private applicants and other non-Federal entities requiring EPA approvals.

(ii) When required, assuring that adequate draft EISs are prepared and distributed at the earliest possible point in EPA's decision-making process, their internal and external review is coordinated, and final EISs are prepared and distributed.

(iii) When an EIS is not prepared, assuring documentation of the decision to grant a categorical exclusion, or assuring that findings of no significant impact (FNSIs) and environmental assessments are prepared and distributed for those actions requiring them.

(iv) Consulting with appropriate officials responsible for other environmental laws set forth in Subpart C.

(v) Consulting with the Office of External Affairs (OEA) on actions involving unresolved conflicts concerning this part or other Federal agencies.

(vi) When required, assuring that public participation requirements are met.

(2) *Office of External Affairs duties include:* (i) Supporting the Administrator in providing EPA policy guidance and assuring that EPA offices establish and maintain adequate administrative procedures to comply with this part.

(ii) Monitoring the overall timeliness and quality of the EPA effort to comply with this part.

(iii) Providing assistance to responsible officials as required, i.e., preparing guidelines describing the scope of environmental information required by private applicants relating to their proposed actions.

(iv) Coordinating the training of personnel involved in the review and preparation of EISs and other associated documents.

(v) Acting as EPA liaison with the Council on Environmental Quality and other Federal and State entities on matters of EPA policy and administrative mechanisms to facilitate external review of EISs, to determine lead agency and to improve the uniformity of the NEPA procedures of Federal agencies.

(vi) Advising the Administrator and Deputy Administrator on projects which involve more than one EPA office, are highly controversial, are nationally significant, or "pioneer" EPA policy, when these projects have had or should have an EIS prepared on them.

(vii) Carrying out administrative duties relating to maintaining status of EISs within EPA, i.e., publication of notices of intent in the FEDERAL REGISTER and making available to the public status reports on EISs and other elements of the environmental review process.

(3) *Office of an Assistant Administrator duties include:* (i) Providing specific policy guidance to their respective offices and assuring that those offices establish and maintain adequate administrative procedures to comply with this part.

(ii) Monitoring the overall timeliness and quality of their respective office's efforts to comply with this part.

(iii) Acting as liaison between their offices and the OEA and between their offices and other Assistant Administrators or Regional Administrators on matters of agencywide policy and procedures.

(iv) Advising the Administrator and Deputy Administrator through the OEA on projects or activities within their respective areas of responsibilities which involve more than one EPA office, are highly controversial, are nationally significant, or "pioneer" EPA policy, when these projects will have or should have an EIS prepared on them.

(v) Pursuant to § 6.102(b) of this subpart, preparing legislative EISs as appropriate on EPA legislative initiatives.

(4) The Office of Policy, Planning, and Evaluation duties include: responsibilities for coordinating the preparation of EISs required on EPA legislative proposals in accordance with § 6.102(b).

(b) *Responsibilities for Subpart E*— (1) *Responsible official.* The responsible official for EPA actions covered by this subpart is the Regional Administrator.

(2) *Assistant Administrator.* The responsibilities of the Assistant Administrator, as described in § 6.103(a)(3), shall be assumed by the Assistant Administrator for Water for EPA actions covered by this subpart.

(c) *Responsibilities for Subpart F*— (1) *Responsible official.* The responsible official for activities covered by this subpart is the Regional Administrator.

(2) *Assistant Administrator.* The responsibilities of the Assistant Administrator, as described in § 6.103(a)(3), shall be assumed by the Assistant Administrator for Enforcement and Compliance Monitoring for EPA actions covered by this subpart.

(d) *Responsibilities for Subpart G.* The Assistant Administrator for Research and Development will be the responsible official for activities covered by this subpart.

(e) *Responsibilities for Subpart H.* The Assistant Administrator for Solid Waste and Emergency Response will be the responsible official for activities covered by this subpart.

(f) *Responsibilities for Subpart I.* The responsible official for new construction and modification of special purpose facilities is as follows:

(1) The Chief, Facilities Engineering and Real Estate Branch, Facilities and Support Services Division, Office of the Assistant Administrator for Administration and Resource Management (OARM) shall be the responsible official on all new construction of special purpose facilities and on all new modification projects for which the Facilities Engineering and Real Estate Branch has received a funding allowance and for all other field components not covered elsewhere in paragraph (f) of this section.

(2) The Regional Administrator shall be the responsible official on all improvement and modification projects for which the regional office has received the funding allowance.

[44 FR 64177, Nov. 6, 1979, as amended at 47 FR 9829, Mar. 8, 1982; 50 FR 26315, June 25, 1985; 51 FR 32609, Sept. 12, 1986]

§ 6.104 Early involvement of private parties.

As required by 40 CFR 1501.2(d) and § 6.103(a)(3)(v) of this regulation, responsible officials must ensure early involvement of private applicants or other non-Federal entities in the environmental review process related to EPA grant and permit actions set forth under Subparts E, F, G, and H. The responsible official in conjunction with OEA shall:

(a) Prepare where practicable, generic guidelines describing the scope and level of environmental information required from applicants as a basis for evaluating their proposed actions, and make these guidelines available upon request.

(b) Provide such guidance on a project-by-project basis to any applicant seeking assistance.

(c) Upon receipt of an application for agency approval, or notification that an application will be filed, consult as required with other appropriate parties to initiate and coordinate the necessary environmental analyses.

[44 FR 64177, Nov. 6, 1979, as amended at 47 FR 9829, Mar. 8, 1982]

§ 6.105 Synopsis of environmental review procedures.

(a) *Responsible official.* The responsible official shall utilize a systematic, interdisciplinary approach to integrate natural and social sciences as well as environmental design arts in planning programs and making decisions which are subject to environmental review. The respective staffs may be supplemented by professionals from other agencies (see 40 CFR 1501.6) or consultants whenever in-house capabilities are insufficiently interdisciplinary.

(b) *Environmental information documents (EID).* Environmental information documents (EIDs) must be prepared by applicants, grantees, or permittees and submitted to EPA as required in Subparts E, F, G, H, and I. EIDs will be of sufficient scope to

enable the responsible official to prepare an environmental assessment as described under § 6.105(d) of this part and Subparts E through I. EIDs will not have to be prepared for actions where a categorical exclusion has been granted.

(c) *Environmental reviews.* Environmental reviews shall be conducted on the EPA activities outlined in § 6.102 of this part and set forth under Subparts E, F, G, H and I. This process shall consist of a study of the action to identify and evaluate the related environmental impacts. The process shall include a review of any related environmental information document to determine whether any significant impacts are anticipated and whether any changes can be made in the proposed action to eliminate significant adverse impacts; when an EIS is required, EPA has overall responsibility for this review, although grantees, applicants, permittees or contractors will contribute to the review through submission of environmental information documents.

(d) *Environmental assessments.* Environmental assessments (i.e., concise public documents for which EPA is responsible) are prepared to provide sufficient data and analysis to determine whether an EIS or finding of no significant impact is required. Where EPA determines that a categorical exclusion is appropriate or an EIS will be prepared, there is no need to prepare a formal environmental assessment.

(e) *Notice of intent and EISs.* When the environmental review indicates that a significant environmental impact may occur and significant adverse impacts can not be eliminated by making changes in the project, a notice of intent to prepare an EIS shall be published in the FEDERAL REGISTER, scoping shall be undertaken in accordance with 40 CFR 1501.7, and a draft EIS shall be prepared and distributed. After external coordination and evaluation of the comments received, a final EIS shall be prepared and disseminated. The final EIS shall list any mitigation measures necessary to make the recommended alternative environmentally acceptable.

(f) *Finding of no significant impact* (FNSI). When the environmental review indicates no significant impacts are anticipated or when the project is altered to eliminate any significant adverse impacts, a FNSI shall be issued and made available to the public. The environmental assessment shall be included as a part of the FNSI. The FNSI shall list any mitigation measures necessary to make the recommended alternative environmentally acceptable.

(g) *Record of decision.* At the time of its decision on any action for which a final EIS has been prepared, the responsible official shall prepare a concise public record of the decision. The record of decision shall describe those mitigation measures to be undertaken which will make the selected alternative environmentally acceptable. Where the final EIS recommends the

alternative which is ultimately chosen by the responsible official, the record of decision may be extracted from the executive summary to the final EIS.

(h) *Monitoring.* The responsible official shall provide for monitoring to assure that decisions on any action where a final EIS has been prepared are properly implemented. Appropriate mitigation measures shall be included in actions undertaken by EPA.

[44 FR 64177, Nov. 6, 1979, as amended at 50 FR 26315, June 25, 1985; 51 FR 32610, Sept. 12, 1986]

§ 6.106 Deviations.

(a) *General.* The Assistant Administrator, OEA, is authorized to approve deviations from these regulations. Deviation approvals shall be made in writing by the Assistant Administrator, OEA.

(b) *Requirements.* (1) Where emergency circumstances make it necessary to take an action with significant environmental impact without observing the substantive provisions of these regulations or the CEQ Regulations, the responsible official shall notify the Assistant Administrator, OEA, before taking such action. The responsible official shall consider to the extent possible alternative arrangements; such arrangements will be limited to actions necessary to control the immediate impacts of the emergency; other actions remain subject to the environmental review process. The Assistant Administrator, OEA, after consulting CEQ, will inform the responsible official, as expeditiously as possible of the disposition of his request.

(2) Where circumstances make it necessary to take action without observing procedural provisions of these regulations, the responsible official shall notify the Assistant Administrator, OEA, before taking such action. If the Assistant Administrator, OEA, determines such a deviation would be in the best interest of the Government, he shall inform the responsible official, as soon as possible, of his approval.

(3) The Assistant Administrator, OEA, shall coordinate his action on a deviation under § 6.106(b) (1) or (2) of this part with the Director, Grants Administration Division, Office of Planning and Management, for any required grant-related deviation under 40 CFR 30.1000, as well as the appropriate Assistant Administrator.

[44 FR 64177, Nov. 6, 1979, as amended at 47 FR 9829, Mar. 8, 1982]

§ 6.107 Categorical exclusions.

(a) *General.* Categories of actions which do not individually, cumulatively over time, or in conjunction with other Federal, State, local, or private actions have a significant effect on the quality of the human environment and which have been identified as having no such effect based on the requirements in § 6.505, may be exempted from the substantive environmental review requirements of this part. Environmental information documents and environmental assessments or environmental impact statements will not be required for excluded actions.

(b) *Determination.* The responsible official shall determine whether an action is eligible for a categorical exclusion as established by general criteria in § 6.107 (d) and (e) and any applicable criteria in program specific subparts of Part 6 of this title. A determination shall be made as early as possible following the receipt of an application. The responsible official shall document the decision to issue or deny an exclusion as soon as practicable following review in accordance with § 6.400(f). For qualified actions, the documentation shall include the application, a brief description of the proposed action, and a brief statement of how the action meets the criteria for a categorical exclusion without violating criteria for not granting an exclusion.

(c) *Revocation.* The responsible official shall revoke a categorical exclusion and shall require a full environmental review if, subsequent to the granting of an exclusion, the responsible official determines that: (1) The proposed action no longer meets the requirements for a categorical exclusion due to changes in the proposed action; or (2) determines from new evidence that serious local or environmental issues exist; or (3) that Federal, State, local, or tribal laws are being or may be violated.

(d) *General categories of actions eligible for exclusion.* Actions consistent with any of the following categories are eligible for a categorical exclusion:

(1) Actions which are solely directed toward minor rehabilitation of existing facilities, functional replacement of equipment, or towards the construction of new ancillary facilities adjacent or appurtenant to existing facilities;

(2) Other actions specifically allowed in program specific subparts of this regulation; or

(3) Other actions developed in accordance with paragraph (f) of this section.

(e) *General criteria for not granting a categorical exclusion.* (1) The full environmental review procedures of this part must be followed if undertaking an action consistent with allowable categories in paragraph (d) of this section may involve serious local or environmental issues, or meets any of the criteria listed below:

(i) The action is known or expected to have a significant effect on the quality of the human environment, either individually, cumulatively over time, or in conjunction with other federal, State, local, tribal or private actions;

(ii) The action is known or expected to directly or indirectly affect:

(A) Cultural resource areas such as archaeological and historic sites in accordance with § 6.301,

(B) Endangered or threatened species and their critical habitats in accordance with § 6.302 or State lists,

(C) Environmentally important natural resource areas such as floodplains, wetlands, important farmlands, aquifer recharge zones in accordance with § 6.302, or

(D) Other resource areas identified in supplemental guidance issued by the OEA;

(iii) The action is known or expected not to be cost-effective or to cause significant public controversy; or

(iv) Appropriate specialized program specific criteria for not granting an exclusion found in other subparts of this regulation are applicable to the action.

(2) Notwithstanding the provisions of paragraph (d) of this section, if any of the conditions cited in paragraph (e)(1) of this section exist, the responsible official shall ensure:

(i) That a categorical exclusion is not granted or, if previously granted, that it is revoked according to paragraph (c) of this section;

(ii) That an adequate EID is prepared; and

(iii) That either an environmental assessment and FNSI or a notice of intent for an EIS and ROD is prepared and issued.

(f) *Developing new categories of excluded actions.* The responsible official, or other interested parties, may request that a new general or specialized program specific category of excluded actions be created, or that an existing category be amended or deleted. The request shall be in writing to the Assistant Administrator, OEA, and shall contain adequate information to support the request. Proposed new categories shall be developed by OEA and published in the FEDERAL REGISTER as a proposed rule, amending paragraph (d) of this section when the proposed new category applies to all eligible programs or, amending appropriate paragraphs in other subparts of this part when the proposed new category applies to one specific program. The publication shall include a thirty (30) day public comment period. In addition to criteria for specific programs listed in other subparts of this part, the following general criteria shall be considered in evaluating proposals for new categories:

(1) Any action taken seldom results in the effects identified in general or specialized program specific criteria identified through the application of criteria for not granting a categorical exclusion;

(2) Based upon previous environmental reviews, actions consistent with the proposed category have not required the preparation of an EIS; and

(3) Whether information adequate to determine if a potential action is consistent with the proposed category will normally be available when needed.

[50 FR 26315, June 25, 1985, as amended at 51 FR 32610, Sept. 12, 1986]

§ 6.108 **Criteria for initiating an EIS.**

The responsible official shall assure that an EIS will be prepared and issued for actions under Subparts E, G, H, and I when it is determined that any of the following conditions exist:

(a) The Federal action may significantly affect the pattern and type of land use (industrial, commercial, agricultural, recreational, residential) or growth and distribution of population;

(b) The effects resulting from any structure or facility constructed or operated under the proposed action may conflict with local, regional or State land use plans or policies;

(c) The proposed action may have significant adverse effects on wetlands, including indirect and cumulative effects, or any major part of a structure or facility constructed or operated under the proposed action may be located in wetlands;

(d) The proposed action may significantly affect threatened and endangered species or their habitats identified in the Department of the Interior's list, in accordance with § 6.302, or a State's list, or a structure or a facility constructed or operated under the proposed action may be located in the habitat;

(e) Implementation of the proposed action or plan may directly cause or induce changes that significantly:

(1) Displace population;

(2) Alter the character of existing residential areas;

(3) Adversely affect a floodplain; or

(4) Adversely affect significant amounts of important farmlands as defined in requirements in § 6.302(c), or agricultural operations on this land.

(f) The proposed action may, directly, indirectly or cumulatively have significant adverse effect on parklands, preserves, other public lands or areas of recognized scenic, recreational, archaeological, or historic value; or

(g) The Federal action may directly or through induced development have a significant adverse effect upon local ambient air quality, local ambient noise levels, surface water or groundwater quality or quantity, water supply, fish, shellfish, wildlife, and their natural habitats.

[50 FR 26315, June 25, 1985, as amended at 51 FR 32611, Sept. 12, 1986]

Subpart B—Content of EISs

§ 6.200 **The environmental impact statement.**

Preparers of EISs must conform with the requirements of 40 CFR Part 1502 in writing EISs.

§ 6.201 **Format.**

The format used for EISs shall encourage good analysis and clear presentation of alternatives, including the proposed action, and their environmental, economic and social impacts. The following standard format for EISs should be used unless the responsible official determines that there is a compelling reason to do otherwise:

(a) Cover sheet;

(b) Executive Summary;

(c) Table of contents;

(d) Purpose of and need for action;

(e) Alternatives including proposed action;

(f) Affected environment;

(g) Environmental consequences of the alternatives;

(h) Coordination (includes list of agencies, organizations, and persons to whom copies of the EIS are sent);

(i) List of preparers;

(j) Index (commensurate with complexity of EIS);

(k) Appendices.

§ 6.202 Executive summary.

The executive summary shall describe in sufficient detail (10–15 pages) the critical facets of the EIS so that the reader can become familiar with the proposed project or action and its net effects. The executive summary shall focus on:

(a) The existing problem;

(b) A brief description of each alternative evaluated (including the preferred and no action alternatives) along with a listing of the environmental impacts, possible mitigation measures relating to each alternative, and any areas of controversy (including issues raised by governmental agencies and the public); and

(c) Any major conclusions.

A comprehensive summary may be prepared in instances where the EIS is unusually long in nature. In accordance with 40 CFR 1502.19, the comprehensive summary may be circulated in lieu of the EIS; however, both documents shall be distributed to any Federal, State and local agencies who have EIS review responsibilities and also shall be made available to other interested parties upon request.

§ 6.203 Body of EISs.

(a) *Purpose and need.* The EIS shall clearly specify the underlying purpose and need to which EPA is responding. If the action is a request for a permit or a grant, the EIS shall clearly specify the goals and objectives of the applicant.

(b) *Alternatives including the proposed action.* In addition to 40 CFR 1502.14, the EIS shall discuss:

(1) *Alternatives considered by the applicant.* This section shall include a *balanced* description of each alternative considered by the applicant. These discussions shall include size and location of facilities, land requirements, operation and maintenance requirements, auxiliary structures such as pipelines or transmission lines, and construction schedules. The alternative of no action shall be discussed and the applicant's preferred alternative(s) shall be identified. For alternatives which were eliminated from detailed study, a brief discussion of the reasons for their having been eliminated shall be included.

(2) *Alternatives available to EPA.* EPA alternatives to be discussed shall include: (i) Taking an action; or (ii) taking an action on a modified or alternative project, including an action not considered by the applicant; and (iii) denying the action.

(3) *Alternatives available to other permitting agencies.* When preparing a joint EIS, and if applicable, the alternatives available to other Federal and/or State agencies shall be discussed.

(4) *Identifying preferred alternative.* In the final EIS, the responsible official shall signify the preferred alternative.

(c) *Affected environment and environmental consequences of the alternatives.* The affected environment on which the evaluation of each alternative shall be based includes, for example, hydrology, geology, air quality, noise, biology, socioeconomics, energy, land use, and archeology and historic subjects. The discussion shall be structured so as to present the total impacts of each alternative for easy comparison among all alternatives by the reader. The effects of a "no action" alternative should be included to facilitate reader comparison of the beneficial and adverse impacts of other alternatives to the applicant doing nothing. A description of the environmental setting shall be included in the "no action" alternative for the purpose of providing needed background information. The amount of detail in describing the affected environment shall be commensurate with the complexity of the situation and the importance of the anticipated impacts.

(d) *Coordination.* The EIS shall include: (1) The objections and suggestions made by local, State, and Federal agencies before and during the EIS review process must be given full consideration, along with the issues of public concern expressed by individual citizens and interested environmental groups. The EIS must include discussions of any such comments concerning our actions, and the author of each comment should be identified. If a comment has resulted in a change in the project or the EIS, the impact statement should explain the reason.

(2) Public participation through public hearings or scoping meetings shall also be included. If a public hearing has been held prior to the publication of the EIS, a summary of the transcript should be included in this section. For the public hearing which shall be held after the publication of the draft EIS, the date, time, place, and purpose shall be included here.

(3) In the final EIS, a summary of the coordination process and EPA responses to comments on the draft EIS shall be included.

[44 FR 64177, Nov. 6, 1979, as amended at 50 FR 26316, June 25, 1985]

§ 6.204 Incorporation by reference.

In addition to 40 CFR 1502.21, material incorporated into an EIS by reference shall be organized to the extent possible into a Supplemental Information Document and be made available for review upon request. No material may be incorporated by reference unless it is reasonably available for inspection by potentially interested persons within the period allowed for comment.

§ 6.205 List of preparers.

When the EIS is prepared by contract, either under direct contract to EPA or through an applicant's or grantee's contractor, the responsible official must independently evaluate the EIS prior to its approval and take responsibility for its scope and contents. The EPA officials who undertake this evaluation shall also be described under the list of preparers.

Subpart C—Coordination With Other Environmental Review and Consultation Requirements

§ 6.300 General.

Various Federal laws and executive orders address specific environmental concerns. The responsible official shall integrate to the greatest practicable extent the applicable procedures in this subpart during the implementation of the environmental review process under Subparts E through I. This subpart presents the central requirements of these laws and executive orders. It refers to the pertinent authority and regulations or guidance that contain the procedures. These laws and executive orders establish review procedures independent of NEPA requirements. The responsible official shall be familiar with any other EPA or appropriate agency procedures implementing these laws and executive orders.

[44 FR 64177, Nov. 6, 1979]

§ 6.301 Landmarks, historical, and archeological sites.

EPA is subject to the requirements of the Historic Sites Act of 1935, 16 U.S.C. 461 *et seq.*, the National Historic Preservation Act of 1966, as amended, 16 U.S.C. 470 *et seq.*, the Archaeological and Historic Preservation Act of 1974, 16 U.S.C. 469 *et seq.*, and Executive Order 11593, entitled "Protection and Enhancement of the Cultural Environment." These statutes, regulations and executive orders establish review procedures independent of NEPA requirements.

(a) *National natural landmarks.* Under the Historic Sites Act of 1935, the Secretary of the Interior is authorized to designate areas as national natural landmarks for listing on the National Registry of Natural Landmarks. In conducting an environmental review of a proposed EPA action, the responsible official shall consider the existence and location of natural landmarks using information provided by the National Park Service pursuant to 36 CFR 62.6(d) to avoid undesirable impacts upon such landmarks.

(b) *Historic, architectural, archeological, and cultural sites.* Under section 106 of the National Historic Preservation Act and Executive Order 11593, if an EPA undertaking affects any property with historic, architectural, archeological or cultural value that is listed on or eligible for listing on the National Register of Historic Places, the responsible official shall comply with the procedures for consultation and comment promulgated by the Advisory Council on Historic Preservation in 36 CFR Part 800. The responsible official must identify properties affected by the undertaking that are potentially eligible for listing on the National Register and shall request a determination of eligibility from the Keeper of the National Register, Department of the Interior, under the procedures in 36 CFR Part 63.

(c) *Historic, prehistoric and archeological data.* Under the Archeological and Historic Preservation Act, if an EPA activity may cause irreparable loss or destruction of significant scientific, prehistoric, historic or archeological data, the responsible official or the Secretary of the Interior is authorized to undertake data recovery and preservation activities. Data recovery and preservation activities shall be conducted in accordance with implementing procedures promulgated by the Secretary of the Interior. The National Park Service has published technical standards and guidelines regarding archeological preservation activities and methods at 48 FR 44716 (September 29, 1983).

[44 FR 64177, Nov. 6, 1979, as amended at 50 FR 26316, June 25, 1985]

§ 6.302 Wetlands, floodplains, important farmlands, coastal zones, wild and scenic rivers, fish and wildlife, and endangered species.

The following procedures shall apply to EPA administrative actions in programs to which the pertinent statute or executive order applies.

(a) *Wetlands protection.* Executive Order 11990, Protection of Wetlands, requires Federal agencies conducting certain activities to avoid, to the extent possible, the adverse impacts associated with the destruction or loss of wetlands and to avoid support of new construction in wetlands if a practicable alternative exists. EPA's Statement of Procedures on Floodplain Management and Wetlands Protection (dated January 5, 1979, incorporated as Appendix A hereto) requires EPA programs to determine if proposed actions will be in or will affect wetlands. If so, the responsible official shall prepare a floodplains/wetlands assessment, which will be part of the environmental assessment or environmental impact statement. The responsible official shall either avoid adverse impacts or minimize them if no practicable alternative to the action exists.

(b) *Floodplain management.* Executive Order 11988, Floodplain Management, requires Federal agencies to evaluate the potential effects of actions they may take in a floodplain to avoid, to the extent possible, adverse effects associated with direct and indirect development of a floodplain. EPA's Statement of Procedures on Floodplain Management and Wetlands Protection (dated January 5, 1979, incorporated as Appendix A hereto), requires EPA programs to determine whether an action will be located in or will affect a floodplain. If so, the responsible official shall prepare a floodplain/wetlands assessment. The assessment will become part of the environmental assessment or environmental impact statement. The responsible official shall either avoid adverse im-

pacts or minimize them if no practicable alternative exists.

(c) *Important farmlands.* It is EPA's policy as stated in the EPA Policy To Protect Environmentally Significant Agricultural Lands, dated September 8, 1978, to consider the protection of the Nation's significant/important agricultural lands from irreversible conversion to uses which result in its loss as an environmental or essential food production resource. In addition the Farmland Protection Policy Act, (FPPA) 7 U.S.C. 4201 *et seq.*, requires federal agencies to use criteria developed by the Soil Conservation Service, U.S. Department of Agriculture, to:

(1) Identify and take into account the adverse effects of their programs on the preservation of farmlands from conversion to other uses; (2) consider alternative actions, as appropriate, that could lessen such adverse impacts; and (3) assure that their programs, to the extent possible, are compatible with State and local government and private programs and policies to protect farmlands. If an EPA action may adversely impact farmlands which are classified prime, unique or of State and local importance as defined in the Act, the responsible official shall in all cases apply the evaluative criteria promulgated by the U.S. Department of Agriculture at 7 CFR Part 658. If categories of important farmlands, which include those defined in both the FPPA and the EPA policy, are identified in the project study area, both direct and indirect effects of the undertaking on the remaining farms and farm support services within the project area and immediate environs shall be evaluated. Adverse effects shall be avoided or mitigated to the extent possible.

(d) *Coastal zone management.* The Coastal Zone Management Act, 16 U.S.C. 1451 *et seq.*, requires that all Federal activities in coastal areas be consistent with approved State Coastal Zone Management Programs, to the maximum extent possible. If an EPA action may affect a coastal zone area, the responsible official shall assess the impact of the action on the coastal zone. If the action significantly affects the coastal zone area and the State has an approved coastal zone management program, a consistency determination shall be sought in accordance with procedures promulgated by the Office of Coastal Zone Management in 15 CFR Part 930.

(e) *Wild and scenic rivers.* (1) The Wild and Scenic Rivers Act, 16 U.S.C. 1274 *et seq.*, establishes requirements applicable to water resource projects affecting wild, scenic or recreational rivers within the National Wild and Scenic Rivers system as well as rivers designated on the National Rivers Inventory to be studied for inclusion in the national system. Under the Act, a federal agency may not assist, through grant, loan, license or otherwise, the construction of a water resources project that would have a direct and adverse effect on the values for which a river in the National System or

study river on the National Rivers Inventory was established, as determined by the Secretary of the Interior for rivers under the jurisdiction of the Department of the Interior and by the Secretary of Agriculture for rivers under the jurisdiction of the Department of Agriculture. Nothing contained in the foregoing sentence, however, shall:

(i) Preclude licensing of, or assistance to, developments below or above a wild, scenic or recreational river area or on any stream tributary thereto which will not invade the area or unreasonably diminish the scenic, recreational, and fish and wildlife values present in the area on October 2, 1968; or

(ii) Preclude licensing of, or assistance to, developments below or above a study river or any stream tributary thereto which will not invade the area or diminish the scenic, recreational and fish and wildlife values present in the area on October 2, 1968.

(2) The responsible official shall:

(i) Determine whether there are any wild, scenic or study rivers on the National Rivers Inventory or in the planning area, and

(ii) Not recommend authorization of any water resources project that would have a direct and adverse effect on the values for which such river was established, as determined by the administering Secretary in request of appropriations to begin construction of any such project, whether heretofore or hereafter authorized, without advising the administering Secretary, in writing of this intention at least sixty days in advance, and without specifically reporting to the Congress in writing at the time the recommendation or request is made in what respect construction of such project would be in conflict with the purposes of the Wild and Scenic Rivers Act and would affect the component and the values to be protected by the Responsible Official under the Act.

(3) Applicable consultation requirements are found in section 7 of the Act. The Department of Agriculture has promulgated implementing procedures, under section 7 at 36 CFR Part 297, which apply to water resource projects located within, above, below or outside a wild and scenic river or study river under the Department's jurisdiction.

(f) *Barrier islands.* The Coastal Barrier Resources Act, 16 U.S.C. 3501 *et seq.*, generally prohibits new federal expenditures or financial assistance for any purpose within the Coastal Barrier Resources System on or after October 18, 1982. Specified exceptions to this prohibition are allowed only after consultation with the Secretary of the Interior. The responsible official shall ensure that consultation is carried out with the Secretary of the Interior before making available new expenditures or financial assistance for activities within areas covered by the Coastal Barriers Resources Act in accord with the U.S. Fish and Wildlife Service published guidelines defining new expenditures and financial assistance, and describing procedures for consultation at 48 FR 45664 (October 6, 1983).

(g) *Fish and wildlife protection.* The Fish and Wildlife Coordination Act, 16 U.S.C. 661 *et seq.,* requires Federal agencies involved in actions that will result in the control or structural modification of any natural stream or body of water for any purpose, to take action to protect the fish and wildlife resources which may be affected by the action. The responsible official shall consult with the Fish and Wildlife Service and the appropriate State agency to ascertain the means and measures necessary to mitigate, prevent and compensate for project-related losses of wildlife resources and to enhance the resources. Reports and recommendations of wildlife agencies should be incorporated into the environmental assessment or environmental impact statement. Consultation procedures are detailed in 16 U.S.C. 662.

(h) *Endangered species protection.* Under the Endangered Species Act, 16 U.S.C. 1531 *et seq.,* Federal agencies are prohibited from jeopardizing threatened or endangered species or adversely modifying habitats essential to their survival. The responsible official shall identify all designated endangered or threatened species or their habitat that may be affected by an EPA action. If listed species or their habitat may be affected, formal consultation must be undertaken with the Fish and Wildlife Service or the National Marine Fisheries Service, as appropriate. If the consultation reveals that the EPA activity may jeopardize a listed species or habitat, mitigation measures should be considered. Applicable consultation procedures are found in 50 CFR Part 402.

[44 FR 64177, Nov. 6, 1979, as amended at 50 FR 26316, June 25, 1985]

§ 6.303 Air quality.

(a) The Clean Air Act, as amended in 1977, 42 U.S.C. 7476(c), requires all Federal projects, licenses, permits, plans, and financial assistance activities to conform to any State Air Quality Implementation Plan (SIP) approved or promulgated under section 110 of the Act. For proposed EPA actions that may significantly affect air quality, the responsible official shall assess the extent of the direct or indirect increases in emissions and the resultant change in air quality.

(b) If the proposed action may have a significant direct or indirect adverse effect on air quality, the responsible official shall consult with the appropriate State and local agencies as to the conformity of the proposed action with the SIP. Such agencies shall include the State agency with primary responsibility for the SIP, the agency designated under section 174 of the Clean Air Act and, where appropriate, the metropolitan planning organization (MPO). This consultation should include a request for a recommenda-

tion as to the conformity of the proposed action with the SIP.

(c) The responsible official shall provide an assurance in the FNSI or the draft EIS that the proposed action conforms with the SIP.

(d) The assurance of conformity shall be based on a determination of the following:

(1) The proposed action will be in compliance with all applicable Federal and State air pollution emission limitations and standards;

(2) The direct and indirect air pollution emissions resulting from the proposed action have been expressly quantified in the emissions growth allowance of the SIP; or if a case-by-case offset approach is included in the SIP, that offsets have been obtained for the proposed action's air quality impacts;

(3) The proposed action conforms to the SIP's provisions for demonstrating reasonable further progress toward attainment of the national ambient air quality standards by the required date;

(4) The proposed action complies with all other provisions and requirements of the SIP.

(e) During the 30-day FNSI and 45-day draft EIS review time periods EPA shall provide an opportunity for the State agency with primary responsibility for the SIP to concur or nonconcur with the determination of conformity. All State notifications of concurrence or nonconcurrence with the EPA conformity determination shall include a record of consultation with the appropriate section 174 agency and, where different, the MPO. There shall be a presumption of State concurrence if no objection is received by EPA during the review time period.

(f) The responsible official shall provide in the FNSI or the final EIS a response to a notification of state nonconcurrence with the EPA conformity determination. This response shall include the basis by which the conformity of the proposed action to the SIP will be assured. If the responsible official finds that the State nonconcurrence with the EPA conformity determination is unjustified, then an explanation of this finding shall be included in the FNSI or the final EIS.

(g) With regard to wastewater treatment works subject to review under Subpart E of this part, the responsible official shall consider the air pollution control requirements specified in section 316(b) of the Clean Air Act, 42 U.S.C. 7616, and Agency implementing procedures.

[44 FR 64177, Nov. 6, 1979, as amended at 50 FR 26317, June 25, 1985]

Subpart D—Public and Other Federal Agency Involvement

§ 6.400 Public involvement.

(a) *General.* EPA shall make diligent efforts to involve the public in the en-

vironmental review process consistent with program regulations and EPA policies on public participation. The responsibile official shall ensure that public notice is provided for in accordance with 40 CFR 1506.6(b) and shall ensure that public involvement is carried out in accordance with EPA Public Participation Regulations, 40 CFR Part 25, and other applicable EPA public participation procedures.

(b) *Publication of notices of intent.* As soon as practicable after his decision to prepare an EIS and before the scoping process, the responsible official shall send the notice of intent to interested and affected members of the public and shall request the OEA to publish the notice of intent in the FEDERAL REGISTER. The responsible official shall send to OEA the signed original notice of intent for FEDERAL REGISTER publication purposes. The scoping process should be initiated as soon as practicable in accordance with the requirements of 40 CFR 1501.7. Participants in the scoping process shall be kept informed of substantial changes which evolve during the EIS drafting process.

(c) *Public meetings or hearings.* Public meetings or hearings shall be conducted consistent with Agency program requirements. There shall be a presumption that a scoping meeting will be conducted whenever a notice of intent has been published. The responsible official shall conduct a public hearing on a draft EIS. The responsible official shall ensure that the draft EIS is made available to the public at least 30 days in advance of the hearing.

(d) *Findings of no significant impact (FNSI).* The responsible official shall allow for sufficient public review of a FNSI before it becomes effective. The FNSI and attendant publication must state that interested persons disagreeing with the decision may submit comments to EPA. The responsible official shall not take administrative action on the project for at least thirty (30) calendar days after release of the FNSI and may allow more time for response. The responsible official shall consider, fully, comments submitted on the FNSI before taking administrative action. The FNSI shall be made available to the public in accordance with the requirements and all appropriate recommendations contained in § 1506.6 of this title.

(e) *Record of Decision (ROD).* The responsible official shall disseminate the ROD to those parties which commented on the draft or final EIS.

(f) *Categorical exclusions.* An applicant who files for and receives a determination of categorical exclusion under § 6.107(a), or has one rescinded under § 6.107(c), shall publish a notice indicating the determination of eligibility or rescission in a local newspaper of community-wide circulation and indicate the availability of the supporting documentation for public inspection. The responsible official shall, concurrent with the publication of the notice: Make the documentation as outlined in § 6.107(b) available to the public; and distribute the notice of the determination to all known interested parties.

[44 FR 64177, Nov. 6, 1979, as amended at 51 FR 32611, Sept. 12, 1986]

§ 6.401 Official filing requirements.

(a) *General.* OEA is responsible for the conduct of the official filing system for EISs. This system was established as a central repository for all EISs which serves not only as means of advising the public of the availability of each EIS but provides a uniform method for the computation of minimum time periods for the review of EISs. OEA publishes a weekly notice in the FEDERAL REGISTER listing all EISs received during a given week. The 45-day and 30-day review periods for draft and final EISs, respectively, are computed from the Friday following a given reporting week. Pursuant to 40 CFR 1506.9, responsible officials shall comply with the guidelines established by OEA on the conduct of the filing system.

(b) *Minimum time periods.* No decision on EPA actions shall be made until the later of the following dates: (1) Ninety (90) days after the date established in § 6.401(a) of this part from which the draft EIS review time period is computed.

(2) Thirty (30) days after the date established in § 6.401(a) of this part from which the final EIS review time period is computed.

(c) *Filing of EISs.* All EISs, including supplements, must be officially filed with OEA. Responsible officials shall transmit each EIS in five (5) copies to the Director, Office of Environmental Review, EIS Filing Section (A-104). OEA will provide CEQ with one copy of each EIS filed. No EIS will be officially filed by OER unless the EIS has been made available to the public. OEA will not accept unbound copies of EISs for filing.

(d) *Extensions or waivers.* The responsible official may independently extend review periods. In such cases, the responsible official shall notify OEA as soon as possible so that adequate notice may be published in the weekly FEDERAL REGISTER report. OEA upon a showing of compelling reasons of national policy may reduce the prescribed review periods. Also, OEA upon a showing by any other Federal agency of compelling reasons of national policy may extend prescribed review periods, but only after consultation with the responsible official. If the responsible official does not concur with the extension of time, OEA may not extend a prescribed review period more than 30 days beyond the minimum prescribed review period.

(e) *Rescission of filed EISs.* The responsible official shall file EISs with OEA at the same time they are transmitted to commenting agencies and made available to the public. The responsible official is required to reproduce an adequate supply of EISs to satisfy these distribution requirements prior to filing an EIS. If the EIS is not made available, OEA will consider retraction of the EIS or revision of the prescribed review periods based on the circumstances.

[44 FR 64177, Nov. 6, 1979, as amended at 47 FR 9829, Mar. 8, 1982]

§ 6.402 Availability of documents.

(a) *General.* The responsible official will ensure sufficient copies of the EIS are distributed to interested and affected members of the public and are made available for further public distribution. EISs, comments received, and any underlying documents should be available to the public pursuant to the provisions of the Freedom of Information Act (5 U.S.C. 552(b)), without regard to the exclusion for interagency memoranda where such memoranda transmit comments of Federal agencies on the environmental impact of the proposed actions. To the extent practicable, materials made available to the public shall be provided without charge; otherwise, a fee may be imposed which is not more than the actual cost of reproducing copies required to be sent to another Federal agency.

(b) *Public information.* Lists of all notices, determinations and other reports/documentation, related to these notices and determinations, involving CEs, EAs, FNSIs, notices of intent, EISs, and RODs prepared by EPA shall be available for public inspection and maintained by the responsible official as a monthly status report. OEA shall maintain a comprehensive list of notices of intent and draft and final EISs provided by all responsible officials for public inspection including publication in the FEDERAL REGISTER. In addition, OEA will make copies of all EPA-prepared EISs available for public inspection; the responsible official shall do the same for any EIS he/she undertakes.

[44 FR 64177, Nov. 6, 1979, as amended at 51 FR 32611, Sept. 12, 1986]

§ 6.403 The commenting process.

(a) *Inviting comments.* After preparing a draft EIS and before preparing a final EIS, the responsible official shall obtain the comments of Federal agencies, other governmental entities and the public in accordance with 40 CFR 1503.1.

(b) *Response to comments.* The responsible official shall respond to comments in the final EIS in accordance with 40 CFR 1503.4.

§ 6.404 Supplements.

(a) *General.* The responsible official shall consider preparing supplements to draft and final EISs in accordance with 40 CFR 1502.9(c). A supplement shall be prepared, circulated and filed in the same fashion (exclusive of scoping) as draft and final EISs.

(b) *Alternative procedures.* In the case where the responsible official wants to deviate from existing procedures, OEA shall be consulted. OEA shall consult with CEQ on any alternative arrangements.

[44 FR 64177, Nov. 6, 1979, as amended at 47 FR 9829, Mar. 8, 1982]

Subpart E—Environmental Review Procedures for Wastewater Treatment Construction Grants Program

SOURCE: 50 FR 26317, June 25, 1985, unless otherwise noted.

§ 6.500 Purpose.

This subpart amplifies the procedures described in Subparts A through D with detailed environmental review procedures for the Municipal Wastewater Treatment Works Construction Grants Program under Title II of the Clean Water Act.

§ 6.501 Definitions.

(a) *"Step 1 facilities planning"* means preparation of a plan for facilities as described in 40 CFR Part 35, Subpart E or I.

(b) *"Step 2"* means a project to prepare design drawings and specifications as described in 40 CFR Part 35, Subpart E or I.

(c) *"Step 3"* means a project to build a publicly owned treatment works as described in 40 CFR Part 35, Subpart E or I.

(d) *"Step 2+3"* means a project which combines preparation of design drawings and specifications as described in § 6.501(b) and building as described in § 6.501(c).

(e) *"Applicant"* means any individual, agency, or entity which has filed an application for grant assistance under 40 CFR Part 35, Subpart E or I.

(f) *"Grantee"* means any individual, agency, or entity which has been awarded wastewater treatment construction grant assistance under 40 CFR Part 35, Subpart E or I.

(g) *"Responsible Official"* means a Federal or State official authorized to fulfill the requirements of this subpart. The responsible federal official is the EPA Regional Administrator and the responsible State official is as defined in a delegation agreement under 205(g) of the Clean Water Act. The responsibilities of the State official are subject to the limitations in § 6.514 of this subpart.

(h) *"Approval of the facilities plan"* means approval of the facilities plan for a proposed wastewater treatment works pursuant to 40 CFR Part 35, Subpart E or I.

§ 6.502 Applicability and limitations.

(a) *Applicability.* This subpart applies to the following actions:

(1) Approval of a facilities plan or an amendment to the plan;

(2) Award of grant assistance for a project where significant change has occurred in the project or its impact

since prior compliance with this part; and

(3) Approval of preliminary Step 3 work prior to the award of grant assistance pursuant to 40 CFR Part 35, Subpart E or I.

(b) *Limitations.* (1) Except as provided in § 6.504(c), all recipients of Step 1 grant assistance must comply with the requirements, steps, and procedures described in this subpart.

(2) As specified in 40 CFR 35.2113, projects that have not received Step 1 grant assistance must comply with the requirements of this subpart prior to submission of an application for Step 3 or Step 2+3 grant assistance.

(3) Except as otherwise provided in § 6.507, no step 3 or 2+3 grant assistance may be awarded for the construction of any component/portion of a proposed wastewater treatment system(s) until the responsible official has:

(i) Completed the environmental review for all complete wastewater treatment system alternatives under consideration for the facilities planning area, or any larger study area identified for the purposes of conducting an adequate environmental review as required under this subpart; and

(ii) Recorded the selection of the preferred alternative(s) in the appropriate decision document (ROD for EISs, FNSI for environmental assessments, or written determination for categorical exclusions).

(4) In accord with § 6.302(f), on or after October 18, 1982, no new expenditures or financial assistance involving the construction grants program can be made within the Coastal Barrier Resource System, or for projects outside the system which would have the effect of encouraging development in the system, other than specified exceptions made by the EPA after consultation with the Secretary of the Interior.

[50 FR 26317, June 25, 1985, as amended at 51 FR 32611, Sept. 12, 1986]

§ 6.503 Overview of the environmental review process.

The process for conducting an environmental review of wastewater treatment construction grant projects includes the following steps:

(a) *Consultation.* The Step 1 grantee or the potential Step 3 or Step 2+3 applicant is encouraged to consult with the State and EPA early in project formulation or the facilities planning stage to determine whether a project is eligible for a categorical exclusion from the remaining substantive environmental review requirements of this part (§ 6.505), to determine alternatives to the proposed project for evaluation, to identify potential environmental issues and opportunities for public recreation and open space, and to determine the potential need for partitioning the environmental review process and/or the need for an Environmental Impact Statement (EIS).

(b) *Determining categorical exclusion eligibility.* At the request of a po-

tential Step 3 or Step 2+3 grant applicant, or a Step 1 facilities planning grantee, the responsible official will determine if a project is eligible for a categorical exclusion in accordance with § 6.505. A Step 1 facilities planning grantee awarded a Step 1 grant on or before December 29, 1981 may request a categorical exclusion at any time during Step 1 facilities planning. A potential Step 3 or Step 2+3 grant applicant may request a categorical exclusion at any time before the submission of a Step 3 or Step 2+3 grant application.

(c) *Documenting environmental information.* If the project is determined to be ineligible for a categorical exclusion, or if no request for a categorical exclusion is made, the potential Step 3 or Step 2+3 applicant or the Step 1 grantee subsequently prepares an Environmental Information Document (EID) (§ 6.506) for the project.

(d) *Preparing environmental assessments.* Except as provided in § 6.506(c)(4) and following a review of the EID by EPA or by a State with delegated authority, EPA prepares an environmental assessment (§ 6.506), or a State with delegated authority (§ 6.514) prepares a preliminary environmental assessment. EPA reviews and finalizes any preliminary assessments. EPA subsequently:

(1) Prepares and issues a Finding of No Significant Impact (FNSI) (§ 6.508); or

(2) Prepares and issues a Notice of Intent to prepare an original or supplemental EIS (§ 6.510) and Record of Decision (ROD) (§ 6.511).

(e) *Monitoring.* The construction and post-construction operation and maintenance of the facilities are monitored (§6.512) to ensure implementation of mitigation measures (§ 6.511) identified in the FNSI or ROD.

[50 FR 26317, June 25, 1985, as amended at 51 FR 32611, Sept. 12, 1986]

§ 6.504 Consultation during the facilities planning process.

(a) *General.* Consistent with 40 CFR 1501.2 and 35.2030(c), the responsible official shall initiate the environmental review process early to identify environmental effects, avoid delays, and resolve conflicts. The environmental review process should be integrated throughout the facilities planning process. Two processes for consultation are described in this section to meet this objective. The first addresses projects awarded Step 1 grant assistance on or before December 29, 1981. The second applies to projects not receiving grant assistance for facilities planning on or before December 29, 1981 and, therefore, subject to the regulations implementing the Municipal Wastewater Treatment Construction Grant Amendments of 1981 (40 CFR Part 35, Subpart I).

(b) *Projects receiving Step 1 grant assistance on or before December 29, 1981.* (1) During facilities planning, the grantee shall evaluate project alternatives and the existence of environmentally important resource areas

including those identified in § 6.108 and § 6.509 of this subpart, and potential for open space and recreation opportunities in the facilities planning area. This evaluation is intended to be brief and concise and should draw on existing information from EPA, State agencies, regional planning agencies, areawide water quality management agencies, and the Step 1 grantee. The Step 1 grantee should submit this information to EPA or a delegated State at the earliest possible time during facilities planning to allow EPA to determine if the action is eligible for a categorical exclusion. The evaluation and any additional analysis deemed necessary by the responsible official may be used by EPA to determine whether the action is eligible for a categorical exclusion from the substantive environmental review requirements of this part. If a categorical exclusion is granted, the grantee will not be required to prepare a formal EID nor will the responsible official be required to prepare an environmental assessment under NEPA. If an action is not granted a categorical exclusion, this evaluation may be used to determine the scope of the EID required of the grantee. This information can also be used to make an early determination of the need for partitioning the environmental review or for an EIS. Whenever possible, the Step 1 grantee should discuss this initial evaluation with both the delegated State and EPA.

(2) A review of environmental information developed by the grantee should be conducted by the responsible official whenever meetings are held to assess the progress of facilities plan development. These meetings should be held after completion of the majority of the EID document and before a preferred alternative is selected. Since any required EIS must be completed before the approval of a facilities plan, a decision whether to prepare an EIS is encouraged early during the facilities planning process. These meetings may assist in this early determination. EPA should inform interested parties of the following:

(i) The preliminary nature of the Agency's position on preparing an EIS;

(ii) The relationship between the facilities planning and environmental review processes;

(iii) The desirability of public input; and

(iv) A contact person for further information.

(c) *Projects not receiving grant assistance for Step 1 facilities planning on or before December 29, 1981.* Potential Step 3 or Step 2+3 grant applicants should, in accordance with § 35.2030(c), consult with EPA and the State early in the facilities planning process to determine the appropriateness of a categorical exclusion, the scope of an EID, or the appropriateness of the early preparation of an environmental assessment or an EIS. The consultation would be most useful during the evaluation of project alternatives prior to the selection of a preferred alternative to assist in resolving any identified environmental problems.

§ 6.505 Categorical exclusions.

(a) *General.* At the request of an existing Step 1 facilities planning grantee or of a potential Step 3 or Step 2+3 grant applicant, the responsible official, as provided for in §§ 6.107(b), 6.400(f) and 6.504(a), shall determine from existing information and document whether an action is consistent with the categories eligible for exclusion from NEPA review identified in § 6.107(d) or § 6.505(b) and not inconsistent with the criteria in § 6.107(e) or § 6.505(c).

(b) *Specialized categories of actions eligible for exclusion.* For this subpart, eligible actions consist of any of the categories in § 6.107(d), or:

(1) Actions for which the facilities planning is consistent with the category listed in § 6.107(d)(1) which do not affect the degree of treatment or capacity of the existing facility including, but not limited to, infiltration and inflow corrections, grant-eligible replacement of existing mechanical equipment or structures, and the construction of small structures on existing sites;

(2) Actions in sewered communities of less than 10,000 persons which are for minor upgrading and minor expansion of existing treatment works. This category does not include actions that directly or indirectly involve the extension of new collection systems funded with federal or other sources of funds;

(3) Actions in unsewered communities of less than 10,000 persons where on-site technologies are proposed; or

(4) Other actions are developed in accordance with § 6.107(f).

(c) *Specialized Criteria for not granting a categorical exclusion.* (1) The full environmental review procedures of this part must be followed if undertaking an action consistent with the categories described in paragraph (b) of this section meets any of the criteria listed in § 6.107(e) or when:

(i) The facilities to be provided will (A) create a new, or (B) relocate an existing, discharge to surface or ground waters;

(ii) The facilities will result in substantial increases in the volume of discharge or the loading of pollutants from an existing source or from new facilities to receiving waters; or

(iii) The facilities would provide capacity to serve a population 30% greater than the existing population.

(d) *Proceeding with grant awards.* (1) After a categorical exclusion on a proposed treatment works has been granted, and notices published in accordance with § 6.400(f), grant awards may proceed without being subject to any further environmental review requirements under this part, unless the responsible official later determines that the project, or the conditions at the time the categorical determination was made, have changed significantly

since the independent EPA review of information submitted by the grantee in support of the exclusion.

(2) For all categorical exclusion determinations:

(i) That are five or more years old on projects awaiting Step 2+3 or Step 3 grant funding, the responsible official shall re-evaluate the project, environmental conditions and public views and, prior to grant award, either:

(A) *Reaffirm*—issue a public notice reaffirming EPA's decision to proceed with the project without need for any further environmental review;

(B) *Supplement*—update the information in the decision document on the categorically excluded project and prepare, issue, and distribute a revised notice in accordance with § 6.107(f); or

(C) *Reassess*—revoke the categorical exclusion in accordance with § 6.107(c) and require a complete environmental review to determine the need for an EIS in accordance with § 6.506, followed by preparation, issuance and distribution of an EA/FNSI or EIS/ROD.

(ii) That are made on projects that have been awarded a Step 2+3 grant, the responsible official shall, at the time of plans and specifications review under § 35.2202(b) of this title, assess whether the environmental conditions or the project's anticipated impact on the environment have changed and, prior to plans and specifications approval, advise the Regional Administrator if additional environmental review is necessary.

[50 FR 26317, June 25, 1985, as amended at 51 FR 32611, Sept. 12, 1986]

§ 6.506 Environmental review process.

(a) *Review of completed facilities plans.* The responsible official shall ensure a review of the completed facilities plan with particular attention to the EID and its utilization in the development of alternatives and the selection of a preferred alternative. An adequate EID shall be an integral part of any facilities plan submitted to EPA or to a State. The EID shall be of sufficient scope to enable the responsible official to make determinations on requests for partitioning the environmental review process in accordance with § 6.507 and for preparing environmental assessments in accordance with § 6.506(b).

(b) *Environmental assessment.* The environmental assessment process shall cover all potentially significant environmental impacts. The responsible official shall prepare a preliminary environmental assessment on which to base a recommendation to finalize and issue the environmental assessment/FNSI. For those States delegated environmental review responsibilities under § 6.514, the State responsible official shall prepare the preliminary environmental assessment in sufficient detail to serve as an adequate basis for EPA's independent NEPA review and decision to finalize and issue an environmental assessment/FNSI or to prepare and issue a notice of intent for an

EIS/ROD. The EPA also may require submission of supplementary information before the facilities plan is approved if needed for its independent review of the State's preliminary assessment for compliance with environmental review requirements. Substantial requests for supplementary information by EPA, including the review of the facilities plan, shall be made in writing. Each of the following subjects outlined below, and requirements of Subpart C of this part, shall be reviewed by the responsible official to identify potentially significant environmental concerns and their associated potential impacts, and the responsible official shall furthermore address these concerns and impacts in the environmental assessment:

(1) *Description of the existing environment.* For the delineated facilities planning area, the existing environmental conditions relevant to the analysis of alternatives, or to determining the environmental impacts of the proposed action, shall be considered.

(2) *Description of the future environment without the project.* The relevant future environmental conditions shall be described. The no action alternative should be discussed.

(3) *Purpose and need.* This should include a summary discussion and demonstration of the need, or absence of need, for wastewater treatment in the facilities planning area, with particular emphasis on existing public health or water quality problems and their severity and extent.

(4) *Documentation.* Citations to information used to describe the existing environment and to assess future environmental impacts should be clearly referenced and documented. These sources should include, as appropriate but not limited to, local, tribal, regional, State, and federal agencies as well as public and private organizations and institutions with responsibility or interest in the types of conditions listed in § 6.509 and in Subpart C of this part.

(5) *Analysis of alternatives.* This discussion shall include a comparative analysis of feasible alternatives, including the no action alternative, throughout the study area. The alternatives shall be screened with respect to capital and operating costs; direct, indirect, and cumulative environmental effects; physical, legal, or institutional constraints; and compliance with regulatory requirements. Special attention should given to: the environmental consequences of long-term, irreversible, and induced impacts; and for projects initiated after September 30, 1978, that grant applicants have satisfactorily demonstrated analysis of potential recreation and open-space opportunities in the planning of the proposed treatment works. The reasons for rejecting any alternatives shall be presented in addition to any significant environmental benefits precluded by rejection of an alternative. The analysis should consider when relevant to the project:

(i) Flow and waste reduction measures, including infiltration/inflow reduction and pretreatment requirements;

(ii) Appropriate water conservation measures;

(iii) Alternative locations, capacities, and construction phasing of facilities;

(iv) Alternative waste management techniques, including pretreatment, treatment and discharge, wastewater reuse, land application, and individual systems;

(v) Alternative methods for management of sludge, other residual materials, including utilization options such as land application, composting, and conversion of sludge for marketing as a soil conditioner or fertilizer;

(vi) Improving effluent quality through more efficient operation and maintenance;

(vii) Appropriate energy reduction measures; and

(viii) Multiple use including recreation, other open space, and environmental education.

(6) *Evaluating environmental consequences of proposed action.* A full range of relevant impacts of the proposed action shall be discussed, including measures to mitigate adverse impacts, any irreversible or irretrievable commitments of resources to the project and the relationship between local short-term uses of the environment and the maintenance and enhancement of long-term productivity. Any specific requirements, including grant conditions and areawide waste treatment management plan requirements, should be identified and referenced. In addition to these items, the responsible official may require that other analyses and data in accordance with Subpart C which are needed to satisfy environmental review requirements be included with the facilities plan. Such requirements should be discussed whenever meetings are held with Step 1 grantees or potential Step 3 or Step 2 + 3 applicants.

(7) *Minimizing adverse effects of the proposed action.* (i) Structural and nonstructural measures, directly or indirectly related to the facilities plan, to mitigate or eliminate adverse effects on the human and natural environments, shall be identified during the environmental review. Among other measures, structual provisions include changes in facility design, size, and location; non-structural provisions include staging facilities, monitoring and enforcement of environmental regulations, and local commitments to develop and enforce land use regulations.

(ii) The EPA shall not accept a facilities plan, nor award grant assistance for its implementation, if the applicant/grantee has not made, or agreed to make, changes in the project, in accordance with determinations made in a FNSI based on its supporting environmental assessment or the ROD for a EIS. The EPA shall condition a grant, or seek other ways, to ensure that the grantee will comply with such environmental review determinations.

(c) *FNSI/EIS determination.* The responsible official shall apply the criteria under § 6.509 to the following:

(1) A complete facilities plan;

(2) The EID;

(3) The preliminary environmental assessment; and

(4) Other documentation, deemed necessary by the responsible official adequate to make an EIS determination by EPA. Where EPA determines that an EIS is to be prepared, there is no need to prepare a formal environmental assessment. If EPA or the State identifies deficiencies in the EID, preliminary environmental assessment, or other supporting documentation, necessary corrections shall be made to this documentation before the conditions of the Step 1 grant are considered satisfied or before the Step 3 or Step 2+3 application is considered complete. The responsible official's determination to issue a FNSI or to prepare an EIS shall constitute final Agency action, and shall not be subject to administrative review under 40 CFR Part 30 Subpart L.

[50 FR 26317, June 25, 1985, as amended at 51 FR 32612, Sept. 12, 1986]

§ 6.507 Partitioning the environmental review process.

(a) *Purpose.* Under certain circumstances the building of a component/portion of a wastewater treatment system may be justified in advance of completing all NEPA requirements for the remainder of the system(s). When there are overriding considerations of cost or impaired program effectiveness, the responsible official may award a construction grant, or approve procurement by other than EPA funds, for a discrete component of a complete wastewater treatment system(s). The process of partitioning the environmental review for the discrete component shall comply with the criteria and procedures described in paragraph (b) of this section. In addition, all reasonable alternatives for the overall wastewater treatment works system(s) of which the component is a part shall have been previously identified, and each part of the environmental review for the remainder of the overall facilities system(s) in the planning area in accordance with § 6.502(b)(3) shall comply with all requirements under § 6.506.

(b) *Criteria for partitioning.* (1) Projects may be partitioned under the following circumstances:

(i) To overcome impaired program effectiveness, the project component, in addition to meeting the criteria listed in paragraph (b)(2) of this section, must immediately remedy a severe public health, water quality or other environmental problem; or

(ii) To significantly reduce direct costs on EPA projects, or other related public works projects, the project component (such as major pieces of equipment, portions of conveyances or small structures) in addition to meeting the criteria listed in paragraph (b)(2) of this section, must achieve a cost savings to the federal government and/or to the grantee's or potential grantee's

overall costs incurred in procuring the wastewater treatment component(s) and/or the installation of other related public works projects funded in coordination with other federal, State, tribal or local agencies.

(2) The project component also must:

(i) Not foreclose any reasonable alternatives identified for the overall wastewater treatment works system(s);

(ii) Not cause significant adverse direct or indirect environmental impacts including those which cannot be acceptably mitigated without completing the entire wastewater treatment system of which the component is a part; and

(iii) Not be highly controversial.

(c) *Requests for partitioning.* The applicant's or State's request for partitioning must contain the following:

(1) A description of the discrete component proposed for construction before completing the environmental review of the entire facilities plan;

(2) How the component meets the above criteria;

(3) The environmental information required by § 6.506 of this subpart for the component; and

(4) Any preliminary information that may be important to EPA in an EIS determination for the entire facilities plan (§ 6.509).

(d) *Approval of requests for partitioning.* The responsible official shall:

(1) Review the request for partitioning against all requirements of this subpart;

(2) If approvable, prepare and issue a FNSI in accordance with § 6.508;

(3) Include a grant condition prohibiting the building of additional or different components of the entire facilities system(s) in the planning area as described in § 6.502(b)(3)(i).

[50 FR 26317, June 25, 1985, as amended at 51 FR 32612, Sept. 12, 1986]

§ 6.508 Finding of No Significant Impact (FNSI) determination.

(a) *Criteria for producing and distributing FNSIs.* If, after completion of the environmental review, EPA determines that an EIS will not be required, the responsible official shall issue a FNSI in accordance with §§ 6.105(f) and 6.400(d). The FNSI will be based on EPA's independent review of the preliminary environmental assessment and any other environmental information deemed necessary by the responsible official consistent with the requirements of § 6.506(c). Following the Agency's independent review, the environmental assessment will be finalized and either be incorporated into, or attached to, the FNSI. The FNSI shall list all mitigation measures as defined in § 1508.20 of this title, and specifically identify those mitigation measures necessary to make the recommended alternative environmentally acceptable.

(b) *Proceeding with grant awards.* (1) Once an environmental assessment has been prepared and the issued FNSI becomes effective for the treatment works within the study area, grant awards may proceed without preparation of additional FNSIs, unless the responsible official later determines that the project or environmental conditions have changed significantly from that which underwent environmental review.

(2) For all environmental assessment/FNSI determinations:

(i) That are five or more years old on projects awaiting Step 2+3 or Step 3 grant funding, the responsible official shall re-evaluate the project, environmental conditions and public views and, prior to grant award, either:

(A) *Reaffirm*—issue a public notice reaffirming EPA's decision to proceed with the project without revising the environmental assessment;

(B) *Supplement*—update information and prepare, issue and distribute a revised EA/FNSI in accordance with §§ 6.105(f) and 6.400(d); or

(C) *Reassess*—withdraw the FNSI and publish a notice of intent to produce an EIS followed by the preparation, issuance and distribution of the EIS/ROD.

(ii) That are made on projects that have been awarded a Step 2+3 grant, the responsible official shall, at the time of plans and specifications review under § 35.2202(b) of this title, assess whether the environmental conditions or the project's anticipated impact on the environment have changed and, prior to plans and specifications approval, advise the Regional Administrator if additional environmental review is necessary.

[51 FR 32612, Sept. 12, 1986]

§ 6.509 Criteria for initiating Environmental Impact Statements (EIS).

(a) *Conditions requiring EISs.* (1) The responsible official shall assure that an EIS will be prepared and issued when it is determined that the treatment works or collector system will cause any of the conditions under § 6.108 to exist, or when

(2) The treated effluent is being discharged into a body of water where the present classification is too lenient or is being challenged as too low to protect present or recent uses, and the effluent will not be of sufficient quality or quantity to meet the requirements of these uses.

(b) *Other conditions.* The responsible official shall also consider preparing an EIS if: The project is highly controversial; the project in conjunction with related Federal, State, local or tribal resource projects produces significant cumulative impacts; or if it is determined that the treatment works may violate federal, State, local or tribal laws or requirements imposed for the protection of the environment.

§ 6.510 Environmental Impact Statement (EIS) preparation.

(a) *Steps in preparing EISs.* In addition to the requirements specified in Subparts A, B, C, and D of this part, the responsible official will conduct the following activities:

(1) *Notice of intent.* If a determination is made that an EIS will be required, the responsible official shall prepare and distribute a notice of intent as required in § 6.105(e) of this part.

(2) *Scoping.* As soon as possible, after the publication of the notice of intent, the responsible official will convene a meeting of affected federal, State and local agencies, or affected Indian tribes, the grantee and other interested parties to determine the scope of the EIS. A notice of this scoping meeting must be made in accordance with § 6.400(a) and 40 CFR 1506.6(b). As part of the scoping meeting EPA, in cooperation with any delegated State, will as a minimum:

(i) Determine the significance of issues for and the scope of those significant issues to be analyzed in depth, in the EIS;

(ii) Identify the preliminary range of alternatives to be considered;

(iii) Identify potential cooperating agencies and determine the information or analyses that may be needed from cooperating agencies or other parties;

(iv) Discuss the method for EIS preparation and the public participation strategy;

(v) Identify consultation requirements of other environmental laws, in accordance with Subpart C; and

(vi) Determine the relationship between the EIS and the completion of the facilities plan and any necessary coordination arrangements between the preparers of both documents.

(3) *Identifying and evaluating alternatives.* Immediately following the scoping process, the responsible official shall commence the identification and evaluation of all potentially viable alternatives to adequately address the range of issues identified in the scoping process. Additional issues may be addressed, or others eliminated, during this process and the reasons documented as part of the EIS.

(b) *Methods for preparing EISs.* After EPA determines the need for an EIS, it shall select one of the following methods for its preparation:

(1) Directly by EPA's own staff;

(2) By EPA contracting directly with a qualified consulting firm;

(3) By utilizing a third party method, whereby the responsible official enters into "third party agreements" for the applicant to engage and pay for the services of a third party contractor to prepare the EIS. Such agreement shall not be initiated unless both the applicant and the responsible official agree to its creation. A third party agreement will be established prior to the applicant's EID and eliminate the need for that document. In proceeding under the third party agreement, the responsible official shall carry out the following practices:

(i) In consultation with the applicant, choose the third party contractor and manage that contract;

(ii) Select the consultant based on ability and an absence of conflict of interest. Third party contractors will be required to execute a disclosure statement prepared by the responsible official signifying they have no financial or other conflicting interest in the outcome of the project; and

(iii) Specify the information to be developed and supervise the gathering, analysis and presentation of the information. The responsible official shall have sole authority for approval and modification of the statements, analyses, and conclusions included in the third party EIS; or

(4) By utilizing a joint EPA/State process on projects within States which have requirements and procedures comparable to NEPA, whereby the EPA and the State agree to prepare a single EIS document to fulfill both federal and State requirements. Both EPA and the State shall sign a Memorandum of Agreement which includes the responsibilities and procedures to be used by both parties for the preparation of the EIS as provided for in 40 CFR 1506.2(c).

§ 6.511 Record of Decision (ROD) for EISs and identification of mitigation measures.

(a) *Record of Decision.* After a final EIS has been issued, the responsible official shall prepare and issue a ROD in accordance with 40 CFR 1505.2 prior to, or in conjunction with, the approval of the facilities plan. The ROD shall include identification of mitigation measures derived from the EIS process including grant conditions which are necessary to minimize the adverse impacts of the selected alternative.

(b) *Specific mitigation measures.* Prior to the approval of a facilities plan, the responsible official must ensure that effective mitigation measures identified in the ROD will be implemented by the grantee. This should be done by revising the facilities plan, initiating other steps to mitigate adverse effects, or including conditions in grants requiring actions to minimize effects. Care should be exercised if a condition is to be imposed in a grant document to assure that the applicant possesses the authority to fulfill the conditions.

(c) *Proceeding with grant awards.* (1) Once the ROD has been prepared on the selected, or preferred, alternative(s) for the treatment works described within the EIS, grant awards may proceed without the preparation of supplemental EISs unless the responsible official later determines that the project or the environmental conditions described within the current EIS have changed significantly from the previous environmental review in accordance with § 1502.9(c) of this title.

(2) For all EIS/ROD determinations:

(i) That are five or more years old on projects awaiting Step 2+3 or Step 3 grant funding, the responsible official shall re-evaluate the project, environmental conditions and public views and, prior to grant award, either:

(A) *Reaffirm*—issue a public notice reaffirming EPA's decision to proceed with the project, and documenting that no additional significant impacts were identified during the re-evaluation which would require supplementing the EIS; or

(B) *Supplement*—conduct additional studies and prepare, issue and distribute a supplemental EIS in accordance with § 6.404 and document the original, or any revised, decision in an addendum to the ROD.

(ii) That are made on projects that have been awarded a Step 2+3 grant, the responsible official shall, at the time of plans and specifications review under § 35.2202(b) of this title, assess whether the environmental conditions or the project's anticipated impact on the environment have changed, and prior to plans and specifications approval, advise the Regional Administrator if additional environmental review is necessary.

[50 FR 26317, June 25, 1985, as amended at 51 FR 32613, Sept. 12, 1986]

§ 6.512 Monitoring for compliance.

(a) *General.* The responsible official shall ensure adequate monitoring of mitigation measures and other grant conditions identified in the FNSI, or ROD.

(b) *Enforcement.* If the grantee fails to comply with grant conditions, the responsible official may consider applying any of the sanctions specified in 40 CFR 30.900.

§ 6.513 Public participation.

(a) *General.* Consistent with public participation regulations in Part 25 of this title, and Subpart D of this part, it is EPA policy that certain public participation steps be achieved before the State and EPA complete the environmental review process. As a minimum, all potential applicants that do not qualify for a categorical exclusion shall conduct the following steps in accordance with procedures specified in Part 25 of this title:

(1) One public meeting when alternatives have been developed, but before an alternative has been selected, to discuss all alternatives under consideration and the reasons for rejection of others; and

(2) One public hearing prior to formal adoption of a facilities plan to discuss the proposed facilities plan and any needed mitigation measures.

(b) *Coordination.* Public participation activities undertaken in connection with the environmental review process should be coordinated with any other applicable public participation program wherever possible.

(c) *Scope.* The requirements of 40 CFR 6.400 shall be fulfilled, and consistent with 40 CFR 1506.6, the responsible official may institute such additional NEPA-related public participation procedures as are deemed necessary during the environmental review process.

[50 FR 26317, June 25, 1985, as amended at 51 FR 32613, Sept. 12, 1986]

§ 6.514 Delegation to States.

(a) *General.* Authority delegated to the State under section 205(g) of the Clean Water Act to review a facilities plan may include all EPA activities under this part except for the following:

(1) Determinations of whether or not a project qualifies for a categorical exclusion;

(2) Determinations to partition the environmental review process;

(3) Finalizing the scope of an EID when required to adequately conclude an independent review of a preliminary environmental assessment;

(4) Finalizing the scope of an environmental assessement, and finalization, approval and issuance of a final environmental assessment;

(5) Determination to issue, and issuance of, a FNSI based on a completed (§ 6.508) or partitioned (§ 6.507(d)(2)) environmental review;

(6) Determination to issue, and issuance of, a notice of intent for preparing an EIS;

(7) Preparation of EISs under § 6.510(b) (1) and (2), final decisions required for preparing an EIS under § 6.510(b)(3), finalizing the agreement to prepare an EIS under § 6.510(b)(4), finalizing the scope of an EIS, and issuance of draft, final and supplemental EISs;

(8) Preparation and issuance of the ROD based on an EIS;

(9) Final decisions under other applicable laws described in subpart C of this part;

(10) Determination following re-evaluations of projects awaiting grant funding in the case of Step 3 projects whose existing evaluations and/or decision documents are five or more years old, or determinations following re-evaluations on projects submitted for plans and specifications review and approval in the case of awarded Step 2+3 projects where the EPA Regional Administrator has been advised that additional environmental review is necessary, in accordance with § 6.505(d)(2), § 6.508(b)(2) or § 6.511(c)(2); and

(11) Maintenance of official EPA monthly status reports as required under § 6.402(b).

(b) *Elimination of duplication.* The responsible official shall assure that maximum efforts are undertaken to minimize duplication within the limits described under paragraph (a) of this section. In carrying out requirements under this subpart, maximum consideration shall be given to eliminating duplication in accordance with § 1506.2 of this title. Where there are State or local procedures comparable to NEPA, EPA should enter into memoranda of understanding with these States concerning workload distribution and responsibilities not specifically reserved to EPA in paragraph (a) of this section for implementing the environmental review and facilities planning process.

[50 FR 26317, June 25, 1985, as amended at 51 FR 32613, Sept. 12, 1986]

Subpart F—Environmental Review Procedures for the New Source NPDES Program

§ 6.600 Purpose.

(a) *General.* This subpart provides procedures for carrying out the environmental review process for the issuance of new source National Pollutant Discharge Elimination System (NPDES) discharge permits authorized under section 306, section 402, and section 511(c)(1) of the Clean Water Act.

(b) *Permit regulations.* All references in this subpart to the "permit regulations" shall mean Parts 122 and 124 of Title 40 of the CFR relating to the NPDES program.

[44 FR 64177, Nov. 6, 1979, as amended at 47 FR 9831, Mar. 8, 1982]

§ 6.601 Definitions.

(a) The term "administrative action" for the sake of this subpart means the issuance by EPA of an NPDES permit to discharge as a new source, pursuant to 40 CFR 124.15.

(b) The term "applicant" for the sake of this subpart means any person who applies to EPA for the issuance of an NPDES permit to discharge as a new source.

[44 FR 64177, Nov. 6, 1979, as amended at 47 FR 9831, Mar. 8, 1982]

§ 6.602 Applicability.

(a) *General.* The procedures set forth under Subparts A, B, C and D, and this subpart shall apply to the issuance of new source NPDES permits, except for the issuance of a new source NPDES permit from any State which has an approved NPDES program in accordance with section 402(b) of the Clean Water Act.

(b) *New Source Determination.* An NPDES permittee must be determined a "new source" before these procedures apply. New source determinations will be undertaken pursuant to the provisions of the permit regulations under § 122.29(a) and (b) of this chapter and § 122.53(h).

[44 FR 64177, Nov. 6, 1979, as amended at 47 FR 9831, Mar. 8, 1982; 51 FR 32613, Sept. 12, 1986]

§ 6.603 Limitations on actions during environmental review process.

The processing and review of an applicant's NPDES permit application shall proceed concurrently with the procedures within this subpart. Actions undertaken by the applicant or EPA shall be performed consistent with the requirements of § 122.29(c) of this chapter.

[47 FR 9831, Mar. 8, 1982, as amended at 51 FR 32613, Sept. 12, 1986]

§ 6.604 Environmental review process.

(a) *New source.* If EPA's initial determination under § 6.602(b) is that the facility is a new source, the responsible official shall evaluate any environmental information to determine if any significant impacts are anticipated and an EIS is necessary. If the permit applicant requests, the responsible official shall establish time limits for the completion of the environmental review process consistent with 40 CFR 1501.8.

(b) *Information needs.* Information necessary for a proper environmental review shall be provided by the permit applicant in an environmental information document. The responsible official shall consult with the applicant to determine the scope of an environmental information document. In doing this the responsible official shall consider the size of the new source and the extent to which the applicant is capable of providing the required information. The responsible official shall not require the applicant to gather data or perform analyses which unnecessarily duplicate either existing data or the results of existing analyses available to EPA. The responsible official shall keep requests for data to the minimum consistent with his responsibilities under NEPA.

(c) *Environmental assessment.* The responsible official shall prepare a written environmental assessment based on an environmental review of either the environmental information document and/or any other available environmental information.

(d) *EIS determination.* (1) When the environmental review indicates that a significant environmental impact may occur and that the significant adverse impacts cannot be eliminated by making changes in the proposed new source project, a notice of intent shall be issued, and a draft EIS prepared and distributed. When the environmental review indicates no significant impacts are anticipated or when the proposed project is changed to eliminate the significant adverse impacts, a FNSI shall be issued which lists any mitigation measures necessary to make the recommended alternative environmentally acceptable.

(2) The FNSI together with the environmental assessment that supports the finding shall be distributed in accordance with § 6.400(d) of this regulation.

(e) *Lead agency.* (1) If the environmental review reveals that the preparation of an EIS is required, the responsible official shall determine if other Federal agencies are involved with the project. The responsible official shall contact all other involved agencies and together the agencies shall decide the lead agency based on the criteria set forth in 40 CFR 1501.5.

(2) If, after the meeting of involved agencies, EPA has been determined to be the lead agency, the responsible official may request that other involved agencies be cooperating agencies. Cooperating agencies shall be chosen and shall be involved in the EIS preparation process in the manner prescribed in the 40 CFR 1501.6(a). If EPA has been determined to be a cooperating agency, the responsible official shall be involved in assisting in the preparation of the EIS in the manner prescribed in 40 CFR 1501.6(b).

(f) *Notice of intent.* (1) If EPA is the

lead agency for the preparation of an EIS, the responsible official shall arrange through OER for the publication of the notice of intent in the FEDERAL REGISTER, distribute the notice of intent and arrange and conduct a scoping meeting as outlined in 40 CFR 1501.7.

(2) If the responsible official and the permit applicant agree to a third party method of EIS preparation, pursuant to § 6.604(g)(3) of this part, the responsible official shall insure that a notice of intent is published and that a scoping meeting is held before the third party contractor begins work which may influence the scope of the EIS.

(g) *EIS method.* EPA shall prepare EISs by one of the following means:

(1) Directly by its own staff;

(2) By contracting directly with a qualified consulting firm; or

(3) By utilizing a third party method, whereby the responsible official enters into a "third party agreement" for the applicant to engage and pay for the services of a third party contractor to prepare the EIS. Such an agreement shall not be initiated unless both the applicant and the responsible official agree to its creation. A third party agreement will be established prior to the applicant's environmental information document and eliminate the need for that document. In proceeding under the third party agreement, the responsible official shall carry out the following practices:

(i) In consultation with the applicant, choose the third party contractor and manage that contract.

(ii) Select the consultant based on his ability and an absence of conflict of interest. Third party contractors will be required to execute a disclosure statement prepared by the responsible official signifying they have no financial or other conflicting interest in the outcome of the project.

(iii) Specify the information to be developed and supervise the gathering, analysis and presentation of the information. The responsible official shall have sole authority for approval and modification of the statements, analyses, and conclusions included in the third party EIS.

(h) *Documents for the administrative record.* Pursuant to 40 CFR 124.9(b)(6) and 124.18(b)(5) any environmental assessment, FNSI EIS, or supplement to an EIS shall be made a part of the administrative record related to permit issuance.

[44 FR 64177, Nov. 6, 1979, as amended at 47 FR 9831, Mar. 8, 1982]

§ 6.605 Criteria for preparing EISs.

(a) *General guidelines.* (1) When determining the significance of a proposed new source's impact, the responsible official shall consider both its short term and long term effects as well as its direct and indirect effects and beneficial and adverse environmental impacts as defined in 40 CFR 1508.8.

(2) If EPA is proposing to issue a number of new source NPDES permits

during a limited time span and in the same general geographic area, the responsible official shall examine the possibility of tiering EISs. If the permits are minor and environmentally insignificant when considered separately, the responsible official may determine that the cumulative impact of the issuance of all these permits may have a significant environmental effect and require an EIS for the area. Each separate decision to issue an NPDES permit shall then be based on the information in this areawide EIS. Site specific EISs may be required in certain circumstances in addition to the areawide EIS.

(b) *Specific criteria.* An EIS will be prepared when:

(1) The new source will induce or accelerate significant changes in industrial, commercial, agricultural, or residential land use concentrations or distributions which have the potential for significant environmental effects. Factors that should be considered in determining if these changes are environmentally significant include but are not limited to: The nature and extent of the vacant land subject to increased development pressure as a result of the new source; the increases in population or population density which may be induced and the ramifications of such changes; the nature of land use regulations in the affected area and their potential effects on development and the environment; and the changes in the availability or demand for energy and the resulting environmental consequences.

(2) The new source will directly, or through induced development, have significant adverse effect upon local ambient air quality, local ambient noise levels, floodplains, surface or groundwater quality or quantity, fish, wildlife, and their natural habitats.

(3) Any major part of the new source will have significant adverse effect on the habitat of threatened or endangered species on the Department of the Interior's or a State's lists of threatened and endangered species.

(4) The environmental impact of the issuance of a new source NPDES permit will have significant direct and adverse effect on a property listed in or eligible for listing in the National Register of Historic Places.

(5) Any major part of the source will have significant adverse effects on parklands, wetlands, wild and scenic rivers, reservoirs or other important bodies of water, navigation projects, or agricultural lands.

§ 6.606 Record of decision.

(a) *General.* At the time of permit award, the responsible official shall prepare a record of decision in those cases where a final EIS was issued in accordance with 40 CFR 1505.2 and pursuant to the provisions of the permit regulations under 40 CFR 124.15 and 124.18(b)(5). The record of decision shall list any mitigation measures necessary to make the recommended alternative environmentally acceptable.

(b) *Mitigation measures.* The mitigation measures derived from the EIS process shall be incorporated as conditions of the permit; ancillary agreements shall not be used to require mitigation.

[44 FR 64177, Nov. 6, 1979, as amended at 47 FR 9831, Mar. 8, 1982]

§ 6.607 Monitoring.

In accordance with 40 CFR 1505.3 and pursuant to 40 CFR 122.66(c) and 122.10 the responsible official shall ensure that there is adequate monitoring of compliance with all NEPA related requirements contained in the permit.

[47 FR 9831, Mar. 8, 1982]

Subpart G—Environmental Review Procedures for Research and Development Programs

§ 6.700 Purpose.

This subpart amplifies the requirements described in Subparts A through D by providing more specific environmental review procedures on research and development programs undertaken by the Office of Research and Development (ORD).

§ 6.701 Definition.

The term "appropriate program official" means the official at each decision level within ORD to whom the Assistant Administrator has delegated responsibility for carrying out the environmental review process.

§ 6.702 Applicability.

The requirements of this subpart apply to administrative actions undertaken to approve intramural and extramural programs under the purview of ORD.

§ 6.703 Criteria for preparing EISs.

(a) The responsible official shall assure that an EIS will be prepared when it is determined that any of the conditions under § 6.108 exist and when:

(1) The project consists of field tests involving the introduction of significant quantities of toxic or polluting agricultural chemicals, animal wastes, pesticides, radioactive materials or other hazardous substances into the environment by ORD, its grantees or its contractors;

(2) The action may involve the introduction of species or subspecies not indigenous to an area;

(3) There is a high probability of an action ultimately being implemented on a large scale, and this implementation may result in significant environmental impacts; or

(4) The project involves commitment to a new technology which is significant and may restrict future viable alternatives;

(b) An EIS will not usually be needed when:

(1) The project is conducted completely within any laboratory or other facility, and external environmental effects have been eliminated by methods for disposal of laboratory wastes and safeguards to prevent hazardous materials entering the environment accidentally; or

(2) The project is a relatively small experiment or investigation that is part of a non-Federally funded activity of the private sector, and it makes no significant new or additional contribution to existing pollution.

[44 FR 64177, Nov. 6, 1979, as amended at 50 FR 26323, June 25, 1985]

§ 6.704 Environmental review process.

Environmental review activities will be integrated into the decision levels of ORD's research planning system to assure managerial control.

(a) *Environmental information.* (1) Environmental information documents shall be submitted with all grant applications and all unsolicited contract proposals. The documents shall contain the same information required for EISs under Subpart B. Guidance on environmental information documents shall be included in all grant application kits and attached to instructions for the submission of unsolicited proposals.

(2) In the case of competitive contracts, environmental information documents need not be submitted by potential contractors since the environmental review procedures must be completed before a request for proposal (RFP) is issued. If there is a question concerning the need for an environmental information document, the potential contractor should contact the official responsible for the contract.

(b) *Environmental review.* (1) At the start of the planning year, an environmental review will be performed for each program plan with its supporting substructures (work plans and projects) before incorporating them into the ORD program planning system, unless they are excluded from review by existing legislation. This review is an evaluation of the potentially adverse environmental effects of the efforts required by the program plan. The criteria in § 6.703 of this part shall be used in conducting this review. Each program plan with its supporting substructures which does not have significant adverse impacts may be dismissed from further current year environmental considerations with a single FNSI. Any supporting substructures of a program plan which cannot be dismissed with the parent plan shall be reviewed at the appropriate subordinate levels of the planning system.

(i) All continuing program plans and supporting substructures, including those previously dismissed from consideration, will be reevaluated annually. An environmental review will coincide with the annual planning cycle and whenever a major redirection of a parent plan is undertaken. All environmental documents will be updated as appropriate.

(ii) Later plans and/or projects, added to fulfill the mission objectives but not identified at the time program plans were approved, will be subjected to the same environmental review.

(2) The responsible official shall assure completion of the EPA Form 5300-23 for each extramural project subject to an environmental review. If the project consists of literature studies, computer studies, or studies in which essentially all work is performed within the confines of the laboratory, the Form 5300-23 may be issued as a finding of no significant impact.

(c) *Notice of intent and EIS.* (1) If the reviews conducted according to § 6.704(b) of this part reveal a potential significant adverse effect on the environment and the adverse impact cannot be eliminated by replanning, the appropriate program official shall issue a notice of intent and through proper organizational channels shall request the Regional Administrator to assist him in the preparation and distribution of the EIS.

(2) As soon as possible after release of the notice of intent, the appropriate program official shall prepare a draft EIS in accordance with Subpart B and distribute the draft EIS in accordance with Subpart D.

(3) All draft and final EISs shall be sent through the proper organizational channels to the Assistant Administrator for ORD for approval.

(d) *Finding of no significant impact.* If an environmental review conducted according to § 6.704(b) of this part reveals that proposed actions will not have significant adverse environmental impacts, the appropriate program official shall prepare a FNSI which lists any mitigation measures necessary to make the recommended alternative environmentally acceptable.

(e) *Timing of action.* Pursuant to § 6.401(b), in no case shall a contract or grant be awarded or intramural activity undertaken until the prescribed 30-day review period for a final EIS has elapsed. Similarly, no action shall be taken until the 30-day comment period for a FNSI is completed.

§ 6.705 Record of decision.

The responsible official shall prepare a record of decision in any case where final EIS has been issued in accordance with 40 CFR 1505.2. It shall be prepared at the time of contract or grant award or before the undertaking of the intramural activity. The record of decision shall list any mitigation measures necessary to make the recommended alternative environmentally acceptable.

Subpart H—Environmental Review Procedures for Solid Waste Demonstration Projects

§ 6.800 Purpose.

This subpart amplifies the procedures described in Subparts A through D by providing more specific environmental review procedures for demonstration projects undertaken by the

Office of Solid Waste and Emergency Response.

[44 FR 64177, Nov. 6, 1979, as amended at 51 FR 32613, Sept. 12, 1986]

§ 6.801 Applicability.

The requirements of this subpart apply to solid waste demonstration projects for resource recovery systems and improved solid waste disposal facilities undertaken pursuant to section 8006 of the Resource Conservation and Recovery Act of 1976.

§ 6.802 Criteria for preparing EISs.

The responsible official shall assure that an EIS will be prepared when it is determined that any of the conditions in § 6.108 exist.

[44 FR 64177, Nov. 6, 1979, as amended at 50 FR 26323, June 25, 1985]

§ 6.803 Environmental review process.

(a) *Environmental information.* (1) Environmental information documents shall be submitted to EPA by grant applicants or contractors. If there is a question concerning the need for a document, the potential contractor or grantee should consult with the appropriate project officer for the grant or contract.

(2) The environmental information document shall contain the same sections specified for EIS's in Subpart B. Guidance alerting potential grantees and contractors of the environmental information documents shall be included in all grant application kits, attached to letters concerning the submission of unsolicited proposals, and included with all requests for proposal.

(b) *Environmental review.* An environmental review will be conducted before a grant or contract award is made. This review will include the preparation of an environmental assessment by the responsible official; the appropriate Regional Administrator's input will include his recommendations on the need for an EIS.

(c) *Notice of intent and EIS.* Based on the environmental review if the criteria in § 6.802 of this part apply, the responsible official will assure that a notice of intent and a draft EIS are prepared. The responsible official may request the appropriate Regional Administrator to assist him in the preparation and distribution of the environmental documents.

(d) *Finding of no significant impact.* If the environmental review indicated no significant environmental impacts, the responsible official will assure that a FNSI is prepared which lists any mitigation measures necessary to make the recommended alternative environmentally acceptable.

(e) *Timing of action.* Pursuant to § 6.401(b), in no case shall a contract or grant be awarded until the prescribed 30-day review period for a final EIS has elapsed. Similarly, no action shall be taken until the 30-day comment period for a FNSI is completed.

§ 6.804 Record of decision.

The responsible official shall prepare a record of decision in any case where final EIS has been issued in accordance with 40 CFR 1505.2. It shall be prepared at the time of contract or grant award. The record of decision shall list any mitigation measures necessary to make the recommended alternative environmentally acceptable.

Subpart I—Environmental Review Procedures for EPA Facility Support Activities

§ 6.900 Purpose.

This subpart amplifies the general requirements described in Subparts A through D by providing environmental procedures for the preparation of EISs on construction and renovation of special purpose facilities.

§ 6.901 Definitions.

(a) The term "special purpose facility" means a building or space, including land incidental to its use, which is wholly or predominantly utilized for the special purpose of an agency and not generally suitable for other uses, as determined by the General Services Administration.

(b) The term "program of requirements" means a comprehensive document (booklet) describing program activities to be accomplished in the new special purpose facility or improvement. It includes architectural, mechanical, structural, and space requirements.

(c) The term "scope of work" means a document similar in content to the program of requirements but substantially abbreviated. It is usually prepared for small-scale projects.

§ 6.902 Applicability.

(a) *Actions covered.* These procedures apply to all new special purpose facility construction, activities related to this construction (e.g., site acquisition and clearing), and any improvements or modifications to facilities having potential environmental effects external to the facility, including new construction and improvements undertaken and funded by the Facilities Engineering and Real Estate Branch, Facilities and Support Services Division, Office of the Assistant Administrator for Administration and Resource Management; or by a regional office .

(b) *Actions excluded.* This subpart does not apply to those activities of the Facilities Engineering and Real Estate Branch, Facilities and Support Services Division, for which the branch does not have full fiscal responsibility for the entire project. This includes pilot plant construction, land acquisition, site clearing and access road construction where the Facilities Engineering and Real Estate Branch's activity is only supporting a project financed by a program office. Responsibility for considering the en-

vironmental impacts of such projects rests with the office managing and funding the entire project. Other subparts of this regulation apply depending on the nature of the project.

[44 FR 64177, Nov. 6, 1979, as amended at 51 FR 32613, Sept. 12, 1986]

§ 6.903 Criteria for preparing EISs.

(a) *Preliminary information.* The responsible official shall request an environmental information document from a construction contractor or consulting architect/engineer employed by EPA if he is involved in the planning, construction or modification of special purpose facilities when his activities have potential environmental effects external to the facility. Such modifications include but are not limited to facility additions, changes in central heating systems or wastewater treatment systems, and land clearing for access roads and parking lots.

(b) *EIS preparation criteria.* The responsible official shall conduct an environmental review of all actions involving construction of special purpose facilities and improvements to these facilities. The responsible official shall assure that an EIS will be prepared when it is determined that any of the conditions in § 6.108 of this part exist.

[44 FR 64177, Nov. 6, 1979, as amended at 50 FR 26323, June 25, 1985]

§ 6.904 Environmental review process.

(a) *Environmental review.* (1) An environmental review shall be conducted when the program of requirements or scope of work has been completed for the construction, improvements, or modification of special purpose facilities. For special purpose facility construction, the Chief, Facilities Engineering and Real Estate Branch, shall request the assistance of the appropriate program office and Regional Administrator in the review. For modifications and improvement, the appropriate responsible official shall request assistance in making the review from other cognizant EPA offices.

(2) Any environmental information documents requested shall contain the same sections listed for EISs in Subpart B. Contractors and consultants shall be notified in contractual documents when an environmental information document must be prepared.

(b) *Notice of intent, EIS, and FNSI.* The responsible official shall decide at the completion of the Environmental review whether there may be any significant environmental impacts. If there could be significant environmental impacts, a notice of intent and an EIS shall be prepared according to the procedures under Subparts A, B, C and D. If there are not any significant environmental impacts, a FNSI shall be prepared according to the procedures in Subparts A and D. The FNSI shall list any mitigation measures necessary to make the recommended alternative environmentally acceptable.

(c) *Timing of action.* Pursuant to § 6.401(b), in no case shall a contract be awarded or construction activities begun until the prescribed 30-day wait period for a final EIS has elapsed. Similarly, under § 6.400(d), no action shall be taken until the 30-day comment period for FNSIs is completed.

§ 6.905 Record of decision.

At the time of contract award, the responsible official shall prepare a record of decision in those cases where a final EIS has been issued in accordance with 40 CFR 1505.2. The record of decision shall list any mitigation measures necessary to make the recommended alternative environmentally acceptable.

Subpart J—Assessing the Environmental Effects Abroad of EPA Actions

AUTHORITY: Executive Order 12114, 42 U.S.C. 4321, note.

SOURCE: 46 FR 3364, Jan. 14, 1981, unless otherwise noted.

§ 6.1001 Purpose and policy.

(a) *Purpose.* On January 4, 1979, the President signed Executive Order 12114 entitled "Environmental Effects Abroad of Major Federal Actions." The purpose of this Executive Order is to enable responsible Federal officials in carrying out or approving major Federal actions which affect foreign nations or the global commons to be informed of pertinent environmental considerations and to consider fully the environmental impacts of the actions undertaken. While based on independent authority, this Order furthers the purpose of the National Environmental Policy Act (NEPA) (42 U.S.C. section 4321 et seq.) and the Marine Protection Research and Sanctuaries Act (MPRSA) (33 U.S.C. section 1401 et seq.). It should be noted, however, that in fulfilling its responsibilities under Executive Order 12114, EPA shall be guided by CEQ regulations only to the extent that they are made expressly applicable by this subpart. The procedures set forth below reflect EPA's duties and responsibilities as required under the Executive Order and satisfy the requirement for issuance of procedures under section 2-1 of the Executive Order.

(b) *Policy.* It shall be the policy of this Agency to carry out the purpose and requirements of the Executive Order to the fullest extent possible. EPA, within the realm of its expertise, shall work with the Department of State and the Council on Environmental Quality to provide information to other Federal agencies and foreign nations to heighten awareness of and interest in the environment. EPA shall further cooperate to the extent possible with Federal agencies to lend special expertise and assistance in the preparation of required environmental documents under the Executive Order. EPA shall perform environmental reviews of activities significantly affecting the global commons and foreign nations as required under Executive Order 12114 and as set forth under these procedures.

§ 6.1002 Applicability.

(a) Administrative actions requiring environmental review. The environmental review requirements apply to the activities of EPA as set forth below:

(1) Major research or demonstration projects which affect the global commons or a foreign nation.

(2) Ocean dumping activities carried out under section 102 of the MPRSA which affect the related environment.

(3) Major permitting or licensing by EPA of facilities which affect the global commons or the environment of a foreign nation. This may include such actions as the issuance by EPA of hazardous waste treatment, storage, or disposal facility permits pursuant to section 3005 of the Resource Conservation and Recovery Act (42 U.S.C. Section 6925), NPDES permits pursuant to section 402 of the Clean Water Act (33 U.S.C. section 1342), and prevention of significant deterioration approvals pursuant to Part C of the Clean Air Act (42 U.S.C. section 7470 et seq.).

(4) Wastewater Treatment Construction Grants Program under section 201 of the Clean Water Act when activities addressed in the facility plan would have environmental effects abroad.

(5) Other EPA activities as determined by OER and OIA (see § 6.1007(c)).

§ 6.1003 Definitions.

As used in this subpart, "environment" means the natural and physical environment and excludes social, economic and other environments; "global commons" is that area (land, air, water) outside the jurisdiction of any nation; and "responsible official" is either the EPA Assistant Administrator or Regional Administrator as appropriate for the particular EPA program. Also, an action "significantly" affects the environment if it does *significant* harm to the environment even though on balance the action may be beneficial to the environment. To the extent applicable, the responsible official shall address the considerations set forth in the CEQ Regulations under 40 CFR 1508.27 in determining significant effect.

§ 6.1004 Environmental review and assessment requirements.

(a) *Research and demonstration projects.* The appropriate Assistant Administrator is responsible for performing the necessary degree of environmental review on research and demonstration projects undertaken by EPA. If the research or demonstration project affects the environment of the global commons, the applicant shall prepare an environmental analysis. This will assist the responsible official in determining whether an EIS is necessary. If it is determined that the action significantly affects the environment of the global commons, then an EIS shall be prepared. If the undertaking significantly affects a foreign nation EPA shall prepare a unilateral, bilateral or multilateral environmental

study. EPA shall afford the affected foreign nation or international body or organization an opportunity to participate in this study. This environmental study shall discuss the need for the action, analyze the environmental impact of the various alternatives considered and list the agencies and other parties consulted.

(b) *Ocean dumping activities.* (1) The Assistant Administrator for Water and Waste Management shall ensure the preparation of appropriate environmental documents relating to ocean dumping activities in the global commons under section 102 of the MPRSA. For ocean dumping site designations prescribed pursuant to section 102(c) of the MPRSA and 40 CFR Part 228, EPA shall prepare an environmental impact statement consistent with the requirements of EPA's Procedures for the Voluntary Preparation of Environmental Impact Statements dated October 21, 1974 (see 39 FR 37419). Also EPA shall prepare an environmental impact statement for the establishment or revision of criteria under section 102(a) of MPRSA.

(2) For individual permits issued by EPA under section 102(b) an environmental assessment shall be made by EPA. Pursuant to 40 CFR Part 221, the permit applicant shall submit with the application an environmental analysis which includes a discussion of the need for the action, an outline of alternatives, and an analysis of the environmental impact of the proposed action and alternatives consistent with the EPA criteria established under section 102(a) of MPRSA. The information submitted under 40 CFR Part 221 shall be sufficient to satisfy the environmental assessment requirement.

(c) *EPA permitting and licensing activities.* The appropriate Regional Administrator is responsible for conducting concise environmental reviews with regard to permits issued under section 3005 of the Resource Conservation and Recovery Act (RCRA permits), section 402 of the Clean Water Act (NPDES permits), and section 165 of the Clean Air Act (PSD permits), for such actions undertaken by EPA which affect the global commons or foreign nations. The information submitted by applicants for such permits or approvals under the applicable consolidated-permit regulations (40 CFR Parts 122 and 124) and Prevention of Significant Deterioration (PSD) regulations (40 CFR Part 52) shall satisfy the environmental document requirement under section 2-4(b) of Executive Order 12114. Compliance with applicable requirements in Part 124 of the consolidated permit regulations (40 CFR Part 124) shall be sufficient to satisfy the requirements to conduct a concise environmental review for permits subject to this paragraph.

(d) *Wastewater treatment facility planning.* 40 CFR 6.506 details the environmental review process for the facilities planning process under the wastewater treatment works construction grants program. For the purpose of these regulations, the facility plan shall also include a concise environmental review of those activities that would have environmental effects abroad. This shall apply only to the Step 1 grants awarded after January 14, 1981, but on or before December 29, 1981, and facilities plans developed after December 29, 1981. Where water quality impacts identified in a facility plan are the subject or water quality agreements with Canada or Mexico, nothing in these regulations shall impose on the facility planning process coordination and consultation requirements in addition to those required by such agreements.

(e) *Review by other Federal agencies and other appropriate officials.* The responsible officials shall consult with other Federal agencies with relevant expertise during the preparation of the environmental document. As soon as feasible after preparation of the environmental document, the responsible official shall make the document available to the Council on Environmental Quality, Department of State, and other appropriate officials. The responsible official with assistance from OIA shall work with the Department of State to establish procedures for communicating with and making documents available to foreign nations and international organizations.

[46 FR 3364, Jan. 14, 1981, as amended at 50 FR 26323, June 25, 1985]

§ 6.1005 Lead or cooperating agency.

(a) *Lead Agency.* Section 3-3 of Executive Order 12114 requires the creation of a lead agency whenever an action involves more than one federal agency. In implementing section 3-3, EPA shall, to the fullest extent possible, follow the guidance for the selection of a lead agency contained in 40 CFR 1501.5 of the CEQ regulations.

(b) *Cooperating Agency.* Under section 2-4(d) of the Executive Order, Federal agencies with special expertise are encouraged to provide appropriate resources to the agency preparing environmental documents in order to avoid duplication of resources. In working with a lead agency, EPA shall to the fullest extent possible serve as a cooperating agency in accordance with 40 CFR 1501.6. When other program commitments preclude the degree of involvement requested by the lead agency, the responsible EPA official shall so inform the lead agency in writing.

§ 6.1006 Exemptions and considerations.

Under section 2-5 (b) and (c) of the Executive Order, Federal agencies may provide for modifications in the contents, timing and availability of documents or exemptions from certain requirements for the environmental review and assessment. The responsible official, in consultation with the Director, Office of Environmental Review (OER), and the Director, Office of International Activities (OIA), may approve modifications for situations described in section 2-5(b). The responsible official, in consulta-

tion with the Director, OER and Director OIA, shall obtain exemptions from the Administrator for situations described in section 2-5(c). The Department of State and the Council on Environmental Quality shall be consulted as soon as possible on the utilization of such exemptions.

§ 6.1007 Implementation.

(a) *Oversight.* OER is responsible for overseeing the implementation of these procedures and shall consult with OIA wherever appropriate. OIA shall be utilized for making formal contacts with the Department of State. OER shall assist the responsible officials in carrying out their responsibilities under these procedures.

(b) *Information exchange.* OER with the aid of OIA, shall assist the Department of State and the Council on Environmental Quality in developing the informational exchange on environmental review activities with foreign nations.

(c) *Unidentified activities.* The responsible official shall consult with OER and OIA to establish the type of environmental review or document appropriate for any new EPA activities or requirements imposed upon EPA by statute, international agreement or other agreements.

APPENDIX A—STATEMENT OF PROCEDURES ON FLOODPLAIN MANAGEMENT AND WETLANDS PROTECTION

Contents:

Section 1 General
Section 2 Purpose
Section 3 Policy
Section 4 Definitions
Section 5 Applicability
Section 6 Requirements
Section 7 Implementation

Section 1   General

a. Executive Order 11988 entitled "Floodplain Management" dated May 24, 1977, requires Federal agencies to evaluate the potential effects of actions it may take in a floodplain to avoid adversely impacting floodplains wherever possible, to ensure that its planning programs and budget requests reflect consideration of flood hazards and floodplain management, including the restoration and preservation of such land areas as natural undeveloped floodplains, and to prescribe procedures to implement the policies and procedures of this Executive Order. Guidance for implementation of the Executive Order has been provided by the U.S. Water Resources Council in its Floodplain Management Guidelines dated February 10, 1978 (see 40 FR 6030).

b. Executive Order 11990 entitled "Protection of Wetlands", dated May 24, 1977, requires Federal agencies to take action to avoid adversely impacting wetlands wherever possible, to minimize wetlands destruction and to preserve the values of wetlands, and to prescribe procedures to implement the policies and procedures of this Executive Order.

c. It is the intent of these Executive Orders that, wherever possible, Federal agencies implement the floodplains/wetlands requirements through existing procedures, such as those internal procedures established to implement the National Environmental Policy Act (NEPA) and OMB A-95 review procedures. In those instances

where the environmental impacts of a proposed action are not significant enough to require an environmental impact statement (EIS) pursuant to section 102(2)(C) of NEPA, or where programs are not subject to the requirements of NEPA, alternative but equivalent floodplain/wetlands evaluation and notice procedures must be established.

Section 2   Purpose

a. The purpose of this Statement of Procedures is to set forth Agency policy and guidance for carrying out the provisions of Executive Orders 11988 and 11990.

b. EPA program offices shall amend existing regulations and procedures to incorporate the policies and procedures set forth in this Statement of Procedures.

c. To the extent possible, EPA shall accommodate the requirements of Executive Orders 11988 and 11990 through the Agency NEPA procedures contained in 40 CFR Part 6.

Section 3   Policy

a. The Agency shall avoid wherever possible the long and short term impacts associated with the destruction of wetlands and the occupancy and modification of floodplains and wetlands, and avoid direct and indirect support of floodplain and wetlands development wherever there is a practicable alternative.

b. The Agency shall incorporate floodplain management goals and wetlands protection considerations into its planning, regulatory, and decisionmaking processes. It shall also promote the preservation and restoration of floodplains so that their natural and beneficial values can be realized. To the extent possible EPA shall:

(1) Reduce the hazard and risk of flood loss and wherever it is possible to avoid direct or indirect adverse impact on floodplains;

(2) Where there is no practical alternative to locating in a floodplain, minimize the impact of floods on human safety, health, and welfare, as well as the natural environment;

(3) Restore and preserve natural and beneficial values served by floodplains;

(4) Require the construction of EPA structures and facilities to be in accordance with the standards and criteria, of the regulations promulgated pursuant to the National Flood Insurance Program;

(5) Identify floodplains which require restoration and preservation and recommend management programs necessary to protect these floodplains and to include such considerations as part of on-going planning programs; and

(6) Provide the public with early and continuing information concerning floodplain management and with opportunities for participating in decision making including the (evaluation of) tradeoffs among competing alternatives.

c. The Agency shall incorporate wetlands protection considerations into its planning, regulatory, and decisionmaking processes. It shall minimize the destruction, loss, or degradation of wetlands and preserve and enhance the natural and beneficial values of wetlands. Agency activities shall continue to be carried out consistent with the Administrator's Decision Statement No. 4 dated February 21, 1973 entitled "EPA Policy to Protect the Nation's Wetlands."

Section 4   Definitions

a. "Base Flood" means that flood which has a one percent chance of occurrence in any given year (also known as a 100-year flood). This term is used in the National Flood Insurance Program (NFIP) to indicate the minimum level of flooding to be used by a community in its floodplain management regulations.

b. "Base Floodplain" means the land area covered by a 100-year flood (one percent chance floodplain). Also see definition of floodplain.

c. "Flood or Flooding" means a general and temporary condition of partial or complete inundation of normally dry land areas from the overflow of inland and/or tidal waters, and/or the unusual and rapid accumulation or runoff of surface waters from any source, or flooding from any other source.

d. "Floodplain" means the lowland and relatively flat areas adjoining inland and coastal waters and other floodprone areas such as offshore islands, including at a minimum, that area subject to a one percent or greater chance of flooding in any given year. The base floodplain shall be used to designate the 100-year floodplain (one percent chance floodplain). The critical action floodplain is defined as the 500-year floodplain (0.2 percent chance floodplain).

e. "Floodproofing" means modification of individual structures and facilities, their sites, and their contents to protect against structural failure, to keep water out or to reduce effects of water entry.

f. "Minimize" means to reduce to the smallest possible amount or degree.

g. "Practicable" means capable of being done within existing constraints. The test of what is practicable depends upon the situation and includes consideration of the pertinent factors such as environment, community welfare, cost, or technology.

h. "Preserve" means to prevent modification to the natural floodplain environment or to maintain it as closely as possible to its natural state.

i. "Restore" means to re-establish a setting or environment in which the natural functions of the floodplain can again operate.

j. "Wetlands" means those areas that are inundated by surface or ground water with a frequency sufficient to support and under normal circumstances does or would support a prevalence of vegetative or aquatic life that requires saturated or seasonally saturated soil conditions for growth and reproduction. Wetlands generally include swamps, marshes, bogs, and similar areas such as sloughs, potholes, wet meadows, river overflows, mud flats, and natural ponds.

Section 5   Applicability

a. The Executive Orders apply to activities of Federal agencies pertaining to (1) acquiring, managing, and disposing of Federal lands and facilities, (2) providing Federally undertaken, financed, or assisted construction and improvements, and (3) conducting Federal activities and programs affecting land use, including but not limited to water and related land resources planning, regulating, and licensing activities.

b. These procedures shall apply to EPA's programs as follows: (1) All Agency actions involving construction of facilities or management of lands or property. This will require amendment of the EPA Facilities Management Manual (October 1973 and revisions thereafter).

(2) All Agency actions where the NEPA process applies. This would include the programs under sections 306/402 of the Clean Water Act pertaining to new source permitting and section 201 of the Clean Water Act pertaining to wastewater treatment construction grants.

(3) All agency actions where there is sufficient independent statutory authority to carry out the floodplain/wetlands procedures.

(4) In program areas where there is no EIS requirement nor clear statutory authority for EPA to require procedural implementation, EPA shall continue to provide lead-

ership and offer guidance so that the value of floodplain management and wetlands protection can be understood and carried out to the maximum extent practicable in these programs.

c. These procedures shall not apply to any permitting or source review programs of EPA once such authority has been transferred or delegated to a State. However, EPA shall, to the extent possible, require States to provide equivalent effort to assure support for the objectives of these procedures as part of the state assumption process.

Section 6   Requirements

a. Floodplain/Wetlands review of proposed Agency actions.

(1) *Floodplain/Wetlands Determination*— Before undertaking an Agency action, each program office must determine whether or not the action will be located in or affect a floodplain or wetlands. The Agency shall utilize maps prepared by the Federal Insurance Administration of the Federal Emergency Management Agency (Flood Insurance Rate Maps or Flood Hazard Boundary Maps), Fish and Wildlife Service (National Wetlands Inventory Maps), and other appropriate agencies to determine whether a proposed action is located in or will likely affect a floodplain or wetlands. If there is no floodplain/wetlands impact identified, the action may proceed without further consideration of the remaining procedures set forth below.

(2) *Early Public Notice*—When it is apparent that a proposed or potential agency action is likely to impact a floodplain or wetlands, the public should be informed through appropriate public notice procedures.

(3) *Floodplain/Wetlands Assessment*—If the Agency determines a proposed action is located in or affects a floodplain or wetlands, a floodplain/wetlands assessment shall be undertaken. For those actions where an environmental assessment (EA) or environmental impact statement (EIS) is prepared pursuant to 40 CFR Part 6, the floodplain/wetlands assessment shall be prepared concurrently with these analyses and shall be included in the EA or EIS. In all other cases, a "floodplain/wetlands assessment" shall be prepared. Assessments shall consist of a description of the proposed action, a discussion of its effect on the floodplain/wetlands, and shall also describe the alternatives considered.

(4) *Public Review of Assessments*—For proposed actions impacting floodplain/wetlands where an EA or EIS is prepared, the opportunity for public review will be provided through the EIS provisions contained in 40 CFR Parts 6, 25, or 35, where appropriate. In other cases, an equivalent public notice of the floodplain/wetlands assessment shall be made consistent with the public involvement requirements of the applicable program.

(5) *Minimize, Restore or Preserve*—If there is no practicable alternative to locating in or affecting the floodplain or wetlands, the Agency shall act to minimize potential harm to the floodplain or wetlands. The Agency shall also act to restore and preserve the natural and beneficial values of floodplains and wetlands as part of the analysis of all alternatives under consideration.

(6) *Agency Decision*—After consideration of alternative actions, as they have been modified in the preceding analysis, the Agency shall select the desired alternative. For all Agency actions proposed to be in or affecting a floodplain/wetlands, the Agency shall provide further public notice announcing this decision. This decision shall be accompanied by a Statement of Findings, not to exceed three pages. This Statement shall include: (i) The reasons why the proposed

action must be located in or affect the floodplain or wetlands; (ii) a description of significant facts considered in making the decision to locate in or affect the floodplain or wetlands including alternative sites and actions; (iii) a statement indicating whether the proposed action conforms to applicable State or local floodplain protection standards; (iv) a description of the steps taken to design or modify the proposed action to minimize potential harm to or within the floodplain or wetlands; and (v) a statement indicating how the proposed action affects the natural or beneficial values of the floodplain or wetlands. If the provisions of 40 CFR Part 6 apply, the Statement of Findings may be incorporated in the final EIS or in the environmental assessment. In other cases, notice should be placed in the FEDERAL REGISTER or other local medium and copies sent to Federal, State, and local agencies and other entities which submitted comments or are otherwise concerned with the floodplain/wetlands assessment. For floodplain actions subject to Office of Management and Budget (OMB) Circular A-95, the Agency shall send the Statement of Findings to State and areawide A-95 clearinghouse in the geographic area affected. At least 15 working days shall be allowed for public and interagency review of the Statement of Findings.

(7) *Authorizations/Appropriations*—Any requests for new authorizations or appropriations transmitted to OMB shall include, a floodplain/wetlands assessment and, for floodplain impacting actions, a Statement of Findings, if a proposed action will be located in a floodplain or wetlands.

b. *Lead agency concept.* To the maximum extent possible, the Agency shall relay on the lead agency concept to carry out the provisions set forth in section 6.a of this appendix. Therefore, when EPA and another Federal agency have related actions, EPA shall work with the other agency to identify which agency shall take the lead in satisfying these procedural requirements and thereby avoid duplication of efforts.

c. *Additional floodplain management provisions relating to Federal property and facilities.*

(1) *Construction Activities*—EPA controlled structures and facilities must be constructed in accordance with existing criteria and standards set forth under the NFIP and must include mitigation of adverse impacts wherever feasible. Deviation from these requirements may occur only to the extent NFIP standards are demonstrated as inappropriate for a given structure or facility.

(2) *Flood Protection Measures*—If newly constructed structures or facilities are to be located in a floodplain, accepted floodproofing and other flood protection measures shall be undertaken. To achieve flood protection, EPA shall, wherever practicable, elevate structures above the base flood level rather than filling land.

(3) *Restoration and Preservation*—As part of any EPA plan or action, the potential for restoring and preserving floodplains and wetlands so that their natural and beneficial values can be realized must be considered and incorporated into the plan or action wherever feasible.

(4) *Property Used by Public*—If property used by the public has suffered damage or is located in an identified flood hazard area, EPA shall provide on structures, and other places where appropriate, conspicuous indicators of past and probable flood height to enhance public knowledge of flood hazards.

(5) *Transfer of EPA Property*—When property in flood plains is proposed for lease, easement, right-of-way, or disposal to non-Federal public or private parties, EPA shall reference in the conveyance those uses that are restricted under Federal, State and local

floodplain regulations and attach other restrictions to uses of the property as may be deemed appropriate. Notwithstanding, EPA shall consider withholding such properties from conveyance.

Section 7 Implementation

a. Pursuant to section 2, the EPA program offices shall amend existing regulations, procedures, and guidance, as appropriate, to incorporate the policies and procedures set forth in this Statement of Procedures. Such amendments shall be made within six months of the date of these Procedures.

b. The Office of External Affairs (OEA) is responsible for the oversight of the implementation of this Statement of Procedures and shall be given advanced opportunity to review amendments to regulations, procedures, and guidance. OEA shall coordinate efforts with the program offices to develop necessary manuals and more specialized supplementary guidance to carry out this Statement of Procedures.

[44 FR 64177, Nov. 6, 1976, as amended at 50 FR 26323, June 25, 1985]

Federal Energy Regulatory Commission
NEPA Regulations
18 C.F.R. §2.80, Pt. 380

§ 2.80 Detailed environmental statement.

(a) It will be the general policy of the Federal Energy Regulatory Commission to adopt and to adhere to the objectives and aims of the National Environmental Policy Act of 1969 (NEPA) in its regulations promulgated for statutes under the jurisdiction of the Commission, including the Federal Power Act, the Natural Gas Act and the Natural Gas Policy Act. The National Environmental Policy Act of 1969 requires, among other things, all Federal agencies to include a detailed environmental statement in every recommendation or report on proposals for legislation and other major Federal actions significantly affecting the quality of the human environment.

(b) Therefore, in compliance with the National Environmental Policy Act of 1969, the Commission staff will make a detailed environmental statement when the regulatory action taken by the Commission under the statutes under the jurisdiction of the Commission will have a significant environmental impact. The specific regulations implementing NEPA are contained in Part 380 of the Commission's regulations.

[Order 486, 52 FR 47910, Dec. 17, 1987]

PART 380—REGULATIONS IMPLEMENTING THE NATIONAL ENVIRONMENTAL POLICY ACT

Sec.
380.1 Purpose.
380.2 Definitions and terminology.
380.3 Environmental information to be supplied by an applicant.
380.4 Projects or actions categorically excluded.
380.5 Actions that require an environmental assessment.
380.6 Actions that require an environmental impact statement.
380.7 Format of an environmental impact statement.
380.8 Preparation of environmental documents.
380.9 Public availability of NEPA documents and public notice of NEPA related hearings and public meetings.
380.10 Participation in Commission proceedings.
380.11 Environmental decisionmaking.

APPENDIX A—GUIDELINES FOR THE PREPARATION OF ENVIRONMENTAL REPORTS FOR APPLICATIONS UNDER THE NATURAL GAS ACT, AS SPECIFIED IN § 380.3 OF THE COMMISSION'S REGULATIONS

AUTHORITY: National Environmental Policy Act of 1969, 42 U.S.C. 4321–4370a (1982); Department of Energy Organization Act, 42 U.S.C. 7101–7352 (1982); E.O. 12009, 3 CFR 1978 Comp., p. 142.

Source: Order 486, 52 FR 47910, Dec. 17, 1987, unless otherwise noted.

§ 380.1 Purpose.

The regulations in this part implement the Federal Energy Regulatory Commission's procedures under the National Environmental Policy Act of 1969. These regulations supplement the regulations of the Council on Environmental Quality, 40 CFR Parts 1500 through 1508 (1986). The Commission will comply with the regulations of the Council on Environmental Quality except where those regulations are inconsistent with the statutory requirements of the Commission.

§ 380.2 Definitions and terminology.

For purposes of this part—

(a) "Categorical exclusion" means a category of actions described in § 380.4, which do not individually or cumulatively have a significant effect on the human environment and which the Commission has found to have no such effect and for which, therefore, neither an environmental assessment nor an environmental impact statement is required. The Commission may decide to prepare environmental assessments for the reasons stated in § 380.4(b).

(b) "Commission" means the Federal Energy Regulatory Commission.

(c) "Council" means the Council on Environmental Quality.

(d) "Environmental assessment" means a concise public document for which the Commission is responsible that serves to:

(1) Briefly provide sufficient evidence and analysis for determining whether to prepare an environmental impact statement or a finding of no significant impact.

(2) Aid the Commission's compliance with NEPA when no environmental impact statement is necessary.

(3) Facilitate preparation of a statement when one is necessary. Environmental assessments must include brief discussions of the need for the proposal, of alternatives as required by section 102(2)(E) of NEPA, of the environmental impacts of the proposed action and alternatives, and a listing of agencies and persons consulted.

(e) "Environmental impact statement" (EIS) means a detailed written statement as required by section 102(2)(C) of NEPA. DEIS means a draft EIS and FEIS means a final EIS.

(f) "Environmental report" or ER means that part of an application submitted to the Commission by an applicant for authorization of a proposed action which includes information concerning the environment, the applicant's analysis of the environmental impact of the action, or alternatives to the action required by this or other applicable statutes or regulations.

(g) "Finding of no significant impact" (FONSI) means a document by the Commission briefly presenting the reason why an action, not otherwise excluded by § 380.4, will not have a significant effect on the human environment and for which an environmental impact statement therefore will not be prepared. It must include the environmental assessment or a summary of it and must note other environmental documents related to it. If the assessment is included, the FONSI need not repeat any of the discussion in the assessment but may incorporate it by reference.

§ 380.3 Environmental information to be supplied by an applicant.

(a) An applicant must submit information as follows:

(1) For any proposed action identified in §§ 380.5 and 380.6, and environmental report with the proposal as prescribed in paragraph (c) of this section.

(2) For any proposal not identified in paragraph (a)(1) of this section, any environmental information that the Commission may determine is necessary for compliance with these regulations, the regulations of the Council, NEPA and other Federal laws such as the Endangered Species Act, the National Historic Preservation Act or the Coastal Zone Management Act.

(b) An applicant must also:

(1) Provide all necessary or relevant information to the Commission;

(2) Conduct any studies that the Commission staff considers necessary or relevant to determine the impact of the proposal on the human environment and natural resources;

(3) Consult with appropriate Federal, regional, State, and local agencies during the planning stages of the proposed action to ensure that all potential environmental impacts are identified. (The specific requirements for consultation on hydropower projects are contained in § 4.38 of this chapter and in section 4(a) of the Electric Consumers Protection Act, Pub. L. No. 99-495, 100 Stat. 1243, 1246 (1986));

(4) Submit applications for all Federal and State approvals as early as possible in the planning process; and

(5) Notify the Commission staff of all other Federal actions required for completion of the proposed action so that the staff may coordinate with other interested Federal agencies.

(c) Content of an applicant's environmental report for specific proposals—(1) Hydropower projects. The information required for specific project applications under Part 4 of this chapter.

(2) Natural gas projects. (i) For any application filed under the Natural Gas Act for any proposed action identified in §§ 380.5 or 380.6, except for prior notice filings under § 157.208, as described in § 380.5(b), the information identified in Appendix A of this part.

(ii) For prior notice filings under § 157.208, the report described by § 157.208(c)(11) of this chapter.

§ 380.4 Projects or actions categorically excluded.

(a) *General rule.* Except as stated in paragraph (b) of this section, neither an environmental assessment nor an environmental impact statement will be prepared for the following projects or actions:

(1) Procedural, ministerial, or internal administrative and management actions, programs, or decisions, including procurement, contracting, personnel actions, correction or clarification of filings or orders, and acceptance, rejection and dismissal of filings;

(2)(i) Reports or recommendations on legislation not initiated by the Commission, and

(ii) Proposals for legislation and promulgation of rules that are clarifying, corrective, or procedural, or that do not substantially change the effect of legislation or regulations being amended;

(3) Compliance and review actions, including investigations (jurisdictional or otherwise), conferences, hearings, notices of probable violation, show cause orders, and adjustments under section 502(c) of the Natural Gas Policy Act of 1978 (NGPA);

(4) Review of grants or denials by the Department of Energy (DOE) of any adjustment request, and review of contested remedial orders issued by DOE;

(5) Information gathering, analysis, and dissemination;

(6) Conceptual or feasibility studies;

(7) Actions concerning the reservation and classification of United States lands as water power sites and other actions under section 24 of the Federal Power Act;

(8) Transfers of water power project licenses and transfers of exemptions under Part I of the Federal Power Act and Part 9 of this chapter;

(9) Issuance of preliminary permits for water power projects under Part I of the Federal Power Act and Part 4 of this chapter;

(10) Withdrawals of applications for certificates under the Natural Gas Act, or for water power project preliminary permits, exemptions, or licenses under Part I of the Federal Power Act and Part 4 of this chapter;

(11) Actions concerning annual charges or headwater benefits, charges for water power projects under Parts 11 and 13 of this chapter and establishment of fees to be paid by an applicant for a license or exemption required to meet the terms and conditions of section 30(c) of the Federal Power Act;

(12) Approval for water power projects under Part I of the Federal Power Act, of "as built" or revised drawings or exhibits that propose no changes to project works or operations or that reflect changes that have previously been approved or required by the Commission;

(13) Surrender and amendment of preliminary permits, and surrender of water power licenses and exemptions where no project works exist or ground disturbing activity has occurred and amendments to water power licenses and exemptions that do not require ground disturbing activity or changes to project works or operation;

(14) Exemptions for small conduit hydroelectric facilities as defined in § 4.30(b)(26) of this chapter under Part I of the Federal Power Act and Part 4 of this chapter;

(15) Electric rate filings submitted by public utilities under sections 205 and 206 of the Federal Power Act, the establishment of just and reasonable rates, and confirmation, approval, and disapproval of rate filings submitted by Federal power marketing agencies under the Pacific Northwest Electric Power Planning and Conservation Act, the Department of Energy Organization Act, and DOE Delegation Order No. 0204-108.

(16) Approval of actions under sections 4(b), 203, 204, 301, 304, and 305 of the Federal Power Act relating to issuance and purchase of securities, acquisition or disposition of property, merger, interlocking directorates, jurisdictional determinations and accounting orders;

(17) Approval of electrical interconnections and wheeling under sections 202(b), 210, 211, and 212 of the Federal Power Act, that would not entail:

(i) Construction of a new substation or expansion of the boundaries of an existing substation;

(ii) Construction of any transmission line that operates at more than 115 kilovolts (KV) and occupies more than ten miles of an existing right-of-way; or

(iii) Construction of any transmission line more than one mile long if located on a new right-of-way;

(18) Approval of changes in land rights for water power projects under Part I of the Federal Power Act and Part 4 of this chapter, if no construction or change in land use is either proposed or known by the Commission to be contemplated for the land affected;

(19) Approval of proposals under Part I of the Federal Power Act and Part 4 of this chapter to authorize use of water power project lands or waters for gas or electric utility distribution lines, radial (sub-transmission) lines, communications lines and cables, storm drains, sewer lines not discharging into project waters, water mains, piers, landings, boat docks, or similar structures and facilities, landscaping or embankments, bulkheads, retaining walls, or similar shoreline erosion control structures;

(20) Action on applications for exemption under section 1(c) of the Natural Gas Act;

(21) Approvals of blanket certificate applications and prior notice filings under § 157.204 and §§ 157.209 through 157.218 of this chapter;

(22) Approvals of blanket certificate applications under §§ 284.221 through 284.224 of this chapter;

(23) Producers' applications for the sale of gas filed under §§ 157.23 through 157.29 of this chapter;

(24) Approval under section 7 of the Natural Gas Act of taps, meters, and regulating facilities located completely within an existing natural gas pipeline right-of-way or compressor station if company records show the land use of the vicinity has not changed since the original facilities were installed, and no significant nonjurisdictional facilities would be constructed in association with construction of the interconnection facilities;

(25) Review of natural gas rate filings, including any curtailment plans other than those specified in § 380.5(b)(5), and establishment of rates for transportation and sale of natural gas under sections 4 and 5 of the Natural Gas Act and sections 311 and 401 through 404 of the Natural Gas Policy Act of 1978;

(26) Review of approval of oil pipeline rate filings under Parts 340 and 341 of this chapter;

(27) Sale, exchange, and transportation of natural gas under sections 4, 5 and 7 of the Natural Gas Act that requires no construction of facilities;

(28) Abandonment in place of a minor natural gas pipeline (short segments of buried pipe of 6-inch inside diameter or less), or abandonment by removal of minor surface facilities such as metering stations, valves, and tops under section 7 of the Natural Gas Act so long as appropriate erosion control and site restoration takes place;

(29) Abandonment of service under any gas supply contract pursuant to section 7 of the Natural Gas Act;

(30) Approval of filing made in compliance with the requirements of a certificate for a natural gas project under section 7 of the Natural Gas Act or a preliminary permit, exemption, license, or license amendment order for a water power project under Part I of the Federal Power Act;

(31) Approval of natural gas import/ export sites under DOE Delegation Order Nos. 0204-26 and 0204-112, if the site does not involve the construction of any facilities.

(b) *Exceptions to categorical exclusions.* (1) In accordance with 40 CFR 1508.4, the Commission and its staff will independently evaluate environmental information supplied in an application and in comments by the public. Where circumstances indicate that an action may be a major Federal action significantly affecting the quality of the human environment, the Commission:

(i) May require an environmental report or other additional environmental information, and

(ii) Will prepare an environmental assessment or an environmental impact statement.

(2) Such circumstances may exist when the action may have an effect on one of the following:

(i) Indian lands;

(ii) Wilderness areas;

(iii) Wild and scenic rivers;

(iv) Wetlands;

(v) Units of the National Park System, National Refuges, or National Fish Hatcheries;

(vi) Anadromous fish or endangered species; or

(vii) Where the environmental effects are uncertain.

However, the existence of one or more of the above will not automatically require the submission of an environmental report or the preparation of an environmental assessment or an environmental impact statement.

[Order 486, 52 FR 47910, Dec. 17, 1987, as amended at 53 FR 8177, Mar. 14, 1988]

§ 380.5 Actions that require an environmental assessment.

(a) An environmental assessment will normally be prepared first for the actions identified in this section. Depending on the outcome of the environmental assessment, the Commission may or may not prepare an environmental impact statement. However, depending on the location or scope of the proposed action, or the resources affected, the Commission may in specific circumstances proceed directly to prepare an environmental impact statement.

(b) The projects subject to an environmental assessment are as follows:

(1) Except as identified in §§ 380.4, 380.6 and 2.55 of this chapter, authorization for the site of new gas import/export facilities under DOE Delegation Order Nos. 0204-26 and 0204-112 and authorization under section 7 of the Natural Gas Act for the construction, replacement, or abandonment of compression, processing, or interconnecting facilities, onshore and offshore pipelines, metering facilities, LNG peak-shaving facilities, or other facilities necessary for the sale, exchange, storage, or transportation of natural gas;

(2) Prior notice filings under § 157.208 of this chapter for the rearrangement of any facility specified in §§ 157.202 (b)(3) and (6) of this chapter or the acquisition, construction, or operation of any eligible facility as specified in §§ 157.202 (b)(2) and (3) of this chapter;

(3) Abandonment or reduction of natural gas service under section 7 of the Natural Gas Act unless excluded under § 380.4 (a)(21), (28) or (29);

(4) Except as identified in § 380.6, conversion of existing depleted oil or natural gas fields to underground storage fields under section 7 of the Natural Gas Act.

(5) New natural gas curtailment plans, or any amendment to an existing curtailment plan under section 4 of the Natural Gas Act and sections 401 through 404 of the Natural Gas Policy Act of 1978 that has a major effect on an entire pipeline system;

(6) Licenses under Part I of the Federal Power Act and Part 4 of this chapter for construction of any water power project—existing dam;

(7) Exemptions under section 405 of the Public Utility Regulatory Policies Act of 1978, as amended, and §§ 4.30(b)(27) and 4.101-4.106 of this chapter for small hydroelectric power projects of 5 MW or less;

(8) Licenses for additional project works at licensed projects under Part I of the Federal Power Act whether or not these are styled license amendments or original licenses;

(9) Licenses under Part I of the Federal Power Act and Part 4 of this chapter for transmission lines only;

(10) Applications for new licenses under section 15 of the Federal Power Act;

(11) Approval of electric interconnections and wheeling under sections 202(b), 210, 211, and 212 of the Federal Power Act, unless excluded under § 380.4(a)(17); and

(12) Regulations or proposals for legislation not excluded under § 380.4(a)(2).

(13) Surrender of water power licenses and exemptions where project works exist or ground disturbing activity has occurred and amendments to water power licenses and exemptions that require ground disturbing activity or changes to project works or operations.

[Order 486, 52 FR 47910, Dec. 17, 1987; Order 486, 53 FR 4817, Feb. 17, 1988; 53 FR 8177, Mar. 14, 1988]

§ 380.6 Actions that require an environmental impact statement.

(a) Except as provided in paragraph (b) of this section, an environmental impact statement will normally be prepared first for the following projects:

(1) Authorization under section 3 or 7 of the Natural Gas Act and DOE Delegation Order Nos. 0204-26 and 0204-112 for the siting, construction, and operation of jurisdictional liquefied natural gas import/export facilities used wholly or in part to liquefy, store, or regasify liquified natural gas transported by water;

(2) Certificate applications under section 7 of the Natural Gas Act to develop an underground natural gas storage facility except where depleted oil or natural gas producing fields are used;

(3) Major pipeline construction projects under section 7 of the Natural Gas Act using right-of-way in which there is no existing natural gas pipeline; and

(4) Licenses under Part I of the Federal Power Act and Part 4 of this chapter for construction of any unconstructed water power project.

(b) If the Commission believes that a proposed action identified in paragraph (a) of this section may not be a major Federal action significantly affecting the quality of the human environment, an environmental assessment, rather than an environmental impact statement, will be prepared first. Depending on the outcome of the environmental assessment, an environmental impact statement may or may not be prepared.

(c) An environmental impact statement will not be required if an environmental assessment indicates that a proposal has adverse environmental affects and the proposal is not approved.

[Order 486, 52 FR 47910, Dec. 17, 1987, as amended at 53 FR 8177, Mar. 14, 1988]

§ 380.7 Format of an environmental impact statement.

In addition to the requirements for an environmental impact statement prescribed in 40 CFR 1502.10 of the regulations of the Council, an environmental impact statement prepared by the Commission will include a section on the literature cited in the environmental impact statement and a staff conclusion section. The staff conclusion section will include summaries of:

(a) The significant environmental impacts of the proposed action;

(b) Any alternative to the proposed action that would have a less severe environmental impact or impacts and the action preferred by the staff;

(c) Any mitigation measures proposed by the applicant, as well as additional mitigation measures that might be more effective;

(d) Any significant environmental impacts of the proposed action that cannot be mitigated; and

(e) References to any pending, completed, or recommended studies that might provide baseline data or additional data on the proposed action.

§ 380.8 Preparation of environmental documents.

The preparation of environmental documents, as defined in § 1508.10 of the regulations of the Council, on hydroelectric projects, is the responsibility of the Commission's Office of Hydropower Licensing, 400 First Street NW., Washington, DC 20426, (202) 376-9171. The preparation of environmental documents on natural gas projects is the responsibility of the Commission's Office of Pipeline and Producer Regulation, (202) 357-8500, 825 North Capitol Street NW., Washington, DC 20426. Persons interested in status reports or information on environmental impact statements or other elements of the NEPA process, including the studies or other information the Commission may require on these projects, can contact these sections.

§ 380.9 Public availability of NEPA documents and public notice of NEPA related hearings and public meetings.

(a)(1) The Commission will comply with the requirements of 40 CFR 1506.6 of the regulations of the Council for public involvement in NEPA.

(2) If an action has effects of primarily local concern, the Commission may give additional notice in a Commission order.

(b) The Commission will make environmental impact statements, environmental assessments, the comments received, and any underlaying documents available to the public pursuant to the provisions of the Freedom of Information Act (5 U.S.C. 552 (1982)). The exclusion in the Freedom of Information Act for interagency memoranda is not applicable where such memoranda transmit comments of Federal agencies on the environmental impact of the proposed action. Such materials will be made available to the public at the Commission's Public Reference Room at 825 North Capitol Street NW., Room 1000, Washington, DC 20426 at a fee and in the manner described in Part 388 of this chapter. A copy of an environmental impact statement or environmental assessment for hydroelectric projects may also be made available for inspection at the Commission's regional office for the region where the proposed action is located.

§ 380.10 Participation in Commission proceedings.

(a) *Intervention proceedings involving a party or parties*—(1) *Motion to intervene.* (i) In addition to submitting comments on the NEPA process and NEPA related documents, any person may file a motion to intervene in a Commission proceeding dealing with environmental issues under the terms of § 385.214 of this chapter. Any person who files a motion to intervene on the basis of a draft environmental impact statement will be deemed to have filed a timely motion, in accordance with § 385.214, as long as the motion is filed within the comment period for the draft environmental impact statement.

(ii) Any person that is granted intervention after petitioning becomes a party to the proceeding and accepts the record as developed by the parties as of the time that intervention is granted.

(2)(i) *Issues not set for trial-type hearing.* An intervenor who takes a position on any environmental issue that has not yet been set for hearing must file a timely motion with the Secretary containing an analysis of its position on such issue and specifying any differences with the position of Commission staff or an applicant upon which the intervenor wishes to be heard at a hearing.

(ii) *Issues set for trial-type hearing.* (A) Any intervenor that takes a position on an environmental issue set for hearing may offer evidence for the record in support of such position and otherwise participate in accordance with the Commission's Rules of Practice and Procedure. Any intervenor must specify any differences from the staff's and the applicant's positions.

(B) To be considered, any facts or opinions on an environmental issue set for hearing must be admitted into evidence and made part of the record of the proceeding.

(b) *Rulemaking proceedings.* Any person may file comments on any environmental issue in a rulemaking proceeding.

§ 380.11 Environmental decisionmaking.

(a) *Decision points.* For the actions which require an environmental assessment or environmental impact statement, environmental consider-

ations will be addressed at appropriate major decision points.

(1) In proceedings involving a party or parties and not set for trial-type hearing, major decision points are the approval or denial of proposals by the Commission or its designees.

(2) In matters set for trial-type hearing, the major decision points are the initial decision of an administrative law judge or the decision of the Commission.

(3) In a rulemaking proceeding, the major decision points are the Notice of Proposed Rulemaking and the Final Rule.

(b) *Environmental documents as part of the record.* The Commission will include environmental assessments, findings of no significant impact, or environmental impact statements, and any supplements in the record of the proceeding.

(c) *Application denials.* Notwithstanding any provision in this Part, the Commission may dismiss or deny an application without performing an environmental impact statement or without undertaking environmental analysis.

Appendix A—Guidelines for the Preparation of Environmental Reports for Applications Under the Natural Gas Act, as Specified in § 380.3 of the Commission's Regulations

These guidelines:

(1) Identify the kinds of information to be supplied by applicants to assist Federal Power Commission staff in an independent assessment of major Federal actions significantly affecting the quality of the human environment;

(2) Pertain to actions under Part 380, Chapter I, Title 18, Code of Federal Regulations;

(3) Provide the basis for the preparation of environmental reports being prepared pursuant to Part 380 by applicants for the construction of pipeline facilities under the jurisdiction of the Commission; and

(4) Provide an insight into the rationale and scope of environmental reports to assure a balanced interdisciplinary analysis of actions significantly affecting the quality of the human environment.

It is the general policy of the Federal Power Commission to expect applicants to take the following actions in carrying out their environmental evaluation responsibilities:

(5) Consult with the appropriate Federal, regional, State, and local entities during the preliminary planning stages of the proposed action to assure that all environmental factors are identified;

(6) Conduct any studies which are necessary to determine the impact of the proposed action on the human and natural resources and the measures which may be necessary to protect the values of the affected area. These analyses of impacts upon living and nonliving elements which make up the environment shall be to the depth necessary for a valid assessment of the impacts;

(7) Utilize a sufficiently imaginative, comprehensive, interdisciplinary approach—utilizing a broad physical, biological, and social overview—during the development of the plans for a project, including the selection of its site, design, and methods of construction, operation/maintenance, and abandonment; and

(8) These guidelines have been prepared to relate to a wide range of possible actions that could come before the Commission for consideration. The applicant is expected to make the detail of the environmental report commensurate with the complexity of the possible environmental impact of the proposed action. It is important to recognize that there is some duplication in the information requested. Often a section asks for an evaluation from a different viewpoint rather than absolutely new information. Upon review of the applicant's environmental report, staff may request additional informaiton.

Components of an Environmental Report

1. *Description of proposed action.*—Provide, as an introductory paragraph, a brief description of the action under application. Then describe fully its:

1.1 *Purpose.*—Describe the primary purpose of the proposed action and such secondary purposes as water supply, navigation, flood control, low flow augmentation, recreation, fish, and wildlife. Describe how these purposes, both primary and secondary, fit into existing and future utility systems or aid in meeting system reliability or regional and national needs. List the increases in productivity and values for each purpose described, e.g., power capacity in kW and generation in kWh/year, navigation in tonnage, recreation in visitor days, water use in ft³/s and af.

1.2 *Location.*—Describe the geographical location of the action as related to other similar programs or developments in the same river basin. Locate the proposed action with respect to State boundaries, counties and major cities and, if necessary, by more specific geographical identification such as township and range; provide a map or maps of the area and such other graphic materials as are needed to locate the action.

1.3 *Land requirements.*—Locate and indicate the area and use of lands to be utilized by the proposed action and any measures, other than construction procedures, involved in its use, including clearing, borrow and spoil areas, rip-rap, settling ponds or basins, relocation or development of roads, recreation and wildlife management programs, drilling of wells for water supply or aquifer recharge, and reserving project lands for future uses. Describe the length and width of all existing, joint, or new rights-of-way required by the proposed action and any land treatment programs proposed thereon, including activities on "adjacent" lands.

1.4 *Proposed facilities.*—Provide dimensions where pertinent.

1.4.1 *Project works.*—Describe and locate on functional drawings the project works proposed for construction, including dams, dikes, reservoirs, spillways, powerhouses, switchyards and transmission facilities, water intakes and outlets and conduits, navigation works, visitor centers and other public use facilities, fish ladders, fish hatcheries, and fish protective facilities. Provide dimensions, elevations, data on geological foundations, and other technical data as necessary to give functional design characteristics for safety and adequacy.

1.4.2 *Reservoir.*—Describe the reservoir and its outlet works giving dimensions in capacity, elevations, area, depth; thermal stratification if present or anticipated; currents, mixing actions, and flow-through of inflowing waters as related to water densities; and locate any water intake structures by elevations and in relation to the occurence of a reservoir thermocline.

1.4.3 *Tailwater features.*—Using a profile drawing, show elevations of the turbine or pump runners, maximum and minimum tailwaters, and of any tailrace excavations.

1.4.4 *Transmission facilities.*—Describe

any transmission lines, rights-of-way, and substations existing or planned for future development, not included as part of the action under application but considered a necessary adjunct thereto.

1.5 *Construction procedures.*—Describe procedures to be taken prior to or during construction of project works such as the relocation of homes and commercial and industrial facilities, clearing, preparation of any diversion works, surveying, land acquisition and environmental planning. Provide a schedule of construction of major project works and how this will meet future power needs and avoid such limiting factors as floods, severe climatic conditions, or migrations of fish. Include schedules for needed relocations or development of transportation and other public use facilities and methods of maintaining service during these activities. Indicate the source of the work forces, numbers involved, and their housing needs in the area.

1.6 *Operational and maintenance procedures.*—Describe the proposed operational modes and the reasons therefor. Show how the water resources of the area are to be utilized (provide usable reservoir storage capacities for respective purposes, area-capacity curves, hydrology data, drawdowns, and flow duration curves applicable to project operation during dry, average, and wet years). Include a discussion of the quantity and quality of water flows as they enter, pass through the project, and are released to maintain the downstream aquatic habitat; and of any diversions of water for other uses including municipal or industrial uses, or fish ladders or hatcheries. For pumped storage projects describe the daily, weekly, and seasonal exchanges of waters between upper and lower reservoirs and the water currents and temperature changes produced by this pseudo-tidal action. Include also a discussion of any pollutants (and their sources) which would be discharged as a result of the proposed action. Describe maintenance of proposed project works under normal conditions; include types of expected maintenance, and how system or area needs will be met during shutdown for maintenance. Describe capacity of project works to withstand both usual and unusual, but possible, natural phenomena and accidents (e.g., earthquakes, floods, hurricanes or tornadoes, slides); describe any related geological or structural problems, and measures to be taken to minimize problems arising from malfunctions and accidents.

1.7 *Future plans.*—Describe plans or potential for future expansion of facilities including land use and the compatibility of these plans with the proposed action.

2. *Description of the existing environment.*—Provide an overall description of existing conditions for resources which might be affected directly and indirectly by the proposed action; include a discussion of such pertinent topics as:

2.1 *Land features and uses.*—Identify present uses and describe the characteristics of the land area.

2.1.1 *Land uses.*—Describe the extent of present uses, as in agriculture, business, industry, recreation, residence, wildlife, and other uses, including the potential for development; locate major nearby transportation corridors, including roads, highways, ship channels, and aviation traffic patterns; locate transmission facilities on or near the lands affected by the proposed action and their placement (underground, surface, or overhead).

2.1.2 *Topography, physiography, and geology.*—Provide a detailed description of the topographic, physiographic, and geologic features within the area of the proposed action. Includes U.S. Geological Survey Topographic Maps, aerial photographs, and other such graphic material.

2.1.3 *Soils.*—Describe the physical and chemical characteristics of the soils. Sufficient detail should be given to allow interpretation of the nature of and fertility of the soil and stability of slopes.

2.1.4 *Geological hazards.*—Indicate the probability of occurrence of geological hazards in the area, such as earthquakes, slumping, landslides, subsidence, permafrost, and erosion.

2.2 *Species and ecosystems.*—Identify those species and ecosystems that will be affected by the proposed action.

2.2.1 *Species.*—List in general categories, by common and scientific names, the plant and wildlife species found in the area of the proposed action and indicate those having commercial and recreational importance.

2.2.2 *Communities and associations.*—Describe the dominant plant and wildlife communities and associations located within the area of the proposed action. Provide an estimate of the population densities of major species. If data are not available for the immediate area of the proposed action, data from comparable areas may be used.

2.2.3 *Unique and other biotic resources.*—Describe unique ecosystems or communities, rare or endangered species, and other biotic resources that may have special importance in the area of the proposed action. Describe any areas of critical environmental concern, e.g., wetlands and estuaries. Summarize findings of any studies conducted thereon.

2.3 *Socioeconomic considerations.*—If the proposed action could have a significant socioeconomic effect on the local area, discuss the socioeconomic future, including population and industrial growth, of the area without the implementation of the proposed action; describe the economic development in the vicinity of the proposed action, particularly the local tax base and per capita income; and identify trends in economic development and/or land use of the area, both from a historical and prospective viewpoint. Describe the population densities of both the immediate and generalized area. Include distances from the site of the proposed action to nearby residences, cities, and urban areas and list their populations. Indicate the number and type of residences, farms, businesses, and industries that will be directly affected and those requiring relocation if the proposed action occurs.

2.4 *Air and water environments.*—Describe the prevailing climate and the quality of the air (including noise) and water environments of the area. Estimate the quality and availability of surface water resources in the proposed project area.

2.4.1 *Climate.*—Describe the historic climatic conditions that prevail in the vicinity of the proposed action; extremes and means of monthly temperatures, precipitation, and wind speed and direction. In addition, indicate the frequency of temperature inversions, fog, smog, icing, and destructive storms such as hurricanes and tornadoes.

2.4.2 *Hydrology and hydrography.*—Describe surface waters, fresh, brackish, or saline, in the vicinity of the proposed action and discuss drainage basins, physical and chemical characteristics, water use, water supplies, and circulation. Describe the ground water situation, water uses and sources, acquifer systems, and flow characteristics.

2.4.3 *Air, noise, and water quality monitoring.*—Provide data on the existing quality of the air and water, indicate the distance(s) from the proposed action site to monitoring stations and the mean and maximum audible noise and radio interference levels at the site boundaries.

2.5 *Unique features.*—Describe unique or unusual features of the area, including historical, archeological, and scenic sites and values.

3. *Environmental impact of the proposed action.*—Describe all known or expected sig-nificant environmental effects and changes, both beneficial and adverse, which will take place should the action be carried out. Include the impacts caused by (a) construction, (b) operation, including maintenance, breakdown, and malfunctions, and (c) termination of activities, including abandonment. Include both direct and primary indirect changes in the existing environment in the immediate area and throughout the sphere of influence of the proposed action. [1]

3.1 *Construction.*

3.1.1 *Land features and uses.*—Assess the impact on present or future land use, including commercial use, mineral resources, recreational areas, public health and safety, and the aesthetic value of the land and its features. Describe any temporary restriction on land use due to construction activities. State the effect of construction related activities upon local traffic patterns, including roads, highways, ship channels, and aviation patterns.

3.1.2 *Species and ecosystems.*—Assess the impact of construction on the terrestrial and aquatic species and habitats in the area, including clearing, excavation, and impoundment. Discuss the possibility of a major alteration to the ecosystem and any potential loss of an endangered species.

3.1.3 *Socioeconomic considerations.*—Discuss the effect on local socioeconomic development in relation to labor, housing, local industry, and public services. Discuss the need for relocations of families and businesses. Describe the beneficial effects, both direct and indirect, of the action on the human environment, such as benefits resulting from the services and products, and other results of the action (include tax benefits to local and State governments, growth in local tax base from new business and housing development and payrolls). Describe the impact on human elements, including the need for increased public services (schools, health facilities, police and fire protection, housing, waste disposal, markets, transportation, communication, energy supplies, and recreational facilities and uses in the proposed project area, including any changes which will occur in recreational use and potential of the local area or region) due to the proposed action; provisions for public access to and use of project lands and waters, including the impacts these uses will have on the area; project lands reserved for future recreation development and the types of facilities which will be or which may need to be provided thereon and how the incremental uses of these lands will affect the area, including the effects of any increased recreational use on the land and water resources and on the public service facilities which presently exist or which would need to be developed to provide for public needs. Discuss the impact of the proposed action on national and local historic and archeological sites, any existing scenic, and cultural values;

3.1.4 *Air and water environment.*—Estimate the qualitative and quantitative effects on air, noise, and water quality, including sedimentation, and whether regulatory standards in effect for the area will be complied with.

[1] *Changes in the Environment Throughout the Sphere of Influence of Proposed Action.*—Direct and indirect effects are those effects which can be discerned as occurring primarily because the proposed action would occur. For example: (1) The impact of a borrow pit would be evaluated to the extent that it would be developed or expanded but the manufacture of conventional trucks to work the pit would not; (2) the impact of construction workers moving into the area would be evaluated but not the impact of their leaving present homes. However, the impact of their subsequent leaving this place must be considered.

3.1.5 *Waste Disposal.*—Discuss the impact of disposal of all waste material such as spoils, vegetation, and construction materials.

3.2 *Operation and maintenance.*

3.2.1 *Land features and uses.*—Outline restrictions on existing and potential land use in the vicinity of the proposed action, including mineral and water resources. State the effect of operation related activities upon local traffic patterns including roads, highways, ship channels, and aviation patterns, and the possible need of new facilities.

3.2.2 *Species and ecosystems.*—Assess the impact of operation upon terrestrial and aquatic species and habitats, including the importance of plant and animal species having economic or aesthetic value to man that would be affected by the action; provide pertinent information on animal migrations, foods, and reproduction in relation to the impacts; and describe any ecosystem imbalances that would be caused by the action and the possibility of major alteration to an ecosystem or the loss of an endangered species. Assess any effects of this action which would be cumulative to those of other similar, existing projects or proposed actions.

3.2.3 *Socioeconomic considerations.*—Discuss the effect on the local socioeconomic development in relation to labor, housing and population growth trends, relocation, local industry and industrial growth, and public service. Describe the beneficial effects, both direct and indirect, of the action on the human environment such as economic benefits resulting from the services and products, energy, and other results of the action (include tax benefits to local and State governments, growth in local tax base from new business and housing developments, and payrolls). Describe impacts on human elements, including any need for increased public service (schools, police and fire protection, housing, waste disposal, markets, transportation, communication and recreational facilities). Indicate the extent to which maintenance of the area is dependent upon new sources of energy or the use of such vital resources as water.

3.2.4 *Air and water environment.*—Assess the impact on present air quality. Assess the impact on present noise levels due to project-related noises. Assess the impact on present water quality, including sedimentation, due to reservoir operations, downstream water releases, power peaking operations, location of outlet works, and sanitary, waste, and process effluents.

3.2.5 *Solid wastes.*—Describe any impacts from accumulation of solid wastes and by-products that will be produced.

3.2.6 *Use of resources.*—Quantify the resources necessary for operational uses; e.g., water (human needs and processes), energy requirements, raw products, and specialized needs. Assess the impact of obtaining and using these resources.

3.2.7 *Maintenance.*—Discuss the impact of maintenance programs, such as subsequent clearing or treatment of rights-of-way. Discuss the potential impact of major breakdowns and shutdowns of the facilities and how service will be maintained during shutdowns.

3.2.8 *Accidents and catastrophes.*—Describe any impacts resulting from accidents and natural catastrophes, which might occur, and provide an analysis of the capability of the area to absorb predicted impacts.

3.3 *Termination and abandonment.*—Discuss the impact on land use and aesthetics of the termination and/or abandonment of facilities resulting from the proposed action.

4. *Measures to enhance the environment or to avoid or mitigate adverse environmental effects.*—Identify all measures which will be undertaken to enhance the environment or eliminate, avoid, mitigate, protect, or compensate for adverse and detrimental aspects of the proposed action, as described under part 3, above, including engineering planning and design, design criteria, contract specifications, selection of materials, construction techniques, monitoring programs during construction and operation, environmental tradeoffs, research and development, and restoration measures which will be taken routinely or as the need arises.

4.1 *Preventative measures and monitoring.*—Discuss provisions for pre- and post-monitoring of significant environmental impacts of the proposed action. Include programs for monitoring changes in operational phases. Describe proposed measures for detecting and modifying noise levels, monitoring air and water quality, inventorying key species in food chains, and detecting induced changes in the weather. Describe measures, including equipment, training procedures, and vector [2] control measures, to be taken for protecting the health and welfare of workers and the public at the project during its construction, operation, and maintenance, including structures to exclude people from hazardous areas or to protect them during changes in operations; include sanitary and solid and liquid waste disposal facilities for workers and the public during construction and operation. Discuss measures to be undertaken to minimize problems arising from malfunctions and accidents (with estimates of probability of occurrence). Identify standard procedures for protecting services and environmental values during maintenance and breakdowns. Discuss proposed and alternative construction timetables to prevent significant environmental impacts and plans for implementation of changes whenever necessary to reduce environmental impact.

4.2 *Environmental restoration and enhancement.*—Discuss all measures to be taken to restore and enhance the environment, including measures for restoration, replacement, or protection of flora and fauna and of scenic, historic, archeological, and other natural values, describe measures to facilitate animal migrations and movements to protect their life processes (e.g., spawning and rearing of fish); describe programs for landscaping and horticultural practices; describe selection and use of any chemicals needed during construction, operation, and maintenance so as to prevent their entry into waters in the area; discuss programs to assist displaced families and businesses in their relocation; describe provisions for public access to, and use of, lands and waters in the area of the proposed action; and discuss the preparation of lands prior to and following their use.

5. *Unavoidable adverse environmental effects.*—Discuss all significant environmental effects which cannot be avoided by measures outlined in section 4 above.

5.1 *Human resources impacted.*—Indicate those human resources and values which will sustain significant, unavoidable adverse effects and discuss whether the impact will be transitory, a one-time but lasting effect, repetitive, continual, incremental, or synergistic to other effects and whether secondary adverse consequences will follow. Focus on the displacement of people by the proposed action and its local, economic, and aesthetic implications; on human health and safety; and on aesthetic and cultural values and standards of living which will be sacrificed or endangered. Where possible provide quantitative evaluations of these effects.

5.2 *Uses preempted and unavoidable changes.*—Discuss all significant, unavoidable environmental impacts on the land and its present use, caused by inundation, clearing, excavation, and fills; losses to wildlife habitat, forests, unique ecosystems, minerals, and farmlands; effects on fish habitat and migrations; on relocation of populations and manmade facilities, such as homes, roads, highways, and trails; on historical, recreational, archeological, and aesthetic values or scenic areas.

5.3 *Loss of environmental quality.*—Discuss any significant, unavoidable adverse changes in the air, including dust and emissions to the air, and noise levels; impacts resulting from solid wastes and their disposal; effects on the water resources of the area, including consumptive uses.

6. *Relationship between local short-term uses of man's environment and the maintenance and enhancement of long-term productivity.*—Compare the benefits to be derived from the immediate or short-term use of the environment, with and without the proposed action, and the long-term consequences of the proposed action. [3] Actions which diminish the diversity of beneficial uses of the environment or preempt the options for future uses or needs require detailed analysis, to assure that shortsighted decisions are not made which may commit future generations to undesirable courses of actions.

6.1 *Short-term uses.*—Assess the local short-term uses of man's environment in terms of the proposed action's benefit to man, land use, alterations to the ecosystem, use of resources, and public health and safety.

6.2 *Long-term productivity.*—Discuss any cumulative long-term effects which may be caused by the proposed action in terms of land use, alterations to the ecosystem, use of resources and public health and safety.

7. *Irreversible and irretrievable commitments of resources.*—Discuss, and quantify when possible, any irrevocable commitments of resources which would be involved in the implementation of the proposed action.

7.1 *Land features and uses.*—Discuss any permanent changes in land features and/or land use.

7.2 *Endangered species and ecosystems.*—Assess the possibility of eliminating any endangered species or the loss or alteration of an ecosystem.

7.3 *Socioeconomic considerations.*—Discuss probable indirect actions (e.g., new highway system or waste water treatment facilities, housing developments, etc.) made economically feasible by the implementation of the proposed action that would likely be triggered and would irrevocably commit other resources under our free enterprise system. Identify the destruction of any historical, archeological, or scenic areas.

7.4 *Resources lost or uses preempted.*—Analyzed the extent to which the proposed action would curtail the range of beneficial uses of the environment. Determine whether, considering presently known technology, the proposed use of resources or any resource extraction method would contaminate other associated resources or foreclose their usage.

7.5 *Finite resources.*—Indicate the irreversible and/or irretrievable resources that would be committed as a result of the proposed action, such as fossil fuels, and construction materials.

8. *Alternatives to the proposed action.*—Discuss the systematic procedure used to

---

[2] Carriers (e.g., ticks, mosquitoes, and rodents) of diseases.

[3] *Duration of Impacts*—Short-term impacts and benefits generally are those which occur during the development and operation of a project. Long-term productivity related to an effect that remains many years (sometimes permanently) after the cause. As examples, strip mining without restoration and land inundation by reservoirs have obvious long-term effects.

arrive at the proposed action, starting with the broadest, feasible objectives of the action and progressively narrowing the alternatives to a specific action at a specific site or right-of-way. This systematic procedure should include the decision criteria used, the information weighed, and an explanation of the conclusion at each decision point. The decision criteria must show how environmental benefits/costs, even if not quantifiable, are weighed against economic benefits/costs and technology and procedural constraints. All realistic alternatives must be discussed even though they may not be within the jurisdiction of the Commission or the responsibilities and capabilities of the applicant. Modification of the proposed action may be among the alternatives. Describe the timeliness and the environmental consequences of each alternative discussed.

8.1 *Objective.*—Explain the need for any proposed new energy supply.

8.2 *Energy alternatives.*—Discuss the potential for accomplishing the proposed objectives through energy conservation and the potential for using realistic energy alternatives, such as natural and artificial gas, oil, and coal. Also discuss realistic electric energy alternatives, such as gas, oil, coal, and nuclear-fueled powerplants, and other conventional and pumped storage hydroelectric plants. Provide an analysis of environmental benefits and costs.

8.3 *Sites and locations.*—Discuss considerations given to alternative sites and locations. Include a description of each site, a summary of environmental factors of each site, the reasons for rejection, and an analysis of environmental benefits and costs.

8.4 *Designs, processes, and operations.*—Describe alternative facility designs, processes (e.g., handling of waste water and solid wastes), and/or operations that were considered and discuss the environmental consequences of each, the reasons for rejection, and an analysis of environmental benefits and costs.

8.5 *No action.*—Discuss the alternative of no action with an evaluation of the consequences of this option on a national, regional, State, or local level, as appropriate. Present a brief perspective of what future use the proposed site (area) may assume if the proposed facilities are not constructed and summarize the environmental benefits and costs.

9. *Permits and compliance with other regulations and codes.*

9.1 *Permits.*—Identify all necessary Federal, regional, State and local permits, licenses, and certificates needed before the proposed action can be completed, such as permits needed from State and local agencies for construction and waste discharges. Describe steps which have been taken to secure these permits and any additional efforts still required.

9.1.1 *Authorities consulted.*—List all authorities consulted for obtaining permits, licenses, and certificates, including zoning approvals needed to comply with applicable statutes and regulations.

9.1.2 *Dates of approval.*—Give dates of consultations and of any approvals received.

9.2 *Compliance with health and safety regulations and codes.*—Identify all Federal, regional, State, and local safety and health regulations and codes which must be complied with in the construction, maintenance, and operation of the proposed project. Also identify other health and safety standards and codes that will be complied with, such as underwriter codes and voluntary industry codes.

9.2.1 *Authorities consulted.*—List all authorities and professional organizations consulted in identifying pertinent regulations and codes.

9.2.2 *Procedures to be followed.*—Describe any specific procedures or actions that will be taken to assure compliance with each such regulation and code.

9.3 *Compliance with other regulations and codes.*—Identify all other Federal, regional, State and local regulations and codes which must be complied with in the construction, maintenance, and operation of the proposed project.

9.3.1 *Authorities consulted.*—List all authorities and professional organizations consulted in identifying pertinent regulations and codes.

9.3.2 *Procedures to be followed.*—Explained the specific procedures or actions that will be taken to assure compliance with each such regulation and code.

10. *Source of information.*

10.1 *Public hearings.*—Describe any public hearings or meetings held, summarize the general tenor of public comments with the proportions of proponents to those in dissent, and include any public records re-

sulting from these meetings. Include a description of the manner in which the public was informed of the time and place of the hearings. Fully discuss efforts made for seeking constructive inputs from affected people and how their concerns were accommodated.

10.2 *Other sources.*—Identify all other sources of information utilized in the preparation of the environmental report, including:

10.2.1 *Meetings with governmental and other entities.*—List meetings held with Federal, regional, State, and local planning, commerce, regulatory, environmental and conservation entities, the subjects discussed (e.g., recreation, fish, wildlife, aesthetics, other natural resources, and values of the area, and economic development), and any environmental conclusions reached as a result of the meeting.

10.2.2 *Studies conducted.*—Identify the studies conducted, including those by consultants, the general nature and major findings of those studies, and the title and availability of any reports thereon.

10.2.3 *Consultants.*—Give the names, addresses, and professional vitae of all consultants who contributed to the environmental report.

10.2.4 *Bibliography.*—Provide a bibliography of the books, other publications, reports, documents, maps, and aerial photographs consulted for background information, including county land use and other planning reports. Indicate by some method, as by asterisks or numbers, those bibliographic references specifically cited in the environmental report.

10.3 *Provide copies of supportive reports.*—Supply at least a single copy of all technical reports prepared in conjunction with the preparation of the environmental report, such as model, heat budget, plankton, fish, and benthic sampling studies.

(Federal Power Act, as amended, 16 U.S.C. 792-828c; Public Utility Regulatory Policies Act of 1978, as amended 16 U.S.C. 2601-2645; Dept. of Energy Organization Act, 42 U.S.C. 7101-7352; E.O. 12009, 3 CFR Part 142 (1979); 5 U.S.C. 553)

[Order 415-C, 38 FR 15949, June 19, 1973. Redesignated by Order 486, 52 FR 47910, Dec. 17, 1987, and amended by Order 486, 52 FR 47914, Dec. 17, 1987]

Federal Highway Administration
NEPA Regulations
23 C.F.R. Pt. 771

Sec.

AUTHORITY: 42 U.S.C. 4321 *et seq.*; 23 U.S.C. 109, 128, 138 and 315; 49 U.S.C. 303(c), 1602(d), 1604(h), 1604(i), and 1610; 40 CFR Part 1500 *et seq.*; 49 CFR 1.48(b) and 1.51.

SOURCE: 52 FR 32660, Aug. 28, 1987, unless otherwise noted.

§ 771.101   Purpose.

This regulation prescribes the policies and procedures of the Federal Highway Administration (FHWA) and the Urban Mass Transportation Administration (UMTA) for implementing the National Environmental Policy Act of 1969 as amended (NEPA), and the regulation of the Council on Environmental Quality (CEQ), 40 CFR Parts 1500–1508. This regulation sets forth all FHWA, UMTA, and Department of Transportation (DOT) requirements under NEPA for the processing of highway and urban mass transportation projects. This regulation also sets forth procedures to comply with 23 U.S.C. 109(h), 128, 138, and 49 U.S.C. 303, 1602(d), 1604(h), 1604(i), 1607a, 1607a–1 and 1610.

§ 771.103   [Reserved]

§ 771.105   Policy.

It is the policy of the Administration that:

(a) To the fullest extent possible, all environmental investigations, reviews, and consultations be coordinated as a single process, and compliance with all applicable environmental requirements be reflected in the environmental document required by this regulation.[1]

---

[1] FHWA and UMTA have supplementary guidance on the format and content of NEPA documents for their programs. This includes a list of various environmental laws, regulations, and Executive orders which may be applicable to projects. The FHWA Technical Advisory T6640.8A, October 30, 1987, and the UMTA supplementary guidance are available from the respective

(b) Alternative courses of action be evaluated and decisions be made in the best overall public interest based upon a balanced consideration of the need for safe and efficient transportation; of the social, economic, and environmental impacts of the proposed transportation improvement; and of national, State, and local environmental protection goals.

(c) Public involvement and a systematic interdisciplinary approach be essential parts of the development process for proposed actions.

(d) Measures necessary to mitigate adverse impacts be incorporated into the action. Measures necessary to mitigate adverse impacts are eligible for Federal funding when the Administration determines that:

(1) The impacts for which the mitigation is proposed actually result from the Administration action; and

(2) The proposed mitigation represents a reasonable public expenditure after considering the impacts of the action and the benefits of the proposed mitigation measures. In making this determination, the Administration will consider, among other factors, the extent to which the proposed measures would assist in complying with a Federal statute, Executive Order, or Administration regulation or policy.

(e) Costs incurred by the applicant for the preparation of environmental documents requested by the Administration be eligible for Federal assistance.

(f) No person, because of handicap, age, race, color, sex, or national origin, be excluded from participating in, or denied benefits of, or be subject to discrimination under any Administration program or procedural activity required by or developed pursuant to this regulation.

[52 FR 32660, Aug. 28, 1987; 53 FR 11065, Apr. 5, 1988]

§ 771.107   Definitions.

The definitions contained in the CEQ regulation and in Titles 23 and 49 of the United States Code are applicable. In addition, the following definitions apply.

(a) *Environmental studies*—The investigations of potential environmental impacts to determine the environmental process to be followed and to assist in the preparation of the environmental document.

(b) *Action*—A highway or transit project proposed for FHWA or UMTA funding. It also includes activities such as joint and multiple use permits, changes in access control, etc., which may or may not involve a commitment of Federal funds.

FHWA and UMTA headquarters and field offices as prescribed in 49 CFR Part 7, Appendices D and G.

(c) *Administration action*—The approval by FHWA or UMTA of the applicant's request for Federal funds for construction. It also includes approval of activities such as joint and multiple use permits, changes in access control, etc., which may or may not involve a commitment of Federal funds.

(d) *Administration*—FHWA or UMTA, whichever is the designated lead agency for the proposed action.

(e) *Section 4(f)*—Refers to 49 U.S.C. 303 and 23 U.S.C. 138.[2]

§ 771.109   Applicability and responsibilities.

(a)(1) The provisions of this regulation and the CEQ regulation apply to actions where the Administration exercises sufficient control to condition the permit or project approval. Actions taken by the applicant which do not require Federal approvals, such as preparation of a regional transportation plan are not subject to this regulation.

(2) This regulation does not apply to, or alter approvals by the Administration made prior to the effective date of this regulation.

(3) Environmental documents accepted or prepared by the Administration after the effective date of this regulation shall be developed in accordance with this regulation.

(b) It shall be the responsibility of the applicant, in cooperation with the Administration to implement those mitigation measures stated as commitments in the environmental documents prepared pursuant to this regulation. The FHWA will assure that this is accomplished as a part of its program management responsibilities that include reviews of designs, plans, specifications, and estimates (PS&E), and construction inspections. The UMTA will assure implementation of committed mitigation measures through incorporation by reference in the grant agreement, followed by reviews of designs and contruction inspections.

(c) The Administration, in cooperation with the applicant, has the responsibility to manage the preparation of the appropriate environmental document. The role of the applicant will be determined by the Administration accordance with the CEQ regulation:

(1) *Statewide agency.* If the applicant is a public agency that has statewide jurisdiction (for example, a State

---

[2] Section 4(f), which protected certain public lands and all historic sites, technically was repealed in 1983 when it was codified, without substantive change, as 49 U.S.C. 303. This regulation continues to refer to section 4(f) because it would create needless confusion to do otherwise; the policies section 4(f) engendered are widely referred to as "section 4(f)" matters. A provision with the same meaning is found at 23 U.S.C. 138 and applies only to FHWA actions.

highway agency or a State department of transportation) or is a local unit of government acting through a state-wide agency, and meets the requirements of section 102(2)(D) of NEPA, the applicant may prepare the environmental impact statement (EIS) and other environmental documents with the Administration furnishing guidance, participating in the preparation, and independently evaluating the document. All FHWA applicants qualify under this paragraph.

(2) *Joint lead agency.* If the applicant is a public agency and is subject to State or local requirements comparable to NEPA, then the Administration and the applicant may prepare the EIS and other environmental documents as joint lead agencies. The applicant shall initially develop substantive portions of the environmental document, although the Administration will be responsible for its scope and content.

(3) *Cooperating agency.* Local public agenices with special expertise in the proposed action may be cooperating agencies in the preparation of an environmental document. An applicant for capital assistance under the Urban Mass Transportation Act of 1964, as amended (UMT Act), is presumed to be a cooperating agency if the conditions in paragraph (c) (1) or (2) of this section do not apply. During the environmental process, the Administration will determine the scope and content of the environmental document and will direct the applicant, acting as a cooperating agency, to develop information and prepare those portions of the document concerning which it has special expertise.

(4) *Other.* In all other cases, the role of the applicant is limited to providing environmental studies and commenting on environmental documents. All private institutions or firms are limited to this role.

§ 771.111 Early coordination, public involvement, and project development.

(a) Early coordination with appropriate agencies and the public aids in determining the type of environmental document an action requires, the scope of the document, the level of analysis, and related environmental requirements. This involves the exchange of information from the inception of a proposal for action to preparation of the environmental document. Applicants intending to apply for funds should notify the Administration at the time that a project concept is identified. When requested, the Administration will advise the applicant, insofar as possible, of the probable class of action and related environmental laws and requirements and of the need for specific studies and findings which would normally be developed concurrently with the environmental document.

(b) The Administration will identify the probable class of action as soon as sufficient information is available to identify the probable impacts of the action. For UMTA, this is normally no later than the review of the transpor-

tation improvement program (TIP) and for FHWA, the approval of the 105 program (23 U.S.C. 105).

(c) When FHWA and UMTA are involved in the development of joint projects, or when FHWA or UMTA acts as a joint lead agency with another Federal agency, a mutually acceptable process will be established on a case-by-case basis.

(d) During the early coordination process, the Administration, in cooperation with the applicant, may request other agencies having special interest or expertise to become cooperating agencies. Agencies with jurisdiction by law must be requested to become cooperating agencies.

(e) Other States, and Federal land management entities, that may be significantly affected by the action or by any of the alternatives shall be notified early and their views solicited by the applicant in cooperation with the Administration. The Administration will prepare a written evaluation of any significant unresolved issues and furnish it to the applicant for incorporation into the environmental assessment (EA) or draft EIS.

(f) In order to ensure meaningful evaluation of alternatives and to avoid commitments to transportation improvements before they are fully evaluated, the action evaluated in each EIS or finding of no significant impact (FONSI) shall:

(1) Connect logical termini and be of sufficient length to address environmental matters on a broad scope;

(2) Have independent utility or independent significance, i.e., be usable and be a reasonable expenditure even if no additional transportation improvements in the area are made; and

(3) Not restrict consideration of alternatives for other reasonably foreseeable transportation improvements.

(g) For major transportation actions, the tiering of EISs as discussed in the CEQ regulation (40 CFR 1502.20) may be appropriate. The first tier EIS would focus on broad issues such as general location, mode choice, and areawide air quality and land use implications of the major alternatives. The second tier would address site-specific details on project impacts, costs, and mitigation measures.

(h) For the Federal-aid highway program:

(1) Each State must have procedures approved by the FHWA to carry out a public involvement/public hearing program pursuant to 23 U.S.C. 128 and 40 CFR Parts 1500–1508.

(2) State public involvement/public hearing procedures must provide for:

(i) Coordination of public involvement activities and public hearings with the entire NEPA process.

(ii) Early and continuing opportunities during project development for the public to be involved in the identification of social, economic, and environmental impacts, as well as impacts associated with relocation of individuals, groups, or institutions.

(iii) One or more public hearings or the opportunity for hearing(s) to be held by the State highway agency at a

convenient time and place for any Federal-aid project which requires significant amounts of right-of-way, substantially changes the layout or functions of connecting roadways or of the facility being improved, has a substantial adverse impact on abutting property, otherwise has a significant social, economic, environmental or other effect, or for which the FHWA determines that a public hearing is in the public interest.

(iv) Reasonable notice to the public of either a public hearing or the opportunity for a public hearing. Such notice will indicate the availability of explanatory information. The notice shall also provide information required to comply with public involvement requirements of other laws, Executive orders, and regulations.

(v) Explanation at the public hearing of the following information, as appropriate:

(A) The project's purpose, need, and consistency with the goals and objectives of any local urban planning,

(B) The project's alternatives, and major design features,

(C) The social, economic, environmental, and other impacts of the project,

(D) The relocation assistance program and the right-of-way acquisition process.

(E) The State highway agency's procedures for receiving both oral and written statements from the public.

(vi) Submission to the FHWA of a transcript of each public hearing and a certification that a required hearing or hearing opportunity was offered. The transcript will be accompanied by copies of all written statements from the public, both submitted at the public hearing or during an announced period after the public hearing.

(3) Based on the reevaluation of project environmental documents required by § 771.129, the FHWA and the State highway agency will determine whether changes in the project or new information warrant additional public involvement.

(4) Approvals or acceptances of public involvement/public hearing procedures prior to the publication date of this regulation remain valid.

(i) Applicants for capital assistance in the UMTA program achieve public participation on proposed projects by holding public hearings and seeking input from the public through the scoping process for environmental documents. For projects requiring EISs, a public hearing will be held during the circulation period of the draft EIS. For all other projects, an opportunity for public hearings will be afforded with adequate prior notice pursuant to 49 U.S.C. 1602(d), 1604(i), 1607a(f) and 1607a-1(d), and such hearings will be held when anyone with a significant social, economic, or environmental interest in the matter requests it. Any hearing on the action must be coordinated with the NEPA process to the fullest extent possible.

(j) Information on the UMTA environmental process may be obtained from: Director, Office of Planning Assistance, Urban Mass Transportation Administration, Washington, DC 20590. Information on the FHWA environmental process may be obtained from: Director, Office of Environmental Policy, Federal Highway Administration, Washington, DC 20590.

§ 771.113 Timing of Administration activities.

(a) The Administration in cooperation with the applicant will perform the work necessary to complete a FONSI or an EIS and comply with other related environmental laws and regulations to the maximum extent possible during the NEPA process. This work includes environmental studies, related engineering studies, agency coordination and public involvement. However, final design activities, property acquisition (with the exception of hardship and protective buying, as defined in § 771.117(d)), purchase of construction materials or rolling stock, or project construction shall not proceed until the following have been completed:

(1)(i) The action has been classified as a categorical exclusion (CE), or

(ii) A FONSI has been approved, or

(iii) A final EIS has been approved and available for the prescribed period of time and a record of decision has been signed;

(2) For actions proposed for FHWA funding, the FHWA Division Administrator has received and accepted the certifications and any required public hearing transcripts required by 23 U.S.C. 128;

(3) For activities proposed for FHWA funding, the programming requirements of 23 CFR Part 450, Subpart B, and 23 CFR Part 630, Subpart A, have been met.

(b) For FHWA, the completion of the requirements set forh in paragraph (a)(1) and (a)(2) of this section is considered acceptance of the general project location and concepts described in the environmental document unless otherwise specified by the approving official. However, such approval does not commit the Administration to approve any future grant request to fund the preferred alternative.

(c) Letters of Intent issued under the authority of section 3(a)(4) of the UMT Act are used by UMTA to indicate an intention to obligate future funds for multi-year capital transit projects. Letters of Intent will not be issued by UMTA until the NEPA process is completed.

[52 FR 32660, Aug. 28, 1987; 53 FR 11066, Apr. 5, 1988]

§ 771.115 Classes of actions.

There are three classes of actions which prescribe the level of documentation required in the NEPA process.

(a) *Class I (EISs)*. Actions that significantly affect the environment require an EIS (40 CFR 1508.27). The following are examples of actions that normally required an EIS:

(1) A new controlled access freeway.

(2) A highway project of four or more lanes on a new location.

(3) New construction or extension of fixed rail transit facilities (e.g., rapid rail, light rail, commuter rail, automated guideway transit).

(4) New construction or extension of a separate roadway for buses or high occupancy vehicles not located within an existing highway facility.

(b) *Class II (CEs)*. Actions that do not individually or cumulative have a significant environmental effect are excluded from the requirement to prepare an EA or EIS. A specific list of CEs normally not requiring NEPA documentation is set forth in § 771.117(c). When appropriately documented, additional projects may also qualify as CEs pursuant to § 771.117(d).

(c) *Class III (EAs)*. Actions in which the significance of the environmental impact is not clearly estabilished. All actions that are not Class I or II are Class III. All actions in this class require the preparation of an EA to determine the appropriate environmental document required.

§ 771.117 Categorical exclusions.

(a) Categorical exclusions (CEs) are actions which meet the definition contained in 40 CFR 1508.4 and, based on past experience with similar actions, do not involve signifícnt environmental impacts. They are actions which: do not induce significant impacts to planned growth or land use for the area; do not require the relocation of significant numbers of people; do not have a significant impact on any natural, cultural, recreational, historic or other resource; do not involve significant air, noise, or water quality impacts; do not have significant impacts on travel patterns; or do not otherwise, either individually or cumulatively, have any significant environmental impacts.

(b) Any action which normally would be classified as a CE but could involve unusual circumstances will require the Administration, in cooperation with the applicant, to conduct appropriate environmental studies to determine if the CE classification is proper. Such unusual circumstances include:

(1) Significant environmental impacts;

(2) Substantial controversy on environmental grounds;

(3) Significant impact on properties protected by section 4(f) of the DOT Act or section 106 of the National Historic Preservation Act; or

(4) Inconsistencies with any Federal, State, or local law, requirement or administrative determination relating to the environmental aspects of the action.

(c) The following actions meet the criteria for CEs in the CEQ regulation (section 1508.4) and § 771.117(a) of this regulation and normally do not require any further NEPA approvals by the Administration:

(1) Activities which do not involve or lead directly to construction, such as planning and technical studies; grants

for training and research programs; research activities as defined in 23 U.S.C. 307; approval of a unified work program and any findings required in the planning process pursuant to 23 U.S.C. 134; approval of statewide programs under 23 CFR Part 630; approval of project concepts under 23 CFR Part 476; engineering to define the elements of a proposed action or alternatives so that social, economic, and environmental effects can be assessed; and Federal-aid system revisions which establish classes of highways on the Federal-aid highway system.

(2) Approval of utility installations along or across a transportation facility.

(3) Construction of bicycle and pedestrian lanes, paths, and facilities.

(4) Activities included in the State's "highway safety plan" under 23 U.S.C. 402.

(5) Transfer of Federal lands pursuant to 23 U.S.C. 317 when the subsequent action is not an FHWA action.

(6) The installation of noise barriers or alterations to existing publicly owned buildings to provide for noise reduction.

(7) Landscaping.

(8) Installation of fencing, signs, pavement markings, small passenger shelters, traffic signals, and railroad warning devices where no substantial land acquisition or traffic disruption will occur.

(9) Emergency repairs under 23 U.S.C. 125.

(10) Acquisition of scenic easements.

(11) Determination of payback under 23 CFR Part 480 for property previously acquired with Federal-aid participation.

(12) Improvements to existing rest areas and truck weigh stations.

(13) Ridesharing activities.

(14) Bus and rail car rehabilitation.

(15) Alterations to facilities or vehicles in order to make them accessible for elderly and handicapped persons.

(16) Program administration, technical assistance activities, and operating assistance to transit authorities to continue existing service or increase service to meet routine changes in demand.

(17) The purchase of vehicles by the applicant where the use of these vehicles can be accommodated by existing facilities or by new facilities which themselves are within a CE.

(18) Track and railbed maintenance and improvements when carried out within the existing right-of-way.

(19) Purchase and installation of operating or maintenance equipment to be located within the transit facility and with no significant impacts off the site.

(20) Promulgation of rules, regulations, and directives.

(d) Additional actions which meet the criteria for a CE in the CEQ regulations (40 CFR 1508.4) and paragraph (a) of this section may be designated as CEs only after Administration approval. The applicant shall submit documentation which demonstrates that the specific conditions or criteria for these CEs are satisfied and that significant environmental effects will not result. Examples of such actions include but are not limited to:

(1) Modernization of a highway by resurfacing, restoration, rehabilitation, reconstruction, adding shoulders, or adding auxiliary lanes (e.g., parking, weaving, turning, climbing).

(2) Highway safety or traffic operations improvement projects including the installation of ramp metering control devices and lighting.

(3) Bridge rehabilitation, reconstruction or replacement or the construction of grade separation to replace existing at-grade railroad crossings.

(4) Transportation corridor fringe parking facilities.

(5) Construction of new truck weigh stations or rest areas.

(6) Approvals for disposal of excess right-of-way or for joint or limited use of right-of-way, where the proposed use does not have significant adverse impacts.

(7) Approvals for changes in access control.

(8) Construction of new bus storage and maintenance facilities in areas used predominantly for industrial or transportation purposes where such construction is not inconsistent with existing zoning and located on or near a street with adequate capacity to handle anticipated bus and support vehicle traffic.

(9) Rehabilitation or reconstruction of existing rail and bus buildings and ancillary facilities where only minor amounts of additional land are required and there is not a substantial increase in the number of users.

(10) Construction of bus transfer facilities (an open area consisting of passenger shelters, boarding areas, kiosks and related street improvements) when located in a commercial area or other high activity center in which there is adequate street capacity for projected bus traffic.

(11) Construction of rail storage and maintenance facilities in areas used predominantly for industrial or transportation purposes where such construction is not inconsistent with existing zoning and where there is no significant noise impact on the surrounding community.

(12) Acquisition of land for hardship or protective purposes; advance land acquisition loans under section 3(b) of the UMT Act.[3] Hardship and protec-

---

[3] Hardship acquisition is early acquisition of property by the applicant at the property owner's request to alleviate particular hardship to the owner, in contrast to others, because of an inability to sell his property. This is justified when the property owner can document on the basis of health, safety or financial reasons that remaining in the property poses an undue hardship compared to others.

Protective acquisition is done to prevent imminent development of a parcel which is needed for a proposed transportation corridor or site. Documentation must clearly demonstrate that development of the land would preclude future transportation use and that such development is imminent. Ad-

---

tive buying will be permitted only for a particular parcel or a limited number of parcels. These types of land acquisition quality for a CE only where the acquisition will not limit the evaluation of alternatives, including shifts in alignment for planned construction projects, which may be required in the NEPA process. No project development on such land may proceed until the NEPA process has been completed.

(e) Where a pattern emerges of granting CE status for a particular type of action, the Administration will initiate rulemaking proposing to add this type of action to the list of categorical exclusions in paragraph (c) or (d) of this section, as appropriate.

[52 FR 32660, Aug. 28, 1987; 53 FR 11066, Apr. 5, 1988]

§ 771.119 Environmental assessments.

(a) An EA shall be prepared by the applicant in consultation with the Administration for each action that is not a CE and does not clearly require the preparation of an EIS, or where the Administration believes an EA would assist in determining the need for an EIS.

(b) For actions that require an EA, the applicant, in consultation with the Administration, shall, at the earliest appropriate time, begin consultation with interested agencies and others to advise them of the scope of the project and to achieve the following objectives: determine which aspects of the proposed action have potential for social, economic, or environmental impact; identify alternatives and measures which might mitigate adverse environmental impacts; and identify other environmental review and consultation requirements which should be performed concurrently with the EA. The applicant shall accomplish this through an early coordination process (i.e., procedures under § 771.111) or through a scoping process. Public involvement shall be summarized and the results of agency coordination shall be included in the EA.

(c) The EA is subject to Administration approval before it is made available to the public as an Administration document. The UMTA applicants may circulate the EA prior to Administration approval provided that the document is clearly labeled as the applicant's document.

(d) The EA need not be circulated for comment but the document must be made available for public inspection at the applicant's office and at the appropriate Administration field offices in accordance with paragraphs (e) and (f) of this section. Notice of availability of the EA, briefly describing the action and its impacts, shall be sent by the applicant to the affected units of Federal, State and local government. Notice shall also be sent to the State intergovernmental review contacts established under Executive Order 12372.

---

vance acquisition is not permitted for the sole purpose of reducing the cost of property for a proposed project.

(e) When a public hearing is held as part of the application for Federal funds, the EA shall be available at the public hearing and for a minimum of 15 days in advance of the public hearing. The notice of the public hearing in local newspapers shall announce the availability of the EA and where it may be obtained or reviewed. Comments shall be submitted in writing to the applicant or the Administration within 30 days of the availability of the EA unless the Administration determines, for good cause, that a different period is warranted. Public hearing requirements are as described in § 771.111.

(f) When a public hearing is not held, the applicant shall place a notice in a newspaper(s) similar to a public hearing notice and at a similar stage of development of the action, advising the public of the availability of the EA and where information concerning the action may be obtained. The notice shall invite comments from all interested parties. Comments shall be submitted in writing to the applicant or the Administration within 30 days of the publication of the notice unless the Administration determines, for good cause, that a different period is warranted.

(g) If no significant impacts are identified, the applicant shall furnish the administration a copy of the revised EA, as appropriate; the public hearing transcript, where applicable; copies of any comments received and responses thereto; and recommend a FONSI. The EA should also document compliance, to the extent possible, with all applicable environmental laws and Executive orders, or provide reasonable assurance that their requirements can be met.

(h) When the Administration expects to issue a FONSI for an action described in § 771.115(a), copies of the EA shall be made available for public review (including the affected units of government) for a minimum of 30 days before the Administration makes its final decision (See 40 CFR 1501.4(e)(2).) This public availability shall be announced by a notice similar to a public hearing notice.

(i) If, at any point in the EA process, the Administration determines that the action is likely to have a significant impact on the environment, the preparation of an EIS will be required.

§ 771.121 Findings of no significant impact.

(a) The Administration will review the EA and any public hearing comments and other comments received regarding the EA. If the Administration agrees with the applicant's recommendations pursuant to § 771.119(g), it will make a separate written FONSI incorporating by reference the EA and any other appropriate environmental documents.

(b) After a FONSI has been made by the Administration, a notice of availability of the FONSI shall be sent by the applicant to the affected units of Federal, State and local government and the document shall be available from the applicant and the Administration upon request by the public. Notice shall also be sent to the State intergovernmental review contacts established under Executive Order 12372.

(c) If another Federal agency has issued a FONSI on an action which includes an element proposed for Administration funding, the Administration will evaluate the other agency's FONSI. If the Administration determines that this element of the project and its environmental impacts have been adequately identified and assessed, and concurs in the decision to issue a FONSI, the Administration will issue its own FONSI incorporating the other agency's FONSI. If environmental issues have not been adequately identified and assessed, the Administration will require appropriate environmental studies.

§ 771.123 Draft environmental impact statements.

(a) A draft EIS shall be prepared when the Administration determines that the action is likely to cause significant impacts on the environment. When the decision has been made by the Administration to prepare an EIS, the Administration will issue a Notice of Intent (40 CFR 1508.22) for publication in the FEDERAL REGISTER. Applicants are encouraged to announce the intent to prepare an EIS by apprpriate means at the local level.

(b) After publication of the Notice of Intent, the Administration, in cooperation with the applicant, will begin a scoping process. The scoping process will be used to identify the range of alternatives and impacts and the significant issues to be addressed in the EIS and to achieve the other objectives of 40 CFR 1501.7. For FHWA, scoping is normally achieved through public and agency involvement procedures required by § 771.111. For UMTA, scoping is achieved by soliciting agency and public responses to the action by letter or by holding scoping meetings. If a scoping meeting is to be held, it should be announced in the Administration's Notice of Intent and by appropriate means at the local level.

(c) The draft EIS shall be prepared by the Administration in cooperation with the applicant or, where permitted by law, by the applicant with appropriate guidance and participation by the Administration. The draft EIS shall evaluate all reasonable alternatives to the action and discuss the reasons why other alternatives, which may have been considered, were eliminated from detailed study. The draft EIS shall also summarize the studies, reviews, consultations, and coordination required by environmental laws or Executive orders to the extent appropriate at this stage in the environmental process.

(d) An applicant which is a "statewide agency" may select a consultant to assist in the preparation of an EIS in accordance with applicable contracting procedures. Where the applicant is a "joint lead" or "cooperating" agency, the applicant may select a consultant, after coordination with the Administration to assure compliance with 40 CFR 1506.5(c). The Administration will select any such consultant for "other" applicants. (See § 771.109(c) for definitions of these terms.)

(e) The Administration, when satisfied that the draft EIS complies with NEPA requirements, will approve the draft EIS for circulation by signing and dating the cover sheet.

(f) A lead, joint lead, or a cooperating agency shall be responsible for printing the EIS. The initial printing of the draft EIS shall be in sufficient quantity to meet requirements for copies which can reasonably be expected from agencies, organizations, and individuals. Normally, copies will be furnished free of charge. However, with Administration concurrence, the party requesting the draft EIS may be charged a fee which is not more than the actual cost of reproducing the copy or may be directed to the nearest location where the statement may be reviewed.

(g) The draft EIS shall be circulated for comment by the applicant on behalf of the Administration. The draft EIS shall be made available to the public and transmitted to agencies for comment no later than the time the document is filed with the Environmental Protection Agency in accordance with 40 CFR 1506.9. The draft EIS shall be transmitted to:

(1) Public officials, interest groups, and members of the public known to have an interest in the proposed action or the draft EIS;

(2) Federal, State and local government agencies expected to have jurisdiction or responsibility over, or interest or expertise in, the action. Copies shall be provided directly to appropriate State and local agencies, and to the State intergovernmental review contacts established under Executive Order 12372; and

(3) States and Federal land management entities which may be significantly affected by the proposed action or any of the alternatives. These copies shall be accompanied by a request that such State or entity advise the Administration in writing of any disagreement with the evaluation of impacts in the statement. The Administration will furnish the comments received to the applicant along with a written assessment of any disagreements for incorporation into the final EIS.

(h) The UMTA requires a public hearing during the circulation period of all draft EISs. FHWA public hearing requirements are as described in § 771.111(h). Whenever a public hearing is held, the draft EIS shall be available at the public hearing and for a minimum of 15 days in advance of the public hearing. The availability of the draft EIS shall be mentioned, and public comments requested, in any public hearing notice and at any public hearing presentation. If a public hearing on an action proposed for FHWA funding is not held, a notice shall be placed in a newspaper similar to a public hearing notice advising where the draft EIS is available for review, how copies may be obtained, and where the comments should be sent.

(i) The FEDERAL REGISTER public availability notice (40 CFR 1506.10) shall establish a period of not less than 45 days for the return of comments on the draft EIS. The notice and the draft EIS transmittal letter shall identify where comments are to be sent.

(j) For UMTA funded major urban mass transportation investments, the applicant shall prepare a report identifying a locally preferred alternative at the conclusion of the Draft EIS circulation period. Approval may be given to begin preliminary engineering on the principal alternative(s) under consideration. During the course of such preliminary engineering, the applicant will refine project costs, effectiveness, and impact information with particular attention to alternative designs, operations, detailed location decisions and appropriate mitigation measures. These studies will be used to prepare the final EIS or, where appropriate, a supplemental draft EIS.

§ 771.125 Final environmental impact statements.

(a)(1) After circulation of a draft EIS and consideration of comments received, a final EIS shall be prepared by the Administration in cooperation with the applicant or, where permitted by law, by the applicant with appropriate guidance and participation by the Administration. The final EIS shall identify the preferred alternative and evaluate all reasonable alternatives considered. It shall also discuss substantive comments received on the draft EIS and responses thereto, summarize public involvement, and describe the mitigation measures that are to be incorporated into the proposed action. Mitigation measures presented as commitments in the final EIS will be incorporated into the project as specified in § 771.109(b). The final EIS should also document compliance, to the extent possible, with all applicable environmental laws and Executive orders, or provide reasonable assurance that their requirements can be met.

(2) Every reasonable effort shall be made to resolve interagency disagreements on actions before processing the final EIS. If significant issues remain unresolved, the final EIS shall identify those issues and the consultations and other efforts made to resolve them.

(b) The final EIS will be reviewed for legal sufficiency prior to Administration approval.

(c) The Administration will indicate approval of the EIS for an action by signing and dating the cover page. Final EISs prepared for actions in the following categories will be submitted to the Administration's Headquarters for prior concurrence:

(1) Any action for which the Administration determines that the final EIS should be reviewed at the Headquarters office. This would typically occur when the Headquarters office determines that (i) additional coordination with other Federal, State or local governmental agencies is needed; (ii) the social, economic, or environmental impacts of the action may need to be more fully explored; (iii) the impacts of the proposed action are unusually great; (iv) major issues remain unresolved; or (v) the action involves national policy issues.

(2) Any action to which a Federal, State or local government agency has indicated opposition on environmental grounds (which has not been resolved to the written satisfaction of the objecting agency).

(3) Major urban mass transportation investments as defined by UMTA's policy on major investments (49 FR 21284; May 18, 1984).

(d) The signature of the UMTA approving official on the cover sheet also indicates compliance with section 14 of the UMT Act and fulfillment of the grant application requirements of sections 3(d)(1) and (2), 5(h), and 5(i) of the UMT Act.

(e) Approval of the final EIS is not an Administration Action (as defined in § 771.107(c)) and does not commit the Administration to approve any future grant request to fund the preferred alternative.

(f) The initial printing of the final EIS shall be in sufficient quantity to meet the request for copies which can be reasonably expected from agencies, organizations, and individuals. Normally, copies will be furnished free of charge. However, with Administration concurrence, the party requesting the final EIS may be charged a fee which is not more than the actual cost of reproducing the copy or may be directed to the nearest location where the statement may be reviewed.

(g) The final EIS shall be transmitted to any persons, organizations, or agencies that made substantive comments on the draft EIS or requested a copy, no later than the time the document is filed with EPA. In the case of lengthy documents, the agency may provide alternative circulation processes in accordance with 40 CFR 1502.19. The applicant shall also publish a notice of availability in local newspapers and make the final EIS available through the mechanism established pursuant to DOT Order 4600.13 which implements Executive Order 12372. When filed with EPA, the final EIS shall be available for public review at the applicant's offices and at appropriate Administration offices. A copy should also be made available for public review at institutions such as local government offices, libraries, and schools, as appropriate.

§ 771.127 Record of decision.

(a) The Administration will complete and sign a record of decision (ROD) no sooner than 30 days after publication of the final EIS notice in the FEDERAL REGISTER or 90 days after publication of a notice for the draft EIS, whichever is later. The ROD will present the basis for the decision as specified in 40 CFR 1505.2, summarize any mitigation measures that will be incorporated in the project and document any required section 4(f) approval in accordance with § 771.135(l). Until any required ROD has been signed, no further approvals may be given except for administrative activities taken to secure further project funding and other activities consistent with 40 CFR 1506.1.

(b) If the Administration subsequently wishes to approve an alternative which was not identified as the preferred alternative but was fully evaluated in the final EIS, or proposes to make substantial changes to the mitigation measures or findings discussed in the ROD, a revised ROD shall be subject to review by those Administration offices which reviewed the final EIS under § 771.125(c). To the extent practicable the approved revised ROD shall be provided to all persons, organizations, and agencies that received a copy of the final EIS pursuant to § 771.125(g).

§ 771.129 Re–evaluations.

(a) A written evaluation of the draft EIS shall be prepared by the applicant in cooperation with the Administration if an acceptable final EIS is not submitted to the Administration within 3 years from the date of the draft EIS circulation. The purpose of this evaluation is to determine whether or not a supplement to the draft EIS or a new draft EIS is needed.

(b) A written evaluation of the final EIS will be required before further approvals may be granted if major steps to advance the action (e.g., authority to undertake final design, authority to acquire a significant portion of the right-of-way, or approval of the plans, specifications and estimates) have not occurred within three years after the approval of the final EIS, final EIS supplement, or the last major Administration approval or grant.

(c) After approval of the EIS, FONSI, or CE designation, the applicant shall consult with the Administration prior to requesting any major approvals or grants to establish whether or not the approved environmental document or CE designation remains valid for the requested Administration action. These consultations will be documented when determined necessary by the Administration.

[52 FR 32660, Aug. 28, 1987; 53 FR 11066, Apr. 5, 1988]

§ 771.130 Supplemental environmental impact statements.

(a) A draft EIS, final EIS, or supplemental EIS may be supplemented at any time. An EIS shall be supplemented whenever the Administration determines that:

(1) Changes to the proposed action would result in significant environmental impacts that were not evaluated in the EIS; or

(2) New information or circumstances relevant to environmental concerns and bearings on the proposed action or its impacts would result in significant environmental impacts not evaluated in the EIS.

(b) However, a supplemental EIS will not be necessary where:

(1) The changes to the proposed action, new information, or new circumstances result in a lessening of adverse environmental impacts evaluated in the EIS without causing other environmental impacts that are significant and were not evaluated in the EIS; or

(2) The Administration decides to approve an alternative fully evaluated in an approved final EIS but not identified as the preferred alternative. In such a case, a revised ROD shall be prepared and circulated in accordance with § 771.127(b).

(c) Where the Administration is uncertain of the significance of the new impacts, the applicant will develop appropriate environmental studies or, if the Administration deems appropriate, an EA to assess the impacts of the changes, new information, or new circumstances. If, based upon the studies, the Administration determines that a supplemental EIS is not necessary, the Administration shall so indicate in the project file.

(d) A supplement is to be developed using the same process and format (i.e., draft EIS, final EIS, and ROD) as an original EIS, except that scoping is not required.

(e) A supplemental draft EIS may be necessary for UMTA major urban mass transportation investments if there is a substantial change in the level of detail on project impacts during project planning and development. The supplement will address site-specific impacts and refined cost estimates that have been developed since the original draft EIS.

(f) In some cases, a supplemental EIS may be required to address issues of limited scope, such as the extent of proposed mitigation or the evaluation of location or design variations for a limited portion of the overall project. Where this is the case, the preparation of a supplemental EIS shall not necessarily:

(1) Prevent the granting of new approvals;

(2) Require the withdrawal of previous approvals; or

(3) Require the suspension of project activities; for any activity not directly affected by the supplement. If the changes in question are of such magnitude to require a reassessment of the entire action, or more than a limited portion of the overall action, the Administration shall suspend any activities which would have an adverse environmental impact or limit the choice of reasonable alternatives, until the supplemental EIS is completed.

§ 771.131 Emergency action procedures.

Requests for deviations from the

procedures in this regulation because of emergency circumstances (40 CFR 1506.11) shall be referred to the Administration's headquarters for evaluation and decision after consultation with CEQ.

§ 771.133 Compliance with other requirements.

The final EIS or FONSI should document compliance with requirements of all applicable environmental laws, Executive orders, and other related requirements. If full compliance is not possible by the time the final EIS or FONSI is prepared, the final EIS or FONSI should reflect consultation with the appropriate agencies and provide reasonable assurance that the requirements will be met. Approval of the environmental document constitutes adoption of any Administration findings and determinations that are contained therein. The FHWA approval of the appropriate NEPA document will constitute its finding of compliance with the report requirements of 23 U.S.C. 128.

§ 771.135 Section 4(f) (49 U.S.C. 303).

(a)(1) The Administration may not approve the use of land from a significant publicly owned public park, recreation area, or wildlife and wildlife refuge, or any significant historic site unless a determination is made that:

(i) There is no feasible and prudent alternative to the use of land from the property; and

(ii) The action includes all possible planning to minimize harm to the property resulting from such use.

(2) Supporting information must demonstrate that there are unique problems or unusual factors involved in the use of alternatives that avoid these properties or that the cost, social, economic, and environmental impacts, or community disruption resulting from such alternatives reach extraordinary magnitudes.

(b) The Administration will determine the application of section 4(f). Any use of lands from a section 4(f) property shall be evaluated early in the development of the action when alternatives to the proposed action are under study.

(c) Consideration under section 4(f) is not required when the Federal, State, or local officials having jurisdiction over a park, recreation area or refuge determine that the entire site is not significant. In the absence of such a determination, the section 4(f) land will be presumed to be significant. The Administration will review the significance determination to assure its reasonableness.

(d) Where Federal lands or other public land holdings (e.g., State forests) are administered under statutes permitting management for multiple uses, and, in fact, are managed for multiple uses, section 4(f) applies only to those portions of such lands which function for, or are designated in the plans of the administering agency as being for, significant park, recreation,

or wildlife and waterfowl purposes. The determination as to which lands so function or are so designated, and the significance of those lands, shall be made by the officials having jurisdiction over the lands. The Administration will review this determination to assure its reasonableness. The determination of significance shall apply to the entire area of such park, recreation, or wildlife and waterfowl refuge sites.

(e) In determining the application of section 4(f) to historic sites, the Administration, in cooperation with the applicant, will consult with the State Historic Preservation Officer (SHPO) and appropriate local officials to identify all properties on or eligible for the National Register of Historic Places (National Register). The section 4(f) requirements apply only to sites on or eligible for the National Register unless the Administration determines that the application of section 4(f) is otherwise appropriate.

(f) The Administration may determine that section 4(f) requirements do not apply to restoration, rehabilitation, or maintenance of transportation facilities that are on or eligible for the National Register when:

(1) Such work will not adversely affect the historic qualities of the facility that caused it to be on or eligible for the National Register, and

(2) The SHPO and the Advisory Council on Historic Preservation (ACHP) have been consulted and have not objected to the Administration finding in paragraph (f)(1) of this section.

(g)(1) Section 4(f) applies to all archeological sites on or eligible for inclusion on the National Register, including those discovered during construction except as set forth in paragraph (g)(2) of this section. Where section 4(f) applies to archeological sites discovered during construction, the section 4(f) process will be expedited. In such cases, the evaluation of feasible and prudent alternatives will take account of the level of investment already made. The review process, including the consultation with other agencies, will be shortened as appropriate.

(2) Section 4(f) does not apply to archeological sites where the Administration, after consultation with the SHPO and the ACHP, determines that the archeological resource is important chiefly because of what can be learned by data recovery and has minimal value for preservation in place. This exception applies both to situations where data recovery is undertaken or where the Administration decides, with agreement of the SHPO and, where applicable, the ACHP not to recover the resource.

(h) Designations of park and recreation lands, wildlife and waterfowl refuges, and historic sites are sometimes made and determinations of significance changed late in the development of a proposed action. With the exception of the treatment of archeological resources in paragraph (g) of this section, the Administration may permit a

project to proceed without consideration under section 4(f) if the property interest in the section 4(f) lands was acquired for transportation purposes prior to the designation or change in the determination of significance and if an adequate effort was made to identify properties protected by section 4(f) prior to acquisition.

(i) The evaluations of alternatives to avoid the use of section 4(f) land and of possible measures to minimize harm to such lands shall be developed by the applicant in cooperation with the Administration. This information should be presented in the draft EIS, EA, or, for a project classified as a CE in a separate document. The section 4(f) evaluation shall be provided for coordination and comment to the officials having jurisdiction over the section 4(f) property and to the Department of the Interior, and as appropriate to the Department of Agriculture and the Department of Housing and Urban Development. A minimum of 45 days shall be established by the Administration for receipt of comments. Uses of section 4(f) land covered by a programmatic section 4(f) evaluation shall be documented and coordinated as specified in the programmatic section 4(f) evaluation.

(j) When adequate support exists for a section 4(f) determination, the discussion in the final EIS, FONSI, or separate section 4(f) evaluation shall specifically address:

(1) The reasons why the alternatives to avoid a section 4(f) property are not feasible and prudent; and

(2) All measures which will be taken to minimize harm to the section 4(f) property.

(k) The final Section 4(f) evaluation will be reviewed for legal sufficiency.

(l) For actions processed with EISs, the Administration will make the section 4(f) approval either in its approval of the final EIS or in the ROD. Where the section 4(f) approval is documented in the final EIS, the Administration will summarize the basis for its section 4(f) approval in the ROD. Actions requiring the use of section 4(f) property, and proposed to be processed with a FONSI or classified as a CE, shall not proceed until notified by the Administration of section 4(f) approval. For these actions, any required section 4(f) approval will be documented separately.

(m) Circulation of a separate section 4(f) evaluation will be required when:

(1) A proposed modification of the alignment or design would require the use of section 4(f) property after the CE, FONSI, draft EIS, or final EIS has been processed;

(2) The Administration determines, after processing the CE, FONSI, draft EIS, or final EIS that section 4(f) applies to a property;

(3) A proposed modification of the alignment, design, or measures to minimize harm (after the original section 4(f) approval) would result in a substantial increase in the amount of section 4(f) land used, a substantial increase in the adverse impacts to sec-

tion 4(f) land, or a substantial reduction in mitigation measures; or

(4) Another agency is the lead agency for the NEPA process, unless another DOT element is preparing the section 4(f) evaluation.

(n) If the Administration determines under section 771.135(m) or otherwise, that section 4(f) is applicable after the CE, FONSI, or final EIS has been processed, the decision to prepare and circulate a section 4(f) evaluation will not necessarily require the preparation of a new or supplemental environmental document. Where a separately circulated section 4(f) evaluation is prepared, such evaluation does not necessarily:

(i) Prevent the granting of new approvals;

(ii) Require the withdrawal of previous approvals; or

(iii) Require the suspension of project activities; for any activity not affected by the section 4(f) evaluation.

(o) An analysis required by section 4(f) may involve different levels of detail where the section 4(f) involvement is addressed in a tiered EIS.

(1) When the first-tier, broad-scale EIS is prepared, the detailed information necessary to complete the section 4(f) evaluation may not be available at that stage in the development of the action. In such cases, an evaluation should be made on the potential impacts that a proposed action will have on section 4(f) land and whether those impacts could have a bearing on the decision to be made. A preliminary determination may be made at this time as to whether there are feasible and prudent locations or alternatives for the action to avoid the use of section 4(f) land. This preliminary determination shall consider all possible planning to minimize harm to the extent that the level of detail available at the first-tier EIS stage allows. It is recognized that such planning at this stage will normally be limited to ensuring that opportunities to minimize harm at subsequent stages in the development process have not been precluded by decisions made at the first-tier stage. This preliminary determination is then incorporated into the first-tier EIS.

(2) A section 4(f) approval made when additional design details are available will include a determination that:

(i) The preliminary section 4(f) determination made pursuant to paragraph (o)(1) of this section is still valid; and

(ii) The criteria of paragraph (a) of this section have been met.

[52 FR 32660, Aug. 28, 1987; 53 FR 11066, Apr. 5, 1988]

§ 771.137 International actions.

(a) The requirements of this part apply to:

(1) Administration actions significantly affecting the environment of a foreign nation not participating in the action or not otherwise involved in the action.

(2) Administration actions outside the U.S., its territories, and possessions which significantly affect natural resources of global importance designated for protection by the President or by international agreement.

(b) If communication with a foreign government concerning environmental studies or documentation is anticipated, the Administration shall coordinate such communication with the Department of State through the Office of the Secretary of Transportation.

Department of the Interior
NEPA Procedures
Departmental Manual, Pt. 516

	Part 516 National Environmental
Environmental Quality	Policy Act of 1969

Protection and Enhancement
Chapter 1   of Environmental Quality   516 DM 1.1

1.1   Purpose. This Chapter establishes the Department's
policies for complying with Title 1 of the National Environ-
mental Policy Act of 1969, as amended (42 U.S.C. 4321-4347)
(NEPA); Section 2 of Executive Order 11514, Protection and
Enhancement of Environmental Quality, as amended by
Executive Order 11991; and the regulations of the Council on
Environmental Quality (CEQ) implementing the procedural pro-
visions of NEPA (40 CFR 1500-1508).

1.2   Policy. It is the policy of the Department:

A. To provide leadership in protecting and enhancing
those aspects of the quality of the Nation's environment
which relate to or may be affected by the Department's
policies, goals, programs, plans, or functions in furtherance of national environmental policy;

B. To use all practicable means, consistent with other
essential considerations of national policy, to improve,
coordinate, and direct its policies, plans, functions,
programs, and resources in furtherance of national environmental goals;

C. To interpret and administer, to the fullest extent
possible, the policies, regulations, and public laws of the
United States administered by the Department in accordance
with the policies of NEPA;

D. To consider and give important weight to environmental factors, along with other essential considerations,
in developing proposals and making decisions in order to .
achieve a proper balance between the development and utilization of natural, cultural, and human resources and the
protection and enhancement of environmental quality;

E. To consult, coordinate, and cooperate with other
Federal agencies and State, local, and Indian tribal
governments in the development and implementation of the
Department's plans and programs affecting environmental
quality and, in turn, to provide to the fullest extent
practicable, these entities with information concerning the
environmental impacts of their own plans and programs;

Department of the Interior

DEPARTMENTAL MANUAL

	Part 516	National Environmental
Environmental Quality		Policy Act of 1969

	Protection and Enhancement	
Chapter 1	of Environmental Quality	516 DM 1.2F

F. To provide, to the fullest extent practicable, timely information to the public to better assist in understanding Departmental plans and programs affecting environmental quality and to facilitate their involvement in the development of such plans and programs; and

G. To cooperate with and assist the CEQ.

1.3 General Responsibilities. The following responsibilities reflect the Secretary's decision that the officials responsible for making program decisions are also responsible for taking the requirements of NEPA into account in those decisions and will be held accountable for that responsibility:

A. Assistant Secretary--Policy, Budget and Administration.

(1) Is the Department's focal point on NEPA matters and is responsible for overseeing the Department's implementation of NEPA.

(2) Serves as the Department's principal contact with the CEQ.

(3) Assigns to the Director, Office of Environmental Project Review, the responsibilities outlined for that Office in this Part.

B. Solicitor. Is responsible for providing legal advice in the Department's compliance with NEPA.

C. Assistant Secretaries.

(1) Are responsible for compliance with NEPA, E.O. 11514, as amended, the CEQ regulations, and this Part for bureaus and offices under their jurisdiction.

(2) Will insure that, to the fullest extent possible, the policies, regulations, and public laws of the United States administered under their jurisdiction are interpreted and administered in accordance with the policies of NEPA.

Department of the Interior

DEPARTMENTAL MANUAL

Environmental Quality	Part 516 National Environmental Policy Act of 1969
Chapter 1	Protection and Enhancement of Environmental Quality	516 DM 1.3D

D. Heads of Bureaus and Offices.

(1) Must comply with the provisions of NEPA, E.O. 11514, as amended, the CEQ regulations and this Part.

(2) Will interpret and administer, to the fullest extent possible, the policies, regulations, and public laws of the United States administered under their jurisdiction in accordance with the policies of NEPA.

(3) Will continue to review their statutory authorities, administrative regulations, policies, programs, and procedures, including those related to loans, grants, contracts, leases, licenses, or permits, in order to identify any deficiencies or inconsistencies therein which prohibit or limit full compliance with the intent, purpose, and provisions of NEPA and, in consultation with the Solicitor and the Legislative Counsel, shall take or recommend, as appropriate, corrective actions as may be necessary to bring these authorities and policies into conformance with the intent, purpose, and procedures of NEPA.

(4) Will monitor, evaluate, and control on a continuing basis their activities so as to protect and enhance the quality of the environment. Such activities will include those directed to controlling pollution and enhancing the environment and designed to accomplish other program objectives which may affect the quality of the environment. They will develop programs and measures to protect and enhance environmental quality and assess progress in meeting the specific objectives of such activities as they affect the quality of the environment.

1.4 Consideration of Environmental Values.

A. In Departmental Management.

(1) In the management of the natural, cultural, and human resources under its jurisdiction, the Department must consider and balance a wide range of economic, environmental, and social objectives at the local, regional, national, and international levels, not all of which are quantifiable in comparable terms. In considering and balancing these objectives, Departmental plans, proposals,

Department of the Interior

DEPARTMENTAL MANUAL

Environmental Quality	Part 516	National Environmental Policy Act of 1969
Chapter 1	Protection and Enhancement of Environmental Quality	516 DM 1.4A(1)

and decisions often require recognition of complements and resolution of conflicts among interrelated uses of these natural, cultural, and human resources within technological, budgetary, and legal constraints.

(2) Departmental project reports, program proposals, issue papers, and other decision documents must carefully analyze the various objectives, resources, and constraints, and comprehensively and objectively evaluate the advantages and disadvantages of the proposed actions and their reasonable alternatives. Where appropriate, these documents will utilize and reference supporting and underlying economic, environmental, and other analyses.

(3) The underlying environmental analyses will factually, objectively, and comprehensively analyze the environmental effects of proposed actions and their reasonable alternatives. They will systematically analyze the environmental impacts of alternatives, and particularly those alternatives and measures which would reduce, mitigate or prevent adverse environmental impacts or which would enhance environmental quality. However, such an environmental analysis is not, in and of itself, a program proposal or the decision document, is not a justification of a proposal, and will not support or deprecate the over-all merits of a proposal or its various alternatives.

B. In Internally Initiated Proposals. Officials responsible for development or conduct of planning and decisionmaking systems within the Department shall incorporate to the maximum extent necessary environmental planning as an integral part of these systems in order to insure that environmental values and impacts are fully considered and in order to facilitate any necessary documentation of those considerations.

C. In Externally Initiated Proposals. Officials responsible for development or conduct of loan, grant, contract, lease, license, permit, or other externally initiated activities shall require applicants, to the extent necessary and practicable, to provide environmental information, analyses, and reports as an integral part of their applications. This will serve to encourage applicants to incorporate environmental considerations into their planning

Department of the Interior

DEPARTMENTAL MANUAL

| | Part 516   National Environmental |
| Environmental Quality | Policy Act of 1969 |

Protection and Enhancement

Chapter 1   of Environmental Quality   516 DM 1.4C

processes as well as provide the Department with necessary
information to meet its own environmental responsibilities.

1.5   Consultation, Coordination, and Cooperation with Other
Agencies and Organizations.

A.   Departmental Plans and Programs.

(1)   Officials responsible for planning or implementing Departmental plans and programs will develop and
utilize procedures to consult, coordinate, and cooperate
with relevant State, local, and Indian tribal governments;
other bureaus and Federal agencies; and public and private
organizations and individuals concerning the environmental
effects of these plans and programs on their jurisdictions
or interests.

(2)   Bureaus and offices will utilize, to the
maximum extent possible, existing notification, coordination
and review mechanisms established by the Office of Management and Budget, the Water Resources Council, and CEQ.
However, use of these mechanisms must not be a substitute
for early and positive consultation, coordination, and
cooperation with others, especially State, local, and
Indian tribal governments.

B.   Other Departmental Activities.

(1)   Technical assistance, advice, data, and
information useful in restoring, maintaining, and enhancing
the quality of the environment will be made available to
other Federal agencies, State, local, and Indian tribal
governments, institutions, and individuals as appropriate.

(2)   Information regarding existing or potential
environmental problems and control methods developed as a
part of research, development, demonstration, test, or
evaluation activities will be made available to other
Federal agencies, State, local, and Indian tribal governments, institutions and other entities as appropriate.

(3)   Recognizing the worldwide and long-range
character of environmental problems, where consistent with
the foreign policy of the United States, appropriate support
will be made available to initiatives, resolutions, and

Department of the Interior

DEPARTMENTAL MANUAL

Environmental Quality	Part 516	National Environmental Policy Act of 1969
	Protection and Enhancement	
Chapter 1	of Environmental Quality	516 DM 1.5B(3)

programs designed to maximize international cooperation in anticipating and preventing a decline in the quality of the world environment.

C. Plans and Programs of Other Agencies and Organizations

(1) Officials responsible for protecting, conserving, developing, or managing resources under the Department's jurisdiction shall coordinate and cooperate with State, local, and Indian tribal governments, other bureaus and Federal agencies, and public and private organizations and individuals, and provide them with timely information concerning the environmental effects of these entities' plans and programs.

(2) Bureaus and offices are encouraged to participate early in the planning processes of other agencies and organizations in order to insure full cooperation with and understanding of the Department's programs and interests in natural, cultural, and human resources.

(3) Bureaus and offices will utilize to the fullest extent possible, existing Departmental review mechanisms to avoid unnecessary duplication of effort and to avoid confusion by other organizations.

1.6 Public Involvement. Bureaus and offices, in consultation with the Office of Public Affairs, will develop and utilize procedures to insure the fullest practicable provision of timely public information and understanding of their plans and programs with environmental impact including information on the environmental impacts of alternative courses of action. These procedures will include, wherever appropriate, provision for public meetings or hearings in order to obtain the views of interested parties. Bureaus and offices will also encourage State and local agencies and Indian tribal governments to adopt similar procedures for informing the public concerning their activities affecting the quality of the environment. (See also 301 DM 2.)

Department of the Interior

DEPARTMENTAL MANUAL

	Part 516 National Environmental
Environmental Quality	Policy Act of 1969

Protection and Enhancement	
Chapter 1 of Environmental Quality	516 DM 1.7

1.7 <u>Mandate</u>.

    A. This Part provides Department-wide instructions for complying with NEPA and Executive Orders 11514, as amended by 11991 (Protection and Enhancement of Environmental Quality) and 12114 (Environmental Effects Abroad of Major Federal Actions).

    B. The Department hereby adopts the regulations of the CEQ implementing the procedural provisions of NEPA (Sec. 102(2)(C)) except where compliance would be inconsistent with other statutory requirements. In the case of any apparent discrepancies between these procedures and the mandatory provisions of the CEQ regulations, the regulations shall govern.

    C. Instructions supplementing the CEQ regulations are provided in Chapters 2-7 of this Part. Citations in brackets refer to the CEQ regulations. Instructions specific to each bureau are appended to Chapter 6. In addition, bureaus may prepare a handbook(s) or other technical guidance for their personnel on how to apply this Part to principal programs.

    D. Instructions implementing Executive Order 12114 will be provided in Chapter 8.

Chapter 2 Initiating the NEPA Process   516 DM 2.1

2.1   Purpose. This Chapter provides supplementary instructions for implementing those portions of the CEQ regulations pertaining to initiating the NEPA process.

2.2   Apply NEPA Early (1501.2).

        A.   Bureaus will initiate early consultation and coordination with other bureaus and any Federal agency which has jurisdiction by law or special expertise with respect to any environmental impact involved, and with appropriate Federal, State, local and Indian tribal agencies authorized to develop and enforce environmental standards.

        B.   Bureaus will also consult early with interested private parties and organizations, including when the Bureau's own involvement is reasonably foreseeable in a private or non-Federal application.

        C.   Bureaus will revise or amend program regulations or directives to insure that private or non-Federal applicants are informed of any environmental information required to be included in their applications and of any consultation with other Federal agencies, and State, local or Indian tribal governments required prior to making the application. A list of these regulations or directives will be included in each Bureau Appendix to Chapter 6.

2.3   Whether to Prepare an EIS (1501.4).

        A.   Categorical Exclusions (CX) (1508.4).

               (1)   The following criteria will be used to determine actions to be categorically excluded from the NEPA process: (a) The action or group of actions would have no significant effect on the quality of the human environment; and (b) The action or group of actions would not involve unresolved conflicts concerning alternative uses of available resources.

               (2)   Based on the above criteria, the classes of actions listed in Appendix 1 to this Chapter are categorically excluded, Department-wide, from the NEPA process. A list of CX specific to Bureau programs will be included in each Bureau Appendix to Chapter 6.

               (3)   The exceptions listed in Appendix 2 to this Chapter apply to individual actions within CX. Environmental documents must be prepared for any actions involving these exceptions.

               (4)   Notwithstanding the criteria, exclusions and exceptions above, extraordinary circumstances may dictate or a responsible Departmental or Bureau official may decide to prepare an environmental document.

        B.   Environmental Assessment (EA) (1508.9). See 516 DM 3.

        C.   Finding of No Significant Impact (FONSI) (1508.13). A FONSI will be prepared as a separate covering document based upon a review of an EA. Accordingly, the words include(d) in Section 1508.13 should be interpreted as attach(ed).

D.   Notice of Intent (NOI) (1508.22).   A NOI will be prepared as soon as practicable after a decision to prepare an environmental impact statement and shall be published in the Federal Register, with a copy to the Office of Environmental Project Review, and made available to the affected public in accordance with Section 1506.6. Publication of a NOI may be delayed if there is proposed to be more than three (3) months between the decision to prepare an environmental impact statement and the time preparation is actually initiated. The Office of Environmental Project Review will periodically publish a consolidated list of these notices in the Federal Register.

E.   Environmental Impact Statement (EIS) (1508.11).   See 516 DM 4. Decisions/actions which would normally require the preparation of an EIS will be identified in each Bureau Appendix to Chapter 6.

2.4   Lead Agencies (1501.5).

A.   The Assistant Secretary-Policy, Budget and Administration will designate lead Bureaus within the Department when Bureaus under more than one Assistant Secretary are involved and will represent the Department in consultations with CEQ or other Federal agencies in the resolution of lead agency determinations.

B.   Bureaus will inform the Office of Environmental Project Review of any agreements to assume lead agency status.

C.   A non-Federal agency will not be designated as a joint lead agency unless it has a duty to comply with a local or State EIS requirement that is comparable to a NEPA statement. Any non-Federal agency may be a cooperating agency by agreement. Bureaus will consult with the Solicitor's Office in cases where such non-Federal agencies are also applicants before the Department to determine relative lead/cooperating agency responsibilities.

2.5   Cooperating Agencies (1501.6).

A.   The Office of Environmental Project Review will assist Bureaus and coordinate requests from non-Interior agencies in determining cooperating agencies.

B.   Bureaus will inform the Office of Environmental Project Review of any agreements to assume cooperating agency status or any declinations pursuant to Section 1501.6(c).

2.6   Scoping (1501.7).

A.   The invitation requirement in Section 1501.7(a)(1) may be satisfied by including such an invitation in the NOI.

B.   If a scoping meeting is held, consensus is desirable; however, the lead agency is ultimately responsible for the scope of an EIS.

2.7   Time Limits (1501.8).   When time limits are established they should reflect the availability of personnel and funds.

Chapter 2 Appendix 1. Departmental Categorical Exclusions

The following actions are categorical exclusions (CX) pursuant to 516 DM 2.3A(2). However, environmental documents will be prepared for individual actions within these CX if the exceptions listed in 516 DM 2, Appendix 2, apply.

1.1 Personnel actions and investigations and personnel services contracts.

1.2 Internal organizational changes and facility and office reductions and closings.

1.3 Routine financial transactions, including such things as salaries and expenses, procurement contracts, guarantees, financial assistance, income transfers, audits, fees, bonds and royalties.

1.4 Law enforcement and legal transactions, including such things as arrests, investigations, patents, claims, legal opinions, and judicial activities including their initiation, processing, settlement, appeal or compliance.

1.5 Regulatory and enforcement actions, including inspections, assessments, administrative hearings and decisions; when the regulations themselves or the instruments of regulations (leases, permits, licenses, etc.) have previously been covered by the NEPA process or are exempt from it.

1.6 Non-destructive data collection, inventory (including field, aerial and satellite surveying and mapping), study, research and monitoring activities.

1.7 Routine and continuing government business, including such things as supervision, administration, operations, maintenance and replacement activities having limited context and intensity; e.g. limited size and magnitude or short-term effects.

1.8 Management, formulation, allocation, transfer and reprogramming of the Department's budget at all levels. (This does not exclude the preparation of environmental documents for proposals included in the budget when otherwise required.)

1.9 Legislative proposals of an administrative or technical nature, including such things as changes in authorizations for appropriations, and minor boundary changes and land transactions; or having primarily economic, social, individual or institutional effects; and comments and reports on referrals of legislative proposals.

1.10 Policies, directives, regulations and guidelines of an administrative, financial, legal, technical or procedural nature; or the environmental effects of which are too broad, speculative or conjectural to lend themselves to meaningful analysis and will be subject later to the NEPA process, either collectively or case-by-case.

1.11 Activities which are educational, informational, advisory or consultative to other agencies, public and private entities, visitors, individuals or the general public.

Chapter 2   Appendix 2. Exceptions to Categorical Exclusions

The following exceptions apply to individual actions within categorical exclusions (CX). Environmental documents must be prepared for actions which may:

2.1   Have significant adverse effects on public health or safety.

2.2   Have adverse effects on such unique geographic characteristics as historic or cultural resources, park, recreation or refuge lands, wilderness areas, wild or scenic rivers, sole or principal drinking water aquifers, prime farmlands, wetlands, floodplains, or ecologically significant or critical areas, including those listed on the Department's National Register of Natural Landmarks.

2.3   Have highly controversial environmental effects.

2.4   Have highly uncertain and potentially significant environmental effects or involve unique or unknown environmental risks.

2.5   Establish a precedent for future action or represent a decision in principle about future actions with potentially significant environmental effects.

2.6   Be directly related to other actions with individually insignificant but cumulatively significant environmental effects.

2.7   Have adverse effects on properties listed or eligible for listing on the National Register of Historic Places.

. 2.8   Have adverse effects on species listed or proposed to be listed on the List of Endangered or Threatened Species, or have adverse effects on designated Critical Habitat for these species.

2.9   Require compliance with Executive Order 11988 (Floodplain Management), Executive Order 11990 (Protection of Wetlands), or the Fish and Wildlife Coordination Act.

2.10   Threaten to violate a Federal, State, local or tribal law or requirement imposed for the protection of the environment.

Environmental Quality

Chapter 3 Environmental Assessments   516 DM 3.1

3.1   Purpose. This Chapter provides supplementary instructions for implementing those portions of the CEQ regulations pertaining to environmental assessments (EA).

3.2   When to Prepare (1501.3).

A.   An EA will be prepared for all actions, except those covered by a categorical exclusion, covered sufficiently by an earlier environmental document, or for those actions for which a decision has already been made to prepare an EIS. The purpose of such an EA is to allow the responsible official to determine whether to prepare an EIS.

B.   In addition, an EA may be prepared on any action at any time in order to assist in planning and decisionmaking.

3.3   Public Involvement.

A.   Public notification must be provided and, where appropriate, the public involved in the EA process (1506.6).

B.   The scoping process may be applied to an EA (1501.7).

3.4   Content.

A.   At a minimum, an EA will include brief discussions of the need for the proposal, of alternatives as required by Section 102(2)(E) of NEPA, of the environmental impacts of the proposed action and such alternatives, and a listing of agencies and persons consulted (1508.9(b)).

B.   In addition, an EA may be expanded to describe the proposal, a broader range of alternatives, and proposed mitigation measures if this facilitates planning and decisionmaking.

C.   The level of detail and depth of impact analysis should normally be limited to that needed to determine whether there are significant environmental effects.

D.   An EA will contain objective analyses which support its environmental impact conclusions. It will not, in and of itself, conclude whether or not an EIS will be prepared. This conclusion will be made upon review of the EA by the responsible official and documented in either a NOI or FONSI.

3.5   Format.

A.   An EA may be prepared in any format useful to facilitate planning and decisionmaking.

B.   An EA may be combined with any other planning or decisionmaking document; however, that portion which analyzes the environmental impacts of the proposal and alternatives will be clearly and separately identified and not spread throughout or interwoven into other sections of the document.

3.6   Adoption.

A.   An EA prepared for a proposal before the Department by another agency, entity or person, including an applicant, may be adopted if, upon independent evaluation by the responsible official, it is found to comply with this Chapter and relevant provisions of the CEQ regulations.

B.   When appropriate and efficient, a responsible official may augment such an EA when it is essentially but not entirely in compliance in order to make it so.

C.   If such an EA or augmented EA is adopted, the responsible official must prepare his/her own NOI or FONSI which also acknowledges the origin of the EA and takes full responsibility for its scope and content.

Environmental Quality

Part 516 National Environmental
Policy Act of 1969

Chapter 4   Environmental Impact Statements   516 DM 4.1

4.1   Purpose. This Chapter provides supplementary instructions for implementing those portions of the CEQ regulations pertaining to environmental impact statements (EIS).

4.2   Statutory Requirements (1502.3). NEPA requires that an EIS be prepared by the responsible Federal official. This official is normally the lowest-level official who has overall responsibility for formulating, reviewing, or proposing an action or, alternatively, has been delegated the authority or responsibility to develop, approve, or adopt a proposal or action. Preparation at this level will insure that the NEPA process will be incorporated into the planning process and that the EIS will accompany the proposal through existing review processes.

4.3   Timing (1502.5).

        A.   The feasibility analysis (go/no-go) stage, at which time an EIS is to be completed, is to be interpreted as the stage prior to the first point of major commitment to the proposal. For example, this would normally be at the authorization stage for proposals requiring Congressional authorization, the location or corridor stage for transportation, transmission, and communication projects, and the leasing stage for mineral resources proposals.

        B.   An EIS need not be commenced until an application is essentially complete; e.g., any required environmental information is submitted, any consultation required with other agencies has been conducted, and any required advance funding is paid by the applicant.

4.4   Page Limits (1502.7). Where the text of an EIS for a complex proposal or group of proposals appears to require more than the normally prescribed limit of 300 pages, bureaus will insure that the length of such statements is no greater than necessary to comply with NEPA, the CEQ regulations, and this Chapter.

4.5   Supplemental Statements (1502.9).

        A.   Supplements are only required if such changes in the proposed action or alternatives, new circumstances, or resultant significant effects are not adequately analyzed in the previously prepared EIS.

        B.   A bureau and/or the appropriate program Assistant Secretary will consult with the Office of Environmental Project Review and the Office of the Solicitor prior to proposing to CEQ to prepare a final supplement without preparing an intervening draft.

        C.   If, after a decision has been made based on a final EIS, a described proposal is further defined or modified and if its changed effects are minor or still within the scope of the earlier EIS, an EA and FONSI may be prepared for subsequent decisions rather than a supplement.

4.6   Format (1502.10).

A.   Proposed departures from the standard format described in the CEQ regulations and this Chapter must be approved by the Office of Environmental Project Review.

B.   The section listing the preparers of the EIS will also include other sources of information, including a bibliography or list of cited references, when appropriate.

C.   The section listing the distribution of the EIS will also briefly describe the consultation and public involvement processes utilized in planning the proposal and in preparing the EIS, if this information is not discussed elsewhere in the document.

D.   If CEQ's standard format is not used or if the EIS is combined with another planning or decisionmaking document, the section which analyzes the environmental consequences of the proposal and its alternatives will be clearly and separately identified and not interwoven into other portions of or spread throughout the document.

4.7   Cover Sheet (1502.11). The cover sheet will also indicate whether the EIS is intended to serve any other environmental review or consultation requirements pursuant to Section 1502.25.

4.8   Summary (1502.12). The emphasis in the summary should be on those considerations, controversies, and issues which significantly affect the quality of the human environment.

4.9   Purpose and Need (1502.13). This section may introduce a number of factors, including economic and technical considerations and Departmental or bureau statutory missions, which may be beyond the scope of the EIS. Care should be taken to insure an objective presentation and not a justification.

4.10   Alternatives Including the Proposed Action (1502.14).

A.   As a general rule, the following guidance will apply:

(1)   For internally initiated proposals; i.e., for those cases where the Department conducts or controls the planning process, both the draft and final EIS shall identify the bureaus' proposed action.

(2)   For externally initiated proposals; i.e., for those cases where the Department is reacting to an application or similar request, the draft and final EIS shall identify the applicant's proposed action and the bureau's preferred alternative unless another law prohibits such an expression.

Environmental Quality

Part 516   National Environmental
Policy Act of 1969

Chapter 4   Environmental Impact Statements   516 DM 4.10A(3)

(3)   Proposed departures from this guidance must be approved by the Office of Environmental Project Review and the Office of the Solicitor.

B.   Mitigation measures are not necessarily independent of the proposed action and its alternatives and should be incorporated into and analyzed as a part of the proposal and appropriate alternatives. Where appropriate, major mitigation measures may be identified and analyzed as separate alternatives in and of themselves where the environmental consequences are distinct and significant enough to warrant separate evaluation.

4.11   Appendix (1502.18). If an EIS is intended to serve other environmental review or consultation requirements pursuant to Section 1502.25, any more detailed information needed to comply with these requirements may be included as an appendix.

4.12   Incorporation by Reference (1502.21). Citations of specific topics will include the pertinent page numbers. All literature references will be listed in the bibliography.

4.13   Incomplete or Unavailable Information (1502.22). The references to overall costs in this section are not limited to market costs, but include other costs to society such as social costs due to delay.

4.14   Methodology and Scientific Accuracy (1502.24). Conclusions about environmental effects will be preceded by an analysis that supports that conclusion unless explicit reference by footnote is made to other supporting documentation that is readily available to the public.

4.15   Environmental Review and Consultation Requirements (1502.25).

A.   A list of related environmental review and consultation requirements is available from the Office of Environmental Project Review.

B.   If the EIS is intended to serve as the vehicle to fully or partially comply with any of these requirements, the associated analyses, studies, or surveys will be identified as such and discussed in the text of the EIS and the cover sheet will so indicate. Any supporting analyses or reports will be referenced or included as an appendix and shall be sent to reviewing agencies as appropriate in accordance with applicable regulations or procedures.

4.16   Inviting Comments (1503.1).

A.   Comments from State agencies will be requested through procedures established by the Governor pursuant to Executive Order 12372, and may be requested from local agencies through these procedures to the extent that they include the affected local jurisdictions. See 511 DM.

B.   When the proposed action may affect the environment of an Indian reservation, comments will be requested from the Indian tribe through the tribal governing body, unless the tribal governing body has designated an alternate review process.

4.17   Response to Comments (1503.4).

A.   Preparation of a final EIS need not be delayed in those cases where a Federal agency, from which comments are required to be obtained (1503.1(a)(1)), does not comment within the prescribed time period. Informal attempts will be made to determine the status of any such comments and every reasonable attempt should be made to include the comments and a response in the final EIS.

B.   When other commentors are late, their comments should be included in the final EIS to the extent practicable.

C.   For those EISs requiring the approval of the Assistant Secretary – Policy, Budget and Administration pursuant to 516 DM 6.3, bureaus will consult with the Office of Environmental Project Review when they propose to prepare an abbreviated final EIS (1503.4(c)).

4.18   Elimination of Duplication with State and Local Procedures (1506.2). Bureaus will incorporate in their appropriate program regulations provisions for the preparation of an EIS by a State agency to the extent authorized in Section 102(2)(D) of NEPA. Eligible programs are listed in Appendix 1 to this Chapter.

4.19   Combining Documents (1506.4). See 516 DM 4.6D.

4.20   Departmental Responsibility (1506.5). Following the responsible official's preparation or independent evaluation of and assumption of responsibility for an environmental document, an applicant may print it provided the applicant is bearing the cost of the document pursuant to other laws.

4.21   Public Involvement (1506.6). See 516 DM 1.6 and 301 DM 2.

4.22   Further Guidance (1506.7). The Office of Environmental Project Review may provide further guidance concerning NEPA pursuant to its organizational responsibilities (110 DM 22) and through supplemental directives (381 DM 4.5B).

4.23   Proposals for Legislation (1506.8). The Legislative Counsel, in consultation with the Office of Environmental Project Review, shall:

A.   Identify in the annual submittal to OMB of the Department's proposed legislative program any requirements for and the status of any environmental documents.

B.   When required, insure that a legislative EIS is included as a part of the formal transmittal of a legislative proposal to the Congress.

4.24   Time Periods (1506.10).

A.   The minimum review period for a draft EIS will be sixty (60) days from the date of transmittal to the Environmental Protection Agency.

B.   For those EISs requiring the approval of the Assistant Secretary – Policy, Budget and Administration pursuant to 516 DM 6.3, the Office of Environmental Project Review will be responsible for consulting with the Environmental Protection Agency and/or CEQ about any proposed reductions in time periods or any extensions of time periods proposed by those agencies.

Chapter 4   Appendix 1. Programs of Grants to States in Which Agencies Having Statewide Jurisdiction May Prepare EISs.

1.1   Fish and Wildlife Service.
A. Anadromous Fish Conservation (=15.600).
B. Fish Restoration (=15.605).
C. Wildlife Restoration (=15.611).
D. Endangered Species Conservation (=15.612).
E. Marine Mammal Grant Program (=15.613).
1.2   Bureau of Land Management.
A. Wildlife Habitat Management Technical Assistance (=15.219).
1.3   National Park Service.
A. Historic Preservation Grants-in-Aid (=15.904).
B. Outdoor Recreation—Acquisition. Development and Planning (=15.916).
1.4   Bureau of Reclamation.
A. National Water Research and Development Program (=15.505).
1.5   Office of Surface Mining.
A. Regulation of Surface Coal Mining and Surface Effects of Underground Coal Mining (=15.250).
B. Abandoned Mine Land Reclamation (AMLR) Program (=15.252).
1.6   Office of Territorial and International Affairs.
A. Economic and Political Development of the Territories and the Trust Territory of the Pacific Islands (=15.875).

Note.—Citations in parenthesis refer to the Catalog of Federal Domestic Assistance. Office of Management and Budget. 1983.

Environmental Quality | Part 516 National Environmental Policy Act of 1969

Chapter 5 Relationship to Decisionmaking   516 DM 5.1

5.1 Purpose. This Chapter provides supplementary instructions for implementing those portions of the CEQ regulations pertaining to decisionmaking.

5.2 Predecision Referrals to CEQ [1504.3].

A. Upon receipt of advice that another Federal agency intends to refer a Departmental matter to CEQ, the lead bureau will immediately meet with that Federal agency to attempt to resolve the issues raised and expeditiously notify its Assistant Secretary and the Office of Environmental Project Review.

B. Upon any referral of a Departmental matter to CEQ by another Federal agency, the Office of Environmental Project Review will be responsible for coordinating the Department's position.

5.3 Decisionmaking Procedures [1505.1].

A. Procedures for decisions by the Secretary/Under Secretary are specified in 301 DM 1. Assistant Secretaries should follow a similar process when an environmental document accompanies a proposal for their decision.

B. Bureaus will incorporate in their formal decisionmaking procedures and NEPA handbooks provisions for consideration of environmental factors and relevant environmental documents. The major decision points for principal programs likely to have significant environmental effects will be identified in the Bureau Appendix to Chapter 6.

C. Relevant environmental documents, including supplements, will be included as part of the record in formal rulemaking or adjudicatory proceedings.

D. Relevant environmental documents, comments, and responses will accompany proposals through existing review processes so that Departmental officials use them in making decisions.

E. The decisionmaker will consider the environmental impacts of the alternatives described in any relevant environmental document and the range of these alternatives must encompass the alternatives considered by the decisionmaker.

5.4 Record of Decision [1505.2].

      A. Any decision documents prepared pursuant to
301 DM 1 for proposals involving an EIS may incorporate all
appropriate provisions of Section 1505.2(b) and (c).

      B. If a decision document incorporating these provi-
sions is made available to the public following a decision,
it will serve the purpose of a record of decision.

5.5 Implementing the Decision [1505.3].   The terms
"monitoring" and "conditions" will be interpreted as being
related to factors affecting the quality of the human
environment.

5.6 Limitations on Actions [1506.1]. A bureau will notify
its Assistant Secretary, the Solicitor, and the Office of
Environmental Project Review of any situations described in
Section 1506.1(b).

5.7 Timing of Actions [1506.10]. For those EISs requiring
the approval of the Assistant Secretary--Policy, Budget and
Administration pursuant to 516 DM 6.3, the responsible
official will consult with the Office of Environmental
Project Review before making any request for reducing the
time period before a decision or action.

5.8 Emergencies [1506.11]. In the event of an unantici-
pated emergency situation, a bureau will immediately take
any necessary action to prevent or reduce risks to public
health or safety or serious resource losses and then
expeditiously consult with its Assistant Secretary, the
Solicitor, and the Office of Environmental Project Review
about compliance with NEPA. The Office of Environmental
Project Review and the bureau will jointly be responsible
for consulting with CEQ.

Environmental Quality   Part 516   National Environmental
Policy Act of 1969

Chapter 6   Managing the NEPA Process   516 DM 6.1

6.1 <u>Purpose</u>. This Chapter provides supplementary instructions for implementing those provisions of the CEQ regulations pertaining to procedures for implementing and managing the NEPA process.

6.2 <u>Organization for Environmental Quality</u>.

A. <u>Office of Environmental Project Review</u>. The Director, Office of Environmental Project Review, reporting to the Assistant Secretary--Policy, Budget and Administration (PBA), is responsible for providing advice and assistance to the Department on matters pertaining to environmental quality and for overseeing and coordinating the Department's compliance with NEPA, E.O. 11514, the CEQ regulations, and this Part. (See also 110 DM 22.)

B. <u>Bureaus and Offices</u>. Heads of bureaus and offices will designate organizational elements or individuals, as appropriate, at headquarters and regional levels to be responsible for overseeing matters pertaining to the environmental effects of the bureau's plans and programs. The individuals assigned these responsibilities should have management experience or potential, understand the bureau's planning and decisionmaking processes, and be well trained in environmental matters, including the Department's policies and procedures so that their advice has significance in the bureau's planning and decisions. These organizational elements will be identified in the Bureau Appendix to this Chapter.

6.3 <u>Approval of EISs</u>.

A. A program Assistant Secretary is authorized to approve an EIS in those cases where the responsibility for the decision for which the EIS has been prepared rests with the Assistant Secretary or below. The Assistant Secretary may further assign the authority to approve the EIS if he or she chooses. The Assistant Secretary--PBA will make certain that each program Assistant Secretary has adequate safeguards to assure that the EISs comply with NEPA, the CEQ regulations, and the Departmental Manual.

B.   The Assistant Secretary--PBA is authorized to
approve an EIS in those cases where the decision for which
the EIS has been prepared will occur at a level in the
Department above an individual program Assistant Secretary.

6.4   List of Specific Compliance Responsibilities.

A.   Bureaus and offices shall:

(1)   Prepare NEPA handbooks providing guidance on
how to implement NEPA in principal program areas.

(2)   Prepare program regulations or directives
for applicants.

(3)   Propose categorical exclusions.

(4)   Prepare and approve EAs.

(5)   Decide whether to prepare an EIS.

(6)   Prepare and publish NOIs and FONSIs.

(7)   Prepare and, when assigned, approve EISs.

B.   Assistant Secretaries shall:

(1)   Approve bureau handbooks.

(2)   Approve regulations or directives for
applicants.

(3)   Approve categorical exclusions.

(4)   Approve EISs pursuant to 516 DM 6.3.

C.   The Assistant Secretary--Policy, Budget and
Administration shall:

(1)   Concur with regulations or directives for
applicants.

(2)   Concur with categorical exclusions.

(3)   Approve EISs pursuant to 516 DM 6.3.

Environmental Quality	Part 516 National Environmental Policy Act of 1969

Chapter 6 Managing the NEPA Process	516 DM 6.5

6.5   Bureau Requirements.

A.   Requirements specific to bureaus appear as appendices to this Chapter and include the following:

(1)   Identification of officials and organizational elements responsible for NEPA compliance (516 DM 6.2B).

(2)   List of program regulations or directives which provide information to applicants (516 DM 2.2B).

(3)   Identification of major decision points in principal programs (516 DM 5.3B) for which an EIS is normally prepared (516 DM 2.3E).

(4)   List of categorical exclusions (516 DM 2.3A).

B.   Appendices are attached for the following bureaus:

(1)   Fish and Wildlife Service (Appendix 1).

(2)   Geological Survey (Appendix 2).

(3)   Heritage Conservation and Recreation Service (Appendix 3).

(4)   Bureau of Indian Affairs (Appendix 4).

(5)   Bureau of Land Management (Appendix 5).

(6)   Bureau of Mines (Appendix 6).

(7)   National Park Service (Appendix 7).

(8)   Office of Surface Mining (Appendix 8).

(9)   Water and Power Resources Service (Appendix 9).

C.   The Office of the Secretary and other Departmental Offices do not have separate appendices, but must comply with this Part and will consult with the Office of Environmental Project Review about compliance activities.

Environmental Quality   Part 516 National Environmental
                                                   Policy Act of 1969

Chapter 6 Managing the NEPA Process   516 DM 6.6

6.6 <u>Information About the NEPA Process</u>. The Office of
Environmental Project Review will publish periodically a
Departmental list of contacts where information about the
NEPA process and the status of EISs may be obtained.

Fish and Wildlife Service

519 DM Appendix 1

Fish and Wildlife Service

1.1 *NEPA Responsibility.*

A. The *Director* is responsible for NEPA compliance for Fish and Wildlife Service (FWS) activities.

B. Each *Associate Director* (Wildlife Resources, Fishery Resources, Research, Federal Assistance, and Environment) is responsible for general guidance and compliance in their respective areas of responsibility.

C. The *Associate Director— Environment* has been delegated oversight responsibility for FWS NEPA compliance.

D. The *Office of Environmental Coordination* (Washington), which reports to the Associate Director— Environment, is responsible for internal control of both environmental reviews of documents prepared by other agencies and environmental statements prepared by the various FWS Divisions. This Office is also responsible for preparing FWS NEPA procedures, guidelines, and instructions, and for supplying technical assistance in NEPA matters to FWS entities.

E. Each *Regional Director* and the Alaska Area Director is responsible for NEPA compliance in his/her area of responsibility. An individual in each Regional Office and the Alaska Area Office, named by title and reporting to the Regional or Alaska Area Director, will have NEPA coordination duties at the regional level similar to those of the Office of Environmental Coordination.

F. Each *Area Office* will have an individual with similar NEPA coordination responsibilities.

1.2 *Guidance to Applicants.*

A. *FWS Permits.* The FWS has responsibility for issuing certain permits to Federal and State agencies and private parties for actions which would involve certain wildlife species and/or use of FWS-administered lands.

(1) *Permits for the Taking, Possession, Transportation, Sale, Purchase, Barter, Exportation, or Importation of Certain Wildlife Species.* The Code of Federal Regulations, Part 13, Title 50 (50 CFR 13) contains regulations for General Permit Procedures. Section 13.3 lists types of permits and the pertinent Parts of 50 CFR. These include: Import and Marking (Part 14), Feather Imports (Part 15), Injurious Wildlife (Part 16), Endangered Species (Part 17), Marine Mammals (Part 18), Migratory Birds (Part 21), Eagles (Part 22), and Endangered Species Convention (Part 23). Potential applicants should request information from the Chief, Federal Wildlife Permit Office, U.S. Fish and Wildlife Service, Department of the Interior, Washington, D.C. 20240.

(2) *Federal Lands Managed by the FWS.* The Administration of National Wildlife Refuge System Act (16 U.S.C. 668dd-668ee) allows the granting of public use rights in areas of the National Wildlife Refuge and Fish Hatchery System only when the FWS determines that such use is compatible with the purposes for which the area was established. Detailed procedures an applicant must adhere to are contained in the Code of Federal Regulations, Title 50, Parts 25-29, 31-35, 60, 70-71. These rules and regulations apply to all FWS-administered lands.

B. *Permits and Licenses Reviewed by FWS Under the Fish and Wildlife Coordination Act (FWCA).* Under provisions of the Fish and Wildlife Coordination Act (16 U.S.C. 661-667e; 48 Stat. 401, as amended), the FWS investigates and reports on proposals by any department or agency of the United States, or by any public or private agency under Federal permit or license that may impound, divert, deepen, or otherwise control or modify any stream or other waterbody. Private parties and government agencies' planning activities that may require a permit or license for activities of this kind are encouraged to consult with the FWS at the onset of planning. Applications to other Federal

Fish and Wildlife Service

agencies for these actions will be forwarded to the FWS and reviewed according to the "Guidelines for the Review of Fish and Wildlife Aspects of Proposals in or Affecting Navigable Waters" (40 FR 55809, December 1, 1975, and reprinted in 44 FR 29346, May 18, 1979). The non-Federal works and activities reviewed under the authority of the Fish and Wildlife Coordination Act include:

(1) Works and activities in navigable waters of the United States, permitted by the Corps of Engineers (Corps) or the Coast Guard (CG) under Sections 9 and 10 of the River and Harbor Act of March 3, 1899 (1899 Act).

(2) Works secondarily permitted by the Corps such as mineral exploration and development on the Outer Continental Shelf (OCS) and other public lands, rights-of-way on public lands and activities in wetlands in Guam, the Virgin Islands, and American Samoa.

(3) Discharge of pollutants and the disposal of materials, including:

(a) Discharge of pollutants permitted by the Environmental Protection Agency (EPA) under Section 402 of the Clean Water Act (CWA).

(b) Disposal of dredged and fill material permitted by the Corps under Section 404, CWA.

(c) Ocean dumping of dredged material permitted by EPA under Section 102 of the Marine Protection, Research and Sanctuaries Act of 1972.

(d) Disposal of sewage sludge permitted by EPA under Section 405, CWA.

(4) Construction of powerplants and related facilities permitted or licensed by the Federal Energy Regulatory Commission or the Nuclear Regulatory Commission.

(5) Other federally sanctioned works that affect streams or other water bodies and therefore require a permit from the Corps, CG or EPA. These include most channels, highways, airports, and transmission lines, and dredging, filling, discharge, or disposal related to hydro, steam and nuclear electric generating plants. It also includes permits for oil,

gas, and mineral exploration, drilling, mining, and development on the OCS and public lands, and rights-of-way and other permits issued for works involving Federal lands.

C. *Federal Aid to States.* The FWS administers grant funds to State under the Anadromous Fish and Conservation Act (CFDA #15.600), Sport Fish Restoration Act (CFDA #15.605), Wildlife Restoration Act (CFDA #15.611), and the Endangered Species Conservation Act (CFDA #15.612). Information on how States may request funds through the FWS under these Acts is contained in the Federal Aid Manual. Copies of this Manual have been provided to all State fish and wildlife resource agencies and are regularly updated. Current copies are also available for inspection in each FWS Regional Office as well as the Division of Federal Aid, U.S. Fish and Wildlife Service, Department of the Interior, Washington, D.C. 20240.

1.3 *Major Actions Normally Requiring an EIS.*

A. The following FWS proposals will normally require the preparation of an EIS:

(1) Establishment of new refuges, fish hatcheries, or research stations and major additions to existing installations.

(2) Master plans for major new installations.

(3) Master plans for established installations where major new developments or substantial changes in management practices are proposed.

B. If for any of these proposals it is initially decided not to prepare an EIS, an EA will be prepared and handled in accordance with Section 1501.4(e)(2).

1.4 *Categorical Exclusions:* In addition to the actions listed in the Departmental categorical exlusions outlined in Appendix I of 516 DM 2, many of which the Service also performs, the following FWS actions are designated categorical exclusions unless the action qualifies as an exception under 516 DM 2.3(A)(3):

Fish and Wildlife Service

A. *General:*

(1) Changes or amendments to an approved action when such changes have no potential for causing substantial environmental impact.

(2) Personnel training, environmental interpretation, public safety efforts and other educational activities.

(3) The issuance and modification of procedures, including manuals, orders and field rules, when the impacts are limited to administrative or technological effects.

(4) The acquisition of land in accordance with the Service's procedures, when the acquisition is from a willing seller, the acquistion planning process has been performed in coordination with the affected public and continuance of essentially the exisiting use is planned.

B. *Resource Management:*

(1) Research, inventory and information collection activities directly related to the conservation of fish and wildlife resources which involve negligible animal mortality or habitat destruction, and no introduction of either exotic organisms or contaminants.

(2) The operation, maintenance and management of existing facilities and improvements (i.e., structures, roads), including renovations and replacements which result in no or only minor changes in the capacity, use or purpose of the affected facilities.

(3) The addition of small structures or improvements in the area of exising improvements, which result in no or only minor changes in the capacity, use or purpose of the affected area.

(4) The reintroduction (stocking) of native or established species into suitable habitat within their historic or established range.

(5) Minor changes in the amounts or types of public use on FWS or State-managed lands, in accordance with existing regulations management plans and procedures.

(6) Consultation and technical assistance activities directly related to the conservation of fish and wildlife resources.

C. *Permit and Regulatory Functions:*

(1) The issuance of permits for activities involving fish, wildlife or plants regulated under 50 CFR Chapter 1. Subchapter B, except when such permits involve the killing, the removal from natural habitat or the permanent impairment of reproductive capability of endangered species, threatened species, eagles or marine mammals.

(2) The issuance of special regulations for public use of FWS-managed land, which maintain essentially the permitted level of use and do not continue a level of use that has resulted in adverse environmental effects.

(3) Permitting a limited additional use of an exising right-of-way, such as the addition of new power or telephone lines where no new structures or improvements are required, or the addition of buried lines.

(4) The issuance or reissuance of rights-of-way and special use permits that result in no or negligible environmental disturbance.

(5) The reissuance of grazing or agricultural use permits which do not increase the level of use nor continue a level of use that has resulted in adverse environmental effects.

(6) Activities directly related to the enforcement of fish and wildlife laws.

(7) Actions where FWS has concurrence or coapproval with another bureau and the action is a categorical exclusion for that bureau.

D. *State Grants:*

(1) State planning grants and the administrative determination that State plans wer prepared in accordance with prescribed standards. However, when the plan is submitted for approval, the program proposed by the plan is subject to the NEPA process.

(2) Grants for categorically excluded actions listed in paragraphs A, B and C above.

Geological Survey

Appendix 2

[516 DM 6]

Geological Survey

2.1 NEPA Responsibility

A. *Director* is responsible for NEPA compliance for U.S. Geological Survey (GS) activities.

B. *Assistant Director, Resource Programs,* is responsible for approving or concurring with all EISs for GS actions. The Assistant Director is also responsible for approving reviews of environmental documents prepared by other agencies.

C. *Chief, Environmental Affairs Office* (Reston, VA), is the focal point for all NEPA matters and develops NEPA-related policy and guidance for the GS. The Chief is responsible for: assuring the quality control of environmental documents; monitoring Survey-wide activities to ensure NEPA compliance; reviewing and commenting on other bureaus' and agencies' environmental documents; managing GS personnel assigned to other agencies' EISs; preparing environmental documents at the request of other agencies, assisting in the performance of specialized studies in support of ongoing environmental analyses; and conducting research to improve the NEPA process. Information about GS environmental documents or the NEPA process can be obtained by contacting this office.

D. *Chiefs of Divisions* and *Independent Offices* are responsible within their respective organizations for ensuring compliance with NEPA and other environmental review and consultation requirements.

2.2 Guidance to Applicants

The following regulations and documents of the Survey include information to applicants as to the environmental information required to be submitted as part of or to accompany their applications relating to Federal or Indian mineral leases. The regulations and documents are available upon request from the appropriate regional Conservation Manager.

A. *Oil and Gas*

(1) Onshore—Notice to Lessees and Operators: NTL-6 (Approval of Operations)

(2) Offshore—30 CFR 250.34

—30 CFR 251.6-2

—Guidelines for Preparing Outer Continental Shelf (OCS) Environmental Reports

B. *Geothermal Resources*

—30 CFR 270.34

—Geothermal Resources Operational Order: GRO-4 (General Environmental Protection Requirements)

C. *Coal*

—30 CFR 211.10

D. *Solid Minerals (except coal)*

—30 CFR 231.10

2.3 Major Actions Normally Requiring an EIS

A. The following proposals will normally require the preparation of an EIS:

(1) Approval of studies and investigations that would result in liberation of radioactive tracer materials, or nuclear stimulation.

(2) Approval of an OCS oil and gas development and production plan in any area or region of the OCS, other than the Gulf of Mexico, when the plan is declared to be a major Federal action in accordance with Section 25 of the OCS Land Act Amendments of 1978 (30 CFR 250.34-4).

(3) Approval of a new non-coal surface mine plan which would disturb a total of 640 acres or more.

(4) Approval of a new commercial surface oil shale mine plan, regardless of size.

(5) Approval of a new underground uranium mine plan in which 640 acres or more would be mined.

B. If, for any of these actions, it is proposed not to prepare an EIS, an EA will be prepared and handled in accordance with Section 1501.4(e)(2).

Geological Survey

2.4 Categorical Exclusions

In addition to the actions listed in the Departmental categorical exclusions outlined in Appendix 1 of 516 DM 2, many of which the Survey also performs, the following GS actions are designated categorical exclusions unless the action qualifies as an exception under 516 DM 2.3A(3):

A. *Internal Program Initiatives*

(1) Topographic, land use and land cover, geologic, mineralogic, resource evaluation, and hydrologic mapping activities including aerial topographic surveying, photography, and geophysical surveying.

(2) Rendering formal classification of Federal lands in the United States as to their mineral character and waterpower and waterstorage values.

(3) Collection of data and samples for geologic, paleontologic, mineralogic, geochemcical and geophysical investigations, and resource evaluation, including contracts therefor.

(4) Acquisition of existing geological or geophysical data from otherwise private exploration ventures.

(5) Well logging, aquifer response testing, digital modeling, inventory of existing wells and water supplies, water-sample collection, operation/installation of water-level recording devices in wells, and installation and operation of stream-gaging stations and telemetry systems, including contracts therefor.

(6) Establishment of survey marks, emplacement and operation of field instruments, and installation of any research/monitoring devices.

(7) Exploratory or observation groundwater well drilling operations, including contracts therefor.

(8) Establishment of seasonal and temporary field camps.

(9) Digging of exploratory trenches.

(10) Offroad travel to drilling or data collection or observation sites.

(11) Test or exploration drilling and downhole testing included in a project previously subject to the NEPA process.

(12) Hydraulic fracturing of rock formations included in a project previously subject to the NEPA process.

B. *Permit and Regulatory Functions*

(1) *Administrative and General*

(a) Issuance and modification of regulations, Orders, Standards, Notices to Lessees and Operators, and field rules where the impacts are obviously limited to administrative, economic or technological effects and the environmental impacts are minimal.

(b) Development of reporting forms to collect data required by regulations.

(c) Inspections and investigations.

(d) Decisions made and enforcement actions taken as a result of inspections made to ensure compliance with the applicable laws and regulations. Orders, lease terms, and all requirements imposed as conditions of approval.

(e) Approval of production measurement methods, facilities and procedures.

(f) Approval of off-lease storage in existing facilities.

(g) Determination and designation of logical mining units (LMU's).

(h) Approval of unitization agreements, pooling or communitization agreements.

(i) Approval for commingling of production.

(j) Approval of suspensions of operations and suspensions of production.

(k) Approval of royalty payment procedures and determinations concerning royalty quantities and values, such as audits, royalty reductions, collection procedures, cash handling procedures, reporting procedures, and any actions taken with regard to royalty collections (including similar actions relating to net profit and windfall profit taxes).

(l) Approval of applications for pricing determinations under the Natural Gas Policy Act.

(m) Administrative decisions and actions and recordkeeping, such as:

(i) Approval of royalty oil contracts.

(ii) Approvals of underground gas storage agreements from a presently or formerly productive reservoir.

(iii) Issuance of paying well determinations and participating area approvals.

Geological Survey

(iv) Issuance of drainage determinations.

(n) Reports to Surface Management agencies concerning mineral appraisals and applications for rights-of-way, small tract leases, lease consolidation applications, lease assignments, and bond termination.

(o) Other actions where GS has concurrence or coapproval with another bureau and the action is a categorical exclusion for that bureau.

(2) *Onshore Oil and Gas*

(a) Approval of an Application for Permit to Drill (APD) for exploratory oil and gas wells prior to the first confirmation drilling.

(b) Approval of minor modifications to or minor variances from activities described in approved development/ production plans, such as the relocation of a drill site(s).

(c) Approval of an APD for oil and gas wells subsequent to the first confirmation drilling for which an environmental document is required.

(d) Approval of wells as capable of producing in paying quantities.

(e) Approval of an APD for a new injection or withdrawal well pursuant to an approved gas storage project.

(f) Approval of an APD or equivalent proposal for the enhanced recovery of proven oil and gas resources.

(g) Approval of an APD for a well or approval of a surface facility for the disposal of produced water meeting the standards of NTL–2B (Disposal of Produced Water).

(h) Approval of conversion of an existing oil and gas well for disposal of produced water meeting the standards of NTL–2B.

(i) Approval of an APD for a new water source or observation well.

(j) Approval of conversion of an unsuccessful oil and gas well or an exhausted producer to a water source or observation well.

(k) Approval of Sundry Notices and Reports on Wells.

(3) *Offshore Oil and Gas*

(a) Approval of OCS geological and geophysical exploration activities, except where the proposed activity includes the drilling of deep stratigraphic test holes.

(b) Approval of an OCS exploration or development/production plan in the western Gulf of Mexico (30 CFR 250.2) which does not require an environmental report from an operator pursuant to item 3 of NTL 80–0.

(c) Approval of minor revisions of or minor variances from activities described in an approved OCS exploration or development/production plan.

(d) Approval of an Application for Permit to Drill (APD) an OCS oil and gas exploration or development well when said well and appropriate mitigation measures are described in an approved exploration plan, development plan, or production plan.

(e) Other applicable actions included in paragraph (2) above.

(4) *Geothermal Resources*

(a) Approval of geophysical exploration for geothermal resources.

(b) Approval of a plan of operation for geothermal exploration or development when an environmental document has been prepared at the leasing stage.

(c) Approval of a plan for geothermal production when derived from a plan of utilization which has been covered by an environmental document.

(d) Approval of a plan for injection of geothermal fluids meeting the requirements of GRO–4 (Environmental Protection Requirements).

(e) Approval of conversion of an unsuccessful geothermal well or an exhausted producer to a water source or observation well.

(5) *Minerals*

(a) Approval of a mineral exploration plan on Federal or Indian lands where the preceding permit, lease, or contract has been covered by an environmental document.

(b) Approval of minor modifications to or minor variances from activities described in an approval mineral exploration plan.

(c) Approval of minor modifications to or minor variances from activities described in an approved underground or surface mine plan.

(d) Findings of completeness (30 CFR 211.10) furnished to the Office of Surface Mining for coal mining and operation plans filed under the Surface Mining Control and Reclamation Act.

Bureau of Indian Affairs

4.1 NEPA Responsibility

A. *Commissioner of Indian Affairs.* As chief executive officer, the Commissioner is responsible for the NEPA compliance of Bureau of Indian Affairs (BIA) activities.

B. *Director, Office of Trust Responsibilities,* is responsible for oversight of the BIA program for achieving compliance with NEPA. The Director shall determine the adequacy of all EISs which come before the Commissioner.

C. The *Environmental Services Staff* (Washington), in the Office of Trust Responsibilities, is the focal point for NEPA matters within BIA and is responsible for advising and assisting Area Directors and field support personnel in their environmental activities and acting as the Central Office's liaison with Indian tribal governments on environmental matters. Information about BIA NEPA documents or the NEPA process can be obtained by contacting this staff.

D. Other *Central Office Directors* are responsible for ensuring that the programs and activities within their directorate comply with NEPA.

E. *Area Directors* and *Project Officers* are responsible for conducting all activities under their jurisdiction in compliance with NEPA and providing advice and assistance to Indian tribes on environmental matters; and will provide sufficient staff assistance to ensure that these responsibilities are fulfilled.

F. *Agency Superintendents and Field Unit Supervisors* are responsible, as directed and delegated by the Area Directors, for implementation and enforcement of the Bureau's environmental policy at the Agency or field unit level, including the field inspection, preparation, and approval of environmental documents.

4.2 Guidance to Applicants and Tribal Governments

A. *Relationship with Applicants and Tribal Governments.*

(1) *Types of Applicants.* An "applicant" is any entity which proposes to undertake an activity which will at some point require BIA action. These may include tribal governments, private entities, State and local governments, or Federal agencies.

(2) *Tribal Governments.*

(a) Tribal governments are accorded a special status by BIA. This relationship requires close cooperation and consultation. Tribal governments may be applicants, and/or be affected by a proposed action of BIA or another applicant. In the preparation of environmental documents, tribal governments will be consulted and, if they desire, be a cooperating agency.

(b) Tribal actions that do not require BIA or other Federal approval are not subject to the NEPA process.

B. *Prepared Program Guidance.* Program guidance for surface mining is found in 25 CFR 177 (Surface Exploration, Mining, and Reclamation of Land).

C. *Other Guidance.* Other programs under 25 CFR for which BIA has not yet issued regulations or directives for environmental information from applicants are listed below. These programs may or may not require environmental documents and could involve submission of applicant information. Applicants for these types of programs should contact the nearest affected BIA office for information and assistance:

(1) Indian Business Development Program (25 CFR 80)

(2) Loans to Indians from the Revolving Loan Fund (25 CFR 91)

(3) Loan guaranty, insurance, and interest subsidy (25 CFR 93)

(4) Leasing and permitting (Lands) (25 CFR 131)

(5) Preservation of antiquities (25 CFR 132)

(6) General forest regulations (25 CFR 141)

(7) Sale of lumber and other forest products by Indian enterprises from the forests of Indian reservations (25 CFR 142)

(8) Sale of forest products, Red Lake Indian Reservation, Minn. (25 CFR 144)

(9) General grazing regulations (25 CFR 151)

(10) Navajo grazing regulations (25 CFR 152)

(11) Grazing regulations for former Navajo-Hopi joint use area lands (25 CFR 153)

(12) Rights-of-way over Indian lands (25 CFR 161)

(13) Roads of the Bureau of Indian Affairs (25 CFR 162)

(14) Leasing of tribal lands for mining (25 CFR 171)

(15) Leasing of allotted lands for mining (25 CFR 172)

(16) Leasing of lands on Crow Indian Reservation, Montana, for mining (25 CFR 173)

(17) Leasing of restricted lands of members of Five Civilized Tribes, Oklahoma, for mining (25 CFR 174)

Bureau of Indian Affairs

(18) Leasing of Osage Reservation. Oklahoma, lands for mining, except oil and gas (25 CFR 175)

(19) Lead and zinc mining operations and leases. Quapaw Agency (25 CFR 176)

(20) Leasing of Osage Reservation lands for oil and gas mining (25 CFR 183)

(21) Leasing of certain lands in the Wind River Indian Reservation. Wyoming, for oil and gas mining (25 CFR 184)

(22) Concessions, permits, and leases on lands withdrawn or acquired in connection with Indian irrigation projects (25 CFR 203)

(23) Electric power system—Colorado River Irrigation Project, Arizona (25 CFR 231)

(24) Electric power system—Flathead Indian Irrigation Project. Montana (25 CFR 232)

(25) Off-reservation treaty fishing (25 CFR 256)

(26) Contracts under Indian Self-Determination Act (25 CFR 271)

(27) Grants under the Indian Self-Determination Act (25 CFR 272)

(28) School construction contracts or services for tribally operated previously private schools (25 CFR 274)

(29) School construction contracts for public schools (25 CFR 277)

4.3 Major Actions Normally Requiring an EIS

A. The following BIA actions normally require the preparation of an EIS:

(1) Proposed mining contracts (for other than oil and gas), or the combination of a number of smaller contracts comprising a mining unit, for:

(a) new mines of 640 acres or more, other than surface coal mines.

(b) new surface coal mines of 1,280 acres or more, or having an annual full production level of 5 million tons or more.

(2) Proposed water development projects which would, for example, inundate more than 1,000 acres, or store more than 30,000 acre-feet, or irrigate more than 5,000 acres of undeveloped land.

B. If, for any of these actions, it is proposed not to prepare and EIS, an EA will be prepared and handled in accordance with section 1501.4(e)(2).

4.4 Categorical Exclusions

In addition to the actions listed in the Departmental categorical exclusions outlined in Appendix 1 of 516 DM 2, many of which the BIA also performs, the following BIA actions are designated as categorical exclusions unless the action qualifies as an exception under 516 DM 2.3A(3):

A. *Operation, maintenance, and replacement of existing facilities.* Examples are renovation of buildings, renovation of existing roads, and rehabilitation of irrigation structures.

B. *Transfer of Existing Federal Facilities to Other Entities.* Transfer of the operations and maintenance activities of Federal facilities to tribal groups, water user organizations, or other entities where the anticipated operation and maintenance activities are agreed to in a contract, follow BIA policy, and no major change in operations or maintenance is anticipated.

C. *Human resource programs having primarily socio-economic effects.* Examples are social services, education services, employment assistance, tribal operations, law enforcement, and credit and financing activities.

D. *Administrative actions and other activities relating to trust resources.* Examples are management of trust funds; issuance of such documents as certificates of competency, allotments, and fee patents; renewal of agricultural and other leases when environmental impacts are addressed in an earlier environmental document; and routine research and investigation activities regarding trust resources.

E. *Self-Determination Act Grants and Contracts.*

(1) Self-Determination Act grants.

(2) Self-Determination Act contracts for BIA programs which are listed as categorical exclusions, or for programs in which environmental impacts are adequately addressed in an earlier environmental document.

F. *Rights-of-way.*

(1) Rights-of-way inside another right-of-way or amendments to rights-of-way where minor deviations from or additions to the original right-of-way are involved and where there is an existing environmental document covering the same or similar impacts in the right-of-way area.

(2) Right-of-way for a single-poled power or telephone line to an individual residence, building or well from an existing line where installation will involve no clearance of vegetation from the right-of-way other than for placement of the poles.

G. *Mineral Resources.*

(1) Approval of a mineral prospecting permit or exploration plan when an environmental document has been prepared for the exploration or mining contract.

Bureau of Indian Affairs

(2) Approval of minor modifications to or variances from activities described in an approved underground or surface mine plan.

(3) Approval of geophysical exploration for oil and gas and geothermal resources.

(4) Approval of minor modifications to or variances from activities described in an approved oil and gas or geothermal exploration or development/production plan, such as the relocation of a drill site(s).

(5) Approval of an Application for Permit to Drill (APD) exploratory oil and gas wells prior to the first confirmation drilling.

(6) Approval of an APD for exploratory oil and gas wells subsequent to the first confirmation drilling for which an environmental document is required.

(7) Approval of an APD for a new water source or observation well.

(8) Approval of an APD for a new injection or withdrawal well pursuant to an approved gas storage project.

(9) Approval of an APD or equivalent proposal for the enhanced recovery of proven oil and gas resources.

(10) Approval of conversion of an unsuccessful oil and gas or geothermal well or an exhausted producer to a water source well or observation well.

(11) Approval of conversion of an existing oil and gas well for disposal of produced water meeting the standards of NTL-2B (Disposal of Produced Water).

(12) Approval of surface facilities and wells for the disposal of produced water meeting the standards of NTL-2B.

(13) Approval of a plan for geothermal exploration or development.

(14) Approval of a plan for geothermal production when derived from a plan of utilization previously covered by an environmental document.

(15) Approval of a plan for injection of geothermal fluids meeting the requirements of GRO-4 (Environmental Protection Requirements).

(16) Approval of utilization agreements, pooling or communitization agreements.

(17) Other actions where BIA has concurrence or co-approval with another bureau and the action is a categorical exclusion for that bureau.

Bureau of Land Management

5.4 *Categorical Exclusions*

In addition to the actions listed in the Departmental categorical exclusions outlined in Appendix 1 of 516 DM 2, many of which the Bureau also performs, the following BLM actions are designated categorical exclusions unless the action qualifies as an exception under 516 DM 2.3A(3):

A. *General*

(1) Inventory, data and information collection (including collection of samples), including land use and land cover, geologic, mineralogic and resource evaluation activities, cadastral surveys, geophysical surveys (including contracts therefor) and approval of permits for such activities.

(2) Placing of monitoring equipment (e.g., stream gages).

(3) Non-manipulative research.

(4) Minor routine or preventive operation and maintenance activities on BLM facilities, lands and resource developments.

(5) Actions where BLM has concurrence or co-approval with another Bureau and the action is a categorical exclusion for that Bureau.

(6) Rendering formal classification of Federal lands in the United States as to their mineral character and waterpower and water storage values.

(7) Acquistion of existing geological or geophysical data from otherwise private exploration ventures.

(8) Digging of exploratory trenches.

(9) Offroad vehicle travel to drilling or data collection or observation sites.

(10) Test or exploration drilling and downhole testing included in a project previously subject to the NEPA process.

B. *Realty*

(1) Withdrawal continuations or extensions which would merely establish a specific time period and where there would be essentially no change in use and continuation would not lead to environmental degradation.

(2) Withdrawal continuations or extensions for administrative sites, location of facilities, other proprietary purposes, and roadside areas and buffer zones for other Bureaus and the Forest Service.

(3) Withdrawal continuations or extensions where a report has been prepared which determined that the land contains minerals of no more than nominal value and there has not been serious interest in mineral development expressed, and no new uses would be permitted and existing uses would not lead to environmental degradation under the continuation.

(4) Withdrawal terminations, modifications or revocations if, because of other withdrawals, classifications, management decisions or administrative determinations that will survive the action, the status of the land, insofar as its availability for appropriation under the general land laws, will not be changed.

(5) Withdrawal terminations, modifications or revocations that, because of overlying withdrawals or statutory provisions, involve merely a record clearing procedure.

(6) Withdrawal revocations and opening orders for stock driveways.

(7) Withdrawal terminations, modifications or revocations and classification cancellations and opening orders where the land would be opened to discretionary land laws and where such future discretionary actions would be subject to the NEPA process.

(8) Withdrawal terminations, modifications or revocations and classification cancellations and opening orders where the land would be opened to the operation of the mining laws, if the land does not contain minerals of more than nominal value, as determined in accordance with the established practices and procedures of BLM and there has not been any serious interest in mineral development expressed.

(9) Withdrawal terminations, modifications or revocations and opening orders that the Secretary of the Interior is under a specific statutory directive to execute.

(10) Transfer of lands or interest in land to other Bureaus or to the Secretary of Agriculture pursuant to Sections 205(c) and 206(c) of FLPMA when the land was acquired for that purpose and the acquisition was covered by an environmental document.

Bureau of Land Management

(11) All non-discretionary land actions in Alaska pursuant to the Alaska Native Claims Settlement Act (ANSCA), Alaska Statehood Act and other statutes, including:
  (a) ANSCA grants.
  (b) Native allotments.
  (c) Trade and manufacturing sites.
  (d) Homesites.
  (e) Headquarters sites.
  (f) Homesteads.
  (g) State selections.
(12) Administrative conveyances and leases to the State of Alaska to accommodate airports for which property rights existed prior to the enactment of NEPA.
(13) Continuations of Recreation and Public Purpose Act lands, small tract lands or other land disposal classifications where the surface has been patented and the locatable minerals are reserved to the United States.
(14) Actions taken in conveying mineral interests under Section 209(b) of FLPMA where the intended land use by the non-Federal surface owner would be consistent with surrounding land uses or would cause only minimal environmental impact.
(15) Color of Title cases (Class one).
(16) Recordable disclaimers of interest under Section 315 of FLPMA.
(17) Corrections of patents and other conveyance documents under Section 316 of FLPMA and other applicable statutes.
(18) Assignment of land use authorization (to another party) where the assignment conveys no additional rights beyond those granted in the original authorization.
(19) Transfer of use authorization from one agency to another when an action such as a boundary adjustment necessitates changing a right-of-way from one agency to another (e.g., Forest Service Special Land Use Permit to a BLM Title V Right-of-Way).
(20) Conversion of existing right-of-way grants to Title V grants where no new facilities or other changes are needed.
(21) Rights-of-way inside another right-of-way or amendments to rights-of-way where minor deviations from or additions to the original right-of-way are involved and where there is an existing environmental document covering the same or similar impacts in the right-of-way area.

(22) Buried power or telephone lines in an existing right-of-way using the split trench method.
(23) Upgrading or adding new lines (power or telephone) to existing pole(s) when there is no change in pole configuration.
(24) Right-of-way for a single-poled power or telephone line to an individual residence, building or well from an existing line where installation of the line will involve no clearance of vegetation from the right-of-way other than for placement of the pole.
(25) Rights-of-way for overhead line (no pole or tower on BLM land) crossing over a corner of public land.
(26) Right-of-way which would add another radio transmitter to an approved communication site.
(27) Minor ancillary rights-of-way actions associated with the action of another Bureau or Federal agency, and the action is a categorical exclusion for that Bureau/agency, but only if a cooperative arrangement for the related actions provides for mutually acceptable mitigation measures.
(28) Transfer of land or interest in land to or from other Bureaus or Federal agencies where current management will continue and future changes in management will be subject to the NEPA process.
(29) Easement acquisition, grants of right-of-way, temporary use permits or minor modification to existing grants to use existing improvements, facilities or sites for the same or similar purposes.
(30) Grant of a right-of-way for a pipeline or a terminal transportation road, utility line or drop to an individual residence, well, building or facility adjacent thereto.
(31) Grant of a right-of-way for buried utility distribution line.
(32) Temporary placement of a pipeline above ground.
(33) Designation of existing transportation and utility corridors under Section 503 of FLPMA.
(34) Grant of a right-of-way within a designated corridor, within the intent of the designation.
(35) Renewals, assignments and conversions of existing right-of-way grants.
(36) Grant of temporary use permit for storage sites.

Bureau of Land Management

(37) Authorization of installation of devices to protect human or animal life (e.g., raptor electrocution prevention devices, grates across mines, etc.).

(38) Issuance of land use authorization in Alaska on land which has been selected by and title will vest in State, Native village or regional corporation selected land if the selecting entity does not object to or is promoting the action.

(39) Issuance of rights-of-way for ancillary facilities (gathering or feeder pipelines, tank batteries, access roads, power and communication lines and holding facilities) within an established, unitized or developing oil and gas field which has been covered by either a specific or a programmatic environmental document.

(40) Actions taken in connection with Sections 910 and 1431 of the Alaska National Interest Lands Conservation Act.

C. *Transportation*

(1) Placing of existing roads in BLM road net where no new facilities or other changes are needed.

(2) Installation of routine signs, markers or cattleguards on/or adjacent to existing roads.

(3) Temporary road closures.

(4) Placement of recreational, special designation or information signs, visitor registers, kiosks and portable sanitation devices.

D. *Minerals*

(1) Administration—

(a) Issuance of mineral patents.

(b) Mineral lease adjustments and transfers, including assignments and subleases.

(c) issuance and modification of regulations, orders, standards, notices to lessees and operators and field rules where the impacts are obviously limited to administrative, economic or technological effects and the environmental impacts are minimal.

(d) Development of reporting forms to collect data required by regulations.

(e) Inspections and investigations.

(f) Decisions made and enforcement actions taken as a result of inspections made to ensure compliance with the applicable laws and regulations, orders, lease terms and all requirements imposed as conditions of approval.

(g) Approval of production measurement methods, facilities and procedures.

(h) Approval of off-lease storage in existing facilities.

(i) Determination and designation of logical mining units (L M U's).

(j) Approval of unitization agreements, pooling or communitization agreements.

(k) Approval of commingling of production.

(l) Approval of suspensions of operations and suspensions of production.

(m) Approval of royalty determinations such as royalty rate reduction and operations reporting procedures.

(n) Approval of applications for pricing determinations under the Natural Gas Policy Act.

(o) Administrative decisions and actions and recordkeeping, such as:

(i) Approval of underground gas storage agreements.

(ii) Paying well determinations and participating area approvals.

(iii) Drainage determinations.

(p) Reports to Surface Management Agencies concerning mineral appraisals and applications for rights-of-way, small tract leases, lease consolidation application, lease assignments and bond determination.

(2) Oil and Gas—

(a) Issuance of individual non-competitive oil and gas leases.

(b) Establishment of terms and conditions in Notices of Intent to conduct geophysical exploration of oil and gas pursuant to 43 CFR 3045.

(c) Offering and issuance of upland competitive oil and gas leases where the issuance of the lease is consistent with existing land uses and has been covered by an areawide environmental document.

(d) Approval of an Application for Permit to Drill (APD) for exploratory oil and gas wells prior to the first confirmation drilling.

(e) Approval of minor modifications to or minor variances from activities described in approved development/ production plans, such as the relocation of a drill site(s).

(f) Approval of an APD for oil and gas wells subsequent to the first confirmation drilling for which an environmental document is required.

Bureau of Land Management

(g) Approval of wells as capable of producing in paying quantities.

(h) Approval of an APD for a new injection or withdrawal well pursuant to an approved gas storage project.

(i) Approval of an APD or equivalent proposal for the enhanced recovery of proven oil and gas resources.

(j) Approval of an APD for a well or approval of a surface facility for the disposal of produced water meeting the standards of NTL-2B (Disposal of Produced Water).

(k) Approval of conversion of an existing oil and gas well for disposal of produced water meeting the standards of NTL-2B.

(l) Approval of an APD for a new water source or observation well.

(m) Approval of conversion of an unsuccessful oil and gas well or an exhausted producer to a water source or observation well.

(n) Routine hydraulic fracturing of rock formation to enhance production or injection.

(o) Approval of Sundry Notices and Reports on Wells.

(3) Geothermal Resources—

(a) Approval of Notices of Intent to conduct geothermal resources exploration operations pursuant to 43 CFR 3209 and 30 CFR 270.

(b) Issuance of individual non-competitive geothermal leases where there will be subsequent NEPA compliance prior to development.

(c) Approval of a plan of operation for geothermal exploration or a plan of development when an environmental document has been prepared at the leasing stage.

(d) Approval of a plan for geothermal production when derived from a plan of utilization which has been covered by an environment document.

(e) Approval of a plan for injection of geothermal fluids meeting the requirements of GRO-4 (Environmental Protection Requirements).

(f) Approval of conversion of an unsuccessful geothermal well or an exhausted producer to a water source or observation well.

(4) Solid Minerals—

(a) Findings of completeness furnished to the Office of Surface Mining for coal mining and operation plans filed under the Surface Mining Control and Reclamation Act.

(b) Approval of a mineral exploration plan on Federal or Indian lands where the permit, lease or contract has been covered by an environmental document.

(c) Approval of minor modifications to or minor variances from activities described in an approved mineral exploration plan.

(d) Approval of minor modifications to or minor variances from activities described in an approved underground or surface mine plan.

(e) Disposal of small amounts of mineral materials as authorized by the Act of July 31, 1947, as amended (30 U.S.C. 601, 602).

E. Recreation

(1) Dispersed non-commercial recreation activities such as rock collection, Christmas tree cutting and pine nut gathering.

(2) Issuance of special recreation permits:

(a) To organized groups for search and rescue training, orienteering or similar activities.

(b) For dog trials, endurance horse races and similar events.

(c) Along rivers, trails and other specified areas where use is similar to previous permits for which environmental documents have been prepared and which would not substantially increase the level of use or continue unsatisfactory environmental conditions.

(d) Where uses are consistent with planning decisions or ORV designations, as applicable, or where there will be no surface disturbance.

(3) ORV designations which are the result of planning decisions for which there has been NEPA compliance.

F. Rangeland Management

(1) Issuance of grazing permits and leases and annual use authorizations which are consistent with decisions covered by a grazing management EIS.

(2) Issuance of grazing permits and leases and annual use authorizations in areas scheduled for the preparation of a grazing management EIS which do not increase the level of use or continue

Bureau of Land Management

unsatisfactory environmental conditions.

G. *Forestry*

(1) Land cultivation activities in forest tree nurseries.

(2) Small timber sales for removal of individual trees which are dead, diseased, injured or which constitute a safety hazard, and where the removal requires no more than minor improvement (maintenance) to existing rights-of-way.

(3) Reseeding or reforestation of old timber sales or burn areas where no chemicals are used and there is no conversion of timber type or conversion of non-forested to forested land.

(4) Precommercial thinning activities using small mechanical devices.

H. *Wildlife*

(1) Construction of guzzlers, spring developments and other small water facilities for wildlife water.

(2) Modification of existing fences to provide improved wildlife ingress and egress.

(3) Reintroduction of endemic or native species into their historical habitats, other than endangered or threatening species.

(4) Preparation and implementation of Wildlife Management Plans, cooperatively completed with State agencies under authority of the Sikes Act, Title II, Pub. L. 93–452.

I. *Other*

(1) Issuance of special use or short-term permits not entailing environmental disturbance.

(2) Issuance of authorization for temporary use of small sites for field work camps.

(3) Small sales of sand and gravel, wood products or other materials from authorized sale areas.

(4) Free use of small quantities of sand and gravel, vegetative products or other materials for non-commercial purposes.

(5) Construction of snow fences for safety purposes or to accumulate snow for small water facilities.

(6) Small exclosures constructed for protective purposes, including those to protect reservoirs and springs and those to protect small study areas.

(7) Removal on non-valuable, recent structures and materials (including abandoned automobiles, dumps, fences and buildings) and reclamation of the site.

(8) Issuance of reindeer grazing permits in Alaska which are consistent with an approved land use plan.

(9) Removal of log jams and debris dams using hand labor or small mechanical devices.

[FR Doc. 83–26162 Filed 9–23–83; 8:45 am]
BILLING CODE 4310-84-M

Bureau of Mines

Bureau of Mines

6.1 NEPA Responsibility

A. The *Director* is responsible for NEPA compliance for Bureau of Mines activities.

B. *Assistant Director, Program Development and Evaluation* is operationally responsible to the Director for insuring, on a continuing basis, Bureau-wide compliance with NEPA.

C. *Deputy Director for Minerals Research* will insure that environmental concerns are identified early in the planning stages for all proposed research and development projects.

D. *Special Assistant—Environmental Assessment* is responsible for overall coordination of the Bureau's NEPA activities; providing information, guidance, training, advice, and coordination on NEPA matters as they relate to the Bureau's research and development programs; and reviewing Bureau-proposed legislation and programs for NEPA-related implications. Information about Bureau of Mines NEPA documents or the NEPA process can be obtained by contacting the Special Assistant.

E. *Directors, Minerals Technology Programs* are responsible to the Deputy Director for Minerals Research for integrating the NEPA process into all R&D programs.

F. *Director, Division of Research Center Operations* is responsible to the Deputy Director for Minerals Research for integrating the NEPA process into all activities involving the research centers.

6.2 Guidance to Applicants

The Bureau of Mines has no applicable programs.

6.3 Major Actions Normally Requiring an EIS

A. Approval of construction of a major new research center or test facility will normally require the preparation of an EIS.

B. If it is initially decided not to prepare an EIS, an EA will be prepared and handled in accordance with Section 1501.4(c)(2).

6.4 Categorical Exclusions

In addition to the actions listed in the Departmental categorical exclusions outlined in Appendix 1 of 516 DM 2, many of which the Bureau also performs, the following Bureau of Mines actions are designated categorical exclusions unless the action qualifies as an exception under 516 DM 2.3A(3):

A. Data collection activities and field surveys. Included are reconnaissance-type investigations, research studies to develop new information, stream gaging, well logging, and aquifer response testing.

B. Individual research projects concerning the development or evaluation of mining, metallurgical, or environmental technologies; and the demonstration of associated equipment.

C. Research activities concerning minerals health and safety technology.

D. Research activities that take place in a laboratory where methods for proper disposal of laboratory wastes to prevent environmental pollution have been implemented.

E. Field demonstrations and pilot plants when operated in conjunction with existing facilities of a cooperator or contractor when such facilities provide for effluent and/or emission controls and waste disposal practices that are and will be in compliance with all existing Federal, State, and local standards or regulations.

[FR Doc. 80-40126 Filed 12-24-80; 8:45 am]

BILLING CODE 4310-53-M

National Park Service

516 DM 6, Appendix 7

National Park Service

7.1 NEPA Responsibilities

A. The Director is responsible for NEPA compliance for National Park Service (NPS) activities.

B. Regional Directors are responsible to the Director for integrating the NEPA process into all regional activities and for NEPA compliance in their regions.

C. The Denver Service Center performs most major planning efforts for the National Park Service and integrates NEPA compliance and environmental considerations with project planning, consistent with direction and oversight provided by the appropriate Regional Director.

D. The Environmental Compliance Division (Washington), which reports to the Associate Director—Planning and Development, serves as the focal point for all matters relating to NEPA compliance; coordinates NPS review of NEPA documents prepared by other agencies; and provides policy review and clearance for NPS EISs. Information concerning NPS NEPA documents or the NEPA process can be obtained by contacting this office.

7.2 Guidance to Applicants

Actions in areas of NPS jurisdiction that are initiated by private or non-Federal entities include the following:

A. Minerals. Mineral exploration, leasing and development activities are not permitted in most units of the National Park System. There are exceptions where mineral activities are authorized by law and all mineral activities conducted under these exceptions require consulation with and evaluation by officials of the NPS and are subject to NEPA compliance. Some procedures whereby mineral activities are authorized are outlined below. For site-specific proposals, interested parties should contact the appropriate NPS Regional Director for a determination of whether authorities for conducting other types of mineral activities in particular areas exist and, if so, how to obtain appropriate permits. For further information about NPS minerals policy, interested parties should contact the Energy, **Mining & Minerals** Division (Denver, Colorado).

(1) Mining Claims and Associated Mining Operations.

All units of the National Park System are closed to mineral entry under the 1872 Mining Law, and mining operations associated with mining claims are limited to the exercise of valid prior existing rights. Prior to conducting mining operations on patented or unpatented mining claims within the National Park System, operators must obtain approval of the appropriate NPS Regional Director. The Regional Directors base approval on information submitted by potential operators that discusses the scope of the proposed operations, evaluates the potential impacts on park resources, identifies measures that will be used to mitigate adverse impacts, and meets other requirements contained in 36 CFR Part 9, Subpart A, which governs mining operations on mining claims under the authority of the Mining in the Parks Act of 1976.

(2) Non-Federal Mineral Rights.

Privately-held oil, gas and mineral rights on private land or split estates (Federally-owned surface estate and non-Federally owned subsurface estate) exist within some park unit boundaries. Owners of outstanding subsurface oil and gas rights are granted reasonable access on or across park units through compliance with 36 CFR Part 9, Subpart B. These procedures require an operator to file a plan of operations for approval by the appropriate NPS Regional Director. An approved plan of operations serves as the operator's access permit.

(3) Federal Mineral Leasing and Mineral Operations.

(a) Leasing of Federally-owned minerals is restricted to five national recreation areas in the National Park System, where leasing is authorized in the enabling legislation of the units. According to current regulations (43 CFR 3100.0–3(g)(4); 43 CFR 3500.0–3(c)(7)). These areas are: Lake Mead, Glen Canyon, Ross Lake, Lake Chelan and Whiskeytown National Recreation Areas. However, Lake Chelan was designated in 1981 as an "excepted area" under the regulations and is closed to mineral leasing. The Bureau of Land Management (BLM) issues leases on these lands and controls and monitors operations Applicable general leasing and operating procedures for oil and gas are contained in 43 CFR Part 3100, et seq and for minerals other than oil and gas in 43 CFR Part 3500, et seq.

Within units of the National Park System, the NPS, as the surface management agency, must consent to the permitting and leasing of park lands and concur with operating conditions established in consultation with the BLM. Leases and permits can only be granted upon a finding by the NPS Regional Director that the activities authorized will not have a significant adverse effect on the resources and administration of the unit. The NPS can also require special lease and permit stipulations for protecting the environment and other park resources. In addition, the NPS participates with BLM in preparing environmental analyses of all proposed activities and in establishing reclamation requirements for park unit lands.

(b) Glen Canyon National Recreation Area is the only unit of the National Park System containing special tar sands areas as defined in the Combined Hydrocarbon Leasing Act of 1981. In accordance with the requirements of this Act, the BLM has promulgated regulations governing the conversion of existing oil and gas leases located in special tar sands areas to combined hydrocarbon (oil, gas and tar sands) leases and for instituting a competitive combined hydrocarbon leasing program in the special tar sands areas. Both of these activities, lease conversions and new leasing, may occur within the Glen Canyon NRA provided that they take place commensurate with the unit's minerals management plan and that the Regional Director of the NPS makes a finding of no significant adverse impact on the resources and administration of the unit or on other contiguous units of the National Park System. If the Regional Director does not make such a finding, then the BLM cannot authorize lease conversions or issue new leases within the Glen Canyon NRA. The applicable regulations are contained in 43 CFR 3140.7 and 3141.4-2, respectively. Intra-Departmental procedures for processing conversion applications have been laid out in a Memorandum of Understanding (MOU) between the BLM and the NPS. For additional information about combined hydrocarbon leasing, interested parties should contact the Energy, Mining and Minerals Division (Denver, Colorado).

B. Grazing. Grazing management plans for NPS units subject to legislatively-authorized grazing are normally prepared by the NPS or jointly with the BLM. Applicants for grazing allotments must provide the NPS and/or the BLM with such information as may be required to enable preparation of environmental documents on grazing management plans.

Grazing is also permitted in some NPS areas as a condition of land acquisition in instances where grazing rights were held prior to Federal acquisition. The availability of these grazing rights is limited and information should be sought through individual Park Superintendents.

C. Permits, Rights-of-Way, and Easements for Non-Park Uses. Informational requirements are determined on a case-by-case basis, and applicants should consult with the Park Superintendent before making formal application. The applicant must provide sufficient information on the proposed non-park use, as well as park resources and resource-related values to be affected directly and indirectly by the proposed use in order to allow the Service to evaluate the application, assess the impact of the proposed use on the NPS unit and other environmental values, develop restrictions/stipulations to mitigate adverse impacts, and reach a final decision on issuance of the instrument. Authorities for such permits, rights-of-way, etc., are found in the enabling legislation for individual National Park System units and 16 U.S.C. 5 and 79 and 23 U.S.C. 317. Right-of-way and easement regulations are found at 36 CFR Part 14. Policies concerning regulation of special uses are described in the NPS Management Policies Notebook.

D. Archaeological Permits. Permits for the excavation or removal of archaeological resources on public and Indian lands owned or administered by the Department of the Interior, and by other agencies that may delegate this responsibility to the Secretary, are issued by the Director of the NPS. These permits are required pursuant to the Archaeological Resources Protection Act of 1979 (Pub. L. 96-95) and implementing regulations (43 CFR Part 7), whenever materials of archaeological interest are to be excavated or removed. These permits are not required for

National Park Service

archaeological work that does not result in any subsurface testing and does not result in the collection of any surface or subsurface archaeological materials. Applicants should contact the Departmental Consulting Archeologist in Washington about these permits.

E. Federal Aid. The NPS administers financial and land grants to States, local governments and private organizations/ individuals for outdoor recreation acquisition, development and planning (Catalog of Federal Domestic Assistance (CFDA #15.916), historic preservation (CFDA #15.904), urban park and recreation recovery (CFDA #15.919) and Federal surplus real property for park, recreation and historic monument use (CFDA #15.403).

The following program guidelines and regulations list environmental requirements which applicants must meet:

(1) Land and Water Conservation Fund Grants Manual, Part 650.2;

(2) Historic Preservation Grants-in-Aid Manual, Chapter 4;

(3) Urban Park and Recreation Recovery Guidelines, NPS–37;

(4) Policies and Responsibilities for Conveying Federal Surplus Property (draft) Manual, Part 271.

Copies of documents related to the Land and Water Conservation Fund and the Historic Preservation Fund have been provided to all State Liaison Officers for out/door recreation and all State Historic Preservation Officers. Copies of these and documents related to the Urban Park and Recreation Recovery Program are available for inspection in each NPS Regional Office as well as the NPS Office of Public Affairs in Washington, D.C.

Many State agencies which seek NPS grants may prepare related EISs pursuant to section 102(2)(D) of NEPA. Such agencies should consult with the appropriate NPS Regional Office.

F. Conversion of Acquired and Developed Recreation Lands

The NPS must approve the conversion of certain acquired and developed lands prior to conversion. These include:

(1) All State and local lands and interests therein, and certain Federal lands under lease to the States, acquired or developed in whole or in part with monies from the Land and Water Conservation Fund Act are subject to section 6(f) of the Act which requires approval of conversion of use.

(2) All recreation areas and facilities (as defined in section 1004), developed or improved, in whole or in part, with a grant under the Urban Park and Recreation Recovery Act of 1978 (Pub. L. 95–625, Title 10) are subject to section 1010 of the Act which requires approval for a conversion to other than public recreation uses.

(3) Most Federal surplus real property which has been conveyed to State and local governments for use as recreation demonstration areas, historic monuments or public park and recreation areas (under the Recreation Demonstration Act of 1942 or the Federal Property and Administrative Services Act of 1949, as amended) are subject to approval of conversion of use.

(4) All abandoned railroad rights-of-way acquired by State and local governments for recreational and/or conservation uses with grants under section 809(b) of the Railroad Revitalization and Regulatory Reform Act of 1976, are subject to approval of conversion of use.

Application for approval of conversion of the use of these lands must be submitted to the appropriate Regional Director of the NPS. Early consultation with the Regional Office is encouraged to insure that the application is accompanied by any required environmental documentation. If the property was acquired through the Land and Water Conservation Fund, then the application must be submitted through the appropriate State Liaison Officer for Outdoor Recreation. If the property was acquired under the Federal Property and Administrative Services Act of 1949, as amended, approval of an application for conversion of use must also be concurred in by the General Services Administration.

7.3 Major Actions Normally Requiring Environmental Impact Statements

A. The following types of NPS proposals will normally require the preparation of an EIS:

(1) Wild and Scenic River proposals;

(2) National Trail proposals;

(3) Wilderness proposals;

(4) General Management Plans for major National Park System units;

National Park Service

(5) Grants, including multi-year grants, whose size and/or scope will result in major natural or physical changes, including interrelated social and economic changes and residential and land use changes within the project area or its immediate environs.

(6) Grants which foreclose other beneficial uses of mineral, agricultural, timber, water, energy or transportation resources important to National or State welfare.

B. If for any of these proposals it is initially decided not to prepare an EIS, an EA will be prepared and made available for public review in accordance with section 1501.4(e)(2).

7.4 Categorical Exclusions

In addition to the actions listed in the Departmental categorical exclusions in Appendix 1 of 516 DM 2, many of which the Service also performs, the following NPS actions are designated categorical exclusions unless the action qualifies as an exception under Appendix 2 to 516 DM 2:

A. Actions Related to General Administration (1) Changes or amendments to an approved action when such changes would cause no or only minimal environmental impact.

(2) Land and boundary surveys.

(3) Minor boundary changes.

(4) Reissuance/renewal of permits, rights-of-way or easements not involving new environmental impacts.

(5) Conversion of existing permits to rights-of-way, when such conversions do not continue or initiate unsatisfactory environmental conditions.

(6) Issuances, extensions, renewals, reissuances or minor modifications of concession contracts or permits not entailing new construction.

(7) Commercial use licenses involving no construction.

(8) Leasing of historic properties in accordance with 36 CFR Part 18 and NPS-38.

(9) Preparation and issuance of publications.

(10) Modifications or revisions to existing regulations, or the promulgation of new regulations for NPS-administered areas, provided the modifications, revisions or new regulations do not:

(a) Increase public use to the extent of compromising the nature and character of the area or causing physical damage to it;

(b) Introduce noncompatible uses which might compromise the nature and characteristics of the area, or cause physical damage to it;

(c) Conflict with adjacent ownerships or land uses; or

(d) Cause a nuisance to adjacent owners or occupants.

(II) At the direction of the NPS responsible official, actions where NPS has concurrence or coapproval with another bureau and the action is a categorical exclusion for that bureau.

B. Plans, Studies and Reports (1) Changes or amendments to an approved plan, when such changes would cause no or only minimal environmental impact.

(2) Cultural resources maintenance guides, collection management plans and historic furnishings reports.

(3) Interpretive plans (interpretive prospectuses, audio-visual plans, museum exhibit plans, wayside exhibit plans).

(4) Plans, including priorities, justifications and strategies, for non-manipulative research, monitoring, inventorying and information gathering.

(5) Statements for management, outlines of planning requirements and task directives for plans and studies.

(6) Technical assistance to other Federal, State and local agencies or the general public.

(7) Routine reports required by law or regulation.

(8) Authorization, funding or approval for the preparation of Statewide Comprehensive Outdoor Recreation Plans.

(9) Adoption or approval of surveys, studies, reports, plans and similar documents which will result in recommendations or proposed actions which would cause no or only minimal environmental impact.

(10) Preparation of internal reports, plans, studies and other documents containing recommendations for action which NPS develops preliminary to the process of preparing a specific Service proposal or set of alternatives for decision.

(11) Land protection plans which propose no significant change to existing land or visitor use.

(12) Documents which interpret existing mineral management regulations and policies, and do not recommend action.

National Park Service

C. Actions Related to Development (1) Land acquisition within established park boundaries.

(2) Land exchanges which will not lead to significant changes in the use of land.

(3) Routine maintenance and repairs to non-historic structures, facilities, utilities, grounds and trails.

(4) Routine maintenance and repairs to cultural resource sites, structures, utilities and grounds under an approved Historic Structures Preservation Guide or Cyclic Maintenance Guide; or if the action would not adversely affect the cultural resource.

(5) Installation of signs, displays, kiosks, etc.

(6) Installation of navigation aids.

(7) Establishment of mass transit systems not involving construction, experimental testing of mass transit systems, and changes in operation of existing systems (e.g., routes and schedule changes).

(8) Replacement in kind of minor structures and facilities with little or no change in location, capacity or appearance.

(9) Repair, resurfacing, striping, installation of traffic control devices, repair/replacement of guardrails, etc., on existing roads.

(10) Sanitary facilities operation.

(11) Installation of wells, comfort stations and pit toilets in areas of existing use and in developed areas.

(12) Minor trail relocation, development of compatible trail networks on logging roads or other established routes, and trail maintenance and repair.

(13) Upgrading or adding new overhead utility facilities to existing poles, or replacement poles which do not change existing pole line configurations.

(14) Issuance of rights-of-way for overhead utility lines to an individual building or well from an existing line where installation will not result in significant visual intrusion and will involve no clearance of vegetation other than for placement of poles.

(15) Issuance of rights-of-way for minor overhead utility lines not involving placement of poles or towers and not involving vegetation management or significant visual intrusion in an NPS-administered area.

(16) Installation of underground utilities in previously disturbed areas having stable soils, or in existing utility right-of-way.

(17) Construction of minor structures, including small improved parking lots, in previously disturbed or developed areas.

(18) Construction or rehabilitation in previously disturbed or developed areas, required to meet health or safety regulations, or to meet requirements for making facilities accessible to the handicapped.

(19) Landscaping and landscape maintenance in previously disturbed or developed areas.

(20) Contruction of fencing enclosures or boundary fencing posing no effect on wildlife migrations.

D. Actions Related to Visitor Use (1) Carrying capacity analyses.

(2) Minor changes in amounts or types of visitor use for the purpose of ensuring visitor safety or resource protection in accordance with existing regulations.

(3) Changes in interpretive and environmental education programs.

(4) Minor changes in programs and regulations pertaining to vistor activities.

(5) Issuance of permits for demonstrations, gatherings, ceremonies, concerts, arts and crafts shows, etc., entailing only short-term or readily mitigable environmental disturbance.

(6) Designation of trailside camping zones with no or minimal improvements.

E. Actions Related to Resource Management and Protection (1) Archeological surveys and permits, involving only surface collection or small-scale test excavations.

(2) Day-to-day resource management and research activities.

(3) Designation of environmental study areas and research natural areas.

(4) Stabilization by planting native plant species in disturbed areas.

(5) Issuance of individual hunting and/or fishing licenses in accordance with State and Federal regulations.

(6) Restoration of noncontroversial native species into suitable habitats within their historic range, and elimination of exotic species.

(7) Removal of park resident individuals of non-threatened/endangered species which pose a danger

National Park Service

to visitors, threaten park resources or become a nuisance in areas surrounding a park, when such removal is included in an approved resource management plan.

(8) Removal of non-historic materials and structures in order to restore natural conditions.

(9) Development of standards for, and identification, nomination, certification and determination of eligibility of properties for listing in the National Register of Historic Places and the National Historic Landmark and National Natural Landmark Programs.

F. Actions Related to Grant Programs
(1) Proposed actions essentially the same as those listed in paragraphs A–E above.

(2) Grants for acquisition of areas which will continue in the same or lower density use with no additional disturbance to the natural setting.

(3) Grants for replacement or renovation of facilities at their same location without altering the kind and amount of recreational, historical or cultural resources of the area; or the integrity of the existing setting.

(4) Grants for construction of facilities on lands acquired under a previous NPS or other Federal grant provided that the development is in accord with plans submitted with the acquisition grant.

(5) Grants for the construction of new facilities within an existing park or recreation area, provided that the facilities will not:

(a) Conflict with adjacent ownerships or land use, or cause a nuisance to adjacent owners or occupants; e.g., extend use beyond daylight hours;

(b) Introduce motorized recreation vehicles;

(c) Introduce active recreation pursuits into a passive recreation area;

(d) Increase public use or introduce noncompatible uses to the extent of compromising the nature and character of the property or causing physical damage to it; or

(e) Add or alter access to the park from the surrounding area.

(6) Grants for the restoration, rehabilitation, stabilization, preservation and reconstruction (or the authorization thereof) of properties listed on or eligible for listing on the National Register of Historic Places, at their same location and provided that such actions:

(a) Will not alter the integrity of the property or its setting;

(b) Will not increase public use of the area to the extent of compromising the nature and character of the property; and

(c) Will not cause a nuisance to adjacent property owners or occupants.

[FR Doc. 84-26396 Filed 10-3-84; 8:45 am]
BILLING CODE 4310-70-M

Office of Surface Mining

Appendix 8

[516 DM 6]

OFFICE OF SURFACE MINING

8.1 NEPA Responsibility

A. *Director.* Is responsible for NEPA compliance for Office of Surface Mining (OSM).

B. *Assistant Directors.*

(1) Are responsible to the Director for supervision and coordination of NEPA activities in their program areas of responsibility.

(2) Are responsible, within their program areas, for OSM Headquarters review of EISs for compliance with program area policy guidance.

(3) Are responsible for assuring that environmental concerns are identified early in the planning stages and appropriate policy and program guidance is disseminated.

C. *Regional Directors.*

(1) Are responsible to the Director for integrating the NEPA process into all Regional activities and for NEPA compliance activities in their Regions.

(2) Will designate a staff position to be responsible to the Regional Director for the consistency, adequacy, and quality of all NEPA documents prepared by the Region's staff. The position will also be responsible to the Regional Director for providing information, guidance, training, advice, and coordination on NEPA matters, and for oversight of the Region's NEPA process.

D. *Chief, Branch of Environmental Analysis (Washington).* Is designated by the Director to be responsible for overall policy guidance for NEPA compliance for OSM. Information about OSM NEPA documents or the NEPA process can be obtained by contacting this Branch.

8.2 Guidance to Applicants

OSM personnel are available to meet with all applicants for permits on Federal lands or under a Federal program for a State to provide guidance on the permitting procedures. Permit applications under approved State programs are excluded from NEPA compliance. In addition, OSM's regulations implementing the Surface Mining Control and Reclamation Act of 1977 (SMCRA) provide requirements for applicants to submit environmental information. The following parts of the regulations (30 CFR) describe the information requirements.

A. Parts 770 and 771 outline the content requirements of permit applications on Federal lands or under a Federal program for a State, including: the procedures for coal exploration operations required by 30 CFR 776; the permit application contents for surface coal mining activities required by 30 CFR 778, 779, and 780; the permit application contents for underground coal mining required by 30 CFR 782, 783, and 784; the requirements for special categories of surface coal mining required by 30 CFR 785; and the procedures for review, revision, and renewal of permits and for the transfer, sale, or assignment of rights granted under permits, as required by 30 CFR 788.

B. Part 776 identifies the minimum requirements for coal exploration activities outside the permit area. Part 776 is complemented by Part 815 of Subchapter K which provides environmental protection performance standards applicable to these operations.

C. Part 778 provides the minimum requirements for legal, financial, compliance, and general nontechnical information for surface mining activities applications. Information submitted in permit applications under Part 778 will ber used primarily to enable the regulatory authority and interested members of the public to ascertain the particular nature of the entity which will mine the coal and those entities which have other financial interests and public record ownership interests in both the mining entity and the property which is to be mined.

Office of Surface Mining

D. Part 779 establishes the minimum standards for permit applications regarding information on existing environmental resources that may be impacted by the conduct and location of the proposed surface mining activities. With the information required under Part 779, the regulatory authority is to utilize information provided in mining and reclamation plans under Part 780, in order to determine what specific impacts the proposed surface mining activities will have on the environment.

E. Part 780 establishes the heart of the permit application: the mining operations and reclamation plan for surface mining activities. The regulatory authority will utilize this information, together with the description of the existing environmental resources obtained under Part 779, to predict whether the lands to be mined can be reclaimed as required by the Act.

F. Part 782 contains permit application requirements for underground mining activities. This corresponds to Part 778 for surface mining. As such, Part 782 sets forth the minimum requirements for general, legal, financial, and compliance information required to be contained in applications for permits.

G. Part 783 describes the minimum requirements for information on existing environmental resources required in the permit application for underground mining and corresponds to Part 779 for surface mining activities.

H. Part 784 contains a discussion of the minimum requirements for reclamation and operation plans related to underground mining permit applications and corresponds to Part 780 for surface mining activities.

I. Part 785 contains requirements for permits for special categories of mining, including anthracite, special bituminous, experimental practices, mountaintop removal, steep slope, variances from approximate original contour restoration requirements, prime farmlands, alluvial valley floors, augering operation, and in-situ activities. The provisions of Part 785 are intereulated to the performance standards applicable to the special categories covered in Subchapter K and must be reviewed together with the preamble and text for Parts 818 through 828 of Subchapter K.

J. Part 788 specifies the responsibilities of persons conducting surface coal mining and reclamation operations with respect to changes, modifications, renewals, and revisions of permits after they are originally granted, and of persons who attempt to succeed to rights granted under permits by transfer, sale, or assignment of rights.

8.3 Major Actions Normally Requiring an EIS

A. The following OSM actions will normally require the preparation of an EIS:

(1) Approval of the Abandoned Mine Lands Reclamation Program, (SMCRA, Title IV). *Completed in March 1980.*

(2) Promulgation of the permanent regulatory program for surface coal mining and reclamation operations (SMCRA, Title V). *Completed in February 1979.*

(3) Approval of a proposed mining and reclamation plan that includes any of the following:

(a) Mountaintop removal operations.

(b) Mining within high use recreation areas.

(c) Mining that will cause population increases that exceed the community's ability to absorb the growth.

(d) Mining that would require a major change in existing coal transportation facilities.

(4) Approval of a proposed mining and reclamation plan for a surface mining operation that meets the following:

(a) The environmental impacts of the proposed mining operation are not adequately analyzed in an earlier environmental document covering the specific leases or mining activity; and

(b) The area to be mined is 1280 acres or more, or the annual full production level is 5 million tons or more; and

(c) Mining and reclamation operations will occur for 15 years or more.

B. If for any of these actions it is proposed not to prepare an EIS, an EA will be prepared and handled in accordance with Section 1501.4(e)(2).

Office of Surface Mining

8.4 Categorical Exclusions

A. The following OSM actions are deemed not to be major Federal actions within the meaning of Section 102(2)(C) of NEPA under Sections 501(a) or 702(d) of the SMCRA. They are hereby designated as categorical exclusions from the NEPA process and are exempt from the exceptions under 516 DM 2.3A(3):

(1) Promulgation of interim regulations.

(2) Approval of State programs.

(3) Promulgation of Federal programs where a State fails to submit, implement, enforce, or maintain an acceptable State program.

(4) Promulgation and implementation of the Federal lands program.

B. In addition to the actions listed in the Departmental categorical exclusions outlined in Appendix 1 of 516 DM 2, many of which OSM also performs, the following OSM actions (SMCRA sections are in parentheses) are designated categorical exclusions unless the actions qualify as an exception under 516 DM 2.3A(3):

(1) Monetary allotments to States for mining and mineral resources institutes (301).

(2) Allocation of research funds to institutes (302).

(3) Any research effort associated with ongoing abandoned mine land reclamation projects where the research is coincidential to the reclamation (401(c)(6)).

(4) Collection of reclamation fees from operators (402(a)).

(5) Findings of fact and entries on land adversely affected by past coal mining (407(a)).

(6) Acquisition of particular parcels of abandoned mine lands for reclamation (407(c)).

(7) Filing liens against property adversely affected by past coal mining (408).

(8) Interim regulatory grants (502(e)(4)).

(9) Disapproval of a proposed State program (503(c)).

(10) Review of permits issued under a previously approved State program (504(d)).

(11) Five-year permit renewal on life-of-mine plans under the Federal lands program or the Federal program for a State where the environmental impacts of continued mining are adequately analyzed in a previous environmental document for the mining operation (506(d)).

(12) Small operator assistance program (507(c)).

(13) Issuance of public notices and holding public hearings on permit applications invovling Federal lands or under a Federal program for a State (513).

(14) Routine inspection and enforcement activities (517).

(15) Conflict of interest regulations (517(g)).

(16) Assessment of civil penalties (518).

(17) Releases of performance bonds or deposits for mining on Federal lands or under a Federal program for a State (519).

(18) Issuance of cessation orders for coal mining and reclamation operations (521(a)(2) and (3)).

(19) Suspension or revocation of permits (521(a)(4)).

(20) Federal oversight and enforcement of ineffective State programs (521(b)).

(21) Cooperative agreements between a State and the Secretary to provide for State regulation of surface coal mining and reclamation operations on Federal lands (523(c)).

(22) Development of a program to assure that, with respect to the granting of permits, leases, or contracts for Federally-owned coal, no one shall be unreasonably denied purchase of the mined coal (523(d)).

(23) Annual grants programs to States for program development, administration, and enforcement (705(a)).

(24) Assistance to States in the development, administration, and enforcement of State programs (705(b)).

Office of Surface Mining

(25) Increasing the amount of annual grants to States (705(c)).

(26) Submission of the Secretary's annual report to the Congress (706).

(27) The proposal of legislation to allow Indian tribes to regulate surface coal mining on Indian lands (710(a)).

(28) The certification and training of blasters (719).

(29) Approval of State Reclamation Plans for abandoned mine lands (405).

Bureau of Reclamation

516 DM 6 Appendix 9

Bureau of Reclamation

9.1 *NEPA Responsibility.*

A. *Commissioner.* Is responsible for NEPA compliance for Bureau of Reclamation (BuRec) activities.

B. *Assistant Commissioners.* (1) are responsible to the Commissioner for supervising and coordinating NEPA activities in their assigned areas of responsibility.

(2) are responsible. in assigned area of responsibility. for the Washington level review of EISs prepared in the regions or E&R Center for compliance with program area policy guidance.

(3) provide supervision and coordination in assigned areas of responsibility, to insure that environmental concerns are identified in the planning stages and to see that Regional Directors follow through with environmental commitments during the construction and operation and maintenance stages.

(4) may designate a staff position to be responsible for NEPA oversight and coordination in their assigned areas of responsibility.

C. *Regional Directors.* (1) are fully responsible to the Commissioner for integrating the NEPA compliance activities in their regional area.

(2) will designate a staff position with the full responsibility to the Regional Director for providing direction of the NEPA process including information. guidance. training. advice. consistency. quality. adequacy. oversight. and coordination on NEPA documents or matters.

D. *Division and Office Chiefs in E&R Center.* (1) are responsible for integrating the NEPA process into their activities.

(2) will designate a staff position to be responsible to the division or office chief for providing guidance. advice. consistency. quality. adequacy. oversight. and coordination on NEPA documents for matters originating in the E&R Center.

(3) will provide a technical review within their area of expertise of environmental documents directed to their office for review and comment.

E. *Director. Office of Environmental Affairs (Washington).* Is the position designated by the Commissioner to be responsible for overall policy review of BuRec NEPA compliance. Information about BuRec NEPA documents of the NEPA process can be obtained by contacting this office.

9.2 *Guidance to Applicants.*

A. *Types of Applicants.* (1) Actions that are initiated by private or non-Federal entities through applications include the following: repayment contracts. water service contracts. Small Reclamation Projects Act Loans. Emergency Loans. Rehabilitation and Betterment Loans. Distribution System Loans. land use permits. licenses. easements. crossing agreements. permits for removal of sand and gravel. renewal of grazing. recreation management. or cabin site leases.

(2) Applicants will be provided information by the regional office on what environmental reports. analysis. or information are needed when they initiate their application. The environmental information requested may. of necessity. be related to impacts on private lands or other lands not under the jurisdiction of the Bureau to allow the BuRec to meet its environmental responsibilities.

B. *Prepared Program Guidance for Applicants.* (1) Loans under the Small Reclamation Projects Act of 1956. U.S. Department of the Interior. Bureau of Reclamation. March 1976 (35 pages).

(2) Guidelines for Preparing Applications for Loans and Grants under the Small Reclamation Projects Act. Public Law 84-984. U.S. Department of the Interior. Bureau of Reclamation. December 1973 (121 pages).

Bureau of Reclamation

(3) The Rehabilitation and Betterment Program. U.S. Department of the Interior. Bureau of Reclamation, September 1978 (14 pages).

(4) Guidelines for Preparation of Reports to Support Proposed Rehabilitation and Betterment Programs. U.S. Department of the Interior. Bureau of Reclamation. September 1978 (8 pages).

9.3   *Major Actions Normally Requiring and EIS.*

A. The following types of BuRec proposals will normally require the preparation of an EIS:

(1) Proposed Feasibility Reports on water resources projects.

(2) Proposed Definite Plan Reports (DPR) on water resources projects if not covered by an EIS at the feasibility report stage or if there have been major changes in the project plan which may cause significantly different or additional new impacts.

(3) Proposed repayment contracts and water service contracts or amendments thereof or supplements thereto, for irrigation. municipal, domestic, or industrial water where NEPA compliance has not already been accomplished.

(4) Proposed modifications to existing projects or proposed changes in the programmed operation of an existing project that may cause a significant new impact.

(5) Proposed initiation of construction of a project or major unit thereof, if not already covered by an EIS. or if significant new impacts are anticipated.

(6) Proposed major research projects where there may be significant impacts resulting from experimentation or other such research activities.

B. If, for any of these proposals it is initially decided not to prepare an EIS. and EA will be prepared and handled in accordance with Section 1501.4(e)(2).

9.4 *Categorical Exclusions.* In addition to the actions listed in the Departmental categorical exclusions outlined in Appendix 1 of 516 DM 2. many of which the Bureau also performs. the following Bureau actions are designated categorical exclusions unless the action qualifies as an exception under 516 DM 2.3A(3):

A. General Activities

1. Changes in regulations or policy directives and legislative proposals where the impacts are limited to economic and/or social effects.

2. Training activities of enrollees assigned to the various youth programs. Such training may include minor construction activities for other entities.

3. Research activities. such as nondestructive data collection and analysis. monitoring. modeling. laboratory testing. calibration. and testing of instruments or procedures and nonmanipulative field studies.

B. Planning Activities

1. Routine planning investigation activities where the impacts are expected to be localized. such as land classification surveys. topographic surveys. archeological surveys. wildlife studies. economic studies. social studies. and other study activity during any planning. preconstruction. construction. or operation and maintenance phases.

2. Special. status. concluding. or other planning reports that do not contain recommendations for action. but may or may not recommend further study.

3. Data collection studies that involve test excavations for cultural resources investigations or test pitting. drilling. or seismic investigations for geologic exploration purposes where the impacts will be localized.

C. Project Implementation Activities

1. Classification and certification of irrigable lands.

2. Minor acquisition of land and rights-of-way or easements.

3. Minor construction activities associated with authorized projects which correct unsatisfactory environmental conditions or which merely augment or supplement. or are enclosed within existing facilities.

4. Approval of land management plans where implementation will only result in minor construction activities and resultant increased operation and maintenance activities.

Bureau of Reclamation

D. Operations and Maintenance Activities

1. Maintenance. rehabilitation. and replacement of existing facilities which may involve a minor change in size. location and/or operation.

2. Transfer of the operation and maintenance of Federal facilities to water districts, recreation agencies, fish and wildlife agencies, or other entities where the anticipated operation and maintenance activities are agreed to in a contract or a memorandum of agreement, follow approved Reclamation policy, and no major change in operation and maintenance is anticipated.

3. Administration and implementation of project repayment and water service contracts. including approval of organizational or other administrative changes in contracting entities brought about by inclusion or exclusion of lands in these contracts.

4. Approval, execution, and implementation of water service contracts for minor amounts of long-term water use or tempoarary or interim water use where the action does not lead to long-term changes and where the impacts are expected to be localized.

5. Approval of changes in pumping power and water rates charged contractors by the Bureau for project water service or power.

6. Execution and administration of recordable contracts for disposal of excess lands.

7. Withdrawal termination. modification. or revocation where the land would be opened to discretionary land laws and where such future discretionary actions would be subject to the NEPA process. and disposal or sale of acquired lands where no major change in usage is anticipated.

8. Renewal of existing grazing. recreation management. or cabin site leases which do not increase the level of use or continue unsatisfactory environmental conditions.

9. Issuance of permits for removal of gravel or sand by an established process from existing quarries.

10. Issuance of permits. licenses. easements. and crossing agreements which provide right-of-way over Bureau lands where the action does not allow for or lead to a major public or private action.

11. Implementation of improved appearance and soil and moisture conservation programs where the impacts are localized.

12. Conduct of programs of demonstration. educational. and technical assistance to water user organizations for improvement of project and on-farm irrigation water use and management.

13. Follow-on actions such as access agreements. contractual arrangements. and operational procedures for hydropower facilities which are on or appurtenant to Bureau facilities or lands which are permitted or licensed by the Federal Energy Regulatory Commission (FERC). when FERC has accomplished compliance with NEPA (including actions to be taken by the Bureau) and when the Bureau's environmental concerns have been accommodated in accordance with the Bureau/FERC Memorandum of Understanding of June 22, 1981.

14. Approval, renewal. transfer. and execution of an original, amendatory, or supplemental water service or repayment contract where the only result will be to implement an administrative or financial practice or change.

15. Approval of second party water sales agreements for small amounts of water (usually less than 10 acre-feet) where the Bureau has an existing water sales contract in effect.

16. Approval and execution of contracts requiring the repayment of funds furnished or expended on behalf of an entity pursuant to the Emergency Fund Act of June 26, 1948 (43 U.S.C. 502) where the action taken is limited to the original location of the damaged facility.

17. Minor safety of dams construction activities where the work is confined to the dam. abutment areas, or appurtenant features. and where no major change in reservoir or downstream operation is anticipated as a result of the construction activities.

E. Grant and Loan Activities

1. Rehabilitation and Betterment Act loans and contracts which involve repair, replacement. or modification of equipment in existing structures or minor repairs to existing dams. canals. laterals. drains. pipelines. and similar facilities.

2. Small Reclamation Projects Act grants and loans where the work to be done is confined to areas already impacted by farming or development activities, work is considered minor. and where the impacts are expected to be localized.

3. Distribution System Loans Act loans where the work to be done is confined to areas already impacted by farming or developing activities, work is considered minor. and where the impacts are expected to be localized.

Department of Transportation
NEPA Procedures
Order 5610.1C (as amended July 30, 1985)

SUBJECT: PROCEDURES FOR CONSIDERING ENVIRONMENTAL IMPACTS

INTRODUCTION.

1. PURPOSE. This Order establishes procedures for consideration of environmental impacts in decision making on proposed Department of Transportation (DOT) actions. The Order provides that information on environmental impacts of proposed actions will be made available to public officials and citizens through environmental impact statements, environmental assessments or findings of no significant impact. These documents serve as the single vehicle for environmental findings and coordination.

2. CANCELLATION. DOT 5610.1B, PROCEDURES FOR CONSIDERING ENVIRONMENTAL IMPACTS, dated September 30, 1974.

3. AUTHORITY. This Order provides instructions for implementing Section 102(2) of the National Environmental Policy Act of 1969, as amended, (42 USC 4321-4347, hereinafter "NEPA") and the Regulations for Implementing NEPA issued by the Council on Environmental Quality, 11-29-78 (40 CFR 1500-1508); Sections 2(b) and 4(f) of the Department of Transportation Act of 1966 (49 USC 1653, hereinafter "the DOT Act"); Sections 309 and 176 of the Clean Air Act, as amended (42 USC 7401 et seq.); Section 106 of the National Historic Preservation Act of 1966 (16 USC 470, hereinafter "the Historic Preservation Act"); Sections 303 and 307 of the Coastal Zone Management Act of 1972 (43 USC 1241); Section 2 of the Fish and Wildlife Coordination Act (16 USC 661 et seq.); Section 7 of the Endangered Species Act, as amended (16 USC 1533); the Federal Water Pollution Control Act, as amended (33 USC 1314 et seq.); Executive Order 12114, Environmental Effects Abroad of Major Federal Actions; and various Executive Orders relating to environmental impacts. In addition, the Order provides instructions for implementing, where environmental statements are required, Sections 138 and 109 of Federal-aid highway legislation (Title 23, USC, hereinafter "the Highway Act); Sections 16 and 18(a) of the Airport and Airway Development Act of 1970 (49 USC 1716, 1718, hereinafter "the Airport Act"); and Section 14 of the Urban Mass Transportation Act of 1964 (49 USC Section 1601 et seq., hereinafter "the Urban Mass Transportation Act").

DISTRIBUTION: T-1 (All DOT Office and Regional
              Directors and Above), Including
              Coast Guard
              National Transportation Safety Board (Info)

OPI: Office of
     Environment
     and Safety

DOT 5610.1C Chg 2   Page i (and ii)
7-30-85

TABLE OF CONTENTS

Attachment 1
State and Localities with EIS Requirements

Attachment 2
Form and Content of Environmental Impact Statements

1.   <u>BACKGROUND</u>.

The National Environmental Policy Act (NEPA) establishes a broad
national policy to promote efforts to improve the relationship between
man and his environment. NEPA sets out certain policies and goals
concerning the environment and requires that to the fullest extent
possible, the policies, regulations, and public laws of the United States
shall be interpreted and administered in accordance with those policies
and goals.

Section 102 of NEPA is designed to insure that environmental considerations are given careful attention and appropriate weight in all decisions
of the Federal Government. Section 102(2)(C) requires that all agencies of
the Federal Government shall

> include in every recommendation or report on proposals for legisla-
> tion and other major Federal actions significantly affecting the
> quality of the human environment, a detailed statement by the
> responsible official on —
>
> (i)   the environmental impact of the proposed action,
>
> (ii)   any adverse environmental effects which cannot be avoided
>   should the proposal be implemented,
>
> (iii)   alternatives to the proposed action,
>
> (iv)   the relationship between local short-term uses of man's
>   environment and the maintenance and enhancement of long-
>   term productivity, and
>
> (v)   any irreversible and irretrievable commitments of resources
>   which would be involved in the proposed action should it be
>   implemented.

Section 102(2)(A) requires all agencies of the Federal Government to
"utilize a systematic, interdisciplinary approach which will insure the
integrated use of the natural and social sciences and the environmental
design arts in planning and decision making which may have an impact on
man's environment..."

The Council on Environmental Quality (CEQ) issued regulations for implementation of the procedural provisions of NEPA (40 CFR Parts 1500-1508) on 11-29-78. The CEQ regulations apply uniformly to and are binding upon all Federal agencies, and direct each agency to adopt implementing procedures which relate the CEQ regulations to the specific needs of that agency's programs and operating procedures.

This Order implements the mandate of NEPA, as defined and elaborated upon by CEQ's regulations, within the programs of the Department of Transportation. The Order is not a substitute for the regulations promulgated by CEQ, nor does it repeat or paraphrase the language of those regulations. Rather, the Order supplements the CEQ regulations by applying them to DOT programs. Therefore, all operating administrations and Secretarial Offices shall comply with both the CEQ regulations and the provisions of this Order.

This Order provides instructions for implementation of relevant environmental laws and executive orders in addition to NEPA. The environmental process established by this Order is intended to implement the Department's policy objective of one-stop environmental processing. To the maximum extent possible, a single process shall be used to meet requirements for environmental studies, consultations and reviews.

2.   POLICY AND INTENT.

   a.   It is the policy of the Department of Transportation to integrate national environmental objectives into the missions and programs of the Department and to:

      (1)   avoid or minimize adverse effects wherever possible;

      (2)   restore or enhance environmental quality to the fullest extent practicable;

      (3)   preserve the natural beauty of the countryside and public park and recreation lands, wildlife and waterfowl refuges, and historic sites;

      (4)   preserve, restore and improve wetlands;

      (5)   improve the urban physical, social and economic environment;

(6) increase access to opportunities for disadvantaged persons; and

(7) utilize a systematic, interdisciplinary approach in planning and decision making which may have an impact on the environment.

b. The purpose of the environmental procedures in this Order is to provide Department officials, other decision makers, and the public, as part of the decision making process, with an understanding of the potential effects of proposed actions significantly affecting the quality of the human environment. The environmental review process is to be used to explore and document alternative actions that will avoid or minimize adverse impacts.

c. The environmental impact statement (EIS), finding of no significant impact (FONSI, formerly "negative declaration") and determination that a proposed action is categorically excluded serve as the record of compliance with the policy and procedures of NEPA and the policy and procedures of other environmental statutes and executive orders. To the maximum extent possible, all environmental studies, reviews and consultations shall be coordinated into a single process, and compliance with all applicable environmental requirements shall be reflected in the EIS or FONSI.

3. PLANNING AND EARLY COORDINATION.

a. The identification and evaluation of the social, economic and environmental effects of a proposed action and the identification of all reasonable measures to mitigate adverse impacts shall be initiated in the early planning stages of the action, and shall be considered along with technical and economic studies. Assessment of environmental impacts should be a part of regional transportation system planning and broad transportation program development.

General criteria for identification of social, economic, and environmental impacts in DOT planning programs are set forth in subparagraph 10.e., DOT 1130.4, Intermodal Planning Groups and Unified Planning Work Programs, of 2-12-79. Other guidance may be identified in the implementing procedures of the administrations.

b. Where the DOT action is initiated by a State or local agency or a private applicant, the responsible operating administration shall assure that the applicant is advised of environmental assessment and review requirements and that consultation with appropriate agencies and interested parties is initiated at the earliest possible time. (See paragraph 20.b. below.)

c.   Existing administration procedures for early consultation and citizen participation shall be modified to incorporate the scoping process (CEQ 1501.7). Implementing procedures shall assure that significant issues are identified and that all interested parties have an opportunity to participate in the scoping and early consultation process.

d.   Where the proposed action is initiated by a State and may have significant impacts on a Federal land management entity or any other State, the responsible Federal official shall provide early notice to and solicit the views of that Federal land management entity or other State.

4.   <u>ENVIRONMENTAL PROCESSING CHOICE.</u>

     a.   <u>Actions covered.</u> Except as provided in subparagraph c. below, the requirements of this Order apply to, but are not limited to, the following: all grants, loans, loan guarantees, construction, research activities, rulemaking and regulatory actions, certifications, licenses, permits, approval of policies and plans (including those submitted to the Department by State or local agencies), adoption or implementation of programs, legislation proposed by DOT, and any renewals or reapprovals of the foregoing. (CEQ 1508.18(b).)

     b.   <u>Environmental Impact Statements.</u> An EIS shall be prepared for any proposed major Federal action significantly affecting the environment. (See also: CEQ 1508.27, and paragraphs 7 and 20 of this Order.)

     c.   <u>Categorical Exclusions.</u> The following actions are not Federal actions with a significant impact on the environment, and do not require either an environmental assessment or an environmental impact statement:

         (1)   Administrative procurements (e.g. general supplies) and contracts for personal services;

         (2)   Personnel actions (e.g. promotions, hirings);

         (3)   Project amendments (e.g. increases in costs) which do not significantly alter the environmental impact of the action;

(4) Operating or maintenance subsidies when the subsidy will not result in a change in the effect on the environment; and

(5) Other actions identified by the administrations as categorical exclusions pursuant to paragraph 20.

(6) The following actions relating to economic regulation of airlines:

(a) Actions implementing the essential air service program;

(b) Enforcement proceedings;

(c) Actions approving a carrier agreement; acquisition of control, merger, consolidation, or interlocking relationship;

(d) Finding a carrier fit under section 401 of the Federal Aviation Act of 1958, as amended;

(e) Approving or setting carrier fares or rates;

(f) Route awards involving turboprop aircraft having a capacity of 60 seats or less and a maximum payload capacity of 18,000 pounds or less;

(g) Route awards that do not involve supersonic service and will not result in an increase in commercial aircraft operations of one or more percent;

(h) Determinations on termination of airline employees;

(i) Actions relating to consumer protection, including regulations;

(j) Authorizing carriers to serve airports already receiving the type of service authorized;

(k) Granting temporary or emergency authority;

(l) Negotiating bilateral agreements;

(m) Registration of an air taxi operator pursuant to the Department's Regulations (14 CFR Part 298); and

(n) Granting of charter authority to a U.S. or foreign air carrier under sections 401, 402 or 416 of the Federal Aviation Act or the Department's Economic Regulations.

d. <u>Environmental Assessment</u>. An environmental assessment or EIS shall be prepared for actions normally categorically excluded, but which are likely to involve (1) significant impacts on the environment; (2) substantial controversy on environmental grounds; (3) impacts which are more than minimal on properties protected by section 4(f) and sections 106 of the Historic Preservation Act; or (4) inconsistencies with any Federal, State or local law or administrative determination relating to the environment.

e.   Exemptions. The provisions of this Order do not apply to actions that have
     an impact primarily outside the United States, except for those actions
     significantly affecting the environment of a foreign nation not participa-
     ting in the action, or ecological natural resources designated for protec-
     tion by the President or the Secretary of State, or the global commons.

5.   FINDING OF NO SIGNIFICANT IMPACT.

     a.   The FONSI may be attached to an enviornmental assessment or the environ-
          mental assessment and FONSI may be combined into a single document.

     b.   Except as provided in subparagraph c. below, a FONSI or environmental
          assessemnt need not be coordinated outside the originating office, but must
          be made available to the public upon request. Notice of availability shall
          be provided (see suggestions for public notice in CEQ 1506.6(b)). In all
          cases, notice shall be provided to State and areawide clearinghouses.

     c.   In the circumstances defined in CEQ 1501.4(e)(2), a copy of the environmen-
          tal assessment should be made available to the public for a period of not
          less than 30 days before the finding of no significant impact is made and
          the action is implemented. Consultation with other Federal agencies con-
          cerning section 4(f) of the DOT Act, the Historic Preservation Act,
          section 404 permits and other Federal requirements should be accomplished
          prior to or during this period.

6.   LEAD AGENCIES AND COOPERATING AGENCIES.

     a.   The appropriate Operating Administration or Secretarial Office shall serve
          as the lead agency or joint lead agency for preparing and processing envir-
          onmental documents when that element has the primary Federal responsibility
          for the action.

     b.   An applicant should to the fullest extent possible serve as a joint lead
          agency if the applicant is a State agency with State-wide jurisdiction, or
          is a State or local agency, and the proposed action is subject to State
          requirements comparable to NEPA. (See CEQ 1506.2.)

     c.   Coordination with cooperating agencies shall be initiated early in project
          planning and shall be continued through all stages of development of the
          appropriate environmental document.

     d.   If an agency requested to be a cooperating agency replies that it will not
          participate, the agency shall be provided a copy of the draft EIS. If the
          agency makes adverse comments on the draft EIS (including the adequacy of
          the EIS or consideration of alternatives or of mitigating measures), or if
          the agency indicates that it may delay or withhold action on some aspect
          of the proposal, the matter may be discussed with CEQ.

     e.   Where a DOT element is requested to be a cooperating agency, it shall
          make every effort to participate.

7.   PREPARATION AND PROCESSING OF DRAFT ENVIRONMENTAL STATEMENTS.

     a.   Scope of Statement. The action covered by the statement should have signi-
          ficance, and must be broad enough in scope to avoid segmentation of projects
          and to ensure meaningful consideration of alternatives. The scope of the
          statement should be decided upon during the scoping process. (See also CEQ
          1502.20 and para. 7.g. below.) A general class of actions may be covered in
          a single EIS when the environmental impacts of all the actions are similar.

b. Timing of Preparation of Draft Statements. Draft statements shall
    be prepared at the earliest practical time prior to the first
    significant point of decision in the program or project development
    process. They should be prepared early enough in the process so
    that the analysis of the environmental effects and the exploration of
    alternatives are meaningful inputs to the decision making process.
    The implementing guidance (see paragraph 20) shall specify the point
    at which draft statements should be prepared for each type of
    action.

c. Interdisciplinary Approach and Responsibilities for EIS Preparation.
    An interdisciplinary approach should be used throughout planning
    and preparation of environmental documents to help assure a
    systematic evaluation of reasonable alternative courses of action
    and their potential social, economic, and environmental
    consequences. At a minimum, operating administrations should have
    staff capabilities adequate to evaluate environmental assessments
    and environmental documents so that DOT can take responsibility
    for their content. Secretarial Offices may request assistance from
    P-30. If the necessary disciplines are not represented on the staff
    of the administration, the responsible official should obtain pro-
    fessional services from other Federal, State or local agencies,
    universities, or consulting firms.

d. Preparation of Draft. Draft EISs shall be prepared concurrently
    with and integrated with environmental analyses required by other
    environmental review laws and executive orders. To the maximum
    extent possible, the EIS process shall be used to coordinate all
    studies, reviews and consultations. (See CEQ 1502.25.) The draft
    EIS should reflect the result of the scoping/early consultation
    process. Further guidance on compliance with the various environ-
    mental statutes is included in Attachment 2.

e. Format and Content. Further guidance on the format and content
    of EISs is provided in Attachment 2.

f. Circulation of the Draft Environmental Impact Statement.

    (1) The originating operating administration or Secretarial Office
         shall circulate the draft environmental statement or summary
         to the parties indicated in paragraph 8 below. Copies of the
         draft EIS should be filed with the Environmental Protection
         Agency (EPA). (See also CEQ 1506.9 and 1506.10.)

(2)   If a State agency with statewide jurisdiction is functioning as a joint lead agency and has prepared the draft EIS, the draft statement may be circulated by the State agency after the operating administration has approved it.

g.   Tiering. Tiering of EISs as discussed in CEO 1502.20 is encouraged when it will improve or simplify the environmental processing of proposed DOT actions. Preparation of tiered EISs should be considered for complex transportation proposals (e.g. major urban transportation investments, airport master plans, aid to navigation systems, etc.) or for a number of discrete but closely related Federal actions. The first tier EIS should focus on broad issues such as mode choice, general location and areawide air quality and land use implications of the alternative transportation improvements. System planning activities should encompass environmental studies, as noted in subparagraph 3.a., and the first tier EISs should use information from these system planning studies and appropriate corridor planning and other planning studies. A second tier, site specific EIS should focus on more detailed project impacts and detailed mitigation measures (e.g. addressing detailed location, transit station locations, highway interchange configurations, etc.).

8.   INVITING COMMENTS ON THE DRAFT EIS.

The draft EIS shall be circulated with an invitation to comment to (1) all agencies having jurisdiction by law or special expertise with respect to the environmental impact involved; (2) interested parties; (3) EPA Office of Federal Activities; (4) the Assistant Secretary for Policy and International Affairs (P-1); and (5) other elements of DOT, where appropriate. A reasonable number of copies shall be provided to permit agencies and interested parties to comment expeditiously.

a.   State and Local Review.

(1)   Review of the proposed action by State and local agencies, when appropriate, shall be obtained as follows:

(a)   Where review of draft Federal development projects, and of projects assisted under programs listed in Attachment D to revised OMB Circular A-95 (as implemented by DOT 4600.4C, Evaluation, Review and Coordination of DOT Assistance Programs and Projects, of 4-12-79), takes place prior to preparation of a draft environmental statement, comments of the reviewing agencies on the environmental effects of the proposed project shall be attached to the environmental statement. Copies of the draft and final environmental statements shall be sent to clearinghouses and to the applicant whose project is the subject of the statement.

(b) Project applicants or administrations shall obtain comments directly from appropriate State and local agencies, except where review is secured by agreement through A-95 clearinghouses. Comments shall be solicited from all affected local governments.

(2) At the time a draft or final environmental statement is filed with EPA, the availability of the statement should be announced through advertisements in local newspapers and other effective methods. Copies of EISs shall be provided to the public upon request and made available at appropriate public places.

b. Review of EISs Prepared Pursuant to Section 102(2)(D) of NEPA. If the draft EIS is prepared by a State agency with statewide jurisdiction, and the proposed action will affect another State or Federal land management entity, the draft EIS shall be circulated to the affected State or Federal land management entity.

9. REVIEW OF ENVIRONMENTAL STATEMENTS PREPARED BY OTHER AGENCIES.

The purpose of DOT review and comment on environmental statements drafted by other agencies is to provide a competent and cooperative advisory and consultative service.

a.   Comments should be limited to the impacts on areas within the Department's functional responsibility, jurisdiction by law or expertise.

b.   DOT projects that are environmentally or functionally related to the action proposed in the EIS should be identified so that inter-relationships can be discussed in the final statement. In such cases, the DOT agency should consider serving as a joint lead agency or cooperating agency.

c.   Other agencies will generally be requested to forward their draft environmental statements directly to the appropriate regional offices of the Department. There are several types of proposals, however, that should be referred by regional offices to Departmental headquarters for comment. These generally include the following:

     (1)   Actions with national policy implications;

     (2)   Legislation, regulations having national impacts, or national program proposals.

     Draft EISs in these categories are to be referred to P-1 for preparation of DOT comments and, where appropriate, to the headquarters of the operating administrations. In referring these matters to headquarters, the regional office is encouraged to prepare a proposed Departmental response.

d.   Draft EISs for actions which have impact on only one region or which do not fall within subparagraph c. above should be reviewed by regional offices of DOT administrations. Comments should be forwarded directly to the office designated by the originating agency. If the receiving office believes that another DOT office is in a better position to respond, it should send the statement to that office. If more than one administration is commenting at the regional level, the comments shall be coordinated by the Regional Representative or a designee.

e.   When appropriate, the commenting office should coordinate a response with other Departmental offices having special expertise in the subject matter. For example, comments on projects affecting the transportation of hazardous materials or natural gas and liquid-products pipelines should be coordinated with the Research and Special Programs Administration, Materials Transportation Bureau, and water resources projects should be coordinated with the U.S. Coast Guard, Ports and Waterways Planning Staff (G-WS/73).

f.   Copies of comments on another agency's EIS shall be provided to the requesting agency, to P-1, and to the Regional Representative if the comment is prepared by a regional office.

10.   PREDECISION REFERRALS TO THE COUNCIL ON ENVIRONMENTAL QUALITY.

The following specific procedures apply to referrals involving DOT elements:

a.   DOT Lead Agency Proposals.

(1)   An operating administration or Secretarial Office receiving a notice of intended referral from another agency with respect to a proposed DOT action shall provide P-30 with a copy of the notice. Every effort should be made to resolve the issues raised by the referring agency prior to processing the final EIS. These efforts should be documented in the EIS. P-1 will be available to assist in any such resolution, and should be notified of the results.

(2)   In the event of an actual referral, the lead agency shall obtain P-1's concurrence in the response to CEQ.

b.   DOT Referrals to CEQ on other Agencies' Proposals.

(1)   If upon reviewing a draft from another Federal agency, an operating administration or Secretarial Office believes a referral will be necessary, it should so advise P-30. If P-30 agrees, it will advise the lead agency that DOT intends to refer the proposal to CEQ unless the proposal is changed. P-30 will coordinate DOT comments on the draft EIS, including the notice of intended referral.

(2)   Environmental referrals should be avoided, where possible,
       through efforts to resolve the issues, after providing notice of
       intent to refer and prior to the lead agency's filing the final
       EIS.

(3)   In the event that the issues have not been resolved prior to
       filing of the final EIS with EPA, P-1 will deliver a referral to
       CEQ not later than 25 calendar days after the final EIS is
       made available to EPA, commenting agencies, and the public.

    (a)   Operating administrations and Secretarial Offices should
               submit proposed referrals to P-1 at least 5 days prior to
               the 25-day deadline. The proposed referral should
               include the information specified in section 1504.3(c) of
               the CEQ regulations.

    (b)   P-1 will inform the lead agency of the referral and the
               reasons for it, including a copy of the detailed statement
               developed pursuant to section 1504.3(c).

11.   **FINAL ENVIRONMENTAL IMPACT STATEMENTS.**

    a.   **Preparation.** The final EIS shall identify the preferred alternative,
             including measures to mitigate adverse impacts. In identifying the
             preferred alternative, the DOT element should consider the policies
             stated in paragraph 2 above. Every effort should be made to resolve
             significant issues raised through circulation of the draft EIS, the
             community involvement process and consultation with cooperating
             agencies before the EIS is put into final form for approval by the
             responsible official. The final statement shall reflect such issues,
             consultation and efforts to resolve the issues, including an explana-
             tion of why any remaining issues have not been resolved.

    b.   **Compliance with other Requirements.** The final EIS should reflect
             that there has been compliance with the requirements of all
             applicable environmental laws and orders, e.g. section 4(f)
             of the DOT Act, section 106 of the Historic Preservation Act,
             section 404 of the Clean Water Act, section 7 of the
             Endangered Species Act, the DOT Floodplain Management Order (5650.2)
             and the DOT Wetlands Order (5660.1A). If such compliance
             is not possible by the time of final EIS preparation, the EIS
             should reflect consultation with the appropriate agencies and
             provide reasonable assurance that the requirements can be met.

c.   Legal Review. All final environmental statements shall be reviewed for legal sufficiency by the Chief Counsel of the operating administration concerned, or by a designee. Final environmental statements prepared within the Office of the Secretary (OST) shall be reviewed for legal sufficiency by the General Counsel (C-I).

d.   Approval. Final environmental impact statements may be approved by the Administrator or Secretarial Officer (or a designee) originating the action. For highly controversial final EIS's that require approval or concurrence by the headquarters of the operating administration pursuant to Administration procedures for approval, P-I and C-I shall be notified that the final EIS is under review and will be provided a copy of the summary section contained in the final EIS. P-I and C-I will also be given at least two weeks notice before approval of the final environmental impact statement. For purposes of this paragraph a proposed Federal action is considered highly controversial when the action is opposed on environmental grounds by a Federal, state, or local government agency or by a substantial number of the persons affected by such action.

e.   Availability Pending Approval. Following the initial level of approval by the administration (for example, by the FHWA Division Administrator), proposed final statements should normally be made available for inspection during usual business hours by the public and Federal, State or local agencies. Such statements should carry a notation that the statement is not approved and filed.

f.   Availability of Statements to EPA and the Public. After approval, the originating office shall transmit copies of each final statement to EPA in accordance with instructions from EPA. The originating office shall send copies of the final statement to the applicant, P-I all Federal, State, and local agencies and private organizations which commented substantively on the draft statement or requested copies of the final statement, and to individuals who requested copies.

g.   <u>Implementation of Representations in Environmental Statements.</u> The administrations shall assure, through funding agreements and project review procedures, that applicants carry out any actions to minimize adverse environmental effects set forth in the approved statement. Any significant deviation from prescribed action that may reduce protection to the environment must be submitted for concurrence in accordance with Administration procedures for final EIS approval.

h.   <u>Supplemental Statements.</u> The responsible official shall supplement a draft EIS when either: (1) it is determined that a reasonable alternative which is significantly different from alternatives considered in the draft EIS exists and will be considered, or (2) when environmental conditions or data change significantly from those presented in the statement. A final EIS shall be supplemented when substantial changes are made in the proposed action, when conditions or data change significantly from that presented in the statement, or if the responsible official determines that a supplement is necessary for some other reason. (The development of additional data as a proposal moves through the implementation process would not require a supplement if the data does not materially conflict with the data in the EIS.) A supplemental EIS may be prepared to address detailed information which was not available at the time an EIS was prepared and approved, for example, site or project specific impacts which have been discussed only in general terms in a corridor or program EIS. (See also CEQ 1502.20 and paragraph 7.g.) A supplemental statement should be prepared, circulated and approved in accordance with the provisions of the CEQ regulations and paragraphs 7, 8, and 11 of this Order, unless the responsible official believes there are compelling reasons to do otherwise. In such cases, the operating administration or Secretarial Office should consult with CEQ.

12.   <u>DETERMINATIONS UNDER SECTION 4(f) OF THE DOT ACT.</u>

a.   Any action having more than a minimal effect on lands protected under section 4(f) of the DOT Act will normally require the preparation of an environmental statement. In these cases, the environmental statement shall include the material required by paragraph 4 of Attachment 2. If in the preparation of the final EIS, it is concluded that there is no feasible and prudent alternative to the use of section 4(f) lands, the final EIS shall support a specific determination to that effect, including evidence that there has been all possible planning to minimize harm to the protected lands.

DOT 5610.1C   Page 15
9-18-79

b.   If an environmental statement is not required, the material called for in paragraph 4 of Attachment 2 shall be set forth in a separate document, accompanied by a FONSI or a determination that the section 4(f) involvement is minimal and that the action is categorically excluded. The section 4(f) determination shall be reviewed for legal sufficiency by the Chief Counsel of the operating administration involved, or by a designee. The document must reflect consultation with the Department of the Interior, and where appropriate, the Departments of Agriculture or Housing and Urban Development.

13.   RESPONSIBILITY.

Where an operating administration or Secretarial Office serves as lead agency or joint lead agency, it shall be responsible for the scope, objectivity, accuracy and content of EISs and environmental assessments. The EIS or environmental assessment shall be prepared by the operating administration or secretarial office, by a contractor selected by DOT, or by the applicant, pursuant to the provisions of CEQ 1506.2 and 1506.5. In developing implementing instructions, administrations shall note the distinctions made in the CEQ regulations between State agencies with statewide jurisdiction, State and local agencies which must comply with State or local requirements comparable to NEPA, and other applicants. State and local governments with requirements comparable to NEPA are listed in Attachment 1.

14.   CITIZEN INVOLVEMENT PROCEDURES.

a.   Citizen involvement in the environmental assessment of Departmental actions is encouraged at each appropriate stage of development of the proposed action and should be sought as early as possible. Citizen involvement in the environmental process should be integrated with other citizen involvement procedures to the maximum extent possible. Attempts should be made to solicit the views of the public through hearings, personal contact, press releases, advertisements or notices in newspapers, including minority or foreign language papers, if appropriate, and other methods. A summary of citizen involvement and any environmental issues raised should be documented in the EIS.

b.   The administrations' implementing instructions shall provide (1) that interested parties and Federal, State, and local agencies receive early notification of the decision to prepare an environmental impact statement, including publication of a notice of intent in the Federal Register, and (2) that their comments on the environmental effects of the proposed Federal action are solicited at an early stage in the preparation of the draft impact statement.

c. Administrations are encouraged to develop lists of interested parties at the national, State and local levels. These would include individuals and community, environmental, conservation, public service, education, labor, or business organizations, who are affected by or known to have an interest in the project, or who can speak knowledgeably on the environmental impact of the proposed action.

d. Under OMB Circular A-95, (Revised) Evaluation, Review, and Coordination of Federal Assistance Programs and Projects, and DOT 4600.4C, Evaluation, Review and Coordination of DOT Assistance Programs and Projects, of 4-12-76, a grant applicant must notify the clearinghouse of its intention to apply for Federal program assistance. The administrations' implementing instructions should provide for the solicitation of comments from the clearinghouse on the environmental consequences of the proposed action.

e. Hearings.

    (1) In several instances, a public hearing is required by statute as a condition to Federal approval of a proposed action. Even where not required by statute, an informational hearing or meeting may serve as a useful forum for public involvement.

    (2) If a public hearing is to be held, the draft EIS or environmental assessment (or environmental analysis where the hearing is held by an applicant which is not a joint lead agency) should be made available to the public at least 30 days prior to the hearing.

f. Interested persons can get information on the DOT environmental process and on the status of EISs issued by the Office of the Secretary from: Deputy Director for Environment and Policy Review (P-32), Department of Transportation, Washington, D.C. 20590, telephone 202- 426-4361.

Each administration shall indicate in its implementing instructions where interested persons can get information or status reports on EISs and other elements of the NEPA process.

15. **PROPOSALS FOR LEGISLATION.**

   a. **Preparation.** An EIS shall be prepared and circulated for any
       legislative proc   or for any favorable report on proposed legislation,
       for which DOT is primarily responsible and which involves significant
       environmental impacts. The administration or Secretarial Office
       originating the legislation or developing the Departmental position
       on the report shall prepare the EIS.

   b. **Processing.** The draft EIS shall be cleared with P-1 and submitted
       by the Assistant General Counsel for Legislation (C-40) to the
       Office of Management and Budget for circulation in the normal
       legislative clearance process. The EIS shall be transmitted to
       Congress no later than 30 days after transmittal of the legislative
       proposal, and must be available in time for Congressional hearings.
       Any comments received on the EIS shall be transmitted to Congress.
       Except as provided by CEQ 1506.8(b)(2), there need not be a final
       EIS.

16. **INTERNATIONAL ACTIONS.**

   a. Pursuant to Executive Order 12114, Environmental Effects Abroad of Major
       Federal Actions, the requirements of this Order apply to:

      (1) Major Federal actions significantly affecting the environment
           of the global commons outside the jurisdiction of any nation
           (e.g. the oceans and Antarctica).

      (2) Major Federal actions significantly affecting the environment
           of a foreign nation not participating in the action or otherwise
           involved in the action.

      (3) Major Federal actions significantly affecting the environment
           of a foreign nation which provide a product or a project
           producing a toxic emission or effluent, which is prohibited
           or strictly regulated in the U.S. by Federal law.

      (4) Major Federal actions outside the U.S., its territories and posses-
           sions which significantly affect natural resources of global importance
           designated for protection by the President or by international agreement.

   b. If communication with a foreign government concerning environmental studies
       or documentation is anticipated, the responsible Federal official
       shall coordinate such communication with the State Department,
       through P-1.

17.   TIMING OF AGENCY ACTION.

A decision on the proposed action may not be made sooner than the times specified in CEQ 1506.10(b).

a.   Requests for reasonable extensions of the review period for the draft EISs shall be granted whenever possible, and particularly when warranted by the magnitude and complexity of the statement or the extent of citizen interest.

b.   If an administration or Secretarial Office believes it is necessary to reduce the prescribed time periods for EIS processing, it should request such a reduction from EPA. P-32 should be notified of such a request.

c.   Where emergency circumstances make it necessary to take an action with significant environmental impacts without observing the provisions of this Order and the CEQ regulations, the administration or Secretarial Office should consult with CEQ. P-32 should be notified of such consultation.

18.   EFFECTIVE DATE.

a.   This Order and attachments apply to all draft statements filed by DOT with EPA after 7-30-79, except as provided in paragraph 1506.12 of the CEQ regulations.

b.   For final statements whose drafts are filed by 7-30-79 (for FHWA, 11-30-79), paragraph 11 of this Order applies after 7-30-81. In the interim, final EISs shall be processed in accordance with the provisions of DOT 5610.1B.

19.   TIME IN EFFECT OF STATEMENTS.

a.   The draft EIS may be assumed valid for a period of three years. If the proposed final EIS is not submitted to the approving official within three years from the date of the draft EIS circulation, a written reevaluation of the draft shall be prepared by the responsible Federal official to determine whether the consideration of alternatives, impacts, existing environment and mitigation measures set forth in the draft EIS remain applicable, accurate and valid. If there have been changes in these factors which would be significant in the consideration of the proposed action, a supplement to the draft EIS or a new draft statement shall be prepared and circulated.

DOT 5610.1C
9-18-79

b. If major steps toward implementation of the proposed action (such as the start of construction or substantial acquisition and relocation activities) have not commenced within three years from the date of approval of the final EIS, a written reevaluation of the adequacy, accuracy and validity of the EIS shall be prepared by the responsible Federal official unless tiering of EISs (as discussed in subparagraph 7.g.) is being used. If there have been significant changes in the proposed action, the affected environment, anticipated impacts, or proposed mitigation measures, a new or supplemental EIS shall be prepared and circulated.

c. If major steps toward implementation of the proposed action have not occurred within five years from the date of approval of the final EIS, or within the time frame set forth in the final EIS, the responsible Federal official shall prepare a written reevaluation of the adequacy, accuracy, and validity of the EIS. This reevaluation shall be processed in accordance with subparagraph 11.d.

d. If the proposed action is to be implemented in phases or requires successive Federal approvals, a written reevaluation of the continued adequacy, accuracy and validity of the EIS shall be made prior to Federal approval of each major stage which occurs more than three years after approval of the final EIS, and a new or supplemental EIS prepared, if necessary.

20. <u>IMPLEMENTING INSTRUCTIONS.</u>

a. Operating administrations shall issue instructions implementing this Order using one of the following options:

(1) An operating administration may issue detailed instructions or regulations which incorporate the points of this Order and the CEQ regulations and provide guidance on applying the environmental process to the administration's programs; or

(2) An operating administration may rely on this Order as its implementing procedures, provided it issues supplementary guidance which at a minimum applies the environmental process to the administration's programs, as described in the following subparagraph.

b. Implementing instructions shall include the following information:

   (1) A list of actions which normally require preparation of an EIS.

   (2) A list of actions which are not normally major Federal actions
        significantly affecting the environment and as such do not
        normally require an environmental assessment or an environ-
        mental impact statement (i.e. categorical exclusions). These
        actions may include, but are not limited to, funding or
        authorizing: maintenance and modernization of existing
        facilities; minor safety improvements; equipment purchases;
        operating expenses; and planning grants which do not imply a
        project commitment. Instructions should provide for prepara-
        tion of environmental assessments or EISs, as appropriate, for
        actions which would otherwise be classified as categorically
        excluded, but which are likely to involve: (1) significant
        impacts on the environment; (2) substantial controversy;
        (3) impacts which are more than minimal on properties
        protected by section 4(f) and section 106 of the Historic
        Preservation Act; or (4) inconsistencies with any Federal,
        State, or local law or administrative determination relating
        to the environment.

   (3) Identification of the decision making process, including timing
        for preparation of a draft and final environmental statement
        or a FONSI and designation of officials responsible for
        providing information on the administration's preparation,
        review and approval of environmental documents.

   (4) A description of the public participation process or reference
        to other administration guidance on the public participation
        process. (See paragraph 14, public participation.)

   (5) A description of the processes to be used to insure early
        involvement of DOT, other agencies and the public in the
        environmental review of actions proposed by nonfederal appli-
        cants (CEQ 1501.2(d)).

   (6) A description of the procedures for assuring implementation
        of mitigation measures identified in the EIS and the record
        of decision.

c.   Proposed implementing instructions and any substantial amendments thereto shall be submitted to P-1 for review and concurrence. Consultation with CEQ will be assisted by P-1. Proposed and final implementing instructions shall be published in the Federal Register.

21.   <u>RESPONSIBLE OFFICIAL FOR OFFICE OF THE SECRETARY ACTIONS</u>. For the actions originating within the Office of the Secretary, the official responsible for approval of environmental documents is the Office Director of the office originating the action. The Director, Office of Transportation Regulatory Affairs, is responsible for general oversight and advice on environmental matters in liaison with the Assistant General Counsel for Environmental, Civil Rights, and General Law.

FOR THE SECRETARY OF TRANSPORTATION:

Robert L. Fairman
Deputy Assistant Secretary
for Administration

STATES AND LOCALITIES WITH EIS REQUIREMENTS

1.   States with Comprehensive Statutory Requirements:

      California
      Connecticut
      Hawaii
      Indiana
      Maryland
      Massachusetts
      Minnesota
      Montana
      New York
      New Jersey
      North Carolina
      South Dakota
      Virginia
      Washington
      Wisconsin
      Puerto Rico

2.   States with Comprehensive Executive or Administrative Orders:

      Michigan
      New Jersey
      Texas
      Utah

3.   Local EIS requirements:

      Bowie, Maryland
      New York, New York

Source:

      Memorandum for NEPA Liaisons from the Council on Environmental Quality,
      on agency implementing procedures under CEQ's NEPA regulations, dated
      January 19, 1979.   (Appendix D)

FORMAT AND CONTENT OF ENVIRONMENTAL IMPACT STATEMENTS

1.   Format.

    a.   The format recommended in CEQ 1502.10 should be used for DOT
        EISs:

        (a)   Cover Sheet
        (b)   Summary
        (c)   Table of Contents
        (d)   Purpose and Need for the Action
        (e)   Alternatives Including the Proposed Action
        (f)   Affected Environment
        (g)   Environmental Consequences
        (h)   List of Preparers
        (i)   List of Agencies, Organizations, and Persons to Whom Copies
             of the Statement Are Sent
        (j)   Index
        (k)   Appendices (if any)

    b.   The cover sheet for each environmental impact statement will
        include the information identified in CEQ 1502.11 and will be headed
        as follows:

                  Department of Transportation

                _____
                  (operating administration)

        (Draft/Final) Environmental Impact Statement
          Pursuant to Section 102(2)(C), P.L. 91-190

        As appropriate, the heading will indicate that the EIS also covers
        the requirements of section 4(f) of the DOT Act, section 14 of
        the Mass Transportation Act, and/or sections 16 and 18(a)(4) of
        the Airport Act.

2.   Guidance as to Content of Statements.

   a.   Environmental impact statements shall include the information
         specified in CEQ 1502.11 through 1502.18. The following paragraphs
         of Attachment 2 are intended to be considered, where relevant,
         as guidance regarding the content of environmental statements.

   b.   Additional information contained in research reports, guidance
         on methodology, and other materials relating to consideration
         of environmental factors should be employed as appropriate in
         the preparation of EISs and environmental assessments. Examples
         of such materials include:

            U.S. Department of Transportation, Environmental Assessment
            Notebook Series: Highways, 1975, Report No. DOT P 5600.4,
            available from the U.S. Government Printing Office, Washington,
            D.C. 20402, Stock Number 050-000-00109-1;

            U.S. DOT, Environmental Assessment Notebook Series:
            Airports, 1978, Report Number DOT P 5600.5, available from
            the U.S. Government Printing Office, Washington, D.C.
            20402, Stock Number 050-000-00138-5;

            U.S. DOT, FAA, Environmental Assessment of Airport Development
            Actions, 1977, available from the National Technical Information
            Service, 5284 Port Royal Road, Springfield, Virginia 22161,
            NTIS Catalog Number ADA-039274; and

            U.S. DOT, Guidelines for Assessing the Environmental Impact
            of Public Mass Transportation Projects, 1979, Report Number
            DOT P 79 001, available from the National Technical Information
            Service, Springfield, Virginia 22161.

3.   General Content. The following points are to be covered.

   a.   A description of the proposed Federal action (e.g. "The proposed
         Federal action is approval of location of highway..." or "The proposed
         Federal action is approval of a grant application to construct..."),
         and a statement of its purpose.

   b.   Alternatives, including the proposed action, and including, where
         relevant, those alternatives not within the existing authority of
         the responsible preparing office. Section 102(2)(E) of NEPA requires
         the responsible agency to "study, develop, and describe appropriate
         alternatives to recommended courses of action in any proposal
         which involves unresolved conflicts concerning alternative uses

of available resources." A rigorous exploration and an objective evaluation of the environmental impacts of all reasonable alternative actions, particularly those that might enhance environmental quality or avoid some or all of the adverse environmental effects, are essential. Sufficient analysis of such alternatives and their environmental benefits, costs, and risks should accompany the proposed action through the review process in order not to foreclose prematurely options which might enhance environmental quality or have less detrimental effects. Examples of such alternatives include: the alternative of not taking any action or of postponing action pending further study; alternatives requiring actions of a significantly different nature which would provide similar benefits with different environmental impacts, e.g. low capital intensive improvements, mass transit alternatives to highway construction; alternatives related to different locations or designs or details of the proposed action which would present different environmental impacts. In each case, the analysis should be sufficiently detailed to reveal comparative evaluation of the environmental benefits, costs, and risks of each reasonable alternative, including the proposed action. Where an existing impact statement already contains such an analysis, its treatment of alternatives may be incorporated, provided such treatment is current and relevant to the precise purpose of the proposed action.

c.   Affected environment.

(1)   The statement should succinctly describe the environment of the area affected as it exists prior to a proposed action, including other related Federal activities in the area, their interrelationships, and cumulative environmental impact. The amount of detail provided in such descriptions should be commensurate with the extent and expected impact of the action, and with the amount of information required at the particular level of decision making (planning, feasibility, design, etc.).

(2)   The statement should identify, as appropriate, population and growth characteristics of the affected area and any population and growth assumptions used to justify the project or program or to determine secondary population and growth impacts resulting from the proposed action and its alternatives (see paragraph 3e(2)). In discussing these population aspects, the statement should give consideration to using the rates of growth in the region of the project contained in the projections compiled for the Water Resources Council by the Bureau of Economic Analysis of the Department of Commerce and the Economic Research Service of the Department of Agriculture (the OBERS projection).

d. The relationship of the proposed action and how it may conform
to or conflict with adopted or proposed land use plans, policies,
controls, and goals and objectives as have been promulgated by
affected communities. Where a conflict or inconsistency exists,
the statement should describe the extent of reconciliation and
the reasons for proceeding notwithstanding the absence of full
reconciliation.

e. The probable impact of the proposed action on the environment.

   (1) This requires assessment of the positive and negative effects
        of the proposed action as it affects both national and international
        human environment. The attention given to different environmental
        factors will vary according to the nature, scale, and location
        of proposed actions. Primary attention should be given in
        the statement to discussing those factors most evidently
        impacted by the proposed action.

   (2) Secondary and other foreseeable effects, as well as primary
        consequences for the environment, should be included in
        the analysis. Secondary effects, such as impacts on existing
        community facilities and activities inducing new facilities
        and activities, may often be even more substantial than
        the primary effects of the original action itself. For example,
        the effects of the proposed action on population and growth
        may be among the more significant secondary effects. Such
        population and growth impacts should be estimated and an
        assessment made on their effects upon the resource base,
        including land use, water, and public services, of the area
        in question.

f. Any probable adverse environmental effects which cannot be avoided
(such as water or air pollution, noise, undesirable land use patterns,
or impacts on public parks and recreation areas, wildlife and waterfowl
refuges, or on historic sites, damage to life systems, traffic congestion,
threats to health, or other consequences adverse to the environmental
goals set out in section 101(b) of NEPA). This should be a brief
summary of those effects discussed in paragraph 3c that are adverse and
unavoidable under the proposed action. Included for purposes
of contrast should be a clear statement of how all adverse effects
will be mitigated.

g. The relationship between local short-term uses of man's environment and the maintenance and enhancement of long-term productivity. This discussion should cover the extent to which the proposed action involves tradeoffs between short-term environmental gains at the expense of long-term losses, or vice versa, and a discussion of the extent to which the proposed action forecloses future options.

h. Any irreversible and irretrievable commitments of resources that would be involved in the proposed action should it be implemented. This requires identification of unavoidable impacts and the extent to which the action irreversibly curtails the range of potential uses of the environment. "Resources" means not only the labor and materials devoted to an action but also the natural and cultural resources lost or destroyed.

i. An indication of what other interests and considerations of Federal policy are thought to offset the adverse environmental effects of the proposed action identified pursuant to subparagraphs (e) and (f) of this paragraph. The statement should also indicate the extent to which these stated countervailing benefits could be realized by following reasonable alternatives to the proposed action (as identified in subparagraph (b) of this paragraph) that would avoid some or all of the adverse environmental effects. In this connection, cost-benefit analyses of proposed actions, if prepared, should be attached, or summaries thereof, to the environmental impact statement, and should clearly indicate the extent to which environmental costs have not been reflected in such analyses.

j. A discussion of problems and objections raised by other Federal agencies, State and local entities, and citizens in the review process, and the disposition of the issues involved and the reasons therefor. (This section may be added to the final environmental statement at the end of the review process.)

    (1) The draft and final statements should document issues raised through consultations with Federal, State, and local agencies with jurisdiction or special expertise and with citizens, of actions taken in response to comments, public hearings, and other citizen involvement proceedings.

    (2) Any unresolved environmental issues and efforts to resolve them, through further consultations or otherwise, should be identified in the final statement. For instance, where

an agency comments that the statement has inadequate
analysis or that the agency has reservations concerning
the impacts, or believes that the impacts are too adverse
for approval, either the issue should be resolved or the final
statement should reflect efforts to resolve the issue and
set forth any action that will result.

(3)   The statement should reflect that every effort was made
to discover and discuss all major points of view on the environmental
effects of the proposed action and alternatives in the draft
statement. However, where opposing professional views
and responsible opinion have been overlooked in the draft
statement and are raised through the commenting process,
the environmental effects of the action should be reviewed
in light of those views. A meaningful reference should be
made in the final statement to the existence of any responsible
opposing view not adequately discussed in the draft statement
indicating responses to the issues raised.

(4)   All substantive comments received on the draft (or summaries
of responses from the public which have been exceptionally
voluminous) should be attached to the final statement, whether
or not each such comment is thought to merit individual
discussion in the text of the statement.

k.   <u>Draft statements should indicate at appropriate points in the text</u>
any underlying studies, reports, and other information obtained
and considered in preparing the statement, including any cost-
benefit analyses prepared. In the case of documents not likely
to be easily accessible (such as internal studies or reports), the
statement should indicate how such information may be obtained.
If such information is attached to the statement, care should be
taken to insure that the statement remains an essentially self-
contained instrument, capable of being understood by the reader
without the need for undue cross reference.

4.   <u>Publicly Owned Parklands, Recreational Areas, Wildlife and Waterfowl
Refuges and Historic Sites</u>. The following points are to be covered:

a.   Description of "any publicly owned land from a public park, recreational
area or wildlife and waterfowl refuge" or "any land from an historic
site" affected or taken by the project. This includes its size, available
activities, use, patronage, unique or irreplaceable qualities, relationship
to other similarly used lands in the vicinity of the project, maps,

plans, slides, photographs, and drawings showing in sufficient scale and detail the project. This also includes its impact on park, recreation, wildlife, or historic areas, and changes in vehicular or pedestrian access.

b. Statement of the "national, State or local significance" of the entire park, recreation area, refuge, or historic site "as determined by the Federal, State or local officials having jurisdiction thereof."

  (1) In the absence of such a statement, lands will be presumed to be significant. Any statement of "insignificance" by the official having jurisdiction is subject to review by the Department as to whether such statement is capricious.

  (2) Where Federal lands are administered for multiple uses, the Federal official having jurisdiction over the lands shall determine whether the subject lands are in fact being used for park, recreation, wildlife, waterfowl, or historic purposes.

c. Similar data, as appropriate, for alternative designs and locations, including detailed cost estimates (with figures showing percentage differences in total project costs) and technical feasibility, and appropriate analysis of the alternatives, including any unique problems present and evidence that the cost or community disruptions resulting from alternative routes reach extraordinary magnitudes. This portion of the statement should demonstrate compliance with the Supreme Court's statement in the <u>Overton Park</u> case, as follows:

  "The very existence of the statute indicates that the protection of parklands was to be given paramount importance. The few green havens that are public parks were not to be lost unless there were truly unusual factors present in a particular case or the cost or community disruption resulting from alternative routes reached extraordinary magnitudes. If the statutes are to have any meaning, the Secretary cannot approve the destruction of parkland unless he finds that the alternative routes present unique problems."

d. If there is no feasible and prudent alternative, description of all planning undertaken to minimize harm to the protected area and statement of actions taken or to be taken to implement this planning, including measures to maintain or enhance the natural beauty of the lands traversed.

   (1)   Measures to minimize harm may include replacement of
         land and facilities, providing land or facilities, or provision
         for functional replacement of the facility (see 49 C.F.R.
         25.267).

   (2)   Design measures to minimize harm; e.g. tunneling, cut
         and cover, cut and fill, treatment of embankments, planting,
         screening, maintenance of pedestrian or bicycle paths and
         noise mitigation measures, all reflecting utilization of appropriate
         interdisciplinary design personnel.

e.   Evidence of concurrence or description of efforts to obtain concurrence
     of Federal, State or local officials having jurisdiction over the
     section 4(f) property regarding the action proposed and the measures
     planned to minimize harm.

f.   If Federally-owned properties are involved in highway projects,
     the final statement shall include the action taken or an indication
     of the expected action after filing a map of the proposed use of
     the land or other appropriate documentation with the Secretary
     of the Department supervising the land (23 U.S.C. 317).

g.   If land acquired with Federal grant money (Department of Housing
     and Urban Development open space or Heritage Conservation
     and Recreation Service land and water conservation funds) is involved,
     the final statement shall include appropriate communications
     with the grantor agency.

h.   The General Counsel will determine application of section 4(f)
     to public interests in lands, such as easements, reversions, etc.

i.   A specific statement that there is no feasible and prudent alternative
     and that the proposal includes all possible planning to minimize
     harm to the "section 4(f) area" involved.

5.   <u>Properties and Sites of Historic and Cultural Significance</u>. The statement
     should document actions taken to preserve and enhance districts, sites,
     buildings, structures, and objects of historical, architectural, archaeological,
     or cultural significance affected by the action.

a.   Draft environmental statements should include identification, through
     consulting the State Historic Preservation Officer and the National
     Register and applying the National Register Criteria (36 C.F.R. Part 800), of
     properties that are included in or eligible for inclusion in the National Register

of Historic Places that may be affected by the project. The Secretary of the Interior will advise whether properties not listed are eligible for the National Register (36 C.F.R. Part 63).

b. If application of the Advisory Council on Historic Preservation's (ACHP) Criteria of Effect (36 C.F.R. Part 800) indicates that the project will have an effect upon a property included in or eligible for inclusion in the National Register of Historic Places, the draft environmental statement should document the effect. Evaluation of the effect should be made in consultation with the State Historic Preservation Officer (SHPO) and in accordance with the ACHP's Criteria of Adverse Effect (36 C.F.R. Part 800).

c. Determinations of no adverse effect should be documented in the draft statement with evidence of the application of the ACHP's Criteria of Adverse Effect, the views of the appropriate State Historic Preservation Officer, and submission of the determination to the ACHP for review.

d. If the project will have an adverse effect upon a property included in or eligible for inclusion in the National Register of Historic Places, the final environmental statement should include either an executed Memorandum of Agreement or comments from the Council after consideration of the project at a meeting of the ACHP and an account of actions to be taken in response to the comments of the ACHP. Procedures for obtaining a Memorandum of Agreement and the comments of the Council are found in 36.C.F.R. Part 800.

e. To determine whether the project will have an effect on properties of State or local historical, architectural, archaeological, or cultural significance not included in or eligible for inclusion in the National Register, the responsible official should consult with the State Historic Preservation Officer, with the local official having jurisdiction of the property, and, where appropriate, with historical societies, museums, or academic institutions having expertise with regard to the property. Use of land from historic properties of Federal, State and local significance as determined by the official having jurisdiction thereof involves section 4(f) of the DOT Act and documentation should include information necessary to consider a section 4(f) determination (see paragraph 4).

6.   Impacts of the Proposed Action on the Human Environment Involving
     Community Disruption and Relocation.

     a.   The statement should include a description of probable impact
          sufficient to enable an understanding of the extent of the environmental
          and social impact of the project alternatives and to consider whether
          relocation problems can be properly handled. This would include
          the following information obtainable by visual inspection of the
          proposed affected area and from secondary sources and community
          sources when available.

          (1)   An estimate of the households to be displaced including
                the family characteristics (e.g. minorities, and income levels,
                tenure, the elderly, large families).

          (2)   Impact on the human environment of an action which divides
                or disrupts an established community, including, where pertinent,
                the effect of displacement on types of families and individuals
                affected, effect of streets cut off, separation of residences
                from community facilities, separation of residential areas.

          (3)   Impact on the neighborhood and housing to which relocation
                is likely to take place (e.g. lack of sufficient housing for
                large families, doublings up).

          (4)   An estimate of the businesses to be displaced, and the general
                effect of business dislocation on the economy of the community.

          (5)   A discussion of relocation housing in the area and the ability
                to provide adequate relocation housing for the types of families
                to be displaced. If the resources are insufficient to meet
                the estimated displacement needs, a description of the actions
                proposed to remedy this situation including, if necessary,
                use of housing of last resort.

          (6)   Results of consultation with local officials and community
                groups regarding the impacts to the community affected.
                Relocation agencies and staff and other social agencies
                can help to describe probable social impacts of this proposed
                action.

          (7)   Where necessary, special relocation advisory services to be
                provided the elderly, handicapped and illiterate regarding
                interpretations of benefits, assistance in selecting replacement

housing, and consultation with respect to acquiring, leasing,
and occupying replacement housing.

b.   This data should provide the preliminary basis for assurance of the availability
     of relocation housing as required by DOT 5620.1, Replacement Housing Policy,
     dated 6-24-70, and 49 C.F.R. 25.57.

7.   Considerations Relating to Pedestrians and Bicyclists. Where appropriate,
     the statement should discuss impacts on and consideration to be given
     in the development of the project to pedestrian and bicycle access,
     movement and safety within the affected area, particularly in medium
     and high density commercial and residential areas.

8.   Other Social Impacts. The general social groups specially benefitted
     or harmed by the proposed action should be identified in the statement,
     including the following:

a.   Particular effects of a proposal on the elderly, handicapped, non-drivers, transit
     dependent, or minorities should be described to the extent reasonably
     predictable.

b.   How the proposal will facilitate or inhibit their access to jobs,
     educational facilities, religious institutions, health and welfare
     services, recreational facilities, social and cultural facilities,
     pedestrian movement facilities, and public transit services.

9.   Standards as to Noise, Air, and Water Pollution. The statement shall
     reflect sufficient analysis of the effects of the proposed action on attainment
     and maintenance of any environmental standards established by law
     or administrative determination (e.g. noise, ambient air quality, water
     quality), including the following documentation:

a.   With respect to water quality, there should be consultation with
     the agency responsible for the State water pollution control program
     as to conformity with standards and regulations regarding storm
     sewer discharge, sedimentation control, and other non-point source
     discharges.

b.   The comments or determinations of the offices charged with administration
     of the State's implementation plan for air quality as to the consistency
     of the project with State plans for the implementation of ambient
     air quality standards.

c.   Conformity to adopted noise standards, compatible, if appropriate,
     with different land uses.

10. <u>Energy Supply and Natural Resources Development</u>. Where applicable,
     the statement should reflect consideration of whether the project or
     program will have any effect on either the production or consumption
     of energy and other natural resources, and discuss such effects if they
     are significant.

11. <u>Floodplain Management Evaluation</u>. When an alternative under
     consideration encroaches on a base (100-year) floodplain, the statement
     should describe the anticipated impacts on natural and beneficial floodplain
     values, any risk to or resulting from the transportation action, and the
     degree to which the action facilitates additional development in the
     base floodplain. The necessary measures to address floodplain impacts,
     including an evaluation of alternatives to avoid the encroachment in
     appropriate cases, should be described in compliance with Executive
     Order 11988, "Floodplain Management," and DOT Order 5650.2, "Floodplain
     Management and Protection."

12. <u>Considerations Relating to Wetlands or Coastal Zones</u>. Where wetlands
     or coastal zones are involved, the statement should reflect compliance
     with Executive Order 11990, Protection of Wetlands, and DOT 5660.1A
     and should include:

     a.   Information on location, types, and extent of wetlands areas which
          might be affected by the proposed action.

     b.   An assessment of the impacts resulting from both construction
          and operation of the project on the wetlands and associated wildlife,
          and measures to minimize adverse impacts.

     c.   A statement by the local representative of the Department of
          the Interior, and any other responsible officials with special expertise,
          setting forth his views on the impacts of the project on the wetlands,
          the worth of the particular wetlands areas involved to the community
          and to the Nation, and recommendtions as to whether the proposed
          action should proceed, and, if applicable, along what alternative
          route.

     d.   Where applicable, a discussion of how the proposed project relates
          to the State coastal zone management program for the particular
          State in which the project is to take place.

13.   <u>Construction Impacts</u>. In general, adverse impacts during construction will be of less importance than long-term impacts of a proposal. Nonetheless, statements should appropriately address such matters as the following, identifying any special problem areas:

    a.   Noise impacts from construction and any specifications setting maximum noise levels.

    b.   Disposal of spoil and effect on borrow areas and disposal sites (include specifications where special problems are involved).

    c.   Measures to minimize effects on traffic and pedestrians.

14.   <u>Land Use and Urban Growth</u>. The statement should include, to the extent relevant and predictable:

    a.   The effect of the project on land use, development patterns, and urban growth.

    b.   Where significant land use and development impacts are anticipated, identify public facilities needed to serve the new development and any problems or issues which would arise in connection with these facilities, and the comments of agencies that would provide these facilities.

15.   (Deleted)

16.   <u>Projects under Section 14 of the Mass Transportation Act: Mass Transit Projects with a Significant Impact on the Quality of the Human Environment</u>: The statement should include:

    a.   Evidence of the opportunity that was afforded for the presentation of views by all parties with a significant economic, social or environmental interest.

    b.   Evidence that fair consideration has been given to the preservation and enhancement of the environment and to the interests of the community in which the project is located.

    c.   If there is an adverse environmental effect and there is no feasible and prudent alternative, description of all planning undertaken to minimize such adverse environmental effect and statement of actions taken or to be taken to implement the planning; or a specific statement that there is no adverse environmental effect.

Policy Guidance

Preamble to Proposed CEQ NEPA Regulations
(Council on Environmental Quality May 31, 1978)
43 Fed. Reg. 25230 (June 9, 1978)

MAY 31, 1978.

AGENCY: Council on Environmental Quality, Executive Office of the President.

ACTION: Proposed regulations.

SUMMARY: These proposed regulations implementing procedural provisions of the National Environmental Policy Act are submitted for public comment. These regulations would provide Federal agencies with uniform procedures for implementing the law. The regulations would accomplish three principal aims: to reduce paperwork, to reduce delays, and to produce better decisions.

DATES: Comments must be received by August 11, 1978.

ADDRESSES: Comments should be addressed to: Nicholas C. Yost, General Counsel, Attention: NEPA Comments, Council on Environmental Quality, 722 Jackson Place NW., Washington, D.C. 20006.

FOR FURTHER INFORMATION CONTACT:

Nicholas C. Yost, General Council on Environmental Quality (address same as above), 202-633-7032.

SUPPLEMENTARY INFORMATION:

1. PURPOSE

We are publishing for public review draft regulations to implement the National Environmental Policy Act. Their purpose is to provide all Federal agencies with an efficient, uniform procedure for translating the law into practical action. We expect the new regulations to accomplish three principal aims: To reduce paperwork, to reduce delays, and at the same time to produce better decisions, thereby better accomplishing the law's objective, which is to protect and enhance the quality of the human environment.

These regulations replace the Guidelines issued by previous Councils, under Executive Order 11514 (1970), and apply more broadly. The Guidelines assist Federal agencies in carrying out NEPA's most conspicuous requirement, the preparation of environmental impact statements (EISs). These regulations were developed in response to Executive Order 11991 issued by President Carter in 1977, and implement "the procedural provisions of the Act." They address all nine subdivisions of Section 102(2) of the Act, rather than just the EIS provision covered by the Guidelines, and they carry out the broad purposes and spirit of the Act.

President Carter instructed us that the regulations should be:

* * * designed to make the environmental impact statement more useful to decision-makers and the public; and to reduce paperwork and the accumulation of extraneous background data, in order to emphasize the need to focus on real environmental issues and alternatives.

The President has also signed Executive Order 12044, dealing with regulatory reform. It is our intention that that Order and these NEPA regulations be read together and implemented consistently.

2. SUMMARY OF CHANGES MADE BY THE REGULATIONS

Following this mandate in developing the new regulations, we have kept in mind the threefold objective of less paperwork, less delay, and better decisions.

A. REDUCING PAPERWORK

The measures to reduce paperwork are listed in sec. 1500.4 of the regulations. Neither NEPA nor these regulations impose paperwork requirements on the public. These regulations reduce such requirements on agencies of government.

i. *Reducing the length of environmental impact statements.* Agencies are directed to write concise EISs, which shall normally be less than 150 pages, or, for proposals of unusual scope and complexity, 300 pages.

ii. *Emphasize options among alternatives.* The regulations stress that the environmental analysis is to concentrate on alternatives, which are the heart of the matter; to treat peripheral matters briefly; and to avoid accumulating masses of background data which tend to obscure the important issues.

iii. *Using an early "scoping" process to determine what the important issues are.* To assist agencies in deciding what the central issues are, how long the EIS shall be, and how the responsibility for the EIS will be allocated among the lead agency and cooperating agencies, a new "scoping" procedure is established. Scoping meetings are to be held as early in the NEPA process as possible—in most cases, shortly after the decision to prepare an EIS—and shall be integrated with other planning.

iv. *Writing in plain language.* The regulations strongly advocate writing in plain, direct language.

v. *Following a clear format.* The regulations spell out a standard format intended to eliminate repetitive discussion, stress the major conclusions, highlight the areas of controversy, and focus on the issues to be resolved.

vi. *Requiring summaries of environmental impact statements* to make the document more usable by more people.

vii. *Eliminating duplication.* To eliminate duplication, the regulations provide for Federal agencies to prepare EISs jointly with state and local units of government which have "little NEPA" requirements. They also permit a Federal agency to adopt another agency's EIS.

viii. *Consistent terminology.* The regulations provide a uniform terminology for the implementation of NEPA. For instance, the CEQ requirement for an environmental assessment will replace the following (nonexhaustive) list of comparable existing agency procedures: "survey" (Corps of Engineers), "environmental analysis" (Forest Service), "initial assessment" (Transportation), "normal or special clearance" (HUD), "environmental analysis report" (Interior), and "marginal impact statement" (HEW).)

ix. *Reducing paperwork requirements.* The regulations will reduce reporting paperwork requirements as summarized below. The existing Guidelines issued under Executive Order 11514 cover section 102(2)(C) of NEPA (environmental impact statements), and the new CEQ regulations cover sections 102(2) (A) through (I). The regulations replace not only the requirements of the Guidelines concerning environmental impact statements, but also replace more than 70 different sets of existing agency regulations, although each agency will issue its own implementing procedures to explain how these regulations apply to its particular programs.

Existing Requirements (Applicable Guidelines sections are noted.)	New Requirements (Applicable regulations sections are noted.)
Assessment (optional under Guidelines on a case-by-case basis; currently required, however by most major agencies in practice or in procedures) 1500.6.	*Assessment* (limited requirement: not required where there would not be environmental effects or where an EIS would normally be required) 1501.3, .4.
Notice of intent to prepare impact statement 1500.6.	*Notice of intent* to prepare EIS and commence scoping process 1501.7
Quarterly list of notices of intent 1500.6.	Requirement abolished.
Negative determination (decision not to prepare impact, statement) 1500.6.	*Finding of no significant impact* 1501.4.
Quarterly list of negative determinations 1500.6.	Requirement abolished.
Draft EIS 1500.7	*Draft EIS* 1502.9
Final EIS 1500.6, .10	*Final EIS* 1502.9
EISs on legislative reports ("agency reports on legislation initiated elsewhere") 1500.5(a)(1).	Requirement abolished.
Agency report to CEQ on implementation experience 1500.14(b).	Do.

Existing Requirements (Applicable Guidelines sections are noted.)	New Requirements (Applicable regulations sections are noted.)
Agency report to CEQ on substantive guidance 1500.6(c), .14.	Do.
Record of decision (no Guideline provision but required by many agencies' own procedures and in a wide range of cases generally under the Administrative Procedure Act and OMB Circular A-95, Part I, sec. 6(c) and (d), Part II, sec. 5(b)(4)).	*Record of decision* (brief explanation of decision EIS has been prepared; no circulation requirement) 1505.2.

B. REDUCING DELAY

The measures to reduce delay are listed in § 1500.5 of the regulations.

i. *Time limits on the NEPA process.* The regulations encourage lead agencies to set time limits on the NEPA process and require that they be set when requested by an applicant.

ii. *Integrating EIS requirements with other environmental review requirements.* Often the NEPA process and the requirements of other laws proceed separately, causing delay. The regulations provide for all agencies with jurisdiction over the project to cooperate so that all reviews may be conducted simultaneously.

iii. *Integrating the NEPA process into early planning.* If environmental review is tacked on to the end of the planning process, then the process is prolonged, or else the EIS is written to justify a decision that has already been made, and genuine consideration may not be given to environmental factors.

iv. *Emphasizing interagency cooperation before the EIS is drafted.* The regulations emphasize that other agencies should begin cooperating with the lead agency before the EIS is prepared in order to encourage early resolution of differences. By having the affected agencies cooperate early in preparing a draft EIS, we hope both to produce a better draft and to reduce delays caused by unnecessarily late criticism.

v. *Swift and fair resolution of lead agency disputes.* When agencies differ as to who shall take the lead in preparing an EIS or none is willing to take the lead, the regulations provide a means for prompt resolution of the dispute.

vi. *Prepare EISs on programs and not repeat the same material in project specific EISs.* Material common to many actions may be covered in a broad EIS, and then through "tiering" may be incorporated by reference rather than reiterated in each subsequent EIS.

vii. *Legal delays.* The regulations provide that litigation should come at the end rather than in the middle of the process.

viii. *Accelerated procedures for legislative proposals.* The regulations provide accelerated simplified procedures for environmental analysis of legislative proposals, to fit better with Congressional schedules.

C. BETTER DECISIONS

Most of the features described above will help to improve decisionmaking. This, of course, is the fundamental purpose of the NEPA process, the end to which the EIS is a means. Section 101 of NEPA sets forth the substantive requirements of the Act, the policy to be implemented by the "action-forcing" procedures of Section 102. These procedures must be tied to their intended purpose, otherwise they are indeed useless paper work and wasted time. A central purpose of these regulations is to tie means to ends.

i. *Securing more accurate, professional documents.* The regulations insist upon accurate documents as the basis for sound decisions. The documents should draw upon all the appropriate disciplines from the natural and social sciences, plus the environmental design arts. The lead agency is responsible for the professional integrity of reports, and care should be taken to keep any possible bias from data prepared by applicants out of the environmental analysis. A list of people who helped prepare documents, and their professional qualifications, should be included in the EIS.

ii. *Recording in the decision how the EIS was used.* The new regulations require agencies to point out in the EIS analysis of alternatives which one is preferable on environmental grounds—including the often-overlooked alternative of no action at all. (However, if "no action" is identified as environmentally preferable, a second-best alternative must also be pointed out.)

Agencies must also produce a concise public record, indicating how the EIS was used in arriving at the decision. If the EIS is disregarded, it really is useless paperwork. It only contributes if it is used by the decisionmaker and the pubic. The record must state what the final decision was; whether the environmentally preferable alternative was selected; and if not, what considerations of national policy led to another choice.

iii. *Insure follow-up of agency decisions.* When an agency requires environmentally protective mitigation measures in its decision, the regulations provide for means to ensure that these measures are monitored and implemented.

Taken altogether, the regulations aim for a streamlined process, but one which as a broader purpose than the Guidelines they replace. The Guidelines emphasized a single document, the EIS, while the regulations emphasize the entire NEPA process, from early planning through assessment and EIS preparation through provisions for follow-up. They attempt to gear means to ends—to insure that the action-forcing procedures of sec. 102(2) of NEPA are used by agencies to fulfill the requirements of the Congressionally mandated policy set out in sec. 101 of the Act. Furthermore, the regulations are uniform, applying in the same way to all federal agencies, although each agency will develop its own procedures for implementing the regulations. Our attempt has been with these new regulations to carry out as faithfully as possible the original intent of Congress in enacting NEPA.

3. BACKGROUND

We have been greatly assisted in our task by the hundreds of people who responded to our call for suggestions on how to make the NEPA process work better. In public hearings which we held in June 1977, we invited testimony from a broad array of public officials, organizations, and private citizens, affirmatively involving NEPA's critics as well as its friends.

Among those represented were the U.S. Chamber of Commerce, which coordinated testimony from business; the Building and Construction Trades Department of the AFL–CIO, for labor; the National Conference of State Legislatures, for state and local governments; the Natural Resources Defense Council, for environmental groups. Scientists, scholars, and the general public were there.

There was extraordinary consensus among these diverse witnesses. All, without exception, expressed the view that NEPA benefited the public. Equally widely shared was the view that the process had become needlessly cumbersome and should be trimmed down. Witness after witness said that the length and detail of EIS's made it extremely difficult to distinguish the important from the trivial. The degree of unanimity about the good and bad points of the NEPA process was such that at one point an official spokesman for the oil industry rose to say that he adopted in its entirety the presentation of the President of the Sierra Club.

After the hearings we culled the record to organize both the problems and the solutions proposed by witnesses into a 38-page "NEPA Hearing Questionnaire." The questionnaire was sent to all witnesses, every state governor, all federal agencies, and everyone who responded to an invitation in the FEDERAL REGISTER. We received more than 300 replies, from a broad cross section of groups and individuals. By the comments we received from respondents we gauged our success in faithfully presenting the results of the public hearings. One commenter, an electric utility official, said that for the first time in his life he knew the government was listening to him, because all the suggestions made at the hearing turned up in the questionnaire. We then collated all the responses for use in drafting the regulations.

We also met with every agency of the federal government to discuss what should be in the regulations. Guided by these extensive interactions with government agencies and the public, we prepared draft regulations which were circulated for comment to all federal agencies in December 1977. We then studied agency comments in detail, and consulted numerous federal officials with special experience in implementing the Act. Informal redrafts were circulated to the agencies with greatest experience in preparing environmental impact statements. Improvements from our December 12 draft reflect this process.

At the same time that federal agencies were reviewing the early draft, we continued to meet with, listen to, and brief members of the public, including representatives of business, labor, state and local governments, environmental groups and others. We also considered seriously and proposed in our regulations virtually every major recommendation made by the Commission on Federal Paperwork and the General Accounting Office in their recent studies on the environmental impact statement process. The studies by these two independent bodies were among the most detailed and informed reviews of the paperwork abuses of the impact statement process. In many cases, such as streamlining intergovernmental coordination, the proposed regulations go further than their recommendations.

4. EXCLUSION

It should be noted that the issue of application of NEPA to environmental effects occurring outside the United States is the subject of continued discussions within the government and is not addressed in these regulations. Affected agencies continue to hold different views on this issue. Nothing in these regulations should be construed as asserting that NEPA either does or does not apply in this situation.

5. ANALYSIS AND ASSESSMENT OF THE REGULATIONS

Since Executive Order 12044 became effective on March 23, 1978, after the Council's draft NEPA regulations had completed interagency review, the extent to which Executive Order 12044 applies to the Council's nearly completed process of developing NEPA regulations is not clear. Nevertheless, the requirements of Executive Order 12044 have been undertaken to the fullest extent possible. The analyses required by sections 2 (b), (c), (d), and 3(b), to the extent they may apply

to the Council's proposed NEPA regulations, are available on request.

The Council has prepared a special environmental assessment of these regulations to illustrate the analysis that is appropriate under NEPA. The assessment discusses alternative regulatory approaches. Some regulations lend themselves to an analysis of their environmental impacts, particularly regulations with substantive requirements of those which apply to a physical setting. Although the Council obviously believes that its regulations will work to improve environmental quality, the impacts of procedural regulations of this kind are not susceptible to detailed analysis beyond that set out in the assessment.

Both the analyses under Executive Order 12044 and the assessment described above are available on request. Comments may be made on both documents in the same manner and by the same time as the comments on the regulations.

6. ADDITIONAL SUBJECTS FOR COMMENTS

Several issues have been brought to our attention as appropriate subjects to be covered in the regulations. They are difficult issues on which we particularly solicit thoughtful views.

a. *Data bank.* Many were intrigued by the idea of a national data bank in which information developed in one EIS would be stored and become available for use in a subsequent EIS. Public comment on the questionnaire led us to conclude, reluctantly, that the idea is impractical. In practice most environmental information is

specific to given areas or activities. To assemble a nationwide data bank would demand financial and other resources that are simply beyond the benefits that may be achieved. We have not included a data bank in these regulations but have instead tried to insure that in the scoping process the preparers of one EIS become aware of all related EISs so they can make use of the information in them. We would, however, welcome comment on this subject.

b. *Encouragement for agencies to fund public comments on EISs when an important viewpoint would otherwise not be presented.* The Council has been urged to provide either encouragement or direction to agencies, as part of their routine EIS preparation, to provide funds to responsible groups for public comments when important viewpoints would not otherwise be presented. Although we are acutely aware of the importance of comments to the success of the EIS process, we have not included such a provision. We would welcome comment on this subject also.

CONCLUSION

We look forward to your comments and help. To repeat, comments should be sent by August 11, 1978, to Nicholas C. Yost, General Counsel, Attention: NEPA Comments, Council on Environmental Quality, 722 Jackson Place NW., Washington, D.C. 20006.

Thank you for cooperating with us.

CHARLES WARREN,
Chairman.

Preamble to Final CEQ NEPA Regulations
(Council on Environmental Quality)
43 Fed. Reg. 55978 (Nov. 29, 1978)

AGENCY: Council on Environmental Quality, Exective Office of the President.

ACTION: Final regulations.

SUMMARY: These final regulations establish uniform procedures for implementing the procedural provisions of the National Environmental Policy Act. The regulations would accomplish three principal aims: to reduce paperwork, to reduce delays, and to produce better decisions. The regulations were issued in draft form in 43 FR 25230-25247 (June 9, 1978) for public review and comment and reflect changes made as a result of this process.

EFFECTIVE DATE: July 30, 1979. (See exceptions listed in § 1506.12.)

FOR FURTHER INFORMATION CONTACT:

Nicholas C. Yost, General Counsel, Council on Environmental Quality, Executive Office of the President, 722 Jackson Place NW., Washington, D.C. 20006 (telephone number 202-633-7032 or 202-395-5750).

SUPPLEMENTARY INFORMATION:

1. PURPOSE

We are publishing these final regulations to implement the procedural provisions of the National Environmental Policy Act. Their purpose is to provide all Federal agencies with efficient, uniform procedures for translating the law into practical action. We expect the new regulations to accomplish three principal aims: To reduce paperwork, to reduce delays, and at the same time to produce better decisions which further the national policy to protect and enhance the quality of the human environment.

The Council on Environmental Quality is responsbile for overseeing Federal efforts to comply with the National Environmental Policy Act ("NEPA"). In 1970, the Council issued Guidelines for the preparation of environmental impact statements (EISs) under Executive Order 11514 (1970). The 1973 revised Guidelines are now in effect. Although the Council conceived of the Guidelines as non-discretionary standards for agency decisionmaking, some agencies viewed them as advisory only. Similarly, courts differed over the weight which should be accorded the Guidelines in evaluating agency compliance with the statute.

The result has been an evolution of inconsistent agency practices and interpretations of the law. The lack of a uniform, government-wide approach to implementing NEPA has impeded Federal coordination and made it more difficult for those outside government to understand and participate in the environmental review process. It has also caused unnecessary duplication, delay and paperwork.

Moreover, by the terms of Executive Order 11514, the Guidelines were confined to Subsection (C) of Section 102(2) of NEPA—the requirement for environmental impact statements. The Guidelines did not address Section 102(2)'s other important provisions for agency planning and decisionmaking. Consequently, the environmental impact statement has tended to become an end in itself, rather than a means to making better decisions. Environmental impact statements have often failed to establish the link between what is learned through the NEPA process and how the information can contribute to decisions which further national environmental policies and goals.

To correct these problems, the President issued Executive Order 11991 on May 24, 1977 directing the Council to issue the regulations. The Executive Order was based on the President's Constitutional and statutory authority, including NEPA, the Environmental Quality Improvement Act, and Section 309 of the Clean Air Act. The President has a constitutional duty to insure that the laws are faithfully executed (U.S. Const. art. II, sec. 3), which may be delegated to appropriate officials. (Title 3 U.S.C., Sec. 301). In signing Executive Order 11991, the President delegated this authority to the agency created by NEPA, the Council on Environmental Quality.

In accordance with this directive, the Council's regulations are binding on all Federal agencies, replace some seventy different sets of agency regulations, and provide uniform standards applicable throughout the Federal government for conducting environmental reviews. The regulations also establish formal guidance from the Council on the requirements of NEPA for use by the courts in interpreting this law. The regulations address all nine subdivisions of Section 102(2) of the Act, rather than just the EIS provision covered by the Guidelines. Finally, as mandated by President Carter's Executive Order, the regulations are

" * * * designed to make the environmental impact statement more useful to decisionmakers and the public; and to reduce paperwork and the accumulation of extraneous background data, in order to emphasize the need to focus on real environmental issues and alternatives."

2. SUMMARY OF MAJOR INNOVATIONS IN THE REGULATIONS

Following this mandate in developing the new regulations, we have kept in mind the threefold objective of less paperwork, less delay, and better decisions.

A. REDUCING PAPERWORK

These regulations reduce paperwork requirements on agencies of government. Neither NEPA nor these regulations impose paperwork requirements on the public.

i. *Reducing the length of environmental impact statements.* Agencies are directed to write concise EISs (§ 1502.2(c)), which normally shall be less than 150 pages, or, for proposals of unusual scope or complexity, 300 pages (§ 1502.7).

ii. *Emphasizing real alternatives.* The regulations stress that the environmental analysis is to concentrate on alternatives, which are the heart of the process (§§ 1502.14, 1502.16); to treat peripheral matters briefly (§ 1502.2(b)); and to avoid accumulating masses of background data which tend to obscure the important issues (§§ 1502.1, 1502.15).

iii. *Using an early "scoping" process to determine what the important issues are.* A new "scoping" procedure is established to assist agencies in deciding what the central issues are, how long the EIS shall be, and how the responsibility for the EIS will be allocated among the lead agency and cooperating agencies (§ 1501.7). The scoping process is to begin as early in the NEPA process as possible—in most cases, shortly after the decision to prepare an EIS—and shall be integrated with other planning.

iv. *Using plain language.* The regulations strongly advocate writing in plain language (§ 1502.8).

v. *Following a clear format.* The regulations recommend a standard format intended to eliminate repetitive discussion, stress the major conclusions, highlight the areas of controversy, and focus on the issues to be resolved (§ 1502.10).

vi. *Requiring summaries of environmental impact statements.* The regulations are intended to make the document more usable by more people (§ 1502.12). With some exceptions, a summary may be circulated in lieu of the environmental impact statement if the latter is unusually long (§ 1502.19).

vii. *Eliminating duplication.* Under the regulations Federal agencies may prepare EISs jointly with State and local units of government which have "little NEPA" requirements (§ 1506.2).

They may also adopt another Federal agency's EIS (§ 1506.3).

viii. *Consistent terminology.* The regulations provide uniform terminology for the implementation of NEPA (§ 1508.1). For instance, the CEQ term "environmental assessment" will replace the following (nonexhaustive) list of comparable existing agency procedures: "survey" (Corps of Engineers), "environmental analysis" (Forest Service), "normal or special clearance" (HUD), "environmental analysis report" (Interior), and "marginal impact statement" (HEW) (§ 1508.9).

ix. *Incorporation by reference.* Agencies are encouraged to incorporate material by reference into the environmental impact statement when the material is not of central importance and when it is readily available for public inspection (§ 1502.21).

x. *Specific comments.* The regulations require that comments on environmental impact statements be as specific as possible to facilitate a timely and informative exchange of views among the lead agency and other agencies and the public (§ 1503.3).

xi. *Simplified procedures for making minor changes in environmental impact statements.* If comments on a draft environmental impact statement require only minor changes or factual corrections, an agency may circulate the comments, responses thereto, and the changes from language in the draft statement, rather than rewriting and circulating the entire document as a final environmental impact statement (§ 1506.4).

xii. *Combining documents.* Agencies may combine environmental impact statements and other environmental documents with any other document used in agency planning and decision-making (§ 1506.4).

xiii. *Reducing paperwork involved in reporting requirements.* The regulations will reduce the paperwork involved in reporting requirements as summarized below. In comparing the requirements under the existing Guidelines and the new CEQ regulations, it should be kept in mind that the regulations cover Sections 102(2)(A) through (I) of NEPA, while the Guidelines cover only Section 102(2)(C) (environmental impact statements). CEQ's new regulations will also replace more than 70 different existing sets of individual agency regulations. (Under the new regulations each agency will only issue implementing procedures to explain how the regulations apply to its particular policies and programs (§ 1507.3).)

Existing requirements (Applicable guidelines sections are noted)	New requirements (Applicable regulations sections are noted)
Assessment (optional under Guidelines on a case-by-case basis; currently required, however, by most major agencies in practice or in procedures) Sec. 1500.6.	*Assessment* (limited requirement: not required where there would not be environmental effects or where an EIS will be required) Secs. 1501.3, .4.
Notice of intent to prepare impact statement Sec. 1500.6.	*Notice of intent* to prepare EIS and commence scoping process Sec. 1501.7.
Quarterly list of notices of intent Sec. 1500.6.	Requirement abolished.
Negative determination (decision not to prepare impact statement) Sec. 1500.6.	*Finding of no significant impact* Sec. 1501.4.
Quarterly list of negative determinations Sec. 1500.6.	Requirement abolished.
Draft EIS Sec. 1500.7	*Draft EIS* Sec. 1502.9.
Final EIS Sec. 1500.6, .10	*Final EIS* Sec. 1502.9.
EISs on non-agency legislative reports ("agency reports on legislation initiated elsewhere") Sec. 1500.5(a)(1).	Requirment abolished.
Agency report to CEQ on implementation experience Sec. 1500.14(b).	Requirement abolished.
Agency report to CEQ on substantive guidance Secs. 1500.6(c), .14.	Requirement abolished.
Record of decision (no Guideline provision but required by many agencies' own procedures and in a wide range of cases generally under the Administrative Procedure Act and OMB Circular A-95, Part I. Sec. 6(c) and (d). Part II. Sec. 5(b)(4)).	*Record of decision* (brief explanation of decision based in part on EIS that was prepared: no circulation requirement) Sec. 1505.2.

B. REDUCING DELAY

The measures to reduce delay are listed below.

i. *Time limits on the NEPA process.* The regulations encourage lead agencies to set time limits on the NEPA process and require that time limits be set when requested by an applicant (§§ 1501.7(b)(2), 1501.8).

ii. *Integrating EIS requirements with other environmental review requirements.* Often the NEPA process and the requirements of other laws proceed separately, causing delay. The regulations provide for all agencies with jurisdiction over a proposal to cooperate so that all reviews may be conducted simultaneously (§§ 1501.7, 1502.25).

iii. *Integrating the NEPA process into early planning.* If environmental review is tacked on to the end of the planning process, then the process is prolonged, or else the EIS is written to justify a decision that has already been made and genuine consideration may not be given to environmental factors. The regulations require agencies to integrate the NEPA process

with other planning at the earliest possible time (§ 1501.2).

iv. *Emphasizing interagency cooperation before the EIS is drafted.* The regulations emphasize that other agencies should begin cooperating with the lead agency before the EIS is prepared in order to encourage early resolution of differences (§ 1501.6). We hope that early cooperation among affected agencies in preparing a draft EIS will produce a better draft and will reduce delays caused by unnecessarily late criticism.

v. *Swift and fair resolution of lead agency disputes.* When agencies differ as to who shall take the lead in preparing an EIS, or when none is willing to take the lead, the regulations provide a means for prompt resolution of the dispute (§ 1501.5).

vi. *Preparing EISs on programs and not repeating the same material in project specific EISs.* Material common to many actions may be covered in a broad EIS, and then through "tiering" may be summarized and incorporated by reference rather than reiterated in each subsequent EIS (§§ 1502.4, 1502.20, 1502.21, 1508.28).

vii. *Legal delays.* The regulations provide that litigation, if any, should come at the end rather than in the middle of the process (§ 1500.3).

viii. *Accelerated procedures for legislative proposals.* The regulations provide accelerated, simplified procedures for environmental analysis of legislative proposals, to fit better with Congressional schedules (§ 1506.8).

ix. *Categorical exclusions.* Under the regulations, categories of actions which do not individually or cumulatively have a significant effect on the human environment may be excluded from environmental review requirements (§ 1508.4).

x. *Finding of no significant impact.* If an action has not been categorically excluded from environmental review under § 1508.4, but nevertheless will not significantly affect the quality of the human environment, the agency will issue a finding of no significant impact as a basis for not preparing an EIS (§ 1508.13).

C. BETTER DECISIONS

Most of the features described above will help to improve decisionmaking. This, of course, is the fundamental purpose of the NEPA process the end to which the EIS is a means. Section 101 of NEPA sets forth the substantive requirements of the Act, the policy to be implemented by the "action-forcing" procedures of Section 102. These procedures must be tied to their intended purpose, otherwise they are indeed useless paperwork and wasted time.

i. *Recording in the decision how the EIS was used.* The new regulations require agencies to produce a concise public record, indicating how the EIS was used in arriving at the decision (§ 1505.2). This record of decision must indicate which alternative (or alternatives) considered in the EIS is preferable on environmental grounds. Agencies may also discuss preferences among alternatives based on relevant factors including economic and technical considerations and agency statutory missions. Agencies should identify those "essential considerations of national policy", including factors not related to environmental quality, which were balanced in making the decision.

ii. *Insure follow-up of agency decisions.* When an agency requires environmentally protective mitigation measures in its decisions, the regulations provide for means to ensure that these measures are implemented and monitored (§ 1505.3).

iii. *Securing more accurate, professional documents.* The regulations require accurate documents as the basis for sound decisions. As provided by Section 102(2)(A) of NEPA, the documents must draw upon all the appropriate disciplines from the natural and social sciences, plus the environmental design arts (§ 1502.6). The lead agency is responsible for the professional integrity of environmental documents and requirements are established to ensure this result, such as special provisions regarding the use of data provided by an applicant (§ 1506.5). A list of people who helped prepare documents, and their professional qualifications, shall be included in the EIS to encourage professional responsibility and ensure that an interdisciplinary approach was followed (§ 1502.17).

The regulations establish a streamlined process, and one which has a broader purpose than the Guidelines they replace. The Guidelines emphasized a single document, the EIS, while the regulations emphasize the entire NEPA process, from early planning through assessment and EIS preparation through decisions and provisions for follow-up. They are designed to gear means to ends—to ensure that the action-forcing procedures of Section 102(2) of NEPA are used by agencies to fulfill the requirements of the Congressionally mandated policy set out in Section 101 of the Act. Furthermore, the regulations are uniform, applying in the same way to all Federal agencies, although each agency will develop its own procedures for implementing the regulations. With these new regulations we seek to carry out as faithfully as possible the original intent of Congress in enacting NEPA.

3. BACKGROUND

The Council was greatly assisted by the hundreds of people who responded to our call for suggestions on how to make the NEPA process work better. In all, the Council sought the views of almost 12,000 private organizations, individuals, State and local agencies, and Federal agencies. In public hearings which we held in June 1977, we invited testimony from a broad array of public officials, organizations, and private citizens, affirmatively involving NEPA's critics as well as its friends.

Among those represented were the U.S. Chamber of Commerce, which coordinated testimony from business; the Building and Construction Trades Department of the AFL–CIO, which did so for labor; the National Conference of State Legislatures, for State and local governments; and the Natural Resources Defense Council, for environmental groups. Scientists, scholars, and the general public were also represented.

There was broad consensus among these diverse witnesses. All, without exception, expressed the view that NEPA benefited the public. Equally widely shared was the view that the process had become needlessly cumbersome and should be streamlined. Witness after witness said that the length and detail of EISs made it difficult to distinguish the important from the trivial. The degree of unanimity about the good and bad points of the NEPA process was such that at one point an official spokesperson for the oil inductry rose to say that he adopted in its entirety the presentation of the President of the Sierra Club.

After the hearings we culled the record to organize both the problems and the solutions proposed by witnesses into a 38-page "NEPA Hearing Questionnaire." The questionnaire was sent to all witnesses, every State governor, all Federal agencies, and everyone who responded to an invitation in the FEDERAL REGISTER. We received more than 300 replies, from a broad cross section of groups and individuals. By the comments we received from respondents we gauged our success in faithfully presenting the results of the public hearings. One commenter, an electric utility official, said that for the first time in his life he knew the government was listening to him, because all the suggestions made at the hearing turned up in the questionnaire. We then collated all the responses for use in drafting the regulations.

We also met with every agency of the Federal government to discuss what should be in the regulations. Guided by these extensive interactions with government agencies and the public, we prepared draft regulations which were circulated for comment to all Federal agencies in December, 1977. We then studied agency comments in detail, and consulted numerous Federal officials with special expe-rience in implementing the Act. Informal redrafts were circulated to the agencies with greatest experience in preparing environmental impact statements.

At the same time that Federal agencies were reviewing the early draft, we continued to meet with, listen to, and brief members of the public, including representatives of business, labor, State and local governments, environmental groups, and others. Their views were considered during this early stage of the rulemaking. We also considered seriously and proposed in our regulations virtually every major recommendation made by the Commission on Federal Paperwork and the General Accounting Office in their recent studies on the environmental impact statement process. The studies by these two independent bodies were among the most detailed and informed reviews of the paperwork abuses in the impact statement process. In many cases, such as streamlining intergovernmental coordination, the proposed regulations go further than their recommendations.

On June 9, 1978 the regulations were proposed in draft form (43 FR at pages 25230–25247) and the Council announced that the period for public review of and comment on the draft regulations would extend for two months until August 11, 1978. During this period, the Council received almost 500 written comments on the draft regulations, most of which contained specific and detailed suggestions for improving them. These comments were again broadly representative of the various interests which are involved in the NEPA process.

The Council carefully reevaluated the regulations in light of the comments we received. The Council's staff read and analyzed each of the comments and developed recommendations for responding to them. A clear majority of the comments were favorable and expressed strong support for the draft regulations as a major improvement over the existing Guidelines. Some comments suggested further improvements through changes in the wording of specific provisions. A smaller number expressed more general concerns about the approach and direction taken by the regulations. In continuing efforts to resolve issues raised during the review, staff members conducted numerous meetings with individuals and groups who had offered comments and with representatives of affected Federal agencies. This process continued until most concerns with the proposals were alleviated or satisfied.

When, after discussions and review the Council determined that the comments raised valid concerns, we altered the regulations accordingly. When we decided that reasons supporting the regulations were stronger than those for challenging them, we left the regulations unchanged. Part 4 of the Preamble describes section by section the more significant comments we received, and how we responded to them.

4. COMMENTS AND THE COUNCIL'S RESPONSE

PART 1500—PURPOSE, POLICY AND MANDATE

Comments on § 1500.3: Mandate. Section 1500.3 of the draft regulations stated that it is the Council's intention that judicial review of agency compliance with the regulations not occur before an agency has filed the final environmental impact statement, causes irreparable injury, or has made a finding of no significant impact. Some comments expressed concern that court action might be commenced under this provision following a finding of no significant impact which was only tentative and did not represent a final determination that an environmental impact statement would not be prepared.

The Council made two changes in response to this concern: First, the word "final" was inserted before the phrase "finding of no significant impact." Thus, the Council eliminated the possibility of interpreting this phrase to mean a preliminary or tentative determination. Second, a clarification was added to this provision to indicate the Council's intention that judicial review would be appropriate only where the finding of no significant impact would lead to action affecting the environment.

Several comments on § 1500.3 expressed concern that agency action could be invalidated in court proceedings as the result of trivial departures from the requirements established by the Council's regulations. This is not the Council's intention. Accordingly, a sentence was added to indicate the Council's intention that a trivial departure from the regulations not give rise to an independent cause of action under law.

PART 1501—NEPA AND AGENCY PLANNING

Comments on § 1501.2: Apply NEPA early in process. Section (d)(1) of § 1501.2 stated that Federal agencies should take steps to ensure that private parties and State and local entities initiate environmental studies as soon as Federal involvement in their proposals can be foreseen. Several commenters raised questions concerning the authority of a Federal agency to require that environmental studies be initiated by private parties, for example, even before that agency had become officially involved in the review of the proposal.

The Council's intention in this provision is to ensure that environmental factors are considered at an early stage in the planning process. The Council recognizes that the authority of Federal agencies may be limited before their duty to review proposals initiated by parties outside the Federal government officially begins. Accordingly, the Council altered subsection (d)(1) of § 1501.2 to require that in such cases Federal agencies must ensure that "[p]olicies or designated staff are available to advise potential applicants of studies or other information foreseeably required by later Federal action." The purpose of the amended provision is to assure the full cooperation and support of Federal agencies for efforts by private parties and State and local entities in making an early start on studies for proposals that will eventually be reviewed by the agencies.

Comments on § 1501.3: When to prepare an environmental assessment. One commenter asked whether an environmental assessment would be required where an agency had already decided to prepare an environmental impact statement. This is not the Council's intention. To clarify this point, the Council added a sentence to this provision stating that an assessment is not necessary if the agency has decided to prepare an environmental impact statement.

Comments on § 1501.5: Lead agencies. The Council's proposal was designed to insure the swift and fair resolution of lead agency disputes. Section 1501.5 of the draft regulations established procedures for resolving disagreements among agencies over which of them must take the lead in preparing an environmental impact statement. Under subsection (d) of this section, persons and governmental entities substantially affected by the failure of Federal agencies to resolve this question may request these agencies in writing to designate a lead agency forthwith. If this request has not been met "within a reasonable period of time," subsection (e) authorizes such persons and governmental entities to petition the Council for a resolution of this issue.

Several comments objected to the phrase "within a reasonable time" because it was vague, and left it uncertain when concerned parties could file a request with the Council. The comments urged that a precise time period be fixed instead. The Council adopted this suggestion and substituted 45 days for the phrase "within a reasonable period of time." With this change, the regulations require that a lead agency be designated, if necessary by the Council, within a fixed period following a request from concerned parties that this be done.

Several commenters suggested that the Council take responsibility for designating lead agencies in every case to reduce delay. These commenters recommended that all preliminary steps be dropped in favor of immediate Council action whenever the lead agency issue arose.

The Council determined, however, that individual agencies are in the best position to decide these questions and should be given the opportunity to do so. In view of its limited resources, the Council does not have the capability to make lead agency designations for all proposals. As a result of these factors, the Council determined not to alter this provision.

Several commenters opposed the concept of joint lead agencies authorized by subsection (b) of this section, particularly where two or more of the agencies are Federal. These commenters expressed doubt that Federal agencies could cooperate in such circumstances and stated their view that the environmental review process will only work where one agency is given primary responsibility for conducting it.

In the Council's judgment, however, the designation of joint lead agencies may be the most efficient way to approach the NEPA process where more than one agency plays a significant role in reviewing proposed actions. The Council believes that Federal agencies should have the option to become joint lead agencies in such cases.

Comments on § 1501.6: Cooperating agencies. The Council developed proposals to emphasize interagency cooperation before the environmental impact statement was prepared rather than comments on a completed document. Section 1501.6 stated that agencies with jurisdiction by law over a proposal would be required to become "cooperating agencies" in the preparation of an EIS should the lead agency request that they do so. Under subsection (b) of this provision, "cooperating agencies" could be required to assume responsibility for developing information and analysis within their special competence and to make staff support available to enhance the interdisciplinary capability of the lead agency.

Several comments pointed out that principal authority for environmental matters resides in a small number of agencies in the Federal government. Concern was expressed that these few agencies could be inundated with requests for cooperation in the preparation of EISs and, if required to meet these requests in every case, drained of resources required to fulfill other statutory mandates.

The Council determined that this was a valid concern. Accordingly, it added a new subsection (c) to this section which authorizes a cooperating agency to decline to participate or otherwise limit its involvement in the preparation of an EIS where existing program commitments preclude more extensive cooperation.

Subsection (b)(5) of this section provided that a lead agency shall finance the major activities or analyses it requests from cooperating agencies to the extent available funds permit. Several commenters expressed opposition to this provision on grounds that a lead agency should conserve its funds for the fulfillment of its own statutory mandate rather than disburse funds for analyses prepared by other agencies.

The same considerations apply, however, to cooperating agencies. All Federal agencies are subject to the mandate of the National Environmental Policy Act. This provision of the regulations allows a lead agency to facilitate compliance with this statute by funding analyses prepared by cooperating agencies "to the extent available funds permit." In the Council's view, this section will enhance the ability of a lead agency to meet all of its obligations under law.

Section 1501.7: Scoping. The new concept of "scoping" was intended by the Council and perceived by the great preponderance of the commenters as a means for early identification of what are and what are not the important issues deserving of study in the EIS. Section 1501.7 of the draft regulations established a formal mechanism for agencies, in consultation with affected parties, to identify the significant issues which must be discussed in detail in an EIS, to identify the issues that do not require detailed study, and to allocate responsibilities for preparation of the document. The section provided that a scoping meeting must be held when practicable. One purpose of scoping is to encourage affected parties to identify the crucial issues raised by a proposal before an environmental impact statement is prepared in order to reduce the possibility that matters of importance will be overlooked in the early stages of a NEPA review. Scoping is also designed to ensure that agency resources will not be spent on analysis of issues which none concerned believe are significant. Finally, since scoping requires the lead agency to allocate responsibility for preparing the EIS among affected agencies and to identify other environmental review and consultation requirements applicable to the project, it will set the stage for a more timely, coordinated, and efficient Federal review of the proposal.

The concept of scoping was one of the innovations in the proposed regulations most uniformly praised by members of the public ranging from business to environmentalists. There was considerable discussion of the details of implementing the concept. Some commenters objected to the formality of the scoping process, expressing the view that compliance with this provision in every case would be time-consuming, would lead to legal challenges by citizens and private organizations with objections to the agency's way of conducting the process, and would lead to paperwork since every issue raised during the process would have to be addressed to some extent in the environmental impact statement. These commenters stated further that Federal agencies themselves were in the best position to determine matters of scope, and that public participation in these decisions was unnecessary because any scoping errors that were made by such agencies could be commented upon when the draft EIS was issued (as was done in the past) and corrected in the final document. These commenters urged that scoping at least be more open-ended and flexible and that agencies be merely encouraged rather than required to undertake the process.

Other commenters said that the Council had not gone for enough in imposing uniform requirements. These commenters urged the Council to require that a scoping meeting be held in every case, rather than only when practicable; that a scoping document be issued which reflected the decisions reached during the process; and that formal procedures be established for the resolution of disagreements over scope that arise during the scoping process. These commenters felt that more stringent requirements were necessary to ensure that agencies did not avoid the process.

In developing § 1501.7, the Council sought to ensure that the benefits of scoping would be widely realized in Federal decisionmaking, but without significant disruptions for existing procedures. The Council made the process itself mandatory to guarantee that early cooperation among affected parties would be initiated in every case. However, § 1501.7 left important elements of scoping to agency discretion. After reviewing the recommendations for more flexibility on the one hand, and more formality on the other, and while making several specific changes in response to specific comments, the Council determined that the proper balance had been struck in Section 1501.7 and did not change the basic outline of this provision. The Council did accept amendments to make clear that scoping meetings were permissive and that an agency might make provision for combining its scoping process with its environmental assessment process.

Comments on § 1501.8: Time limits. Reducing delay and uncertainty by the use of time limits is one of the Council's principal changes. Section 1501.8 of the draft regulations established criteria for setting time limits for completion of the entire NEPA process or any part of the process. These criteria include the size of the proposal and its potential for environmental harm, the state of the art, the number of agencies involved, the availability of relevant information and the time required to obtain it. Under this section, if a private applicant requests a lead agency to set time limits for an EIS review, the agency must do so provided that the time limits are consistent with the purposes of NEPA and other essential considerations of national policy. If a Federal agency is the sponsor of a proposal for major action, the lead agency is encouraged to set a timetable for the EIS review.

Several commenters objected to the concept of time limits for the NEPA process. In their opinion, the uncertainties involved in an EIS review and competing demands for limited Federal resources could make it difficult for agencies to predict how much time will be required to complete environmental impact statements on major proposals. These commenters were concerned that time limits could prompt agencies to forego necessary analysis in order to meet deadlines. In their view, the concept of time limits should be dropped from the regulations in favor of more flexible "targets" or "goals" which would be set only after consultation with all concerned parties.

On the other side of the question, the Council received several comments that the provision for time limits was not strict enough. These comments expressed concern that the criteria contained in the draft regulations were vague and would not serve effectively to encourage tight timetables for rapid completion of environmental reviews. The Council was urged to strengthen this section by including definite time limits for the completion of the EIS process in every case or by providing that CEQ itself set such limits for every environmental review, and by setting time limits for the establishment of time limits.

A primary goal of the Council's regulations is to reduce delays in the EIS process. The Council recognizes the difficulties of evaluating in advance the time required to complete environmental reviews. Nevertheless, the Council believes that a provision for time limits is necessary to concentrate agencies' attention on the timely completion of environmental impact statements and to provide private applicants with reasonable certainty as to how long the NEPA process will take. Section 1501.7(c) of the regulations allows revision of time limits if significant new circumstances (including information) arise which bear on the proposal or its impacts.

At the same time, the Council believes that precise time limits to apply uniformly across government would be unrealistic. The factors which determine the time needed to complete an environmental review are various, including the state of the art, the size and complexity of the proposal, the number of Federal agencies involved, and the presence of sensitive ecological conditions. These factors may differ significantly from one proposal to the next. The same law that applies to a Trans-Alaska pipeline may also apply to a modest federally funded building in a historic district. In the Council's judgment, individual agencies are in the best position to perform this function. The Council does not have the resources to weigh these factors for each proposal. Accordingly, the Council determined not to change these provisions of § 1501.8 of the regulations.

PART 1502—ENVIRONMENTAL IMPACT STATEMENT

Comments on Section 1502.5: Timing. Several commenters noted that it has become common practice in informal rulemaking for Federal agencies to issue required draft environmental impact statements at the same time that rules are issued in proposed form. These commenters expressed the view that this procedure was convenient, time-saving and consistent with NEPA, and urged that the regulations provide for it. The Council added a new subsection (d) to § 1502.5 on informal rulemaking stating that this procedure shall normally be followed.

Comments on section 1502.7: Page limits. A principal purpose of these regulations is to turn bulky, often unused EISs into short, usable documents which are in fact used. Section 1502.7 of the draft regulations provided that final environmental impact statements shall normally be less than 150 pages long and, for proposals of unusual scope or complexity, shall normally be less than 300 pages. Numerous commenters expressed strong support for the Council's decision to establish page limits for environmental impact statements.

Several commenters objected to the concept of page limits for environmental impact statements on grounds that it could constrain the thoroughness of environmental reviews. Some said that the limits were too short and would preclude essential analysis; others contended that they were too long and would encourage the inclusion of unnecessary detail. One commenter proposed a "sliding scale" for page limits;

another suggested that a limitation on the number of words would be more effective than a limitation on the number of pages. A number of commenters urged that page limits be simply recommended rather than established as standards that should normally be met.

The usefulness of the NEPA process to decisionmakers and the public has been jeopardized in recent years by the length and complexity of environmental impact statements. In accordance with the President's directive, a primary objective of the regulations is to insure that these documents are clear, concise, and to the point. Numerous provisions in the regulations underscore the importance of focusing on the major issues and real choices facing federal decisionmakers and excluding less important matters from detailed study. Other sections in the regulations provide that certain technical and background materials developed during the environmental review process may be appended but need not be presented in the body of an EIS.

The Council recognizes the tension between the requirement of a thorough review of environmental issues and a limitation on the number of pages that may be devoted to the analysis. The Council believes that the limits set in the regulations are realistic and will help to achieve the goal of more succinct and useful environmental documents. The Council also determined that a limitation on the number of words in an EIS was not required for accomplishing the objective of this provision. The inclusion of the term "normally" in this provision accords Federal agencies latitude if abnormal circumstances exist.

Others suggested that page limits might result in conflict with judicial precedents on adequacy of EISs, that the proverbial kitchen sink may have to be included to insure an adequate document, whatever the length. The Council trusts and intends that this not be the case. Based on its day-to-day experience in overseeing the administration of NEPA throughout the Federal government, the Council is acutely aware that in many cases bulky EISs are not read and are not used by decisionmakers. An unread and unused document quite simply cannot achieve the purpose Congress set for it. The only way to give greater assurance that EISs will be used is to make them usable and that means making them shorter. By way of analogy, judicial opinions are themselves often models of compact treatment of complex subjects. Departmental option documents often provide brief coverage of complicated decisions. Without sacrifice of analytical rigor, we see no reason why the material to be covered in an EIS cannot normally

be covered in 150 pages (or 300 pages in extraordinary circumstances).

Comments on § 1502.10: Recommended format. Section 1502.10 stated that agencies shall normally use a standard format for environmental impact statements. This provision received broad support from those commenting on the draft regulations.

As part of the recommended format, environmental impact statements would be required to describe the environmental consequences of a proposed action before they described the environment that would be affected. Many commenters felt that these elements of the EIS should be reversed so that a description of the environmental consequences of a proposal would follow rather than precede a description of the affected environment. The commenters stated their view that it would be easier for the reader to appreciate the nature and significance of environmental consequences if a description of the affected environment was presented first. The Council concurs in this view and adopted the suggested change.

Comments on § 1502.13: Purpose and need. This section of the draft regulations provided that agencies shall briefly specify—normally in one page or less—the underlying purpose and need to which the agency is responding in proposing alternatives for action. Many commenters stated that in some cases this analysis would require more than one page. The Council responded to these comments by deleting the one page limitation.

Comments on § 1502.14: Alternatives including the proposed action. Subsection (a) of this section of the draft regulations provided, among other things, that agencies shall rigorously explore and objectively evaluate all reasonable alternatives. This provision was strongly supported by a majority of those who commented on the provision.

A number of commenters objected to the phrase "all reasonable alternatives" on the grounds that it was unduly broad. The commenters suggested a variety of ways to narrow this requirement and to place limits on the range and type of alternatives that would have to be considered in an EIS.

The phrase "all reasonable alternatives" is firmly established in the case law interpreting NEPA. The phrase has not been interpreted to require that an infinite or unreasonable number of alternatives be analyzed. Accordingly, the Council determined not to alter this subsection of the regulations.

Subsection (c) requires Federal agencies to consider reasonable alternatives not within the jurisdiction of the lead agency. Subsection (d) requires consideration of the no action alternative. A few commenters inquired into the basis for these provisions. Subsections (c) and (d) are declaratory of existing law.

Subsection (e) of this section required Federal agencies to designate the "environmentally preferable alternative (or alternatives, if two or more are equally preferable)" and the reasons for identifying it. While the purpose of NEPA is better environmental decisionmaking, the process itself has not always successfully focused attention on this central goal. The objective of this requirement is to ensure that Federal agencies consider which course of action available to them will most effectively promote national environmental policies and goals. This provision was strongly supported in many comments on the regulations.

Some commenters noted that a wide variety of decisionmaking procedures are employed by agencies which are subject to NEPA and recommended flexibility to accommodate these diverse agency practices. In particular, the commenters recommended that agencies be given latitude to determine at what stage in the NEPA process—from the draft EIS to the record of decision—the environmentally preferable alternative would be designated.

The Council adopted this recommendation and deleted this requirement from the EIS portion of the regulations (§ 1502.14), while leaving it in § 1505.2 regarding the record of decision. Nothing in these regulations would preclude Federal agencies from choosing to identify the environmentally preferable alternative or alternatives in the environmental impact statement.

Comments on § 1502.15: Environmental consequences. Subsection (e) of this section requires an environmental impact statement to discuss energy requirements and conservation potential of various alternatives and mitigation measures. One commenter asked whether the subsection would require agencies to analyze total energy costs, including possible hidden or indirect costs, and total energy benefits of proposed actions. The Council intends that the subsection be interpreted in this way.

Several commenters suggested that the regulations expressly mention the quality of the urban environment as an environmental consequence to be discussed in an environmental impact statement. The Council responded by adding a new subsection (g) to this section requiring that EISs include a discussion of urban quality, historic and cultural resources, and the design of the built environment, including the reuse and conservation potential of various alternatives and mitigation

measures. Section 1502.15 has been renumbered as § 1502.16.

Comments on § 1502.17: List of preparers. Section 1502.17 provided that environmental impact statements shall identify and describe the qualifications and professional disciplines of those persons who were primarily involved in preparing the document and background analyses. This section has three principal purposes: First, Section 102(2)(A) of NEPA requires Federal agencies to "utilize a systematic, interdisciplinary approach which will insure the integrated use of the natural and social sciences and the environmental design arts in planning and decisionmaking which may have an impact on man's environment." The list of preparers will provide a basis for evaluating whether such a "systematic interdisciplinary approach" was used in preparing the EIS. Second, publication of a list of preparers increases accountability for the analyses appearing in the EIS and thus tends to encourage professional competence among those preparing them. Finally, publication of the list will enhance the professional standing of the preparers by giving proper attribution to their contributions, and making them a recognized part of the literature of their disciplines. This provision received broad support from those commenting on the regulations.

Some commenters felt that a list of preparers would be used as a list of witnesses by those challenging the adequacy of an EIS in court proceedings. However, this information would ordinarily be available anyway through normal discovery proceedings.

Section 1502.17 was also criticized for failing expressly to mention expertise and experience as "qualifications" for preparing environmental impact statements. The Council added these two terms to this section to insure that the term "qualifications" would be interpreted in this way.

Some commenters suggested that the list of preparers should also specify the amount of time that was spent on the EIS by each person identified. These commenters felt that such information was required as a basis for accurately evaluating whether an interdisciplinary approach had been employed. While the Council felt there was much to be said for this suggestion, it determined that the incremental benefits gained from this information did not justify the additional agency efforts that would be required to provide it.

Comments on § 1502.19: Circulation of the environmental impact statement. If an EIS is unusually long, Section 1502.19 provided, with certain exceptions, that a summary can be circulated in lieu of the entire document. Several commenters suggested that

private applicants sponsoring a proposal should receive the entire environmental impact statement in every case in view of their interest and probable involvement in the NEPA process. The Council concurs and altered this provision accordingly.

Comments on § 1502.20: Tiering. Section 1502.20 encouraged agencies to tier their environmental impact statements to eliminate repetitive discussions and to focus on the actual issues ripe for decision at each level of environmental review. Some commenters objected to tiering on grounds that it was not required by NEPA and would add an additional unauthorized layer to the environmental review process.

Section 1502.20 authorizes tiering of EISs; it does not require that it be done. In addition, the purpose of tiering is to simplify the EIS process by providing that environmental analysis completed at a broad program level not be duplicated for site-specific project reviews. Many agencies have already used tiering successfully in their decisionmaking. In view of these and other considerations, the Council determined not to alter this provision.

Comments on § 1502.22: Incomplete or unavailable information. Section 1502.22 provided, among other things, that agencies prepare a worst case analysis of the risk and severity of possible adverse environmental impacts when it proceeds with a proposal in the face of uncertainty. This provision received strong support from many commenters.

Several commenters expressed concern that this requirement would place undue emphasis on the possible occurence of adverse environmental consequences regardless of how remote the possiblity might be. In response, the Council added a phrase designed to ensure that the improbability as well as the probability of adverse environmental consequences would be discussed in worst case analyses prepared under this section.

Section 1502.22 stated that if information is essential to a reasoned choice among alternatives and is not known and the costs of obtaining it are not exorbitant, the agency shall include the information in the environmental impact statement. Some commenters inquired into the meaning of the term "costs." The Council intends for this word to be interpreted as including financial and other costs and adopted the phrase "overall costs" to convey this meaning.

PART 1503—COMMENTING

Comments on § 1503.1: Inviting comments. Section 1503.1 set forth the responsibility of Federal agencies to solicit comments on environmental impact statements. Several commenters observed that may Federal agencies solicit comments from State and local environmental agencies through procedures established by Office of Management and Budget Circular A-95 and suggested that the Council confirm this approach in the regulations. The Council adopted this suggestion by adding an appropriate paragraph to the section.

Comments on § 1503.2: Duty to comment. Section 1503.2 set forth the responsibilities of Federal agencies to comment on environmental impact statements. Several commenters suggested reinforcing the requirement that Federal agencies are subject to the same time limits as those outside the Federal government in order to avoid delays. The Council concurred in this suggestion and amended the provision accordingly. The Council was constrained from further changes by the requirement of Section 102(2)(C) of NEPA that agencies "consult with and obtain" the comments of specified other agencies.

Comments on § 1503.3: Specificity of comments. Section 1503.3 of the draft regulations elaborated upon the responsibilities of Federal agencies to comment specifically upon draft environmental impact statements prepared by other agencies. Several commenters suggested that cooperating agencies should assume a particular obligation in this regard. They noted that cooperating agencies which are themselves required independently to evaluate and/or approve the proposal at some later stage in the Federal review process are uniquely qualified to advise the lead agency of what additional steps may be required to facilitate these actions. In the opinion of these commenters, cooperating agencies should be required to provide this information to lead agencies when they comment on draft EISs so that the final EIS can be prepared with further Federal involvement in mind.

The Council adopted this suggestion and amended § 1503.3 through the addition of new subsections (c) and (d). The new subsections require cooperating agencies, in their comments on draft EISs, to specify what additional information, if any, is required for them to fulfill other applicable environmental review and consultation requirements, and to comment adequately on the site-specific effects to be expected from issuance of subsequent Federal approvals for the proposal. In addition, if a cooperating agency criticizes the proposed action, this section now requires that it specify the mitigation measures which would be necessary in order for it to approve the proposal under its independent statutory authority.

Comments on § 1504.3: Procedure for referrals and response. Several commenters noted that § 1504.3 did not establish a role for members of the public or applicants in the referral process. The Council determined that such persons and organizations were entitled to a role and that their views would be helpful in reaching a proper decision on the referral. Accordingly, the Council added subsection (e) to this section, authorizing interested persons including the applicant to submit their views on the referral, and any response to the referral, in writing to the Council.

Subsection (d) of this section provided that the Council may take one of several actions within 25 days after the referral and agency responses to the referral, if any, are received. Several commenters observed, however, that this subsection did not establish a deadline for final action by the Council in cases where additional discussions, public meetings, or negotiations were deemed appropriate. These commenters expressed concern that the absence of a deadline could lead to delays in concluding the referral process. The Council concurred. Accordingly, the Council added subsection (g) to this section which requires that specified actions be completed within 60 days.

Several commenters noted that the procedures established by Section 1504.3 may be inappropriate for referrals which involve agency determinations required by statute to be made on the record after opportunity for public hearing. The Council agrees. The Council added subsection (h) to this section requiring referrals in such cases to be conducted in a manner consistent with 5 U.S.C. 557(d). Thus, communications to agency officials who made the decision which is the subject of the referral must be made on the public record and after notice to all parties to the referral proceeding. In other words, ex parte contacts with agency decisionmakers in such cases are prohibited.

PART 1505—NEPA AND AGENCY DECISIONMAKING

Comments on Section 1501.1: Agency decisionmaking procedures. Some commenters asked whether this or other sections of the regulations would allow Federal agencies to place responsibility for compliance with NEPA in the hands of those with decisionmaking authority at the field level. Nothing in the regulations would prevent this arrangement. By delegating authority in this way, agencies can avoid multiple approvals of environmental documents and enhance the role of those most directly involved in their preparation and use. For policy oversight and quality control, an environmental quality review office at the national level can, among other things, establish general procedures and guidance for NEPA compliance, monitor agency performance through periodic review of selected environmental documents, and facilitate coordination among agency subunits involved in the NEPA process.

Comments on § 1505.2: Record of decision in those cases requiring environmental impact statements. Section 1505.2 provided that in cases where an environmental statement was prepared, the agency shall prepare a concise public record stating what its final decision was. If an environmentally preferable alternative was not selected, § 1505.2 required the record of decision to state why other specific considerations of national policy overrode those alternatives.

This requirement was the single provision most strongly supported by individuals and organizations commenting on the regulations. These commenters stated, among things, that the requirement for a record of decision would be the most significant improvement over the existing process, would procedurally link NEPA's documentation to NEPA's policy, would relate the EIS process to agency decisionmaking, would ensure that EISs are actually considered by Federal decisionmakers, and was required as sound administrative practice.

As noted above, the Council decided that agencies shall identify the environmentally preferable alternative and the reasons for identifying it in the record of decision. *See* Comments on § 1502.14. The Council's decision does not involve the preparation of additional analysis in the EIS process; it simply affects where the analysis will be presented.

Some commenters objected to the concept of a public record of decision on actions subject to NEPA review. In the Council's opinion, however, a public record of decision is essential for the effective implementation of NEPA. As previously noted, environmental impact statement preparation has too often become an end in itself with no necessary role in agency decisionmaking. One serious problem with the administration of NEPA has been the separation between an agency's NEPA process and its decisionmaking process. In too many cases bulky EISs have been prepared and transmitted but not used by the decisionmaker. The primary purpose of requiring that a decisionmaker concisely record his or her decision in those cases where an EIS has been prepared is to tie means to ends, to see that the decisionmaker considers and pays attention to what the NEPA process has shown to be an environmentally sensitive way of doing things. Other factors may, on balance, lead the decisionmaker to decide that other policies outweigh the environmental ones, but at least the record of decision will have achieved the original Congressional purpose of ensuring that environmental factors are integrated into the agency's decisionmaking.

Some commenters expressed the opinion that it could be difficult for Federal agencies to identify the environmentally preferable alternative or alternatives because of the multitude of factors that would have to be weighed in any such determination and the subjective nature of the balancing process. By way of illustration, commenters asked: Is clean water preferable to clean air, or the preservation of prime farmland in one region preferable to the preservation of wildlife habitat in another?

In response, the Council has amended the regulations to permit agencies to identify more than one environmentally preferable alternative, regardless of whether they are "equally" preferable, as originally proposed. Moreover, the "environmentally preferable alternative" will be that alternative which best promotes the national environmental policy as expressed in Section 101 of NEPA and most specifically in Section 101(b). Section 101(a) stresses that the policy is concerned with man and nature, to see that they exist in productive harmony and that the social, economic, and other requirements of present and future generations of Americans are fulfilled. Section 101(c) recognizes the need for a healthy environment and each person's responsibility to contribute to it. Section 101(b) contemplates Federal actions which will enable the Nation to fulfill the responsibilities of each generation as trustee for the environment for succeeding generations; to attain the widest range of beneficial uses of the environment; to preserve important historic, cultural and natural aspects of our national heritage; and to accomplish other important goals. The Council recognizes that the identification of the environmentally preferable alternative or alternatives may involve difficult assessments in some cases. The Council determined that the benefits of ensuring that decisionmakers consider and take account of environmental factors outweigh these difficulties. To assist agencies in developing and determining environmentally preferable alternatives, commenters on impact statements may choose to provide agencies with their views on this matter.

Several commenters expressed concern that the regulations did not authorize Federal agencies to express preferences based on factors other than environmental quality. In the opinion of these commenters, this emphasis on environmental considerations was misplaced and not consistent with the factors that agencies are

expected to consider in decisionmaking.

The Council responded to these comments by reference to the statute, recognizing that Title II of NEPA and especially Section 101 clearly contemplate balancing of essential considerations of national policy. We provided that agencies may discuss preferences they have among alternatives based on relevant factors, including economic and technical considerations and agency statutory mission. Agencies should identify those considerations, including factors not related to environmental quality, which were balanced in making the decision. Nothing in the final regulations precludes Federal agencies from choosing to discuss these preferences and identifying these factors in the environmental impact statement.

Some commenters objected to the word "overrode" in this provision. The language of the Act and its legislative history make clear that Federal agencies must act in an environmentally responsible fashion and not merely consider environmental factors. NEPA requires that each Federal agency use "all practicable means and measures" to protect and improve the environment "consistent with other essential considerations of national policy." Section 101(b). The Council determined to tie this provision of the regulations to NEPA's statutory provision in place of the "overrode" language.

Several commenters expressed concern that the phrase "national policy" would not allow agencies to refer to state and local policies in the record of decision. "National policy" is the phrase used by Congress in NEPA. However, in many cases specific statutory provisions require that Federal agencies adhere to or pay heed to State and local policies.

Finally, some commenters expressed concern that the requirement for a concise record of decision would involve additional agency efforts. The intention is not to require new efforts, but to see that environmental considerations are built into existing processes. Preparing such decision records is recognized as good administrative practice and the benefits of this requirement outweigh the difficulties of building environmental considerations into the decisionmaking process.

Subsection (c) of § 1505.2 states that for any mitigation adopted a monitoring and enforcement program where applicable shall be adopted and summarized in the record of decision. One commenter asked what the term "summarized" was intended to mean in this context. The Council intends this word to be interpreted as requiring a brief and concise statement describing the monitoring and enforcement program which has been adopted.

Comments on § 1505.3: Implementing the decision. Section 1505.3 provides for mitigation of adverse environmental effects. Several commenters expressed concern that this provision would grant broad authority to the lead agency for mandating that other agencies undertake and monitor mitigation measures without their consent. This is not the Council's intention and the language of the provision does not support this interpretation.

PART 1506—OTHER REQUIREMENTS OF NEPA

Comments on §1506.1: Limitations on actions during NEPA process. Section 1506.1 placed limitations on actions which can be taken before completion of the environmental review process because of the possibility of prejudicing or foreclosing important choices. Some commenters expressed concern that these limitations would impair the ability of those outside the Federal government to develop proposals for agency review and approval. Accordingly, the Council added a new paragraph (d) to this section which authorizes certain limited activities before completion of the environmental review process.

Comments on § 1506.2: Elimination of duplication with State and local procedures. This section received strong support from many commenters. Several commenters sought clarification of the procedures established by this section. It provides for coordination among Federal, State and local agencies in several distinct situations. First, subsection (a) of this section simply confirms that Federal agencies funding State programs have been authorized by Section 102(2)(D) of NEPA to cooperate with certain State agencies with statewide jurisdiction in conducting environmental reviews. Second, subsection (b) provides generally for Federal cooperation with all States in environmental reviews such as joint planning processes, joint research, joint public hearings, and joint environmental assessments. Third, subsection (c) specifically provides for Federal cooperation with those States and localities which administer "little NEPA's." The Federal agencies are directed to the fullest extent possible to reduce duplication between NEPA and comparable State and local requirements. Approximately half the states now have some sort of environmental impact statement requirement either legislatively adopted or administratively promulgated. In these circumstances, Federal agencies are required to cooperate in fulfilling these requirements as well as those of Federal laws so that one document will comply with all applicable laws. Finally, subsection (d) provides that Federal agencies generally shall in environmental impact statements discuss any inconsistency between a proposed action and any approved State or local plan or laws, regardless of whether the latter are Federally sanctioned.

Comments on § 1506.3: Adoption. Section 1506.3 authorized one Federal agency to adopt an environmental impact statement prepared by another in prescribed circumstances, provided that the statement is circulated for public comment in the same fashion as a draft EIS. Several commenters stated their view that recirculation was unnecessary if the actions contemplated by both agencies were substantially the same. The Council concurs and added a new paragraph (b) which provides that recirculation is not required in these circumstances.

Comments on § 1506.4: Combining documents. Section 1506.4 provided for the combination of environmental documents with other agency documents. Some commenters expressed the view that this section should enumerate the types of agency documents which could be combined under this provision. The Council concluded that such a list was not necessary and that such matters were better left to agency discretion. Thus, agencies may choose to combine a regulatory analysis review document, an urban impact analysis, and final decision or option documents with environmental impact statements.

Comments on § 1506.5: Agency responsibility. NEPA is a law which imposes obligations on Federal agencies. This provision is designed to insure that agencies meet those obligations and to minimize the conflict of interest inherent in the situation of those outside the government coming to the government for money, leases or permits while attempting impartially to analyze the environmental consequences of their getting it. § 1506.5 set forth the responsibility of Federal agencies for preparing environmental documents, and addressed the role of those outside the Federal government. As proposed, subsection (b) of this section provided that environmental impact statements shall be prepared either by Federal agencies or by parties under contract to and chosen solely by Federal agencies. The purpose of this provision is to ensure the objectivity of the environmental review process.

Some commenters expressed the view that requiring Federal agencies to be a formal party to every contract for the preparation of an environmental impact statement was not necessary to ensure objectivity so long as the contractor was chosen solely by Federal agencies. These commenters contended that a requirement for formal Federal involvement in all such contracts could cause delay. The Council concurs and deleted the phrase "under contract" from this provision.

Several commenters noted that the existing procedures for a few Federal programs are not consistent with § 1506.5. The Council recognizes that this provision will in a few cases require additional agency efforts where, for example, agencies have relied on applicants for the preparation of environmental impact statements. The Council determined that such efforts were justified by the goal of this provision.

Several commenters expressed concern that environmental information provided by private applicants would not be adequately evaluated by Federal agencies before it was used in environmental documents. Other commenters wanted to insure that applicants were free to submit information to the agencies. Accordingly, the Council amended subsection (a) to allow receipt of such information while requiring Federal agencies to independently evaluate the information submitted and to be responsible for its accuracy. In cases where the information is used in an environmental impact statement, the persons responsible for that evaluation must be identified in the list of preparers required by § 1502.17.

Several commenters expressed the view that applicants should be allowed to prepare environmental assessments. These commenters noted that the number of assessments prepared each year is far greater than the number of environmental impact statements; that such authority was necessary to ensure environmental sensitivity was built into actions, which while ultimately Federal were planned outside the Federal government; that assessments are much shorter and less complex than EISs; and that it would be considerably less difficult for Federal agencies independently to evaluate the information submitted for an environmental assessment than for an environmental impact statement.

The Council concurs and has added a new subsection (b) to this section which authorizes the preparation of environmental assessments by applicants. The Council intends that this provision enable private and State and local applicants to build the environment into their own planning processes, while the Federal agency retains the obligation for the ultimate EIS. The Council emphasizes, however, that Federal agencies must independently evaluate the information submitted for environmental assessments and assume responsibility for its accuracy; make their own evaluation of environmental issues; and take responsibility for the scope and content of environmental assessments.

Comments on § 1506.6: Public involvement. Subsection (b)(3) of this section listed several means by which Federal agencies might provide notice of actions which have effects primarily of local concern. Several commenters urged that such notices be made mandatory, rather than permissive; other commenters felt these methods of public notice should not be listed at all. Some commenters suggested that additional methods be included in this subsection; others urged that one or more methods be deleted.

Subsection (b) of this section required agencies to provide public notice by means calculated to inform those persons and agencies who may be interested or affected. Paragraph 3 of the subsection merely identified alternative techniques that might be used for this purpose at the local level. Paragraph 3 is not intended to provide an exhaustive list of the means of providing adequate public notice. Nor are the measures it lists mandatory in nature. On the basis of these considerations, the Council determined not to alter this provision.

As proposed, subsection (f) of this section required Federal agencies to make comments on environmental impact statements available to the public. This subsection repeated the existing language on the subject that has been in the Guidelines since 1973 (40 CFR 1500.11(d)) relative to the public availability of comments. On the basis of comments received, the Council altered this provision to state that intra-agency documents need not be made available when the Freedom of Information Act allows them to be withheld.

Several commenters observed that subsection (f) did not establish limitations on charges for environmental impact statements as the Council's Guidelines had. Accordingly, the Council incorporated the standard of the Guidelines into this subsection. The standard provides that such documents shall be provided to the public without charge to the extent practicable, or at a fee which is not more than the actual costs incurred.

Comments on § 1506.8: Proposals for legislation. Section 1506.8 established modified procedures for the preparation of environmental impact statements on legislative proposals. Except in prescribed circumstances, this section provided for the transmittal of a single legislative EIS to the Congress and to Federal, State and local agencies and the public for review and comment. No revised EIS is required in such cases.

A few commenters objected to these procedures and urged that draft and final environmental impact statements be required for all legislative proposals. These commenters said that the conventional final environmental impact statement, including an agency's response to comments, was no less important in this context than in a purely administrative setting.

However, the Council views legislative proposals as different from proposed actions to be undertaken by agencies, in several important respects. Unlike administrative proposals, the timing of critical steps (hearings, votes) is not under the control of the administrative agency. Congress will hold its hearings or take its votes when it chooses, and if an EIS is to influence those actions, it must be there in time. Congress may request Federal agencies to provide any additional environmental information it needs following receipt of a legislative EIS. Administration proposals are considered alongside other proposals introduced by members of Congress and the final product, if any, may be substantially different from the proposal transmitted by the Federal agency. Congress may hold hearings on legislative proposals and invite testimony on all aspects of proposed legislation including its environmental impacts. On the basis of these considerations, the Council determined that it would be overly burdensome and unproductive to require draft and final legislative environmental impact statements for all legislation, wherever it originates.

Several commenters also expressed concern about the requirement that the legislative environmental impact statement actually accompany legislative proposals when they are transmitted to Congress. These commenters noted that such proposals are often transmitted on an urgent basis without advance warning. Accordingly, the Council amended this section to provide for a period of thirty days for transmittal of legislative environmental impact statements, except that agencies must always transmit such EISs before the Congress begins formal deliberations on the proposal.

Comments on § 1506.10: Timing of agency action. Subsection (c) of this section provided that agencies shall allow not less than 45 days for comments on draft environmental impact statements. Several commenters felt that this period was too long; others thought it too short.

The Council recognizes that a balance must be struck between an adequate period for public comment on draft EIS's and timely completion of the environmental review process. In the Council's judgment, 45 days has proven to be the proper balance. This period for public comment was established by the Guidelines in 1973, and the Council determined not to alter it. Subsection (e) of this section authorizes the Environmental Protection Agency to reduce time periods for

agency action for compelling reasons of national policy.

Comments on § 1506.11: Emergencies. Section 1506.11 provided for agency action in emergency circumstances without observing the requirements of the regulations. The section required the Federal agency "proposing to take the action" to consult with the Council about alternative arrangements.

Several commenters expressed concern that use of the phrase "proposing to take the action" would be interpreted to mean that agencies consult with the Council before emergency action was taken. In the view of these commenters, such a requirement might be impractical in emergency circumstances and could defeat the purpose of the section. The Council concurs and substituted the phrase "taking the action" for "proposing to take the action." Similarly, the Council amended the section to provide for consultation "as soon as feasible" and not necessarily before emergency action.

PART 1507—AGENCY COMPLIANCE

Comments on § 1507.2: Agency capability to comply. Section 1507.2 provided, among other things, that a Federal agency shall itself have "sufficient capability" to evaluate any analysis prepared for it by others. Several commenters expressed concern that this could be interpreted to mean that each agency must employ the full range of professionals including geologists, biologists, chemists, botanists and others to gain sufficient capability for evaluating work prepared by others. This is not the Council's intention. Agency staffing requirements will vary with the agency's mission and needs including the number of EIS's for which they are responsible.

Comments on § 1507.3: Agency procedures. Subsection (a) of § 1507.3 provided that agencies shall adopt procedures for implementation of the regulations within eight months after the regulations are published in the FEDERAL REGISTER. Several commenters noted that State and local agencies participating in the NEPA process under certain statutory highway and community development programs would also require implementing procedures but could not finally begin to develop them until the relevant Federal agencies had completed this task. Accordingly, the Council amended this provision to allow such state and local agencies an additional four months for the adoption of implementing procedures.

Several commenters suggested that agencies with similar programs should establish similar procedures, especially for the submission of information by applicants. The Council concurs and added a new sentence to subsection (a)

stating that agencies with similar programs should consult with each other and the Council to coordinate their procedures, especially for programs requesting similar information from applicants.

Several commenters suggested that a committee be established to review agency compliance with these regulations. Under subsection (a), the Council will review agency implementing procedures for conformity with the Act and the regulations. Moreover, the Council regularly consults with Federal agencies regarding their implementation of NEPA and conducts periodic reviews on how the process is working. On the basis of these considerations, the Council determined that a committee for the review of agency compliance with NEPA should not be established.

PART 1508—TERMINOLOGY AND INDEX

Comments on § 1508.8: Effects. Several commenters urged that the term "effects" expressly include aesthetic, historic and cultural impacts. The Council adopted this suggestion and altered this provision accordingly.

Comments on § 1508.12: Federal agency. Several commenters urged that States and units of general local government assuming NEPA responsibilities under Section 104(h) of the Housing and Community Development Act of 1974 be expressly recognized as Federal agencies for purposes of these regulations. The Council adopted this suggestion and amended this provision accordingly.

Comments on § 1508.14: Human environment. In its proposed form, § 1508.14 stated that the term "human environment" shall be interpreted comprehensively to include the natural and physical environment and the interaction of people with that environment. A few commenters expressed concern that this definition could be interpreted as being limited to the natural and physical aspects of the environment. This is not the Council's intention. See § 1508.8 (relating to effects) and our discussion of the environment in the portion of this Preamble relating to § 1505.2. The full scope of the environment is set out in Section 101 of NEPA. Human beings are central to that concept. In § 1508.14 the Council replaced the work "interaction" with the work "relationship" to ensure that the definition is interpreted as being inclusive of the human environment.

The only line we draw is one drawn by the cases. Section 1508.14 stated that economic or social effects are not intended by themselves to require preparation of an environmental impact statement. A few commenters sought further explanation of this provision. This provision reflects the

Council's determination, which accords with the case law, that NEPA was not intended to require an environmental impact statement where the closing of a military base, for example, only affects such things as the composition of the population or the level of personal income in a region.

Comments on § 1508.16: Legislation. Section 1508.16 defined legislation to exclude requests for appropriations. Some commenters felt that this exclusion was inappropriate. Others noted that environmental reviews for requests for appropriations had not been conducted in the eight years since NEPA was enacted. On the basis of traditional concepts relating to appropriations and the budget cycle, considerations of timing and confidentiality, and other factors, the Council decided not to alter the scope of this provision. The Council is aware that this is the one instance in the regulations where we assert a position opposed to that in the predecessor Guidelines. Quite simply, the Council in its experience found that preparation of EISs is ill-suited to the budget preparation process. Nothing in the Council's determination, however, relieves agencies of responsibility to prepare statements when otherwise required on the underlying program or other actions. (We note that a petition for certiorari on this issue is now pending before the Supreme Court.) This section was renumbered as § 1508.17.

Comments on § 1508.17: Major Federal action. Section 1508.17 of the draft regulations addressed the issue of NEPA's application to Federal programs which are delegated or otherwise transferred to State and local government. Some commenters said that the application of NEPA in such circumstances is a highly complicated issue; that its proper resolution depends on a variety of factors that may differ significantly from one program to the next and should be weighed on a case-by-case basis; and that agencies themselves should be accorded latitude in resolving this issue, subject to judicial review. The Council concurs and determined not to address this issue in this context at the present time. This determination should not be interpreted as a decision one way or the other on the merits of the issue.

Section 1508.17 also stated that the term "major" reinforces but does not have a meaning independent of the term "significantly" in NEPA's phrase "major Federal action significantly affecting the quality of the human environment." A few commenters noted that courts have differed over whether these terms should have independent meaning under NEPA. The Council determined that any Federal action which significantly affects the quality of the human environment is "major"

for purposes of NEPA. The Council's view is in accord with *Minnesota PIRG* v. *Butz*, 498 F. 2d 1314 (8th Cir., 1974). Section 1508.17 was renumbered as § 1508.18.

Comments on § 1508.22: Proposal. Section 1508.22 stated that a proposal exists when an agency is "actively considering" alternatives and certain other factors are present. Several commenters expressed the view that this phrase could be interpreted to mean that a proposal exists too early in planning and decisionmaking, before there is any likelihood that the agency will be making a decision on the matter. In response to this concern, and to emphasize the link between EISs and actual agency decisions, the Council deleted the phrase "actively considering" and replaced it with the phrase "actively preparing to make a decision on" alternatives. The Council does not intend the change to detract from the importance of integrating NEPA with agency planning as provided in § 1501.2 of the regulations.

This section was renumbered as § 1508.23.

OTHER COMMENTS

Comments on the application of NEPA abroad. Several commenters urged that the question of whether NEPA applies abroad be resolved by these regulations. However, the President has publicly announced his intention to address this issue in an Executive Order. The Executive Order, when issued, will represent the position of the Administration on that issue.

Comments on the role of Indian tribes in the NEPA process. Several commenters stated that the regulations should clarify the role of Indian Tribes in the NEPA process. Accordingly, the Council expressly identified Indian Tribes as participants in the NEPA process in §§ 1501.2(d)(2), 1501.7(a)(1), 1502.15(c) and 1503.1(a)(2)(ii).

Comments on the Council's special environmental assessment for the NEPA regulations. The Council prepared a special environmental assessment for these regulations and announced in the preamble to the draft regulations that the document was available to the public upon request. Some commenters expressed the view that it did not contain an adequate evaluation of the effects of the regulations. For the reasons set out in the assessment, and the preamble to the proposed regulations, the Council confirmed its earlier determination that the special environmental assessment did provide an adequate evaluation for these procedural regulations.

Comments on the President's authority to issue Executive Order 11991 and the Council's authority to issue regula-

tions. A few commenters questioned the authority of the President to issue Executive Order 11991, and the authority of the Council to issue the regulations. The President is empowered to issue regulations implementing the procedural provisions of NEPA by virtue of the authority vested in him as President of the United States under Article II, Section 3 of the Constitution and other provisions of the Constitution and laws of the United States. The President is empowered to delegate responsibility for performing this function to the Council on Environmental Quality under Section 301 of Title 3 of the United States Code and other laws of the United States.

Comments on the responsibilities of Federal agencies in the NEPA process. Agency responsibilities under the regulations often depend upon whether they have "jurisdiction by law" or "special expertise" with respect to a particular proposal. Several commenters noted that these terms were not defined in the regulations and could be subject to varying interpretations. Accordingly, the Council added definitions for these terms in §§ 1508.15 and 1508.26.

Comments on the role of State and areawide clearinghouses. At the request of several States, the Council recognized the role of state and areawide clearinghouses in distributing Federal documents to appropriate recipients. *See* e.g. §§ 1501.4(e)(2), 1503.1(2)(iii), and 1506.6(b)(3)(i).

Comments on the concept of a national data bank. When the Council issued the proposed regulations, it invited comment on the concept of a national data bank. The purpose of a data bank would be to provide for the storage and recall of information developed in one EIS for use in subsequent EISs. Most commenters expressed reservations about the idea on grounds of cost and practicality. The Council, while still intrigued by the concept did not change its initial conclusion that the financial and other resources that would be required are beyond the benefits that might be achieved.

Comments on Federal funding of public comments on EISs. The Council also invited comment on a proposal for encouraging Federal agencies to fund public comments on EISs when an important viewpoint would otherwise not be presented. Several commenters supported this proposal on grounds that it would broaden the range and improve the quality of public comments on EISs. Others doubted that the expenditure of Federal funds for this purpose would be worthwhile. Some felt that Congress should decide the question. The Council determined not to address the issue of Federal funding for public comments on EISs in the regulations, but to leave the matter to individual agencies' discretion.

5. REGULATORY ANALYSES

The final regulations implement the policy and other requirements of Executive Order 12044 to the fullest extent possible. We intend agencies in implementing these regulations to minimize burdens on the public. The determinations required by Section 2(d) of the Order have been made by the Council and are available on request.

It is our intention that a Regulatory Analysis required by Section 3 of the Order be undertaken concurrently with and, where appropriate, integrated with an environmental impact statement required by NEPA and these regulations.

6. CONCLUSION

We could not, of course, adopt every suggestion that was made on the regulations. We have tried to respond to the major concerns that were expressed. In the process, we have changed 74 of the 92 sections, making a total of 340 amendments to the regulations. We are confident that any issues which arise in the future can be resolved through a variety of mechanisms that exists for improving the NEPA process.

We appreciate the efforts of the many people who participated in developing the regulations and look forward to their cooperation as the regulations are implemented by individual agencies.

CHARLES WARREN,
Chairman.

Preamble to Final Rule Withdrawing Worst Case Analysis Requirement
(Council on Environmental Quality)
43 Fed. Reg. 15619 (Apr. 25, 1986)

Background

The National Environmental Policy Act, signed into law by President Nixon on January 1, 1970, articulated national policy and goals for the nation, established the Council on Environmental Quality, and, among other federal agencies to assess the environmental impacts of and, among other things, required all federal agencies to assess the environmental impacts of and alternatives to proposals for major federal actions significantly affecting the quality of the human environment. The Council on Environmental Quality, charged with the duty of overseeing the implementation of NEPA, developed guidelines to aid federal agencies in assessing the environmental impacts of their proposals. A combination of agency practice, judicial decisions and CEQ guidance resulted in the development of what is commonly referred to as "the NEPA process", which includes the preparation of environmental impact statements for certain types of federal actions.

Because of complaints about paperwork and delays in projects caused by the NEPA process, and a perception that the problem was caused in part by lack of a uniform, binding authority, CEQ was directed in 1977 to promulgate binding regulations implementing the procedural provisions of NEPA. (Executive Order 11991, 3 CFR 123 (1978). Council was directed to specifically: "make the environmental impact statement process more useful to decisionmakers and the public; and to reduce paperwork and the accumulation of extraneous background data, in order to emphasize the need to focus on real environmental issues and alternatives." After undertaking an extensive process of review and comment with federal, state and local governmental officials, private citizens, business and industry representatives, and public interest organizations, the Council issued the NEPA regulations on November 29, 1978. 40 CFR 1500–1508 (1958). The regulations were hailed as a "significant improvement on prior EIS guidelines", (Letter, Chamber of Commerce of the United States, January 8, 1979), and became effective for, and binding upon, most federal agencies on July 30, 1979, and for all remaining federal agencies on November 29, 1979.

Since promulgation of the NEPA regulations, the Council has continually reviewed the regulations to identify areas where further interpretation or

guidance is required.[1] No broad support for amendment of the regulations surfaced during review under the 1981 Vice President's Regulatory Relief Task Force; indeed, some recommended that. "CEQ's streamlining regulations for the implementation of NEPA requirements should receive full support from the Administration and the federal agencies". (Letter, National League of Cities, May 14, 1981). Although continual attention is required to ensure that the mandate of the regulations is being fulfilled, the regulations appear to be generally working well.

During the past two and a half years, however, the Council has received numerous requests from both government agencies and private parties to review and amend the regulation which addresses "incomplete or unavailable information" in the EIS process. That regulation currently reads as follows:

"Section 1502.22. Incomplete or unavailable information.

"When an agency is evaluating significant adverse effects on the human environment in an environmental impact statement and there are gaps in relevant information or scientific uncertainty, the agency shall always make clear that such information is lacking or that uncertainty exists.

"(a) If the information relevant to adverse impacts is essential to a reasoned choice among alternatives and is not known and the overall costs of obtaining it are not exorbitant, the agency shall include the information in the environmental impact statement.

"(b) If (1) the information relevant to adverse impacts is essential to a reasoned choice among alternatives and is not known and the overall costs of obtaining it are exorbitant or (2) the information relevant to adverse impacts is important to the decision and the means to obtain it are not known (e.g., the means for obtaining it are beyond the state of the art) the agency shall weigh the need for the action against the risk and severity of possible adverse impacts were the action to proceed in the face of uncertainty. If the agency proceeds, it shall include a worst case analysis and an indication of the probability or improbability of its occurrence." 40 CFR 1502.22.

On August 11, 1983, the Council

proposed guidance regarding the "worst case analysis" requirement and asked for comments on the proposed guidance 48 FR 36486 (1983). The draft guidance suggested that an initial threshold of probability should be crossed before the requirements in 40 CFR 1502.22 became applicable. Although some commentators agreed with the guidance, others believed that the proposed threshold would weaken analysis of low probability and severe consequences impacts. Other writers suggested different approaches to the issue, or advocated amendment of the regulation rather than guidance. After reviewing the comments received in response to that proposal, the Council withdrew the proposed guidance, stating its intent to give the matter additional examination before publishing a new proposal. 49 FR 4803 (1984).

After many discussions with federal agency representatives and other interested parties in state governments, public interest groups, and business and industry, the Council published an Advance Notice of Proposed Rulemaking (ANPRM) for 40 CFR 1502.22, and stated that it was considering the need to amend the regulation. 49 FR 50744 (1984). The ANPRM posed five questions about the issue of incomplete or unavailable information in an EIS and asked for thoughtful written responses to the questions. The Council received 161 responses to the ANPRM. A majority of the commentators cited problems with the "worst case analysis" requirement, but recognized the need to address potential impacts in the face of incomplete or unavailable information. Many commentators thought that either the regulation itself or recent judicial decisions required agencies to go beyond the "rule of reason". These commentators suggested that the "rule of reason" should be made specifically applicable to the requirements of the regulation. A minority of commentators felt strongly that the original regulation was adequate and should not be amended.

On March 18, 1985, the Council held a meeting, open to the public, to discuss the comments received in response to the Advance Notice of Proposed Rulemaking. 50 FR 9535 (1985). Shortly after that meeting, the Council voted to amend the regulation. On August 9, 1985, CEQ published a proposed amendment to 40 CFR 1502.22 which read as follows:

"Section 1502.22. Incomplete or unavailable information.

"In preparing an environmental impact statement, the agency shall make reasonable efforts, in light of overall

---

[1] See, *Forty Most Asked Questions Concerning CEQ's National Environmental Policy Act Regulations,* 46 FR 18026 (1981); *Memorandum for General Counsels, NEPA Liaisons and Participants in Scoping,* April 30, 1981 (available upon request from the General Counsel's office, CEQ); *Guidance Regarding NEPA Regulations,* 48 FR 34263 (1983).

costs and state of the art, to obtain missing information which, in its judgment, is important to evaluating significant adverse impacts on the human environment that are reasonably foreseeable. If, for the reasons stated above, the agency is unable to obtain this missing information, the agency shall include within the environmental impact statement (a) a statement that such information is missing, (b) a statement of the relevance of the missing information to evaluating significant adverse impacts on the human environment, (c) a summary of existing credible scientific evidence which is relevant to evaluating the significant adverse impacts on the human environment, and (d) the agency's evaluation of such evidence. 'Reasonably foreseeable' includes impacts which have catastrophic consequences, even if their probability of occurrence is low, provided that they have credible scientific support, are not based on pure conjecture, and are within the rule of reason." 50 FR 32238 (1985).

The Council received 184 comments in response to the proposed amendment: 81 comments from business and industry; 39 comments from private citizens; 30 comments from public interest groups; 15 comments from federal agencies; 14 comments from state governments; 4 comments from local governments; and one comment from a Member of Congress.

A majority of the commentators favored an amendment to the regulation, and supported the general approach of the proposed amendment. However, many of these writers offered specific suggestions for improving the proposal. Many commentators asked for definitions of terms used in the proposal, particularly for the phrase "credible scientific evidence." Some commentators wanted the Council to specify a particular methodology, such as risk assessment, as a substitute for a worst case analysis. Many commentators had specific comments about particular words or phrases used in the proposed amendment. Many commentators asked CEQ to provide further guidance or monitoring after the regulation was issued in final form.

A minority of commentators strongly opposed the amendment. Some of these writers were concerned over perceived changes in the first two paragraphs of the original regulation—requirements to disclose the fact that information is missing, and to obtain that information, if possible. Some commentators opposed deletion of the "worst case analysis" requirement. Other commentators believed that the proposed amendment did not require agencies to analyze or evaluate impacts in the face of incomplete or unavailable information. These comments, and others, will be

discussed below in the section "Comments and the Council's Response".

On January 9, 1986, CEQ held a meeting, open to the public, to discuss the comments received in response to the proposed amendment. 50 FR 53061 (1985). A summary of the presentation made at that meeting is available from the Office of the General Counsel. Shortly after that meeting, the Council voted to proceed to final amendment of the regulation.

Purpose and Analysis of Final Amendment

CEQ is amending this regulation because it has concluded that the new requirements provide a wiser and more manageable approach to the evaluation of reasonably foreseeable significant adverse impacts in the face of incomplete or unavailable information in an EIS. The new procedure for analyzing such impacts in the face of incomplete or unavailable information will better inform the decisionmaker and the public. The Council's concerns regarding the original wording of 40 CFR 1502.22 are discussed at length in the preamble to the proposed amendment. 50 FR 32234 (1985). It must again be emphasized that the Council concurs in the underlying goals of the original regulation—that is, disclosure of the fact of incomplete or unavailable information; acquisition of that information if reasonably possible; and evaluation of reasonably foreseeable significant adverse impacts even in the absence of all information. These goals are based on sound public policy and early NEPA case law.[2] Rather, the need for amendment is based upon the Council's perception that the "worst case analysis" requirement is an unproductive and ineffective method of achieving those goals; one which can breed endless hypothesis and speculation.

The amended regulation applies when a federal agency is preparing an EIS on a major federal action significantly affecting the quality of the human environment and finds that there is incomplete or unavailable information relating to reasonably foreseeable significant adverse impacts on the environment. It retains the legal requirements of the first paragraph and subsection (a) of the environment and finds that there is incomplete or unavailable information relating to reasonably foreseeable significant adverse impacts on the environment. It retains the legal requirements of the first paragraph and subsection (a) of the original regulation. Thus, when preparing an EIS, agencies must disclose

the fact that there is incomplete or unavailable information. The term "incomplete information" refers to information which the agency cannot obtain because the overall costs of doing so are exorbitant. The term "unavailable information" refers to information which cannot be obtained because the means to obtain it are not known. If the incomplete information relevant to adverse impacts is essential to a reasoned choice among alternatives and the overall costs of obtaining it are not exorbitant, the agency must include the information in the EIS. The first paragraph and subsection (a) of the original regulation have been amended only insofar as the phrases "incomplete or unavailable information" (title of the original regulation) or "incomplete information" are substituted for synonymous phrases and the term "reasonably foreseeable" is added to modify "significant adverse impacts". These changes are made for consistency, clarity and readability.

Subsection (b) is amended to require federal agencies to include four items in an EIS if the information relevant to reasonably foreseeable significant adverse impacts remains unavailable because the overall costs of obtaining it are exorbitant or the means to obtain it are not known. The first step is disclosure of the fact that such information is incomplete or unavailable; that is, "a statement that such information is incomplete or unavailable". The second step is to discuss why this incomplete or unavailable information is relevant to the task of evaluating reasonably foreseeable significant adverse impacts; thus, "a statement of the relevance of the incomplete or unavailable information to evaluating reasonably foreseeable relevant to evaluating the reasonably foreseeable significant adverse impacts, impacts on the human environment". Fourth, the agency must use sound scientific methods to evaluate the potential impacts; or in the words of the regulation, "the agency's evaluation of such impacts based upon theoretical approaches or research methods generally accepted in the scientific community".

The regulation also makes clear that the reasonably foreseeable potential impacts which the agency must evaluate include those which have a low probability of occurrence but which would be expected to result in catastrophic consequences if they do occur. However, the regulation specifies that the analysis must be supported by credible scientific evidence, not based on pure conjecture, and be within the rule of reason.

Subsection (b) deletes two substantive requirements from the same subsection of the original regulation,

[2] See, for example, *Scientists' Institute for Public Information, Inc. v. Atomic Energy Commission*, 481 F.2d 1079 (D.C. Cir. 1973).

promulgated in 1978. First, it eliminates the requirement for agencies to "weigh the need for the action against the risk and severity of possible adverse impacts were the action to proceed in the face of uncertainty" while in the process of preparing an EIS. The Council believes that the weighing of risks and benefits for the particular federal proposal at hand is properly done after completion of the entire NEPA process, and is reflected in the Record of Decision. Nothing, of course, prohibits a decisionmaker from withdrawing a proposal during the course of EIS preparation.

Second, the regulation eliminates the "worst case analysis" requirement. It does not, however, eliminate the requirement for federal agencies to evaluate the reasonably foreseeable significant adverse impacts of an action, even in the face of unavailable or incomplete information. Rather, it specifies that the evaluation must be carefully conducted, based upon credible scientific evidence, and must consider those reasonably foreseeable significant adverse impacts which are based upon scientific evidence. The requirement to disclose all credible scientific evidence extends to responsible opposing views which are supported by theoretical approaches or research methods generally accepted in the scientific community (in other words, credible scientific evidence).

The regulation also requires that analysis of impacts in the face of unavailable information be grounded in the "rule of reason". The "rule of reason" is basically a judicial device to ensure that common sense and reason are not lost in the rubric of regulation. The rule of reason has been cited in numerous NEPA cases for the proposition that, "An EIS need not discuss remote and highly speculative consequences. . . . This is consistent with the (CEQ) Council on Environmental Quality Guidelines and the frequently expressed view that adequacy of the content of the EIS should be determined through use of a rule of reason." *Trout Unlimited* v. *Morton*, 509 F.2d 1276, 1283 (9th Cir. 1974). In the seminal case which applied the rule of reason to the problem of unavailable information, the court stated that, "[NEPA's] requirement that the agency describe the anticipated environmental effects of a proposed action is subject to a rule of reason. The agency need not foresee the unforeseeable, but by the same token, neither can it avoid drafting an impact statement simply because describing the environmental effects of alternatives to particular agency action involves some degree of forecasting . . . 'The statute must be construed in the light of reason if it is not to demand what is, fairly

speaking, not meaningfully possible . . .' " *Scientists' Institute for Public Information, Inc.* v. *Atomic Energy Commission*, 481 F.2d 1079, 1092 (D.C. 1973), citing *Calvert Cliffs' Coordinating Committee* v. *Atomic Energy Commission*, 499 F.2d 1109, 1114 (D.C. Cir. 1971). The Council's amendment supports and conforms with this direction.

The evaluation of impacts under § 1502.22 is an integral part of an EIS and should be treated in the same manner as those impacts normally analyzed in an EIS. The information included in the EIS to fulfill the requirements of § 1502.22 is properly a part of the "Environmental Consequences" section of the EIS (40 CFR 1502.16). As with other portions of the EIS, material substantiating the analysis fundamental to the evaluation of impacts may properly be included in an appendix to the EIS.

Comments and the Council's Response

Comment: CEQ does not make clear the fact that the first paragraph and paragraph (a) of 1502.22 would be eliminated in the proposed amendment. The preamble says nothing about radical changes in the research requirements of the existing regulation.

Response: The changes to the first paragraph and subsection (a) of the existing regulation in the proposed amendment were made primarily for the purpose of attempting to clarify and simplify the existing requirements. However, in response to a number of concerns regarding perceived changes in the legal requirements of these paragraphs, the Council has chosen to retain the original format of the regulation. The Council intends that the substitution of the phrase "incomplete or unavailable information" and "incomplete information" are taken from the title of the regulation itself, and are being inserted for the sake of consistency of terms and clarity.

Comment: The term "reasonable efforts" should be defined.

Response: The term "reasonable efforts" does not appear in the final regulation.

Comment: The proposed amendment drops the standard of "exorbitant costs" and substitutes "overall costs." Substantively, the current standard should be retained. It is a purposefully high standard, intended to counter agencies' demonstrated reluctance to seek out information. The proposed standard is lax and undefined.

Response: The final regulation retains the original standard.

Comment: The term "state of the art" should be replaced with "the availability of adequate scientific or other analytical techniques or equipment".

Response: The term has been deleted in the final regulation, and the phrase "the means to obtain it are not known" is substituted. That phrase is meant to include circumstances in which the unavailable information cannot be obtained because adequate scientific knowledge, expertise, techniques or equipment do not exist.

Comment: The regulation should make clear that "overall costs" include, among other things, all economic costs and delays in timing. The "overall cost" requirement needs to be further defined to reflect items such as comparing low cost/high cost risk (and vice versa), costs of time in obtaining information, costs of delaying projects, benefit/cost ratio and outyear impact cost.

Response: CEQ intends that the term "overall costs" encompasses financial costs and other costs such as costs in terms of time (delay) and personnel. It does not intend that the phrase be interpreted as a requirement to weigh the cost of obtaining the information against the severity of the impacts, or to perform a cost-benefit analysis. Rather, it intends that the agency interpret "overall costs" in light of overall program needs.

Comment: The term "missing information" should be clarified or changed.

Response: The term "missing information" is deleted in the final regulation, and is replaced with the terms "incomplete or unavailable information" and "incomplete information". These terms are consistent with the title of the regulation.

Comment: The word "material" should be substituted for the word "significant" because the word "significant" is a term of art and incorporates consideration of controversy surrounding a proposal. The word "material" would be more appropriate.

Response: The final regulation retains the term "significant". "Significant" is indeed a term of art which connotes the type of environmental impact which the agency is obligated to analyze in an EIS. Consideration of controversy is one of many factors which must be considered in determining whether an impact is "significant"; others include the degree to which the proposed action affects public health or safety, unique characteristics of the geographic area such as wetlands, wild and scenic rivers, etc., the degree to which the possible effects on the human environment are highly uncertain or involve unique or unknown risks, the cumulative impacts of an action, whether the action may adversely affect an endangered species or critical habitat, the degree to which an action may adversely affect historic areas, and whether the proposed action would violate another federal, state or local environmental law. 40 CFR 1508.27. The 1978 CEQ regulations differed from the earlier CEQ Guidelines in stating that the fact of controversy does not, alone, require preparation of an EIS; rather, it is one of many factors which the responsible official must bear in mind in judging the context and intensity of the potential impacts.

Comment: The term "in its judgment" gives agencies the administrative discretion to limit the data needed to prepare an EIS. It gives too much discretionary authority to agency officials to decide if they need to obtain the information. Suggest deleting "in its judgment" or adding "and with the concurrence of appropriate federal or state resource agencies".

Related Comment: It is important to allow an agency discretion to determine the extent of the investigation required to obtain information.

Response: The term "in its judgment" is deleted from the final regulation. However, deletion of that phrase is not intended to change the discretion currently vested in the agencies to determine the extent of the investigation required to obtain information. The agency's discretion must be used to make judgments about cost and scientific availability of the information.

Comment: The proposed amendment's definition of "reasonably foreseeable" should be strengthened or clarified or the use of this phrase should be changed.

Response: The term "reasonably foreseeable" has a long history of use in the context of NEPA law, and is included elsewhere in the CEQ NEPA regulations. 40 CFR 1508.8(b). Generally, the term has been used to describe what kind of environmental impacts federal agencies must analyze in an EIS; for example, ". . . if the [agency] makes a good faith effort in the survey to describe the *reasonably foreseeable* environmental impact of the program, alternatives to the program and their *reasonably foreseeable* environmental impact, and the irreversible and irretrievable commitment of resources the program involves, we see no reason why the survey will not fully satisfy the requirements of [NEPA] section 102(C)." *Sierra Club* v. *Morton,* 379 F. Supp. 1254, 1259 (D. Col. 1974) (emphasis added). *See also, Town of Orangetown* v. *Gorsuch,* 718 F.2d 29, 34 (2d Cir. 1983); *NRDC* v. *NRC,* 685 F.2d 459, 476 (D.C. Cir. 1982). The term has also been used in the context of incomplete or unavailable information. *See Scientists' Institute for Public Information* v. *Atomic Energy Commission,* 481 F.2d 1079, 1092 (D.C. Cir. 1973).

Because of the controversy and nature of this particular regulation, CEQ has specified that in the context of 40 CFR 1502.22, the term "reasonably foreseeable" includes low probability/ severe consequence impacts, provided that the analysis of such impacts is supported by credible scientific evidence, is not based on pure conjecture, and is within the rule of reason.

Comment: To prevent confusion, the proposed amendment should use either the term "credible scientific evidence" or "credible scientific support"—not both.

Response: The final regulation uses the term "credible scientific evidence" and deletes the term "credible scientific support".

Comment: The term "credible scientific evidence" should be defined. (A number of commentators offered specific suggestions for such a definition).

Response: The final regulation states that the agency's evaluation of impacts in the face of incomplete or unavailable information should be based upon theoretical approaches or research methods generally accepted in the scientific community. While this is admittedly a broad and general direction, CEQ is concerned that a narrow definition of "credible scientific evidence" would prove inappropriate in some circumstances, given the wide variety of actions which potentially fall under the auspices of this regulation. In many cases, the Council expects that "theoretical approaches or research methods generally accepted in the scientific community" will include commonly accepted professional practices such as literature searches and peer review.

Comment: The term "credible" should be deleted from the regulation, and all information should be considered.

Response: The definition of the word "credible" is, "capable of being believed". *Webster's II New Riverside University Dictionary,* 1984. Information which is unworthy of belief should not be included in an EIS.

Comment: The term "scientific" is overly restrictive since measurement of an action's environmental effects may be grounded in, among other things, economic, historical or sociological information.

Response: In an EIS, federal agencies are responsible for analysis of significant environmental effects which include "ecological, aesthetic, historic, cultural, economic, social, or health, whether direct, indirect, or cumulative." 40 CFR 1508.8(b). The requirement to analyze these potential impacts or effects are not modified in any manner by the qualified "scientific evidence" in 40 CFR 1502.22. Rather, the term "scientific" is meant to imply that the evidence presented about the possibility of a certain impact should be based upon methodological activity, discipline or study. *Webster's II New Riverside University Dictionary,* 1984.

Comment: The amendment should include some recognized scientific method for evaluating uncertainty, such as, perhaps, a risk assessment approach.

Response: Because of the wide variety of types of incomplete or unavailable information which may potentially fall within the scope of this regulation, CEQ does not choose to specify a particular methodology. Rather, each agency should select that approach which best meets the goals of evaluating potential impacts in the face of unavailable information. Further, a requirement that a particular methodology be utilized might be soon outdated by scientific developments in a particular field.

Comment: The draft preamble states that the summary of credible scientific evidence must include all information from all sources, including minority or opposing viewpoints. What are "minority views" as they relate to credible scientific evidence?

Response: The preamble to the proposed amendment states that the requirement to disclose all credible scientific evidence extends to those views which are generally regarded as "minority views" within the scientific community. The final preamble adopts the term "responsible opposing views" as the preferred term, consistent with 40 CFR 1502.9(b). The requirement to include responsible opposing views reflects the belief that many times, particularly when dealing with questions of incomplete or unavailable information, there will be more than one point of view about potential environmental impacts which has scientific credibility. The regulation requires an agency to include information about such views which have scientific credibility, rather than simply selecting one concept which supports its particular view. The responsible opposing views, must, of course, meet the criteria set out in subsection (b) of the regulation. Once such information is set out in the EIA, the agency must then use its own judgment and discretion to determine which viewpoint it believes is the most worthy of acceptance.

Comment: CEQ should indicate in the preamble that along with available scientific evidence, the views and conclusions of other government agencies and departments may be considered.

Response: The views and conclusion of other government agencies and departments are appropriately considered throughout the EIS process, beginning with the scoping process. Section 1502.22 does not limit involvement by other federal agencies in that process. Special attention should be paid to the views of those agencies with special expertise or jurisdiction by law in a particular field of inquiry. 40 CFR 1503.1(a)(1). The views of the public, and indeed all interested parties, are, of course also to be considered throughout the EIS process.

Comment: It should be made clear that the summary should be limited to credible scientific evidence only.

Response: This is precisely the requirement of the regulation itself. Again, credible scientific evidence includes both majority views and responsible opposing views, so long as these views meet the criteria in the regulation.

Comment: The regulation should require agencies to state the probability or improbability of the occurrence of the impacts which are identified.

Response: Although this requirement is not part of the final regulation, agencies are free to include this information in the EIS. The Council encourages the inclusion of such data when it is relatively reliable and when such information would help to put the analysis in perspective for the decisionmaker and other persons who read and comment on the EIS.

Comment: The fourth requirement, to include the agency's "evaluation" of the scientific evidence is vague. Presumably, what is meant is not a critique of the evidence, but an application of the evidence to predict impacts.

Response: The fourth requirement has been reworded so that it is clear that the agency is required to evaluate reasonably foreseeable significant adverse impacts which significantly affect the quality of the human environment.

Comment: There is no requirement for the agencies to analyze impacts—the basic purpose of the regulation.

Response: The fourth requirement clearly states a requirement for the agencies to evaluate the reasonably foreseeable significant adverse impacts.

Comment: The final amendment should require agencies to address high probability/low or chronic impacts, as well as low probability/catastrophic impacts.

Response: If there is a high probability of an impact occurring, an agency is probably not in the realm of incomplete or unavailable information; hence, the impacts would be analyzed under the ordinary requirements in the "Environmental consequences" section. This section includes the analysis of the environmental impacts of the proposal and the environmental impacts of alternatives to the proposed action. 40 CFR 1502.16.

Comment: The preamble to the draft amendment errs in asserting that case law has established a precedent to go beyond the rule of reason and it ignores subsequent Ninth Circuit case law which applies the rule of reason to find that agencies properly refused to prepare a worst case analysis.

Response: The Ninth Circuit decision referred to in this comment held that a worst case analysis was not required because the lead agency had obtained the information which it needed; thus there was no incomplete or unavailable information to trigger the worst case analysis requirement. *Friends of Endangered Species v. Jantzen,* 760 F.2d 976 (9th Cir. 1985).

Comment: The threshold triggering the agency's responsibility to comply with 40 CFR 1502.22(b) is actually the existance of incomplete or unavailable information. "Scientific credibility" is not a threshold, but rather a standard to be applied to the analysis once the duty to comply is triggered.

Response: This comment is correct.

Comment: The Council should make clear in the regulation itself that "scientific credibility" is the threshold which triggers the regulation.

Response: "Scientific credibility" is the criterion for the evidence which should be used to evaluate impacts in the face of incomplete or unavailable information. The trigger to comply with the regulation itself is incomplete or unavailable information.

Comment: If the phrase "worst case analysis" is unacceptable, the Council should consider replacing the term with its functional equivalent, "spectrum of events".

Response: In the final regulation, a lead agency is required to evaluate "impacts". "Impacts" or "effects" (the two are synonymous under CEQ regulations) are the subject of analysis in an EIS, not "events". Indeed, the event to be anticipated is the proposed action itself.

Under the final regulation, agencies are required to evaluate impacts for which there is credible scientific evidence. In implementing this section, agencies will have to determine the appropriate range of analysis based on the unique facts of each particular proposal. In some cases, this may amount to a spectrum or range of impacts. In other cases, the scope of suggested impacts may be much more limited. Credible scientific evidence should determine the scope of the analysis, as opposed to a pre-determined number of impacts.

Comment: A careful reading of the case law reveals that neither the Ninth Circuit nor any other circuit has required worst case analysis in the absence of scientific opinion, evidence, and experience, as alleged in the draft preamble.

Response: Although CEQ was asked to consider this question by various persons who were concerned about the effect in future cases of possible interpretations of judicial decisions involving the worst case analysis requirement, CEQ has amended the

regulation because it believes, based on further review, that the worst case analysis requirement is flawed, and the new requirements provide a better and more logical means of dealing with the analysis of impacts in the face of incomplete or unavailable information in an EIS.

Comment: Deletion of the worst case requirement will weaken environmental protection.

Response: This assertion is incorrect. The amended regulation establishes a better approach to dealing with the issue of incomplete and unavailable information in an EIS. It is a less sensational approach, but one which is a more careful and professional approach to the analysis of impacts in the face of incomplete or unavailable information. It should improve the quality of the EIS and the decision which follows, and, hence, strengthen environmental protection, in conformance with the purpose and goals of NEPA. 42 U.S.C. 4321, 4331. It will provide the public and the decisionmaker with an improved and more informed basis for the decision.

Comment: Before eliminating the term "worst case analysis", the Council should determine whether a worst case analysis is really impossible to prepare, or whether it is being resisted by agencies unwilling to learn because they do not want to admit the adverse impacts of their preferred programs.

Response: The Council does not maintain that a worst case analysis is impossible to prepare; however, it does view the worst case analysis requirement as a flawed technique to analyze impacts in the face of incomplete or unavailable information. The new requirement will provide more accurate and relevant information about reasonably foreseeable significant adverse impacts. To the extent that agencies were reluctant to discuss such impacts under the requirements of the original regulation, the amended regulation will not offer them an escape route.

Comment: The expressed need for clarification can be met by simply adding the "rule of reason" to the existing regulation.

Response: While the "rule of reason" is indeed added to the language of the regulation, CEQ believes that it is also important to amend the requirement to prepare a worst case analysis. The requirement that the analysis of impacts be based on credible scientific evidence is viewed as a specific component of the "rule of reason".

Comment: The proposal inappropriately removes the obligation to weigh the need for an action against its potential impacts.

Response: The regulation deletes this requirement because it is more properly accomplished at the conclusion of the entire NEPA process. A decisionmaker may, of course, decide to withdraw a proposal at any stage of the NEPA process for any reason, including the belief that the paucity of information undermines the wisdom of proceeding in the face of possibly severe impacts. However, such weighing and balancing in the middle of EIS preparation is a matter of policy, not law.

It is clear that, "one of the costs that must be weighed by decisionmakers is the cost of uncertainty—i.e., the costs of proceeding without more and better information." *Alaska v. Andrus*, 580 F.2d 465, 473 (D.C. Cir. 1978). However, that weighing takes place after completion of the EIS process, including the public comment process. Indeed, it would seem that the results of such a weighing process would naturally be more informed and wiser after the agency has completed the requirements of § 1502.22 to evaluate the potential impacts in the face of incomplete or unavailable information. After completion of the EIS process, the responsible decisionmaker must then weigh the costs of proceeding in the face of uncertainty, "and where the responsible decision-maker has decided that it is outweighed by the benefits of proceeding with the project without further delay . . ." he may proceed to do so. *Id.* Similarly, he or she may also decide, with the benefit of the best possible information, to delay the project until further information is obtained or to cancel the project altogether.

Comment: CEQ should provide additional guidance about the new regulation, and oversee and actively monitor its implementation.

Response: CEQ plans to provide additional guidance about the new regulation in the form of an amended question 20 of *Forty Most Asked Questions Concerning CEQ's National Environmental Policy Act Regulations.* CEQ also plans to actively monitor the implementation of the amended regulation, and evaluate its effectiveness after it has been implemented for a sufficient period of time to make a reasonable assessment.

Comment: It is unclear in which situations the new rule would apply, and what specific information it mandates. CEQ should apply the rule to actual or hypothetical situations and explain how the rule will apply and how the agencies' obligations differ under the new rule from those of the old. Request the Council provide such an analysis for particular fact patterns.

Response: CEQ plans to provide specific examples of the application of the rule to hypothetical situations in its guidance, following issuance of the final rule. The amended regulation will apply, of course, to the very same situations to which the original regulation applies;

that is, the existence of incomplete or unavailable information related to significant adverse impacts on the human environment. The modifications to the regulation are designed to better articulate the precise requirements with which an agency must comply once it finds itself in this situation.

Comment: It is essential to mention the Committee of Scientists which was instrumental in development of the proposed regulation.

Response: The writer is probably referring to a proposed Advisory Committee on Worst Case Analysis, which would have included scientists. The Committee was never formed, and thus had no role in developing the amended regulation. Instead, the Council sought public comment through the process of asking questions in the Advance Notice of Proposed Rulemaking.

Comment: CEQ should state that this analysis is to be done only in conjunction with an EIS, as opposed to an environmental assessment.

Response: Section 1502.22 is part of the set of regulations which govern the EIS process, as opposed to the preparation of an environmental assessment. *It is only appropriate to require this level of analysis when an agency is preparing an EIS.* The type of analysis called for in § 1502.22 is clearly much more sophisticated and detailed than the scope of an environmental assessment. Environmental assessments should be concise public documents which *briefly* provide sufficient analysis for determining whether to prepare an EIS, and aid in an agency's compliance with NEPA when no EIS is necessary. "Since the EA [environmental assessment] is a concise document, it should not contain long descriptions or detailed data which the agency may have gathered". The Council's suggested page limit for environmental assessments are ten to fifteen pages. *Forty Most Asked Questions Concerning CEQ's National Environmental Policy Act Regulations,* Question 36a, 46 FR 18026, 18037 (1981).

Comment: CEQ should state clearly that the amendment is intended to repudiate and overrule the Ninth Circuit decisions on worst case analysis.

Response: The Ninth Circuit opinions are based on the requirements of former § 1502.22, or agency reflections thereof, and are inapplicable to this revision. The regulation is being amended to provide a better approach to the problem of analyzing environmental impacts in the face of incomplete or unavailable information. Because the requirements of the amended regulation are more clearly articulated and manageable than the "worst case analysis" requirement, CEQ expects that there will be less litigation based on § 1502.22 than the former version of

§ 1502.22 interpreted by the Ninth Circuit.

Comment: CEQ should withdraw the guidance contained in the 1981 publication, *Forty Most Asked Questions about CEQ's NEPA Regulations,* relating to worst case analysis.

Response: That guidance is withdrawn by this publication.

Comment: CEQ has not complied with its duties to assert its substantive powers over federal agencies to comply with NEPA, to coordinate programs, and to issue instructions to agencies, but has instead succumbed to pressure from defendant agencies and their attorneys to amend the regulation. Further, CEQ is collaterally estopped from overruling the Ninth Circuit decisions.

Response: CEQ manifests its oversight of the NEPA process in a number of ways on a daily basis; for example, review of agency NEPA procedures, resolving referrals of proposals of major federal actions, and assisting parties on an individual basis in resolving difficulties with the NEPA process. The requirements of the amended regulation are a more productive use of the agencies' resources than attempting to prepare a worst case analysis. Collateral estoppel is a doctrine by which a party may be barred from relitigating a question decided in a prior case. It does not bar an agency from changing a regulation that the courts have interpreted.

Comment: Agencies should be required to present an evaluation of the existing evidence of the most likely outcome.

Response: Step four of subsection (b) requires agencies to evaluate potential impacts. The lead agency may wish to specify which of the impacts are the most likely to occur, and the Council encourages inclusion of such data when it is reliable information which would be useful to the decisionmaker and the public.

Comment: Case law required worst case analysis prior to adoption of 40 CFR 1502.22.

Response: This assertion is incorrect. Case law prior to the adoption of 40 CFR 1502.22 *did* require agencies to make a "good faith effort . . . to describe the reasonably foreseeable environmental impact(s)" of the proposal and alternatives to the proposal in the face of incomplete or unavailable information, consistent with the "rule of reason". *Scientists' Institute for Public Information* v. *Atomic Energy Commission,* 481 F.2d 1079, 1092 (D.C. Cir. 1973). The "worst case analysis" requirement was a technique adopted by CEQ as a means of achieving the goals enunciated in such case law. The "worst case" requirement itself, however, was clearly a "major innovation". Comment.

New Rules for the NEPA Process: CEQ Establishes Uniform Procedures to Improve Implementation, 9 Envt'l L.Rep. 10,005, 10,008 (1979). The U.S. Court of Appeals for the Fifth Circuit,

interpreting the "worst case analysis" requirement for the first time in a litigation context, recognized that it was an innovation of CEQ. *Sierra Club* v. *Sigler,* 695 F.2d 957, 972 (5th Cir. 1983).

CEQ has since observed difficulties with the technique of "worst case analysis" and is replacing it with a better approach to the problem of incomplete or unavailable information in an EIS.

Memorandum: Questions and Answers About the NEPA Regulations

(Council on Environmental Quality Mar. 17, 1981)

46 Fed. Reg. 18026 (Mar. 23, 1981), as amended, 51 Fed. Reg. 15618 (Apr. 25, 1986)

Questions and Answers About the NEPA Regulations (1981)

1a. Q. What is meant by "range of alternatives" as referred to in Sec. 1505.1(e)? [1]

A. The phrase "range of alternatives" refers to the alternatives discussed in environmental documents. It includes all reasonable alternatives, which must be rigorously explored and objectively evaluated, as well as those other alternatives, which are eliminated from detailed study with a brief discussion of the reasons for eliminating them. Section 1502.14. A decisionmaker must not consider alternatives beyond the range of alternatives discussed in the relevant environmental documents. Moreover, a decisionmaker must, in fact, consider all the alternatives discussed in an EIS. Section 1505.1(e).

1b. Q. How many alternatives have to be discussed when there is an infinite number of possible alternatives?

A. For some proposals there may exist a very large or even an infinite number of possible reasonable alternatives. For example, a proposal to designate wilderness areas within a National Forest could be said to involve an infinite number of alternatives from 0 to 100 percent of the forest. When there are potentially a very large number of alternatives, only a reasonable number of examples, covering the *full spectrum* of alternatives, must be analyzed and compared in the EIS. An appropriate series of alternatives might include dedicating 0, 10, 30, 50, 70, 90, or 100 percent of the Forest to wilderness. What constitutes a reasonable range of alternatives depends on the nature of the proposal and the facts in each case.

2a. Q. If an EIS is prepared in connection with an application for a permit or other federal approval, must the EIS rigorously analyze and discuss alternatives that are outside the capability of the applicant or can it be limited to reasonable alternatives that can be carried out by the applicant?

A. Section 1502.14 requires the EIS to examine all reasonable alternatives to the proposal. In determining the scope of alternatives to be considered, the emphasis is on what is "reasonable" rather than on whether the proponent or applicant likes or is itself capable of

carrying out a particular alternative. Reasonable alternatives include those that are *practical or feasible* from the technical and economic standpoint and using common sense, rather than simply *desirable* from the standpoint of the applicant.

2b. Q. Must the EIS analyze alternatives outside the jurisdiction or capability of the agency or beyond what Congress has authorized?

A. An alternative that is outside the legal jurisdiction of the lead agency must still be analyzed in the EIS if it is reasonable. A potential conflict with local or federal law does not necessarily render an alternative unreasonable, although such conflicts must be considered. Section 1506.2(d). Alternatives that are outside the scope of what Congress has approved or funded must still be evaluated in the EIS if they are reasonable, because the EIS may serve as the basis for modifying the Congressional approval or funding in light of NEPA's goals and policies. Section 1500.1(a).

3. Q. What does the "no action" alternative include? If an agency is under a court order or legislative command to act, must the EIS address the "no action" alternative?

A. Section 1502.14(d) requires the alternatives analysis in the EIS to "include the alternative of no action." There are two distinct interpretations of "no action" that must be considered, depending on the nature of the proposal being evaluated. The first situation might involve an action such as updating a land management plan where ongoing programs initiated under existing legislation and regulations will continue, even as new plans are developed. In these cases "no action" is "no change" from current management direction or level of management intensity. To construct an alternative that is based on no management at all would be a useless academic exercise. Therefore, the "no action" alternative may be thought of in terms of continuing with the present course of action until that action is changed. Consequently, projected impacts of alternative management schemes would be compared in the EIS to those impacts projected for the existing plan. In this case, alternatives would include management plans of both greater and lesser intensity, especially greater and lesser levels of resource development.

The second interpretation of "no action" is illustrated in instances involving federal decisions on proposals for projects. "No action" in such cases would mean the proposed activity would not take place, and the resulting

---

[1] References throughout the document are to the Council on Environmental Quality's Regulations For Implementing The Procedural Provisions of the National Environmental Policy Act. 40 CFR Parts 1500–1508.

environmental effects from taking no action would be compared with the effects of permitting the proposed activity or an alternative activity to go forward.

Where a choice of "no action" by the agency would result in predictable actions by others, this consequence of the "no action" alternative should be included in the analysis. For example, if denial of permission to build a railroad to a facility would lead to construction of a road and increased truck traffic, the EIS should analyze this consequence of the "no action" alternative.

In light of the above, it is difficult to think of a situation where it would *not* be appropriate to address a "no action" alternative. Accordingly, the regulations require the analysis of the no action alternative even if the agency is under a court order or legislative command to act. This analysis provides a benchmark, enabling decisionmakers to compare the magnitude of environmental effects of the action alternatives. It is also an example of a reasonable alternative outside the jurisdiction of the agency which must be analyzed. Section 1502.14(c). See Question 2 above. Inclusion of such an analysis in the EIS is necessary to inform the Congress, the public, and the President as intended by NEPA. Section 1500.1(a).

4a. Q. What is the "agency's preferred alternative"?

A. The "agency's preferred alternative" is the alternative which the agency believes would fulfill its statutory mission and responsibilities, giving consideration to economic, environmental, technical and other factors. The concept of the "agency's preferred alternative" is different from the "environmentally preferable alternative," although in some cases one alternative may be both. See Question 6 below. It is identified so that agencies and the public can understand the lead agency's orientation.

4b. Q. Does the "preferred alternative" have to be identified in the Draft EIS and the Final EIS or just in the Final EIS?

A. Section 1502.14(e) requires the section of the EIS on alternatives to "identify the agency's preferred alternative if one or more exists, in the draft statement, and identify such alternative in the final statement . . ." This means that if the agency has a preferred alternative at the Draft EIS stage, that alternative must be labeled or identified as such in the Draft EIS. If the responsible federal official in fact has no preferred alternative at the Draft EIS stage, a preferred alternative need not be identified there. By the time the Final EIS is filed, Section 1502.14(e) presumes the existence of a preferred alternative and requires its identification in the Final EIS "unless

another law prohibits the expression of such a preference."

4c. Q. Who recommends or determines the "preferred alternative?"

A. The lead agency's official with line responsibility for preparing the EIS and assuring its adequacy is responsible for identifying the agency's preferred alternative(s). The NEPA regulations do not dictate which official in an agency shall be responsible for preparation of EISs, but agencies can identify this official in their implementing procedures, pursuant to Section 1507.3.

Even though the agency's preferred alternative is identified by the EIS preparer in the EIS, the statement must be objectively prepared and not slanted to support the choice of the agency's preferred alternative over the other reasonable and feasible alternatives.

5a. Q. Is the "proposed action" the same thing as the "preferred alternative"?

A. The "proposed action" may be, but is not necessarily, the agency's "preferred alternative." The proposed action may be a proposal in its initial form before undergoing analysis in the EIS process. If the proposed action is internally generated, such as preparing a land management plan, the proposed action might end up as the agency's preferred alternative. On the other hand the proposed action may be granting an application to a non-federal entity for a permit. The agency may or may not have a "preferred alternative" at the Draft EIS stage (see Question 4 above). In that case the agency may decide at the Final EIS stage, on the basis of the Draft EIS and the public and agency comments, that an alternative other than the proposed action is the agency's "preferred alternative."

5b. Q. Is the analysis of the "proposed action" in an EIS to be treated differently from the analysis of alternatives?

A. The degree of analysis devoted to each alternative in the EIS is to be substantially similar to that devoted to the "proposed action." Section 1502.14 is titled "Alternatives including the proposed action" to reflect such comparable treatment. Section 1502.14(b) specifically requires "substantial treatment" in the EIS of each alternative including the proposed action. This regulation does not dictate an *amount* of information to be provided, but rather, prescribes a *level of treatment*, which may in turn require varying amounts of information, to enable a reviewer to evaluate and compare alternatives.

6a. Q. What is the meaning of the term "environmentally preferable alternative" as used in the regulations with reference to Records of Decision? How is the term "environment" used in the phrase?

A. Section 1505.2(b) requires that, in cases where an EIS has been prepared,

the Record of Decision (ROD) must identify all alternatives that were considered, ". . . specifying the alternative or alternatives which were considered to be environmentally preferable." The environmentally preferable alternative is the alternative that will promote the national environmental policy as expressed in NEPA's Section 101. Ordinarily, this means the alternative that causes the least damage to the biological and physical environment; it also means the alternative which best protects, preserves, and enhances historic, cultural, and natural resources.

The Council recognizes that the identification of the environmentally preferable alternative may involve difficult judgments, particularly when one environmental value must be balanced against another. The public and other agencies reviewing a Draft EIS can assist the lead agency to develop and determine environmentally preferable alternatives by providing their views in comments on the Draft EIS. Through the identification of the environmentally preferable alternative, the decisionmaker is clearly faced with a choice between that alternative and others, and must consider whether the decision accords with the Congressionally declared policies of the Act.

6b. Q. Who recommends or determines what is environmentally preferable?

A. The agency EIS staff is encouraged to make recommendations of the environmentally preferable alternative(s) during EIS preparation. In any event the lead agency official responsible for the EIS is encouraged to identify the environmentally preferable alternative(s) in the EIS. In all cases, commentors from other agencies and the public are also encouraged to address this question. The agency must identify the environmentally preferable alternative in the ROD.

7. Q. What is the difference between the sections in the EIS on "alternatives" and "environmental consequences"? How do you avoid duplicating the discussion of alternatives in preparing these two sections?

A. The "alternatives" section is the heart of the EIS. This section rigorously explores and objectively evaluates all reasonable alternatives including the proposed action. Section 1502.14. It should include relevant comparisons on environmental and other grounds. The "environmental consequences" section of the EIS discusses the specific environmental impacts or effects of each of the alternatives including the proposed action. Section 1502.16. In order to avoid duplication between these two sections, most of the "alternatives" section should be devoted to describing and comparing the alternatives. Discussion of the environmental impacts of these alternatives should be limited to a concise descriptive summary of such impacts in a comparative form, including charts or tables, thus sharply defining the issues and providing a clear basis for choice among options. Section 1502.14. The "environmental consequences" section should be devoted largely to a scientific analysis of the direct and indirect environmental effects of the proposed action and of each of the alternatives. It forms the analytic basis for the concise comparison in the "alternatives" section.

8. Q. Section 1501.2(d) of the NEPA regulations requires agencies to provide for the early application of NEPA to cases where actions are planned by private applicants or non-Federal entities and are, at some stage, subject to federal approval of permits, loans, loan guarantees, insurance or other actions. What must and can agencies do to apply NEPA early in these cases?

A. Section 1501.2(d) requires federal agencies to take steps toward ensuring that private parties and state and local entities initiate environmental studies as soon as federal involvement in their proposals can be foreseen. This section is intended to ensure that environmental factors are considered at an early stage in the planning process and to avoid the situation where the applicant for a federal permit or approval has completed planning and eliminated all alternatives to the proposed action by the time the EIS process commences or before the EIS process has been completed.

Through early consultation, business applicants and approving agencies may gain better appreciation of each other's needs and foster a decisionmaking process which avoids later unexpected confrontations.

Federal agencies are required by Section 1507.3(b) to develop procedures to carry out Section 1501.2(d). The procedures should include an "outreach program", such as a means for prospective applicants to conduct pre-application consultations with the lead and cooperating agencies. Applicants need to find out, in advance of project planning, what environmental studies or other information will be required, and what mitigation requirements are likely, in connecton with the later federal NEPA process. Agencies should designate staff to advise potential applicants of the agency's NEPA information requirements and should publicize their pre-application procedures and information requirements in newsletters or other media used by potential applicants.

Complementing Section 1501.2(d), Section 1506.5(a) requires agencies to assist applicants by outlining the types of information required in those cases where the agency requires the applicant to submit environmental data for possible use by the agency in preparing an EIS.

Section 1506.5(b) allows agencies to authorize preparation of environmental assessments by applicants. Thus, the procedures should also include a means for anticipating and utilizing applicants' environmental studies or "early corporate environmental assessments" to fulfill some of the federal agency's NEPA obligations. However, in such cases the agency must still evaluate independently the environmental issues and take responsibility for the environmental assessment.

These provisions are intended to encourage and enable private and other non-federal entities to build environmental considerations into their own planning processes in a way that facilitates the application of NEPA and avoids delay.

9. Q. To what extent must an agency inquire into whether an applicant for a federal permit, funding or other approval of a proposal will also need approval from another agency for the same proposal or some other related aspect of it?

A. Agencies must integrate the NEPA process into other planning at the earliest possible time to insure that planning and decisions reflect environmental values, to avoid delays later in the process, and to head off potential conflicts. Specifically, the agency must "provide for cases where actions are planned by . . . applicants," so that designated staff are available to advise potential applicants of studies or other information that will foreseeably be required for the later federal action; the agency shall consult with the applicant if the agency foresees its own involvement in the proposal; and it shall insure that the NEPA process commences at the earliest possible time. Section 1501.2(d). (See Question 8.)

The regulations emphasize agency cooperation early in the NEPA process. Section 1501.6. Section 1501.7 on "scoping" also provides that all affected Federal agencies are to be invited to participate in scoping the environmental issues and to identify the various environmental review and consultation requirements that may apply to the proposed action. Further, Section 1502.25(b) requires that the draft EIS list all the federal permits, licenses and other entitlements that are needed to implement the proposal.

These provisions create an affirmative obligation on federal agencies to inquire early, and to the maximum degree possible, to ascertain whether an applicant is or will be seeking other federal assistance or approval, or whether the applicant is waiting until a proposal has been substantially developed before requesting federal aid or approval.

Thus, a federal agency receiving a request for approval or assistance should determine whether the applicant has filed separate requests for federal approval or assistance with other federal agencies. Other federal agencies that are likely to become involved should then be contacted, and the NEPA process coordinated, to insure an early and comprehensive analysis of the direct and indirect effects of the proposal and any related actions. The agency should inform the applicant that action on its application may be delayed unless it submits all other federal applications (where feasible to do so), so that all the relevant agencies can work together on the scoping process and preparation of the EIS.

10a. Q. What actions by agencies and/or applicants are allowed during EIS preparation and during the 30-day review period after publication of a final EIS?

A. No federal decision on the proposed action shall be made or recorded until at least 30 days after the publication by EPA of notice that the particular EIS has been filed with EPA. Sections 1505.2 and 1506.10. Section 1505.2 requires this decision to be stated in a public Record of Decision.

Until the agency issues its Record of Decision, no action by an agency or an applicant concerning the proposal shall be taken which would have an adverse environmental impact or limit the choice of reasonable alternatives. Section 1506.1(a). But this does not preclude preliminary planning or design work which is needed *to support an application* for permits or assistance. Section 1506.1(d).

When the impact statement in question is a program EIS, no major action concerning the program may be taken which may significantly affect the quality of the human environment, unless the particular action is justified independently of the program, is accompanied by its own adequate environmental impact statement and will not prejudice the ultimate decision on the program. Section 1506.1(c).

10b. Q. Do these limitations on action (described in Question 10a) apply to state or local agencies that have statutorily delegated responsibility for preparation of environmental documents required by NEPA, for example, under the HUD Block Grant program?

A. Yes, these limitations do apply, without any variation from their application to federal agencies.

11. Q. What actions must a lead agency take during the NEPA process when it becomes aware that a non-federal applicant is about to take an action within the agency's jurisdiction that would either have an adverse environmental impact or limit the choice of reasonable alternatives (e.g., prematurely commit money or other

resources towards the completion of the proposal)?

A. The federal agency must notify the applicant that the agency will take strong affirmative steps to insure that the objectives and procedures of NEPA are fulfilled. Section 1506.1(b). These steps could include seeking injunctive measures under NEPA, or the use of sanctions available under either the agency's permitting authority or statutes setting forth the agency's statutory mission. For example, the agency might advise an applicant that if it takes such action the agency will not process its application.

12a. Q. What actions are subject to the Council's new regulations, and what actions are grandfathered under the old guidelines?

A. The effective date of the Council's regulations was July 30, 1979 (except for certain HUD programs under the Housing and Community Development Act, 42 U.S.C. 5304(h), and certain state highway programs that qualify under Section 102(2)(D) of NEPA for which the regulations became effective on November 30, 1979). All the provisions of the regulations are binding as of that date, including those covering decisionmaking, public participation, referrals, limitations on actions, EIS supplements, etc. For example, a Record of Decision would be prepared even for decisions where the draft EIS was filed before July 30, 1979.

But in determining whether or not the new regulations apply to the preparation of a *particular environmental document,* the relevant factor is the date of filing of the draft of that document. Thus, the new regulations do not require the redrafting of an EIS or supplement if the draft EIS or supplement was filed before July 30, 1979. However, a supplement prepared after the effective date of the regulations for an EIS issued in final before the effective date of the regulations would be controlled by the regulations.

Even though agencies are not required to apply the regulations to an EIS or other document for which the draft was filed prior to July 30, 1979, the regulations encourage agencies to follow the regulations "to the fullest extent practicable," i.e., if it is feasible to do so, in preparing the final document. Section 1506.12(a).

12b. Q. Are projects authorized by Congress before the effective date of the Council's regulations grandfathered?

A. No. The date of Congressional authorization for a project is not determinative of whether the Council's regulations or former Guidelines apply to the particular proposal. No incomplete projects or proposals of any kind are grandfathered in whole or in part. Only certain environmental documents, for which the draft was issued before the effective date of the regulations, are grandfathered and subject to the Council's former Guidelines.

12c. Q. Can a violation of the regulations give rise to a cause of action?

A. While a trivial violation of the regulations would not give rise to an independent cause of action, such a cause of action would arise from a substantial violation of the regulations. Section 1500.3.

13. Q. Can the scoping process be used in connection with preparation of an environmental assessment, i.e., before both the decision to proceed with an EIS and publication of a notice of intent?

A. Yes. Scoping can be a useful tool for discovering alternatives to a proposal, or significant impacts that may have been overlooked. In cases where an environmental assessment is being prepared to help an agency decide whether to prepare an EIS, useful information might result from early participation by other agencies and the public in a scoping process.

The regulations state that the scoping process is to be preceded by a Notice of Intent (NOI) to prepare an EIS. But that is only the minimum requirement. Scoping may be initiated earlier, as long as there is appropriate public notice and enough information available on the proposal so that the public and relevant agencies can participate effectively.

However, scoping that is done before the assessment, and in aid of its preparation, cannot *substitute* for the normal scoping process after publication of the NOI, unless the earlier public notice stated clearly that this possibility was under consideration, *and* the NOI expressly provides that written comments on the scope of alternatives and impacts will still be considered.

14a. Q. What are the respective rights and responsibilities of lead and cooperating agencies? What letters and memoranda must be prepared?

A. After a lead agency has been designated (Sec. 1501.5), that agency has the responsibility to solicit cooperation from other federal agencies that have jurisdiction by law or special expertise on any environmental issue that should be addressed in the EIS being prepared. Where appropriate, the lead agency should seek the cooperation of state or local agencies of similar qualifications. When the proposal may affect an Indian reservation, the agency should consult with the Indian tribe. Section 1508.5. The request for cooperation should come at the earliest possible time in the NEPA process.

After discussions with the candidate cooperating agencies, the lead agency and the cooperating agencies are to determine by letter or by memorandum which agencies will undertake cooperating responsibilities. To the extent possible at this stage,

responsibilities for specific issues should be assigned. The allocation of responsibilities will be completed during scoping. Section 1501.7(a)(4).

Cooperating agencies must assume responsibility for the development of information and the preparation of environmental analyses at the request of the lead agency. Section 1501.6(b)(3). Cooperating agencies are now required by Section 1501.6 to devote staff resources that were normally primarily used to critique or comment on the Draft EIS after its preparation, much earlier in the NEPA process—primarily at the scoping and Draft EIS preparation stages. If a cooperating agency determines that its resource limitations preclude any involvement, or the degree of involvement (amount of work) requested by the lead agency, it must so inform the lead agency in writing and submit a copy of this correspondence to the Council. Section 1501.6(c).

In other words, the potential cooperating agency must decide early if it is able to devote any of its resources to a particular proposal. For this reason the regulation states that an agency may reply to a request for cooperation that "other program commitments preclude any involvement or the degree of involvement requested in the *action* that is the subject of the environmental impact statement." (Emphasis added). The regulation refers to the "action," rather than to the EIS, to clarify that the agency is taking itself out of all phases of the federal action, not just draft EIS preparation. This means that the agency has determined that it cannot be involved in the later stages of EIS review and comment, as well as decisionmaking on the proposed action. For this reason, cooperating agencies with jurisdiction by law (those which have permitting or other approval authority) cannot opt out entirely of the duty to cooperate on the EIS. See also Question 15, relating specifically to the responsibility of EPA.

14b. Q. How are disputes resolved between lead and cooperating agencies concerning the scope and level of detail of analysis and the quality of data in impact statements?

A. Such disputes are resolved by the agencies themselves. A lead agency, of course, has the ultimate responsibility for the content of an EIS. But it is supposed to use the environmental analysis and recommendations of cooperating agencies with jurisdiction by law or special expertise to the maximum extent possible, consistent with its own responsibilities as lead agency. Section 1501.6(a)(2).

If the lead agency leaves out a significant issue or ignores the advice and expertise of the cooperating agency, the EIS may be found later to be inadequate. Similarly, where cooperating agencies have their own decisions to make and they intend to adopt the environmental impact statement and base their decisions on it, one document should include all of the information necessary for the decisions by the cooperating agencies. Otherwise they may be forced to duplicate the EIS process by issuing a new, more complete EIS or Supplemental EIS, even though the original EIS could have sufficed if it had been properly done at the outset. Thus, both lead and cooperating agencies have a stake in producing a document of good quality. Cooperating agencies also have a duty to participate fully in the scoping process to ensure that the appropriate range of issues is determined early in the EIS process.

Because the EIS is not the Record of Decision, but instead constitutes the *information* and *analysis* on which to base a decision, disagreements about conclusions to be drawn from the EIS need not inhibit agencies from issuing a joint document, or adopting another agency's EIS, if the analysis is adequate. Thus, if each agency has its own "preferred alternative," both can be identified in the EIS. Similarly, a cooperating agency with jurisdiction by law may determine in its own ROD that alternative A is the environmentally preferable action, even though the lead agency has decided in its separate ROD that Alternative B is environmentally preferable.

14c. Q. What are the specific responsibilities of federal and state cooperating agencies to review draft EISs?

A. Cooperating agencies (i.e., agencies with jurisdiction by law or special expertise) and agencies that are authorized to develop or enforce environmental standards, must comment on environmental impact statements within their jurisdiction, expertise or authority. Sections 1503.2, 1508.5. If a cooperating agency is satisfied that its views are adequately reflected in the environmental impact statement, it should simply comment accordingly. Conversely, if the cooperating agency determines that a draft EIS is incomplete, inadequate or inaccurate, or it has other comments, it should promptly make such comments, conforming to the requirements of specificity in section 1503.3.

14d. Q. How is the lead agency to treat the comments of another agency with jurisdiction by law or special expertise which has failed or refused to cooperate or participate in scoping or EIS preparation?

A. A lead agency has the responsibility to respond to all substantive comments raising significant issues regarding a draft EIS. Section 1503.4. However, cooperating agencies are generally under an obligation to raise issues or otherwise participate in

the EIS process during scoping and EIS preparation if they reasonably can do so. In practical terms, if a cooperating agency fails to cooperate at the outset, such as during scoping, it will find that its comments at a later stage will not be as persuasive to the lead agency.

15. Q. Are EPA's responsibilities to review and comment on the environmental effects of agency proposals under Section 309 of the Clean Air Act independent of its responsibility as a cooperating agency?

A. Yes. EPA has an obligation under Section 309 of the Clean Air Act to review and comment in writing on the environmental impact of any matter relating to the authority of the Administrator contained in proposed legislation, federal construction projects, other federal actions requiring EISs, and new regulations. 42 U.S.C. Sec. 7609. This obligation is independent of its role as a cooperating agency under the NEPA regulations.

16. Q. What is meant by the term "third party contracts" in connection with the preparation of an EIS? See Section 1506.5(c). When can "third party contracts" be used?

A. As used by EPA and other agencies, the term "third party contract" refers to the preparation of EISs by contractors paid by the applicant. In the case of an EIS for a National Pollution Discharge Elimination System (NPDES) permit, the applicant, aware in the early planning stages of the proposed project of the need for an EIS, contracts directly with a consulting firm for its preparation. See 40 C.F.R. 6.604(g). The "third party" is EPA which, under Section 1506.5(c), must select the consulting firm, even though the applicant pays for the cost of preparing the EIS. The consulting firm is responsible to EPA for preparing an EIS that meets the requirements of the NEPA regulations and EPA's NEPA procedures. It is in the applicant's interest that the EIS comply with the law so that EPA can take prompt action on the NPDES permit application. The "third party contract" method under EPA's NEPA procedures is purely voluntary, though most applicants have found it helpful in expediting compliance with NEPA.

If a federal agency uses "third party contracting," the applicant may undertake the necessary paperwork for the solicitation of a field of candidates under the agency's direction, so long as the agency complies with Section 1506.5(c). Federal procurement requirements do not apply to the agency because it incurs no obligations or costs under the contract, nor does the agency procure anything under the contract.

17a. Q. If an EIS is prepared with the assistance of a consulting firm, the firm must execute a disclosure statement.

What criteria must the firm follow in determining whether it has any "financial or other interest in the outcome of the project" which would cause a conflict of interest?

A. Section 1506.5(c), which specifies that a consulting firm preparing an EIS must execute a disclosure statement, does not define "financial or other interest in the outcome of the project." The Council interprets this term broadly to cover any known benefits other than general enhancement of professional reputation. This includes any financial benefit such as a promise of future construction or design work on the project, as well as indirect benefits the consultant is aware of (e.g., if the project would aid proposals sponsored by the firm's other clients). For example, completion of a highway project may encourage construction of a shopping center or industrial park from which the consultant stands to benefit. If a consulting firm is aware that it has such an interest in the decision on the proposal, it should be disqualified from preparing the EIS, to preserve the objectivity and integrity of the NEPA process.

When a consulting firm has been involved in developing initial data and plans for the project, but does not have any financial or other interest in the outcome of the decision, it need not be disqualified from preparing the EIS. However, a disclosure statement in the draft EIS should clearly state the scope and extent of the firm's prior involvement to expose any potential conflicts of interest that may exist.

17b. Q. If the firm in fact has no promise of future work or other interest in the outcome of the proposal, may the firm later bid in competition with others for future work on the project if the proposed action is approved?

A. Yes.

18. Q. How should uncertainties about indirect effects of a proposal be addressed, for example, in cases of disposal of federal lands, when the identity or plans of future landowners is unknown?

A. The EIS must identify all the indirect effects that are known, and make a good faith effort to explain the effects that are not known but are "reasonably foreseeable." Section 1508.8(b). In the example, if there is total uncertainty about the identity of future land owners or the nature of future land uses, then of course, the agency is not required to engage in speculation or contemplation about their future plans. But, in the ordinary course of business, people do make judgments based upon reasonably foreseeable occurrences. It will often be possible to consider the likely purchasers and the development trends in that area or similar areas in recent years; or the likelihood that the land will be used for an energy project, shopping center, subdivision, farm or factory. The agency has the responsibility to make an informed judgment, and to estimate future impacts on that basis, especially if trends are ascertainable or potential purchasers have made themselves known. The agency cannot ignore these uncertain, but probable, effects of its decisions.

19a. Q. What is the scope of mitigation measures that must be discussed?

A. The mitigation measures discussed in an EIS must cover the range of impacts of the proposal. The measures must include such things as design alternatives that would decrease pollution emissions, construction impacts, esthetic intrusion, as well as relocation assistance, possible land use controls that could be enacted, and other possible efforts. Mitigation measures must be considered even for impacts that by themselves would not be considered "significant." Once the proposal itself is considered as a whole to have significant effects, all of its specific effects on the environment (whether or not "significant") must be considered, and mitigation measures must be developed where it is feasible to do so. Sections 1502.14(f), 1502.16(h), 1508.14.

19b. Q. How should an EIS treat the subject of available mitigation measures that are (1) outside the jurisdiction of the lead or cooperating agencies, or (2) unlikely to be adopted or enforced by the responsible agency?

A. All relevant, reasonable mitigation measures that could improve the project are to be identified, even if they are outside the jurisdiction of the lead agency or the cooperating agencies, and thus would not be committed as part of the RODs of these agencies. Sections 1502.16(h), 1505.2(c). This will serve to alert agencies or officials who *can* implement these extra measures, and will encourage them to do so. Because the EIS is the most comprehensive environmental document, it is an ideal vehicle in which to lay out not only the full range of environmental impacts but also the full spectrum of appropriate mitigation.

However, to ensure that environmental effects of a proposed action are fairly assessed, the probability of the mitigation measures being implemented must also be discussed. Thus the EIS and the Record of Decision should indicate the likelihood that such measures will be adopted or enforced by the responsible agencies. Sections 1502.16(h), 1505.2. If there is a history of nonenforcement or opposition to such measures, the EIS and Record of Decision should acknowledge such opposition or nonenforcement. If the necessary

mitigation measures will not be ready for a long period of time, this fact, of course, should also be recognized.

20. Withdrawn

21. Q. Where an EIS or an EA is combined with another project planning document (sometimes called "piggybacking"), to what degree may the EIS or EA refer to and rely upon information in the project document to satisfy NEPA's requirements?

A. Section 1502.25 of the regulations requires that draft EISs be prepared concurrently and integrated with environmental analyses and related surveys and studies required by other federal statutes. In addition, Section 1506.4 allows any environmental document prepared in compliance with NEPA to be combined with any other agency document to reduce duplication and paperwork. However, these provisions were not intended to authorize the preparation of a short summary or outline EIS, attached to a detailed project report or land use plan containing the required environmental impact data. In such circumstances, the reader would have to refer constantly to the detailed report to understand the environmental impacts and alternatives which should have been found in the EIS itself.

The EIS must stand on its own as an analytical document which fully informs decisionmakers and the public of the environmental effects of the proposal and those of the reasonable alternatives. Section 1502.1. But, as long as the EIS is clearly identified and is self-supporting, it can be physically included in or attached to the project report or land use plan, and may use attached report material as technical backup.

Forest Service environmental impact statements for forest management plans are handled in this manner. The EIS identifies the agency's preferred alternative, which is developed in detail as the proposed management plan. The detailed proposed plan accompanies the EIS through the review process, and the documents are appropriately cross-referenced. The proposed plan is useful for EIS readers as an example, to show how one choice of management options translates into effects on natural resources. This procedure permits initiation of the 90-day public review of proposed forest plans, which is required by the National Forest Management Act.

All the alternatives are discussed in the EIS, which can be read as an independent document. The details of the management plan are not repeated in the EIS, and vice versa. This is a reasonable functional separation of the documents: the EIS contains information relevant to the choice among alternatives; the plan is a detailed description of proposed management activities suitable for use by the land

managers. This procedure provides for concurrent compliance with the public review requirements of both NEPA and the National Forest Management Act.

Under some circumstances, a project report or management plan may be totally merged with the EIS, and the one document labeled as both "EIS" and "management plan" or "project report." This may be reasonable where the documents are short, or where the EIS format and the regulations for clear, analytical EISs also satisfy the requirements for a project report.

22. Q. May state and federal agencies serve as joint lead agencies? If so, how do they resolve law, policy and resource conflicts under NEPA and the relevant state environmental policy act? How do they resolve differences in perspective where, for example, national and local needs may differ?

A. Under Section 1501.5(b), federal, state or local agencies, as long as they include at least one federal agency, may act as joint lead agencies to prepare an EIS. Section 1506.2 also strongly urges state and local agencies and the relevant federal agencies to cooperate fully with each other. This should cover joint research and studies, planning activities, public hearings, environmental assessments and the preparation of joint EISs under NEPA and the relevant "little NEPA" state laws, so that one document will satisfy both laws.

The regulations also recognize that certain inconsistencies may exist between the proposed federal action and any approved state or local plan or law. The joint document should discuss the extent to which the federal agency would reconcile its proposed action with such plan or law. Section 1506.2(d). (See Question 23).

Because there may be differences in perspective as well as conflicts among federal, state and local goals for resources management, the Council has advised participating agencies to adopt a flexible, cooperative approach. The joint EIS should reflect all of their interests and missions, clearly identified as such. The final document would then indicate how state and local interests have been accommodated, or would identify conflicts in goals (e.g., how a hydroelectric project, which might induce second home development, would require new land use controls). The EIS must contain a complete discussion of scope and purpose of the proposal, alternatives, and impacts so that the discussion is adequate to meet the needs of local, state and federal decisionmakers.

23a. Q. How should an agency handle potential conflicts between a proposal and the objectives of Federal, state or local land use plans, policies and controls for the area concerned? See Sec. 1502.16(c).

A. The agency should first inquire of other agencies whether there are any potential conflicts. If there would be immediate conflicts, or if conflicts could arise in the future when the plans are finished (see Question 23(b) below), the EIS must acknowledge and describe the extent of those conflicts. If there are any possibilities of resolving the conflicts, these should be explained as well. The EIS should also evaluate the seriousness of the impact of the proposal on the land use plans and policies, and whether, or how much, the proposal will impair the effectiveness of land use control mechanisms for the area. Comments from officials of the affected area should be solicited early and should be carefully acknowleged and answered in the EIS.

23b. Q. What constitutes a "land use plan or policy" for purposes of this discussion?

A. The term "land use plans," includes all types of formally adopted documents for land use planning, zoning and related regulatory requirements. Local general plans are included, even though they are subject to future change. Proposed plans should also be addressed if they have been formally proposed by the appropriate government body in a written form, and are being actively pursued by officials of the jurisdiction. Staged plans, which must go through phases of development such as the Water Resources Council's Level A, B and C planning process should also be included even though they are incomplete.

The term "policies" includes formally adopted statements of land use policy as embodied in laws or regulations. It also includes proposals for action such as the initiation of a planning process, or a formally adopted policy statement of the local, regional or state executive branch, even if it has not yet been formally adopted by the local, regional or state legislative body.

23c. Q. What options are available for the decisionmaker when conflicts with such plans or policies are identified?

A. After identifying any potential land use conflicts, the decisionmaker must weigh the significance of the conflicts, among all the other environmental and non-environmental factors that must be considered in reaching a rational and balanced decision. Unless precluded by other law from causing or contributing to any inconsistency with the land use plans, policies or controls, the decisionmaker retains the authority to go forward with the proposal, despite the potential conflict. In the Record of Decision, the decisionmaker must explain what the decision was, how it was made, and what mitigation measures are being imposed to lessen adverse environmental impacts of the

proposal, among the other requirements of Section 1505.2. This provision would require the decisionmaker to explain any decision to override land use plans, policies or controls for the area.

24a. Q. When are EISs required on policies, plans or programs?

A. An EIS must be prepared if an agency proposes to implement a specific policy, to adopt a plan for a group of related actions, or to implement a specific statutory program or executive directive. Section 1508.18. In addition, the adoption of official policy in the form of rules, regulations and interpretations pursuant to the Administrative Procedure Act, treaties, conventions, or other formal documents establishing governmental or agency policy which will substantially alter agency programs, could require an EIS. Section 1508.18. In all cases, the policy, plan, or program must have the potential for significantly affecting the quality of the human environment in order to require an EIS. It should be noted that a proposal "may exist in fact as well as by agency declaration that one exists." Section 1508.23.

24b. Q. When is an area-wide or overview EIS appropriate?

A. The preparation of an area-wide or overview EIS may be particularly useful when similar actions, viewed with other reasonably foreseeable or proposed agency actions, share common timing or geography. For example, when a variety of energy projects may be located in a single watershed, or when a series of new energy technologies may be developed through federal funding, the overview or area-wide EIS would serve as a valuable and necessary analysis of the affected environment and the potential cumulative impacts of the reasonably foreseeable actions under that program or within that geographical area.

24c. Q. What is the function of tiering in such cases?

A. Tiering is a procedure which allows an agency to avoid duplication of paperwork through the incorporation by reference of the general discussions and relevant specific discussions from an environmental impact statement of broader scope into one of lesser scope or vice versa. In the example given in Question 24b, this would mean that an overview EIS would be prepared for all of the energy activities reasonably foreseeable in a particular geographic area or resulting from a particular development program. This impact statement would be followed by site-specific or project-specific EISs. The tiering process would make each EIS of greater use and meaning to the public as the plan or program develops, without duplication of the analysis prepared for the previous impact statement.

25a. Q. When is it appropriate to use

appendices instead of including information in the body of an EIS?

A. The body of the EIS should be a succinct statement of all the information on environmental impacts and alternatives that the decisionmaker and the public need, in order to make the decision and to ascertain that every significant factor has been examined. The EIS must explain or summarize methodologies of research and modeling, and the results of research that may have been conducted to analyze impacts and alternatives.

Lengthy technical discussions of modeling methodology, baseline studies, or other work are best reserved for the appendix. In other words, if only technically trained individuals are likely to understand a particular discussion then it should go in the appendix, and a plain language summary of the analysis and conclusions of that technical discussion should go in the text of the EIS.

The final statement must also contain the agency's responses to comments on the draft EIS. These responses will be primarily in the form of changes in the document itself, but specific answers to each significant comment should also be included. These specific responses may be placed in an appendix. If the comments are especially voluminous, summaries of the comments and responses will suffice. (See Question 29 regarding the level of detail required for responses to comments.)

25b. Q. How does an appendix differ from incorporation by reference?

A. First, if at all possible, the appendix accompanies the EIS, whereas the material which is incorporated by reference does not accompany the EIS. Thus the appendix should contain information that reviewers will be likely to want to examine. The appendix should include material that pertains to preparation of a particular EIS. Research papers directly relevant to the proposal, lists of affected species, discussion of the methodology of models used in the analysis of impacts, extremely detailed responses to comments, or other information, would be placed in the appendix.

The appendix must be complete and available at the time the EIS is filed. Five copies of the appendix must be sent to EPA with five copies of the EIS for filing. If the appendix is too bulky to be circulated, it instead must be placed in conveniently accessible locations or furnished directly to commentors upon request. If it is not circulated with the EIS, the Notice of Availability published by EPA must so state, giving a telephone number to enable potential commentors to locate or request copies of the appendix promptly.

Material that is not directly related to preparation of the EIS should be incorporated by reference. This would include other EISs, research papers in the general literature, technical background papers or other material that someone with technical training could use to evaluate the analysis of the proposal. These must be made available, either by citing the literature, furnishing copies to central locations, or sending copies directly to commentors upon request.

Care must be taken in all cases to ensure that material incorporated by reference, and the occasional appendix that does not accompany the EIS, are in fact available for the full minimum public comment period.

26a. Q. How detailed must an EIS index be?

A. The EIS index should have a level of detail sufficient to focus on areas of the EIS of reasonable interest to any reader. It cannot be restricted to the most important topics. On the other hand, it need not identify every conceivable term or phrase in the EIS. If an agency believes that the reader is reasonably likely to be interested in a topic, it should be included.

26b. Q. Is a keyword index required?

A. No. A keyword index is a relatively short list of descriptive terms that identifies the key concepts or subject areas in a document. For example it could consist of 20 terms which describe the most significant aspects of an EIS that a future researcher would need: type of proposal, type of impacts, type of environment, geographical area, sampling or modelling methodologies used. This technique permits the compilation of EIS data banks, by facilitating quick and inexpensive access to stored materials. While a keyword index is not required by the regulations, it could be a useful addition for several reasons. First, it can be useful as a quick index for reviewers of the EIS, helping to focus on areas of interest. Second, if an agency keeps a listing of the keyword indexes of the EISs it produces, the EIS preparers themselves will have quick access to similar research data and methodologies to aid their future EIS work. Third, a keyword index will be needed to make an EIS available to future researchers using EIS data banks that are being developed. Preparation of such an index now when the document is produced will save a later effort when the data banks become operational.

27a. Q. If a consultant is used in preparing an EIS, must the list of preparers identify members of the consulting firm as well as the agency NEPA staff who were primarily responsible?

A. Section 1502.17 requires identification of the names and qualifications of persons who were primarily responsible for preparing the EIS or significant background papers, including basic components of the statement. This means that members of a consulting firm preparing material that is to become part of the EIS must be identified. The EIS should identify these individuals even though the consultant's contribution may have been modified by the agency.

27b. Q. Should agency staff involved in reviewing and editing the EIS also be included in the list of preparers?

A. Agency personnel who wrote basic components of the EIS or significant background papers must, of course, be identified. The EIS should also list the technical editors who reviewed or edited the statements.

27c. Q. How much information should be included on each person listed?

A. The list of preparers should normally not exceed two pages. Therefore, agencies must determine which individuals had *primary* responsibility and need not identify individuals with minor involvement. The list of preparers should include a very brief identification of the individuals involved, their qualifications (expertise, professional disciplines) and the specific portion of the EIS for which they are responsible. This may be done in tabular form to cut down on length. A line or two for each person's qualifications should be sufficient.

28. Q. May an agency file xerox copies of an EIS with EPA pending the completion of printing the document?

A. Xerox copies of an EIS may be filed with EPA prior to printing only if the xerox copies are simultaneously made available to other agencies and the public. Section 1506.9 of the regulations, which governs EIS filing, specifically requires Federal agencies to file EISs with EPA no earlier than the EIS is distributed to the public. However, this section does not prohibit xeroxing as a form of reproduction and distribution. When an agency chooses xeroxing as the reproduction method, the EIS must be clear and legible to permit ease of reading and ultimate microfiching of the EIS. Where color graphs are important to the EIS, they should be reproduced and circulated with the xeroxed copy.

29a Q. What response must an agency provide to a comment on a draft EIS which states that the EIS's methodology is inadequate or inadequately explained? For example, what level of detail must an agency include in its response to a simple postcard comment making such an allegation?

A. Appropriate responses to comments are described in Section 1503.4. Normally the responses should result in changes in the text of the EIS, not simply a separate answer at the back of the document. But, in addition, the agency must state what its response was, and if the agency decides that no substantive response to a comment is necessary, it must explain briefly why.

An agency is not under an obligation to issue a lengthy reiteration of its methodology for any portion of an EIS if the only comment addressing the methodology is a simple complaint that the EIS methodology is inadequate. But agencies must respond to comments, however brief, which are specific in their criticism of agency methodology. For example, if a commentor on an EIS said that an agency's air quality dispersion analysis or methodology was inadequate, and the agency had included a discussion of that analysis in the EIS, little if anything need be added in response to such a comment. However, if the commentor said that the dispersion analysis was inadequate because of its use of a certain computational technique, or that a dispersion analysis was inadequately explained because computational techniques were not included or referenced, then the agency would have to respond in a substantive and meaningful way to such a comment.

If a number of comments are identical or very similar, agencies may group the comments and prepare a single answer for each group. Comments may be summarized if they are especially voluminous. The comments or summaries must be attached to the EIS regardless of whether the agency believes they merit individual discussion in the body of the final EIS.

29b. Q. How must an agency respond to a comment on a draft EIS that raises a new alternative not previously considered in the draft EIS?

A. This question might arise in several possible situations. First, a commentor on a draft EIS may indicate that there is a possible alternative which, in the agency's view, is not a reasonable alternative. Section 1502.14(a): If that is the case, the agency must explain why the comment does not warrant further agency response, citing authorities or reasons that support the agency's position and, if appropriate, indicate those circumstances which would trigger agency reappraisal or further response. Section 1503.4(a). For example, a commentor on a draft EIS on a coal fired power plant may suggest the alternative of using synthetic fuel. The agency may reject the alternative with a brief discussion (with authorities) of the unavailability of synthetic fuel within the time frame necessary to meet the need and purpose of the proposed facility.

A second possibility is that an agency may receive a comment indicating that a particular alternative, while reasonable, should be modified somewhat, for example, to achieve certain mitigation benefits, or for other reasons. If the modification is reasonable, the agency should include a discussion of it in the final EIS. For example, a commentor on a draft EIS on a proposal for a pumped storage power facility might suggest that the applicant's proposed alternative should be enhanced by the addition of certain reasonable mitigation measures, including the purchase and setaside of a wildlife preserve to substitute for the tract to be destroyed by the project. The modified alternative including the additional mitigation measures should be discussed by the agency in the final EIS.

A third slightly different possibility is that a comment on a draft EIS will raise an alternative which is a minor variation of one of the alternatives discussed in the draft EIS, but this variation was not given any consideration by the agency. In such a case, the agency should develop and evaluate the new alternative, if it is reasonable, in the final EIS. If it is qualitatively within the spectrum of alternatives that were discussed in the draft, a supplemental draft will not be needed. For example, a commentor on a draft EIS to designate a wilderness area within a National Forest might reasonably identify a specific tract of the forest, and urge that it be considered for designation. If the draft EIS considered designation of a range of alternative tracts which encompassed forest area of similar quality and quantity, no supplemental EIS would have to be prepared. The agency could fulfill its obligation by addressing that specific alternative in the final EIS.

As another example, an EIS on an urban housing project may analyze the alternatives of constructing 2,000, 4,000, or 6,000 units. A commentor on the draft EIS might urge the consideration of constructing 5,000 units utilizing a different configuration of buildings. This alternative is within the spectrum of alternatives already considered, and, therefore, could be addressed in the final EIS.

A fourth possibility is that a commentor points out an alternative which is not a variation of the proposal or of any alternative discussed in the draft impact statement, and is a reasonable alternative that warrants serious agency response. In such a case, the agency must issue a supplement to the draft EIS that discusses this new alternative. For example, a commentor on a draft EIS on a nuclear power plant might suggest that a reasonable alternative for meeting the projected need for power would be through peak load management and energy conservation programs. If the permitting agency has failed to consider that approach in the Draft EIS, and the approach cannot be dismissed by the agency as unreasonable, a supplement to the Draft EIS, which discusses that alternative, must be prepared. (If necessary, the same supplement should

also discuss substantial changes in the proposed action or significant new circumstances or information, as required by Section 1502.9(c)(1) of the Council's regulations.)

If the new alternative was not raised by the commentor during scoping, but could have been, commentors may find that they are unpersuasive in their efforts to have their suggested alternative analyzed in detail by the agency. However, if the new alternative is discovered or developed later, and it could not reasonably have been raised during the scoping process, then the agency must address it in a supplemental draft EIS. The agency is, in any case, ultimately responsible for preparing an adequate EIS that considers all alternatives.

30. Q. When a cooperating agency with jurisdiction by law intends to adopt a lead agency's EIS and it is not satisfied with the adequacy of the document, may the cooperating agency adopt only the part of the EIS with which it is satisfied? If so, would a cooperating agency with jurisdiction by law have to prepare a separate EIS or EIS supplement covering the areas of disagreement with the lead agency?

A. Generally, a cooperating agency may adopt a lead agency's EIS without recirculating it if it concludes that its NEPA requirements and its comments and suggestions have been satisfied. Section 1506.3(a), (c). If necessary, a cooperating agency may adopt only a portion of the lead agency's EIS and may reject that part of the EIS with which it disagrees, stating publicly why it did so. Section 1506.3(a).

A cooperating agency with jurisidiction by law (e.g., an agency with independent legal responsibilities with respect to the proposal) has an independent legal obligation to comply with NEPA. Therefore, if the cooperating agency determines that the EIS is wrong or inadequate, it must prepare a supplement to the EIS, replacing or adding any needed information, and must circulate the supplement as a draft for public and agency review and comment. A final supplemental EIS would be required before the agency could take action. The adopted portions of the lead agency EIS should be circulated with the supplement. Section 1506.3(b). A cooperating agency with jurisdiction by law will have to prepare its own Record of Decision for its action, in which it must explain how it reached its conclusions. Each agency should explain how and why its conclusions differ, if that is the case, from those of other agencies which issued their Records of Decision earlier.

An agency that did not cooperate in preparation of an EIS may also adopt an EIS or portion thereof. But this would

arise only in rare instances, because an agency adopting an EIS for use in its own decision normally would have been a cooperating agency. If the proposed action for which the EIS was prepared is substantially the same as the proposed action of the adopting agency, the EIS may be adopted as long as it is recirculated as a final EIS and the agency announces what it is doing. This would be followed by the 30-day review period and issuance of a Record of Decision by the adopting agency. If the proposed action by the adopting agency is not substantially the same as that in the EIS (i.e., if an EIS on one action is being adapted for use in a decision on another action), the EIS would be treated as a draft and circulated for the normal public comment period and other procedures. Section 1506.3(b).

31a. Q. Do the Council's NEPA regulations apply to independent regulatory agencies like the Federal Energy Regulatory Commission (FERC) and the Nuclear Regulatory Commission?

A. The statutory requirements of NEPA's Section 102 apply to "all agencies of the federal government." The NEPA regulations implement the procedural provisions of NEPA as set forth in NEPA's Section 102(2) for all agencies of the federal government. The NEPA regulations apply to independent regulatory agencies, however, they do not direct independent regulatory agencies or other agencies to make decisions in any particular way or in a way inconsistent with an agency's statutory charter. Sections 1500.3, 1500.6, 1507.1, and 1507.3.

31b. Q. Can an Executive Branch agency like the Department of the Interior adopt an EIS prepared by an independent regulatory agency such as FERC?

A. If an independent regulatory agency such as FERC has prepared an EIS in connection with its approval of a proposed project, an Executive Branch agency (e.g., the Bureau of Land Management in the Department of the Interior) may, in accordance with Section 1506.3, adopt the EIS or a portion thereof for its use in considering the same proposal. In such a case the EIS must, to the satisfaction of the adopting agency, meet the standards for an adequate statement under the NEPA regulations (including scope and quality of analysis of alternatives) and must satisfy the adopting agency's comments and suggestions. If the independent regulatory agency fails to comply with the NEPA regulations, the cooperating or adopting agency may find that it is unable to adopt the EIS, thus forcing the preparation of a new EIS or EIS Supplement for the same action. The NEPA regulations were made applicable to all federal agencies in order to avoid this result, and to achieve uniform application and efficiency of the NEPA process.

32. Q. Under what circumstances do old EISs have to be supplemented before taking action on a proposal?

A. As a rule of thumb, if the proposal has not yet been implemented, or if the EIS concerns an ongoing program, EISs that are more than 5 years old should be carefully reexamined to determine if the criteria in Section 1502.9 compel preparation of an EIS supplement.

If an agency has made a substantial change in a proposed action that is relevant to environmental concerns, or if there are significant new circumstances or information relevant to environmental concerns and bearing on the proposed action or its impacts, a supplemental EIS must be prepared for an old EIS so that the agency has the best possible information to make any necessary substantive changes in its decisions regarding the proposal. Section 1502.9(c).

33a. Q. When must a referral of an interagency disagreement be made to the Council?

A. The Council's referral procedure is a *pre-decision* referral process for interagency disagreements. Hence, Section 1504.3 requires that a referring agency must deliver its referral to the Council not later than 25 days after publication by EPA of notice that the final EIS is available (unless the lead agency grants an extension of time under Section 1504.3(b)).

33b. Q. May a referral be made after this issuance of a Record of Decision?

A. No, except for cases where agencies provide an internal appeal procedure which permits simultaneous filing of the final EIS and the record of decision (ROD). Section 1506.10(b)(2). Otherwise, as stated above, the process is a pre-decision referral process. Referrals must be made within 25 days after the notice of availability of the final EIS, whereas the final decision (ROD) may not be made or filed until after 30 days from the notice of availability of the EIS. Sections 1504.3(b), 1506.10(b). If a lead agency has granted an extension of time for another agency to take action on a referral, the ROD may not be issued until the extension has expired.

34a. Q. Must Records of Decision (RODs) be made public? How should they be made available?

A. Under the regulations, agencies must prepare a "concise *public* record of decision," which contains the elements specified in Section 1505.2. This public record may be integrated into any other decision record prepared by the agency, or it may be separate if decision documents are not normally made public. The Record of Decision is intended by the Council to be an environmental document (even though it is not explicitly mentioned in the

definition of "environmental document" in Section 1508.10). Therefore, it must be made available to the public through appropriate public notice as required by Section 1506.6(b). However, there is no specific requirement for publication of the ROD itself, either in the Federal Register or elsewhere.

34b. Q. May the summary section in the final Environmental Impact Statement substitute for or constitute an agency's Record of Decision?

A. No. An environmental impact statement is supposed to inform the decisionmaker before the decision is made. Sections 1502.1, 1505.2. The Council's regulations provide for a 30-day period after notice is published that the final EIS has been filed with EPA before the agency may take final action. During that period, in addition to the agency's own internal final review, the public and other agencies can comment on the final EIS prior to the agency's final action on the proposal. In addition, the Council's regulations make clear that the requirements for the summary in an EIS are not the same as the requirements for a ROD. Sections 1502.12 and 1505.2.

34c. Q. What provisions should Records of Decision contain pertaining to mitigation and monitoring?

A. Lead agencies "shall include appropriate conditions [including mitigation measures and monitoring and enforcement programs] in grants, permits or other approvals" and shall "condition funding of actions on mitigation." Section 1505.3. Any such measures that are adopted must be explained and committed in the ROD.

The reasonable alternative mitigation measures and monitoring programs should have been addressed in the draft and final EIS. The discussion of mitigation and monitoring in a Record of Decision must be more detailed than a general statement that mitigation is being required, but not so detailed as to duplicate discussion of mitigation in the EIS. The Record of Decision should contain a concise summary identification of the mitigation measures which the agency has committed itself to adopt.

The Record of Decision must also state whether all practicable mitigation measures have been adopted, and if not, why not. Section 1505.2(c). The Record of Decision must identify the mitigation measures and monitoring and enforcement programs that have been selected and plainly indicate that they are adopted as part of the agency's decision. If the proposed action is the issuance of a permit or other approval, the specific details of the mitigation measures shall then be included as appropriate conditions in whatever grants, permits, funding or other approvals are being made by the federal agency. Section 1505.3 (a), (b). If the

proposal is to be carried out by the federal agency itself, the Record of Decision should delineate the mitigation and monitoring measures in sufficient detail to constitute an enforceable commitment, or incorporate by reference the portions of the EIS that do so.

34d. Q. What is the enforceability of a Record of Decision?

A. Pursuant to generally recognized principles of federal administrative law, agencies will be held accountable for preparing Records of Decision that conform to the decisions actually made and for carrying out the actions set forth in the Records of Decision. This is based on the principle that an agency must comply with its own decisons and regulations once they are adopted. Thus, the terms of a Record of Decision are enforceable by agencies and private parties. A Record of Decision can be used to compel compliance with or execution of the mitigation measures identified therein.

35. Q. How long should the NEPA process take to complete?

A. When an EIS is required, the process obviously will take longer than when an EA is the only document prepared. But the Council's NEPA regulations encourage streamlined review, adoption of deadlines, elimination of duplicative work, eliciting suggested alternatives and other comments early through scoping, cooperation among agencies, and consultation with applicants during project planning. The Council has advised agencies that under the new NEPA regulations even large complex energy projects would require only about 12 months for the completion of the entire EIS process. For most major actions, this period is well within the planning time that is needed in any event, apart from NEPA.

The time required for the preparation of program EISs may be greater. The Council also recognizes that some projects will entail difficult long-term planning and/or the acquisition of certain data which of necessity will require more time for the preparation of the EIS. Indeed, some proposals should be given more time for the thoughtful preparation of an EIS and development of a decision which fulfills NEPA's substantive goals.

For cases in which only an environmental assessment will be prepared, the NEPA process should take no more than 3 months, and in many cases substantially less, as part of the normal analysis and approval process for the action.

36a. Q. How long and detailed must an environmental assessment (EA) be?

A. The environmental assessment is a concise public document which has three defined functions. (1) It briefly provides sufficient evidence and analysis for determining whether to prepare an EIS; (2) it aids an agency's compliance with NEPA when no EIS is necessary, i.e., it helps to identify better alternatives and mitigation measures; and (3) it facilitates preparation of an EIS when one is necessary. Section 1508.9(a).

Since the EA is a concise document, it should not contain long descriptions or detailed data which the agency may have gathered. Rather, it should contain a brief discussion of the need for the proposal, alternatives to the proposal, the environmental impacts of the proposed action and alternatives, and a list of agencies and persons consulted. Section 1508.9(b).

While the regulations do not contain page limits for EA's, the Council has generally advised agencies to keep the length of EAs to not more than approximately 10–15 pages. Some agencies expressly provide page guidelines (e.g., 10–15 pages in the case of the Army Corps). To avoid undue length, the EA may incorporate by reference background data to support its concise discussion of the proposal and relevant issues.

36b. Q. Under what circumstances is a lengthy EA appropriate?

A. Agencies should avoid preparing lengthy EAs except in unusual cases, where a proposal is so complex that a concise document cannot meet the goals of Section 1508.9 *and* where it is extremely difficult to determine whether the proposal could have significant environmental effects. In most cases, however, a lengthy EA indicates that an EIS is needed.

37a. Q. What is the level of detail of information that must be included in a finding of no significant impact (FONSI)?

A. The FONSI is a document in which the agency briefly explains the reasons why an action will not have a significant effect on the human environment and, therefore, why an EIS will not be prepared. Section 1508.13. The finding itself need not be detailed, but must succinctly state the reasons for deciding that the action will have no significant environmental effects, and, if relevant, must show which factors were weighted most heavily in the determination. In addition to this statement, the FONSI must include, summarize, or attach and incorporate by reference, the environmental assessment.

37b. Q. What are the criteria for deciding whether a FONSI should be made available for public review for 30 days before the agency's final determination whether to prepare an EIS?

A. Public review is necessary, for example, (a) if the proposal is a borderline case, i.e., when there is a reasonable argument for preparation of an EIS; (b) if it is an unusual case, a new kind of action, or a precedent setting case such as a first intrusion of even a minor development into a pristine area; (c) when there is either scientific or public controversy over the proposal; or (d) when it involves a proposal which is or is closely similar to one which normally requires preparation of an EIS. Sections 1501.4(e)(2), 1508.27. Agencies also must allow a period of public review of the FONSI if the proposed action would be located in a floodplain or wetland. E.O. 11988, Sec. 2(a)(4); E.O. 11990, Sec. 2(b).

38. Q. Must (EAs) and FONSIs be made public? If so, how should this be done?

A. Yes, they must be available to the public. Section 1506.6 requires agencies to involve the public in implementing their NEPA procedures, and this includes public involvement in the preparation of EAs and FONSIs. These are public "environmental documents" under Section 1506.6(b), and, therefore, agencies must give public notice of their availability. A combination of methods may be used to give notice, and the methods should be tailored to the needs of particular cases. Thus, a **Federal Register** notice of availability of the documents, coupled with notices in national publications and mailed to interested national groups might be appropriate for proposals that are national in scope. Local newspaper notices may be more appropriate for regional or site-specific proposals.

The objective, however, is to notify all interested or affected parties. If this is not being achieved, then the methods should be reevaluated and changed. Repeated failure to reach the interested or affected public would be interpreted as a violation of the regulations.

39. Q. Can an EA and FONSI be used to impose enforceable mitigation measures, monitoring programs, or other requirements, even though there is no requirement in the regulations in such cases for a formal Record of Decision?

A. Yes. In cases where an environmental assessment is the appropriate environmental document, there still may be mitigation measures or alternatives that would be desirable to consider and adopt even though the impacts of the proposal will not be "significant." In such cases, the EA should include a discussion of these measures or alternatives to "assist agency planning and decisionmaking" and to "aid an agency's compliance with [NEPA] when no environmental impact statement is necessary." Section 1501.3(b), 1508.9(a)(2). The appropriate mitigation measures can be imposed as enforceable permit conditions, or adopted as part of the agency final decision in the same manner mitigation measures are adopted in the formal Record of Decision that is required in EIS cases.

40. Q. If an environmental assessment indicates that the environmental effects of a proposal are significant but that, with mitigation, those effects may be reduced to less than significant levels, may the agency make a finding of no significant impact rather than prepare an EIS? Is that a legitimate function of an EA and scoping?

A. Mitigation measures may be relied upon to make a finding of no significant impact only if they are imposed by statute or regulation, or submitted by an applicant or agency as part of the original proposal. As a general rule, the regulations contemplate that agencies should use a broad approach in defining significance and should not rely on the possibility of mitigation as an excuse to avoid the EIS requirement. Sections 1508.8, 1508.27.

If a proposal appears to have adverse effects which would be significant, and certain mitigation measures are then developed during the scoping or EA stages, the existence of such *possible* mitigation does not obviate the need for an EIS. Therefore, if scoping or the EA identifies certain mitigation possibilities without altering the nature of the overall proposal itself, the agency should continue the EIS process and submit the proposal, and the potential mitigation, for public and agency review and comment. This is essential to ensure that the final decision is based on all the relevant factors and that the full NEPA process will result in enforceable mitigation measures through the Record of Decision.

In some instances, where the proposal itself so integrates mitigation from the beginning that it is impossible to define the proposal without including the mitigation, the agency may then rely on the mitigation measures in determining that the overall effects would not be significant (e.g., where an application for a permit for a small hydro dam is based on a binding commitment to build fish ladders, to permit adequate down stream flow, and to replace any lost wetlands, wildlife habitat and recreational potential). In those instances, agencies should make the FONSI and EA available for 30 days of public comment before taking action. Section 1501.4(e)(2).

Similarly, scoping may result in a redefinition of the entire project, as a result of mitigation proposals. In that case, the agency may alter its previous decision to do an EIS, as long as the agency or applicant resubmits the entire proposal and the EA and FONSI are available for 30 days of review and comment. One example of this would be where the size and location of a proposed industrial park are changed to avoid affecting a nearby wetland area.

Memorandum: Scoping Guidance
(Council on Environmental Quality Apr. 30, 1981)

I. Introduction

A. Background of this document

In 1978, with the publication of the proposed NEPA regulations (since adopted as formal rules, 40 C.F.R. Parts 1500-1508), the Council on Environmental Quality gave formal recognition to an increasingly used term—scoping. Scoping is an idea that has long been familiar to those involved in NEPA compliance: In order to manage effectively the preparation of an environmental impact statement (EIS), one must determine the scope of the document—that is, what will be covered, and in what detail. Planning of this kind was a normal component of EIS preparation. But the consideration of issues and choice of alternatives to be examined was in too many cases completed outside of public view. The innovative approach to scoping in the regulations is that the process is open to the public and state and local governments, as well as to affected federal agencies. This open process gives rise to important new opportunities for better and more efficient NEPA analyses, and simultaneously places new responsibilities on public and agency participants alike to surface their concerns early. Scoping helps insure that real problems are identified early and properly studied; that issues that are of no concern do not consume time and effort; that the draft statement when first made public is balanced and thorough; and that the delays occasioned by re-doing an inadequate draft are avoided. Scoping does not create problems that did not already exist; it ensures that problems that would have been raised anyway are identified early in the process.

Many members of the public as well as agency staffs engaged in the NEPA process have told the Council that the open scoping requirement is one of the most far-reaching changes engendered by the NEPA regulations. They have predicted that scoping could have a profound positive effect on environmental analyses, on the impact statement process itself, and ultimately on decisionmaking.

Because the concept of open scoping was new, the Council decided to encourage agencies' innovation without unduly restrictive guidance. Thus the regulations relating to scoping are very simple. They state that "there shall be an early and open process for determining the scope of issues to be addressed" which "shall be termed scoping," but they lay down few specific requirements. (Section 1501.7*). They require an open process with public notice; identification of significant and insignificant issues; allocation of EIS preparation assignments; identification of related analysis requirements in order to avoid duplication of work; and the planning of a schedule for EIS preparation that meshes with the agency's decisionmaking schedule. (Section 1501.7(a)). The regulations encourage, but do not require, setting time limits and page limits for the EIS, and holding scoping meetings. (Section 1501.7(b)). Aside from these general outlines, the regulations left the agencies on their own. The Council did not believe, and still does not, that it is necessary or appropriate to dictate the specific manner in which over 100 federal agencies should deal with the public. However, the Council has received several requests for more guidance. In 1980 we decided to investigate the agency and public response to the scoping requirement, to find out what was working and what was not, and to share this with all agencies and the public.

The Council first conducted its own survey, asking federal agencies to report some of their scoping experiences. The Council then contracted with the American Arbitration Association and Clark McGlennon Associates to survey the scoping techniques of major agencies and to study several innovative methods in detail.** Council staff conducted a two-day workshop in Atlanta in June 1980, to discuss with federal agency NEPA staff and several EIS contractors what seems to work best in scoping of different types of proposals, and discussed scoping with federal, state and local officials in meetings in all 10 federal regions.

This document is a distillation of all the work that has been done so far by many people to identify valuable scoping techniques.

It is offered as a guide to encourage success and to help avoid pitfalls. Since scoping methods are still evolving, the Council welcomes any comments on this guide, and may add to it or revise it in coming years.

B. What scoping is and what it can do

Scoping is often the first contact between proponents of a proposal and the public. This fact is the source of the power of scoping and of the trepidation that it sometimes evokes. If a scoping meeting is held, people on both sides of an issue will be in the same room and, if all goes well, will speak to each other. The possibilities that flow from this situation are vast. Therefore, a large portion of this document is devoted to the productive management of meetings and the de-fusing of possible heated disagreements.

Even if a meeting is not held, the scoping process leads EIS preparers to think about the proposal early on, in order to explain it to the public and affected agencies. The participants respond with their own concerns about significant issues and suggestions of alternatives. Thus as the draft EIS is prepared, it will include, from the beginning, a reflection or at least an acknowledgement of the cooperating agencies' and the public's concerns. This reduces the need for changes after the draft is finished, because it reduces the chances of overlooking a significant issue or reasonable alternative. It also in many cases increases public confidence in NEPA and the decisionmaking process, thereby reducing delays, such as from litigation, later on when implementing the decisions. As we will discuss further in this document, the public generally responds positively when its views are taken seriously, even if they cannot be wholly accommodated.

But scoping is not simply another "public relations" meeting requirement. It has specific and fairly limited objectives: (a) to identify the affected public and agency concerns; (b) to facilitate an efficient EIS preparation process, through assembling the cooperating agencies, assigning EIS writing tasks, ascertaining all the related permits and reviews that must be scheduled concurrently, and setting time or page limits; (c) to define the issues and alternatives that will be examined in detail in the EIS while simultaneously devoting less attention and time to issues which cause no concern; and (d) to save time in the overall process by helping to ensure that draft statements adequately address relevant issues, reducing the possibility that new comments will cause a statement to be rewritten or supplemented.

Sometimes the scoping process enables early identification of a few serious problems with a proposal, which can be changed or solved because the proposal is still being developed. In these cases, scoping the EIS can actually lead to the solution of a conflict over the proposed action itself. We have found that this extra benefit of scoping occurs fairly frequently. But it cannot be expected in most cases, and scoping can still be considered successful when conflicts are clarified but not solved. This guide does not presume that resolution of conflicts over proposals is a principal goal of scoping, because it is only possible in limited circumstances. Instead, the Council views the principal goal of scoping to be an adequate and efficiently prepared EIS. Our suggestions and recommendations are aimed at reducing the conflicts among affected interests that impede this limited objective. But we are aware of the possibilities of more general conflict resolution that are inherent in any productive discussions among interested parties. We urge all participants in scoping processes to be alert to this larger context, in which scoping could prove to be the first step in environmental problem-solving.

Scoping can lay a firm foundation for the rest of the decisionmaking process. If the EIS can be relied upon to include all the necessary information for formulating policies and making rational choices, the agency will be better able to make a sound and prompt decision. In addition, if it is clear that all reasonable alternatives are being seriously considered, the public will usually be more satisfied with the choice among them.

II. Advice for Government Agencies Conducting Scoping

A. General context

Scoping is a process, not an event or a meeting. It continues throughout the planning for an EIS, and may involve a series of meetings, telephone conversations, or written comments from different interested groups. Because it is a process, participants must

*All citations are to the NEPA regulations, 40 C.F.R. Parts 1500-1508 unless otherwise specified.

**The results of this examination are reported in "Scoping the Content of EISs: An Evaluation of Agencies' Experiences," which is available from the Council or the Resource Planning Analysis Office of the U.S. Geological Survey, 750 National Center, Reston, Va. 22092.

remain flexible. The scope of an EIS occasionally may need to be modified later if a new issue surfaces, no matter how thorough the scoping was. But it makes sense to try to set the scope of the statement as early as possible.

Scoping may identify people who already have knowledge about a site or an alternative proposal or a relevant study, and induce them to make it available. This can save a lot of research time and money. But people will not come forward unless they believe their views and materials will receive serious consideration. Thus scoping is a crucial first step toward building public confidence in a fair environmental analysis and ultimately a fair decisionmaking process.

One further point to remember: the lead agency cannot shed its responsibility to assess each significant impact or alternative even if one is found after scoping. But anyone who hangs back and fails to raise something that reasonably could have been raised earlier on will have a hard time prevailing during later stages of the NEPA process or if litigation ensues. Thus a thorough scoping process does provide some protection against subsequent lawsuits.

B. Step-by-step through the process

1. Start scoping after *you have enough information*

Scoping cannot be useful until the agency knows enough about the proposed action to identify most of the affected parties, and to present a coherent proposal and a suggested initial list of environmental issues and alternatives. Until that time there is no way to explain to the public or other agencies *what* you want them to get involved *in*. So the first stage is to gather preliminary information from the applicant, or to compose a clear picture of your proposal, if it is being developed by the agency.

2. Prepare an information packet

In many cases, scoping of the EIS has been preceded by preparation of an environmental assessment (EA) as the basis for the decision to proceed with an EIS. In such cases, the EA will, of course, include the preliminary information that is needed.

If you have not prepared an EA, you should put together a brief information packet consisting of a description of the proposal, an initial list of impacts and alternatives, maps, drawings, and any other material or references that can help the interested public to understand what is being proposed. The proposed work plan of the EIS is not usually sufficient for this purpose. Such documents rarely contain a description of the goals of the proposal to enable readers to develop alternatives.

At this stage, the purpose of the information is to enable participants to make an intelligent contribution to scoping the EIS. Because they will be helping to plan what will be examined during the environmental review, they need to know where you are now in that planning process.

Include in the packet a brief explanation of what scoping is, and what procedure will be used, to give potential participants a context for their involvement. Be sure to point out that you want comments from participants on very specific matters. Also reiterate that no decision has yet been made on the contents of the EIS, much less on the proposal itself. Thus, explain that you do not yet have a preferred alternative, but that you may identify the preferred alternative in the draft EIS. (See Section 1502.14(e)). This should reduce the tendency of participants to perceive the proposal as already a definite plan. Encourage them to focus on recommendations for improvements to the various alternatives.

Some of the complaints alleging that scoping can be a waste of time stem from the fact that the participants may not know what the proposal is until they arrive at a meeting. Even the most intelligent among us can rarely make useful, substantive comments on the spur of the moment. Don't expect helpful suggestions to result if participants are put in such a position.

3. Design the scoping process for each project

There is no established or required procedure for scoping. The process can be carried out by meetings, telephone conversations, written comments, or a combination of all three. It is important to tailor the type, the timing and the location of public and agency comments to the proposal at hand.

For example, a proposal to adopt a land management plan for a National Forest in a sparsely populated region may not lend itself to calling a single meeting in a central location. While people living in the area and elsewhere may be interested, any meeting place will be inconvenient for most of the potential participants. One solution is to distribute the information packet, solicit written comments,

list a telephone number with the name of the scoping coordinator, and invite comments to be phoned in. Otherwise, small meetings in several locations may be necessary when face-to-face communication is important.

In another case, a site-specific construction project may be proposed. This would be a better candidate for a central scoping meeting. But you must first find out if anyone would be interested in attending such a meeting. If you simply assume that a meeting is necessary, you may hire a hall and a stenographer, assemble your staff for a meeting, and find that nobody shows up. There are many proposals that just do not generate sufficient public interest to cause people to attend another public meeting. So a wise early step is to contact known local citizens groups and civic leaders.

In addition, you may suggest in your initial scoping notice and information packet that all those who desire a meeting should call to request one. That way you will only hear from those who are seriously interested in attending.

The question of where to hold a meeting is a difficult one in many cases. Except for site specific construction projects, it may be unclear where the interested parties can be found. For example, an EIS on a major energy development program may involve policy issues and alternatives to the program that are of interest to public groups all over the nation, and to agencies headquartered in Washington, D.C., while the physical impacts might be expected to be felt most strongly in a particular region of the country. In such a case, if personal contact is desired, several meetings would be necessary, especially in the affected region and in Washington, to enable all interests to be heard. —

As a general guide, unless a proposal has no site specific impacts, scoping meetings should not be *confined* to Washington. Agencies should try to elicit the views of people who are closer to the affected regions.

The key is to be flexible. It may not be possible to plan the whole scoping process at the outset, unless you know who all the potential players are. You can start with written comments, move on to an informal meeting, and hold further meetings if desired.

There are several reasons to hold a scoping meeting. First, some of the best effects of scoping stem from the fact that all parties have the opportunity to meet one another and to listen to the concerns of the others. There is no satisfactory substitute for personal contact to achieve this result. If there is any possibility that resolution of underlying conflicts over a proposal may be achieved, this is always enhanced by the development of personal and working relationships among the parties.

Second, even in a conflict situation people usually respond positively when they are treated as partners in the project review process. If they feel confident that their views were actually heard and taken seriously, they will be more likely to be satisfied that the decisionmaking process was fair even if they disagree with the outcome. It is much easier to show people that you are listening to them if you hold a face-to-face meeting where they can see you writing down their points, than if their only contact is through written comments.

If you suspect that a particular proposal could benefit from a meeting with the affected public at any time during its review, the best time to have the meeting is during this early scoping stage. The fact that you are willing to discuss openly a proposal before you have committed substantial resources to it will often enhance the chances for reaching an accord.

If you decide that a public meeting is appropriate, you still must decide what type of meeting, or how many meetings, to hold. We will discuss meetings in detail below in "Conducting a Public Meeting." But as part of designing the scoping process, you must decide between a single meeting and multiple ones for different interest groups, and whether to hold a separate meeting for government agency participants.

The single large public meeting brings together all the interested parties, which has both advantages and disadvantages. If the meeting is efficiently run, you can cover a lot of interests and issues in a short time. And a single meeting does reduce agency travel time and expense. In some cases it may be an advantage to have all interest groups hear each others' concerns, possibly promoting compromise. It is definitely important to have the staffs of the cooperating agencies, as well as the lead agency, hear the public views of what the significant issues are; and it will be difficult and expensive for the cooperating agencies to attend several meetings. But if there are opposing groups of citizens who feel strongly on both sides of an issue, the setting of the large meeting may needlessly create tension and an emotional confrontation between the groups. Moreover, some people may feel intimidated in such a setting, and won't express themselves at all.

The principal drawback of the large meeting, however, is that it is generally unwieldy. To keep order, discussion is limited, dialogue is difficult, and often all participants are frustrated, agency and public alike. Large meetings can serve to identify the interest groups for future discussion, but often little else is accomplished. Large meetings often become "events" where grandstanding substitutes for substantive comments. Many agencies resort to a formal hearing-type format to maintain control, and this can cause resentments among participants who come to the meeting expecting a responsive discussion.

For these reasons, we recommend that meetings be kept small and informal, and that you hold several, if necessary, to accommodate the different interest groups. The other solution is to break a large gathering into small discussion groups, which is discussed below. Using either method increases the likelihood that participants will level with you and communicate their underlying concerns rather than make an emotional statement just for effect.

Moreover, in our experience, a separate meeting for cooperating agencies is quite productive. Working relationships can be forged for the effective participation of all involved in the preparation of the EIS. Work assignments are made by the lead agency, a schedule may be set for production of parts of the draft EIS, and information gaps can be identified early. But a productive meeting such as this is not possible at the very beginning of the process. It can only result from the same sort of planning and preparation that goes into the public meetings. We discuss below the special problems of cooperating agencies, and their information needs for effective participation in scoping.

4. Issuing the public notice

The preliminary look at the proposal, in which you develop the information packet discussed above, will enable you to tell what kind of public notice will be most appropriate and effective.

Section 1501.7 of the NEPA regulations requires that a notice of intent to prepare an EIS must be published in the Federal Register prior to initiating scoping.* This means that one of the appropriate means of giving public notice of the upcoming scoping process could be the same Federal Register notice. And because the notice of intent must be published anyway, the scoping notice would be essentially free. But use of the Federal Register is not an absolute requirement, and other means of public notice often are more effective, including local newspapers, radio and TV, posting notice in public places, etc. (See Section 1506.6 of the regulations.)

What is important is that the notice actually reach the affected public. If the proposal is an important new national policy in which national environmental groups can be expected to be interested, these groups can be contacted by form letter with ease. (See the *Conservation Directory* for a list of national groups.**) Similarly, for proposals that may have major implications for the business community, trade associations can be helpful means of alerting affected groups. The Federal Register notice can be relied upon to notify others that you did not know about. But the Federal Register is of little use for reaching individuals or local groups interested in a site specific proposal. Therefore notices in local papers, letters to local government officials and personal contact with a few known interested individuals would be more appropriate. Land owners abutting any proposed project site should be notified individually.

Remember that issuing press releases to newspapers, and radio and TV stations is not enough, because they may not be used by the media unless the proposal is considered "newsworthy." If the proposal is controversial, you can try alerting reporters or editors to an upcoming scoping meeting for coverage in special weekend sections used by many papers. But placing a notice in the legal notices section of the paper is the only guarantee that it will be published.

5. Conducting a public meeting

In our study of agency practice in conducting scoping, the most interesting information on what works and doesn't work involves the conduct of meetings. Innovative techniques have been developed, and experience shows that these can be successful.

One of the most important factors turns out to be the training and experience of the moderator. The U.S. Office of Personnel Management and others give training courses on how to run a meeting effectively. Specific techniques are taught to keep the meeting on course and to deal with confrontations. These techniques are sometimes called "meeting facilitation skills."

When holding a meeting, the principle thing to remember about scoping is that it is a process to initiate preparation of an EIS. It is not concerned with the ultimate decision on the proposal. A fruitful scoping process leads to an adequate environmental analysis, including all reasonable alternatives and mitigation measures. This limited goal is in the interest of all the participants, and thus offers the possibility of agreement by the parties on this much at least. To run a successful meeting you must keep the focus on this *positive* purpose.

At the point of scoping therefore, in one sense all the parties involved have a common goal, which is a thorough environmental review. If you emphasize this in the meeting you can stop any grandstanding speeches without a heavy hand, by simply asking the speaker if he or she has any concrete suggestions for the group on issues to be covered in the EIS. By frequently drawing the meeting back to this central purpose of scoping, the opponents of a proposal will see that you have not already made a decision, and they will be forced to deal with the real issues. In addition, when people see that you are genuinely seeking their opinion, some will volunteer useful information about a particular subject or site that they may know better than anyone on your staff.

As we stated above, we found that informal meetings in small groups are the most satisfactory for eliciting useful issues and information. Small groups can be formed in two ways: you can invite different interest groups to different meetings, or you can break a large number into small groups for discussion.

One successful model is used by the Army Corps of Engineers, among others. In cases where a public meeting is desired, it is publicized and scheduled for a location that will be convenient for as many potential participants as possible. The information packet is made available in several ways, by sending it to those known to be interested, giving a telephone number in the public notices for use in requesting one, and providing more at the door of the meeting place as well. As participants enter the door, each is given a number. Participants are asked to register their name, address and/or telephone number for use in future contact during scoping and the rest of the NEPA process.

The first part of the meeting is devoted to a discussion of the proposal in general, covering its purpose, proposed location, design, and any other aspects that can be presented in a lecture format. A question and answer period concerning this information is often held at this time. Then if there are more than 15 or 20 attendees at the meeting, the next step is to break it into small groups for more intensive discussion. At this point, the numbers held by the participants are used to assign them to small groups by sequence, random drawing, or any other method. Each group should be no larger than 12, and 8-10 is better. The groups are informed that their task is to prepare a list of significant environmental issues and reasonable alternatives for analysis in the EIS. These lists will be presented to the main group and combined into a master list, after the discussion groups are finished. The rules for how priorities are to be assigned to the issues identified by each group should be made clear before the large group breaks up.

Some agencies ask each group member to vote for the 5 or 10 most important issues. After tallying the votes of individual members, each group would only report out those issues that received a certain number of votes. In this way only those items of most concern to the members would even make the list compiled by each group. Some agencies go further, and only let each group report out the top few issues identified. But you must be careful not to

---

*Several agencies have found it useful to conduct scoping for environmental assessments. EAs are prepared where answering the question of whether an EIS is necessary requires identification of significant environmental issues; and consideration of alternatives in an EA can often be useful even where an EIS is not necessary. In both situations scoping can be valuable. Thus the Council has stated that scoping may be used in connection with preparation of an EA, that is, before publishing any notice of intent to prepare an EIS. As in normal scoping, appropriate public notice is required, as well as adequate information on the proposal to make scoping worthwhile. But scoping at this early stage cannot *substitute* for the normal scoping process unless the earlier public notice stated clearly that this would be the case, *and* the notice of intent expressly provides that written comments suggesting impacts and alternatives for study will still be considered.

**The Conservation Directory is a publication of the National Wildlife Federation, 1421 16th St., N.W., Washington, D.C. 20036, $4.00.

ignore issues that may be considered a medium priority by many people. They may still be important, even if not in the top rank. Thus instead of simply voting, the members of the groups should rank the listed issues in order of perceived importance. Points may be assigned to each item on the basis of the rankings by each member, so that the group can compile a list of its issues in priority order. Each group should then be asked to assign cut-off numbers to separate high, medium and low priority items. Each group should then report out to the main meeting all of its issues, but with priorities clearly assigned.

One member of the lead agency or cooperating agency staff should join each group to answer questions and to listen to the participants' expressions of concern. It has been the experience of many of those who have tried this method that it is better not to have the agency person lead the group discussions. There does need to be a leader, who should be chosen by the group members. In this way, the agency staff member will not be perceived as forcing his opinions on the others.

If the agency has a sufficient staff of formally trained "meeting facilitators," they may be able to achieve the same result even where agency staff people lead the discussion groups. But absent such training, the staff should not lead the discussion groups. A good technique is to have the agency person serve as the recording secretary for the group, writing down each impact and alternative that is suggested for study by the participants. This enhances the neutral status of the agency representative, and ensures that he is perceived as listening and reacting to the views of the group. Frequently, the recording of issues is done with a large pad mounted on the wall like a blackboard, which has been well received by agency and public alike, because all can see that the views expressed actually have been heard and understood.

When the issues are listed, each must be clarified or combined with others to eliminate duplication or fuzzy concepts. The agency staff person can actually lead in this effort because of his need to reflect on paper exactly what the issues are. After the group has listed all the environmental impacts and alternatives and any other issues that the members wish to have considered, they are asked to discuss the relative merits and importance of each listed item. The group should be reminded that one of its tasks is to eliminate insignificant issues. Following this, the members assign priorities or vote using one of the methods described above.

The discussion groups are then to return to the large meeting to report on the results of their ranking. At this point further discussion may be useful to seek a consensus on which issues are really insignificant. But the moderator must not appear to be ruthlessly eliminating issues that the participants ranked of high or medium importance. The best that can usually be achieved is to "deemphasize" some of them, by placing them in the low priority category.

6. What to do with the comments

After you have comments from the cooperating agencies and the interested public, you must evaluate them and make judgments about which issues are in fact significant and which ones are not. The decision of what the EIS should contain is ultimately made by the lead agency. But you will now know what the interested participants consider to be the principal areas for study and analysis. You should be guided by these concerns, or be prepared to briefly explain why you do not agree. Every issue that is raised as a priority matter during scoping should be addressed in some manner in the EIS, either by in-depth analysis, or at least a short explanation showing that the issue was examined, but not considered significant for one or more reasons.

Some agencies have complained that the time savings claimed for scoping have not been realized because after public groups raise numerous minor matters, they cannot focus the EIS on the significant issues. It is true that it is always easier to add issues than it is to subtract them during scoping. And you should realize that trying to *eliminate* a particular environmental impact or alternative from study may arouse the suspicions of some people. Cooperating agencies may be even more reluctant to eliminate issues in their areas of special expertise than the public participants. But the way to approach it is to seek consensus on which issues are less important. These issues may then be deemphasized in the EIS by a brief discussion of why they were not examined in depth.

If no consensus can be reached, it is still your responsibility to select the significant issues. The lead agency cannot abdicate its role and simply defer to the public. Thus a group of participants at a scoping meeting should not be able to "vote" an insignificant matter into a big issue. If a certain issue is raised and in your professional judgment you believe it is not significant, explain clearly and briefly in the EIS why it is not significant. There is no need to devote time and pages to it in the EIS if you can show that it is not relevant or important to the proposed action. But you should address in some manner all matters that were raised in the scoping process, either by an extended analysis or a brief explanation showing that you acknowledge the concern.

Several agencies have made a practice of sending out a post-scoping document to make public the decisions that have been made on what issues to cover in the EIS. This is not a requirement, but in certain controversial cases it can be worthwhile. Especially when scoping has been conducted by written comments, and there has been no face-to-face contact, a post-scoping document is the only assurance to the participants that they were heard and understood until the draft EIS comes out. Agencies have acknowledged to us that "letters instead of meetings seem to get disregarded easier." Thus a reasonable quid pro quo for relying on comment letters would be to send out a post-scoping document as feedback to the commentors.

The post-scoping document may be as brief as a list of impacts and alternatives selected for analysis; it may consist of the "scope of work" produced by the lead and cooperating agencies for their own EIS work or for the contractor; or it may be a special document that describes all the issues and explains why they were selected.

7. Allocating work assignments and setting schedules

Following the public participation in whatever form, and the selection of issues to be covered, the lead agency must allocate the EIS preparation work among the available resources. If there are no cooperating agencies, the lead agency allocates work among its own personnel or contractors. If there are cooperating agencies involved, they may be assigned specific research or writing tasks. The NEPA regulations require that they normally devote their own resources to the issues in which they have special expertise or jurisdiction by law. (Sections 1501.6(b)(3), (5), and 1501.7(a)(4)).

In all cases, the lead agency should set a schedule for completion of the work, designate a project manager and assign the reviewers, and must set a time limit for the entire NEPA analysis if requested to do so by an applicant. (Section 1501.8).

8. A few ideas to try

a. Route design workshop

As part of a scoping process, a successful innovation by one agency involved route selection for a railroad. The agency invited representatives of the interested groups (identified at a previous public meeting) to try their hand at designing alternative routes for a proposed rail segment. Agency staff explained design constraints and evaluation criteria such as the desire to minimize damage to prime agricultural land and valuable wildlife habitat. The participants were divided in to small groups for a few hours of intensive work. After learning of the real constraints on alternative routes, the participants had a better understanding of the agency's and applicant's viewpoints. Two of the participants actually supported alternative routes that affected their own land because the overall impacts of these routes appeared less adverse.

The participants were asked to rank the five alternatives they had devised and the top two were included in the EIS. But the agency did not permit the groups to apply the same evaluation criteria to the routes proposed by the applicant or the agency. Thus public confidence in the process was not as high as it could have been, and probably was reduced when the applicant's proposal was ultimately selected.

The Council recommends that when a hands-on design workshop is used, the assignment of the group be expanded to include evaluation of the reasonableness of all the suggested alternatives.

b. Hotline

Several agencies have successfully used a special telephone number, essentially a hotline, to take public comments before, after, or instead of a public meeting. It helps to designate a named staff member to receive these calls so that some continuity and personal relationships can be developed.

c. Videotape of sites

A videotape of proposed sites is an excellent tool for explaining site differences and limitations during the lecture-format part of a scoping meeting.

d. Videotape meetings

One agency has videotaped whole scoping meetings. Staff found that the participants took their roles more seriously and the taping appeared not to precipitate grandstanding tactics.

e. Review committee

Success has been reported from one agency which sets up review committees, representing all interested groups, to oversee the scoping process. The committees help to design the scoping process. In cooperation with the lead agency, the committee reviews the materials generated by the scoping meeting. Again, however, the final decision on EIS content is the responsibility of the lead agency.

f. Consultant as meeting moderator

In some hotly contested cases, several agencies have used the EIS consultant to actually run the scoping meeting. This is permitted under the NEPA regulations and can be useful to de-fuse a tense atmosphere if the consultant is perceived as a neutral third party. But the responsible agency officials must attend the meetings. There is no substitute for developing a relationship between the agency officials and the affected parties. Moroever, if the responsible officials are not prominently present, the public may intepret that to mean that the consultant is actually making the decisions about the EIS, and not the lead agency.

g. Money saving tips

Remember that money can be saved by using conference calls instead of meetings, tape-recording the meetings instead of hiring a stenographer, and finding out whether people want a meeting before announcing it.

C. Pitfalls

We list here some of the problems that have been experienced in certain scoping cases, in order to enable others to avoid the same difficulties.

1. Closed meetings

In response to informal advice from CEQ that holding separate meetings for agencies and the public would be permitted under the regulations and could be more productive, one agency scheduled a scoping meeting for the cooperating agencies some weeks in advance of the public meeting. Apparently, the lead agency felt that the views of the cooperating agencies would be more candidly expressed if the meeting were closed. In any event, several members of the public learned of the meeting and asked to be present. The lead agency acquiesced only after newspaper reporters were able to make a story out of the closed session. At the meeting, the members of the public were informed that they would not be allowed to speak, nor to record the proceedings. The ill feeling aroused by this chain of events may not be repaired for a long time. Instead, we would suggest the following possibilities:

a. Although separate meetings for agencies and public groups may be more efficient, there is no magic to them. By all means, if someone insists on attending the agency meeting, let him. There is nothing as secret going on there as he may think there is if you refuse him admittance. Better yet, have your meeting of cooperating agencies *after* the public meeting. That may be the most logical time anyway, since only then can the scope of the EIS be decided upon and assignments made among the agencies. If it is well done, the public meeting will satisfy most people and show them that you are listening to them.

b. Always permit recording. In fact, you should suggest it for public meetings. All parties will feel better if there is a record of the proceeding. There is no need for a stenographer, and tape is inexpensive. It may even be better then a typed transcript, because staff and decisionmakers who did not attend the meeting can listen to the exchange and may learn a lot about public perceptions of the proposal.

c. When people are admitted to a meeting, it makes no sense to refuse their requests to speak. However, you can legitimately limit their statements to the subject at hand—scoping. You do not have to permit some participants to waste the others' time if they refuse to focus on the impacts and alternatives for inclusion in the EIS. Having a tape of the proceedings could be useful after the meeting if there is some question that speakers were improperly silenced. But it takes an experienced moderator to handle a situation like this.

d. The scoping stage is the time for building confidence and trust on all sides of a proposal, because this is the only time when there is a common enterprise. The attitudes formed at this stage can carry through the project review process. Certainly it is difficult for things to get better. So foster the good will as long as you can by listening to what is being said during scoping. It is possible that out of that dialogue may appear recommendations for changes and mitigation measures that can turn a controversial fight into an acceptable proposal.

2. Contacting interested groups

Some problems have arisen in scoping where agencies failed to contact all the affected parties, such as industries or state and local governments. In one case, a panel was assembled to represent various interests in scoping an EIS on a wildlife-related program. The agency had an excellent format for the meeting, but the panel did not represent industries that would be affected by the program or interested state and local governments. As a result, the EIS may fail to reflect the issues of concern to these parties.

Another agency reported to us that it failed to contact parties directly because staff feared that if they missed someone they would be accused of favoritism. Thus they relied on the issuance of press releases which were not effective. Many people who did not learn about the meetings in time sought additional meeting opportunities, which cost extra money and delayed the process.

In our experience, the attempt to reach people is worth the effort. Even if you miss someone, it will be clear that you tried. You can enlist a few representatives of an interest group to help you identify and contact others. Trade associations, chambers of commerce, local civic groups, and local and national conservation groups can spread the word to members.

3. Tiering

Many people are not familiar with the way environmental impact statements can be "tiered" under the NEPA regulations, so that issues are examined in detail at the stage that decisions on them are being made. See Section 1508.28 of the regulations. For example, if a proposed program is under review, it is possible that site specific actions are not yet proposed. In such a case, these actions are not addressed in the EIS on the program, but are reserved for a later tier of analysis. If tiering is being used, this concept must be made clear at the outset of any scoping meeting, so that participants do not concentrate on issues that are not going to be addressed at this time. If you can specify when these other issues *will* be addressed it will be easier to convince people to focus on the matters at hand.

4. Scoping for unusual programs

One interesting scoping case involved proposed changes in the Endangered Species Program. Among the impacts to be examined were the effects of this conservation program *on user activities* such as mining, hunting, and timber harvest, instead of the other way around. Because of this reverse twist in the impacts to be analyzed, some participants had difficulty focusing on useful issues. Apparently, if the subject of the EIS is unusual, it will be even harder than normal for scoping participants to grasp what is expected of them.

In the case of the Endangered Species Program EIS, the agency planned an intensive 3 day scoping session, successfully involved the participants, and reached accord on several issues that would be important for the future implementation of the program. But the participants were unable to focus on impacts and program alternatives for the EIS. We suggest that if the intensive session had been broken up into 2 or 3 meetings separated by days or weeks, the participants might have been able to get used to the new way of thinking required, and thereby to participate more productively. Programmatic proposals are often harder to deal with in a scoping context than site specific projects. Thus extra care should be taken in explaining the goals of the proposal and in making the information available well in advance of any meetings.

D. Lead and Cooperating Agencies

Some problems with scoping revolve around the relationship between lead and cooperating agencies. Some agencies are still uncomfortable with these roles. The NEPA regulations, and the *40 Questions and Answers about the NEPA Regulations,* 46 Fed. Reg. 18026, (March 23, 1981) describe in detail the way agencies are now asked to cooperate on environmental analyses. (See Questions 9,

14, and 30.) We will focus here on the early phase of that cooperation.

It is important for the lead agency to be as specific as possible with the cooperating agencies. Tell them what you want them to contribute during scoping: environmental impacts and alternatives. Some agencies still do not understand the purpose of scoping.

Be sure to contact and involve representatives of the cooperating agencies who are responsible for NEPA-related functions. The lead agency will need to contact staff of the cooperating agencies who can both help to identify issues and alternatives *and* commit resources to a study, agree to a schedule for EIS preparation, or approve a list of issues as sufficient. In some agencies that will be at the district or state office level (e.g., Corps of Engineers, Bureau of Land Management, and Soil Conservation Service) for all but exceptional cases. In other agencies you must go to regional offices for scoping comments and commitments (e.g., EPA, Fish and Wildlife Service, Water and Power Resources Service). In still others, the field offices do not have NEPA responsibilities or expertise and you will deal directly with headquarters (e.g., Federal Energy Regulatory Commission, Interstate Commerce Commission). In all cases you are looking for the office that can give you the answers you need. So keep trying until you find the organizational level of the cooperating agency that can give you useful information and that has the authority to make commitments.

As stated in *40 Questions and Answers about the NEPA Regulations,* the lead agency has the ultimate responsibility for the content of the EIS, but if it leaves out a significant issue or ignores the advice and expertise of the cooperating agency, the EIS may be found later to be inadequate. (46 Fed. Reg. 18030, Question 14b.) At the same time, the cooperating agency will be concerned that the EIS contain material sufficient to satisfy its decisionmaking needs. Thus, both agencies have a stake in producing a document of good quality. The cooperating agencies should be encouraged not only to participate in scoping but also to review the decisions made by the lead agency about what to include in the EIS. Lead agencies should allow any information needed by a cooperating agency to be included, and any issues of concern to the cooperating agency should be covered, but it usually will have to be at the expense of the cooperating agency.

Cooperating agencies have at least as great a need as the general public for advance information on a proposal before any scoping takes place. Agencies have reported to us that information from the lead agency is often too sketchy or comes too late for informed participation. Lead agencies must clearly explain to all cooperating agencies what the proposed action is conceived to be at this time, and what present alternatives and issues the lead agency sees, before expecting other agencies to devote time and money to a scoping session. Informal contacts among the agencies before scoping gets underway are valuable to establish what the cooperating agencies will need for productive scoping to take place.

Some agencies will be called upon to be cooperators more frequently than others, and they may lack the resources to respond to the numerous requests. The NEPA regulations permit agencies without jurisdiction by law (i.e., no approval authority over the proposal) to decline the cooperating agency role. (Section 1501.6(c)). But agencies that do have jurisdiction by law cannot opt out entirely and may have to reduce their cooperating effort devoted to each EIS. (See Section 1501.6(c) and *40 Questions and Answers about the NEPA Regulations,* 46 Fed. Reg. 18030, Question 14a.) Thus, cooperators would be greatly aided by a priority list from the lead agency showing which proposals most need their help. This will lead to a more efficient allocation of resources.

Some cooperating agencies are still holding back at the scoping stage in order to retain a critical position for later in the process. They either avoid the scoping sessions or fail to contribute, and then raise objections in comments on the draft EIS. We cannot emphasize enough that the whole point of scoping is to avoid this situation. As we stated in *40 Questions and Answers about the NEPA Regulations,* "if the new alternative [or other issue] was not raised by the commentor during scoping, but could have been, commentors may find that they are unpersuasive in their efforts to have their suggested alternative analyzed in detail by the [lead] agency." (46 Fed. Reg. 18035, Question 29b.)

III. Advice for Public Participants

Scoping is a new opportunity for you to enter the earliest phase of the decisionmaking process on proposals that affect you. Through this process you have access to public officials before decisions are made and the right to explain your objections and concerns. But this opportunity carries with it a new responsibility. No longer may individuals hang back until the process is almost complete and then spring forth with a significant issue or alternative that might have been raised earlier. You are now part of the review process, and your role is to inform the responsible agencies of the potential impacts that should be studied, the problems a proposal may cause that you foresee, and the alternatives and mitigating measures that offer promise.

As noted above, and in *40 Questions and Answers,* no longer will a comment raised for the first time after the draft EIS is finished be accorded the same serious consideration it would otherwise have merited if the issue had been raised during scoping. Thus you have a responsibility to come forward early with known issues.

In return, you get the chance to meet the responsible officials and to make the case for your alternative before they are committed to a course of action. To a surprising degree this avenue has been found to yield satisfactory results. There's no guarantee, of course, but when the alternative you suggest is really better, it is often hard for a decisionmaker to resist.

There are several problems that commonly arise that public participants should be aware of:

A. Public input is often only negative

The optimal timing of scoping within the NEPA process is difficult to judge. On the one hand, as explained above (Section II.B.1.), if it is attempted too early, the agency cannot explain what it has in mind and informed participation will be impossible. On the other, if it is delayed, the public may find that significant decisions are already made, and their comments may be discounted or will be too late to change the project. Some agencies have found themselves in a tactical cross-fire when public criticism arises before they can even define their proposal sufficiently to see whether they have a worthwhile plan. Understandably, they would be reluctant after such an experience to *invite* public criticism early in the planning process through open scoping. But it is in your interest to encourage agencies to come out with proposals in the early stage because that enhances the possibility of your comments being used. Thus public participants in scoping should reduce the emotion level wherever possible and use the opportunity to make thoughtful, rational presentations on impacts and alternatives. Polarizing over issues too early hurts all parties. If agencies get positive and useful public responses from the scoping process, they will more frequently come forward with proposals early enough so that they can be materially improved by your suggestions.

B. Issues are too broad

The issues that participants tend to identify during scoping are much too broad to be useful for analytical purposes. For example, "cultural impacts"—what does this mean? What precisely are the impacts that should be examined? When the EIS preparers encounter a comment as vague as this they will have to make their own judgment about what you meant, and you may find that your issues are not covered. Thus, you should refine the broad general topics, and specify which issues need evaluation and analysis.

C. Impacts are not identified

Similarly, people (including agency staff) frequently identify "causes" as issues but fail to identify the principal "*effects*" that the EIS should evaluate in depth. For example, oil and gas development is a cause of many impacts. Simply listing this generic category is of little help. You must go beyond the obvious causes to the specific effects that are of concern. If you want scoping to be seen as more than just another public meeting, you will need to put in extra work.

IV. Brief Points For Applicants

Scoping can be an invaluable part of your early project planning. Your main interest is in getting a proposal through the review process. This interest is best advanced by finding out early where the problems with the proposal are, who the affected parties are, and where accommodations can be made. Scoping is an ideal meeting place for all the interest groups if you have not already contacted them. In several cases, we found that the compromises made at this stage allowed a project to move efficiently through the permitting process virtually unopposed.

The NEPA regulations place an affirmative obligation on agencies to "provide for cases where actions are planned by private applicants'' so that designated staff are available to consult with the applicants, to advise applicants of information that will be required during review, and to insure that the NEPA process commences at the earliest possible time. (Section 1501.2(d)). This section of the regulations is intended to ensure that environmental factors are considered at an early stage in the applicant's planning process. (See *40 Questions and Answers about the NEPA Regulations,* 46 Fed. Reg. 18028, Questions 8 and 9.)

Applicants should take advantage of this requirement in the regulations by approaching the agencies early to consult on alternatives, mitigation requirements, and the agency's information needs. This early contact with the agency can facilitate a prompt initiation of the scoping process in cases where an EIS will be prepared. You will need to furnish sufficient information about your proposal to enable the lead agency to formulate a coherent presentation for cooperating agencies and the public. But don't wait until your choices are all made and the alternatives have been eliminated (Section 1506.1).

During scoping, be sure to attend any of the public meetings unless the agency is dividing groups by interest affiliation. You will be able to answer any questions about the proposal, and even more important, you will be able to hear the objections raised, and find out what the real concerns of the public are. This is, of course, vital information for future negotiations with the affected parties.

Memorandum: Guidance Regarding NEPA Regulations

(Council on Environmental Quality July 22, 1983)
48 Fed. Reg. 34263 (July 28, 1983)

The Council on Environmental Quality (CEQ) regulations implementing the National Environmental Policy Act (NEPA) were issued on November 29, 1978. These regulations became effective for, and binding upon, most federal agencies on July 30, 1979, and for all remaining federal agencies on November 30, 1979.

As part of the Council's NEPA oversight responsibilities it solicited through an August 14, 1981, notice in the **Federal Register** public and agency comments regarding a series of questions that were developed to provide information on the manner in which federal agencies were implementing the CEQ regulations. On July 12, 1982, the Council announced the availability of a document summarizing the comments received from the public and other agencies and also identifying issue areas which the Council intended to review. On August 12, 1982, the Council held a public meeting to address those issues and hear any other comments which the public or other interested agencies might have about the NEPA process. The issues addressed in this guidance were identified during this process.

There are many ways in which agencies can meet their responsibilities under NEPA and the 1978 regulations. The purpose of this document is to provide the Council's guidance on various ways to carry out activities under the regulations.

Scoping

The Council on Environmental Quality (CEQ) regulations direct federal agencies which have made a decision to prepare an environmental impact statement to engage in a public scoping process. Public hearings or meetings, although often held, are not required; instead the manner in which public input will be sought is left to the discretion of the agency.

The purpose of this process is to determine the scope of the EIS so that preparation of the document can be effectively managed. Scoping is intended to ensure that problems are identified early and properly studied, that issues of little significance do not consume time and effort, that the draft EIS is thorough and balanced, and that delays occasioned by an inadequate draft EIS are avoided. The scoping process should identify the public and agency concerns; clearly define the environmental issues and alternatives to be examined in the EIS including the elimination of nonsignificant issues; identify related issues which originate

from separate legislation, regulation, or Executive Order (e.g. historic preservation or endangered species concerns); and identify state and local agency requirements which must be addressed. An effective scoping process can help reduce unnecessary paperwork and time delays in preparing and processing the EIS by clearly identifying all relevant procedural requirements.

In April 1981, the Council issued a "Memorandum for General Counsels, NEPA Liaisons and Participants in Scoping" on the subject of Scoping Guidance. The purpose of this guidance was to give agencies suggestions as to how to more effectively carry out the CEQ scoping requirement. The availability of this document was announced in the **Federal Register** at 46 FR 25461. It is still available upon request from the CEQ General Counsel's office.

The concept of lead agency (§ 1508.16) and cooperating agency (§ 1508.5) can be used effectively to help manage the scoping process and prepare the environmental impact statement. The lead agency should identify the potential cooperating agencies. It is incumbent upon the lead agency to identify any agency which may ultimately be involved in the proposed action, including any subsequent permitting actions. Once cooperating agencies have been identified they have specific responsibility under the NEPA regulations (40 CFR 1501.6). Among other things cooperating agencies have responsibilities to participate in the scoping process and to help identify issues which are germane to any subsequent action it must take on the proposed action. The ultimate goal of this combined agency effort is to produce an EIS which in addition to fulfilling the basic intent of NEPA, also encompasses to the maximum extent possible all the environmental and public involvement requirements of state and federal laws, Executive Orders, and administrative policies of the involved agencies. Examples of these requirements include the Fish and Wildlife Coordination Act, the Clean Air Act, the Endangered Species Act, the National Historic Preservation Act, the Wild and Scenic Rivers Act, the Farmland Protection Policy Act, Executive Order 11990 (Protection of Wetlands), and Executive Order 11998 (Floodplain Management).

It is emphasized that cooperating agencies have the responsibility and obligation under the CEQ regulations to participate in the scoping process. Early involvement leads to early identification

of significant issues, better decisionmaking, and avoidance of possible legal challenges. Agencies with "jurisdiction by law" must accept designation as a cooperating agency if requested (40 CFR 1501.6).

One of the functions of scoping is to identify the public involvement/public hearing procedures of all appropriate state and federal agencies that will ultimately act upon the proposed action. To the maximum extent possible, such procedures should be integrated into the EIS process so that joint public meetings and hearings can be conducted. Conducting joint meetings and hearings eliminates duplication and should significantly reduce the time and cost of processing an EIS and any subsequent approvals. The end result will be a more informed public cognizant of all facets of the proposed action.

It is important that the lead agency establish a process to properly manage scoping. In appropriate situations the lead agency should consider designating a project coordinator and forming an interagency project review team. The project coordinator would be the key person in monitoring time schedules and responding to any problems which may arise in both scoping and preparing the EIS. The project review team would be established early in scoping and maintained throughout the process of preparing the EIS. This review team would include state and local agency representatives. The review team would meet periodically to ensure that the EIS is complete, concise, and prepared in a timely manner.

A project review team has been used effectively on many projects. Some of the more important functions this review team can serve include: (1) A source of information, (2) a coordination mechanism, and (3) a professional review group. As an information source, the review team can identify all federal, state, and local environmental requirements, agency public meeting and hearing procedures, concerned citizen groups, data needs and sources of existing information, and the significant issues and reasonable alternatives for detailed analysis, excluding the non-significant issues. As a coordination mechanism, the team can ensure the rapid distribution of appropriate information or environmental studies, and can reduce the time required for formal consultation on a number of issues (e.g., endangered species or historic preservation). As a professional review group the team can assist in establishing and monitoring a tight time schedule for preparing the EIS by identifying critical points in the process, discussing and recommending solutions to the lead agency as problems arise, advising whether a requested analysis or information item is relevant to the issues under consideration, and providing timely and substantive review comments on any preliminary reports or analyses that may be prepared during the process. The presence of professionals from all scientific disciplines which have a significant role in the proposed action could greatly enhance the value of the team.

The Council recognizes that there may be some problems with the review team concept such as limited agency travel funds and the amount of work necessary to coordinate and prepare for the periodic team meetings. However, the potential benefits of the team concept are significant and the Council encourages agencies to consider utilizing interdisciplinary project review teams to aid in EIS preparation. A regularly scheduled meeting time and location should reduce coordination problems. In some instances, meetings can be arranged so that many projects are discussed at each session. The benefits of the concept are obvious: timely and effective preparation of the EIS, early identification and resolution of any problems which may arise, and elimination, or at least reduction of, the need for additional environmental studies subsequent to the approval of the EIS.

Since the key purpose of scoping is to identify the issues and alternatives for consideration, the scoping process should "end" once the issues and alternatives to be addressed in the EIS have been clearly identified. Normally this would occur during the final stages of preparing the draft EIS and before it is officially circulated for public and agency review.

The Council encourages the lead agency to notify the public of the results of the scoping process to ensure that all issues have been identified. The lead agency should document the results of the scoping process in its administrative record.

The NEPA regulations place a new and significant responsibility on agencies and the public alike during the scoping process to identify all significant issues and reasonable alternatives to be addressed in the EIS. Most significantly, the Council has found that scoping is an extremely valuable aid to better decisionmaking. Thorough scoping may also have the effect of reducing the frequency with which proposed actions are challenged in court on the basis of an inadequate EIS. Through the techniques identified in this guidance, the lead agency will be able to document that an open public involvement process was conducted,

that all reasonable alternatives were identified, that significant issues were identified and non-significant issues eliminated, and that the environmental public involvement requirements of all agencies were met, to the extent possible, in a single "one-stop" process.

Categorical Exclusions

Section 1507 of the CEQ regulations directs federal agencies when establishing implementing procedures to identify those actions which experience has indicated will not have a significant environmental effect and to categorically exclude them from NEPA review. In our August 1981 request for public comments, we asked the question "Have categorical exclusions been adequately identified and defined?".

The responses the Council received indicated that there was considerable belief that categorical exclusions were not adequately identified and defined. A number of commentators indicated that agencies had not identified all categories of actions that meet the categorical exclusion definition (§ 1508.4) or that agencies were overly restrictive in their interpretations of categorical exclusions. Concerns were expressed that agencies were requiring too much documentation for projects that were not major federal actions with significant effects and also that agency procedures to add categories of actions to their existing lists of categorical exclusions were too cumbersome.

The National Environmental Policy Act and the CEQ regulations are concerned primarily with those "major federal actions significantly affecting the quality of the human environment" (42 U.S.C. 4332). Accordingly, agency procedures, resources, and efforts should focus on determining whether the proposed federal action is a major federal action significantly affecting the quality of the human environment. If the answer to this question is yes, an environmental impact statement must be prepared. If there is insufficient information to answer the question, an environmental assessment is needed to assist the agency in determining if the environmental impacts are significant and require an EIS. If the assessment shows that the impacts are not significant, the agency must prepare a finding of no significant impact. Further stages of this federal action may be excluded from requirements to prepare NEPA documents.

The CEQ regulations were issued in 1978 and most agency implementing regulations and procedures were issued shortly thereafter. In recognition of the experience with the NEPA process that agencies have had since the CEQ regulations were issued, the Council believes that it is appropriate for agencies to examine their procedures to

insure that the NEPA process utilizes this additional knowledge and experience. Accordingly, the Council strongly encourages agencies to re-examine their environmental procedures and specifically those portions of the procedures where "categorical exclusions" are discussed to determine if revisions are appropriate. The specific issues which the Council is concerned about are (1) the use of detailed lists of specific activities for categorical exclusions, (2) the excessive use of environmental assessments/findings of no significant impact and (3) excessive documentation.

The Council has noted some agencies have developed lists of specific activities which qualify as categorical exclusions. The Council believes that if this approach is applied narrowly it will not provide the agency with sufficient flexibility to make decisions on a project-by-project basis with full consideration to the issues and impacts that are unique to a specific project. The Council encourages the agencies to consider broadly defined criteria which characterize types of actions that, based on the agency's experience, do not cause significant environmental effects. If this technique is adopted, it would be helpful for the agency to offer several examples of activities frequently performed by that agency's personnel which would normally fall in these categories. Agencies also need to consider whether the cumulative effects of several small actions would cause sufficient environmental impact to take the actions out of the categorically excluded class.

The Council also encourages agencies to examine the manner in which they use the environmental assessment process in relation to their process for identifying projects that meet the categorical exclusion definition. A report(1) to the Council indicated that some agencies have a very high ratio of findings of no significant impact to environmental assessments each year while producing only a handful of EIS's. Agencies should examine their decisionmaking process to ascertain if some of these actions do not, in fact, fall within the categorical exclusion definition, or, conversely, if they deserve full EIS treatment.

As previously noted, the Council received a number of comments that agencies require an excessive amount of environmental documentation for projects that meet the categorical exclusion definition. The Council believes that sufficient information will usually be available during the course of normal project development to determine the need for an EIS and further that the agency's administrative record will clearly document the basis for its decision. Accordingly, the Council strongly discourages procedures that would require the preparation of additional paperwork to document that an activity has been categorically excluded.

Categorical exclusions promulgated by an agency should be reviewed by the Council at the draft stage. After reviewing comments received during the review period and prior to publication in final form, the Council will determine whether the categorical exclusions are consistent with the NEPA regulations.

Adoption Procedures

During the recent effort undertaken by the Council to review the current NEPA regulations, several participants indicated federal agencies were not utilizing the adoption procedures as authorized by the CEQ regulations. The concept of adoption was incorporated into the Council's NEPA Regulations (40 CFR 1506.3) to reduce duplicative EISs prepared by Federal agencies. The experiences gained during the 1970's revealed situations in which two or more agencies had an action relating to the same project; however, the timing of the actions was different. In the early years of NEPA implementation, agencies independently approached their activities and decisions. This procedure lent itself to two or even three EISs on the same project. In response to this situation the CEQ regulations authorized agencies, in certain instances, to adopt environmental impact statements prepared by other agencies.

In general terms, the regulations recognize three possible situations in which adoption is appropriate. One is where the federal agency participated in the process as a cooperating agency. (40 CFR 1506.3(c)). In this case, the cooperating agency may adopt a final EIS and simply issue its record of decision.(2) *However,* the cooperating agency must independently review the EIS and determine that its own NEPA procedures have been satisfied.

A second case concerns the federal agency which was not a cooperating agency, but is, nevertheless, undertaking an activity which was the subject of an EIS. (40 CFR 1506.3(b)). This situation would arise because an agency did not anticipate that it would be involved in a project which was the subject of another agency's EIS. In this instance where the proposed action is substantially the same as that action described in the EIS, the agency may adopt the EIS and recirculate (file with EPA and distribute to agencies and the public) it as a final EIS. However, the agency must independently review the EIS to determine that it is current and that its own NEPA procedures have been satisfied. When recirculating the final EIS the agency should provide

information which identifies what federal action is involved.

The third situation is one in which the proposed action is not substantially the same as that covered by the EIS. In this case, any agency may adopt an EIS or a portion thereof by circulating the EIS as a draft or as a portion of the agency's draft and preparing a final EIS. (40 CFR 1506.3(a)). Repetitious analysis and time consuming data collection can be easily eliminated utilizing this procedure.

The CEQ regulations specifically address the question of adoption only in terms of preparing EIS's. However, the objectives that underlie this portion of the regulations—i.e., reducing delays and eliminating duplication—apply with equal force to the issue of adopting other environmental documents. Consequently, the Council encourages agencies to put in place a mechanism for adopting environmental assessments prepared by other agencies. Under such procedures the agency could adopt the environmental assessment and prepare a Finding of No Significant Impact based on that assessment. In doing so, the agency should be guided by several principles:

—First, when an agency adopts such an analysis it must independently evaluate the information contained therein and take full responsibility for its scope and content.
—Second, if the proposed action meets the criteria set out in 40 CFR 1501.4(e)(2), a Finding of No Significant Impact would be published for 30 days of public review before a final determination is made by the agency on whether to prepare an environmental impact statement.

Contracting Provisions

Section 1506.5(c) of the NEPA regulations contains the basic rules for agencies which choose to have an environmental impact statement prepared by a contractor. That section requires the lead or cooperating agency to select the contractor, to furnish guidance and to participate in the preparation of the environmental impact statement. The regulation requires contractors who are employed to prepare an environmental impact statement to sign a disclosure statement stating that they have no financial or other interest in the outcome of the project. The responsible federal official must independently evaluate the statement prior to its approval and take responsibility for its scope and contents.

During the recent evaluation of comments regarding agency implementation of the NEPA process, the Council became aware of confusion and criticism about the provisions Section 1506.5(c). It appears that a great deal of misunderstanding exists

regarding the interpretation of the conflict of interest provision. There is also some feeling that the conflict of interest provision should be completely eliminated.(3)

Applicability of § 1506.5(c)

This provision is only applicable when a federal lead agency determines that it needs contractor assistance in preparing an EIS. Under such circumstances, the lead agency or a cooperating agency should select the contractor to prepare the EIS.(4)

This provision does not apply when the lead agency is preparing the EIS based on information provided by a private applicant. In this situation, the private applicant can obtain its information from any source. Such sources could include a contractor hired by the private applicant to do environmental, engineering, or other studies necessary to provide sufficient information to the lead agency to prepare an EIS. The agency must independently evaluate the information and is responsible for its accuracy.

Conflict of Interest Provisions

The purpose of the disclosure statement requirement is to avoid situations in which the contractor preparing the environmental impact statement has an interest in the outcome of the proposal. Avoidance of this situation should, in the Council's opinion, ensure a better and more defensible statement for the federal agencies. This requirement also serves to assure the public that the analysis in the environmental impact statement has been prepared free of subjective, self-serving research and analysis.

Some persons believe these restrictions are motivated by undue and unwarranted suspicion about the bias of contractors. The Council is aware that many contractors would conduct their studies in a professional and unbiased manner. However, the Council has the responsibility of overseeing the administration of the National Environmental Policy Act in a manner most consistent with the statute's directives and the public's expectations of sound government. The legal responsibilities for carrying out NEPA's objectives rest solely with federal agencies. Thus, if any delegation of work is to occur, it should be arranged to be performed in as objective a manner as possible.

Preparation of environmental impact statements by parties who would suffer financial losses if, for example, a "no action" alternative were selected, could easily lead to a public perception of bias. It is important to maintain the public's faith in the integrity of the EIS process, and avoidance of conflicts in the preparation of environmental impact statements is an important means of achieving this goal.

The Council has discovered that some agencies have been interpreting the conflicts provision in an overly burdensome manner. In some instances, multidisciplinary firms are being excluded from environmental impact statements preparation contracts because of links to a parent company which has design and/or construction capabilities. Some qualified contractors are not bidding on environmental impact statement contracts because of fears that their firm may be excluded from future design or construction contracts. Agencies have also applied the selection and disclosure provisions to project proponents who wish to have their own contractor for providing environmental information. The result of these misunderstandings has been reduced competition in bidding for EIS preparation contracts, unnecessary delays in selecting a contractor and preparing the EIS, and confusion and resentment about the requirement. The Council believes that a better understanding of the scope of § 1506.5(c) by agencies, contractors and project proponents will eliminate these problems.

Section 1506.5(c) prohibits a person or entity entering into a contract with a federal agency to prepare an EIS when that party has at that time and during the life of the contract pecuniary or other interests in the outcomes of the proposal. Thus, a firm which has an agreement to prepare an EIS for a construction project cannot, at the same time, have an agreement to perform the construction, nor could it be the owner of the construction site. However, if there are no such separate interests or arrangements, and if the contract for EIS preparation does not contain any incentive clauses or guarantees of any future work on the project, it is doubtful that an inherent conflict of interest will exist. Further, § 1506.5(c) does not prevent an applicant from submitting information to an agency. The lead federal agency should evaluate potential conflicts of interest prior to entering into any contract for the preparation of environmental documents.

Selection of Alternatives in Licensing and Permitting Situations

Numerous comments have been received questioning an agency's obligation, under the National Environmental Policy Act, to evaluate alternatives to a proposed action developed by an applicant for a federal permit or license. This concern arises from a belief that projects conceived and developed by private parties should not be questioned or second-guessed by the government. There has been discussion of developing two standards

to determining the range of alternatives to be evaluated: The "traditional" standard for projects which are initiated and developed by a Federal agency, and a second standard of evaluating only those alternatives presented by an applicant for a permit or license.

Neither NEPA nor the CEQ regulations make a distinction between actions initiated by a Federal agency and by applicants. Early NEPA case law, while emphasizing the need for a rigorous examination of alternatives, did not specifically address this issue. In 1981, the Council addressed the question in its document, "Forty Most Asked Questions Concerning CEQ's National Environmental Policy Act Regulations".(5) The answer indicated that the emphasis in determining the scope of alternatives should be on what is "reasonable". The Council said that, "Reasonable alternatives include those that are *practical or feasible* from the technical and economic standpoint and using common sense rather than simply *desirable* from the standpoint of the applicant."

Since issuance of that guidance, the Council has continued to receive requests for further clarification of this question. Additional interest has been generated by a recent appellate court decision. *Roosevelt Campobello International Park Commission* v. *E.P.A.*(6) dealt with EPA's decision of whether to grant a permit under the National Pollutant Discharge Elimination System to a company proposing a refinery and deep-water terminal in Maine. The court discussed both the criteria used by EPA in its *selecting* of alternative sites to evaluate, and the substantive standard used to *evaluate* the sites. The court determined that EPA's choice of alternative sites was "focused by the primary objectives of the permit applicant . . ." and that EPA had limited its consideration of sites to only those sites which were considered feasible, given the applicant's stated goals. The court found that EPA's criteria for selection of alternative sites was sufficient to meet its NEPA responsibilities.

This decision is in keeping with the concept that an agency's responsibilities to examine alternative sites has always been "bounded by some notion of feasibility" to avoid NEPA from becoming "an exercise in frivolous boilerplate".(7) NEPA has never been interpreted to require examination of purely conjectural possibilities whose implementation is deemed remote and speculative. Rather, the agency's duty is to consider "alternatives as they exist and are likely to exist."(8) In the *Roosevelt Campobello* case, for example, EPA examined three alternative sites and two alternative modifications of the project at the

preferred alternative site. Other factors to be developed during the scoping process—comments received from the public, other government agencies and institutions, and development of the agency's own environmental data—should certainly be incorporated into the decision of which alternatives to seriously evaluate in the EIS. There is, however, no need to disregard the applicant's purposes and needs and the common sense realities of a given situation in the development of alternatives.

Tiering

Tiering of environmental impact statements refers to the process of addressing a broad, general program, policy or proposal in an initial environmental impact statement (EIS), and analyzing a narrower site-specific proposal, related to the initial program, plan or policy in a subsequent EIS. The concept of tiering was promulgated in the 1978 CEQ regulations; the preceding CEQ guidelines had not addressed the concept. The Council's intent in formalizing the tiering concept was to encourage agencies, "to eliminate repetitive discussions and to focus on the actual issues ripe for decisions at each level of environmental review."(9)

Despite these intentions, the Council perceives that the concept of tiering has caused a certain amount of confusion and uncertainty among individuals involved in the NEPA process. This confusion is by no means universal; indeed, approximately half of those commenting in response to our question about tiering (10) indicated that tiering is effective and should be used more frequently. Approximately one-third of the commentators responded that they had no experience with tiering upon which to base their comments. The remaining commentators were critical of tiering. Some commentators believed that tiering added an additional layer of paperwork to the process and encouraged, rather than discouraged, duplication. Some commentators thought that the inclusion of tiering in the CEQ regulations added an extra legal requirement to the NEPA process. Other commentators said that an initial EIS could be prepared when issues were too broad to analyze properly for any meaningful consideration. Some commentators believed that the concept was simply not applicable to the types of projects with which they worked; others were concerned about the need to supplement a tiered EIS. Finally, some who responded to our inquiry questioned the courts' acceptance of tiered EISs.

The Council believes that misunderstanding of tiering and its place in the NEPA process is the cause of much of this criticism. Tiering, of course, is by no means the best way to handle all proposals which are subject to NEPA analysis and documentation. The regulations do not require tiering; rather, they authorize its use when an agency determines it is appropriate. It is an option for an agency to use when the nature of the proposal lends itself to tiered EIS(s).

Tiering does not add an additional legal requirement to the NEPA process. An environmental impact statement is required for proposals for legislation and other major Federal actions significantly affecting the quality of the human environment. In the context of NEPA, "major Federal actions" include adoption of official policy, formal plans, and programs as well as approval of specific projects, such as construction activities in a particular location or approval of permits to an outside applicant. Thus, where a Federal agency adopts a formal plan which will be executed throughout a particular region, and later proposes a specific activity to implement that plan in the same region, both actions need to be analyzed under NEPA to determine whether they are major actions which will significantly affect the environment. If the answer is yes in both cases, both actions will be subject to the EIS requirement, whether tiering is used or not. The agency then has one of two alternatives: Either preparation of two environmental impact statements, with the second repeating much of the analysis and information found in the first environmental impact statement, or tiering the two documents. If tiering is utilized, the site-specific EIS contains a summary of the issues discussed in the first statement and the agency will incorporate by reference discussions from the first statement. Thus, the second, or site-specific statement, would focus primarily on the issues relevant to the specific proposal, and would not duplicate material found in the first EIS. It is difficult to understand, given this scenario, how tiering can be criticized for adding an unnecessary layer to the NEPA process; rather, it is intended to streamline the existing process.

The Council agrees with commentators who stated that there are stages in the development of a proposal for a program, plan or policy when the issues are too broad to lend themselves to meaningful analysis in the framework of an EIS. The CEQ regulations specifically define a "proposal" as existing at, "that stage in the development of an action when an agency subject to [NEPA] has a goal and is actively preparing to make a decision on one or more alternative means of accomplishing the goal *and the effects can be meaningfully evaluated.'*(11) Tiering is not intended to force an agency to prepare an EIS before this stage is reached; rather, it is a technique to be used once meaningful analysis can be performed. An EIS is not required before that stage in the development of a proposal, whether tiering is used or not.

The Council also realizes that tiering is not well suited to all agency programs. Again, this is why tiering has been established as an *option* for the agency to use, as opposed to a requirement.

A supplemental EIS is required when an agency makes substantial changes in the proposed action relevant to environmental concerns, or when there are significant new circumstances or information relevant to environmental concerns bearing on the proposed action, and is optional when an agency otherwise determines to supplement an EIS.(12) The standard for supplementing an EIS is not changed by the use of tiering; there will no doubt be occasions when a supplement is needed, but the use of tiering should reduce the number of those occasions.

Finally, some commentators raised the question of courts' acceptability of tiering. This concern is understandable, given several cases which have reversed agency decisions in regard to a particular programmatic EIS. However, these decisions have never invalidated the concept of tiering, as stated in the CEQ regulations and discussed above. Indeed, the courts recognized the usefulness of the tiering approach in case law before the promulgation of the tiering regulation. Rather, the problems appear when an agency determines not to prepare a site-specific EIS based on the fact that a programmatic EIS was prepared. In this situation, the courts carefully examine the analysis contained in the programmatic EIS. A court may or may not find that the programmatic EIS contains appropriate analysis of impacts and alternatives to meet the adequacy test for the site-specific proposal. A recent decision by the Ninth Circuit Court of Appeals (13) invalidated an attempt by the Forest Service to make a determination regarding wilderness and non-wilderness designations on the basis of a programmatic EIS for this reason. However, it should be stressed that this and other decisions are not a repudiation of the tiering concept. In these instances, in fact, tiering has *not* been used; rather, the agencies have attempted to rely exclusively on programmatic or "first level" EISs which did not have site-specific information. No court has found that the tiering process as provided for in the CEQ regulations is an improper manner of implementing the NEPA process.

In summary, the Council believes that tiering can be a useful method of reducing paperwork and duplication when used carefully for appropriate types of plans, programs and policies which will later be translated into site-specific projects. Tiering should not be viewed as an additional substantive requirement, but rather a means of accomplishing the NEPA requirements in an efficient manner as possible.

Footnotes

(1) Environmental Law Institute, *NEPA In Action Environmental Offices in Nineteen Federal Agencies*, A Report To the Council on Environmental Quality, October 1981.

(2) Records of decision must be prepared by each agency responsible for making a decision, and cannot be adopted by another agency.

(3) The Council also received requests for guidance on effective management of the third-party environmental impact statement approach. However, the Council determined that further study regarding the policies behind this technique is warranted, and plans to undertake that task in the future.

(4) There is no bar against the agency considering candidates suggested by the applicant, although the Federal agency must retain its independence. If the applicant is seen as having a major role in the selection of the contractor, contractors may feel the need to please both the agency and the applicant. An applicant's suggestion, if any, to the agency regarding the choice of contractors should be one of many factors involved in the selection process.

(5) 46 FR 18026 (1981).

(6) 684 F.2d 1041 (1st Cir. 1982).

(7) *Vermont Yankee Nuclear Power Corp. v. NRDC*, 435 U.S. 519, 551 (1978).

(8) *Monarch Chemical Works, Inc. v. Exon*, 466 F.Supp. 639, 650 (1979), quoting *Carolina Environmental Study Group v. U.S.*, 510 F.2d 796, 801 (1975).

(9) Preamble, FR, Vol. 43, No. 230, p. 55984, 11/29/78.

(10) "Is tiering being used to minimizes repetition in an environmental assessment and in environmental impact statements?", 46 FR 41131, August 14, 1981.

(11) 40 CFR 1508.23 (emphasis added).

(12) 40 CFR 1502.9(c).

(13) *California v. Block*, 18 ERC 1149 (1982).

Policy and Procedures for the Review of Federal Actions Impacting the Environment

(Environmental Protection Agency: Office of External Affairs, Office of Federal Activities, Oct. 3, 1984)

Table of Contents

CHAPTER 1 - PURPOSE, POLICY, AND MANDATES

1. PURPOSE.

a. This Manual establishes policies and procedures for carrying out the Environmental Protection Agency's (EPA's) responsibilities to review and comment on Federal actions affecting the quality of the environment. EPA has general statutory authority under the National Environmental Policy Act of 1969 and the Council on Environmental Quality's implementing regulations, and has specific authority and responsibility under Section 309 of the Clean Air Act to conduct such reviews, comment in writing, and make those comments available to the public. These responsibilities have been combined into one process and are referred to throughout this Manual as the "Environmental Review Process."

b. This Manual contains EPA's policies and procedures for carrying out the Environmental Review Process, assigns specific responsibilities, and outlines mechanisms for resolving problems that arise in the Environmental Review Process. This Manual is supplemented by, and should be read in conjunction with, the following manuals, which are also prepared, distributed, and maintained by the Office of Federal Activities:

(1) Office of Federal Activities Policies and Procedures Manual. Contains current guidance and detailed information related to the Environmental Review Process; and

(2) Environmental Review Process Data Management Manual. Contains detailed guidance and reporting requirements for the national level computerized tracking system.

2. STATUTORY AUTHORITIES.

a. The National Environmental Policy Act of 1969 (NEPA), as amended, (42 U.S.C. 4321 et seq., Public Law 91-190, 83 Stat. 852), requires that all Federal agencies proposing legislation and other major actions significantly affecting the quality of the human environment consult with other agencies having jurisdiction by law or special expertise over such environmental considerations, and thereafter prepare a detailed statement of these environmental effects. The Council on Environmental Quality (CEQ) has published regulations and associated guidance to implement NEPA (40 CFR Parts 1500-1508).

b. Section 309 of the Clean Air Act, as amended, (42 U.S.C. 7609, Public Law 91-604 12(a), 84 Stat. 1709), requires the EPA to review and comment in writing on the environmental impact of any matter relating to the duties and responsibilities granted pursuant to the Act or other provisions of the authority of the Administrator, contained in any: (1) legislation proposed by a Federal department or agency; (2) newly authorized Federal projects for construction and any major Federal action, or actions, other than a project for construction, to which Section 102(2)(C) of Public Law 91-190 applies; and (3) proposed regulations published by any department or agency of the Federal Government. Such written comments must be made public at the conclusion of any review. In the event such legislation, action, or regulation is determined to be unsatisfactory from the standpoint of public health, welfare, or environmental quality, the determination will be published and the matter referred to the CEQ.

c. Federal environmental laws require, in most circumstances, facilities of the Executive Branch of the Federal Government to comply with Federal, State, and local pollution control requirements promulgated pursuant to, or effective under, those statutes. The review of proposed Federal projects for compliance with these national environmental standards is the responsibility of the EPA through the Environmental Review Process and the Federal Facilities Compliance Program. In addition to these general statutory authorities, the reviews required under Section 1424(e) of the Safe Drinking Water Act (42 U.S.C. 300 h-3, Public Law 93-523, 88 Stat. 1678) and Section 404(r) of the Federal Water Pollution Control Act (Clean Water Act) (33 U.S.C. 1344(r), Public Law 92-500, Public Law 95-217, 86 Stat. 884, 91 Stat 1600) are integrated into the Environmental Review Process.

3. **POLICY.**

a. The objective of the Environmental Review Process is to foster the goals of the NEPA process by ensuring that the EPA's environmental expertise, as expressed in its comments on Federal actions and other interagency liaison activity, is considered by agency decisionmakers. It is EPA's policy to carry out the Environmental Review Process in conjunction with EPA's other authorities to:

(1) Participate in interagency coordination early in the planning process to identify significant environmental issues that should be addressed in completed documents;

(2) Conduct follow-up coordination on actions where EPA has identified significant environmental impacts to ensure a full understanding of the issues and to ensure implementation of appropriate corrective actions; and

(3) Identify environmentally unsatisfactory proposals and consult with other agencies, including the CEQ, to achieve timely resolution of the major issues and problems.

b. In implementing this policy, EPA will assist Federal agencies in:

(1) Achieving the goals set forth in the NEPA;

(2) Meeting the objectives and complying with the requirements of the laws and regulations administered by the EPA; and

(3) Developing concise, well-reasoned decision documents which identify project impacts, a range of project alternatives, and mitigation measures that will avoid or minimize adverse effects on the environment.

CHAPTER 2 - MANAGEMENT OF THE ENVIRONMENTAL REVIEW PROCESS

1. GENERAL RESPONSIBILITIES. The EPA Administrator has delegated responsibility for carrying out the Environmental Review Process to the Assistant Administrator for External Affairs and the Regional Administrators but has retained the responsibility to refer matters to the CEQ. The Assistant Administrator, Office of External Affairs, has in turn delegated program management to the Director, Office of Federal Activities, but has retained the responsibility for concurring on proposed comment letters that have the potential for referral to the CEQ.

2. OFFICE OF FEDERAL ACTIVITIES. The Office of Federal Activities (OFA) within the Office of External Affairs (OEA) is the program manager for the Environmental Review Process and for the overall coordination and policy development for activities associated with this process. To carry out these responsibilities, the OFA will maintain management support functions consisting of Federal Agency Liaison staff assigned to coordinate with the Headquarters offices of all Federal agencies and a Management Information Unit. The Director, Federal Agency Liaison Division, working through the Director, OFA, has overall policy development and management oversight responsibility for the Environmental Review Process.

a. Federal Agency Liaisons. Each Federal Agency Liaison (FAL), working through their Division Director and other appropriate elements within the OFA, has the following responsibilities:

(1) Conduct Headquarters-level liaison with other Federal agencies to identify those actions that should be reviewed and to provide information on how the EPA can most effectively review other agencies' proposed actions pursuant to the Environmental Review Process;

(2) Provide management oversight of regional review actions carried out under the requirements of this Manual, and provide policy guidance on the Environmental Review Process to Headquarters program offices and regional EIS reviewers;

(3) Ensure appropriate Headquarters involvement and support for actions that are elevated under these procedures; and

(4) Coordinate the EPA review of proposed regulations, national level Environmental Impact Statements (EIS's), and other national level activities and other national level actions.

b. Management Information Unit.

(1) The Management Information Unit (MIU) is responsible for the operation of a centralized data management and reporting system for the Environmental Review Process, and for the public availability of comments pursuant to Section 309 of the Clean Air Act. The procedures and requirements for this centralized data system are described in the Environmental Review

Process Data Management Manual. The MIU is also responsible for the official filing of all EIS's in accordance with 40 CFR Section 1506.9.

(2) The MIU is responsible for preparing the following reports to inform EPA officials and the public of EIS's and other Federal actions received by the EPA for review and comment.

(a) COMDATE. This weekly computerized report contains a list of all EIS's filed, pursuant to 40 CFR Section 1506.9, during the previous week. COMDATE lists, in part, the EIS title, official filing date, EPA control numbers, location, Federal Register notice date (40 CFR 1506.10(a)), date comments are due to the lead agency, and regional assignment. Other relevant information is also noted such as overall extensions of time granted by lead agencies and EPA ratings of previously filed draft EIS's.

(b) CEQ Notice of EIS Availability. A Notice of Availability is published in the Federal Register each Friday for EIS's filed during the previous week, pursuant to 40 CFR Section 1506.10(a). The minimum periods for review of the EIS's are calculated from the Federal Register date of this notice.

(c) Notice of Availability of EPA Comments. A notice will be published weekly announcing the availability of EPA comments on EISs, regulations, and any other action for which an unsatisfactory determination has been made. The notice will include, in part, the title, a summary of comments, and the rating (if applicable) of each review completed.

3. REGIONAL OFFICE. Each EPA regional office is responsible for carrying out the Environmental Review Process in accordance with the policies and procedures of this Manual for proposed Federal actions affecting its region. Each EPA regional office will designate a regional environmental review coordinator who has overall management responsibility for the Environmental Review Process in that region. It is the responsibility of the regional environmental review coordinator to:

a. Ensure that the region is maintaining effective liaison with other Federal agencies at the regional level;

b. Carry out lead responsibilities for the review of proposed EIS's and other Federal actions assigned to the coordinator's region or other actions for which it has lead responsibility (see paragraph 6 of this chapter); and

c. Ensure that the region is maintaining the official agency files and is properly tracking correspondence generated under the regional Environmental Review Process.

4. PROGRAM OFFICES. EPA program offices are responsible for providing technical assistance and policy guidance on review actions directly related to their areas of responsibility. When acting as principal or associate reviewer

in accordance with paragraph 5 of this chapter, program offices will follow the policies and procedures set forth in this Manual.

5. <u>SPECIFIC REVIEW MANAGEMENT RESPONSIBILITIES</u>.

   a. <u>Headquarters and Regional Environmental Review Coordinators</u>. The term Environmental Review Coordinator (ERC) is used in this Manual to mean either a regional environmental review coordinator or the OFA Division Director managing FAL responsibilities for a particular action agency. It is the ERC's responsibility to manage the environmental review of actions to ensure EPA compliance with the procedures in this Manual and to:

   (1) Ensure the timely receipt of all assigned EIS's listed in COMDATE, and ensure completion of MIU reporting requirements;

   (2) Designate a principal reviewer for each assigned action;

   (3) Coordinate determination of the level of participation in EIS scoping efforts and manage participation efforts;

   (4) Coordinate determination of EPA's involvement as a cooperating agency under Section 1501.6 of the CEQ regulations;

   (5) Determine the case-by-case need for reviewing the adequacy of the contents of draft EIS's;

   (6) Determine the case-by-case need for preparation of comments on final EIS's;

   (7) Determine the appropriate rating to be assigned to each draft EIS in the comment letter;

   (8) Determine the need for preparation of comments on non-EIS actions;

   (9) Ensure timely distribution and public availability of comments; and

   (10) Initiate and manage agency follow-up efforts on comment letters identifying significant problem areas.

   b. <u>Principal Reviewer</u>. The principal reviewer (PR) is a person desig- nated by the ERC to coordinate the review of the action and to prepare the EPA comment letter on the proposed Federal action. The PR will be responsible for ensuring that the views of other EPA offices are adequately represented in the comment letter, and that the comment letter is consistent with agency policy and reflects all applicable EPA environmental responsibilities. In general, the PR for Headquarters lead reviews will be the FAL assigned to the lead agency. The PR will have the responsibility to:

(1) Select associate reviewers (AR's) ensuring that all appropriate regional and Headquarters EPA offices are asked to participate;

(2) Set due dates for AR comments that will ensure adequate time for review by the signing official;

(3) Coordinate with AR's to ensure timely receipt of comments and timely resolution of disagreements or inconsistencies between reviewers;

(4) Review and assure the validity of all comments included in the final EPA response;

(5) Resolve and record the disposition of any disagreements with or between AR comments in accordance with subparagraph d, below;

(6) Ensure consistency of EPA comments with any previous comments on the action;

(7) Recommend the most appropriate rating of the environmental impacts of the proposal and/or the adequacy of the EIS, and include the rating in all draft EIS comment letters; and

(8) Ensure the distribution of copies of the signed comment letter to all AR's and other appropriate parties.

c. Associate Reviewer. The associate reviewer (AR) is a person designated by the PR to provide technical and policy advice in specific review areas and to provide the views of the office in which the AR is located. AR's will have the responsibility to:

(1) Review assigned actions within their areas of responsibility taking into account the policies and procedures of this Manual;

(2) Submit comments to the PR on actions in a timely manner;

(3) Obtain the appropriate level of concurrence on comments submitted;

(4) If significant issues are identified, assist the PR in determining the most appropriate rating for the proposed action; and

(5) Upon the request of the PR, and within the limits of available resources, provide liaison with, and technical assistance to, the agency that initiated the EIS or other Federal action.

d. Consolidation of Comments. The PR will consider all AR comments during preparation of the EPA comment letter. If the PR disagrees with substantive AR comments, the PR will attempt to resolve the differences directly with the

AR. If this is not possible, the ERC will be informed and will coordinate
resolution of the issue. On comment letters where substantive changes are
made to comments generated by an AR, the PR will obtain AR concurrence on the
final letter. If major policy issues are involved, the ERC should be informed
and policy level concurrence by the AR office should be obtained. All AR
comments, with applicable PR notations on disposition of the specific issue,
will be retained in the official project file.

6. <u>ROUTING AND LEAD RESPONSIBILITY OF EIS'S AND OTHER FEDERAL ACTIONS.</u>

     a. Distribution of EIS's should be accomplished by lead agencies on or
before the EIS filing date. To ensure that all EIS's are properly distributed,
the ERC will check the weekly COMDATE report to make sure that all assigned
EIS's have been received. If the ERC has not received an EIS identified in
COMDATE, the ERC will inform the MIU immediately and work with the MIU to
obtain the EIS. If appropriate, a request for a time extension due to lack of
availability of the EIS will be coordinated by the MIU at that time. The
following table represents the normal routing and lead responsibility assignment of review actions.

Action	Directed to
Legislation (not accompanied by EIS)	Office of Legislative Analysis
Policy statements, regulations, procedures, and legislation accompanied by an EIS	Office of Federal Activities
Actions that embody a high degree of national controversy or significance, or pioneer Agency policy	Office of Federal Activities
All other actions	Appropriate regional office

     b. In general, a regional office will have the lead responsibility for
reviewing all EIS's and other Federal actions it receives. Specific
exceptions occur where:

     (1) The EIS or other Federal action pertains to an action that is to
take place in another region. In such cases, that regional office will have
the lead, the MIU will be informed immediately, and the EIS will be forwarded to
the lead region.

     (2) The EIS pertains to more than one region. In this case, the
affected regions should refer to COMDATE to determine which is the lead region
and which is an AR. If there is a disagreement with the COMDATE assignments,
the designated lead region will inform the MIU.

     (3) The EIS or other Federal action pertains primarily to national
EPA policy, regulations, or procedures, or to an action which does not have a

geographical focus (e.g., overlapping several regions), or to an action concerning areas in which the regional office does not have adequate expertise. If the ERC suspects this to be the case, the ERC will contact the appropriate FAL to determine lead responsibility. Unless otherwise agreed upon, such cases will be forwarded immediately to the MIU for reassignment of the action.

c. A regional or Headquarters office may at any time request that a particular EIS or other Federal action be evaluated by the OFA to determine lead responsibility.

CHAPTER 3 - PRE-EIS REVIEW ACTIVITIES

1. **POLICY.** It is EPA's policy to participate early in the NEPA compliance efforts of other Federal agencies to the fullest extent practicable in order to identify EPA matters of concern with proposed agency actions and to assist in resolving these concerns at the earliest possible stage of project development. The ERC will make a concerted effort to resolve project concerns through early coordination, where possible, rather than rely on submission of critical comments on completed documents.

2. **GENERAL LIAISON.**

   a. The regional environmental review coordinator and the FAL's will establish and maintain contact at the appropriate levels of other agencies in order to foster an effective working relationship between agencies, to understand the agencies' programs and policies, and to be kept informed of projects of interest to the EPA.

   b. To the fullest extent practicable, the ERC will assist the action agencies in:

      (1) Early identification of potential project impacts and the need to prepare assessments or EIS's;

      (2) Identification of appropriate environmental assessment techniques and methodologies; and

      (3) Incorporation of all reasonable alternatives and impact mitigation measures in the planning and development of projects.

3. **EPA'S PARTICIPATION IN SCOPING.**

   a. **General.** Scoping is the formal early coordination process required by CEQ's 1979 Regulations (40 CFR 1501.7) and is intended to ensure that problems are identified early and are properly studied, that issues of little significance do not consume time and effort, that the draft EIS is thorough and balanced, and that delays occasioned by an inadequate draft EIS are avoided. To help achieve these objectives, EPA will participate in scoping processes to the fullest extent practicable, emphasizing attendance at scoping meetings.

   b. **Responding to Scoping Requests.**

      (1) The ERC will review and respond by letter to all scoping requests specifically made to the EPA. Although **Federal Register** Notices of Intent to prepare an EIS are not considered specific, the ERC is responsible for being aware of all relevant scoping requests and for participating in those of special interest to the EPA. Responses to these non-EPA specific scoping requests may be made by telephone, but a record of the communication must be kept in the official project file.

(2) Scoping letters can be either a form letter of acknowledgment with a list of generic concerns (related to project type or project area), or a letter with detailed action-specific comments. A generic scoping letter or telephone response must define EPA's anticipated level of participation in the scoping process and include at least the following information:

(a) For the general type of project being proposed:

<u>1</u> A list of all EPA permits that might be required;

<u>2</u> Significant environmental issues that should be emphasized in preparation of the EIS; and

<u>3</u> References to publications, including guidelines and current research, that would be useful in analyzing the environmental impacts of various alternatives.

(b) A statement regarding EPA's intention to carry out its independent environmental review responsibilities under Section 309 of the Clean Air Act; and

(c) The name, title, and telephone number of the appropriate working-level contact in the EPA.

(3) The level of EPA participation in scoping processes will be determined by the ERC on a case-by-case basis, taking into account the following factors:

(a) EPA's statutory responsibility;

(b) Severity of potential environmental impacts;

(c) Priority concerns identified in the Administrator's <u>Agency Operating Guidance</u>; and

(d) Available staff and travel resources.

c. <u>Input to the Scoping Process</u>. For those scoping requests where the ERC determines that more substantive EPA participation is warranted, the generic information listed in subparagraph 3b(2) should be supplemented with further detailed guidance to the lead agency. Such guidance will, to the extent possible, include:

(1) Specific environmental issues that should be analyzed;

(2) Specific information or data related to the area of interest;

(3) Specific assessment techniques and methodologies that EPA program offices use or have approved for use;

(4) Reasonable alternatives to the proposed action that may avoid potential adverse impacts, including suggestions for an environmentally preferred alternative; and

(5) Mitigation measures that should be considered to reduce or substantially eliminate adverse environmental impacts.

4. EPA AS A COOPERATING AGENCY.

a. General. Under 40 CFR 1501.6, the lead agency may request any other Federal agency to serve as a cooperating agency if it has jurisdiction or special expertise (statutory responsibility, agency mission, or related program experience) regarding any environmental issue that should be addressed in the statement. EPA may also request that the lead agency designate it as a cooperating agency. The ERC is responsible for determining whether the EPA will become a cooperating agency. The ERC is encouraged to accept cooperating agency status as often as possible, taking into account the criteria in subparagraph 3b(3).

b. Responding to Requests To Be a Cooperating Agency.

(1) If EPA determines in response to a formal request or makes an independent request to be a cooperating agency, the ERC must inform the lead agency of this decision in writing. The response must clearly state that every effort will be made to raise and resolve issues during scoping and EIS preparation, but that EPA has independent obligations under Section 309 of the Clean Air Act to review and comment on every draft EIS. EPA's response to a request to become a cooperating agency should clearly outline EPA's role in the preparation of the EIS. EPA's participation may range from participation in the scoping process and reviewing the scope of work, any preliminary drafts, or technical documents to assuming responsibility for developing information, preparing environmental analyses, and actually drafting portions of the EIS.

(2) If the ERC determines that resource limitations preclude any involvement in the preparation of another agency's EIS, or preclude the degree of involvement requested by the lead agency, it must inform the lead agency in writing (40 CFR 1501.6(c)). The letter should clearly state that EPA's status as a cooperating agency does not affect its independent responsibilities under Section 309 of the Clean Air Act to review and comment on other agencies' EIS's. A copy of this reply will be submitted to the CEQ.

c. Providing Guidance as a Cooperating Agency. Information and/or guidance should be given to the lead agency in those areas where the EPA has special expertise as related to EPA's duties and responsibilities and in those subject areas described in subparagraph 3c. Specific guidance will be given in those areas where the EPA intends to exercise regulatory responsibility.

5. <u>EPA AS LEAD AGENCY</u>.

a. <u>Determining Lead Agency</u>. When, in accordance with 40 CFR Part 6, EPA has an action which is subject to 102(2)(C) of NEPA and the action involves another Federal agency, the ERC and the other Federal agency will determine the lead agency status in accordance with the guidance contained in 40 CFR 1501.5(c), taking into account any relevant Memorandum of Understanding which EPA has executed with the Federal agency in question. Selection of the lead agency should be made at the earliest possible time. If the EPA is the lead agency, EPA will not review the EIS under the Environmental Review Process.

6. <u>REPORTING AND CONTROL</u>. All responses related to scoping, cooperating, or lead agency issues, together with follow-up correspondence must be made a part of the official project file. Copies of letters in which EPA declines an agency's request to become a cooperating agency must be sent to the CEQ.

CHAPTER 4 - REVIEW OF DRAFT ENVIRONMENTAL IMPACT STATEMENTS

1. POLICY. It is EPA's policy to review and comment in writing on all draft EIS's officially filed with the EPA, to provide a rating of the draft EIS which summarizes EPA's level of concern, and to meet with the lead agency to resolve significant issues. The EPA review will be primarily concerned with identifying and recommending corrective action for the significant environmental impacts associated with the proposal. Review of the adequacy of the information and analysis contained in the draft EIS's will be done as needed to support this objective.

2. DRAFT EIS REVIEW MANAGEMENT. Except as noted below, the review management procedures and responsibilities given in chapter 2 apply to the review of draft EIS's.

   a. Establishing Deadlines and Time Extensions.

      (1) Deadlines. Unless a different deadline is officially established for receiving comments, EPA will provide comments on a draft EIS to the lead agency within 45 days from the start of the official review period. The official EIS due dates are listed in COMDATE. The PR will set internal deadlines to ensure EPA's comments are received within the official comment period.

      (2) Time Extensions. Requests for extensions of review periods on draft EIS's should be kept to a minimum. In general, review period extensions on draft EIS's should not be requested unless important environmental issues are involved, and detailed substantive comments are being prepared. Time extensions should normally not exceed 15 days.

   b. Categorization and Agency Notification System for Draft EIS's.

      (1) After completing the review of a draft EIS, the PR will categorize or "rate" the EIS according to the alpha numeric system described below and in paragraph 4 of this chapter, and include the designated rating in the comment letter. In general, the rating will be based on the lead agency's preferred alternative. If, however, a preferred alternative is not identified, or if the preferred alternative has significant environmental problems that could be avoided by selection of another alternative, or if there is reason to believe that the preferred alternative may be changed at a later stage, the reviewer should rate individual alternatives. The purpose of the rating system is to synthesize the level of EPA's overall concern with the proposal and to define the associated follow-up that will be conducted with the lead agency.

      (2) The alphabetical categories LO, EC, EO, and EU signify EPA's evaluation of the environmental impacts of the proposal. Numerical categories 1, 2, and 3 signify an evaluation of the adequacy of the draft EIS. A summary of the rating definitions and the associated follow-up action is given in

figure 4-1 at the end of this chapter. This figure should be attached to draft EIS comment letters when the lead agency may be unfamiliar with the EPA rating system. To the maximum extent possible, assignments of the alphabetical rating will be based on the overall environmental impact of the proposed project or action, including those project impacts that are not adequately addressed in the draft EIS. When there is insufficient information in the draft EIS, the determination of potential project impact may be based on other documents, information, or on-site surveys. The comment letter should clearly identify the source of information used by the EPA in evaluating the proposal.

(3) The rating of a draft EIS will consist of one of the category combinations shown in the table below. As noted in the table and described in chapter 5, the ERC must follow up with the lead agency in those cases where significant problem areas are identified.

Category	Lead Agency Pre-Notification	Follow-up on Draft EIS Comment Letter
LO	None	None
EC-1, EC-2	None	Phone Call
EO-1, EO-2	Phone call	Meeting
EO-3, EU-1, EU-2, EU-3, 3	Meeting	Meeting

(4) For categories EO, EU, or 3, the ERC will ensure that the lead agency is notified of the general EPA concerns prior to receipt of EPA's comment letter. For categories EU and 3, the ERC must attempt to meet with the lead agency to discuss EPA's concerns prior to submission of the comment letter to the lead agency. The purposes of such a meeting are to describe the specific EPA concerns and discuss ways to resolve those concerns, to ensure that the EPA review has correctly interpreted the proposal and supporting information, and to become aware of any ongoing lead agency actions that might resolve the EPA concerns. To assure the objectivity and independence of the EPA review responsibility, the EPA comment letter itself and the assigned rating are not subject to negotiation and should not be changed on the basis of the meeting unless errors are discovered in EPA's understanding of the issues. However, the reviewer may add in the letter an acknowledgment of any relevant new lead agency activities that the reviewer believes could resolve the EPA concerns.

3. SCOPE OF COMMENTS ON THE DRAFT EIS.

    a. General. In general, EPA's comments will focus on the proposal but will, if necessary, review the complete range of alternatives, identifying those that are environmentally unacceptable to EPA and identifying EPA's preferred alternative. EPA's comment letter on the draft EIS will reflect all of EPA's environmental responsibilities that may bear on the action. The review will include EPA's assessment of the expected environmental impacts of the action and, if substantive impacts are identified, an evaluation of the adequacy of the supporting information presented in the EIS with suggestions

4-2

for additional information that is needed. The EPA comment letter on draft
EIS's will:

      (1) Explicitly reference EPA's review responsibilities under NEPA/
Section 309;

      (2) Acknowledge positive lead agency responses to EPA scoping suggestions
or early coordination efforts;

      (3) Provide a clear and concise description of EPA's substantive
concerns and recommendations with supporting details given in attachments;

      (4) Include a rating of the proposal and, if appropriate, the adequacy
of the EIS in accordance with the criteria established in paragraphs 2 and 4 of
this chapter; and

      (5) Give the name and phone number of an appropriate EPA contact
person.

     b. <u>Mitigation (40 CFR 1508.20)</u>. EPA's comments should include measures
to avoid or minimize damage to the environment, or to protect, restore, and
enhance the environment. Suggestions for mitigation should be oriented
towards selection of mitigation measures that are technically feasible, of
long-term effectiveness, and have a high likelihood of being implemented.

     c. <u>Statutory Authorities</u>. Special efforts should be made to identify
project impacts that may lead to possible violation of national environmental
standards or that might preclude or bias future issuance of EPA related environmental permits. EPA comments regarding potential violations of standards
must be clearly stated in the letter, and an offer should be made to work with
the proposing agency to develop appropriate measures to reduce impacts.

     d. <u>Alternatives</u>. If significant impacts are associated with the proposal
and they cannot be adequately mitigated, EPA's comments should suggest an
environmentally preferable alternative, including if necessary, a new alternative. The suggested alternatives should be both "reasonable" and "feasible."
In this context, such an alternative is one that is practical in the technical,
economic, and social sense, even if the alternative is outside the jurisdiction
of the lead agency.

     e. <u>Purpose and Need</u>. If a detailed review of alternatives is required,
the reviewer may have to address the purpose of and need for the proposed
action in order to determine to what degree an alternative would meet project
objectives. In these cases, the reviewer may comment on the technical
adequacy and accuracy of the EIS's methods for estimating the need for the
proposed action in cases where this affects the definition of reasonable and
feasible alternatives. Within the context of reviewing purpose and need, the
EPA may also comment on the economic justification of the project, and the

relationship between the lead agency's economic analysis and any unquantified environmental impacts, values, and amenities. The comments may also address the technical validity and adequacy of the supporting data for the EIS's economic analyses.

f. **Projects Subject to Section 404(r) of the Clean Water Act.** The Section 404 Coordinator will serve as an associate reviewer for those projects for which an agency is seeking an exemption under Section 404(r), and shall concur with the EPA comment letter. Section 404(r) provides that discharges of dredged or fill material which are part of Federal construction projects specifically authorized by Congress are not subject to regulation under Sections 301, 402, or 404 of the Clean Water Act if the information on the effects of such discharge including consideration of the Section 404(b)(1) Guidelines, is included in the EIS for the project, and the EIS has been submitted to Congress before the discharge occurs and before the authorization for the project occurs. In accordance with the CEQ's guidance of November 17, 1980, EPA's comments on the EIS will serve as the vehicle for informing the agency of EPA's determination whether the proposed Section 404(r) exemption will be in compliance with the requirements of the Section 404(b)(1) Guidelines. The comments should reference the CEQ Memorandum for Heads of Agencies, which provides guidance on applying Section 404(r) and should include EPA's determination regarding:

(1) Whether the EIS contains requisite information on the proposed discharges and other effects; and

(2) Whether the proposal is consistent with Section 404(b)(1) Guidelines.

g. **Projects Potentially Affecting a Designated "Sole Source" Aquifer Subject to Section 1424(e) of the Safe Drinking Water Act.**

(1) The regional office responsible for implementing the Safe Drinking Water Act (SDWA) will act as an AR on any EIS for a project potentially affecting a "sole source" aquifer designated under Section 1424(e) of the SDWA. EPA's comments on the draft EIS will serve as EPA's preliminary comments for the groundwater impact evaluation required under Section 1424(e), which stipulates that no commitment to a project of Federal financial assistance may be made, if the Administrator determines that a project has the potential to contaminate a designated aquifer, so as to create a significant hazard to public health. (Rules proposed to implement 1424(e) are found at 42 FR 51620, September 29, 1977.)

(2) If it is determined that a project may contaminate the aquifer through the recharge zone so as to create a significant hazard to public health, the ERC will, in consultation with the drinking water staff, prepare a briefing memorandum and comment letter for the Regional Administrator. Copies of the briefing memorandum and the proposed comment letter shall first be sent to the appropriate FAL, who will coordinate concurrence by the appropriate Headquarters offices. The comment letter should cite EPA's authorities under Section 309/

NEPA and Section 1424(e) of SDWA, and state that the project is a candidate for both referral to the CEQ and a Section 1424(e) determination.

4. <u>RATING SYSTEM CRITERIA</u>.

    a. <u>Rating the Environmental Impact of the Action</u>.

        (1) <u>LO (Lack of Objections)</u>. The review has not identified any potential environmental impacts requiring substantive changes to the preferred alternative. The review may have disclosed opportunities for application of mitigation measures that could be accomplished with no more than minor changes to the proposed action.

        (2) <u>EC (Environmental Concerns)</u>. The review has identified environmental impacts that should be avoided in order to fully protect the environment. Corrective measures may require changes to the preferred alternative or application of mitigation measures that can reduce the environmental impact.

        (3) <u>EO (Environmental Objections)</u>. The review has identified significant environmental impacts that should be avoided in order to adequately protect the environment. Corrective measures may require substantial changes to the preferred alternative or consideration of some other project alternative (including the no action alternative or a new alternative). The basis for environmental objections can include situations:

            (a) Where an action might violate or be inconsistent with achievement or maintenance of a national environmental standard;

            (b) Where the Federal agency violates its own substantive environmental requirements that relate to EPA's areas of jurisdiction or expertise;

            (c) Where there is a violation of an EPA policy declaration;

            (d) Where there are no applicable standards or where applicable standards will not be violated but there is potential for significant environmental degradation that could be corrected by project modification or other feasible alternatives; or

            (e) Where proceeding with the proposed action would set a precedent   r future actions that collectively could result in significant environmental impacts.

        (4) <u>EU (Environmentally Unsatisfactory)</u>. The review has identified adverse environmental impacts that are of sufficient magnitude that EPA believes the proposed action must not proceed as proposed. The basis for an environmentally unsatisfactory determination consists of identification of

environmentally objectionable impacts as defined above and one or more of the following conditions:

(a) The potential violation of or inconsistency with a national environmental standard is substantive and/or will occur on a long-term basis;

(b) There are no applicable standards but the severity, duration, or geographical scope of the impacts associated with the proposed action warrant special attention; or

(c) The potential environmental impacts resulting from the proposed action are of national importance because of the threat to national environmental resources or to environmental policies.

b. **Adequacy of the Impact Statement.**

(1) "1" (Adequate). The draft EIS adequately sets forth the environmental impact(s) of the preferred alternative and those of the alternatives reasonably available to the project or action. No further analysis or data collection is necessary, but the reviewer may suggest the addition of clarifying language or information.

(2) "2" (Insufficient Information). The draft EIS does not contain sufficient information to fully assess environmental impacts that should be avoided in order to fully protect the environment, or the reviewer has identified new reasonably available alternatives that are within the spectrum of alternatives analyzed in the draft EIS, which could reduce the environmental impacts of the proposal. The identified additional information, data, analyses, or discussion should be included in the final EIS.

(3) "3" (Inadequate). The draft EIS does not adequately assess the potentially significant environmental impacts of the proposal, or the reviewer has identified new, reasonably available, alternatives, that are outside of the spectrum of alternatives analyzed in the draft EIS, which should be analyzed in order to reduce the potentially significant environmental impacts. The identified additional information, data, analyses, or discussions are of such a magnitude that they should have full public review at a draft stage. This rating indicates EPA's belief that the draft EIS does not meet the purposes of NEPA and/or the Section 309 review, and thus should be formally revised and made available for public comment in a supplemental or revised draft EIS.

5. **APPROVING AND DISTRIBUTING COMMENTS ON DRAFT EIS'S.**

a. Categories LO, EC, EO, 1, or 2. For draft EIS's rated LO, EC, EO, 1, or 2 the comments will be signed by the appropriate regional or Headquarters official and the ERC will distribute EPA's comments in accordance with subparagraph 5c of this chapter.

b. Categories EU or 3. For draft EIS's where the ERC is proposing a rating of EU or 3, the EPA comment letter must be cleared by the Assistant Administrator for External Affairs prior to release. If the review is a regional action, the draft letter will be submitted through the OFA for ·clearance. The draft comment letter must be submitted at least 5 working days prior to the due date and the proposed rating must have been approved by the regional signing official. In every case where a draft statement has been rated EU or 3, the Assistant Administrator, OEA, will send a copy of the EPA comment letter to the CEQ. In addition, where the EPA has commented to a regional office of the originating agency, appropriate officials within the headquarters office of the originating agency will also be informed. If a communications strategy has been developed for the action, the release of information should follow that strategy.

c. Checklist for Distribution of Agency Comments on the Draft EIS.*

Addressee	Number of Copies
Agency submitting statement	Original
CEQ (if EU or 3) with transmittal letter	1 copy
Office of Public Affairs (if comments are rated EU or 3)	1 copy
EPA offices which served as associate reviewers	1 copy
Office of Federal Activities· Attn: MIU	2 copies

6. **REPORTING AND CONTROL.** All draft EIS's under review, all time extensions, and all comment letters on draft EIS's will be entered in the MIU data management system. All EPA comment letters and associated correspondence on draft EIS's will be retained in the official project file.

---

*To the maximum extent practicable, the comment letter should not be distributed to parties outside of the EPA until after the original has been received by the lead agency.

SUMMARY OF RATING DEFINITIONS
AND FOLLOW-UP ACTION*

Environmental Impact of the Action

LO--Lack of Objections
The EPA review has not identified any potential environmental impacts
requiring substantive changes to the proposal. The review may have disclosed
opportunities for application of mitigation measures that could be
accomplished with no more than minor changes to the proposal.

EC--Environmental Concerns
The EPA review has identified environmental impacts that should be avoided in
order to fully protect the environment. Corrective measures may require
changes to the preferred alternative or application of mitigation measures
that can reduce the environmental impact. EPA would like to work with the
lead agency to reduce these impacts.

EO--Environmental Objections
The EPA review has identified significant environmental impacts that must be
avoided in order to provide adequate protection for the environment. Corrective
measures may require substantial changes to the preferred alterna tive or
consideration of some other project alternative (including the no action
alternative or a new alternative). EPA intends to work with the lead
agency to reduce these impacts.

EU--Environmentally Unsatisfactory
The EPA review has identified adverse environmental impacts that are of
sufficient magnitude that they are unsatisfactory from the standpoint of
public health or welfare or environmental quality. EPA intends to work with
the lead agency to reduce these impacts. If the potential unsatisfactory
impacts are not corrected at the final EIS stage, this proposal will be
recommended for referral to the CEQ.

Adequacy of the Impact Statement

Category 1--Adequate
EPA believes the draft EIS adequately sets forth the environmental impact(s)
of the preferred alternative and those of the alternatives reasonably avail
able to the project or action. No further analysis or data collection is
necessary, but the reviewer may suggest the addition of clarifying language or
information.

Category 2--Insufficient Information
The draft EIS does not contain sufficient information for EPA to fully assess
environmental impacts that should be avoided in order to fully protect the
environment, or the EPA reviewer has identified new reasonably available
alternatives that are within the spectrum of alternatives analyzed in the
draft EIS, which could reduce the environmental impacts of the action. The
identified additional information, data, analyses, or discussion should be
included in the final EIS.

Category 3--Inadequate
EPA does not believe that the draft EIS adequately assesses potentially
significant environmental impacts of the action, or the EPA reviewer has
identified new, reasonably available alternatives that are outside of the
spectrum of alternatives analyzed in the draft EIS, which should be analyzed
in order to reduce the potentially significant environmental impacts. EPA
believes that the identified additional information, data, analyses, or
discussions are of such a magnitude that they should have full public review
at a draft stage. EPA does not believe that the draft EIS is adequate for the
purposes of the NEPA and/or Section 309 review, and thus should be formally
revised and made available for public comment in a supplemental or revised
draft EIS. On the basis of the potential significant impacts involved, this
proposal could be a candidate for referral to the CEQ.

*From EPA Manual 1640 Policy and Procedures for the Review of Federal Actions
 Impacting the Environment.

Figure 4-1

CHAPTER 5 - POST-DRAFT EIS FOLLOW-UP

1. <u>POLICY</u>. It is EPA's policy to conduct follow-up discussions with the lead agency to ensure that EPA's concerns raised at the draft EIS stage are fully understood and considered by the lead agency. To the extent resources allow, follow-up efforts should exceed the minimum required by this chapter and paragraph 2b(3) of chapter 4.

2. <u>POST-DRAFT CONSULTATIONS</u>. In cases where a draft EIS is rated EO, EU, or 3, the ERC must initiate consultation with the lead agency. Agency consultation will continue at increasing levels of management, through the EPA Assistant Administrator level, as appropriate, until EPA's concerns are resolved or further negotiations are pointless. For those actions where the region is the PR, the ERC will work through the appropriate FAL to coordinate the consultation efforts at the regional and Headquarters levels. The ERC and/or FAL should be prepared to review the project in the field, to develop additional information, and/or to work with the agency to improve the proposed action and the supporting final EIS. When substantive consultation meetings are held, the ERC must document the outcome and, as appropriate, respond in writing to the lead agency to acknowledge any points of agreement, and to restate any unresolved issues.

3. <u>STATUS REPORTS</u>.

   a. After consulting or meeting with the lead agency concerning draft EIS's rated EU or 3, the ERC will prepare a status memorandum for the Assistant Administrator, OEA, through the Director, OFA, and, if it is a regional action, for the Regional Administrator. This memorandum should summarize: (1) the progress of the consultations; (2) the remaining unresolved issues; (3) the positions of other affected Federal agencies; and (4) a prognosis for the resolution of remaining issues.

   b. The ERC will periodically assess the lead agency's progress in responding to EPA's concerns on draft EIS's rated EU or 3. It is the ERC's responsibility to anticipate, and make early preparation for, those final EIS's which will be so unresponsive to EPA's concerns that a recommendation for referral of the final EIS to the CEQ will be required.

4. <u>REPORTING AND CONTROL</u>. All correspondence regarding post-draft consultations and agreements must be retained in the official project file. For all draft EIS's which have been rated EU or 3, the official file must also contain all material that may be needed for a formal referral package.

CHAPTER 6 – REVIEW OF FINAL EIS'S

1. POLICY. It is EPA's policy to conduct detailed reviews of those final EIS's which had significant issues raised by the EPA at the draft EIS stage. Each final EIS will be checked to determine whether the statement adequately resolves the problems identified in the EPA review of the draft EIS, or whether there has been a substantive change in the proposal. A detailed review and submission of comments on the final EIS will be done for those actions rated EO, EU, or 3 at the draft stage. A detailed review on other final EIS's may be done if the ERC determines that conditions warrant it.

2. FINAL EIS REVIEW MANAGEMENT. Except as noted below, the review management procedures and responsibilities given in chapter 2 apply to the review of final EIS's.

   a. Designating Lead Responsibility and Principal and Associate Reviewers. Lead responsibility for the final EIS will be the same as for the draft EIS unless other arrangements have been made with the MIU. If possible, the same principal and associate reviewers who dealt with the draft EIS will be assigned to review the final EIS.

   b. Establishing Deadlines and Time Extensions.

      (1) Deadlines. Unless a different deadline is officially established for receiving comments, EPA will respond to a final EIS within 30 days from the start of the official review period. The official EIS due dates are listed in COMDATE. The PR will set internal deadlines to ensure EPA's comments are received within the official comment period. All final EIS's which are candidates for referral to the CEQ, will be given priority review in accordance with the internal deadlines specified in chapter 9.

      (2) Time Extensions. Requests for extensions of review periods on final EIS's should be kept to a minimum. In general, review period extensions on final EIS's should not be requested unless important environmental issues are involved and detailed substantive comments are being prepared. Time extensions should normally not exceed 15 days. Time extensions for a referral deadline will be requested in accordance with the procedures in chapter 9.

   c. Categorizing Final EIS's. The alpha numeric rating system used for draft EIS's will be applied to final EIS's for internal management purposes only (see chapter 4, paragraph 4). The EPA rating is not to be included in comment letters on final EIS's. Instead, the comments will rely wholly on narrative explanations to describe the environmental impact of the proposed action or the responsiveness or unresponsiveness of the EIS. The PR will include the assigned rating when entering the action into the MIU data management system.

3. SCOPE OF COMMENTS ON FINAL EIS'S.

    a. General.

       (1) Except in unusual circumstances, the review of final EIS's will be directed to the major unresolved issues, focusing on the impacts of the project rather than on the adequacy of the statement. Except in unusual circumstances, the scope of review will be limited to issues raised in EPA's comments on the draft EIS that have not been resolved in the final EIS, and any new, potentially significant impacts that have been identified as a result of information made available after publication of the draft EIS.

       (2) Within 5 days after the start of the review period for the final EIS, the PR will make a preliminary determination as to whether the action meets the criteria for "environmentally unsatisfactory" as set forth in chapter 4, paragraph 4 of this Manual. If the action is determined to be environmentally unsatisfactory, the procedures set forth in chapter 9 of this Manual will be followed.

       (3) For final EIS's which had drafts categorized as LO, the PR may decide that no formal comments on the final EIS will be submitted to the lead agency. Written comments will be prepared in other cases and when the agency has made substantive modifications in the proposed action in comparison to the draft EIS. In addition, written comments will be prepared for final EIS's that involve Section 404(r) or Section 1424(e) issues.

       (4) In those cases involving significant mitigation requirements or where the proposed agency action is not clear, EPA's comments on the final EIS will also include a request for a copy of the Record of Decision.

    b. Mitigation Measures. If a final EIS identifies for the first time, or modifies the agency's preferred alternative, EPA's review should include consideration of any additional specific mitigation measures necessary to reduce any adverse impacts of that alternative. When mitigation measures are recommended, the comment letter should suggest that the lead agency include these measures in their Record of Decision as specific conditions on their permits or grants. Where mitigation measures are directly related to the acceptability of the action, the comment letter should include a request that the lead agency keep EPA informed of progress in carrying out the mitigation measures proposed by the EPA.

    c. Projects Under Section 404(r) of the Clean Water Act.

       (1) The Section 404 Coordinator will serve as an associate reviewer on all final EIS's involving a potential 404 permit. In order to satisfy the provisions of Section 404(r), the EIS process must be completed before Congress approves requests for authorizations and appropriations. Pursuant to the CEQ Memorandum for Heads of Agencies, November 17, 1980, completion of the EIS process includes resolution of any pre-decision referrals.

(2) The comment letter on a final EIS seeking a 404(r) exemption will include EPA's determination regarding: (a) whether the EIS contains requisite information on the proposed discharges and other effects, and (b) whether the proposal is consistent with the 404(b)(1) Guidelines.

(3) If a negative determination on either (2)(a) or (b) is made, the appropriate FAL will be informed and will coordinate with the lead agency to ensure that the required statement of EPA's determination is included in the lead agency's congressional submission. The FAL will also ensure that EPA's views regarding an exemption are effectively represented in the Office of Management and Budget's (OMB's) legislative and budget processes.

　　　d. Projects Subject to Groundwater Evaluation Under Section 1424(e) of the SDWA.

(1) The regional drinking water program staff will serve as an AR on the review of any EIS for a project potentially affecting a designated "sole source" aquifer and will be responsible for the preliminary determination of project compliance with the requirements of Section 1424(e) of the SDWA.

(2) If the regional drinking water program staff determines that a project may contaminate the aquifer through the recharge zone so as to create a significant hazard to public health, the ERC will, in consultation with the regional drinking water staff and appropriate Headquarters FAL, prepare a briefing memorandum and comment letter for the Regional Administrator. Upon approval, the Regional Administrator shall submit the package to the Director, OFA, who shall coordinate the appropriate Headquarters approval and submission to the Administrator for action.

4.　UNRESPONSIVE FINAL EIS.

(1) If the lead agency prepares a final EIS rather than a supplement or revised draft EIS in response to an EPA "3" rating, or if there are significant new circumstances or information relevant to areas of significant environmental impact, the review should follow the procedures of chapter 4 to determine if the proposal is either "environmentally unsatisfactory" or "inadequate." If it is determined that either of these situations apply, the procedures of chapter 9 should be initiated to determine if a referral of the proposal to the CEQ is warranted.

(2) If a refferal is not warranted, but the EIS contains insufficient information to assess potentially significant environmental impacts of the proposed action, a request should be made for the agency to prepare a supplemental EIS. In such cases, the EPA comment letter must demonstrate that the final EIS is unresponsive to EPA's comments on the draft EIS and state EPA's belief that the final EIS is inadequate to meet the purposes of the NEPA and/or the EPA review, and therefore should be formally supplemented (40 CFR 1502.9(c)).

5. <u>DISTRIBUTION OF THE FINAL EIS COMMENT LETTER</u>. The ERC will coordinate distribution of the final EIS comment letter in accordance with chapter 4, paragraph 5 of this Manual (or in the case of a referral, chapter 9, paragraph 5) and any applicable communications strategy. To the maximum extent practicable, the comment letter will not be distributed externally until after the lead agency has received the original.

6. <u>REPORTING AND CONTROL</u>. All final EIS's, comment letters, no comment memoranda, and correspondence related to time extensions will be entered in the MIU data management system and retained in the official project file. The final EIS rating must also be entered into the MIU system (even if no comment letter was sent).

CHAPTER 7 - MONITORING AND FOLLOW-UP

1. <u>POLICY</u>. It is EPA's policy to conduct, on a selected basis, follow-up activities on comments on final EIS's to ensure that: (1) the EPA participates as fully as possible in any post-EIS efforts designed to assist agency decisionmaking; (2) agreed upon mitigation measures are identified in the Record of Decision; and (3) the agreed upon mitigation measures are fully implemented (e.g., permit conditions, operating plan stipulations, etc.).

2. <u>MONITORING AND FOLLOW-UP</u>.

    a. After transmittal of EPA's comments on the final EIS, the PR will, as appropriate, ensure that:

        (1) EPA receives a copy of the Record of Decision;

        (2) The lead agency has incorporated into the Record of Decision all agreed upon mitigation and other impact reduction measures; and

        (3) The lead agency has included all agreed upon measures as conditions in grants, permits, or other approvals, where appropriate.

    b. Officials who could be subsequently involved in the proposed action should be informed of the final EPA position on the EIS (e.g., regional or State enforcement officials for NPDES permitting, regional enforcement officials for Section 404 enforcement, regional air program or enforcement officials for transportation control strategy compliance and State implementation plan requirements).

    c. Where resources allow, the ERC is encouraged to assess the level of compliance and effectiveness of Federal agency mitigation measures. The ERC is responsible for determining when and how EPA's final EIS follow-up and monitoring should be carried out.

3. <u>REVIEW OF THE RECORD OF DECISION</u>.

    a. The PR should review the Record of Decision on all final EIS's on which the EPA has expressed environmental objections, and/or those where the EPA has negotiated mitigation measures or changes in project design.

    b. The ERC will bring problems or discrepancies between the Record of Decision and agreed upon mitigation measures to the attention of the lead agency. Any unresolved issues should be coordinated with the appropriate FAL, and, through the FAL, with the lead agency's headquarters office, and if appropriate, with the CEQ.

4. <u>REPORTING AND CONTROL</u>. All correspondence regarding the Record of Decision will be recorded in the official project file.

CHAPTER 8 - REVIEW OF DOCUMENTS OTHER THAN EIS'S

1.   POLICY.   The Environmental Review Process will include review of those proposed Federal agency actions, legislation, regulations, and notices which may not be contained in an EIS, but which could lead to or have significant environmental impacts.

2.   GENERAL REVIEW PROCEDURES.

    a.   Lead Responsibility for Review of Other Actions.   Lead responsibilities for non-EIS actions are, in general, as defined below but may be adjusted in accordance with the procedures in chapter 2 of this Manual.

       (1)   The OFA will have lead responsibility on all regulation reviews and the appropriate FAL will determine which proposed regulations should be reviewed;

       (2)   The Office of Legislative Analysis (OLA), within the Office of External Affairs, will have lead responsibility on all non-EIS legislation reviews and will determine when the EPA will prepare formal comments on legislation; and

       (3)   Overall management of the review of non-EIS agency actions, including environmental assessments and Findings of No Significant Impact (FONSI's), license applications, etc., is the responsibility of the ERC managing the liaison activity that involves the action.

    b.   Conducting Reviews of Other Actions.   The ERC will follow the review coordination procedures of chapter 2 to ensure that EPA's comments are coordinated and comprehensive and are received by the originating agency within its decisionmaking period.   If the ERC believes that an EIS is needed on the proposed action, the procedures found in paragraph 6 of this chapter should be followed.

    c.   Rating Other Federal Actions.   Except for the referral criteria, the rating system for draft impact statements pursuant to chapter 4 of this Manual will not be used for non-EIS actions.   If the PR determines that a Federal agency action covered by this chapter is environmentally unsatisfactory in accordance with the criteria listed in chapter 4, thus warranting a referral to the CEQ, then the procedures found in paragraph 7 of this chapter will apply.

3.   LEGISLATION REVIEWS.   The OLA has lead responsibility on all proposed legislation not accompanied by an EIS.   The OLA is responsible for coordinating with other EPA program and regional offices, and for preparing EPA's comments on all legislation.   Any ERC receiving proposed legislation from another Federal agency should forward it directly to the OLA for action.

4. <u>REGULATION REVIEWS</u>. The FAL's will monitor the <u>Federal Register</u> regularly to determine which environmental regulations proposed by their assigned Federal agencies are significant and should be reviewed. FAL's will normally act as PR's for regulations proposed by the agencies assigned to them. The Director, OFA, will be the signatory official for comments on these regulations. The FAL will be responsible for ensuring that the regions and EPA program offices impacted by the regulations will be designated as AR's.

5. <u>OTHER AGENCY ACTION REVIEWS</u>. The ERC may determine that other non-EIS Federal actions such as environmental assessments (40 CFR 1508.9), FONSI's (40 CFR 1508.13), issue papers, or technical support documents should be reviewed. The ERC's decision to review these actions will take into account the relationship of the proposed action to other Federal actions and how the document fits into the overall decisionmaking process.

6. <u>DETERMINING THE NEED FOR AN EIS</u>. Whenever the ERC determines on the basis of investigating a public inquiry, reviewing a regulation or environmental assessment/FONSI, or by other means, that a Federal agency has not or does not intend to prepare an EIS on an action that the EPA believes could significantly affect the quality of the human environment, the following procedures pertain.

    a. If it is a regional action, the ERC will immediately contact the appropriate FAL and develop a coordinated regional/headquarters approach for working with the lead agency.

    b. The ERC will initiate consultation with the Federal agency responsible for the major action to explore the necessity for EIS preparation. Discussions with the agency will be couched in terms of suggested action for the Federal agency's consideration rather than as an EPA requirement. It is the lead agency's responsibility to decide if an EIS will be prepared.

    c. If, after such consultation, the ERC believes that the requirements of Section 102(2)(C) of NEPA are applicable, the PR will prepare a comment letter to the Federal agency responsible for the proposed action. The comment letter should include EPA's assessment of the action and reasons why the EPA believes the agency should prepare an EIS.

7. <u>ENVIRONMENTALLY UNSATISFACTORY ACTIONS</u>. If the ERC determines that a non-EIS action is environmentally unsatisfactory at the draft stage (in accordance with the EU criteria specified in chapter 4), the proposed comment letter must be cleared by the Assistant Administrator, OEA, prior to release. The procedures of chapter 4 must be followed in obtaining this clearance. At the time of the clearance request, or if the non-EIS action is a final action, the ERC and/or appropriate FAL will set up internal consultation and referral procedures similar to those outlined in chapter 9 of this Manual. The procedures will also consider the option of requesting an EIS. The procedures will ensure that the referral will take place no later than 5 days before the "final" lead agency action. For example, in the case of proposed regulations, the referral must occur prior to publication of the final rule.

8. <u>REPORTING AND CONTROL</u>. Regulations under review and the resulting comment letters, as well as comment letters on any other non-EIS action determined to be environmentally unsatisfactory, will be entered into the MIU data management system. All agency comment letters and official agency actions related to the Environmental Review Process will be retained in the official project file.

CHAPTER 9 - REFERRALS TO THE COUNCIL ON ENVIRONMENTAL QUALITY

1. **POLICY.** The EPA authority for referring proposed regulations or major
Federal actions to the Council on Environmental Quality (40 CFR 1504 and
Section 309 of the Clean Air Act) will be used only when significant environmental issues are involved and only after every effort to resolve these issues
at the agency level has been exhausted.

2. **CRITERIA FOR REFERRAL.** In order to meet a determination of "unsatisfactory
from the standpoint of public health or welfare or environmental quality," the
proposed action must satisfy the "environmentally unsatisfactory" criteria
given in chapter 4.

3. **REFERRAL PROCEDURES.**

    a. The CEQ has established a 25-day time period, starting from the date
of the Notice of Availability of the final EIS in the Federal Register, for
referring final EIS's (40 CFR 1504.3(b)). Extensions of EIS referral periods
can be granted only by the lead agency (40 CFR 1504.3(b)) and must be specific
to the 25-day referral period rather than the overall comment period.

    b. Since EPA has authority under Section 309 of the Clean Air Act to
refer proposed regulations and major Federal actions for which no EIS has been
prepared, the intent of the 25-day deadline is incorporated in the procedures
of this section by requiring all EPA referrals to be made no later than 5 days
before the end of the comment period or, in any case, 5 days before the final
action takes place.

4. **REFERRAL PACKAGE DEVELOPMENT SEQUENCE.**

    a. The objective of the referral package development sequence require-
ments in this section is to ensure that the referral package is ready within
the rigid 25-day time limit and, simultaneously, allow for a final attempt to
resolve EPA's concerns with the lead agency. The key elements in this
sequence are:

        (1) Early identification of the potential referral action by the
PR/ERC;

        (2) Approval of the referral action by the Regional Administrator (if
a regional action) and the Assistant Administrator, OEA;

        (3) An attempt to meet with the lead agency and work out EPA's
concerns; and

        (4) Preparation of the referral package to preserve the referral
option if discussions with the lead agency do not resolve EPA's concerns.

    b. Specific procedures for the referral development sequence are described
below. To facilitate this description, it is assumed that the referral action

is taken by a region. The same procedures apply where Headquarters has the referral action except there would be no regional requirements.

(1) Within 5 days after the beginning of the review period the PR, in consultation with the ERC, will make a preliminary determination as to whether the action is unsatisfactory from the standpoint of public health, welfare, or environmental quality in accordance with the EU criteria in chapter 4. If a referral is indicated, the ERC will notify the appropriate FAL and proceed with development of the materials described below.

(2) Within 10 days from the start of the 25-day referral period, the ERC, in consultation with the FAL, will prepare and submit to the Regional Administrator and the Assistant Administrator, OEA, through the Director, OFA, a briefing memorandum and interim response to the lead agency. The interim response will state that the EPA is considering a referral to the CEQ and will request a meeting and time extension to allow for a resolution of EPA's concerns. The briefing memorandum will contain the following information:

(a) Brief description of the proposed action;

(b) Reason the action is environmentally unsatisfactory;

(c) Description of the attempts to resolve differences with the lead agency;

(d) Positions of other affected Federal agencies, groups, and public officials; and

(e) Recommended strategy for resolution of remaining issues.

(3) If the lead agency grants a time extension, EPA negotiations will take place and, if necessary, the referral package will be developed according to the extended referral time period. If the lead agency grants a time extension of the referral period by phone, the ERC will immediately prepare a letter to the lead agency documenting the agreement. If a time extension is not granted, the referral preparation will proceed on the basis of the original referral deadline.

(4) No later than 10 days before the referral deadline, the FAL will prepare a short information memorandum for the Administrator describing potential referral and the status of unresolved issues; a one-page "talking points" paper; and an outline of a communication strategy for notifying all interested groups of EPA's action. Development of the communication strategy is to be coordinated with the immediate Office of the Assistant Administrator for External Affairs.

(5) No later than 7 days before the referral deadline, the final referral package, prepared in accordance with paragraph 6 of this chapter and approved by the Regional Administrator, will be forwarded to the Director, OFA.

(6) No later than 5 days before the referral deadline, the Director, OFA, will ensure that the referral package is in final form with all letters and appropriate concurrences ready for the Administrator's signature, and working through the Assistant Administrator for OEA, to ensure that a briefing has been arranged for the Administrator.

5. CONTENT AND ORGANIZATION OF THE REFERRAL PACKAGES.

a. Administrator's Referral Package. The referral package for the Administrator will include the package to be submitted to the CEQ and the lead agency, and the following:

(1) An action memorandum to the Administrator (not to exceed two pages) briefly outlining the proposed action, EPA's concerns with the proposed action, and positions of other affected Federal agencies, public interest groups, and congressional delegations.

(2) A communications strategy for notifying all interested groups of the referral. This strategy will be coordinated with the immediate Office of the Assistant Administrator for External Affairs and will follow the established strategy development format.

b. CEQ Referral Package. The CEQ referral package will consist of a letter for the Administrator's signature to the Chairman of the CEQ setting forth the basis of EPA's determination and the lead agency referral package described below.

c. Lead Agency Referral Package. This package will consist of the following:

(1) A letter for the Administrator's signature to the head of the lead agency informing the lead agency of EPA's unsatisfactory determination, and of the referral of the matter to the CEQ. The letter should request that no action be taken on the proposed action until the CEQ acts on the matter.

(2) Detailed comments supporting EPA's conclusion that the matter is unsatisfactory from the standpoint of public health, welfare, or environmental quality. The detailed comments will include the following information:

(a) The unacceptable impacts related to EPA's areas of jurisdiction or expertise;

(b) The reasons EPA believes the matter is unsatisfactory;

(c) Description of those national resources or environmental policies that would be adversely affected;

(d)   Identification of environmentally preferable alternatives;

(e)   Identification of agreed upon facts;

(f)   Identification of material facts in controversy; and

(g)   Brief review of attempts by the EPA to resolve the concerns with the lead agency.

6.   APPROVING AND DISTRIBUTING THE REFERRAL PACKAGE.   After the Administrator signs the referral comment letters to the lead agency and to the CEQ, the letters will be hand-carried to the addressees.   The appropriate FAL will then ensure follow-up distribution of the CEQ referral package as follows and/or in accordance with the communications strategy:

Addressee	Number of Copies
Lead agency	3 copies
CEQ	4 copies
EPA Administrator	2 copies
Assistant Administrator, OEA	2 copies
Headquarters Office of Public Affairs	2 copies
Appropriate regional office	3 copies
Appropriate regional Office of Public Affairs	2 copies
Director, OFA	1 copy
Management Information Unit, OFA	1 copy
EPA offices which served as associate reviewers	1 copy
Appropriate elected officials	Determined by the Office of Congressional Liaison

7.   REPORTING AND CONTROL.

The referral package, all related correspondence, and documentation of time extensions will be retained in the official project file.   Time extensions will be entered into the MIU data management system.

Guidance for the Administrative Aspects of the Environmental Impact Statement Filing Process

(Environmental Protection Agency) 54 Fed. Reg. 9592 (Mar. 7, 1989)

Preamble

In 1978, the Council of Environmental Quality (CEQ) and the Environmental Protection Agency (EPA) entered into a Memorandum of Agreement on the allocation of responsibilities of the two agencies for assuring the government-wide implementation of the National Environmental Policy Act of 1969 (NEPA). These responsibilities are consistent with the 1978 CEQ NEPA-Implementing Regulations (40 CFR Parts 1500-1508).

The Memorandum of Agreement transferred to EPA operational duties associated with the administrative aspects of the environmental impact statement (EIS) filing process. The Office of Federal Activities has been designated the official recipient in EPA of all EISs. It should be noted that the operational duties associated with the administrative aspects of the EIS process are totally separate from the substantive EPA reviews performed pursuant to both NEPA and section 309 of the Clean Air Act.

The purposes of the EPA Filing System paper is to provide guidance to federal agencies on filing EISs, including draft, final, and supplemental EISs. Information is provided on (1) Where to file; (2) number of copies required; (3) information required in the transmittal letter; (4) steps to follow when a federal agency is adopting an EIS or when an EIS is being withdrawn, delayed or reopened; (5) review periods; (6) notice of availability in the *Federal Register*; and, (7) retention of filed EIS.

On August 10, 1988, following consultation with CEQ, EPA sent the draft paper to 26 federal agencies for comment prior to its submission to the *Federal Register* for formal publication and implementation. EPA received comment letters from 16 agencies. Although this preamble does not respond to each comment individually all were carefully considered. A synopsis of the comments, other than editorial, and EPA's response follow:

Section 3—Filing an EIS-Draft, Final and Supplemental

As requested, clarification has been made that completion of the transmittal of an EIS is accomplished simultaneously with the filing with EPA.

It was recommended that the cover letter include the official issuing agency number for the EIS being filed. EPA does not use an agency's number for the EIS being filed; therefore, it is not needed in the cover letter. An agency may, if it wishes, include the number because of internal requirements.

Information has been added to clarify that, in the case of filing an EIS that is not hand carried, the cover letter should state that transmittal has been completed. In addition, EPA will telephone the filing agency to verify that EPA has received the EIS.

At the recommendation of a commenter, EPA will now include a reference in the Notice of Availability when an agency adopts an EIS that does not require recirculation. This will not reopen the public comment period, but will complete the public record.

Several agencies commented on EPA's role in checking an EIS for "completeness and compliance." In response the specific subsection of the CEQ Regulations that recommends the standard format that an agency should follow unless the agency determines that there is a compelling reason to do otherwise has been identified—§1502.*10* of the CEQ Regulations—for clarification. EPA's review is to assure that the document meets certain minimum administrative requirements, i.e., there is a cover sheet, a summary of the statement, a table of contents, the name, address and telephone number of the agency is included, cooperating agencies are listed, etc. The format and explanation of each is found in §1502.10 of the CEQ regulations. The review does *not* address the quality of the document's substance. Further, it is totally independent of EPA's review on environmental impacts under Section 309 of the Clean Air Act.

One commenting agency suggested deleting the sentence concerning reopening an EIS review period after a substantial amount of time has passed since the original review period closed. The commenting agency objected to the use of the word "substantial" without defining the term. EPA believes that the word substantial stands on its own merits and suggests that agencies use their best judgment in deciding what is reasonable. The intent is to keep the public

informed. EISs reopened for review will be published in the Notice of Availability to inform all interested parties and to keep the public record current.

Section 4—Notice in the Federal Register

Language has been added to clarify that the Notice of Availability is published each Friday in the *Federal Register* for those EISs filed during the preceding week—e.g., the notice is published on January 13th for EISs filed between January 2nd and January 6th.

The last paragraph of this section has been deleted at the request of CEQ. CEQ will remain solely responsible for notification to the public of referral actions due to the process timeframes called for in the current CEQ Regulations.

Section 5—Time Periods

The section heading and opening paragraph have been edited to address many comments requesting clarification of time periods for draft and final EISs. The time period for review and comment on draft EISs shall not be less than 45 "calendar" days. CEQ Regulations do not address a review period for a final EIS. It is a 30 "calendar" day wait period during which no decision may be made to proceed with the proposed action.

Additional information has been added to address the question concerning calculated time periods ending on non-work days. When a calculated time period ends on a non-working day, the assigned time period will be the next working day.

Section 1506.10(b) of the CEQ Regulations allows for an exception to the rules of timing. Language has been included on exceptions relating to cases of an agency decision which is subject to a formal internal appeal. When exceptions are made by an agency, it is important to inform EPA so that it is accurately reflected in the Notice of Availability.

It was requested that the paper cite examples where both extensions and reductions of time periods have been granted by EPA and where CEQ has approved special cases. EPA appreciates the point but has declined to present examples since these are done on a case-by-case basis and each case is considered on its individual merits.

One commenting agency was concerned with having to request reductions and extensions of time periods in writing to EPA. The agency felt this put too much stress on a formal, and possibly time-consuming, process. Language has been added indicating EPA will accept these requests by telephone, but agencies should follow up in writing to ensure that EPA can maintain a complete record of the decision-making process.

One commenting agency requested that guidance be provided for filing of non-federal EISs, i.e, those prepared by state and local governments where federal statutes specifically identify these governments as the "federal official for the purposes of NEPA compliance." EPA's position is that EISs prepared by state and local governments for these federal programs are considered "federal" EISs by virtue of the fact that they are prepared in response to a federal statute—NEPA. Therefore, the same filing procedures apply to the filing of these "non-federal EISs" as those that apply to filing of federal EISs.

General Comments

EPA appreciates the comment concerning the length of the guidance and that it "burdens rather than provides useful guidance." However, EPA believes that the narrative format is easier to follow and more useful as a reference than a step by step outline or flow diagram of the process.

As indicated by one commenter, it should be noted that this guidance is intended only to improve the internal management of the Executive branch and is not intended to create any right or benefit, substantive or procedural, enforceable at law by a party against the United States, its agencies, its officials, or any person.

Dated February 28, 1989.

Richard E. Sanderson,
Director, Office of Federal Activities.

EPA Filing System Guidance

1. Purpose

These guidelines provide information on filing environmental impact statements (EISs) required by the National Environmental Policy Act (NEPA) and the Council on Environmental Quality (CEQ) regulations (40 CFR Parts 1500-1508) for implementing the procedural provisions of NEPA. Sections 1506.9 and 1506.10 of the CEQ regulations set forward EPA's basic responsibilities for the filing process and authorize the Agency to issue guidelines to implement its responsibilities under these sections. The process of filing includes the following: (a) Reviewing and recording of the EISs so that information on them can be incorporated into EPA's computerized data base; (b) establishing the beginning and ending dates when draft and final EISs are officially available to the public; (c) publishing these dates in a "Notice of Availability" in the *Federal Register*; (d) retaining the EISs in a central repository; and (e) determining whether time periods can be lengthened or shortened for "compelling reasons of national policy."

EPA duties do not include responsibility for the distribution of EISs or for providing additional copies of already distributed EISs. These are the obligation of the lead agency preparing an EIS and are not addressed in this guidance. Nevertheless, EPA will assist the public and other federal agencies by providing agency contacts on, and information about, EISs.

2. Background

The official EIS filing system was transferred from the Council on Environmental Quality (CEQ) to the Environmental Protection Agency (EPA) effective December 5, 1977, as part of the reorganization of the Executive Office of the President. The functions of the filing system were further delineated by a Memorandum of Understanding between CEQ and EPA, dated March 29, 1978. CEQ promulgated its regulations for implementing the National Environmental Policy Act (NEPA) on November 29, 1978 (see 43 FR 55978).

The EPA filing system was created to provide an official log and public announcement of EISs received by EPA and to guarantee that the requirements of NEPA and the CEQ regulations are satisfied. It is a complete and separate filing system from the Environmental Review Process System which fulfills separate requirements under section 309 of the Clear Air Act for EPA to review an comment on EISs (and other actions) of federal agencies.

3. Filing an EIS—draft, final and supplemental

Federal agencies are required to prepare EISs in accordance with section 1502 of the Regulations and to file the EISs with EPA as specified in §1506.9. The EISs must be filed no earlier than they are transmitted to commenting agencies and made available to the public. If an EIS is hand carried to EPA, the person delivering the document must complete a form stating that transmittal to all agencies is being made simultaneously with the filing with EPA. This will assure that the EIS is received by all interested parties by the time the EPA Notice of Availability appears in the *Federal Register*, and therefore allows for the full minimum review periods prescribed in §1506.10. EPA will acknowledge by a phone call to the sender that it has received an EIS forwarded by means other than hand carried.

If EPA receives a request to file an EIS and transmittal of that EIS is not complete, the EIS will not be filed until assurances have been given that the transmittal process is complete. Similarly, if EPA discovers that a filed EIS has not been transmitted, EPA will retract the EIS from filing and not re-file the EIS until the transmittal process is completed. Once the agency has fulfilled the requirements of §1506.9 and has completed the transmittal process, EPA will reestablish the filing date and the minimum time period, and will publish this information in the next Notice of Availability. Requirements for circulation of EISs appear in §1502.19 of the regulations.

Federal agencies file an EIS by providing EPA with five (5) copies, including appendices. Material which is incorporated into the EIS by reference is not required to be filed with EPA. The agency filing the EIS (usually the lead agency if more than one is involved) should prepare a letter of transmittal to accompany the five copies of the EIS. The letter should identify the name and telephone number of the official responsible for both the distribution and con-

tents of the EIS; should state that the transmittal has been completed; and should be addressed to:

U.S. Environmental Protection Agency,
　Attention, Office of Federal Activities,
　EIS Filing Section (Mail Code A-104),
　Room 2119 Waterside Mall, 401 M Street SW,
　Washington, DC 20460.

Telephone inquiries can be made to (202) 382-5076 or FTS 382-5076.

EPA should be notified in writing of all situations where a federal agency is adopting an EIS, whether the document is recirculated and filed or adopted under the provision of §1506.3(c) of the regulations. If a federal agency chooses to adopt an EIS written by another agency and it was not a cooperating agency in the preparation of the original EIS, then the EIS must be re-transmitted and filed with EPA according to the requirements set forth in §1506.3 of the CEQ regulations. In those cases where an agency can adopt an EIS without recirculating it, there is no necessity to file the EIS again with EPA. EPA should be notified, however, in order to ensure that the official log is accurate, and to include this information as a separate section within the Notice of Availability. This will not establish a comment period, but will complete the public record.

EPA also should be notified of all situations where an agency has decided to withdraw, delay or reopen a review period on an EIS. All such notices to EPA will be published in the *Federal Register*. In the case of reopening EIS review periods, the lead agency should notify EPA as to what measures will be taken to ensure that the EIS is available to all interested parties. This is especially important for EIS reviews that are being reopened after a substantial amount of time has passed since the original review period closed.

Once received by EPA, each EIS is stamped with an official filing date and checked for completeness and compliance with §1502.10 of the CEQ regulations. If the EIS is not "complete" (i.e., if the documents do not contain those elements outlined in §1502.10 of the regulations), EPA will contact the lead agency to obtain the omitted information or to resolve any problems prior to publication of the Notice of Availability in the *Federal Register*.

Agencies often publish (either in their EISs or individual notices to the public) a date by which all comments on an EIS are to be received. Agencies should ensure that the date they use is based on the date of publication of the Notice of Availability in the *Federal Register*. If the published date gives reviewers less than the minimum review time computed by EPA, then EPA will send the agency contact a letter explaining how the review period is calculated and the correct date by which comments are due back to the lead agency. This letter also encourages agencies to notify all reviewers and interested parties of the corrected review periods.

4. Notice in the Federal Register

EPA will prepare a weekly report of all EISs filed during the preceding week for publication each Friday under a Notice of Availability in the *Federal Register*. At the time EPA sends its weekly report for publication in the *Federal Register*, the report will also be sent to the CEQ. Information included in the report for each EIS is the same as the data entered in EPA's computerized data file. This includes an EIS Accession number (created by EPA), EIS status (draft, final, supplemental), date filed with EPA, the agency or bureau that filed the EIS, the state and county of the action that prompted the EIS, the title of the EIS, the date comments are due and the agency contact. Amended notices may be added to the Notice of Availability to include corrections, changes in time periods of previously filed EISs, withdrawals of EISs by lead agencies, and recision of EISs by EPA. A recision including nullifying the date the EIS was filed can occur, as explained earlier, if, after a filed EIS is published in the *Federal Register*, EPA is subsequently informed that the EIS has not been made available to commenting agencies and the public by the lead agency.

5. Time Periods

The minimum time periods set forth in §1506.10(b), (c), and (d) are calculated from the date EPA publishes the Notice of Availability in the *Federal Register*. Review periods for draft EISs, draft supplements, and revised draft EISs shall extend 45 calendar days unless the lead agency extends the prescribed period or a reduction of the period has been granted. The wait periods for final EISs and final supplements shall extend for 30 calendar days unless the lead agency extends the period or a reduction or extension in the period has been granted. If a calculated time period would end on a non-working day, the assigned time period will be the next working day (i.e., time periods will not end on weekends or federal holidays).

It should be noted that §1506.10(b) allows for an exception to the rules of timing. An exception may be made in the case of an agency decision which is subject to a formal internal appeal. Agencies should assure that EPA is informed so that the situation is accurately reflected in the Notice of Availability.

Under §1506.10(d) EPA has the authority to both extend and reduce the time periods on draft and final EISs based on a demonstration of "compelling reasons of national policy." A lead agency request to EPA to reduce time periods or another federal agency request to formally extend a time period normally takes the form of a letter to the Director, Office of Federal Activities (OFA), EPA, outlining the reasons for the request. EPA will accept telephone requests; however, agencies should follow up such requests in writing so that the documentation supporting the decision is complete. A meeting to discuss the consequences for the project and any decision to change time periods may be necessary. For this reason EPA asks that it be made aware of any intent to submit requests of this type as early as possible in the NEPA process. This is to prevent the possibility of the time frame for the decision on the time period modification from interfering with the lead agency's schedule for the EIS. EPA will notify CEQ of any reduction or extension granted.

CEQ has the authority under section 1502.9(c)(4) to approve alternative procedures for preparing, circulating and filing supplemental draft and final EISs. The council will notify EPA of any such alternative procedures that are granted.

6. Retention

Filed EISs are retained in the EPA/OFA office for a period of two years and are made available for reviewing only. After two years the EISs are sent to the National Records Center. However, the EPA Library, Room 2904 Waterside Mall, 401 M Street, SW., Washington, DC 20460, houses a microfiche collection of final EISs issued from 1970 through 1977 and all draft, final and supplemental EISs filed from 1978 to the present time. Facilities for limtied reproduction of the EISs are available.

A comprehensive collection of EISs is available for viewing and individual EISs are available on a loan basis at:

Northwestern University, Transportation Library—NEPA, 1935 North Sheridan Road, Evanston, Illinois 60201, Telephone: (312) 492-2913.

Final EISs prepared from 1970 through 1977, and any draft, final or supplemental EIS prepared from 1978 to the present time may be purchased in either microfiche or hardback copy from:

Information Resources Press, Herner and Company, 1700 North Moore Street, Arlington, Virginia 22209, Telephone: (703) 558-8275.

Agency NEPA Contacts
Courtesy of the Council on Environmental Quality (June 1989)

Mr. Charles Terrell, Asst. Secretary   202-447-4925
National Environmental Coordinator
Soil Conservation Service
Department of Agriculture
Ecological Science Division
P.O. Box 2890
Washington, D.C.   20013

Dr. William Tallent   202-447-3973
Assistant Administrator for
  Cooperative Interactions
Room 358A
Department of Agriculture
Agriculture Administration Building
14th and Independence Avenue
Washington, D.C.   20250

D. Rex. Wright, Chief   202-447-3264
Planning & Eval Branch
Agriculture Stabilization
  & Conservation Service
Department of Agriculture
Rm 4714, P.O. Box 2415
14th & Independence Ave., SW
Washington, D.C.   20013

Terry Medley, Attorney   301-436-7602
Animal & Plant Health
  Inspection Service
Department of Agriculture
Rm 600, Federal Building
6505 Belcrest Road
Hyattsville, MD   20782

Dr. John A. Miranowski, Dir.   202-786-1455
Resources & Technology Division
Economic Research Service
Department of Agriculture
Room 524 NYA
1301 New York Avenue, N.W.
Washington, D.C.   20005

John A. Vance   202-447-7947
Natural Resources & Rural
  Development Extention Service
Department of Agriculture
Room 3909 South Agriculture Building
14th & Independence Ave., SW
Washington, D.C.   20250-0900

John Hansel   202-382-9619
Environmental Protection Specialist
Program Support Staff
Farmers Home Administration
Department of Agriculture
Rm 6309 South Agriculture Building
14th & Independence Ave., SW
Washington, D.C.   20250

Ralph Stafko, Director   202-447-6735
Policy Office
Food Safety & Inspection Service
Department of Agriculture
Rm 2940-S Agriculture Bldg
12th & Independence Ave., SW
Washington, D.C.   20250

David Ketcham, Director   202-447-4708
Env. Coordination Staff
U.S. Forest Service
Department of Agriculture
Rm 4204 S. Agriculture Bldg
14th & Independence Ave., SW
Washington, D.C.   20013

Kenneth Kumor   202-382-0097
Environmental Policy Specialist
Engineering Standards Division
Rural Electrification Administration
Department of Agriculture
Rm 1257-S Agriculture Building
14th and Independence Avenue, SW
Washington, D.C.   20250

Peter Smith   202-447-2587
Ecological Sciences Division
Soil Conservation Service
Department of Agriculture
Rm 6155-S Agriculture Bldg
14th & Independence Ave, SW
P.O. Box 2890
Washington, D.C.   20013

David Cottingham, Chief   202-377-5181
Ecology & Conservation Division
Office of Policy & Planning
National Oceanic & Atmospheric Administration
Department of Commerce
Rm HCHB 6222
14th & Constitution Ave, NW
Washington, D.C.   20230

David S. Maney   202-377-5181
Associate Director for Environment
Economic Development Administration
Department of Commerce
Rm 7319 Herbert Hoover Bldg
14th & Constitution Ave, NW
Washington, D.C.   20230

David Cottingham, Chief   202-377-5181
Ecology & Conservation Division
Office of Policy & Planning
National Oceanic & Atmospheric Administration
Department of Commerce
Rm HCHB 6222
14th & Constitution Ave., NW
Washington, D.C.   20230

Christina Ramsey   202-325-2215
NEPA & Natural Resources
Department of Defense
Room 3D833
The Pentagon
Washington, D.C.   20301

Chris F. Potomas   202-274-6124
Staff Director
Installation Services
& Environmental Protection
Cameron Station Room 4D446
Defense Logistics Agency
Department of Defense
Alexandria, Virginia   22304

Gary D. Vest, Deputy   202-697-9297
Environment & Safety
Office of the Deputy Assistant
Secretary for Installations
Department of Defense
Room 4C916
The Pentagon
Washington, D.C.   20330

Ray Clark   202-695-7824
Assistant for
 Environmental Projects
Department of the Army
Room 2E577 Attn: OASA (I & L)
The Pentagon
Washington, D.C.   20310

Dick Makinen   202-272-0166
Environmental Policy Analyst
Office of Environmental Policy
Corps of Engineers
Room 7119C Pulaski Building
20 Massachusetts Avenue, NW
Washington, D.C.   20314

Tom Peeling   703-325-7350
Naval Facilities   703-325-7353
 Engineering Command
Code 20Y, Rm 10567 Hoffman #2
200 Stovall Street
Department of the Navy
Alexandria, Virginia   22332

Col. Neil J. Bross, Head   202-697-1890
Land Use & Military
 Construction Branch
Marine Corps Headquarters
Commonwealth Bldg, Code LFL
Rm 628, 1300 Wilson Blvd
Rosslyn, Virginia   22209

Carole Borgstrom   202-586-4600
Acting Director
Office of NEPA Project
 Assistance
Department of Energy
Rm 3E-080
1000 Independence Ave, SW
Washington, D.C.   20585

Paul S. Cromwell, Environmental Officer   202-245-6162
Office of Assistant Secretary for
 Manangement Analysis & Systems
Department of Health and Human Services
542 E, Hubert H. Humphrey Bldg
200 Independence Avenue, SW
Washington, D.C.   20201

Dr. David E. Clapp, Chief   404-452-4257 or
Environmental Affairs Group   FTS-236-4257
Center for Environmental Health
Center for Disease Control
Department of Health and Human Services
Room 1015 Bldg: Chamblee-9
1600 Clifton Road
Atlanta, Georgia   30333

John C. Matheson, III   301-443-1880
Chief Environmental Impact
 Staff (HFV-152)
Food and Drug Administration
Department of Health and Human Services
Parklawn Bldg, Room 8-70
5600 Fishers Lane
Rockville, Maryland 20857

Gary J. Hartz, Director   301-443-1043
Environmental Health Branch
Indian Health Service
Health Resources & Services Administration
Department of Health and Human Services
Parklawn Bldg Room 6A-54
5600 Fishers Lane
Rockville, MD 20857

Harvey Rogers   301-496-3537
Chief
Environmental Protection Branch
National Institutes of Health
Department of Health and Human Services
Building 13, Room 2E63
9000 Rockville Pike
Bethesda, Maryland 20892

Spencer Lott, Director   202-475-0418
State Project Assistance
Office of Community Services
Department of Health & Human Services
330 C Street SW
Room 2038 MES
Washington, D.C. 20201

Richard H. Broun, Director   202-755-7894
Office of Environment & Energy
Department of Housing &
 Urban Development
Room 7154 HUD Bldg
451 Seventh Street, SW
Washington, D.C. 20410

Bruce Blanchard, Director   202-343-3891
Office of Environmental
 Project Review
Department of the Interior
Room 4260 Interior Bldg
18th and C Streets, NW
Washington, D.C. 20240

Don Peterson   703-235-2418
Environmental Coordinator
Branch of Federal Activities
US Fish & Wildlife Service
Department of the Interior
Room 621
18th & C Streets, NW
Washington, D.C.   20240

Cliford Houpt   703-648-6826
Chief
Environmental Affairs Program
US Geological Survey
Department of Interior
Mail Stop 423 National Center
Reston Virginia   22092

George R. Farris, Chief   202-343-6574
Environmental Services Staff
Office of Trust & Economic Development
Bureau of Indian Affairs
Department of Interior
Room 343 Interior South
1951 Constitution Avenue, N.W.
Washington, D.C.   20240

David Williams, Chief   202-653-8830
Office of Planning and
 Environmental Coordination
Bureau of Land Management
Department of Interior
Room 906 Premier Bldg
1725 I Street, N.W.
Washington, D.C.   20240

John T. Goll, Chief   703-648-7739
Offshore Environmental Assessment Division
Minerals Management Service
Department of the Interior
6A316 USGS Bldg, Mail Stop 644
12203 Sunrise Valley Drive
Reston, Virginia   22091

John Stone   202-634-1117
Physical Scientist
Regulatory Projects Coordination
Bureau of Mines
Department of the Interior
2401 E Street, NW
Mail Stop 1050, Rm 1027
Washington, D.C.   20241

Jacob Hoogland, Chief   202-343-2163
Environmental Compliance Division
National Park Service
Department of the Interior
Room 1210 Interior Building
18th and C Streets, NW
Washington, D.C.   20240

Dick Porter, Chief   202-343-5104
Environment and Planning
Bureau of Reclamation
Department of the Interior
Room 7455 Interior Bldg
18th and C Streets, NW
Washington, D.C.   20240

Len Richeson, Chief   202-343-5150
Branch of Economic &
 Environmental Analysis
Office of Surface Mining
 Reclamation and Enforcement
Department of the Interior
Rm 5121, 1100 L Street, NW
Washington, D.C.   20240

William M. Cohen, Chief   202-272-6851
General Litigation Section
Land & Natural Resources Div
Department of Justice
601 Pennsylvania Avenue
8th Floor, Room 870
Washington, D.C.   20530

William J. Patrick, Chief   202-724-6535
Office of Facilities
 Development & Operations
Bureau of Prisons
Department of Justice
320 First Street, NW
Washington, D.C.   20534

John W. Gunn, Jr.   202-633-1211
Deputy Assistant Administrator
Office of Science & Technology
Drug Enforcement Administration
Department of Justice
1405 Eye Street NW
Washington, D.C.   20537

Victoria Kingslien   202-633-4448
Director
Facilities & Engineering
Immigration & Natural Service
Department of Justice
425 Eye Street, NW
Washington, D.C.   20536

Charles P. Smith, Director   202-724-5933
Bureau of Justice Assistance
Room 1042
Department of Justice
633 Indiana Avenue, NW
Washington, D.C.   20531

Steven R. Schlesinger   202-724-7765
Director
Bureau of Justice Statistics
Room 1142
Department of Justice
633 Indiana Avenue, NW
Washington, D.C.   20531

Charles J. Cooper   202-633-2041
Assistant Attorney General
Office of Legal Counsel
Department of Justice
Rm 5214 Justice Building
10th & Constitution Ave, NW
Washington, D.C.   20530

Robert E. Copeland, Director   202-523-6197
Office of Regulatory Economics
Assistant Secretary for Policy
Department of Labor
S-2312 Frances Perkins Building
200 Constitution Ave, NW
Washington, D.C.   20210

Jeffrey B. Doranz   703-235-1910
Acting Director
Office of Standards
Mine Safety & Health Administration
Department of Labor
Rm 627 Ballston Tower #3
4015 Wilson Blvd
Arlington, Virginia   22203

Dr. Hugh Conway, Director   202-523-9690
Office of Regulatory Analysis
Occupational Safety & Health Administration
Department of Labor
N-3627 Frances Perkins Building
200 Constitution Ave., NW
Washington, D.C.   20210

Andrew Sens   202-632-9266
Director
Office of Environment & Health
Department of State
Rm 4325 State Department Building
21st and C Streets, NW
Washington, D.C.   20520

Joseph F. Canny, Director   202-366-4220
Office of Transportation
 Regulatory Affairs
Department of Transportation
Rm 9222 Nassif Building
400 Seventh St, SW
Washington, D.C.   20590

James E. Densmore, Director   202-267-3576
Office of Environment
 and Energy (AEE-1)
Federal Aviation Administration
Department of Transportation
Room 432C
800 Independence Ave., SW
Washington, D.C.   20591

Ali F. Sevin, Director   202-366-2045
Office of Environmental
 Policy (HEV-1)
Federal Highway Administration
Department of Transportation
Rm 3222 Nassif Building
400 Seventh Street, SW
Washington, D.C.   20590

Director   202-426-7391
Attn: Marilyn Klein
Office of Economic Analysis
Federal Railroad Administration
Department of Transportation
Rm 8300 Nassif Building
400 Seventh Street, SW
Washington, D.C.   20590

Daniel W. Leubecker   202-366-5470
Office of Port & Intermodal Development
Maritime Administration
Department of Transportation
Rm 7201 Code 830
Department of Transportation
400 Seventh St, SW
Washington, D.C.   20590

Kathleen C. DeMeter   202-426-1834
Assistant Chief Counsel/General Law
National Highway Traffic
 Safety Administration (NOA-33)
Department of Transportation
Rm 5219 Nassif Bldg
400 Seventh Street, SW
Washington, D.C.   20590

Alfred E. Barrington, Chief   617-494-2018,
Environmental Technology Division   FTS-837-2018
Research/Special Programs Administration
Department of Transportation
Transportation Systems Center
Room 355 Kendall Square
Cambridge, MA   02142

John B. Adams, Executive Assistant   315-764-3233,
St. Lawrence Seaway   315-953-0233
 Development Corporation
Seaway Administration Building
Department of Transportation
180 Andrews Street
Box 520
Massena, New York   13662

T.J. Granito, Chief   202-267-1120
Environment Section (G-ECV-2B)
Office of Engineering & Devlopment
Civil Engineering Division
U.S. Coast Guard
Department of Transportation
2100 2nd Street, SW Rm 6503
Washington, D.C.   20593

Samuel L. Zimmerman   202-366-2360
Deputy Director
Office of Planning Assistance (UGM-20)
Urban Mass Transportation Administration
Department of Transportation
Room 9311 Nassif Building
400 Seventh Street, SW
Washington, D.C.   20590

Anthony V. DiSilvestre   202-634-2438
Environmental Protection
 Specialist
Department of Treasury
1730 K Street, Room 420
Washington, D.C.   20220

Willard Hoing, Assistant Director   202-634-9212
Planning, Budget
 & Management Division
Action
Room P401
806 Connecticut Avenue, NW
Washington, D.C.   20525

Thomas F. King, Director   202-786-0505
Cultural Resource Preservation
Advisory Council on
 Historic Preservation
Old Post Office Building, #803
1100 Pennsylvania Ave, NW
Washington, D.C.   20004

Geraldine Storm-Gevanthor   202-673-7845
Director
Division of Housing &
 Community Development
Appalachian Regional Commission
1666 Connecticut Ave, NW
Washington, D.C.   20235

Thomas Graham, Jr.   202-632-3582
General Counsel
Arms Control and
 Disarmament Agency
Room 5534
320 21st Street, NW
Washington, D.C.   20451

Stephen Lemberg
Assistant General Counsel
Office of the General Counsel
Consumer Product Safety Commission
Washington, D.C.   20207

301-492-6550

Gerald M. Hansler
Executive Director
Delaware River Basin Commission
25 State Police Drive
P.O. Box 7360
W Trenton, New Jersey 08628

609-883-9500,
FTS-483-2077

Dick Sanderson, Director
Office of Federal
 Activities (A-104)
Environmental Protection Agency
Room 2119-I
401 M Street, SW
Washington, D.C.   20460

202-382-5053

Hart Fessenden
General Counsel
Export-Import Bank
 of the United States
Room 947 Lafayette Building
811 Vermont Avenue, NW
Washington, D.C.   20571

202-566-8334

David Baer
Director
Office of Examination
Farm Credit Administration
1501 Farm Credit Drive
McLean, Virginia   22102

703-883-4160

Holly Berland, Staff Attorney
Legal Counsel Division
Office of General Counsel
Federal Communications Commission
Room 616
1919 Street NW
Washington, D.C.   20554

202-632-6990

Stanley J. Poling, Director   202-898-6944
Division of Accounting
 & Corporate Services
Federal Deposit Insurance Corporation
Room 6124
550 Seventeenth Street, NW
Washington, D.C.   20429

Susan K. Bank   202-646-3973
Associate General Counsel
**Federal Emergency
 Management Agency**
Room 840
500 C Street, SW
Washington, D.C.   20472

Michael Schopf   202-357-8002
Enforcement, General Law
 and Rulemaking
**Federal Energy and
 Regulatory Commission**
825 No. Capitol Street, NE
Washington, D.C.   20426

Richard R. Hoffman, Chief   202-357-8098
Environmental Evaluation
Pipeline & Producer Regulation
Federal Energy Regulatory Commission
Room 7102A
825 North Capitol Street, NE
Washington, D.C.   20426

Dean L. Shumway, Director   202-376-1768
Division of Environmental Analysis
Office of Hydropower Licensing
Federal Energy Regulatory Commission
308 Railway Labor Building
400 First Street, NW
Washington, D.C.   20426

V. Gerard Comizio, Director   202-377-6411
Corporate & Securities Division
Office of General Counsel
Federal Home Loan Bank Board
East Wing
1700 G Street, NW
Washington, D.C.   20552

Edward R. Meyer   202-523-5835
Office of Special Studies
Federal Maritime Commission
Suite 11305
1100 L Street, NW
Washington, D.C.   20573

Mrs. Kay Bondehagan   202-452-2067
Senior Attorney
Legal Division
Federal Reserve Board
Room B-1016
20th & Constitution Ave., NW
Washington, D.C.   20551

Jerold D. Cummins   202-326-2471
Deputy Assistant General Counsel
Federal Trade Commission
Room 582
6th St & Pennsylvania Ave., NW
Washington, D.C.   20580

Bob Tuch, Director   202-523-1594
Environmental Protection Specialist
Office of Facility Planning
Policy & Analysis Division
General Services Administration
Mail Stop PLP, Room 6323
18th and F Streets, NW
Washington, D.C.   20405

George R. Baumli   915-534-6703,
Principal Engineer   FTS-570-6703
Planning and Hydrographic
International Boundary & Water Commission
United States Section
4171 North Mesa, Suite C316
El Paso, Texas   79902

Carl P. Bausch, Chief   202-275-0800
Section of Energy & Environment
Office of Transportation Analysis
Interstate Commerce Commission
Room 4143
12th & Constitution Ave, NW
Washington, D.C.   20423

Michael L. Gosliner   202-653-6237
General Counsel
Marine Mammal Commission
Room 307
1625 Eye Street, NW
Washington, D.C. 20006

Dr. James Reisa   202-334-3060
Acting Director
Board of Environmental Studies & Technology
National Academy of Sciences
Mail Code MH354
2101 Constitution Ave., NW
Washington, D.C. 20418

Lewis E. Andrews   202-453-1958
Environmental Compliance Office
Facilities Engineer Division (NXG)
Nat'l Aeronautics & Space Administration
Room 5031
400 Maryland Avenue, SW
Washington, D.C. 20546

Environmental/Energy Officer   202-724-0179
Division of Planning Services
National Capital Planning
 Commission
Room 1024
1325 G Street, NW
Washington, D.C. 20576

Robert M. Fenner   202-357-1030
General Counsel
Department of Legal Services
National Credit Union Administration
Room 6261
1776 G Street, NW
Washington, D.C. 20456

Adair F. Montgomery   202-357-9889
Earth and Ocean Sciences
Chairman & Staff Associate
Committee on Environmental Matters
National Science Foundation
Room 644, 1800 G Street, NW
Washington, D.C. 20550

Thomas Murley   301-492-1270
Director
Office of Nuclear Reactor
 Regulation
Nuclear Regulatory Commission
12D1
Washington, D.C.   20555

Richard E. Cunningham   301-492-3426
Director
Division of Industrial &
 Medical Nuclear Safety
Nuclear Regulatory Commission
Mail Stop 6H3
Washington, D.C.   20555

James Rich   202-724-9068
Director of Development
Pennsylvania Avenue
 Development Corporation
Room 1220N
1331 Pennsylvania Ave., NW
Washington, D.C.   20004

Sidney L. Cimmit   202-272-7340
Senior Special Counsel
Public Utility Regulation
Securities & Exchange Commission
Room 7002
450 Fifth Street, NW
Washington, D.C.   20549

Everett Shell   202-653-6470
Director
Office of Business Loans
Small Business Administration
Room 804-C
1441 L Street, NW
Washington, D.C.   20416

Robert J. Bielo   717-238-0422
Executive Director
Susquehanna River Basin
 Commission
1721 North Front Street
Harrisburg, PA   17102

M. Paul Schmierbach   615-632-6578,
Manager   FTS-856-6578
Environmental Quality Staff
Tennessee Valley Authority
201 Summer Place Building
309 Walnut Street
Knoxville, TN 37902

R. Wallace Stewart   202-485-7979
Assistant General Counsel
United States Information Agency
Room 700
301 Fourth Street, Sw
Washington, D.C. 20547

Norman Cohen   202-647-9620
AID, Environmental Coordinator
US Agency for International Development
5883 New State Building C/AID
Department of State
320 Twenty-First Street, NW
Washington, D.C. 20523

Harvey A. Himberg   202-457-7139
Director for Development Policy
 & Environmental Affairs
Office of Development
Overseas Private Investment Corporation
US Agency for International Development
1615 M Street, NW
Washington, D.C. 20527

Rainer J. Hengst, Director   202-268-3124
Facilities Planning & Management
Real Estate & Buildings Department
US Postal Service
Room 4126
475 L'Enfant Plaza West, SW
Washington, D.C. 20260

Susan Livingston   202-233-2192
Director
Environmental Affairs
Veterans Administration
Code 005, 810 Vermont Ave., NW
Washington, D.C. 20420

Abstracts of Supreme Court Litigation Under NEPA

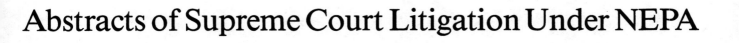

Supreme Court Cases Under the National Environmental Policy Act

Robertson v. Methow Valley Citizens Council, No. 87-1703, 19 ELR 20743 (U.S. May 1, 1989) (EIS need not include final detailed mitigation plan or worst case analysis)

Marsh v. Oregon Natural Resources Council, No. 87-1704, 19 ELR 20749 (U.S. May 1, 1989) (agency decision on preparing supplemental EIS is reviewable under arbitrary and capricious standard)

Baltimore Gas & Electric Co. v. Natural Resources Defense Council, Inc., 462 U.S. 87, 13 ELR 20544 (1983) (NRC complied with NEPA in adopting generic rules on consideration in nuclear reactor licensing decisions of environmental impacts of nuclear fuel cycle)

Metropolitan Edison Co. v. People Against Nuclear Energy, 460 U.S. 766, 13 ELR 20515 (1983) (NEPA does not require NRC to consider potential psychological harm to local residents before authorizing resumption of power generation at Three Mile Island)

Weinberger v. Catholic Action of Hawaii/Peace Education Project, 454 U.S. 139, 12 ELR 20098 (1981) (Navy not required to prepare EIS for classified nuclear weapons storage project)

Strycker's Bay Neighborhood Council, Inc. v. Karlen, 444 U.S. 223, 10 ELR 20079 (1980) (per curiam)

(HUD complied with NEPA in considering environmental consequences of siting low-income housing project)

Andrus v. Sierra Club, 442 U.S. 347, 9 ELR 20390 (1979) (agencies not required to prepare EISs for appropriations requests)

Vermont Yankee Nuclear Power Corp. v. Natural Resources Defense Council, Inc., 435 U.S. 519, 8 ELR 20288 (1978) (NRC complied with NEPA in licensing two nuclear power plants)

Kleppe v. Sierra Club, 427 U.S. 390, 6 ELR 20532 (1976) (agency not required to prepare EIS for coal leasing when it is not proposing regional coal development)

Flint Ridge Development Co. v. Scenic Rivers Ass'n of Oklahoma, 426 U.S. 776, 6 ELR 20528 (1976) (EIS not required when there is "clear and unavoidable conflict" between requirements of NEPA and another statute)

Aberdeen & Rockfish Railroad Co. v. Students Challenging Regulatory Agency Procedures (SCRAP II), 422 U.S. 289, 5 ELR 20418 (1975) (ICC complied with NEPA in assessing environmental impacts on recycling industry of general railroad freight rate increase)

Robertson v. Methow Valley Citizens Council

No. 87-1703 (U.S. May 1, 1989)

The Court rules that an environmental impact statement (EIS) need not include a final detailed mitigation plan or a worst case analysis. The U.S. Forest Service had issued a development permit based on an EIS that, in discussing mitigation of off-site effects, mostly recommended general steps that state and local agencies might take. The Court first rules that the National Environmental Policy Act (NEPA) and regulations issued by the Council on Environmental Quality (CEQ) establish a procedural requirement that an EIS discuss mitigation in enough detail to ensure that environmental consequences have been fairly evaluated, but not a substantive requirement that it formulate and adopt a complete mitigation plan. Moreover, the off-site effects of this development cannot be mitigated unless state and local agencies act, and the Court holds that the Forest Service need not delay action until those agencies have decided on mitigation measures. The Court rules that NEPA does not require that measures be taken to mitigate the adverse effects of major federal actions, or that every EIS include a detailed explanation of those measures.

The Court next holds that NEPA does not require that an EIS address uncertainty through worst case analysis. A CEQ regulation requiring such analysis has been rescinded, and the Court holds that the regulation is not still applicable as a codification of previous judicial decisions. Those decisions merely required agencies to describe uncertain environmental impacts, not to conduct worst case analyses. Moreover, the regulation replacing the worst case requirement is entitled to substantial deference because there appear to have been good reasons for the change. The prior regulation was much criticized, and the new regulation is designed to focus the EIS process on significant rather than speculative risks.

The Court also holds that failure to develop a complete mitigation plan did not violate Forest Service regulations requiring permits to include mitigation measures. The on-site mitigation recommendations were sufficiently clear, and the Court holds that the regulations do not condition permit issuance on consideration and implementation of off-site mitigation measures. The regulations are based on recreational land use authorities, not environmental quality concerns. The Court holds that the Forest Service could reasonably construe its regulations not to extend to potential off-site state or county actions, and that this interpretation is controlling.

[The lower court opinions are published at 16 ELR 20932 and 18 ELR 20163. A related opinion by the Supreme Court appears at 19 ELR 20749.]

Marsh v. Oregon Natural Resources Council

No. 87-1704 (U.S. May 1, 1989)

The Court rules that an agency's decision on whether to prepare a supplemental environmental impact statement (EIS) should be reviewed under the arbitrary and capricious standard, and upholds the Army Corps of Engineers' decision not to supplement an EIS for a dam in Oregon. The Court first holds that the EIS was not defective for failure to include a complete mitigation plan or a worst-case analysis. The Court then holds that EIS supplementation based on new information is sometimes required by the purposes of the National Environmental Policy Act (NEPA) and by regulations issued by the Council on Environmental Quality and the Corps. Applying a rule of reason, an agency must supplement an EIS when new information shows that future major federal action on the project will significantly affect the quality of the human environment in a manner or to an extent not previously considered. The Court next holds that review of an agency's decision on whether to supplement an EIS is governed by the arbitrary and capricious standard of Administrative Procedure Act §706(2)(A). The dispute over the significance of the new information is factual, not legal, so the Court will review the decision carefully but give deference to the agency's expertise and discretion. The Court notes that the difference between the arbitrary and capricious standard and the reasonableness standard applied by some courts is not of great practical consequence, and that its ruling therefore will not require substantial changes in established NEPA law. The Court then holds that the Corps did not act arbitrarily and capriciously in deciding not to supplement the EIS based on receipt of an internal state agency memorandum arguing that the dam would adversely affect fishing

and a soil survey suggesting that it might increase turbidity. The Corps carefully considered these materials and responded to the claim that they required EIS supplementation. Moreover, there are indications that they did not convey significant new information. No one suggested that the information was highly significant until this lawsuit was filed. The agency whose staff wrote the memorandum did not adopt its position or deem it significant enough to transmit to the Corps, and independent experts found it significantly flawed. Moreover, despite the soil survey, the Corps legitimately concluded that the existing turbidity predictions were accurate. It was not arbitrary and capricious for the Corps to find that the information which was new and accurate was not significant and that the information which was significant was not new or accurate.

[The opinions below are published at 16 ELR 20475 and 20826 and 18 ELR 20321 and 20033. A related opinion by the Supreme Court appears at 19 ELR 20743.]

Baltimore Gas & Electric Co. v. Natural Resources Defense Council, Inc.

Nos. 82-524, -545, -551 (U.S. June 6, 1983)

The Supreme Court, reversing the D.C. Circuit's decision, 12 ELR 20465, rules that the Nuclear Regulatory Commission (NRC) complied with the National Environmental Policy Act (NEPA) and was not arbitrary and capricious in adopting generic rules—the "S-3 Table"—dictating how nuclear reactor licensing decisions take into account the environmental impacts of the nuclear fuel cycle. The D.C. Circuit had ruled that the NRC violated NEPA by determining, in spite of substantial uncertainty, that licensing boards should assume that the long-term storage of nuclear wastes has no significant environmental impact and thus should not be considered in individual licensing decisions. The Court rules that the NRC reasonably evaluated the environmental impacts of the fuel cycle. It is clear from the record that the NRC considered all the data on long-term storage and disclosed the substantial uncertainty concerning its safety. Furthermore, the NRC reasonably chose to prepare a generic rather than a plant-specific EIS of long-term storage, since the environmental impacts of much of the fuel cycle are not plant-specific but are common to all nuclear power plants. The NRC also did not act arbitrarily or capriciously in generically deciding that the uncertainties surrounding fuel storage were insufficient to affect individual licensing decisions. The Court points out that the S-3 Table and the "zero-release assumption" were developed for the limited purpose of considering the risks of the most likely long-term waste disposal method as they affect individual licensing decisions. Furthermore, the uncertainties concerning the zero-release assumption, a single figure in the entire table, are offset by conservative assumptions reflected in other values in the table. Finally, the Court notes that it must generally defer to agency expertise at the frontiers of science. The Court rules that the NRC's zero-release assumption was not arbitrary and capricious under the Administrative Procedure Act. The NRC considered and revealed the uncertainties of long-term storage and even those commissioners dissatisfied with the zero-release assumption were convinced that the environmental impacts should be considered in other proceedings.

In addition, the Court rules that the S-3 Table does not preclude consideration in individual licensing decisions of the human health, socioeconomic, or cumulative impacts of fuel cycle activities. Although ambiguities existed in earlier regulations, the Court finds no basis for the D.C. Circuit's conclusion that the NRC ever precluded a licensing board from considering these effects.

Metropolitan Edison Co. v. People Against Nuclear Energy

No. 81-2399 (U.S. Apr. 19, 1983)

The Supreme Court, reversing the D.C. Circuit, 12 ELR 20546, rules that the National Environmental Policy Act (NEPA) does not require the Nuclear Regulatory Commission to consider the potential psychological harm to local residents before authorizing the resumption of power generation at the sister unit to the damaged Three Mile Island nuclear reactor. The Court finds that NEPA's sweeping goals to enhance human health and welfare are ends that Congress chose to pursue by means of protecting the physical environment. NEPA requires a reasonably close causal relationship between a change in the physical environment and the effect at issue. Although the Court agrees that human health is cognizable under NEPA and that human health includes psychological health, agencies need only consider such effects when caused by federally induced changes in the physical environment. The Court rules that the risk of nuclear accident is not an effect on the physical environment and thus NEPA does not apply to any resulting damage to psychological health. In addition, it is unreasonably difficult for agencies to distinguish between disagreement with governmental policies that cause severe anxiety and stress and "genuine" claims of psychological health damage. The D.C. Circuit erred in concluding that the unusual severity of the psychological impacts of Three Mile Island made a distinction possible, because the key question is whether the impacts are environmental in nature, not how serious they may be. Moreover, NEPA does not address past effects of past federal actions, only future effects of future actions. Finally, the Court rules that since there were no environmental effects requiring NEPA consideration, the agency was not required to consider secondary community effects.

Weinberger v. Catholic Action of Hawaii/Peace Education Project

No. 80-1377 (U.S. Dec. 1, 1981)

Reversing a decision of the Ninth Circuit, 10 ELR 20683, the Supreme Court upholds the Navy's failure to prepare an environmental impact statement (EIS) for a classified nuclear weapons storage project. The Court first holds that the Ninth Circuit incorrectly interpreted §102(2)(C) of the National Environmental Policy Act (NEPA) by requiring preparation of a "hypothetical" EIS. It notes that public disclosure of an EIS is expressly governed by the Freedom of Information Act (FOIA). Exemption 1 of FOIA exempts from disclosure national defense or foreign policy matters that are properly classified pursuant to executive order. Since information on whether nuclear weapons will be stored at the project site is classified, an EIS premised on nuclear weapons storage would be exempt from disclosure. The Court also holds that the Navy is not required to prepare, for internal use only, an EIS premised on nuclear weapons storage at the facility. The obligation to prepare an EIS requires a proposal for action. Because of security regulations, however, the storage of nuclear weapons at the site was not shown to have been formally proposed. Thus, for practical purposes the Navy's compliance with NEPA in this case is beyond judicial scrutiny.

In a concurring opinion, two members of the court emphasize that classified proposals are not exempt from NEPA's EIS requirement. Where feasible, EISs should be organized so that unclassified portions can be made available to the public.

Strycker's Bay Neighborhood Council, Inc. v. Karlen

Nos. 79-168, -181, -184 (U.S. Jan. 7, 1980)

In a per curiam order, the Supreme Court reverses the decision of the Second Circuit Court of Appeals in *Karlen v. Harris*, 9 ELR 20001. At issue was a plan by the Department of Housing and Urban Development (HUD) to redesignate a site in New York City for a proposed low-income housing project. The Court concludes that HUD complied with the National Environmental Policy Act (NEPA) in considering the environmental consequences of its decision. In addition, the Court, relying on its decision two years ago in *Vermont Yankee Nuclear Power Corp. v. NRDC*, 8 ELR 20288, rejects the Second Circuit's conclusion that NEPA required the agency, in selecting a course of action, to elevate environmental concerns over other appropriate considerations.

In dissent, Justice Marshall rejects the notion that a reviewing court's duty under NEPA is limited to ensuring that an agency has followed the requisite procedures in considering environmental consequences, arguing that the questions of whether HUD's decision was arbitrary, capricious, or an abuse of discretion and

whether the agency gave a "hard look" at the environmental consequences are sufficiently difficult and important to merit plenary consideration.

Andrus v. Sierra Club

No. 78-625 (U.S. June 11, 1979)

The Supreme Court rules that the National Environmental Policy Act (NEPA) does not require federal agencies to prepare environmental impact statements (EISs) to accompany appropriations requests. Unanimously reversing a decision of the United States Court of Appeals for the District of Columbia Circuit, 8 ELR 20490, the Court holds that neither "routine" budget requests nor those which result from a "painstaking review of an ongoing program" are to be considered "proposals for legislation" within the meaning of §102(2)(C) of NEPA for which an EIS must be prepared. In reaching this conclusion, the Court relies on the Council on Environmental Quality's new NEPA implementation regulations, which interpret the phrase "proposals for legislation" to exclude appropriations requests, and the traditional congressional distinction between "legislation" and "appropriation." The Court likewise rejects the court of appeals' conclusion that appropriations requests which envision significant revisions in ongoing programs constitute proposals for "major Federal action" under NEPA. Such requests do not themselves propose actions but instead seek funding for actions already proposed. Moreover, a contrary ruling would lead to unnecessary redundancy since an EIS must in any event be prepared for the underlying programmatic decision. Because §102(2)(C) of NEPA has no application to appropriations requests, the court of appeals' further ruling requiring the Office of Management and Budget to adopt regulations for the implementation of its NEPA obligations was also incorrect.

Vermont Yankee Nuclear Power Corp. v. Natural Resources Defense Council, Inc.

Nos. 76-419, -528 (U.S. Apr. 3, 1978)

On review of two cases in which plaintiffs challenged the Nuclear Regulatory Commission's (NRC's) licensing of two nuclear power plants, the Supreme Court unanimously reverses the court of appeals' invalidation of the licenses, announcing that the role of the judiciary in the nuclear licensing process must be carefully limited to avoid unauthorized intrusions into the domain of the administrative agency. In the first case (No. 419), the Court of Appeals for the District of Columbia Circuit had sustained respondent's contention that NRC provided for an inadequate ventilation of the issues under the National Environmental Policy Act (NEPA) when it decided to consider the issue of nuclear waste disposal in a separate, non-adjudicatory hearing, the results of which would be applied retroactively to petitioner's license, rather than in the licensing proceeding itself. Disagreeing with that holding, the Supreme Court held the case law and the legislative history of the Administrative Procedure Act (APA) to support the proposition that as long as an agency complies with the APA's minimum requirements, as had the NRC in this case, it is free to adopt or to decline to adopt additional, more complex procedures. The lower court's invalidation, for procedural inadequacy, of the spent fuel cycle rule which emerged from the separate hearing is also rejected by the Court. Because of the absence from this case of circumstances compelling judicial imposition of more exacting procedural safeguards, the court of appeals erred in not judging the procedural adequacy of that proceeding by the rule-making standards set out in §553 of the APA. This issue is remanded, not for a reassessment of procedures, but for a determination whether, under the APA, the adopted rule is supported by substantial evidence produced at the hearing. With respect to the second case (No. 528) the Court holds that the court of appeals was again wrong in reversing the issuance of the construction license because of the NRC's refusal to explore the question of energy conservation as an alternative to construction of the plant. Where, as in this case, the adoption of a project alternative is merely suggested by a party without at least a minimal showing as to the advantages or wisdom of adopting it, the agency is not required to research and analyze exhaustively the issue; the agency was justified in requiring a showing of sufficient force to require reasonable minds to inquire further. The Court also reverses the appellate court's holding that the Atomic Safety and Licensing Appeals Board should have returned the safety report submitted by the Advisory Committee on Reactor Safeguards for analysis of other issues in terms understandable to a layman. This ruling misinterpreted the Committee's purpose and function and demonstrates an inadequate regard for the resources and time that have been invested in this project. In conclusion, the Court notes that the nation's experiment with nuclear power represents a legislative policy decision which cannot be second-guessed by the judiciary, and that NEPA does not authorize the courts to substitute their judgment for that of Congress or the executive branch.

KLEPPE v. SIERRA CLUB, No. 75-552 (U.S. June 28, 1976)

The Supreme Court reverses the Court of Appeals for the D.C. Circuit, 514 F.2d 856, 5 ELR 20463, and holds that NEPA does not require preparation of an environmental impact statement for coal leasing in the Northern Great Plains region absent an agency proposal for regional coal development. There has been no regional proposal; all proposals have been of local or national scope. Nor can a regional impact statement be prepared for practical reasons, since there would be no factual predicate for analysis. The court of appeals erred in holding that agency "contemp!.._ :" of controlling coal development requires an impact statement. The agencies' procedural duty to prepare impact statements for proposals is precise; the court of appeals mistakenly departed from the statutory language by requiring a four-part balancing test for impact statement preparation. In addition, the court of appeals improperly enjoined further coal leasing pending preparation of an impact statement since the equities lay on the side of the lessees and their consumers. Although comprehensive impact statements are often necessary for related proposals, the determination of the relevant geographical region covered by the statement falls within the informed discretion of the responsible agency.

A partial concurrence and dissent argues that the court of appeals' four-part balancing test would implement NEPA's goals by allowing court intervention prior to solidification of an agency's environmental position, rather than fostering wasted effort through belated injunctive relief. The lower court's test merely restricts judicial review to a small number of proper instances where the agency is violating NEPA through nonpreparation of an impact statement. It is no answer to say that such a test invites litigation, if that litigation is brought to redress agency non-compliance with NEPA's mandates. Furthermore, NEPA's legislative history belies the majority's assertion that the Act's requirements are "precise."

FLINT RIDGE DEVELOPMENT CO. v. SCENIC RIVERS ASSOCIATION OF OKLAHOMA, Nos. 75-510, 75-545 (U.S. June 24, 1976)

In a challenge to the Department of Housing and Urban Development (HUD) for allowing a disclosure statement required by the Interstate Land Sales Disclosure Act to become effective without first filing an environmental impact statement, the Supreme Court holds that NEPA's impact statement requirement is inapplicable whenever a "clear and unavoidable conflict" between the requirements of NEPA and another statute occurs. Moreover, HUD's action on the disclosure statement is not a "major federal action significantly affecting the human environment" because HUD has no "ability to react to the environmental consequences" of the disclosure. Absent incompleteness in the statement, the Secretary of HUD has no discretion to extend the 30-day time period after which disclosure statements automatically become effective. The court of appeals decision, 5 ELR 20536, is reversed.

ABERDEEN & ROCKFISH RAILROAD CO. v. STUDENTS CHALLENGING REGULATORY AGENCY PROCEDURES (SCRAP), No. 73-1966 (U.S. Sup. Ct. June 24, 1975)

The Supreme Court reverses a three-judge district court decision that held inadequate the ICC's compliance with NEPA in assessing the environmental impact of a general railroad freight rate increase on the recycling industry. Relying on the long-established and limited character of the ICC's "general revenue proceeding" at which such increases are approved, and emphasizing that the ICC was investigating in a "more appropriate proceeding" the existing rate structure's discrimination against recyclables which the general increase exacerbated, the court finds that the ICC was justified in limiting the scope of the impact statement largely to the effect of the increase rather than including an extended environmental examination of the underlying rate structure. The across-the-board percentage increase in freight rates is facially neutral in its environmental effect, and the ICC need not "start over again" its decision-making process in order to reflect a wholly new environmental assessment. In a case such as this where a federal agency is not proposing an action but is instead considering a proposal by a nonfederal party which requires federal approval, the first point at which an impact statement must be prepared is when a recognizable "recommendation or report" for federal action (i.e., approval) appears.

Justice Douglas dissents, arguing that the majority's ruling excuses a history of foot-dragging by the ICC on NEPA compliance, and pointing out that the "more appropriate proceeding" investigating the environmental effects of the underlying rate structure may go on indefinitely while irreparable environmental damage occurs. For the district court ruling, here reversed, see 4 ELR 20267.

Sample NEPA Documents

Note: The FONSI, EIS, ROD, and CEQ referral are samples, not models. NEPA documents must always be tailored to the circumstances of individual cases.

Finding of No Significant Impact: Storm Damage Reduction Study for Myrtle Beach and Vicinity, Horry and Georgetown Counties, S.C.
(Army Corps of Engineers, June 1988)

Based upon the attached environmental assessment and in consideration of other pertinent documents, I conclude that the environmental effects of the proposed beach erosion control project are not significant and the preparation of an Environmental Impact Statement is not warranted. Specific factors considered in making the determination include the following:

1. Beach nourishment activities would be scheduled during the winter months to reduce disruption of the tourist oriented economy and minimize adverse effects on fish and invertebrate populations.

2. Trucking fill materials rather than hydraulically pumping them from offshore areas would also reduce adverse effects on fish and invertebrate populations.

3. Wetland areas would not be significantly affected.

4. No significant cultural resource would be affected.

5. No threatened or endangered species would be adversely affected.

6. No significant land use changes would occur.

7. Air quality would not be significantly affected.

8. Fish and wildlife resources would not be significantly affected.

9. No environmentally significant habitats would be adversely affected.

10. Water quality would not be significantly affected.

Stewart H. Bornhoft / 9 Jun 88

STEWART H. BORNHOFT
LTC, Corps of Engineers
Commanding

Final Environmental Impact Statement: Bayou La Batre Navigation Improvements
(Army Corps of Engineers)

TABLE OF CONTENTS

*Comments to which no response was necessary omitted. Ed.

TABLE OF CONTENTS

LIST OF TABLES

LIST OF FIGURES*

*Figures omitted. *Ed.*

FINAL
ENVIRONMENTAL IMPACT STATEMENT
BAYOU LA BATRE
NAVIGATION IMPROVEMENTS

The responsible lead agency is the U. S. Army Engineer District Mobile.

Abstract. The Mobile District has investigated public concerns of the Bayou La Batre study area related to providing increased width and depth in the Bayou La Batre navigation channel. Of the plans initially formulated, 18 were selected for detailed study along with the "No Action" alternative. All plans considered for detailed study included provision of a 14- by 75- foot channel from the turning basin to the Highway 188 bridge, a channel 12- by 75-foot for a distance of 1500 feet above the bridge, a channel in Snake Bayou 14- by 50-foot from the junction with Bayou La Batre for 500 feet then 12- by 50-foot for a distance of 800 feet, a 18- by 100-foot channel south from the turning basin to the mouth of the bayou, a 18- by 120-foot channel from the mouth of the bayou into Mississippi Sound to the Gulf Intracoastal Waterway (GIWW). Two alignments from this point to deep water in the Gulf were considered. One southward through Petit Bois Pass, with dimensions of 18 by 120 feet in the Sound and 19 by 150 feet through the Pass into the Gulf, and one westward along the GIWW alignment, with a dimension of 18 by 120 feet, to it's intersection with the Pascagoula Ship Channel. Disposal options which are considered include: upland disposal, including a new and the existing disposal area, for new work and maintenance material dredged from Bayou La Batre and Snake Bayou; wetland establishment, open water disposal or berm construction in Mississippi Sound in depths greater than 12 feet and Gulf disposal of new work from the Mississippi Sound portion; open water disposal in water greater than 12 feet in depth of maintenance material from the sound portion; littoral and Gulf disposal for new work and maintenance material from the Petit Bois Pass alignment; open water, littoral, or Gulf disposal for new work from the GIWW alignment; and open water disposal for maintenance material from this alignment. Based on economic and environmental considerations, Plan XI has been recommended as the National Economic Development (NED) plan. This plan includes deepening and widening the channels including the GIWW alignment as described above and the following disposal alternatives: establishment and use of a new 107 acre upland disposal area and use of the existing 70 acre disposal area for new work and maintenance materials dredged from the Bayou portion of the project; establishment of an emergent berm along the northeastern shore of Isle aux Herbes and direct placement in water with depths greater than 12 feet in Mississippi Sound of new work material from the Mississippi Sound channel and thin layer placement of maintenance material from this channel; and direct placement of new work material and thin layer placement of maintenance material 5000 feet south of the GIWW channel. Impacts to significant resources due to the recommended plan have been minimized through planning and avoidance. Remaining impacts have been determined to be negligible and therefore no additional mitigation is proposed.

If you would like further
information to this
statement, please contact
Dr. Susan Ivester Rees
U. S. Army Engineer District Mobile
P. O. Box 2288
Mobile, Alabama 36628-0001
(205) 690-2724

NOTE: Information, displays, maps, etc., discussed in the Bayou La Batre
Main Report are incorporated by reference in the FEIS.

ENVIRONMENTAL IMPACT STATEMENT

BAYOU LA BATRE, ALABAMA
NAVIGATION CHANNEL IMPROVEMENTS

1.0   Summary.

1.1   **Major Conclusions and Findings.** Alternative Plan XI at the 18-foot
depth interval with the Snake Bayou channel segment and channel
improvements above the turning basin in Bayou La Batre was designated as
the National Economic Development (NED) plan because it provides for
economically efficient improved navigational capabilities at Bayou La
Batre, Alabama.

Placement of dredged materials in the open water sites within Mississippi
Sound has been evaluated following the 404(b)(1) Guidelines, in compliance
with the Clean Water Act of 1977, 33 U.S.C. 1251 et.seq. (See Appendix D to
the Main Report). State water quality certification under Section 401 of
the Clean Water Act will be obtained prior to the disposal of dredged
material into waters of the U. S. The recommended plan is consistent to
the maximum extent practicable with the Coastal Zone Management Programs of
the States of Alabama and Mississippi.

1.2   **Areas of Controversy.** Historically the Federal and state
environmental agencies have recommended that open water disposal of dredged
material in Mississippi Sound be stopped. Their preference has been: 1)
the use of suitable upland disposal areas, or 2) placement in deep water
sites in the Gulf of Mexico. All efforts have been made to fully utilize
upland disposal areas for the proposed navigation improvements at Bayou La
Batre, however this option will not accommodate all the dredged material
associated with the proposed improvements. Placement of new work material
in the ocean dredged material disposal site at Pascagoula, while
economically feasible, is not the preferred alternative because of the
additional cost associated with this method and the lack of environmental
benefits for this method compared with the proposed open water placement
methods. Placement of maintenance material in the ocean disposal site is
not economically feasible at this time. Although differences in opinion
still exists relative to the degree of long-term impacts associated with
the disposal of dredged material in open water, coordination efforts among
the Federal and state agencies has resulted in development of an acceptable
disposal plan at Bayou La Batre which results in the beneficial use of the
dredged material as shoreline protection for emergent wetlands.

1.3   **Unresolved Issues.** The utilization of all 2 million cubic yards of
new work material from the Mississippi Sound Channel segment for shoreline
protection at Isle aux Herbes as recommended by the U. S. Environmental
Protection Agency and the Fish and Wildlife Service is an unresolved issue.
Additional studies will be undertaken during Preconstruction Engineering
and Design in an effort to to utilize all this material as recommended.

1.4 **Relationship to Environmental Requirements.** The recommended plan as well as the other alternatives are in compliance with applicable statutes and executive orders, as provided on Table EIS-1, for this stage of planning.

1.5 **The draft Environmental Impact Statement (FEIS) was filed with EPA 22 July 1988** and the Final Eis was sent to EPA _____.

TABLE EIS-1

Environmental Statutes and Executive Orders

Federal Statutes

Archeological and Historic Preservation Act, as amended, 16 USC 469, et. seq.
Clean Air Act, as amended, 42 USC 1857h-7, et seq.
Clean Water Act, as amended, (Federal Water Pollution Control Act) 33 USC 1251, et seq.
Coastal Zone Management Act, as amended, 17 USC 1451, et seq.
Endangered Species Act, as amended, 16 USC 1531 et seq.
Estuary Protection Act, 16 USC 1221, et seq.
Federal Water Project Recreation Act, as amended, 16 USC 460-1(12), et seq.
Fish and Wildlife Coordination Act, as amended, 16 USC 661, et seq.
Land and Water Conservation Fund Act, as amended, 16 USC 4601-4601-11, et seq.
Marine Protection, Research and Sanctuaries Act, 33 USC 1401, et seq.
National Historic Preservation Act, as amended, 16 USC 470a, et seq.
National Environmental Policy Act, as amended, 42 USC 4321, et seq.
Rivers and Harbors Act, 33 USC 401 et seq.
Watershed Protection and Flood Prevention Act, 16 USC 1001, et seq.
Wild and Scenic Rivers Act, as amended, 16 USC 1271, et seq.
Uniform Relocation Assistance and Real Property Acquisition Policies Act of 1970 (PL 91-646)
The Gulf Islands National Seashore (GIN) System (PL 91-660)
Coastal Barrier Resources Act (PL 97-348)

Executive Orders, Memoranda, etc.

Flood Plain Management (E.O. 11988)
Protection of Wetlands (E.O. 11990)
Environmental Effects Abroad of Major Federal Actions (E.O. 12114)
Analysis of Impacts on Prime and Unique Farmland (CEQ Memorandum, 11 Aug 80)

2.0 Need For and Objectives of Action.

2.1 **Study Authority.** Authority for this study is contained in House
Public Works Committee Resolution adopted on October 10, 1974. The
resolution requested feasibility studies to determine if modifications to
the existing navigation project at Bayou La Batre, Alabama, are warranted.

2.2 **Public Concerns.** The potential for development of the Bayou La Batre
area is related to its historical development as a major fishing port on
the gulf coast as well as its present day national ranking among commercial
fishing harbors. In addition, more recent development of the boat building
industry within the bayou has played an important role in expanding the
economic base of Bayou La Batre and south Mobile County. Public concerns
considered in the proposed study primarily center around the need for
improved waterborne transportation facilities to support changing
commercial vessel types, changes in commercial fishing activities,
prospects for offshore oil and gas exploration service vessel activity,
porting of small ships, and construction of vessels with a draft greater
than 12 feet, the existing project depth. Public concerns were also
expressed concerning the maintenance and or enhancement of the environment
within the study area. The Main Report examines, in detail, the problems,
needs, and opportunities of the study area at Bayou La Batre, Alabama.

2.3 **Planning Objectives.** The planning objectives listed below are the
basis from which alternative plans were formulated.

Increase the diversity of the fleet which could utilize the channel
for commercial purposes.

Increase the economic efficiency of the interactive system of vessels,
facilities, and navigational requirements by improving the channel to
accommodate the existing fleet and larger, more cost effective vessels.

Improve navigational safety and reduce the risk of vessel groundings
and damages.

Provide an adequate and acceptable dredged material disposal plan for
project modifications and continued maintenance of the Bayou La Batre
channel.

Coordinate dredging and disposal alternatives so that no conflicts
arise with existing management plans for Gulf Islands National Seashore
properties on Petit Bois and Horn Islands and the Coastal Area Management
Programs of the State of Alabama and the State of Mississippi.

Avoid irreversible commitments of resources to future uses.

Maintain or enhance environmental quality of the bayou and Mississippi
Sound.

Utilize dredged material for beneficial purposes such as erosion
protection or habitat establishment.

EIS-5

3.0 Alternatives.

3.1 **Plans Eliminated from Further Study.** A large array of channel depths and widths and disposal sites were initially considered for implementation for the Bayou La Batre project, including those suggested by the public, State and local agencies, and Federal agencies as well as those conceived by the Corps of Engineers. These alternatives are discussed in detail in the Main Report. A number of these concepts were eliminated from further study during preliminary stages of the formulation process. Alternative concepts which were retained were subjected to more detailed analysis and of these, eleven concepts were carried forward as the final array of detailed alternatives. The alternatives discussed below were eliminated from further study in the intermediate stage of formulation.

3.1.1 **Channel Depth and Width.** Initial investigations had included depths of 13, 14, 15, 16, 17, 18, 20, and 22 feet. During the intermediate stage 13-, 15-, and 17-foot depths were eliminated. Widths from 100 to 200 feet were considered for the Mississippi Sound and entrance portions of the channel. All widths were eliminated except for 100 feet for the channel segment in the bayou and 120 feet for the channel segments in Mississippi Sound or westward along the GIWW alignment to the Pascagoula Ship Channel, and 150 feet through Petit Bois Pass into the Gulf of Mexico,. A summary of the economics for each channel segment is presented in Appendix E to the Main Report.

3.1.2 **Alternative Disposal Concepts.** The use of diked areas 'Alpha' and 'Beta' on the west side of the bayou were eliminated due to their limited size and the wetland nature of a portion of 'Beta'. One of the main considerations used in determining the suitability of an upland site is it's role in a long-term dredged material disposal plan. This plan which is being developed in conjunction with the improvements to the Bayou La Batre channel will provide disposal capacity for the bayou portion of the channel for a 50 year period. In addition, the maintenance needs for the bayou portion of the Bayou Coden channel are also being considered in this plan. Because of it's small size site 'Alpha' did not fit into the scheme for a long-term plan. In addition to restricted size, the dikes around site 'Beta' have deteriorated and permitted for tidal exchange into a portion of the site with a consequent development of wetland vegetation.

Upland disposal of material dredged from the entire length of the proposed channel, both new work and maintenance, was eliminated from consideration for economic and engineering considerations. The quantity of material to be dredged from the entire project over the 50 year project life is in excess of 16 million cubic yards. Disposal of this quantity of material would require approximately 1000 acres of upland to be purchased by the local sponsor. In addition, the proposed channel extends approximately 13 miles from the mainland shoreline. Pumping of dredged materials for this distance would result in excessive costs in light of the benefits to be gained from improving the channel.

Expansion of the existing disposal area, 'Charlie', through the addition of 20 acres on the west of the site was also eliminated from further consideration. With the enlarged area maintenance materials dredged from Station 30+00, approximately midway between the turning basin and the mouth, to approximately Station 220+00 in Mississippi Sound would be placed in the site. Pumping to the site from the channel segment within Mississippi Sound would require the addition of a booster pump. To break even with the costs associated with the booster pump approximately 210,000 cubic yards would have to be placed in the site every 3 years. Placing this quantity of material within the 90 acre site would result in attaining the design capacity of the site in approximately 30 years which is not consistent with the long term management goal of 50 years. The alternative of placing less than 210,000 cubic yards in the site, to achieve the long term goal, is not cost effective.

Island construction in Mississippi Sound was eliminated due to the lack of quantity of material for an island. Direct nourishment of the barrier islands was eliminated due to the costs associated with this disposal alternative. Disposal on the north side of Petit Bois Island was also eliminated. Extensive grassbeds are known to occur in the areas north of the barrier islands and disposal in these areas could result in significant impacts to this important habitat.

Open water disposal of new work material in waters less than 12 feet deep was eliminated due to the possibility of mounding and subsequent impacts on circulation. Impacts such as these have been observed in other areas, e.g. Pascagoula area, and it was determined that the impacts could be avoided by using deeper waters within Mississippi Sound. Open water disposal of maintenance material into these waters was also eliminated due to the proximity of the significant estuarine nursery areas of Portersville and Grand Bays and the possible impacts due to increased turbidity associated with this disposal alternative.

Gulf disposal of maintenance material from the Mississippi Sound portion of the channel was eliminated due to operational constraints. The size of the channel requires that a cutterhead or mechanical dredge preform the dredging, with material being placed in dump scows or hopper barges for transport to the Gulf. In order to gain an economical load these scows or barges would be overflowed until such a load was obtained. Recent experience with this type barge overflow operation in Mobile Bay has demonstrated that barge loading cannot be enhanced with the type maintenance material present in the Mobile Channel and with equipment presently available within the dredging industry. Studies of maintenance material from the Bayou La Batre channel indicate that it is of a similar nature and therefore Gulf disposal would not be economically feasible at this time. Gulf disposal of maintenance material from an alignment west to the Pascagoula Harbor Channel was eliminated due to the small quantity of material estimated to be removed and the excessive costs associated with removing small quantities and transport to the Gulf.

3.2 **Plans Considered in Detail.** Evaluations performed in the intermediate stage identified eleven conceptual channel segment/disposal alternative combinations which merited further study. Table EIS-2 presents a description of each of the disposal concepts on a channel segment basis.

TABLE EIS-2
Channel Segment/Disposal Alternatives

BAYOU CHANNEL SEGMENT

BA   New work and maintenance material to upland disposal
areas Delta and existing Charlie.

MISSISSIPPI SOUND CHANNEL SEGMENT[1]

SA   New work material split between Point aux Pins and open water
deeper than 12 feet. Maintenance material to open water
greater than 12 feet deep.

SB   New work material split between Isle aux Herbes and open water
deeper than 12 feet. Maintenance material to open water
greater than 12 feet deep.

SC   New work material to Isle aux Herbes. Maintenance material to
open water greater than 12 feet deep.

SD   New work and maintenance material to open water greater than 12
feet deep.

SE   New work material to Gulf of Mexico (ODMDS), only in
conjunction with PB or GB. Maintenance material to open
water greater than 12 feet deep.

PETIT BOIS PASS CHANNEL SEGMENT

PA   New work material in littoral zone. Maintenance material
disposal rotating between littoral zone and ODMDS on an 18-
month cycle.

PB   New work material to ODMDS, alone or in conjunction with SE.
Maintenance material disposal rotating between littoral zone
and ODMDS on an 18-month cycle.

GIWW CHANNEL SEGMENT[2]

GA   New work and maintenance material to open water approximately
5000 feet south of channel.

GB   New work material to Pascagoula ODMDS, only in conjunction with
SE. Maintenance material to open water approximately 5000
feet south of channel.

GC   New work material in littoral zone 10,000 feet south of
channel. Maintenance material to open water approximately
5000 feet south of channel.

[1]Options for open water disposal include:
direct placement approximately 2500 feet west of channel
thin-layer placement approximately 2500 feet west of channel
berm construction

[2]Options for open water disposal include:
direct placement
thin-layer

EIS-8

Combination of these channel/disposal concepts results in eighteen
alternative plans as presented on Table EIS-3. It should be noted that
each of the openwater disposal concepts can be modified depending on the
technique of disposal utilized. The cost of the disposal concept would not
change with change in technique, however the impacts associated with the
use of the different technique are different. In addition five different
depths, 14, 16, 18, 20, and 22 feet, are considered for each of the
eighteen alternative plans. These alternatives, including the "No Action"
alternative, make up the final array of alternatives. Table EIS-4
summarizes information contained in the Main Report related to plan
economics for each depth considered. Based on this table the greatest net
benefits are attained with an 18-foot channel (For more detail refer to
Plan Formulation Section of the Main Report). In order to simplify the
discussion in the EIS, the detailed alternatives analysis is made utilizing
the 18-foot depth alternative. Table EIS-5 summarizes information related
to plan economics for the 18-foot depth alternative. See Appendix B to the
Main Report for more detailed discussion on the economic analysis.

TABLE EIS-3

Alternative Plans

ALTERNATIVE PLAN I	BA+SA+PA	ALTERNATIVE PLAN X	BA+SA+GA
ALTERNATIVE PLAN II	BA+SB+PA	ALTERNATIVE PLAN XI	BA+SB+GA
ALTERNATIVE PLAN III	BA+SC+PA	ALTERNATIVE PLAN XII	BA+SC+GA
ALTERNATIVE PLAN IV	BA+SD+PA	ALTERNATIVE PLAN XIII	BA+SD+GA
ALTERNATIVE PLAN V	BA+SA+PB	ALTERNATIVE PLAN XIV	BA+SE+GB
ALTERNATIVE PLAN VI	BA+SB+PB	ALTERNATIVE PLAN XV	BA+SA+GC
ALTERNATIVE PLAN VII	BA+SC+PB	ALTERNATIVE PLAN XVI	BA+SB+GC
ALTERNATIVE PLAN VIII	BA+SD+PB	ALTERNATIVE PLAN XVII	BA+SC+GC
ALTERNATIVE PLAN IX	BA+SE+PB	ALTERNATIVE PLAN XVIII	BA+SD+GC

3.2.1 "No Action" Alternative. Maintenance of the existing project
provides waterborne transportation via: a 12- by 100-foot channel from the
12-foot contour in Mississippi Sound to a point about 2,800 feet below the
State Highway 188 bridge, thence a channel 12 by 75 feet upstream to the
bridge, for a total channel length of about 6.3 miles. A turning basin is
provided about 0.6 mile below the bridge. Approximately 100,000 cubic
yards of maintenance material removed from the bayou portion of the project
is pumped to a 70 acre confined disposal site (Charlie) approximately
midway between the communities of Bayou La Batre and Coden. Material
removed from the Mississippi Sound portion of the project by hydraulic
pipeline/cutterhead dredge is pumped to six 75 acre open water disposal
sites along the western side of the channel (See Figure EIS-1). These
sites range in depth from 3.5 to 10.5 feet in depth. Typically, 50,000
cubic yards of maintenance material is pumped to each of the sites on a 3
year basis.

TABLE EIS-4

Average Annual Costs and Benefits
by Channel Segment and Depth[1]

Channel Segment (Depth)	Total Average Annual Benefits	Total Average Annual Costs[2]	Net Benefits	B/C Ratio
Sound, Pass, and Bayou to Turning Basin				
14 feet	1,445.8	1,843.0	(397.2)	0.78
16 feet	1,628.1	2,314.3	(686.2)	0.70
18 feet	**4,059.5**	**2,444.6**	**1,614.9**	**1.66**
20 feet	4,072.3	2,800.6	1,271.7	1.45
22 feet	4,072.3	3,015.2	1,057.1	1.35
Sound, GIWW, and Bayou to Turning Basin				
14 feet	1,348.8	1,229.3	119.5	1.10
16 feet	1.530.5	1,599.4	(68.9)	0.96
18 feet	**3,961.9**	**1,757.6**	**2,204.3**	**2.25**
20 feet	3,974.7	2,059.2	1,915.5	1.93
22 feet	3,974.7	2,277.7	1,697.0	1.75
Snake Bayou[3]	365.1	39.8	325.3	
Turning Basin to 1500' above Bridge[3]	574.8	391.5	183.3	

[1]These data are applicable to the most economical alternative plan, i.e., Plan II and Plan XI. Costs and Benefits are 1,000.

[2]These are net average annual costs and are composed of (Construction dredging + Maintenance dredging + Bulkhead replacement + Utility relocations) - (Bulkhead replacement without project + Maintenance dredging without project).

[3]Positive net benefits indicate channel segment feasibility.

TABLE EIS-5

Summary of Selected Features of Alternative Plans
at 18-Foot Depth[1]

	Economic Data[2]			Plan Designation
Plan	Annual Costs	Annual Benefits	B/C Ratio	
I	2,500.8	4,059.5	1.62	
II	2,444.6	4,059.5	1.66	
III	2,522.3	4,059.5	1.61	
IV	2,469.5	4,059.5	1.64	
V	2,624.1	4,059.5	1.55	
VI	2,567.9	4,059.5	1.58	
VII	2,645.6	4,059.5	1.53	
VIII	2,592.8	4,059.5	1.57	
IX	2,862.1	4,059.5	1.44	
X	1,813.8	3,961.9	2.18	
XI	1,757.6	3,961.9	2.25	NED
XII	1,835.3	3,961.9	2.16	EQ
XIII	1.782.5	3,961.9	2.22	
XIV	2,031.3	3,961.9	1.95	
XV	1,846.1	3,961.9	2.15	
XVI	1,789.9	3,961.9	2.21	
XVII	1,867.6	3,961.9	2.12	
XVIII	1,814.8	3,961.9	2.18	

[1]Including Snake Bayou and Turning Basin to 1500 feet above Bridge segments

[2]Costs and benefits are 1,000

The principal difficulties stemming from inadequate widths and depths throughout the existing channel would not be alleviated under this alternative. In addition to this economic handicap this alternative would not alleviate the safety problems associated with utilizing the channel.

3.2.2 **Channel Modification Alternatives.** All alternatives considered in detail included providing a 14- by 75-foot channel from the turning basin (Station 30+00) northward to the Highway 188 bridge (Station 0+00) then 12- by 75-foot to a point approximately 1500 feet above the Highway 188 bridge (Station -15+00). In addition the plan would provide a channel in Snake Bayou, 14- by 50-foot from the junction with Bayou La Batre to Station 5+33 then 12- by 50-foot to Station 13+47. Deepening of the existing 100-foot wide channel from the mouth of the bayou (Station 130+00) to the turning

basin to 14-, 16-, 18-, 20-, and 22-foot depths was considered. Widening
to 120 feet and deepening within Mississippi Sound to 14-, 16-, 18-, 20-,
and 22-foot depths was considered in detail. Two channel alignments to the
Gulf of Mexico were considered: 1) from Station 536+00 (GIWW crossing)
southward through Petit Bois Pass and 2) from Station 536+00 westward to
the Pascagoula Ship Channel. The dimensions considered for the channel
through Petit Bois Pass included 150-foot wide at 15-, 17-, 19-, 21-, 23-
foot depths. The dimensions of the channel west along the GIWW were 120-
foot wide at 14-, 16-, 18-, 20-, and 22-foot depths. The depths indicated
are nominal depths, actual depth would include 1-foot advanced maintenance
and 1-foot allowable overdepth (See Figure EIS-2). For a more detailed
description refer to the Main Report.

Dredging of the channels in Snake Bayou and above the Highway 188 bridge
would impact approximately 1.5 and 2.6 acres of bayou bottoms,
respectively. These bottoms have not been previously dredged. Dredging
within the Bayou south of the bridge would impact approximately 29 acres of
bottoms which are currently dredged on a 3 year cycle. Provision of a 14-
foot channel would impact approximately 126 acres within Mississippi Sound
north of the GIWW. No dredging would be required if the GIWW alignment
were followed, approximately 51 acres south of the GIWW would be dredged
with the Petit Bois Pass alignment. Provision of the 16-foot channel would
impact 173 acres north of the GIWW and 73 acres south of the GIWW for the
Petit Bois Pass alignment. Minimal dredging would be required for the GIWW
alignment. Provision of an 18-foot channel would require dredging on 201
acres north of the GIWW, 140 acres south of the GIWW for the Petit Bois
Pass Channel, or 159 acres in Mississippi Sound with the GIWW alignment.
Similarly the 20-foot channel requires dredging 223 acres north of the
GIWW, 170 acres south of the GIWW or 185 acres in Mississippi Sound for the
GIWW alignment. The 22-foot channel requires dredging 245 acres north of
the GIWW, 188 acres south of the GIWW, or 211 acres in Mississippi Sound
along the GIWW alignment. As discussed in Section 3.2 a comparison of the
average annual incremental costs and average annual benefits associated
with each depth increment indicated that the greatest net benefits are
achieved with the 18-foot depth increment, therefore this depth is analyzed
in greatest detail in the following paragraphs.

The channel modification alternatives considered in detail utilize various
combinations of disposal areas and are presented in comparative format in
Table EIS-6 and described in detail below and in the Main Report (Figures
EIS-2 and EIS-3).

3.2.3 DREDGED MATERIAL PLACEMENT ALTERNATIVES.

3.2.3.1 Upland Disposal Areas 'Charlie' and 'Delta'. Approximately
395,800 cubic yards of new work and approximately 3 million cubic yards of
maintenance material, over the 50 year project life, dredged from Station
90+45 to Station -15+10 within the bayou and Snake Bayou would be placed
into the new 107 acre upland disposal area 'Delta' (Figure EIS-3).
Approximately 171,500 cubic yards of new work and 1,360,000 cubic yards of
maintenance material dredged from the mouth of the bayou to Station 90+45
would be disposed in the existing 70 acre disposal area 'Charlie'. This

Table EIS-6 Comparison of Alternative Plans

Segment		No Action	Plan I	Plan II	Plan III	Plan IV	Plan V
Bayou Channel	NW	N/A	DA Charlie and Delta	DA Charlie and Delta	DA Charlie and Delta	DA Charlie and Delta	DA Charlie and Delta
	OM	DA Charlie	DA Charlie and Delta	DA Charlie and Delta	DA Charlie and Delta	DA Charlie and Delta	DA Charlie and Delta
Mississippi Sound	NW	N/A	Pt Aux Pins & OW > 12'	Isle a'Herbes & OW >12'	Isle Aux Herbes	Open Water >12'	Point Aux Pins & OW >12'
	OM	Open Water >12'	Open Water >12'	Open Water >12'	Open Water > 12'	Open Water >12'	Open Water >12'
Petit Bois Pass	NW	N/A	Littoral Disposal	Littoral Disposal	Littoral Disposal	Littoral Disposal	ODMDS
	OM	N/A	Littoral Disposal + ODMDS, 18 Month Cyc	Littoral Disposal + ODMDS, 18 Month Cyc	Littoral Disposal + ODMDS, 18 Month Cyc	Littoral Disposal + ODMDS, 18 Month Cyc	Littoral Disposal + ODMDS, 18 Month Cyc
GIWW		N/A	N/A	N/A	N/A	N/A	N/A

Segment		No Action	Plan VI	Plan VII	Plan VIII	Plan IX	Plan X
Bayou Channel	NW	N/A	DA Charlie and Delta	DA Charlie and Delta	DA Charlie and Delta	DA Charlie and Delta	DA Charlie and Delta
	OM	DA	DA Charlie and Delta	DA Charlie and Delta	DA Charlie and Delta	DA Charlie and Delta	DA Charlie and Delta
Mississippi Sound	NW	N/A	Isle a'Herbes & OW > 12'	Isle a'Herbes & OW > 12'	Open Water > 12'	ODMDS	Point Aux Pins & OW > 12'
	OM	Open Water > 12'	Open Water > 12'	Open Water > 12'	Open Water > 12'	Open Water > 12'	Open Water > 12'
Petit Bois Pass	NW	N/A	ODMDS	ODMDS	ODMDS	ODMDS	N/A
	OM	N/A	Littoral Disposal + OSDMS, 18 Month Cyc	Littoral Disposal + OSDMS, 18 Month Cyc	Littoral Disposal + OSDMS, 18 Month Cyc	Littoral Disposal + OSDMS, 18 Month Cyc	N/A
GIWW	NW	N/A	N/A	N/A	N/A	N/A	OW 5000'S of Channel
	OM	N/A	N/A	N/A	N/A	N/A	OW 5000'S of Channel

TABLE EIS-6 (cont.) Comparison of Alternative Plans

Segment		NO Action	Plan XI	Plan XII	Plan XIII	Plan XIV	Plan XV
Bayou Channel	NW	N/A	DA Charlie and Delta	DA Charlie and Delta	DA Charlie and Delta	DA Charlie and Delta	DA Charlie and Delta
	OM	DA Charlie	DA Charlie and Delta	DA Charlie and Delta	DA Charlie and Delta	DA Charlie and Delta	DA Charlie and Delta
Mississippi Sound	NW	N/A	Isle a'Herbes & OW > 12'	Isle Aux Herbes	Open Water > 12'	ODMDS	Point a'Pins & OW > 12'
	OM	Open Water > 12'	Open Water > 12'	Open Water > 12'	Open Water > 12'	Open Water > 12'	Open Water > 12'
Petit Bois Pass	NW	N/A	N/A	N/A	N/A	N/A	N/A
	OM	N/A	N/A	N/A	N/A	N/A	N/A
GIWW	NW	N/A	OW 5000 ft S of Channel	OW 5000 Ft S of Channel	Open Water 5000 Ft S	Pascagoula ODMDS	Littoral 10000 Ft S
	OM	NA	Open Water 5000 Ft S of Channel	Open Water 5000 Ft S of Channel	Open Water 5000 Ft S of Channel	Open Water 5000 Ft S of Channel	Open Water 5000 Ft S of Channel

Segment		NO Action	Plan XVI	Plan XVII	Plan XVIII
Bayou Channel	NW	N/A	DA Charlie and Delta	DA Charlie and Delta	DA Charlie and Delta
	OM	DA Charlie	DA Charlie and Delta	DA Charlie and Delta	DA Charlie and Delta
Mississippi Sound	NW	N/A	Isle a'Harbes & OW > 12'	Isle Aux Herbes	Open Water > 12'
	OM	Open Water > 12'	Open Water > 12'	Open Water > 12'	Open Water > 12'
Petit Bois Pass	NW	N/A	N/A	N/A	N/A
	OM	N/A	N/A	N/A	N/A
GIWW	NW	N/A	Littoral 10000 Ft S	Littoral 10000 Ft S	Littoral 10000 Ft S
	OM	N/A	Open Water 5000 Ft S	Open Water 5000 Ft S	Open Water 5000 Ft S

dredging would be accomplished by cutterhead/pipeline dredge. Maintenance would occur on a 3 year cycle, with approximately 175,000 and 80,000 cubic yards being placed in 'Delta' and 'Charlie', respectively. This alternative is represented by the symbol **BA** and is common to all plans considered in detail.

3.2.3.2 **Point aux Pins and Placement in Open Water Greater than 12 Feet in Depth.** Approximately 2 million cubic yards of new work material would be dredged by cutterhead/pipeline dredge from the mouth of the bayou south to the GIWW. Approximately 1.3 million yards of this material would be used to reestablish the eroded shoreline in the Point aux Pins/Isle aux Dames area (Figure EIS-4). The remaining material would be disposed in open water greater than 12 feet in depth on the western side of the channel (Figure EIS-2). This material could be: 1) used to create a submerged berm, 6 feet high x 40 feet wide on the crest and 1250 feet wide at the base x 4500 feet long, in the vicinity of the 12-foot contour on the west side of the channel; 2) placed on approximately 600 acres of estuarine bottoms approximately 2500 feet west of the channel; or 3) placed in a thin-layer, 1-foot thick or less, over approximately 750 acres of bottoms west of the channel. Approximately 430,000 cubic yards of maintenance material would be dredged by cutterhead/pipeline dredge every 3 years and disposed in open water greater than 12 feet deep for a total of 7.3 million cubic yards over the life of the project. This material could be placed directly on approximately 330 acres or placed in a thin layer over approximately 415 acres.

Approximately 260 acres south of the Point aux Pins/Isle aux Dames shoreline would be utilized in the creation of wetlands and provision of erosion protection. As shown on Figure EIS-4, a double row of hay bales, one bale high, would be placed along approximately 8000 feet of shoreline extending from the western tip of Point aux Pins eastward through the remanent of the Isle aux Dames. A double row of hay bales, two bales high, would be established from the ends of the first row extending southward for a distance of approximately 1500 feet. A third row of hay bales would be placed along this outer limit in water approximately 3 feet deep MLW. The placement of materials would begin at the Point aux Pins shoreline with discharge oriented toward the south. As material builds in this area the discharge line would be moved to the east and south. Wetland vegetation, Spartina alterniflora and Juncus roemerianus, would be planted on approximately 160 acres following disposal. Spartina alterniflora, in the form of plant rolls, would be installed on approximately 60 acres along the southern edge. The remainder of the 160 acre area would be sprigged on 3 foot centers using S. alterniflora or J. roemerianus as appropriate. Discharge would require approximately 3 months and would be accomplished between November and March to take advantage of low water levels. Planting would begin as soon after placement as possible but no later than April - May.

This placement alternative is represented by the symbol **SA** and is a component of alternative plans I, V, X, and XV.

3.2.3.3 Isle aux Herbes Placement Concept A and Placement in Open Water Greater than 12 Feet in Depth. Approximately 2 million cubic yards of new work material would be dredged by cutterhead/pipeline dredge from the mouth of the bayou south to the GIWW. Approximately 1.3 million yards of this material would be used to create an emergent berm along the northeastern shore of the Isle aux Herbes, east of the Bayou La Batre channel (Figure EIS-5). The remaining material would be disposed in open water greater than 12 feet in depth on the western side of the channel (Figure EIS-2). This material could be: 1) used to create a submerged berm, 6 feet high x 40 feet wide on the crest and 1250 feet wide at the base x 4500 feet long, in the vicinity of the 12-foot contour on the west side of the channel; 2) placed on approximately 600 acres of estuarine bottoms approximately 2500 feet west of the channel; or 3) placed in a thin-layer, 1-foot thick or less, over approximately 750 acres of bottoms west of the channel. Approximately 430,000 cubic yards of maintenance material would be dredged by cutterhead/pipeline dredge every 3 years and disposed in open water greater than 12 feet deep for a total of 7.3 million cubic yards over the life of the project. This material could be placed directly on approximately 330 acres or placed in a thin layer over approximately 415 acres.

Approximately 160 acres adjacent to the northeast shore of Isle aux Herbes would be utilized during the disposal of new work material. During the detailed design any change in the proposed area due to long-term management activities of the Bayou Coden Channel will be taken into account. As shown on Figure EIS-5, a double row of hay bales, two bales high, would be established east of the 3-foot contour and a single row of bales would be placed east of the existing shoreline. The placement of materials would generally be along the 3-foot contour, beginning in the north and proceeding southward. The emergent berm would be approximately 6 feet high (3 feet above MLW), 10-foot wide at the crest, 1000-foot wide at the base, and approximately 6,000 feet long. A swale would be created between the existing shoreline and the crest of the berm. Discharge would require approximately 3 months and would be accomplished between November and March to take advantage of low water levels.

This alternative placement concept is represented by the symbol **SB** and is a component of alternative plans II, VI, XI, XVI.

3.2.3.4 Isle aux Herbes Placement Concept B and Placement in Open Water Greater than 12 Feet in Depth. Approximately 2 million cubic yards of new work material would be dredged by cutterhead/pipeline dredge from the mouth of the bayou south to the GIWW. This material would be used to create an emergent berm along the eastern shore of the Isle aux Herbes, east of the Bayou La Batre channel (Figure EIS-6). Approximately 430,000 cubic yards of maintenance material would be dredged by cutterhead/pipeline dredge every 3 years and disposed in open water greater than 12 feet deep for a total of 7.3 million cubic yards over the life of the project (Figure EIS-2). This material could be placed directly on approximately 330 acres or placed in a thin layer over approximately 415 acres.

Approximately 240 acres adjacent to the eastern shore of Isle aux Herbes would be utilized during the disposal of new work material. During the detailed design any change in the proposed area due to long-term management activities of the Bayou Coden Channel will be taken into account. As shown on Figure EIS-6, a double row of hay bales, two bales high, would be established east of the 3-foot contour and a single row of bales would be placed east of the existing shoreline. The placement of materials would generally be along the 3-foot contour, pipeline routes would be located around the northern end of the island, through the cut in the center of the island, and around the southern end of the island. The emergent berm would be approximately 6 feet high (3 feet above MLW), 10-foot wide at the crest, 1000-foot wide at the base, and approximately 9,500 feet long. A swale would be created between the existing shoreline and the crest of the berm. Discharge would require approximately 6 months to complete and would be accomplished between October and March to take advantage of low water levels..

This alternative placement concept is represented by the symbol **SC** and is a component of alternative plans III, VII, XII, and XVII.

3.2.3.5 **Placement in Open Water Greater than 12 Feet in Depth.**

Approximately 2 million cubic yards of new work material dredged from the Mississippi Sound Channel segment would be disposed in open water greater than 12 feet in depth (Figure EIS-2). Disposal of this material could be utilized to create an underwater berm approximately 6 feet high x 40 feet wide on the crest x 1250 feet wide at the base x 8400 feet long feet long (approximately 240 acres). This material could also be placed directly on approximately 1100 acres of bottoms, or placed in a thin-layer over approximately 1400 acres of bottoms. Approximately 430,000 cubic yards of maintenance material would be dredged by cutterhead/pipeline dredge every 3 years and disposed in open water greater than 12 feet deep for a total of 7.3 million cubic yards over the life of the project. This material could be placed directly on approximately 330 acres or placed in a thin layer over approximately 415 acres. This alternative placement concept is represented by the symbol **SD** and is a component of alternative plans IV, VIII, XIII, and XVIII.

3.2.3.6 **Placement in an Ocean Dredged Material Disposal Site in the Gulf of Mexico and in Open Water Greater than 12 Feet in Depth.**

Approximately 2 million cubic yards of new work material would be dredged by cutterhead/pipeline dredge from the Mississippi Sound Channel and transported in hopper barges for placement in either the Mobile North ODMDS or the Pascagoula ODMDS (Figure EIS-2). Approximately 430,000 cubic yards of maintenance material would be dredged by cutterhead/pipeline dredge every 3 years and disposed in open water greater than 12 feet deep for a total of 7.3 million cubic yards over the life of the project. This material could be placed directly on approximately 330 acres or placed in a thin layer over approximately 415 acres. This alternative placement concept is represented by the symbol **SE** and can only occur in combination with **PB** or **GB** as discussed below. Alternative plan IX includes this placement option in conjunction with **PB**, alternative plan XIV includes this placement option in conjunction with **GB**.

3.2.3.7 Placement in the Petit Bois Pass Littoral Zone and Mobile North ODMDS. Approximately 872,000 cubic yards of new work material would be dredged by cutterhead/pipeline dredge from the channel through Petit Bois Pass between the GIWW and the Gulf of Mexico and disposed in the littoral zone of Petit Bois Pass, west of the channel (Figure EIS-2). Approximately 525,000 cubic yards of maintenance material would be dredged from this area every 18 months for a total of 17 million cubic yards over the project life. This material would be dredged by hopper dredge and disposed in the Mobile North Ocean Dredged Material Disposal Site (ODMDS) and by cutterhead/pipeline dredge and disposed in the littoral zone on a 18 month basis. The cutterhead/pipeline dredge would be utilized when the remainder of the project was maintained. The hopper dredge would be utilized during off year maintenance. This placement alternative is represented by the symbol **PA** and is a component of alternative plans I, II, III, and IV.

3.2.3.8 Placement in the Mobile North ODMDS and Petit Bois Pass Littoral Zone. Approximately 872,000 cubic yards of new work material would be dredged by hopper dredge from the channel through Petit Bois Pass between the GIWW and the Gulf of Mexico and transported to the Mobile North ODMDS for disposal (Figure EIS-2). Approximately 525,000 cubic yards of maintenance material would be dredged from this area every 18 months for a total of 17 million cubic yards over the project life. This material would be dredged by hopper dredge and disposed in the Mobile North Ocean Dredged Material Disposal Site (ODMDS) and by cutterhead/pipeline dredge and disposed in the littoral zone on a 18 month basis. The cutterhead/pipeline dredge would be utilized when the remainder of the project was maintained. The hopper dredge would be utilized during off year maintenance. This placement alternative is represented by the symbol **PB** and is a component of alternative plans V, VI, VII, VIII, and IX.

3.2.3.9 Open Water Placement Approximately 5000 Feet South of the GIWW Channel. Approximately 485,554 cubic yards of new work material and 90,000 cubic yards of maintenance material would be dredged from Station 536+00 to Station 1185+45 along the GIWW alignment and disposed in open water approximately 5000 feet south of the channel in depths of approximately 18 feet (Figure EIs-2). Maintenance would occur on a three cycle for a total of approximately 1.5 million cubic yards over the 50 year life of the project. The new work material could either be placed directly or in a thin layer less than 1-foot thick on approximately 330 or 400 acres, respectively. Placement of maintenance material would impact 70 or 90 acres utilizing direct placement or thin layer, respectively. This placement concept is represented by the symbol **GA** and is a component of alternative plane X, XI, XI1, and XIII.

3.2.3.10 Placement in the Pascagoula ODMDS and Open Water Approximately 5000 Feet South of the GIWW Channel. Approximately 485,554 cubic yards of new work material from Station 536+00 to Station 1185+00 along the GIWW alignment would be dredged by cutterhead/pipeline dredge and transported in hopper barges to the Pascagoula ODMDS for disposal (Figure EIS-2). Approximately 90,000 cubic yards of maintenance material would be dredged from this channel segment every three years and placed in open water 5000 feet south of the channel for a total of 1.5 million cubic yards over the project life. Direct placement of this material would impact approximately 70 acres whereas placement in a thin layer would impact approximately 90 acres. This placement concept, represented by the symbol **GB**, is only viable in conjunction with **SE** described above and is a component of alternative plan XIV.

3.2.3.11 Open Water Placement Approximately 10000 Feet and 5000 South of the GIWW Channel. Approximately 485,554 cubic yards of new work material would be dredged from Station 536+00 to Station 1185+45 along the GIWW alignment and disposed in open water approximately 10000 feet south of the channel in depths of approximately 18 feet (Figure EIS-2). This material could either be placed directly or in a thin layer less than 1-foot thick on approximately 330 or 400 acres, respectively. Approximately 90,000 cubic yards of maintenance material would be dredged from this channel segment every three years and placed in open water 5000 feet south of the channel for a total of 1.5 million cubic yards over the project life. Direct placement of this material would impact approximately 70 acres whereas placement in a thin layer would impact approximately 90 acres. This placement concept is represented by the symbol **GC** and is a component of alternative plans XV, XVI, XVII, and XVIII.

3.2.4 RECOMMENDED PLAN. Features of the the plan recommended for the improvement of the Bayou La Batre channel include:

o Provision of a 18-foot channel from the mouth of Bayou La Batre to the turning basin.

o Provision of a 14- x 75-foot channel from the turning basin to approximately 1500 feet above the Highway 188 bridge.

o Provision of a 14- x 50-foot channel in Snake Bayou for a distance of 500 feet, then a 12- x 50-foot channel for approximately 850 feet.

o Provision of a 18- x 120-foot channnel from the mouth of the bayou into Mississippi Sound, south to the existing Gulf Intracoastal Waterway (GIWW) alignment then westward along the GIWW alignment to it's intersection with the Pascagoula Ship Channel.

o New work and maintenance materials dredged from Snake Bayou and the bayou proper channel will be disposed in upland disposal areas 'Charlie' and 'Delta'.

o The disposal of the new work material from the Mississippi Sound channel segment will be split between Isle aux Herbes and open water greater than 12 feet deep. The disposal at Isle aux Herbes will result in a 6,000 foot emergent berm along the northeast shore to provide protection to the existing wetlands in that area. The disposal of new work material in open water west of the channel will be placed on approximately 600 acres of estuarine bottoms. Maintenance material from this channel segment will be disposed in a thin-layer on approximately 415 acres on a three year cycle.

o The disposal of the new work and maintenance material dredged from the GIWW segment will be disposed in a thin-layer on approximately 400 and 90 acres, respectively, approximately 5,000 feet south of the channel alignment.

3.2.4.1 **BULKHEAD/PIER REPLACEMENT.** Both Bayou La Batre and Snake Bayou are extensively bulkheaded and numerous piers occur on both sides of the bayous (See Plates 5, 6, and 7 of the main report). From a point about midway between the mouth of the bayou (Station 130+00) and the turning basin (Station 30+00) to the study limits of the bayou (Station -15+00), the bayou is almost solidly bulkheaded on each side of the existing channel. There are presently over 20,000 linear feet of bulkhead and over 9,000 linear feet of pier within the bayous. Construction of the proposed channel would require replacement of approximately 6,300 linear feet of existing bulkhead to avoid potential bulkhead failure causing channel obstruction or damage to adjacent buildings or other infrastructure. In addition, approximately 1,800 linear feet of existing pier would need to be replaced. An additional 2,100 linear feet of bulkhead is needed to provide property protection for properties adjacent to the bayou that are currently without bulkheads and could be substantially affected by the side slopes of an improved channel. Replacement of existing bulkheads and piers and provision of new bulkheads is a responsibility of the local sponsor and/or individual property owner. Replacement of existing structures would be accomplished adjacent to the existing structures and utilizing, for the most part, materials similar to those currently in use. For new bulkheads, the most favorably 50-year cost results from use of anchored concrete bulkheads at all dredge line elevations. For additional information refer to Section IV, Engineering Analyses, of the Main Report and Appendix E, Engineering Data and Cost Estimates.

3.2.4.2 **UTILITY RELOCATIONS.** Utility relocations are required for two force mains, one 6-inch cast iron and one 6-inch PVC, which cross the channel below the Highway 188 bridge (See Plate 2 of the Main Report). The relocations of these force mains is a responsibility of the local sponsor and would be accomplished through directional drilling. Finished top of pipe elevations for the relocated force mains would be -10 feet MLW and -22 feet MLW for the PVC and cast iron line, respectively.

4.0 Affected Environment.

4.1 **General Environmental Conditions.** The Bayou La Batre navigation
project is located in Mobile County in south Alabama. Bayou La Batre is a
tidal stream about 10 miles long which empties into Mississippi Sound 30
miles southwest of Mobile, Alabama. The City of Bayou La Batre although
small in population, 2,162 persons in the 1984 census, serves as a major
port in the U. S. for commercial fishery landings. The Bayou La Batre
study area consists of land and water bodies which may be directly or
indirectly affected by the construction of a deeper channel at Bayou La
Batre. This area includes the City of Bayou La Batre, pertinent portions
of Mobile County, Mississippi Sound, and the Gulf of Mexico. For
environmental aspects, a tiered study area is used such that the area or
resources directly impacted by the construction of the channel are
considered in more detail than those resources indirectly affected. The
area which would be directly impacted includes the mainland region from the
City of Bayou La Batre westward to the Alabama/Mississippi state line; that
portion of Mississippi Sound between Isle aux Herbes and the Pascagoula,
Mississippi Ship Channel approximately 30 miles to the west; and portions
of the nearshore Gulf of Mexico and it's fishery resources. The channel
under study is divided into four segments: 1) the Bayou Channel Segment
from Station -15+10 upstream of the Highway 188 bridge to Station 130+00 at
the mouth of the bayou and also including Snake Bayou; 2) the Mississippi
Sound Channel Segment from Station 130+00 at the mouth to Station 536+00
which is in the vicinity of the Gulf Intracoastal Waterway (GIWW); 3) the
Petit Bois Pass Channel Segment from Station 536+00 south through Petit
Bois Pass to the 26-foot contour in the Gulf of Mexico; and 4) the GIWW
Channel Segment from Station 536+00 west to Station 1185+45 at the junction
with the Pascagoula Ship Channel (Figure 13, Main Report). Although
referenced in this document the Gulf Intracoastal Waterway and the
Pascagoula Ship Channel are not part of this study.

The major biotic communities within the project area are nearshore Gulf of
Mexico, estuarine open waters, emergent wetlands, aquatic beds, wetland and
upland forests, and urban areas. Numerous game animals and migratory
waterfowl utilize the diverse habitats of the study area. Commercial
fisheries utilize the wetland and open water areas throughout their life
cycles. A number of threatened or endangered species may occur within the
study area.

4.2 **Significant Resources.** The following paragraphs summarize the
significant resources occurring within the study area which may be impacted
by the proposed action. For a more detailed discussion, the reader is
referred to the Existing Conditions Section of the Main Report and to the
Mississippi Sound and Adjacent Areas Study (USACE, 1984).

4.2.1 **Vegetation.** Emergent wetlands comprise about 16 percent of the
habitats in the study area. Most of these emergent wetlands are located
along the shoreline of Point aux Chenes Bay, Portersville Bay (Point aux
Pins area) and on Isle aux Herbes, and Petit Bois and Dauphin Islands.
These wetlands are typically brackish or saline and are dominated by black
needlerush with smooth cordgrass locally abundant along open water margins.

Salt flats occur within the saline marshes and are characterized by barren areas interspersed with glasswort and sea bite. Aquatic grassbeds comprise about 1 percent of the habitats of the study area. These are most dominant in shallow waters near the southeasternmost end of Portersville Bay, north shores of the barrier islands, and along the western and eastern shores of the Point aux Pins.

Forested wetlands comprise approximately 5000 acres of the study area. These areas may be moist pine savannahs/pitcher plant bogs characterized by a slash pine overstory with an understory of insectivorous plants such as pitcher plants and sundew in wetter areas and wax myrtle in drier areas. Floodplain swamps are also found within the general study area. These are characterized by sweet bay, swamp tupelo, water oak. Open thickets within the floodplain swamps are characterized by black titi and swamp cyrilla.

4.2.2 **Aquatic Resources.** Estuarine and Gulf of Mexico open water areas dominate the delineated study area. These areas range in depth from less than 1-foot MLW to depths greater than 60 feet and contain a variety of resources important to the functioning of the ecosystem.

Intertidal and subtidal bottoms are populated by communities of macrofauna whose structure is dependent upon substrate, salinity, temperature, depth, and ecological relationships. Of the five benthic communities which have been identified within the study area, the open sound, muddy-sand community occupies over 70% of the study area. Although there are no oyster reefs within the study area, the Cedar Point reef, the largest in Alabama, is just east of the study area. In addition oyster reefs were historically located in both Portersville and Grand Bays however with the widening of Petit Bois Pass salinities increased in these areas and influx of oyster predators resulted in almost total decline of these reefs. A recent shell planting activity resulted in the planting of approximately 2700 barrels of shell in the area adjacent to the northeast shoreline of the Isle aux Herbes.

The major fisheries of the study area include menhaden, mullet, croakers, brown and white shrimp, blue crab, and oysters. The Bayou La Batre area ranks in the top 20 for value of fishery landed at major U. S. ports. Seven-year average (1980-86) of landings and value were 20.2 million pounds and 31.8 million dollars. Shrimp, the dominant fishery landed in the bayou, accounted for approximately 90% of the total value. These species and others landed in the bayou are estuarine dependent, i.e., they spend part or all of their lives in estuaries. A typical estuarine dependent species spawns in the Gulf of Mexico, and the larvae are then carried into the estuaries where they mature. The stage from the egg to juvenile, during which transport from offshore waters to low salinity areas is accomplished, is probably the most critical of all in the life histories of the important fishery organisms of the northern Gulf of Mexico. The threat to individuals during this time may be broken down into three distinct phases: (1) transport from the offshore waters to the vicinity of the tidal passes; (2) transport through the passes into the estuaries; and (3) distribution within the estuaries after entrance has been obtained (Gunter, 1967). Since these forms are typically incapable of sustained locomotion,

any significant increase or decrease in flow through the barrier island
pass could impact the migration of these forms.

The mainland margins of the Sound, the margins of Dauphin and Petit Bois
Islands, and the grassbeds around these islands and Point aux Pins serve as
the dominant nursery grounds during the spring and summer months. In
autumn these areas are still important, but usage is not as heavy due to
the seaward migration of many late juveniles (Benson, 1982 and USACE,
1984).

4.2.3 **Wildlife Resources.** A number of amphibians and reptiles occur in
the diverse habitats of the study area including salamanders, frogs, toads,
snakes, and turtles. Five species of sea turtles are found in nearshore
Gulf waters. The coastal marshes, swamps, islands, and beaches of the
study area support large populations of passerine birds, waterfowl, wading
birds, and shore birds. Several active nesting sites are located within
the study area including an egret rookery on Petit Bois Island, a heron
rookery on Isle aux Herbes, and a large rookery on Cat Island to the east.
A number of marine mammals may be found within the study area including 3
species of whales, dolphins, and an occasional manatee. Coastal mammals
common to the area include squirrel, nutria, muskrat, white-tail deer,
raccoon and others.

4.2.4 **Endangered and Threatened Species.** In April, 1987, threatened and
endangered species information for the vicinity of Bayou La Batre was
requested from the Fish and Wildlife Service and the National Marine
Fisheries Service. The Fish and Wildlife Service has indicated that the
western population of the gopher tortoise (Gopherus polyphemus), a
threatened species, occurs from the Tombigbee and Mobile Rivers in Alabama
to southeastern Louisiana. Habitat for the gopher tortoise is well-
drained sandy soils in transitional areas and it is commonly associated
with a pine overstory with grass and forb groundcover and sunny areas for
nesting.

The National Marine Fisheries Service indicated that a number of threatened
and endangered species may occur off the coast of Alabama including: the
finback whale (Balaenoptera physalus), humpback whale (Megaptera
novaeangliae), sei whale (B. borealis), green sea turtle (Chelonia mydas),
Kemp's (Atlantic) ridley sea turtle (Lepidochelys kempi), leatherback sea
turtle (Dermochelys coriacea), and the loggerhead sea turtle (Caretta
caretta).

Finback whales are cosmopolitan and occur in all oceans. In the Gulf of
Mexico this species is present through the year and sightings at sea have
been recorded in the northern Gulf between 28 and 30 latitude and 86 and
88 longitude. Strandings have been recorded along Florida, Texas, and
Louisiana (Schmidly 1981). Humpback whales also occur in all oceans,
however prior to 1981 the only recent record for the Gulf of Mexico was in
April 1962 at the mouth of Tampa Bay (Layne 1965). Other sightings have
been in deep water (>200 meters) off the Alabama/Florida coast. Sei whales
strandings have been recorded from the coasts of Mississippi and Louisiana
in the vicinity of the Mississippi River Delta (Schmidly 1981).

Although marine turtles occasionally enter estuaries (Behler and King 1979), they generally prefer higher salinity waters such as those of the Gulf of Mexico. Nesting may occur throughout the range but most nesting occurs on restricted areas of beach that the turtles return to each nesting season. Foraging areas are often very far from nesting beaches and in order to nest, turtles may migrate long distances. Mating generally takes place in offshore waters near the nesting beach and males rarely come ashore (Fuller 1978).

Green turtles are most abundant between 35 north and 35 south latitudes, particularly in the Caribbean. Immature turtles are found along the Florida west coast (Carr and Caldwell, 1956) and have been known to nest on the barrier islands of the northern Gulf coast in the past.

Only a small portion of loggerhead nesting occurs in the Gulf. About 90 percent of the total nesting effort in the United States occurs on the south Atlantic coast of Florida (Carr and Carr 1977). Christmas and Waller (1973) reported loggerhead nestings on the beaches of the Mississippi Sound barrier islands. Ogren (1977) stated that historically the loggerhead nested on the remote beaches of Cat, Ship, Horn, Petit Bois, and Dauphin Islands. Human disturbance, natural predation, and island development have reduced the use of the barrier islands for nestings. Normally 1 to 2 loggerhead crawls are noted on the Mississippi barrier islands each year. One nesting attempt was noted on June 7, 1987, on east Ship Island which represents the only confirmed nesting attempt on the Mississippi Islands in the last four years (T. Simons personal communication).

The leatherback is probably the most oceanic of all sea turtles, preferring deep waters (Rebel 1974). It occasionally enters shallow waters and estuaries usually in the more northern waters of it's range (Barbour 1972). Leatherbacks are frequently seen in the Gulf of Mexico and are seasonally abundant off the Florida coast near Panama City (Pritchard 1976).

Kemp's ridley sea turtles are probably the most endangered of the sea turtles in the Gulf of Mexico. Their nesting is restricted to a small stretch of beach near Rancho Nuevo, Ramaulipas, Mexico. Immature ridley's are regularly encountered (strandings) in the Mississippi Sound and adjacent to the barrier islands (R. Smith, National Park Service). Ogren (personal communication) indicated that this species tends to congregate in shallow water vegetated areas within the estuaries.

4.2.5 **Air Quality.** Air quality for the entire state of Alabama is considered good. Recently problems with air quality in Bayou la Batre have arisen due to emissions from the seafood byproduct processing plant located near the southern end of the bayou. Efforts are underway to correct this problem.

4.2.6 **Water Quality.** Surface water quality in the study area is highly variable depending on several factors including nonpoint and point source municipal and industrial loadings and their respective quality, rainfall, urbanization and concentration, and degree of dilution and /or mixing with estuarine waters. The water quality of the study is generally classified

for recreation, fish and wildlife, and shellfish harvesting. However, the
bayou proper and nearshore Mississippi Sound have poor water quality due to
a currently malfunctioning sewage treatment facility, runoff from the
industrial yards, and activities associated with the fishing fleet. Due to
these degraded water quality conditions, especially elevated fecal coliform
bacteria counts, the bayou and adjacent waters are closed to shellfish
harvest.

The major problem with the sewage treatment facility is caused by
regulations that require the seafood processing houses to put process
waters into the sewage collection and treatment system. These waters are
characterized by extremely high biological oxygen demand and organic
content. When the houses are operating, the volume of water supplied to
the treatment system is in excess of design capacity. In an effort to
remedy this problem one private entity has constructed an outfall line into
Mississippi Sound for the process water from their facilities. A second
line is under construction which will be operated and maintained by the
City. This line has an interim design and ultimate load capacity of 2.3
and 7.2 million gallons, respectively. In addition to alternatives for
process waters, the City has recently awarded contracts for the upgrading
of the treatment facility with the addition of sludge drying beds.

A detailed discussion of water quality within Bayou La Batre, Mississippi
Sound, and the nearshore Gulf of Mexico is presented in the Existing
Conditions Section of the Main Report.

4.2.7 **Circulation.** Circulation patterns within the study are controlled
by astronomical tides, winds, and to a small degree freshwater discharge.
In Mississippi Sound and adjacent gulf waters the tidal variation is
diurnal with an average period of 24.8 hours. The effect of wind on
circulation in this area is significant not only in controlling circulation
patterns but also in affecting water surface elevation. Analysis of wind
records and sea level elevation for the period (1974-83) for coastal
Alabama indicated that the passage of winter cold fronts during October
through March caused significant perturbations in sea level (Schroeder and
Wiseman, 1985). As these fronts move through the area an abrupt reversal
of prefrontal conditions (southerly winds, falling barometric pressure, and
warm moist air) was noted. Most significant during and immediately after
passage is rising barometric pressure and wind direction shift to
northerly. The seas and sea level, set up by the prefrontal southerly
winds, are set down by the strong northerly winds and rising pressure.
Schroeder and Wiseman detected differences in sea level elevation between
prefrontal set up and post-frontal set down of 2.5 to 3.0 feet NGVD over
periods of 12 to 24 hours.

Water velocities range between 0 to 3 feet per second (fps) in the barrier
island passes and between 0 to 0.8 fps in the sound. Wave intensity on the
Alabama/Mississippi shelf is low to moderate with wave periods ranging from
three to eight seconds and wave heights rarely over 7 feet. Hurricane or
storm conditions, however, may produce larger waves (USACE, 1984).

4.2.8 Sediment Quality. Soils within the bayou portion of the project consist of inorganic clays of high plasticity, poorly-graded sands, sand-silt mixtures, and sandy-clay mixtures. In this area the upper 2 to 5 feet of material consists of very soft, black to dark gray clay. This material has the consistency of grease, a very high percentage of water by weight, and contains organic material in concentrations of 8 to 24% by weight. Most of the material below -18 MLLW in this area consists of higher quality soils including sands and sand-silt-clay mixtures. Soils within Mississippi Sound consist of inorganic clays of high plasticity, poorly graded sands, sand-clay mixtures, sand-silt mixtures, and inorganic clays of low to medium plasticity. Sands and sandy mixtures decrease greatly in significance from the mouth of the bayou southward for a distance of approximately 28,000 feet. Clays increase in significance along this reach and become dominant between 28,000 and 53,500 feet. Sandy material begins to show up in the soil profile in this area (8300 feet south of the Gulf Intracoastal Waterway) and becomes dominant through the tidal pass into the Gulf of Mexico. Firm to stiff clays are encountered throughout the channel at depths of -18 MLLW in the northern portion of the sound to -22 MLLW in the vicinity of the Gulf Intracoastal Waterway.

Past studies of sediments from within the bayou and in Mississippi Sound indicated highly variable concentrations of nutrients, heavy metals, high molecular hydrocarbons, and pesticides. Mercury, arsenic, copper, zinc, cadmium, and lead were found to occur in concentrations greater than crustal abundance. In addition pesticides such as chlordane, DDD, DDT, and dieldrin, and PCB's had been reported from the area. Toxicity and bioaccumulation studies were performed by the Environmental Protection Agency as part of this feasibility study. Results of these studies indicated that the toxicity of the samples tested were minimal and that bioaccumulation of contaminants by the organisms tested was not significantly different between reference and test animals. These studies indicate that the materials to be dredged from the proposed project are suitable from a contaminant standpoint for disposal in open water. (For more details see the Existing Conditions Section of the Main Report and Section 2 of Appendix D to the Main Report.

4.2.9 Groundwater Resources. The principal sources of groundwater in Mobile County are the Miocene-Pliocene and alluvial aquifers. Wells tapping the Miocene-Pliocene aquifer range in depth from 100 to 800 feet and produce water that is generally soft and low in dissolved solids. In some instances this water may contain excessive levels of iron and be sufficiently acidic to be corrosive. The alluvial aquifer produces water generally suitable for most uses but may contain excessive levels of iron and be corrosive. In areas close to Mississippi Sound water may have dissolved solids in excess of 1,000 mg/l, a sulfurous odor, and chlorides in excess of 500 mg/l (Reed and McCain, 1972). The City of Bayou La Batre water system currently has capacity of up to 2 million gallons per day supplied from wells. Process water for the seafood processing houses is normally supplied by individual wells, however city water may sometimes be used.

4.2.10 Land Resource and Use. Of the land area within the designated study area, approximately 4000 acres are non-forested wetland, 4100 acres are forested wetland, and 900 acres are forested uplands. Approximately 1610 acres are designated as developed/urbanized lands (U.S. Army Corps of Engineers, 1984). Much of the development in the Bayou La Batre area is centered around the bayou and it's tributaries.

The barrier islands of the northern Gulf of Mexico are in an erosion/deposition cycle which results in the westward migration of the islands through time. This is especially evident with Petit Bois Island. Early in the 18th Century, Dauphin and Petit Bois Islands were one island. In about 1848 the island was breached and Petit Bois Pass has widened and migrated westward since this time (Hardin et al., 1975). In addition the mainland shoreline, particularly in the Point aux Pins area and the shoreline of Isle aux Herbes experience significant erosion.

4.2.11 Demography. From the time of incorporation in 1955, bayou la Batre has maintained a relatively stable population except for the late 1970's and early 1980's. In 1984, the population of Bayou La Batre was 2,162 persons representing an increase of 9 percent over 1980 and a decrease of approximately 25 percent from 1970. This out-migration is probably due to a slump in the oil exploration industry. In addition, the City has not actively expanded it's limits to include much of the new housing within it's trade area.

4.2.12 Economy. Seafood harvesting and processing have traditionally been the primary source of employment and income for the area. Total annual employment is estimated to be 4500 persons. The major employers within the city include the ten major seafood processors (900 - 1200 annually), sixteen major shipbuilders (700 - 1000 annually), and an apparel manufacturer (500 annually). The remaining employment is in other marine related industries such as net making, trawl board manufacturing, outrigging, and small retail seafood houses.

In 1986, approximately 53.6 million pounds of seafood worth 100 million was handled at Bayou La Batre. Shipbuilding and vessel repair account for approximately 90 and 4 million annually. This represents sales of about 100 vessels a year and repairs to over 1000 vessels.

4.2.13 Community Cohesion. Two very generalized types of cohesion are exhibited by the citizens of the Bayou La Batre area. The first is a traditional type, based on long and cherished friendships, kinship ties, religious ties, and a sense of community developed out of many years of close interaction and interdependence. The second is much less important and is a more formalized economic type of cohesion.

4.2.14 Recreational Opportunities. The Alabama coast offers a diversity of recreational and cultural activities including fishing, hunting, boating, and beach activities. One public boat launching facility is currently under construction in the bayou.

4.2.15 **Noise.** Noise problems are those associated with day-to-day activities, such as traffic, construction, and shipbuilding. Noise levels are much higher in the vicinity of shipbuilding activities than in outlying areas.

4.2.16 **Aesthetics.** The aesthetic quality of the area ranges from excellent in the region of the barrier islands and Mississippi Sound to poor along the bayou proper. Much of the rest of the study area is variable in nature with well-kept residential neighborhoods to less aesthetically pleasing commercial areas.

4.2.17 **Transportation.** The Bayou La Batre area is supplied by Alabama State Highway 188 which connects with the Dauphin Island Parkway at Alabama Port to the east and US Highway 90 to the north and a number of small county maintained roads. The commercial air terminal at Mobile is approximately 30 miles north of the city and Interstate Highway 10 is approximately 20 north.

4.2.18 **Public Facilities and Services.** Alabama Power Company provides electricity to the study area from their generating plant on Blakeley Island, northeast of the city of Mobile. Water, sewer, and natural gas are supplied by the Utilities Board of Bayou La Batre. As discussed in Section 4.2.6 the existing sewage treatment facility is being upgraded.

4.2.19 **Cultural Resources.** The National Register of Historic Places has been consulted and there are no properties listed on or eligible for inclusion on the National Register that would be affected by the proposed navigation improvements. A number of locations within the general area of the proposed new disposal area have been surveyed and no archeological or historic properties were identified. As a result of consultations with the Alabama State Historic Preservation Officer, it was determined that the proposed new upland disposal area should be surveyed for cultural resources. The survey was conducted by Mobile District archeologists on September 2, 1988. No archeological sites or historic structures were identified. The Alabama State Historic Preservation Officer has concurred with the negative report of these investigations.

Documentary research conducted in 1986 to assess the potential for submerged properties along the Petit Bois Pass channel alignment revealed that there is very little potential for shipwrecks or other submerged properties in the vicinity of Bayou La Batre (Mistovich, 1987). The Alabama State Historic Preservation Officer has agreed that improving the Bayou La Batre channel through Petit Bois Pass will not affect cultural resources.

In 1983 documentary research for submerged cultural resources was conducted as part of the cultural resources investigations for the navigation improvements at Pascagoula Harbor, Mississippi. The Gulf Intracoastal Waterway (GIWW) alternative channel alignment in Alabama and Mississippi under consideration for the Bayou La Batre study was included in this literature search. The only reported wrecks identified in the vicinity of

the GIWW were recorded since 1950 (Mistovich, <u>et al</u>., 1983).   Thus, it is
believed that the potential for significant submerged cultural resources is
extremely low.   Consultation with the Mississippi and Alabama State
Historic Preservation Officers concerning the potential for effects to
submerged cultural resources along the GIWW channel alignment has been
initiated.

5.0 Environmental Effects. The following paragraphs describe the effects of each detailed plan on the previously described significant resources.

5.1 **Vegetation.** Under the "No Action" alternative any vegetation growing within existing disposal area Charlie would be impacted during maintenance activities every 3 years. Similar impacts would occur with implementation of each of the alternative plans. In addition approximately 107 acres of upland pine forest would be impacted during construction activities at new disposal area Delta with implementation of each of the alternative plans.

No emergent wetlands or submersed grass beds would be directly impacted by implementation of any of the alternatives. Implementation of plans I, V, X, and XV could indirectly affect the wetlands along the southern shore of Point aux Pins and the grassbeds along the eastern and western sides of the Point. These plans were formulated in an effort to utilize the new work material to be dredged from the Mississippi Sound Channel in a beneficial way by providing these areas with some measure of protection from the predominant wave approach. implementation of any of these plans would result in the construction of a fan-shaped emergent/submergent area south of the Point aux Pins/Isle aux Dames shoreline (See Figure EIS-4). Approximately 160 acres of emergent wetland habitat would be established as part of the protection for the existing resources. Adverse impacts to the existing vegetative resources could occur from the increased turbidity associated with the disposal operation however extensive efforts have been taken to reduce the possibility of these impacts and it is believed that the benefits associated with protecting existing resources and providing additional resources outweighs the possible costs.

Currently undeveloped wetland areas adjacent to the bayou could be impacted by water dependent development with or without the construction of the recommended plan. Approximately 6.8 acres of wetlands along the east bank below Station 108+00; 0.4 acre of wetlands along the west bank above Station 106+75, including Snake Bayou; and 5.9 acres on the west bank below Station 106+75 are expected to come under development within the life of the project (See Figure 10, Main Report). Development of these areas, either through dredging or filling, would require individual Department of the Army permits. Mitigation for the impacts associated with filling these wetlands would be determined on a case-by-case basis at the time of application. Other wetland areas along the bayou have been exempted from development consideration at this time. These areas are typically pristine in nature; some are remote from the bayou and therefore not suitable for water dependent industry; and some serve as natural drainageways. Future development of these areas would be based on the need for the proposed development as well as the lack of practicable alternatives sites.

Implementation of any of alternative plans II, III, VI, VII, XI, XII, XV, or XVI would provide some protection to the wetland habitats along the eastern shore of Isle aux Herbes (See Figures EIS-5 and EIS-6). Implementation of any of these plans would not conflict with marsh establishment efforts associated with the long-term maintenance of the Bayou Coden Channel. Alternatives II, VI, XI, or XVI would provide protection for approximately 6,000 linear feet of shoreline while alternatives III, VII, XII, or XVI would provide protection for approximately 9,500 linear feet of shoreline. Implementation of these alternatives would not provide additional emergent wetland habitat.

5.2 Aquatic Resources. Under the "No Action" alternative, the macroinfaunal resources of the channel bottoms would continue to be disrupted by dredging on a 3 year cycle. In addition, the resources of the 4 shallow water disposal areas would be covered with 1 - 1.5 feet of dredged material (see Figure EIS-1). Although many of the organisms would be smothered, some would be able to migrate through this material. Other forms would migrate into the area or settle as larvae from the overlying water column such that repopulation of these areas would occur within 12 to 18 months. Motile aquatic resources such as shrimp, crabs and fish would tend to avoid the area where dredging and disposal options were ongoing. Larval and young age class aquatic organisms may become entrained during the dredging and disposal process due to their inability to avoid the area of operation. The degree of these impacts would vary with the location and temporal setting of the operations. Impacts would be expected to be most severe in spring/summer in the nearshore areas of Mississippi Sound. The impacts to the overall fishery of Mississippi Sound however, are unknown. No oyster resources are impacted under this alternative.

Dredging and disposal associated with the proposed navigation improvements would cause many of the same impacts described for the "No Action" alternative. Construction dredging within the Bayou Channel segment would result in the disruption of approximately 2.6 and 1.5 acres of undisturbed bottoms above the Highway 188 bridge and in Snake Bayou, respectively. Similar to the "No Action" alternative these bottoms and the 29 acres of bottoms encompassed by the existing project would continue to be disrupted every 3 years following construction. Within Mississippi Sound south to the GIWW, approximately 200 acres would be dredged. Of these 100 acres are currently disrupted during maintenance of the existing project. Dredging would result in the deepening of the bottoms to 18 feet, however since the open sound muddy sand habitat ranges from 6 feet to deeper than 18 feet there would be no change in habitat type. The major impact would be with the actual disruption, however the area should repopulate within 12 to 18 months and since the acreage is small in comparison to the total habitat available these impacts are not considered significant. These impacts are common to all plans considered in detail.

Alternative plans I - IX would result in the dredging of approximately 140 acres between the GIWW, through Petit Bois Pass to the 21-foot contour in the Gulf of Mexico. This area is naturally variable in depth and since the benthic community is controlled primarily by sediment texture and salinity no change in community structure is expected with depth increase. The major impact would be with the actual disruption, however the area should repopulate within 12 to 18 months and since the acreage is small in comparison to the total habitat available these impacts are not considered significant.

Alternative plans X - XVIII would result in the dredging of approximately 160 acres of bottoms in Mississippi Sound which currently range in depth from 16 to 18 feet. No change in community structure would occur with implementation of any of these alternatives. The major impact would be with the actual disruption, however the area should repopulate within 12 to 18 months and since the acreage is small in comparison to the total habitat available these impacts are not considered significant.

The disposal of approximately 1.3 million cubic yards of new work material from the Mississippi Sound Channel segment as proposed in plans I, V, X, and XV would result in the conversion of approximately 260 acres of shallow bottoms south of Point aux Pins/Isle aux Dames shoreline to emergent wetlands. The disposal of the remaining new work material would be disposed into waters greater of 12 feet deep which are characterized as open sound muddy sands. Construction of a submerged berm would convert approximately 130 acres to bottoms approximately 6 feet shallower. Since open sound muddy sand habitats are located in depths of 6 feet to greater than 18 feet there would be no change in habitat type. Construction of the berm could conflict with shrimp trawling in the area and could possibly result in a hazard to navigation.

Direct placement of the new work dredged material in areas approximately 2500 feet west of the channel would cover approximately 600 acres with a layer of dredged material approximately 2 feet thick. Some benthic organisms would be capable of migrating through 2 feet of dredged material, however most would be smothered. Studies have indicated that these communities are able to recover through migration and settlement of larvae within 12 to 18 months.

Thin layer disposal of the new work material would utilize approximately 750 acres with a final placement thickness of 1-foot or less. A larger number of benthic organisms are capable of migrating through a thinner layer of dredged such as that produced during thin layer disposal. Studies at Fowl River, Alabama and Gulfport, Mississippi indicate that recovery from thin layer deposition begins as early as 6 weeks after disposal operations were completed and that within 20 weeks there are no significant difference between disposal and reference areas (TAI, 1987,1988).

The disposal of approximately 1.3 million cubic yards of new work material from the Mississippi Sound Channel segment as proposed in plans II, VI, XI, and XVI would impact approximately 160 acres of shallow bottoms along the northeast shoreline of Isle aux Herbes. Of this area, approximately 60 acres would be converted to emergent bar while the remainder would become intertidal to shallow submerged in nature. The 2700 barrels of oyster shell planted along the northeast shore of the island would be relocated to deeper water in Portersville Bay. The disposal of the remaining new work material would occur in areas of Mississippi Sound with depths of 12 feet or more. The impacts associated with this portion of these alternatives would be similar to those described above for alternative plans I, V, X, XV.

The disposal of approximately 2 million cubic yards of new work material from the Mississippi Sound channel segment as proposed in plans III, VII, XII, XVII would impact approximately 240 acres of shallow bottoms along the northeast shoreline of Isle aux Herbes. Of this area, approximately 90 acres would be converted to emergent bar while the remainder would become intertidal to shallow submerged in nature. The 2700 barrels of oyster shell planted along the northeast shore of the island would be relocated to deeper water in Portersville Bay.

Alternative plans III, VII, XII, or XVII require the disposal of approximately 2 million cubic yards of new work material into areas of Mississippi Sound with depths of 12 feet or greater. Construction of a submerged berm with this material would convert approximately 240 acres to bottoms approximately 6 feet shallower. Since open sound muddy sand habitats are located in depths of 6 feet to greater than 18 feet there would be no change in habitat type. Direct placement of the dredged material in areas approximately 2500 feet west of the channel would cover approximately 1100 acres with a layer of dredged material 2 feet or less. Thin layer disposal would impact approximately 1400 acres with a final placement thickness of 1-foot or less. Recovery would be similar to that described for similar options in alternative plans II, VI, XI, XVI, however in the center of the disposal areas recovery may be somewhat slower due to the distance organisms would be required to migrate to these areas. Settlement of larvae from the water column should not be impacted by the size of the area impacted. Recovery may also be slowed compared to that described above due to the length of time required to complete construction of the channel with all disposal occurring in open water, i.e. 6 months vs. 3 months.

Implementation of alternative plans I thru IX and XIV would result in the disruption of an unknown acreage of bottoms within the Mobile North or Pascagoula Ocean Dredged Material Disposal Sites (ODMDS), respectively. The severity and duration of these impacts are not well known however historical use of this sites has not resulted in unacceptable impacts to the human environment.

Disposal of maintenance material dredged from the Mississippi Sound Channel segment involves deposition of approximately 430,000 cubic yards on a 3 year cycle. This material would be placed in waters greater than 12 feet in areas 2,500 feet west of the channel. Direct placement of the maintenance material would impact approximately 330 acres along the channel with dredged material approximately 2 feet thick. Placing the material in a thickness of 1-foot or less would impact about 415 acres. The impacts of these operations would be similar to those described for open water new work disposal, however due to the nature of the maintenance material a greater number of organisms would be expected to migrate through the dredged material. Studies have shown that benthic systems are able to recover from pertubations such as dredged material disposal within from as little as 6 weeks to as much as 18 months. This recovery period is highly dependent upon the level of disturbance, time of disturbance, and most importantly the type of benthic community being disturbed. In addition, during the period of recovery, the productivity from an area is still available to the estuarine system and the level of productivity from an area may shift during this recovery period. After disuturbance of an area, early stage succession typically begins within a few days with the arrival of swimming crustaceans (i.e., amphipods and cumaceans) and more motile polychaetes and echinoderms (i.e., nereids and nephtyids and large ophiuroids) which immigrate into the disturbed area as adults from adjacent areas. More importantly however, the larvae of relatively opportunistic polychaetes and bivalve molluscs settle onto the new substratum from the overlying water column. These opportunistic species (Group I colonizers, McCall 1978) are characterized by short generation times, small size, high fecundity, and high larval availability. These species most commonly experience high mortality and may disappear as a result of competition and/or predation from the more motile immigrants. Later phases of succession are usually characterized by the gradual reestablishment of Group III species which are represented by the less mobile crustaceans, molluscs, and less opportunistic polychaetes. These species, in contrast to Group I colonizers, maintain more or less constant, relatively low population densities, are usually larger in size and exhibit lower fecundity and recruitment potential. Group II colonizers are intermediate in their life strategies.

Information collected during the Mississippi Sound and Adjacent Areas Study (Vittor and Associates 1982) indicates that in the areas generally considered for open water disposal of dredged material only Group I and II colonizers are present. Based on this information recovery in the areas in question would be relatively rapid and that the overall impact to the benthic system would be short-term and that the disposal of dredged materials on a three year cycle at these areas would not result in significant impacts to the estuarine system.

Construction of the channel through Petit Bois Pass requires dredging of approximately 872,000 cubic yards of new work material and approximately 525,000 cubic yards of maintenance material on an 18 month frequency. Deposition of new work material in the littoral zone of Petit Bois Island as described in plans I, II, III, and IV would impact an unquantifiable acreage of clean sand tidal pass habitat, however the organisms which inhabit these areas are adapted to very variable environmental conditions including wave and storm transport of sediments. In addition the placement of material into the littoral zone would act to continue the supply of sand to Petit Bois. Deposition of new work material in the Mobile North ODMDS as described in alternative plans V, VI, VII, VIII, and IX would result in the disruption of the benthic community occupying the disposal area. Historical use of similar ODMDS for placement of sandy material has not resulted in unacceptable impacts. Deposition of maintenance material (all plans considered in detail) would occur on a rotating basis between the littoral zone and ODMDS therefore impacts would occur to each area every three years.

Alternative plans X, XI, XII, and XIII consider the deposition of new work material dredged from the GIWW Channel segment in areas 5000 feet south of the channel. Direct placement of this material would impact approximately 330 acres of open sound muddy bottoms. Thin layer deposition of this material would impact approximately 400 acres. The impacts to the benthic resources and their recovery would be similar to that described for open water disposal associated with the Mississippi Sound Channel segment.

Alternative plan XIV considers transportation of the new work material to the Pascagoula ODMDS in conjunction with material from Mississippi Sound. These impacts have been described above. Placement of the new work material in areas 10,000 feet south of the channel (littoral zone) as considered in alternatives XV, XVI, XVII, and XVIII would result in impacts similar to those described for open water disposal and for littoral zone disposal. Disposal of maintenance material from the GIWW segment (plans X thru XVIII) would impact 70 to 90 acres approximately 5,000 feet south the channel utilizing direct placement or thin layer placement, respectively. Impacts associated with this action would be similar to those described earlier for open water disposal of maintenance material and would occur on a three year cycle.

Due to the narrow bank-to-bank confines of the bayou in the upper reaches and the existing waterfront development, there are only about 3.5 acres of shallow waterbottoms (less than 4 feet MLW) in the bayou above Station 106+75 (See Main Report, Plates 1, 2, and 3 for station locations). Approximately 7 acres of shallow water habitat is located adjacent to the west bank below Station 106+75. Repair or replacement of existing bulkheads and construction of additional bulkheads for property protection associated with the improvement of the channel would not impact these resources. Future development, however, could result in the dredging or filling of these areas for water dependent industry. Due to the highly industrialized and confined nature of the bayou, these activities would not result in significant impacts to the aquatic resources of Mississippi Sound.

None of the plans considered in detail would impact any native oyster reefs, aquatic mammals, or reptiles.

Implementation of any of the alternative plans, although increasing efficiencies associated with the commercial fishing industry, is not expected to impact fishery resources of the Gulf of Mexico because of existing regulations promulgated by the Gulf of Mexico Fishery Management Council and State agencies. The development of the butterfish industry is an effort to tap a known resource in the Gulf. Should this industry prove profitable Gulfwide regulations may be required as have been proposed for the Atlantic butterfish.

5.3 **Wildlife Resources.** Under the "No Action" alternative, those wildlife species utilizing the existing upland disposal site would be impacted on a 3 year basis during maintenance of the existing project.

In addition to the impacts associated with the "No Action" alternative, implementation of any of the plans considered in detail would.impact wildlife resources utilizing the proposed upland disposal area. These species would be displaced from the 107 acres, however there is adjacent acreage available in which they may relocate.

5.4 **Endangered and Threatened Species.** The "No Action" alternative would not impact any endangered or threatened species.

Endangered species coordination was initiated in April 1987. Lists of endangered and threatened species which may occur in the study area have been received from the US Fish and Wildlife Service (dated April 20, 1987) and the National Marine Fisheries Service (dated May 1, 1987). As required under Section 7 of the Endangered Species Act of 1973, as amended, the DEIS constituted the biological assessment.

The Fish and Wildlife Service indicated that the gopher tortoise (Gopherus polyphemus), which was at that time proposed for listing, could occur in the study area. Since the receipt of their letter this species has been listed as threatened. Habitat for the gopher tortoise is well-drained sandy soils in transitional (forest and grassy) areas and it is commonly associated with a pine overstory and open understory with a grass and forb groundcover and sunny areas for nesting. The proposed upland disposal area has soils of the Escambia series which consist of somewhat poorly drained soils with a highly weathered mixture of clay with quartz and other diluents formed from loamy marine sediments and therefore does not meet the habitat requirements of this species. No further consultation under the Endangered Species Act is required, unless circumstances relative to the recommended plan change. The Fish and Wildlife Service has concurred with this determination (See Appendix D, Section 6).

The National Marine Fisheries Service indicated that three species of whales and four species of marine turtles may be present in the study area. As indicated in Section 4.2.4 of this FEIS, whales are primarily restricted to open gulf waters and therefore would not be impacted by implementation of the recommended plan. Sea turtles may occur within the Mississippi Sound and may nest on the gulf beaches of the barrier islands as indicated in Section 4.2.4. Of prime importance is the Kemp's (Atlantic) ridley turtle which is considered to be the most endangered of the species listed for this area. This turtle is known from the Mississippi Sound and is typically associated with shallow vegetated habitats. The recommended plan does not require dredging or disposal near any shallow vegetated habitats therefore no impacts to this species are expected to occur. The other species occur less frequently within the sound and therefore would not be impacted by the proposed action. The National Marine Fisheries Service, by letter dated September 13, has concurred with the no impact assessment. No further consultation under the Endangered Species Act is required, unless circumstances relative to the recommended plan change.

5.5 **Air Quality.** For the "No Action" alternative the existing air quality within the project area would remain unchanged. The activities associated with dredging or disposal in all alternative plans would temporarily reduce local air quality levels due to exhaust emissions of the equipment used. The construction of the dikes around the new disposal area Delta would also temporarily reduce air quality in these areas due to exhaust emissions. These impacts are considered to be insignificant and would be limited to the immediate construction area. Any induced development into the area by the project improvement would be subject to State and Federal regulatory procedures to control emissions and protect the air quality.

5.6 **Water Quality.** For the "No Action" alternative, the existing water

quality within the project area would remain the same or possibly improve
in some areas while declining in other areas in the future. The completion
of the seafood processing wash water outfall line and the upgrading of the
sewage facility are expected to result in improvements in water quality.
Open water disposal at the existing sites in Mississippi Sound would result
in temporary localized increased in turbidity and nutrients and decreased
in dissolved oxygen within the water column. Continued use of sites 7, 8,
or 9 could result in shallowing of these areas with subsequent impacts to
circulation and water quality (Figure EIS-1).

Return waters from existing disposal area Charlie cause temporary localized
increases in turbidity and nutrients and decreases in dissolved oxygen
within the water column in the vicinity of the outfall. Short term
localized effects of this nature would also be present at the dredge
cutterhead during maintenance operations.

The impact of disposal of sediments from the Bayou la Batre channels in
open water on marine organisms has been evaluated by the Environmental
Protection Agency (1988) following standard toxicity and bioaccumulation
procedures. Results of these evaluations indicate that the toxicity of the
materials proposed for disposal are minimal. In addition residues of
selected pesticides and PCB's were not detected in either sediments or
animal tissue before or after exposure. Some heavy metals were detected,
especially in sediments from the bayou proper and organisms exposed to
these sediments. Petroleum hydrocarbon residues were also detected in
tissue samples from organisms exposed to sediments, however levels were not
significantly different from organisms not exposed to the sediments.

Use of the upland disposal sites for materials from the Bayou Channel
segment would have similar impacts to the "No Action" alternative. The
return water from the new upland disposal and existing disposal area
Charlie would cause short term localized impacts on turbidity, nutrient
concentrations, and dissolved oxygen levels within the water column in the
vicinity of the outfalls. Short term localized effects of this nature
would also be present at the dredge cutterhead. Although sediments from
the bayou portion of the project have been shown to contain varying levels
of contaminants, these sediments do not produce unacceptable toxic impacts
to marine organisms.

The disposal of new work and maintenance materials within open water sites
in Mississippi Sound would result in short term increases in turbidity and
nutrients and decreases in dissolved oxygen. These impacts would be
localized to the vicinity of the disposal areas and would be rapidly
dissipated with increasing distance from tne discharge point. The
increases in turbidity expected are well within the natural range of
turbidity experienced in the Mississippi Sound area. Similar impacts would
be expected to occur within the vicinity of the dredge cutterhead. As
indicated above no toxic impacts would result from the deposition of these
materials. The disposal in open water areas greater than 12 feet deep on
the western side of the Mississippi Sound channel and south of the GIWW
channel have been evaluated following the Sec 404(b)(1) Guidelines and this
evaluation is included in Appendix D to the Main Report. State water

quality certification, under Section 401 of the Clean Water Act, will be obtained prior to any discharge of dredged material in open waters of Mississippi Sound.

Disposal of materials in the Mobile North or Pascagoula ODMDS would probably not result in significant impacts to water quality. Short term increases in turbidity and nutrient levels would be expected to occur in the vicinity of the dump zone. Decreases in near bottom dissolved oxygen levels would probably occur in this zone as well. Due to the depths within these sites mounding is not expected to pose a problem.
Improvements to the channel as proposed in alternatives I – IX could result in a wedge of salt water moving landward in the channel and possibly impacting groundwater resources. Implementation of any of alternatives X – XVIII would not be expected to have this impact since a direct channel into the higher salinity waters of the Gulf of Mexico would not be constructed.

5.7 **Circulation.** Circulation patterns in the area are controlled primarily by astronomical tides. Under the "No Action" alternative changes in circulation of the nearshore region could occur with continued use of open water disposal sites 7, 8, or 9 (Figure EIS-1).

Dredging within the bayou would have no impact on circulation. Deepening and widening the channels within Mississippi Sound could cause slight changes in velocities within the channels themselves but these changes are not considered significant. Provision of a channel through Petit Bois Pass in alternative plans I – IX could have a significant effect on circulation structure within the pass. Additional studies would be required to determine the magnitude of these impacts.

Direct placement of new work material adjacent to the Mississippi Sound Channel segment, as proposed in alternatives I, II, IV, V, VI, VIII, X, XI, XIII, XV, XVI, and XVIII could cause localized impacts on circulation. Evidence of this type impact has been observed at Pascagoula, Mississippi, where new work material mounded and consolidated causing shallowing of the bottoms. Since disposal is planned for areas greater than 12 feet in depth, areas which are remote from the mainland shoreline, these impacts should not cause significant changes in existing circulation patterns.

Disposal of maintenance materials within Mississippi Sound as proposed in all the alternatives would have no significant impact on circulation. Studies done during the Mississippi Sound and Adjacent Areas Study (USACE, 1984) indicate that circulation is predominately toward the west in this area therefore all disposal areas have been located west of the Mississippi Sound Channel segment and Petit Bois Pass Channel segment.

Disposal of new work material from the Mississippi Sound Channel segment or the GIWW Channel segment or new work and maintenance material from the Petit Bois Pass Channel segment in either the Mobile North or Pascagoula ODMDS would have no impact on circulation of the nearshore Gulf of Mexico.

5.8 **Sediment Quality.** Clay sediments, similar to those present in the Bayou La Batre study area, have a high capacity for retaining pollutants discharged into the water column. Removal of these sediments and their bound contaminants during dredging would improve the sed.ment quality, especially within the bayou proper. This enhancement occurs under the "No Action" alternative and would continue with implementation of any of the alternative plans. Although contaminants have been shown to be present in the sediments of Bayou La Batre, the potential for toxic effects to marine organisms or bioaccumulation within these organisms is low.

All of the alternatives considered in detail would result in a large quantity of both new work and maintenance material from the bayou proper being placed in upland disposal areas.

Gulf disposal of materials in alternative plans IX and XIV would have no effect on the resources of the ODMDS.

5.9 **Groundwater Resources.** Under the "No Action" alternative groundwater resources in the area would continue to be highly variable. Some increase in demand would be expected as seafood processors continue and expand the practice of trucking shrimp from other states to their houses for processing. The lands adjacent to the bayou are already highly developed and undeveloped areas are in short supply. Future development of these areas for water dependent industry, therefore, would be expected to occur with or without the project.

Improvements to the channel as proposed in alternatives I -IX could result in a wedge of salt water moving landward in the channel and possibly impacting groundwater resources. Implementation of any of alternatives X - XVIII would not be expected to have this impact since a direct channel into the higher salinity waters of the Gulf of Mexico would not be constructed. Increased efficiency at existing seafood processors would occur, however, increased use of the resource is expected without the project since the seafood processors currently truck additional shrimp to their facilities for processing.

5.10 **Land Resource and Use.** All plans could induce further growth in the Bayou La Batre area. Currently undeveloped wetland areas adjacent to the bayou could be impacted by water dependent development induced by the improved project. Approximately 6.8 acres of wetlands along the east bank below Station 108+00; 0.4 acre of wetlands along the west bank above Station 106+75, including Snake Bayou; and 5.9 and 7.0 acres of wetlands and shallow water bottoms, respectively, on the west bank below Station 106+75 are expected to come under development within the life of the project (See Figure 10, Main Report). Development of these areas, either through dredging or filling, would require individual Department of the Army permits. Mitigation for the impacts associated with filling these wetlands would be determined on a case-by-case basis at the time of application. Other wetland areas along the bayou have been exempted from development consideration at this time. These areas are typically pristine in nature; some are remote from the bayou and therefore not suitable for water dependent industry; and some serve as natural drainage ways. Future development of these areas would be based on the need for the proposed development as well as the lack of practicable alternatives sites.

Implementation of plans I, V, X, or XV would tend to alleviate the erosion of the Point aux Pins area. This area, which has been shown to have an erosion rate of approximately 6.7 feet per year contains extensive wetland and submersed vegetative resources.

Implementation of plans II, VI, XI, or XVI and III, VII, XII, or XVII would tend to alleviate the erosion of the eastern shoreline of Isle aux Herbes. Plans II, VI, XI, or XVI would provide protection to approximately 4,500 feet of shoreline while plans III, VII, XII, or XVII would provide protection to approximately 9,500 feet of shoreline. Like the Point aux Pins area, Isle aux Herbes contains extensive wetland resources which are currently being eroded by natural forces.

Implementation of plans I through IX would provide a sediment source to the eastern end of Petit Bois Island, however provision of the channel through Petit Bois Pass in these same plans could disrupt the natural littoral drift of sediments from Dauphin Island to the east. In addition, Petit Bois Pass is located within the Dauphin Islands Coastal Barrier Resources System Unit. Provision of a channel through this area is in conflict with the management activities of the Coastal Barrier Resources Act and additional coordination would be required prior to any construction in this area.

5.11 **Demography.** None of the plans considered in detail would have a significant impact on the demographic characteristics of the area.

5.12 **Economy.** Under the "No Action" alternative the economy would be expected to fluctuate in response to factors affecting the commercial fishing industry, shipbuilding, and the oil industry. Since the economy of Bayou La Batre is almost totally dependent upon fishing and shipbuilding implementation of any of the alternative plans would enhance the economic outlook for the area.

5.13 **Community Cohesion.** None of the plans considered in detail would have an effect on community cohesion.

5.14 **Recreational Opportunities.** Under the "No Action" alternative recreational opportunities would continue to be available. Implementation of any of the proposed plans would not impact recreational opportunities.

5.15 **Noise.** For the "No Action" alternative the existing noise levels in the project area would remain the same. Construction and maintenance of any of the alternative plans considered in detail would cause elevated background noise levels due to the equipment used. The elevated noise levels would be of a temporary nature and since much of the area is highly developed in nature or removed from inhabited areas the elevated noise levels should not be significant. There would be no long-term noise impact on wildlife.

5.16 **Aesthetics.** Under the "No Action" alternative the aesthetics of the area would remain in a similar condition to that existing currently. The presence of the dredge and attendant equipment would continue to cause a temporary degradation in aesthetics during each 3 year maintenance cycle. Implementation of any of the alternative plans would have similar impacts to the "No Action" alternative and would tend to enhance aesthetics in the immediate area of the bayou due to the requirement of bulkhead replacement for those currently in dilapidated condition. Use of the new disposal area would change that area from pine forest to disposal area, however with proper management of the facility the area can be aesthetically neutral.

5.17 **Transportation.** Under the "No Action" alternative transportation into Bayou La Batre would continue to be restricted by the 12-foot channel. Implementation of any of the alternatives would greatly enhance waterborne transportation into the port. Other transportation facilities would not be adversely affected by any of the plans.

5.18 **Public Facilities and Services.** Public facilities and services in Bayou La Batre would not be adversely affected by any of the plans considered in detail.

5.19 **Cultural Resources.** As stated in paragraph 4.2.19, the new proposed upland disposal site was inspected for cultural resources in September 1988. No archeological sites or historic structures were identified within the area. The Alabama State Historic Preservation Officer has concurred that the use of the proposed upland site would have no effect to cultural resources within this area. Implementation of any of the alternative plans would have no effect on submerged cultural resources in Alabama and Mississippi (See Appendix D, Section 8).

6.0 **Summary of mitigation measures.** Throughout the planning for the navigation improvements for Bayou La Batre, efforts have been made to incorporate "mitigation" into the project. As defined in the CEQ's Regulations for Implementing the Procedural Provisions of the National Environmental Policy Act (NEPA), "mitigation" includes: (a) avoiding the impact altogether by not taking a certain action or parts of an action; (b) minimizing impacts by limiting the degree or magnitude of the action and its implementation; (c) rectifying the impact by repairing, rehabilitating, or restoring the affected environment; (d) reducing or eliminating the impact over time by preservation and maintenance operations during the life of the action; (e) compensating for the impact by replacing or providing substitute resources or environments (40 CFR 1500- 1508). Paragraph 6.1 summarizes measures which have been incorporated into the design of the project to enhance the environment or minimize impacts.

6.1 As a result of past coordination efforts with the Federal and state environmental agencies in which they stressed the importance of shallow estuarine bottoms to the productivity of the estuarine system, all plan formulation efforts associated with open water disposal were restricted to waters greater than 12 feet in depth. In addition plans were developed which maximized the use of upland disposal areas for both new work and maintenance materials.

Beneficial use of the new work dredged material was also considered a high priority during the formulation process. Although limited in quantity compared to maintenance materials the construction material has characteristics which would allow mounding in terms of berm construction or ease of containment for wetland creation.

6.2 As a result of these efforts impacts to significant resources due to the recommended plan have been minimized through planning and avoidance. Remaining impacts have been determined to be negligible therefore no mitigation is proposed.

7.0 List of Preparers

Name	Expertise	Experience	Role in FEIS Preparation
G. Ashford	Engineering, Environmental	5 years, Compliance Mobile District District	Environmental Compliance Manager
D. Gibbens	Archeology	5 years, Cultural Resource Mgmt. Mobile District	Effects on Cultural Resources
K. Graham	Landscape Architect	16 years, Study Management, Mobile District	Study Manager, Formulation of Alternatives
W. Mears	Engineering, Civil	10 years, Planning Engineering, Operations, Mobile District	Formulation of Alternatives
D. Nester	Biology	10 years, EIS Studies, Mobile District	Effects on Water Quality
S. Ivester Rees	Oceanography	6 years, Assistant Professor, Univ. Alabama, 7 years EIS Studies, Mobile District	EIS Coordinator

8.0 Public Involvement

8.1 **Public Involvement Program.** A history of public involvement is
discussed in the Main Report and in Appendix A to the Main Report.

8.2 **Required Coordination.** Coordination for this study began in February
1984. Principal Federal agencies with which coordination has been
conducted include the Fish and Wildlife Service, National Marine Fisheries
Service, Gulf of Mexico Fishery Management Council, Gulf Islands National
Seashore (National Park Service) and Environmental Protection Agency. At
the State level coordination has been through the Alabama State Historic
Preservation Officer, Alabama Department of Conservation and Natural
Resources, Division of Marine Resources and Alabama Department of
Environmental Management. Additional coordination is required with the
State of Mississippi Department of Wildlife Conservation, Bureau of Marine
Resources, Mississippi Department of Natural Resources, Bureau of Pollution
Control, and Mississippi State Historic Preservation Officer.

8.3 **Statement Recipients.** This FEIS is being sent to the following:

Governor Guy Hunt
Senator Howell Heflin
Senator Richard Shelby
Representative H. L. 'Sonny' Callahan

Governor Ray Mabius

Advisory Council on Historic Preservation
Federal Highway Administration
Food and Drug Administration
Heritage Conservation and Recreation Service
Department of Interior
   Fish and Wildlife Service
   National Park Service
Department of Commerce
   National Marine Fisheries Service
Department of Transportation
   Coast Guard
Department of Health and Human Services
Department of Energy
Department of Housing and Urban Development
Soil Conservation Service
Environmental Protection Agency
Federal Maritime Commission
Federal Highway Administration
Federal Aviation Administration
Federal Railroad Administration
Federal Emergency Management Administration
Forest Service

Alabama-Mississippi Sea Grant Consortium

Alabama Department of Environmental Management
Alabama Department of Conservation and Natural Resources
Alabama Department of Economic and Community Affairs
Alabama State Conservationist
Alabama Forestry Commission
Alabama State Historic Preservation Officer
Geological Survey of Alabama
Dauphin Island Sea Lab

Mississippi Department of Natural Resources
Mississippi Department of Wildlife Conservation
Mississippi Department of Archives and History
State Conservation Service
Gulf Coast Research Laboratory

Public Interests

8.4 The major comments received on the DEIS are concerned with the following topics:

Detailed design of the disposal plan for the proposed Isle aux Herbes disposal area.

Long-term impacts associated with open water disposal.

Possible conflict with the long-term management plan for the Bayou Coden channel.

The non-selection of Isle aux Herbes Option B as the tentatively selected plan.

Development of currently undeveloped areas adjacent to Bayou La Batre.

All comments have been appropriately responded to and necessary changes have been made to the text of the EIS as specifically indicated in the Public Views and Responses Section (paragraph 8.5).

8.5 Public Views and Responses. A total of eleven letters of comment were received concerning the DEIS. Copies of these letters follow. Comments were received from the following:

<table>
<tr><td></td><td>FEIS Page Number
of Letter</td></tr>
<tr><td>U. S. Department of the Interior</td><td>EIS-47</td></tr>
<tr><td>U. S. Environmental Protection Agency</td><td>EIS-53</td></tr>
<tr><td>U. S. Department of Commerce
National Ocean Survey
National Oceanic and Atmospheric Administration</td><td>EIS-58</td></tr>
<tr><td>U. S. Department of Health and Human Services,
Public Health Service, Centers for Disease Control</td><td>EIS-67</td></tr>
<tr><td>U. S. Department of Housing and Urban Development</td><td>EIS-69</td></tr>
<tr><td>U. S. Department of Transportation,
Federal Highway Administration</td><td>EIS-71</td></tr>
<tr><td>Alabama Department of Environmental Management</td><td>EIS-73</td></tr>
<tr><td>Alabama Department of Economic and Community Affairs</td><td>EIS-76</td></tr>
<tr><td>Alabama Historical Commission</td><td>EIS-79</td></tr>
<tr><td>State of Alabama Highway Department</td><td>EIS-81</td></tr>
<tr><td>South Alabama Regional Planning Commission</td><td>EIS-84</td></tr>
</table>

United States Department of the Interior

OFFICE OF ENVIRONMENTAL PROJECT REVIEW
RICHARD B. RUSSELL FEDERAL BUILDING, SUITE 1320
75 SPRING STREET, S.W.
ATLANTA, GEORGIA 30303

SEP 2 1988

ER-88/679

Colonel Larry Bonine
District Engineer
U,S, Army Corps of Engineers
Post Office Box 2288
Mobile, Alabama 36628-0001

Dear Colonel Bonine:

We have reviewed the Draft Environmental Statement and Feasibility Report
for Navigation Improvement at Bayou La Batre, Mobile County, Alabama, and
have the following comments,

General Comments

The Draft Environmental Impact Statement (EIS) and Feasibility Report provide
a satisfactory discussion of the fish and wildlife resources within the
project area and, except for a few points, the expected impacts of the
various proposed alternatives, However, we have concerns regarding the
chosen dredged material disposal option,

In March of 1988, the Daphne, Alabama, Fish and Wildlife Service (Service)   1
Field Office, forwarded to the Corps of Engineers a draft Fish and Wildlife
Coordination Act report addressing the proposed impact area and project
alternatives, The Service also related concerns that the disposal of dredged
material should be conducted in a manner that minimizes impacts to fish and
wildlife resources and encouraged investigation into the possibility of
utilizing the dredged material to benefit fish and wildlife resources,

Specific Comments

Page 90, Part F; paragraph 1 - There should be a discussion of the
possibility of dredged material directly covering the marsh, - A buffer zone
has been considered and should be described in this section, Elsewhere in
the EIS (Fig, 5 and 6), it appears that the dike would meet the island at   2
both ends which would defeat plans for tidal flushing of the area,
Additionally, a discussion should be included of potential impacts to the
marsh if the Bayou Coden maintenance material and marsh-establishment efforts
are completed prior to improvement of the Bayou La Batre channel,

Page 90, Part F; paragraph 2 - The chance of significant intertidal flow
within the diked area would be minimal if the dike meets the existing marsh   3
at both ends, The dike should be opened at the south end to provide tidal
influx,

<u>Page 90, Part F; paragraph 5</u> - It should be recognized that long-term impacts to benthic invertebrates would occur, Though the area of disposal would recolonize to a certain extent within 18 months, every 3 years periodic maintenance dredging would redisturb 500 acres of the 600 acres of waterbottoms that would be covered; i,e,, for only 12 months of every 3 years would the benthic population be stable, Consequently, it would be at least 50 years before the benthic population of the waterbottom would be able to return to preproject conditions,

4

It should also be noted that the referenced studies were conducted on maintenance material and may not be applicable to new work dredged material,

5

<u>Pages EIS-49 and EIS-50</u> - Figures EIS-5 and EIS-6 illustrate proposed deposition areas along Coffee Island; however, the figures show fill occurring at the tidal gut that bisects Coffee Island and at the marsh where the dike would meet the island, These impacts are not described in the text,

6

<u>Page EIS-36; paragraphs 5,9 and 5,10</u> - These two sections are contradictory in that paragraph 5,9 states that channel improvements would not induce additional development along the bayou; yet, paragraph 5,10 discusses the wetland areas that would likely be subject to development if the channel is improved, We believe that channel improvement could induce development of all of the remaining wetland areas along Bayou La Batre; including the 20,1 acres identified in the EIS and the wetland acreage exempted from consideration,

7

Fish and Wildlife Coordination Act Comments

The draft documents estimate that at least 20,1 acres of wetlands adjacent to Bayou La Batre could be developed as a result of the proposed channel improvements, These actions would have to be authorized via the Corps' Section 10/404 regulatory program, The Service, as well as other natural resource management agencies, would review each proposed development action and base our recommendations on the significance of the proposal's expected impacts to fish and wildlife and compliance of the work with various Federal statutes including the Endangered Species Act and the Section 404(b)(1) guidelines of the Clean Water Act, Where the least damaging practicable project alternative would involve unavoidable fish and wildlife impacts, denial of the permit or inclusion of adequate and appropriate compensation measures in the permit conditions might be recommended,

8

Summary Comments

The Service has coordinated with the Corps throughout the planning process, Potential project impacts have been significantly reduced through coordination and the resultant consideration of fish and wildlife resources of the Bayou La Batre area, There are, however, additional measures that should be incorporated into project plans to further reduce impacts to fish and wildlife resources, In general, dredging should be scheduled to occur

9

during late October to February to minimize impacts to spawning fish and shellfish. The project alternative offering the most promise is Plan XII which involves placement of the entire 2 million cubic yards of new work material along the east side of Coffee Island. Our position is based on information that indicates the marshes of Coffee Island have been and are continuing to erode at a significant rate, and that the new work material would be suitable for constructing a protective berm. Additionally, we do not expect that the opportunity to use such quality material will be available in the future. Plan XII, however, needs substantially more definition and refinement. We are concerned that no fill occur in the tidal inlets or the marsh. Also, the proposed dike should not meet the island on its south end so that the disposal area would be intertidal. Furthermore, the potential conflict between disposal or dredged material from maintenance of the Bayou Coden channel and dredged material from the Bayou La Batre channel improvements should be discussed and resolved in the final project documents. Further coordination regarding these issues is necessary. To facilitate such discussions, contact the Field Supervisor of the Fish and Wildlife Service, Daphne Field Office, P.O. Drawer 1190, Daphne, Alabama 36526 or telephone 205/690-2181.

Thank you for the opportunity to comment on these reports.

Sincerely yours,

James H. Lee
Regional Environmental Officer

Response to U. S. Department of the Interior, Regional Environmental
   Officer

1. Comment noted. We appreciate the effort expended by the Daphne Field
Office of the Fish and Wildlife Service in helping us meet our schedules
relative to this project. We also greatly appreciate the cooperative
manner in which they have approached the planning of an environmentally
acceptable plan for improving the Bayou La Batre navigation project.

2. Comment noted. The description of the tentatively selected plan (See
Section 3.2.3.3 of the DEIS, page EIS-16) indicated that a single row of
hay bales would be placed just of the seaward existing shoreline of Isle
aux Herbes. This barrier would provide protection to the existing wetland
areas of the island from dredged material and/or related mud flows. A
detailed design for the hay bale containment feature will be produced
during the Preconstruction Engineering and Design (PED) phase of this
project. We will continue to coordinate these aspects with the Fish and
Wildlife Service (FWS) during PED to ensure the Service's concerns are
alleviated.

We agree that from Figures EIS-5 and EIS-6 it appears that the dike would
join the island at both ends. These figures were for the purpose of
illustrating the general concept being proposed. The actual construction
however, would not regult in a diked containment area as is illustrated on
the figures. As described in Sections 3.2.3.3 and 3.2.3.4 of the DEIS and
as shown on the 'Section A-A'' inserts on Figures EIS-5 and EIS-6, a swale
would remain between the existing shoreline and the crest of the berm.
After construction this area would be subject to tidal flushing and any
tidal creeks emptying on the east side of the island in this area would
retain their natural characteristics. These details will be coordinated
with the FWS and other Federal and state agencies during PED.

Planning associated with Isle aux Herbes Options A and B was done with full
cognizance of the proposed plans for long-term maintenance at Bayou Coden
and in fact was the result of discussions with the interagency team
involved with the Bayou Coden effort. A statement has been added to FEIS
Sections 3.2.3.3 and 3.2.3.4 to address this concern and to indicate that
the detailed design during PED will take into account any change in the
area due to Bayou Coden activities. In addition, a statement has been
added to Section 5.1 of the FEIS to indicate that the implementation of the
Isle aux Herbes disposal will not conflict with any ongoing Bayou Coden
activities and therefore result in no adverse impact to the marsh
establishment efforts.

3. See response to your comment numbered 2.

4. Comment noted. Studies have shown that benthic systems are able to
recover from pertubations such as dredged material disposal within from as
little as 6 weeks to as much as 18 months. This recovery period is highly
dependent upon the level of disturbance, time of disturbance, and most
importantly the type of benthic community being disturbed. In addition,
during the period of recovery, the productivity from an area is still

available to the estuarine system and the level of productivity from an area may shift during this recovery period. After disuturbance of an area, early stage succession typically begins within a few days with the arrival of swimming crustaceans (i.e., amphipods and cumaceans) and more motile polychaetes and echinoderms (i.e., nereids and nephtyids and large ophiuroids) which immigrate into the disturbed area as adults from adjacent areas. More importantly however, the larvae of relatively opportunistic polychaetes and bivalve molluscs settle onto the new substratum from the overlying water column. These opportunistic species (Group I colonizers, McCall 1978) are characterized by short generation times, small size, high fecundity, and high larval availability. These species most commonly experience high mortality and may disappear as a result of competition and/or predation from the more motile immigrants. Later phases of succession are usually characterized by the gradual reestablishment of Group III species which are represented by the less mobile crustaceans, molluscs, and less opportunistic polychaetes. These species, in contrast to Group I colonizers, maintain more or less constant, relatively low population densities, are usually larger in size and exhibit lower fecundity and recruitment potential. Group II colonizers are intermediate in their life strategies.

Information collected during the Mississippi Sound and Adjacent Areas Study (Vittor and Associates 1982) indicates that in the areas generally considered for open water disposal of dredged material only Group I and II colonizers are present. Based on this information recovery in the areas in question would be relatively rapid and that the overall impact to the benthic system would be short-term and that the disposal of dredged materials on a three year cycle at these areas would not result in significant impacts to the estuarine system. This information has been added to Section 5.2 of the FEIS to address your concern.

5. Comment noted. The thin-layer monitoring program at Gulfport, Mississippi, referred to in the DEIS, was conducted utilizing 50,000 cubic yards of new work or virgin material. The results of this study would be indirectly applicable to determining the impacts of the recommended plan on benthic and fishery resources.

6. See response to your comment numbered 2.

7. As indicated in Section V.F. on page 91 of the main report and Section 5.10 of the DEIS (page EIS-28) currently undeveloped wetland areas adjacent to the bayou could be impacted by water dependent development induced by the improved project. This has been revised to indicate that these areas are likely to be considered for development with or without the proposed project. As described in Section III.C. of the Draft Feasibility Report (page 62), this assumption is based on the fact that suitable areas for additional water dependent activities at BLB are in short supply. This assumption is supported by _____ permit and _____ pre-application for _____ of the acreages described.

Those impacts associated with actions required of the local sponsor as part of the LCA; i.e., repair or replacement of existing bulkheads and provision of bulkheads for property protection, have been addressed in the overall impact assessment for the proposed project. Additionally, the upland disposal areas have been planned to contain material originating from deepening of berthing areas by those facilities along the bayou which directly benefit from the proposed project as well as material which may be removed from other berthing areas during the life of the project.

The District believes it likely that future development of the 20.1 acres of wetlands identified in the DEIS will occur, but agrees that this development would have to be separately authorized via the Corps' permit program. The requirement for wetland compensation in permitting this development will be addressed through the permit/public notice coordination process.

Section 5.9 of the FEIS has been revised to remove any apparent contradiction.

8. See response to your comment numbered 7.

9. Comment noted. We agree that project impacts have been significantly reduced through planning and coordination efforts.

In an effort to take advantage of natural low water level conditions in Mississippi Sound and to minimize the impact to species utilizing the wetlands of Isle aux Herbes as spawning areas, every effort will be taken to schedule the disposal at Isle aux Herbes between November and March. Sections 3.2.3.3 and 3.2.3.4 of the FEIS have been revised to reflect this. The construction dredging activities of the rest of the project and maintenance operations associated with the channel would have no impact on spawning activities since the areas associated with these operations are not in or adjacent to known spawning areas.

Plan XII has been designated as the Environmental Quality (EQ) Plan. We agree that the use of construction dredged material at Isle aux Herbes will be of benefit to the wetlands in that area and will, during the development of more detailed engineering studies for the project, investigate the potential for placement of additional material in that location. Should it be found that greater quantities of material can be placed at Isle aux Herbes without increasing the construction costs for the project, this provision will be made a part of project construction. There is ample provision, however, in both law and policy for a local or State Goverment to pay the difference in the increased cost of dredging or material disposal if a use for the material other than the least-cost disposal is desired. This is a matter than can be worked out during the PED phase of the project. Coordination on this matter will be continued during this phase in an effort to realize all the environmental benefits associated with the new work material.

Please refer to responses to your comments numbered 2 for additional information.

UNITED STATES ENVIRONMENTAL PROTECTION AGENCY

REGION IV

345 COURTLAND STREET
ATLANTA, GEORGIA 30365

AUG 22 1988

4PM-EA/GJM

Mr. Hugh A. McClellan, Acting Chief
Environment and Resources Branch
ATTN: Coastal Environment Section
U.S. Army Corps of Engineers, Mobile
P.O. Box 2288
Mobile, Alabama   36628-0001

SUBJECT: Draft Environmental Impact Statement for Navigation Improvements
          at Bayou La Batre (Mobile County), Alabama
          EPA LOG NO.:   D-COE-E32068-AL

Dear Mr. McClellan:

Pursuant to Section 309 of the Clean Air Act and Section 102(2)(c) of the
National Environmental Policy Act, EPA, Region IV has reviewed the subject
document. EPA technical staff have had a relatively long and comprehensive
previous involvement with this project during the feasibility phase to
include performing toxicity and bioaccumulation tests on the sediments in
the navigation channel. In addition to these tests and extensive discussions with our review staff, two onsite inspections were made. This
onsite experience, especially the boat trip you provided to the Isle of
Herbes, was valuable in that it provided us with a more precise determination of the physical elements of the proposal than otherwise would have
been the case. In general, the design elements of the tentatively selected
alternative and the array of options noted in the document tracked the
discussions we had during the coordination meetings on the project.

1

In addition to upgrading the navigational capacities of Bayou La Batre
the proposed channel deepening will provide a source of "new-work" material
which could be used to provide some temporary relief to the erosion of
the wetlands on adjacent shoreline/nearshore features. Exactly how and
where this material will be placed remains a matter of debate among the
involved principals of the various agencies. From our perspective Concept
B (EIS-50) which makes maximum use of this dredged material to protect the
eroding shoreline of Isle Aux Herbes merits re-examination. The opportunity to secure this volume of proximate, suitable material to protect
this barrier feature and its accompanying marsh is unlikely to occur
again in the foreseeable future.

2

The cost/benefit ratio of the tentatively selected alternative and Option
XII are relatively close, 2.19 vs 2.12 respectively, under the current
criteria. However, if the value to the environment of protecting the
marsh and providing some degree of storm surge protection to the Bayou La
Batre and Bayou Coden development were factored into the equation, Concept
B might well become the NED plan. In our opinion the value of the marsh
and storm surge protection aspects should be inserted into the calculations
to arrive at a more complete assessment of the overall impacts of the
project.

3

-2-

It has been mentioned that the loss of shallow bottoms to the increased deposition of Concept B would be a negative environmental factor. However, given the shifting nature of the subject sandy bottoms, the research literature suggests the biological perturbation should be within acceptable limits. Export of detrital material from and interface of the marsh with the marine environment would be somewhat more limited by a complete berm alignment, but the western margin of the island remains unobstructed and should be competent to maintain satisfactory interaction. Further, the area in question appears to have been until quite recently an emergent part of the island. Unless it can be demonstrated in some fashion that the sacrifice of this type of shallow habitat materially limits productivity in the area, we believe the action to protect the entire marsh community on the island rather than just a part of same makes good sense. The mitigation for the total project is currently being coordinated by the principals and should compensate for any other unavoidable losses.

4

The placement of dredged material in the Point aux Pins/Isle aux Dames area has prompted interest among your staff to lessen shoreline erosion. However, certain resource agencies and local academics have expressed reservations to this proposal since there are vascular "seagrass" beds in the immediate area. These taxa could be adversely impacted by immediate inundation or drift of dredged material during or after construction. However, if this area continues to erode and wave energy results in increased erosion, what will happen to the "grass" beds? It appears that these taxa are colonizing an area once vegetated by emergent marsh. However, if the sheltering effect of the Point is lost, would these "beds" be adversely affected? A case could be made for any number of eventual scenarios. It seems that the risks and benefits of this option should be examined in greater detail before a reasoned decision can be made to accept or reject this alternative.

5

Alternative methods to handle process water from the seafood houses are being developed so effluent discharges will not continue to violate water quality standards. Since increased fishery's processing is one of the stated goals of this channel upgrade, elevated BOD loadings are a given. Therefore, we would like to see some definitive results on the efficacy of the new treatment facilities, e.g., sludge drying beds, before additional processors become operational.

6

In a related matter it was clearly noted in the DEIS that future development is likely to occur in wetlands within the port environs. We wish to go on record now as indicating that each of these proposed developments will be viewed on their individual environmental merits and not as an integral, necessary part of this project. Further, any unavoidable losses from the former will have to be functionally compensated prior to any fill via Section 404 action.

7

-3-

On the basis of our evaluation a rating of EC-2 was assigned. That is, we are concerned that an opportunity will be lost to positively impact the environment if full use is not made of this new work material to retard the erosion currently being experienced in the project area. In fact, we have pronounced environmental reservations (ER) to unnecessarily placing this material in deep open water given the obvious need for the material in the nearshore zone, the potential that its loss would have on exacerbating erosion there, and biological losses that occur from dredge spoil deposition even when the "thin-layer" technique is used. Regardless, of which option is ultimately selected some additional information will have to be developed for the final document.

Should you have any questions concerning our comments, or if we can be of any further assistance, please do not hesitate to contact Dr. Gerald J. Miller at 404 347-5014.

Sincerely yours,

Heinz J. Mueller, Acting Chief
NEPA Review Staff
Environmental Assessment Branch

Response to U. S. Environmental Protection Agency, Region IV

1. Comment noted. We appreciate the efforts expended by Region IV of the Environmental Protection Agency during the planning and coordination of this project.

2. Refer to response to comment numbered 9 in Department of Interior letter dated September 2, 1988.

3. Traditionally, an economic value for marsh or other environmental features have not been established and, therefore, not utilized in the economic analysis for this project. Until agreement is reached relative to such values, we cannot address issues such as you raise except in a qualitative fashion. The potential storm surge protection offered by the placement of construction dredged materail at Isle aux Herbes would be minimal. The average elevation of Isle aux Herbes, even with the proposed placement, is approximately 3 feet NGVD. The results from the Sea, Lake, and Overland Surges from Hurricanes (SLOSH) model for the Mobile Bay basin indicate that the potential for overtopping of the island even in a minimal hurricane, thereby negating any potential for surge protection. We agree that the use of construction dredged material at Isle aux Herbes will be of benefit to the wetlands in that area and will, during the development of more detailed engineering studies for the project, investigate the potential for placement of additional material in that location. Should it be found that greater quantities of material can be placed at Isle aux Herbes without increasing the construction costs for the project, this provision will be made a part of project construction. There is ample provision, however, in both law and policy for a local or State Goverment to pay the difference in the increased cost of dredging or material disposal if a use for the material other than the least-cost disposal is desired.

4. Comment noted. We agree that the benefits associated with the provision of erosion protection to the wetlands of Isle aux Herbes greatly outweigh the impacts associated with the filing of the shallow bottoms associated with the proposed disposal area.

It has been determined that the potential project impacts have been significantly reduced through coordination and the resultant consideration of fish and wildlife resources in the Bayou La Batre area. Remaining impacts have been determined to be negligible therefore no mitigation is proposed.

5. Comment noted. Although we believe significant environmental benefits could be gained via the restoration of the Point aux Pins/Isle aux Dames shoreline, we are not able to quantify the benefits at this time. Without these additional benefits this alternative does not meet the requirements of the National Economic Development Plan. Should additional interest in this alternative be forth coming, we will be more than willing to do further studies during the PED phase of the project to investigate the risks and benefits as you suggest.

6. The total seafood processing infrastructure within Bayou La Batre is currently operating at about 50 percent capacity. The city recently completed the construction of a new $1.2 million wastewater outfall line to service the seafood processing facilities. This facility was designed to accommodate existing facilities with provision for additional facilities as well.

7. Refer to response to comment numbered 7 in Department of Interior letter dated September 2, 1988.

8. Comment noted. No response necessary.

UNITED STATES DEPARTMENT OF COMMERCE
The Chief Scientist
National Oceanic and Atmospheric Administration
Washington, D.C. 20230

August 29, 1988

Mr. Hugh A. McClellan
Department of the Army
Mobile District, Army Corps of Engineers
Mobile, Alabama 36628-0001

Dear Mr. McClellan:

This is in reference to your Draft Supplemental Environmental
Impact Statement on the Navigation Improvements, Bayou La Batre,
Alabama. Enclosed are comments from the National Oceanic and
Atmospheric Administration.

We hope our comments will assist you. Thank you for giving us an
opportunity to review the document.

Please note the change in our address for future environmental   1
impact statements:

                    Director
                    Department of Commerce
                    NOAA/CS/EC/Room 6222
                    14th & Constitution Avenue, N.W.
                    Washington, D.C. 20230

                              Sincerely,

                              David Cottingham
                              Ecology and Environmental
                                Conservation Office

Enclosure

UNITED STATES DEPARTMENT OF COMMERCE
National Oceanic and Atmospheric Administration
NATIONAL OCEAN SERVICE
OFFICE OF CHARTING AND GEODETIC SERVICES
ROCKVILLE, MARYLAND 20852

AUG 22 1988

MEMORANDUM FOR: David Cottingham
                          Ecology and Environmental Conservation Office
                          Office of the Chief Scientist

FROM: Rear Admiral Wesley V. Hull, NOAA
                          Director, Charting and Geodetic Services

SUBJECT: DEIS 8807.09 - Navigation Improvements, Bayou
                          La Batre, Alabama

The subject statement has been reviewed within the areas of
Charting and Geodetic Services' (C&GS) responsibility and
expertise. Since safety of navigation is one of C&GS' primary
missions, this proposal was examined with that in mind and any
other impact it may have on C&GS' activities and projects.

The proposed deepening and extensions of the channels serving
Bayou La Batre and the surrounding area are considered to be
significant improvements. C&GS considers the establishment or
improvement of navigation channels to be extremely important for
the safe and efficient operation of vessels and welcomes any
plans to accomplish this purpose.

The project area is covered on NOS nautical chart 11374 and, to a
lesser extent, on chart 11373. Any changes affecting navigation
as a result of this proposed project would be reflected on the
chart. If appropriate, the information would be disseminated
through chartlets or Notice to Mariners, or both.

In addition, a review of C&GS records has indicated that there
are no geodetic control monuments in the immediate vicinity of
the proposed project. Should there be need for information about
geodetic control monuments in adjacent areas, please contact the
National Geodetic Information Branch, N/CG17, Rockwall Bldg.,
room 20, National Geodetic Survey, NOAA, Rockville, Maryland
20852, telephone 301-443-8631

Should there be any need for further information about the
navigation comments contained in this response, please contact
the Chart Planning and Technology Group, N/CG22x2, WSC1,
room 804, Nautical Charting Division, NOAA, Rockville, Maryland
20852, telephone 301-443-8742.

2

cc:
N/CG1x10/33 - Rindal
N/CG17 - Spencer
N/CG22x2 - Frey

EIS-59

75 Years Stimulating America's Progress ★ 1913-1988

UNITED STATES DEPARTMENT OF COMMERCE
National Oceanic and Atmospheric Administration
NATIONAL MARINE FISHERIES SERVICE

Southeast Regional Office
9450 Koger Boulevard
St. Petersburg, FL 33702

August 23, 1988   F/SER1:AM

Colonel Larry S. Bonine
District Engineer, Mobile District
Department of the Army, Corps of Engineers
P.O. Box 2288
Mobile, Alabama 36628-0001

Dear Colonel Bonine:

The National Marine Fisheries Service (NMFS) has reviewed the Draft
Environmental Impact Statement (DEIS) on Navigation Improvements At
Bayou La Batre dated July 1988. The following comments are offered
for your consideration.

General Comments:

The DEIS adequately describes fishery resources and wetland habitats within
the study area. However, there are numerous assumptions that concern the NMFS
because they are not supported by sound scientific data.   3

The Corps of Engineers (COE) assumes that the 20.1 acres of productive
wetlands that would come under increased development pressures within the
project area would be protected or compensated for under existing federal
permit programs. Data compiled by NMFS regarding existing COE regulatory
programs within the southeast contradict this assumption. Further, even when
mitigation is incorporated into issued permits, it usually is not monitored
for success. We are especially concerned that mitigation is mostly   4
unsuccessful. Even when vegetation is established, preliminary NMFS research
indicates that created marshes, even after many years, do not produce the type
and amount of fishery resources produced by natural marshes. We would,
therefore, recommend the COE more adequately address secondary impacts
associated with channel improvements, and incorporate some means of protection
or compensation for the wetlands within the overall project design.

Table VII on page 45 indicates that 73.6% of the Bayou La Batre resident fleet
as well as 91% of the transient vessels using the harbor have a draft of
10 feet or less. The assumption conveyed on page 65, paragraph 4, is that
since there is almost no land available along the bayou to accommodate new or
induced commercial activity, that, "Economic growth, therefore, is in the   5
gradual shift to larger, more efficient, commercial fishing vessels in order
for Bayou La Batre to maintain its current market share within the Gulf of
Mexico." A similar trend would be seen in the shipbuilding industry along the
bayou.

EIS-60

2

The assumption is that a deeper channel alone would sustain the Bayou La Batre commercial fishery and shipbuilding operations. There is no discussion about the displacement of smaller vessels to other areas nor is there a discussion relative to the unit cost for one of the design vessels used to calculate channel dimensions. Cost estimates provided by two local shipbuilders capable of building a 100 net ton (192 feet long x 40 feet wide x 16 feet draft) vessel ranged from 2.5 to 4.0 million dollars depending on electronics and operational equipment. The COE should determine what percentage of the resident fleet that currently drafts less than 10 feet would be able to expend this kind of monetary resources to maintain a market share. Further, where will these shallow draft vessels relocate to and what impact will this relocation have on adjacent harbors?

5

The document states on page 66, paragraph 1, "...the needs of commercial enterprises at Bayou La Batre is a deeper and wider channel in order to maximize operational efficiency within the project." Since there is no economical means available to widen the channel within Bayou La Batre, the question remains how to maximize operational efficiency within the harbor. Deepening the channel to 18 feet + one foot advanced maintenance + one foot overdredge does nothing to increase dockage space or increase operational area within Bayou La Batre. If anything, the increase in numbers of larger vessels would adversely affect operational efficiency within Bayou La Batre due to crowding.

6

The inference that marsh will be created naturally on dredged material adjacent to Isle Aux Herbes is not supported by any data. The placement of dredged material adjacent to Isle Aux Herbes during the past (Bayou Coden maintenance dredging) three dredging cycles, and the failure of any substantial area to become vegetated naturally in a 6-year period, would negate any conclusions that marsh would become established on dredged material areas without intensive plantings of marsh species.

7

Further, we do not consider the building of a berm six feet high (three feet above mean low water), 10 feet wide at the crest, 1,000 feet wide at the base, and approximately 6,000 feet long to be a very good opportunity. The description indicates that the area will be completely diked, thereby eliminating tidal exchange, will isolate the marsh/open water interface adjacent the island, and will isolate tidal cuts in the island that provide additional interface between the marsh and fishery resources. Further, the swale between the berm and island is and will continue to be used on a 3-year cycle as a dredged material disposal area for maintenance material from the Bayou Coden navigation project. What is described is a diked disposal area adjacent Isle Aux Herbes with limited (one row of hay bales) protection from mud flows and spill over for black needlerush and smooth cordgrass wetlands on the island. We believe a more adequate description of what is intended for this area is needed in the final document.

8

The DEIS implies on page 90 that long-term impacts to benthic populations are not expected to occur from open-water dredged material disposal. This statement is based on studies that indicate repopulation occurs within 18 months under normal operations and within as little as six weeks following thin layer placement. We accept the numerous long-term studies that indicate an 18 month recovery period under normal conditions. This fact coupled with a 3-year dredging cycle results in recovery of benthic populations occurring 50% of the time over the life of the project. This would effectively remove these areas from productivity for 25 years. If one considers all the open-water disposal areas within Mississippi Sound the cumulative effect could become significant to benthic populations and higher trophic levels.

9

The reference to thin-layer disposal techniques, which appears to be the preferred means as indicated on page 87, has not been adequately shown to be less damaging. The two short-term studies accomplished to date have only provided minimal data and have not demonstrated long-term impacts. If the COE intends to utilize thin-layer disposal on future projects, we would strongly suggest that a long-term (one year pre-, two years post-dredging minimum) study of thin layer disposal be implemented as part of this project design.

10

Specific Comments:

Page 32, Figure 10 - This figure is difficult to interpret because of poor reproduction.

11

Page 33, Figure 11 - Same as figure 10.

12

Page 34, Figure 12 - Same as figures 10 and 11.

13

Page 89, Figure 19 - This figure depicts the wrong disposal configuration adjacent to Isle Aux Herbes and does not show the area of proposed marsh nourishment.

14

Page EIS-16, Section 3.2 3.3 - The acreage figures given for the thin layer disposal area do not correspond with the amount of material being dredged. For example, if 700,000 cubic yards of material are to be placed in an area to a depth of one foot then only 433 acres should be covered. The report indicates that 750 acres would be impacted. Further, the maintenance material 430,000 cubic yards should only cover 266 acres one foot deep rather than the 415 acres indicated. Are the increased acreage figures meant to imply that the boundaries for the disposal area used for thin layering cannot be accurately marked or is the COE trying to reduce the depth of disposal by increasing the area?

15

4

It also is interesting that 7.3 million cubic yards of material is expected to
be dredged over the life of the project. This is enough material to cover
4,525 acres of Mississippi Sound one foot deep or the indicated 415 acres
10.9 feet deep. This assumes that the material remains within the disposal
area over the life of the project. We doubt this will occur. In all
probability a significant area of Mississippi Sound bottoms will be impacted
by thin layer disposal. The major question is how significant is the impact
and how large is the area of impact. Only long-term studies can answer these
and other questions regarding thin-layer disposal within Mississippi Sound.

16

Sincerely yours,

Andreas Mager, Jr.
Acting Assistant Regional Director
Habitat Conservation Division

Response to U. S. Department of Commerce, Ecology and Environmental
  Conservation Office

1. Thank you for your comments. Our mailing list has been revised to
reflect your change in address.

2. Thank you for your comments. No response is required.

3. Comment noted.

4. Refer to response to comment numbered 7 in Department of Interior
letter dated September 2, 1988.

5. The vessel dimensions and costs noted in your comment are not those of
a commercial fishing vessel but a large research vessel. The trend in the
Gulf of Mexico commercial fishing fleet and the Bayou La Batre fleet is
toward larger vessels, based on data received from the NMFS office in Bayou
La Batre and field interviews, and that trend is expected to continue into
the future. In addition, the number of vessels within the Bayou La Batre
commercial fishing fleet has remained relatively stable. Therefore, we do
not expect any displacement of smaller vessels to other ports from Bayou La
Batre due to a deepened channel. However, over time and consistent with
historic trends, some owners of commercial fishing vessels will replace
their vessels with those of larger size. The financial data required to
quantify the numbers and sizes of these replacement vessels and the times
of replacement is not available. Historic trends were used to project
future increases in operational inefficiencies associated with the existing
channel in order to calculate economic benefits for a deepened channel.
This trend is currently 1.91 percent annually and is expected to continue
until the year 2001, at which time the maximum probable catch for shrimp
within the Gulf of Mexico is expected to be reached.

6. It is not expected that the increase in vessel sizes for commercial
fishing vessels and those constructed by the shipbuilding industry at Bayou
La Batre will have significant impact to existing docking space within the
bayou. The vessels constructed within the bayou are not docked for long
periods of time but are sold and transported to other locations. Also, the
vessels comprising the commercial fishing fleet come into the bayou at
intervals to unload catch and to refuel and resupply. Consequently, all of
the commercial fishing vessels are not competing for dock space within the
bayou at the same time.

7. Comment noted. We fail to find any inference to the fact that marsh
will be created naturally in dredged material adjacent to Isle aux Herbes.
To the contrary, Section 5.1 of the DEIS (pages EIS 28-29) states that
implementation of any one of several alternatives, included the tentatively
selected plan, would provide some protection to the wetland habitats along
the eastern shore of the island but that no additional emergent wetland
habitat would be provided.

8. Refer to response to comment numbered 2 in Department of Interior
letter dated September 2, 1988.

9. Refer to response to comment numbered 4 in Department of Interior
letter dated September 2, 1988.

10. We disagree with the reviewers' comments relative to the impacts
associated with thin-layer disposal. Two extensive studies of 54-week
duration have been performed to assess the impacts of thin layer disposal
on aquatic resources. One study, at Fowl River, Alabama, addressed the
impacts associated with disposal of maintenance material. The other study,
at Gulfport, Mississippi, addressed the impacts associated with disposal of
new work or virgin material. The study plan for each of these studies was
the result of interagency coordination and was designed to address short-
term (less than one year) impacts. As such, data related to fishery and
benthic resources were collected two weeks prior to the disposal operation
and at 2-, 6-, 20-, and 52-week intervals following disposal. The results
of these studies have been coordinated with the NMFS and other interested
Federal and state agencies for their review and comment, and were
summarized in Section 5.2, page EIS-30, of the draft report.

While these studies did not address long-term impacts (greater than one
year) studies in areas which have historically been utilized for disposal
of dredged material (reference Gulfport, MS) have not shown significant
changes in aquatic resources. Please refer to response to comment numbered
4 in Department of Interior letter dated September 2, 1988 for additional
information. This information, coupled with an understanding of the
physical and biological nature of the proposed disposal areas (i.e., a
system that is physically controlled) provides the basis of our statements
relative to the severity of impacts associated with thin layer disposal.

The paragraph relative to the impacts of thin layer disposal of maintenance
material (see Section 5.2, page EIS-31) has been revised to discuss this
rationale.

11. Comment noted, Figure 10 has been reproduced in the Final Report.

12. Comment noted, Figure 11 has been reproduced in the Final Report.

13. Comment noted, Figure 12 has been reproduced in the Final Report.

14. Comment noted. Figure 19 has been revised in the Final Report to
reflect Isle aux Herbes Disposal Option A. As described in Section 3.2.3.3
of the DEIS, the new work material would be utilized to create an emergent
bar east of the Isle aux Herbes shoreline. Section 5.1 (page.EIS-28 of the
draft EIS) indicated that implementation of a number of alternatives,
including the tentatively selected plan, would provide protection to the
shoreline but would not provide additional emergent wetland habitat.

15. During the dredging process, water is added to the material being
dredged such that the slurry volume, that volume of material reaching the
floor of the disposal area, is greater than the in-situ volume of material

being dredged. This difference results in a bulking factor which is dependent primarily on the type of material being dredged; e.g., sandy material has a very low bulking factor while fine grained material may be one and one-half times or more. Our estimates presented in the DEIS assume a bulking factor of 1.8 which results in a very conservative estimate of total acreage which may be impacted.

:6. Comment noted. We agree that the material placed in the open water disposal areas will be transported from these areas in time. As discussed in response to your comment 10, the Mississippi Sound is a physically dominated estuary. Wind-wave resuspension of bottom sediments, transport of sediment by currents, and the influx of sediments via freshwater inflows play a significant role in determining the overall biological structure of this estuary. Because of the physical nature of this estuary, organisms are adapted to movement of sediments as well as the highly turbid nature of the water. Based on this information, we believe the disposal of dredged material over the life of the proposed BLB project will result in impacts within the natural range of variability of the system and therefore will not result in significant long-term impacts to Mississippi Sound.

ALABAMA
DEPARTMENT OF ENVIRONMENTAL MANAGEMENT

Guy Hunt
Governor

Leigh Pegues, Director

1751 Federal Drive
Montgomery, AL
36130
205/271-7700

Field Offices:

Unit 806, Building 8
225 Oxmoor Circle
Birmingham, AL
35209
205/942-6168

P.O. Box 953
Decatur, AL
35602
205/353-1713

2204 Perimeter Road
Mobile, AL
36615
205/479-2336

Colonel Larry S. Bonine, District Engineer
Mobile District Corps of Engineers
P. O. Box 2288
Mobile, Alabama 36628-0001

RE: Draft Feasibility Report and Environmental Impact
Statement for navigation improvements at
Bayou La Batre, Alabama.

Dear Colonel Bonine:

The Alabama Department of Environmental Management has
reviewed the Draft Feasibility Report and EIS regarding Bayou La
Batre navigation improvements. This agency will be requested to
make a determination as to the project's consistency with the Alabama
Coastal Area Management Program and state water quality law and
regulations. The following comments are offered for your consideration:

A. Isle aux Herbes Disposal Site

1. The tentatively selected plan for disposal sites in Mississippi
Sound is described and illustrated on page EIS-51 and includes
disposal only at Isle aux Herbes' northeast sector. Figure 19
of the Main Report (p. 89) illustrates the disposal site as including
the entire east side of Isle aux Herbes. An apparent discrepancy
exists.

2. Detailed information regarding the s ze of the disposal area,
capacity, anticipated height of disposed materials, conduciveness
to revegetation, and fate of existing tidal channels on the east
side of the island will need to be provided.

3. At the August 24, 1988 project public meeting, one commenter
pointed out the existence of bottom leases and presence of oysters
at or near the disposal area. Additional information regarding
this potential problem should be provided.

4. Disposal of maintenance material dredged from the Bayou
Coden federal project channel has been proposed at Isle aux
Herbes. How will the disposal needs of both projects be
accommodated and interfaced?

Colonel Larry S. Bonine
Page Two

B. Open Water Disposal of Dredged Materials

In this agency's April 16, 1987 feasibility study comment letter, it was suggested that a quantitative assessment of the disposal area's productivity and impacts of open-water disposal be made. In the Draft Report submitted for our review, a qualitative analysis of anticipated impacts is provided. The EIS states that the disposal area will recolonize within 12-18 months. Considering the additional disposal of maintenance dredged material approximately every three years, what changes in species diversity and population can be anticipated when comparing pre-project and post-maintenance disposal area populations?

6

Thank you for this opportunity to provide our comments and concerns. Please contact me at your convenience if you have any questions.

Sincerely,

Bradley W. Gane
Environmental Scientist

BWG/jls

Response to Alabama Department of Environmental Management

1. Comment noted. The determination has been made that the recommended plan is consistent with the Alabama Coastal Management Program to the maximum extent practicable. As required by Section 401 of the Clean Water Act of 1972, state water quality certification will be obtained prior to discharge of dredged materials into waters of the U. S. The 404(b)(1) Evaluation is included in Appendix D to the Main Report.

2. See response to comment numbered 14 in U. S. Department of Commerce letter dated August 29, 1988.

3. Information relative to size of the disposal area, capacity, and design of the proposed disposal area was provided in Section 3.2.3.3 of the DEIS. This information may also be found in this section of the FEIS. For additional information relative to fate of the existing tidal channels refer to response to comment numbered 2 in U. S. Department of Interior letter dated September 2, 1988. For information relative to revegetation refer to response to comment numbered 14 in U. S. Department of Commerce letter dated August 29, 1988.

4. Coordination with Mr. Hugh Swingle of the Alabama Department of Conservation and Natural Resources, Marine Resources Division, has been undertaken relative to the oyster shell planting activities that have been occurring along the eastern shore of Isle aux Herbes. Future planting of shells in this area will be restricted and provision has been made to have oyster resources present in this area removed prior to disposal. This has been agreed upon by Mr. Nelson, who was the commenter at the public meeting. This information has been included in Sections 4.2 and 5.2 of the FEIS.

5. Refer to response to comment numbered 1 in U. S. Department of Interior letter dated September 2, 1988.

6. Refer to response to comment numbered 4 in U. S. Department of Interior letter dated September 2, 1988.

Alabama Department of Economic And Community Affairs

Spetember 8, 1988

GUY HUNT
GOVERNOR

FRED O BRASWELL III
DIRECTOR

TO: Mr. Hugh A. McClellan, Acting Chief
        Environment and Resources Branch, Dept. of The
           The Army, Mobile District, Corps of Engineers
        Post Office Box 2288
        Mobile, Alabama 36628-0001

FROM: State Single Point of Contact
        Alabama State Clearinghouse
        Planning and Economic Development Division, ADECA

SUBJECT: PLANS, STUDIES, AND OTHER DOCUMENTS--REVIEW COMPLETE**

        Applicant: Mobile District, Corps of Engineers

        Project: Draft Feasibility Report and Draft Environmental
                   Impact Statement (DEIS) for navigation improvements
                   at Bayou La Batre, Mobile County

        State Application Identifier Number: OSP-050-88

        The above document has been reviewed by the appropriate agencies in
        accordance with Executive Order No. 12372.

        Any comments received from the reviewing agencies are attached.
        Please give any comments from our review agencies due
        consideration when compiling you final document.

        If you need assistance, please feel free to contact us at
        (205) 284-8905.

        OSP/05

        Agencies contacted for comment:
               South AL Regional Planning Commission
               Conservation & Natural Resources - White
               Highway Department
               Historical Commission
               Soil & Water Conservation
               Forestry Commission
               AL Dept. of Environmental Management

        **PLEASE GIVE CAREFUL CONSIDERATION TO THE ATTACHED COMMENTS.

                                EIS-76

STATE OF ALABAMA

ALABAMA HISTORICAL COMMISSION

725 MONROE STREET

MONTGOMERY, ALABAMA 36130-5101

F LAWERENCE OAKS
EXECUTIVE DIRECTOR

TELEPHONE NUMBER
261-3184

July 27, 1988

Hugh A. McClellan
Acting Chief, Environment and
  Resources Branch
Department of the Army
Mobile District, Corps of Engineers
P. O. Box 2288
Mobile, AL 36628-0001

                    Re: Draft Feasibility Report
                         and Environmental Impact Statement
                         for Navigation Improvements at
                         Bayou La Batre, AL
                         Mobile County, AL

Dear Mr. McClellan:

    Thank you for forwarding the Draft Environmental Impact Statement for our
review. As the section on cultural resources states, we concur with the
dredging areas. However, we request that a cultural resource assessment be
conducted for the spoil deposition area.

    Should you have any questions, please contact our office.

                         Sincerely,

                         F. Lawerence Oaks
                         State Historic Preservation Officer

FLO/GCR/cds

Response to Alabama Historical Commission

1.   Comment noted. The survey was conducted by Mobile District
archeologists on September 2, 1988. No archeological sites or historic
structures were identified. The negative report of these investigations
has been filed with your office and the National Park Service.

Record of Decision for Oil and Gas Exploration Within the Coastal Plain of the Arctic National Wildlife Refuge, Alaska
(Fish and Wildlife Service)
48 Fed. Reg. 16870 (Apr. 19, 1983)

SUMMARY: This notice makes available to the public the Record of Decision (ROD) on oil and gas exploration within the coastal plain of the Arctic National Wildlife Refuge in Alaska. The ROD was prepared in accordance with Council on Environmental Quality regulations, 40 CFR 1505.2. The ROD reflects the recommendations of the Fish and Wildlife Service to the Assistant Secretary for Fish and Wildlife and Parks for implementing Section 1002(d) of the Alaska National Interest Lands Conservation Act (ANILCA). The recommendations of the Fish and Wildlife Service were based on the information contained in: the Final Environmental Impact Statement, which was filed with the Environmental Protection Agency on February 23, 1983, and became available to the public on March 4, 1983; the Baseline Study Reports published in April, 1982, and January, 1983, as required by Section 1002(c) of ANILCA; other pertinent scientific and technical data; and public comments received on the proposal. The ROD selects Alternative 3 of the proposal as the best alternative for implementing Section 1002(d)(1) of ANILCA. The regulatory guidelines representing Alternative 3 are being published separately also in Part IV of this same issue of the Federal Register as Final Rules under 50 CFR Part 37.

The Fish and Wildlife Service will hold a workshop for those interested parties wishing to submit applications for a permit to conduct exploratory activities on the coastal plain of the Arctic National Wildlife Refuge. The purpose of the workshop is to clarify application procedures and information requirements consistent with the provisions specified in 50 CFR Part 37. This workshop wil be conducted in Anchorage, Alaska approximately one week from the publication of this Notice in the Federal Register. For specific date(s), place, and time contact Mr. Doug Fruge of the Fish and Wildlife Service Regional Office at the address listed below.

FOR FURTHER INFORMATION CONTACT: Mr. Doug Fruge, 1011 East Tudor Road, Anchorage, Alaska, 99503, (907) 786-3381.

SUPPLEMENTARY INFORMATION: The Record of Decision follows:

Section 1002 of the Alaska National Interest Lands Conservation Act, Pub. L 96-487 (ANILCA) provides for: a comprehensive and continuing baseline inventory and assessment of the fish and wildlife resources of the Arctic National Wildlife Refuge's coastal plain; an analysis of the impacts of oil and gas exploration, development and production; and authorization of surface exploration for oil and gas in a manner that avoids significant adverse effects on the fish and wildlife, their habitats, or the environment. Exploratory drilling is specifically excluded from this exploration program. The Secretary of the Interior is required to establish, by regulation, initial guidelines governing the conduct of these exploratory activities. The guidelines are to be based on the results of the baseline study and other information available to the Secretary, and are to be accompanied by an Environmental Impact Statement (EIS) on exploratory activities. The initial report of the baseline study was published in April 1982, and the first update was published in January 1983. The final EIS was filed with the Environmental Protection Agency (EPA) on February 23, 1983, and EPA's Notice of its availability was published in the Federal Register on March 4, 1983.

The Fish and Wildlife Service (FWS) has recommended adoption of Alternative 3 of the final EIS. The regulations proposed to implement this alternative reflect a moderate level of regulatory guidance and are designed to provide limitations and environmental safeguards to prevent significant adverse effects while allowing applicants a choice among geological and geophysical exploratory methods and techniques. The applicant's exploration plan must satisfy the requirements of the regulations and Section 1002 before approval to conduct exploration activities will be given.

Alternatives Considered

The following alternative regulatory strategies were considered in reaching a decision:

1. Regulations authorizing government-prescribed operations. These would provide the most detailed guidance and strongest governmental control of the alternatives considered by specifying which exploration methods and techniques are to be used when and where within the coastal plain.

2. Regulations authorizing applicant-defined operations. These would provide only general guidance to ensure environmental protection within the broad standards of Section 1002 by leaving it to each applicant to devise protection strategies to assure avoidance of significant adverse effects with a minimum of guidance as to which particular resources are considered important or sensitive.

3. Regulations as proposed reflecting an intermediate level of guidance and control. This alternative represents a mix of the regulatory strategies outlined in Alternatives 1 and 2 inasmuch as these regulations provide performance standards for assuring avoidance of significant adverse effects which will aid in the design of exploratory plans.

4. No Action Alternative. This would be the decision not to establish guidelines by regulation for oil and gas exploration on the ANWR coastal plain. It would result in a continuation of the fish and wildlife management programs currently being practiced on the ANWR coastal plain as a part of the National Wildlife Refuge System. Surface exploration for oil and gas resources within the coastal plain would not occur under this alternative and, therefore, the oil and gas resource information sought by Congress would not be provided.

Basis for the Decision

Under Alternative 1 all exploratory activities would be controlled on the basis of the impacts which would occur in the most sensitive areas until more information becomes known in order to avoid any significant adverse effects, with the attendant closure of areas to exploration as a precautionary measure and the possible absence of adequate data on which to base the required assessment of the coastal plain's oil and gas resources. It is believed that operations conducted under this alternative could result in essentially the same types, though fewer or less severe, of environmental impacts that would occur under the proposed alternative. This alternative would prevent the flexibility necessary to quickly alter exploratory activities as field experience is gained or as conditions change with respect to protective cover and animal distribution and abundance. Imposing detailed, site-specific guidance could constrain applicants in terms of the types of exploratory methods and techniques, equipment, and support facilities that could be used and the time frames permitted for work. The Service believes this, in turn, would undermine the FWS's goal of fostering sound decisionmaking on the future use of the ANWR and the congressional intent that the Department make use of the private sector's expertise and experience in obtaining the quality of data and information needed. This alternative would be administratively more burdensome and require an increase in current levels of personnel and funding to design the detailed and site-specific guidelines that would be necessary for permittees to carry out government-prescribed field operations and to monitor their activities.

Under Alternative 2 the absence of specific guidance inherent in the omission of specific performance standards under this alternative could impose a greater burden on the applicant to design an exploration plan that would assure avoidance of significant adverse effects. At the same time this would give the Regional Director less control over his consistency determinations and ultimately result in the approval of more plans. Operations permitted under this regulatory alternative would result in essentially the same types of impacts as those under Alternative 3, but the numbers and magnitude of these impacts could be greater. For this reason and because enforcement of the Section 1002 standard of no significant adverse effect under this regulatory approach would necessarily rely on more on-site monitoring rather than on initial avoidance, Alternative 2 risks a greater potential for impacts approaching or crossing the limits of the no significant adverse effects standard before enforcement action could be taken.

The EIS analysis indicates that Alternative 3 provides a reasonable balance between the data collection and environmental protection requirements of Section 1002. This moderate regulatory scheme reflects a mix of prohibitions, restrictions, and performance standards necessary to prevent significant adverse impacts to fish and wildlife, their habitats, or the environment, while ensuring that quality data can reasonably be acquired, within

the time frame allotted by Congress. by enabling the private sector to utilize its exploration expertise in designing exploration plans subject to the constraints imposed by the FWS.

The No Action Alternative (Alternative 4) presents an option for decision that precludes any impact to the surface resources of the coastal plain of the ANWR from exploration activities. This is the environmentally preferable alternative. However, Congress has not set a standard of "no impacts" to the resources of the coastal plain resulting from the proposed activity, but rather has set a standard of "no significant adverse effect". Also, selection of the No Action Alternative precludes the gathering of seismic data and information on the oil and gas resources which are necessary to make the report to Congress required by Section 1002(h).

The FWS believes that the statutory standard of no significant adverse effect to the fish and wildlife, their habitats, and the environment can be met together with its goal for data collection on the oil and gas resources under the proposed regulatory approach of Alternative 3. The FWS considers Alternative 3 as the preferred alternative since it will best achieve the aims of Congress by producing the quality of data and information needed to reach sound and lasting decisions on the future use of ANWR while preventing significant adverse effects on the fish and wildlife, their habitats and the environment of the coastal plain. I concur in these judgments. All practicable means to avoid or minimize harm that might result from allowing applicants a choice of geological and geophysical exploration methods and techniques, provided that they meet the FWS's performance standards, have

been built into the guidelines developed to implement this regulatory approach.

Terms and Conditions for Implementing Decision

The FWS will implement Alternative 3 by administering the regulations developed for that purpose in the manner described in the preamble to the regulations and the EIS. This will include a monitoring program, with the objective of ensuring compliance with the specific requirements of the exploration plan, regulations, any site-specific stipulations imposed as a condition of the special use permits, and any additional orders that may be issued The results of monitoring activities will be used to determine the necessity to suspend and/or modify operations for ensuring prevention of significant adverse effects. Acquisition of baseline information relative to vegetation, fish and wildlife, and other resources of the coastal plain of the ANWR will be ongoing, and will be formally summarized annually in interim baseline reports which will be available to the public. Geological and geophysical data and information obtained under this program will be made available to the public in the manner described in the regulations.

Conclusion

Based on a careful review and consideration of Section 1002, the results of the baseline study, the EIS public comments on both the EIS and the proposed regulations, and other relevant factors, I am selecting Alternative 3 as the best alternative for implementing Section 1002(d)(1) of ANILCA.

Dated: April 4, 1983.

G. Ray Arnett,

Assistant Secretary for Fish and Wildlife and Parks.

CEQ Referral
(Department of the Interior, Sept. 28, 1981)

United States Department of the Interior

OFFICE OF THE SECRETARY
WASHINGTON, D.C. 20240

SEP 28 1981

Honorable A. Alan Hill, Chairman
Council on Environmental Quality
Executive Office of the President
722 Jackson Place, N.W.
Washington, D.C. 20006

Dear Mr. Hill:

The Department of the Interior has reviewed the Final Environmental Impact Statement (FEIS) for the U.S. Army Corps of Engineers' Dickey-Lincoln School Lakes Project, Maine. In our opinion, severe long-term adverse environmental impacts will occur if this project is implemented as proposed. Project-induced losses include the large-scale destruction of terrestrial and aquatic resources and the elimination of an important wilderness recreational area. Mitigation of these losses has not been adequately addressed, and those mitigation measures proposed are not an integral part of the project but the subject of a separate authorization. Furthermore, the FEIS does not address alternatives that would allow the development of the hydroelectric potential of the St. John River Basin while maintaining its unique natural resource and recreational values.

It should be noted that Secretary Watt has consistently opposed this project on environmental grounds while holding previous positions in the Federal Government. I also have longstanding familiarity with this project and hydropower projects in general because of my experience with the Bonneville Power Administration and share the Secretary's concern.

We have maintained close coordination with the Corps since 1975. In spite of our extensive efforts, disagreements persist with the Corps over our longstanding concerns about both the serious environmental effects and the lack of adequate mitigation. Since filing of the FEIS signifies an intent to proceed with the project as proposed, we believe action by the Council is appropriate. We have advised the Corps of our intention to refer this matter to you.

The enclosed statement supports our conclusions. We are prepared to discuss the issues with you at your earliest convenience.

Sincerely,

Donald Paul Hodel

Acting SECRETARY

Enclosure

United States Department of the Interior

OFFICE OF THE SECRETARY
WASHINGTON, D.C. 20240

SEP 28 1981

Lieutenant General J. K. Bratton
Chief of Engineers
U.S. Army Corps of Engineers
20 Massachusetts Avenue, N.W.
Washington, D. C. 20314

Dear General Bratton:

The Department of the Interior has reviewed the Final Environmental
Impact Statement (FEIS) for the U.S. Army Corps of Engineers' Dickey-
Lincoln School Lakes Project, Maine. In our opinion, severe long-term
adverse environmental impacts will occur if this project is implemented
as proposed. Project-induced losses include the large-scale destruction
of terrestrial and aquatic resources and the elimination of an important
wilderness recreational area. Mitigation of these losses has not been
adequately addressed, and those mitigation measures proposed are not an
integral part of the project but the subject of a separate authorization.
Furthermore, the FEIS does not address alternatives that would allow the
development of the hydroelectric potential of the St. John River Basin
while maintaining its unique natural resource and recreational values.

It should be noted that Secretary Watt has consistently opposed this
project on environmental grounds while holding previous positions in the
Federal Government. I also have longstanding familiarity with this
project and hydropower projects in general because of my experience with
the Bonneville Power Administration and share the Secretary's concern.

The administrative record indicates that our two respective Departments
are at an impasse in resolving these conflicts. Therefore, we are
referring this matter to the Council on Environmental Quality in accordance with procedures specified in 40 CFR 1504. A copy of our supporting
documentation is enclosed. We request that you take no action to implement
this proposal until the Council acts upon the referral.

We look forward to working with you in the further planning and analysis
of this project.

Sincerely,

Donald Paul Hodel

Acting SECRETARY

Enclosure

Statement of the U.S. Department of Interior
concerning the
Dickey-Lincoln School Lakes Project, Maine - U.S. Army Corps of Engineers

During review of the draft, revised draft, and supplemental draft EIS's
for this project, the Department of the Interior as well as other
Federal agencies pointed out an array of deficiencies. On most points
the Final Environmental Impact Statement (FEIS) does not respond satisfactorily to our concerns. One of the most serious deficiencies is the
failure to address adequately mitigation of unavoidable project-induced
losses of fish and wildlife and recreational resources.

A. Completion of the project as proposed by the U.S. Army Corps of
Engineers, will permanently and adversely alter the aquatic and terrestrial ecosystem of the St. John River valley. The project will result
in:

    1. The inundation of 278 miles of streams and rivers in the basin,
        66 miles of which are along the main stem of the St. John
        River.

    2. The inundation of 80,455 acres of terrestrial habitat (excluding
        waterways, lakes and ponds).

    3. Construction of 386 miles of transmission lines through
        northwestern Maine, northern New Hampshire, and Vermont.

The FEIS filed with the Environmental Protection Agency on August 28, 1981,
recognizes most of the adverse impacts but, in our opinion, underestimates
their severity and long-term nature. The Corps concludes that the
environmental losses are offset by the economic gains to be derived from
hydroelectric generation. We do not agree.

The Corps states that their proposed mitigation plan would replace 100
percent of the wildlife habitat productivity lost due to project implementation. We do not believe this to be the case as stated in our letters to
the Corps on May 13, 1980, and December 29, 1980.

B. The project as proposed appears to be inconsistent with the following
environmental requirements and policies.

    1. The Fish and Wildlife Coordination Act. - The Corps is not
        proposing adequate mitigation for unavoidable project induced
        losses. Further, there is no guarantee that any mitigation
        will ever be accomplished since the Corps is requesting
        separate authorization for mitigation. We believe the Fish
        and Wildlife Coordination Act authorizes the Corps to mitigate
        for project induced losses.

    2. National Environmental Policy Act. - Section 102e of NEPA
        requires the action agency to study, develop, and describe
        appropriate alternatives to recommended courses of action in any

proposal that involves unresolved conflicts concerning
alternative uses of available resources. The FEIS fails to
study less damaging alternatives that would allow development of
the hydroelectric potential of the St. John basin while protecting
the unique natural resource and recreational values of this basin.

3. Council on Environmental Quality Guidelines for Interagency
Consultation to Avoid or Mitigate Adverse Effects on Rivers
in the Nationwide Inventory. - The project will permanently
alter sections of the St. John River, the Big Black River,
and the Little Black River listed by the Department of the
Interior in July 1981 in the Nationwide Inventory of potential
Wild and Scenic Rivers.

C. The Department of the Interior believes the project, as proposed, is
environmentally unsatisfactory as:

1. It would permanently alter the aquatic ecosystem of 278 miles
of streams and rivers.

2. It would destroy 80,455 acres of terrestrial habitat (excluding
waterways, lakes and ponds), and associated wildlife resources.

3. It would eliminate over 1300 acres of wetlands used as breeding
habitat by black duck, a species whose population is in decline,
and important summer foraging area for moose.

4. It would destroy 36,893 acres of deer wintering areas affecting
50 percent of the deer within the St. John Region's 684,500 acres.
The mitigation proposed by the Corps would compensate for less
than half of this habitat loss.

5. It would destroy critical riparian habitats which support several
unusual plants including the endangered Furbish lousewort.

6. It would permanently alter 55 miles of the St. John River, plus
29 miles of the Big Black River, plus 27 miles of the Little
Black River all of which were listed in July 1981 by the
Department of the Interior as meeting the criteria for designation
as potential wild and scenic rivers. The St. John River is the
largest and longest undeveloped river in the northeast, and
the largest river in one of the largest, least accessible and
most primitive geographical units east of the Mississippi River.
The Big Black and Little Black Rivers are listed as two of the ten
least developed rivers within the entire northeast region.

D. The project as proposed will result in degradation of a nationally
significant environmental resource. Project-induced losses include the
large-scale destruction of terrestrial and aquatic resources, and elimination
of an important wilderness recreational area.

E. The Fish and Wildlife Service has worked closely with the Corps of
Engineers on the project since 1975. We have recommended against project
construction since January 4, 1978. We first advised the Corps of our possible
intention to refer this project to the Council on Environmental Quality in our
March 1, 1979, comments on the Revised Draft EIS. We have continually
recommended what we feel is adequate mitigation for project-induced losses
in the event the project is constructed over our objections. Although we
accept some of the mitigation recommendations of the Board of Engineers for
Rivers and Harbors, the portions of the proposal that will cause major long
term adverse impacts have not been modified or adequately mitigated.

Following are the major steps taken since 1975 by the Department to resolve
the issues:

1. Since April 20, 1976, a series of reports has been submitted by
    the Department of the Interior to the Corps to assist in their
    planning.

2. The Department of the Interior made extensive comments on the
    various draft environmental impact statements, revised draft
    environmental impact statements, and draft supplement environmental
    impact statements. We have consistently recommended against
    project construction. We have continually recommended what we
    feel is adequate mitigation if the project is constructed over
    our objections. We have informed the Corps and the Department
    of Energy of our possible referral intentions in letters of
    March 1, 1979, May 13, 1980, and December 11, 1980.

3. Fish and Wildlife Service representatives met with staff of
    the Board of Engineers for Rivers and Harbors on June 4, 1980,
    to discuss fish and wildlife mitigation plans and to clarify
    why we felt that the Corps' proposed mitigation was inadequate.
    In our comments on the proposed report of the Chief of Engineers
    on Fish and Wildlife Mitigation (December 29, 1980), we stated
    that we agreed with part of the Corps mitigation plan but that
    we felt that the wildlife mitigation plan was unacceptable.
    We maintained our recommendation that the project not be
    constructed and reiterated our possible referral intentions.

4. In addition, there have been numerous field level contacts and
    meetings between Corps of Engineers and Fish and Wildlife Service
    personnel.

F. The Department of the Interior recommends that CEQ become involved in
discussions with us and the Corps with the objective of mediating our
differences.

The goals should be to:

1. Have the Corps withdraw its EIS on this project and have the
    Corps and the Department of Interior, with other agencies as
    appropriate, work together in developing a plan that preserves

the unique natural resource and recreational values of the upper St. John while providing hydroelectric power. Such a solution could be developed by eliminating Dickey Dam and concentrating on low head hydro development.

2. Have the President recommend amending the project authorization as needed to accomplish the above goals and to provide for appropriate mitigating measures.

Model NEPA Complaint*
(for failure to prepare adequate environmental impact statement)

	Civil Action No.
Caption)	
_____)	COMPLAINT FOR
_____)	DECLARATORY AND
)	INJUNCTIVE RELIEF

INTRODUCTION

1. [The introductory paragraph should describe the nature of the action.]

JURISDICTION

2. This action arises under the National Environmental Policy Act of 1969, as amended ("NEPA"), 42 U.S.C. §4321 *et seq.*, and its implementing regulations, adopted by the Council on Environmental Quality ("CEQ") and applicable to all agencies ("CEQ NEPA Regulations"), 40 C.F.R. Parts 1500-1508. [Here you may cite any applicable agency NEPA procedures. Also cite the legal authority for the action alleged to be subject to NEPA.] Judicial review is sought pursuant to §10 of the Administrative Procedure Act ("APA"), 5 U.S.C. §§701-706, authorizing judicial review of all agency actions. This Court has jurisdiction over this action pursuant to 28 U.S.C. §§1311 and 1361, and may grant declaratory judgment and further relief pursuant to 28 U.S.C. §§2201 and 2202.

PLAINTIFFS

3. Plaintiff _____ is a non-profit, public benefit membership corporation organized under the laws of the State of _____. Its principal office is located at _____. Its other offices are located in _____. [Plaintiff's] members are scientists and other citizens of the United States. [Plaintiff] has a nationwide membership in excess of _____ persons, including some _____ members in the State of _____, many of whom use [the affected area—here a water body] for swimming, fishing, boating, birdwatching, and scientific studies, and whose uses of [the water body] will be damaged and impaired by [the action alleged to cause significant environmental impact]. [Plaintiff] exists to promote research and action, and to take action itself, to protect and enhance the environment, including the preservation of estuaries, rivers, wetlands, and fish and wildlife resources. Through participation in numerous legislative, administrative, and judicial proceedings, [plaintiff] has demonstrated its strong interest in the effective conservation of the nation's estuarine and coastal resources and the proper implementation of laws designed to protect these resources.
[Follow with an appropriate paragraph for each plaintiff.]

4. Members of each of the Plaintiff organizations (hereinafter referred to collectively as "members") live in the vicinity of [the water body] (hereinafter sometimes referred to as the "affected waters")]. Plaintiffs' members use and enjoy the resources in and around [the affected waters] for [food, sportfishing, wildlife viewing and education, photography, scientific study, recreation, boating, swimming, other beach and water related activities, and general aesthetic and spiritual enjoyment]. Plaintiffs and their members will be adversely affected and injured by Defendants' actions in issuing a permit for [the action alleged to cause significant environmental impact], as set forth more fully below. Plaintiffs' representatives and members have taken part in administrative proceedings concerning [the action alleged to cause significant environmental impact] in the affected area, including testifying at the public hearings held by [the agency]. Plaintiffs' interests in this action fall squarely within the zone of interests protected by the laws sought to be enforced in this action.

DEFENDANTS

5. Defendant [U.S. official] is sued in his official capacity as [position occupied]. In that capacity, he is responsible for the activities of [the agency] in [taking the action alleged to require NEPA compliance]. [Cite the legal authority for the agency action.]
[Follow with a similar paragraph for each defendant.]

*Complaint drafted by Nicholas C. Yost. *Ed.*

THE PROPOSALS

[Describe the proposed action alleged to require an EIS, giving both a chronology and a description of the alleged environmental impacts. These paragraphs form the heart of your factual showing.]

APPLICABLE LAW

6. The National Environmental Policy Act §102(2)(C), 42 U.S.C. §4322(2)(C), requires "responsible [federal] officials" to prepare environmental impact statements ("EISs") on proposals for legislation and other "major Federal actions significantly affecting the quality of the human environment."

It is this section and this requirement which are the heart of this case. As described in detail below, permitting by a federal agency (here [the agency]), is a "Federal action" subject to the EIS requirement. Under NEPA, an agency must prepare an EIS when an "action" *may* have a significant environmental effect. 40 C.F.R. §1508.3. It is Plaintiffs' contention that in this case [the agency's] action *may*, and indeed in some cases *will*, have a significant environmental effect and that therefore as a matter of law an EIS must be prepared.

7. The National Environmental Policy Act establishes a national policy to "prevent or eliminate damage to the environment and biosphere." NEPA §2, 42 U.S.C. §4321. The Act recognizes "the critical importance of restoring and maintaining environmental quality," declares that the federal government has a continuing responsibility to use "all practicable means" to minimize environmental degradation and directs that "to the fullest extent possible . . . the policies, regulations and public laws of the United States shall be interpreted and administered in accordance with the policies set forth in this Act." NEPA §§101(a), 102(1), 42 U.S.C. §§4331(a), 4332(1). The Act further recognizes the right of each person to enjoy a healthful environment. NEPA §101(c), 42 U.S.C. §4331(c).

8. Under Executive Order 11514 (March 5, 1970), as amended by Executive Order 11991 (May 24, 1977), §§2(g) and 3(h), the CEQ has issued regulations binding on all federal agencies for the implementation of the procedural provisions of NEPA. Those regulations (fully entitled "Regulations for Implementing the Procedural Provisions of the National Environmental Policy Act") became effective in 1979 and binding upon [the agency] as of that date. 43 *Fed. Reg.* 55978-56007 (1978), 40 C.F.R. Parts 1500-1508. Each agency was required by the CEQ NEPA Regulations to adopt "procedures" to supplement those regulations. 40 C.F.R. §1507.3.

9. Pursuant to the CEQ's directive, [the agency] adopted ____C.F.R. Part____. [Here cite any applicable agency NEPA procedures.]

[Add paragraphs discussing any particular statutory or regulatory provisions specifically applicable to the particular case. For instance, it may be appropriate to cite to the applicable subsections of 40 C.F.R. §1508.27, which set out the criteria for "significance" of environmental impact and therefore determine the need for an EIS.]

10. For the reasons stated in paragraphs _____ above, Defendants' proposals may and in some cases will significantly affect the quality of the human environment.

11. For the reasons stated in paragraphs _____ above and _____ below, Defendants' proposals will cause irreparable injury.

VIOLATIONS OF LAW

COUNT I

Violation of §102(2)(C) of NEPA, 42 U.S.C. §4332(2)(C)—Failure to Prepare EIS

12. Plaintiffs repeat and incorporate by reference the allegations contained in paragraphs _____ through _____ above.

13. The National Environmental Policy Act of 1969, as amended, 42 U.S.C. §4321 *et seq.*, requires all federal agencies to prepare a detailed EIS on every proposal for a major federal action significantly affecting the quality of the human environment. 42 U.S.C. §4332(2)(C). That EIS must always contain a detailed discussion of environmental impacts (40 C.F.R. §1502.16) and of alternatives (40 C.F.R. §1502.14).

14. The proposal to [describe the action alleged to require NEPA compliance] is a major federal action significantly affecting the quality of the human environment for which Defendants must prepare an EIS. It is an action requiring an EIS because:

(a) The [action] may or will have a significant environmental effect.
(b) By the criteria set out in the CEQ NEPA Regulations (see [paragraphs following paragraph 9 above]), there may or will be such significant effects.

COUNT II

Violations of Administrative Procedure Act, 5 U.S.C. §§701-706

15. Plaintiffs repeat and incorporate by reference the allegations contained in paragraphs _____ through _____ above.

16. Due to Defendants' knowing and conscious failure to comply with NEPA, Plaintiffs have suffered legal wrongs because of agency action and are adversely affected and aggrieved by agency action within the meaning of the APA, 5 U.S.C. §702.

17. Defendants' knowing and conscious failure to comply with NEPA is arbitrary, capricious, and an abuse of discretion, not in accordance with law, in excess of statutory jurisdiction, and without observance of procedure required by law within the meaning of the APA, 5 U.S.C. §706(2), and should therefore be declared unlawful and set aside by this court.

PRAYER FOR RELIEF

WHEREFORE, Plaintiffs respectfully request that this Court:

1. Declare that Defendants' actions in [taking the action alleged to require an EIS] without first having prepared a detailed statement on the environmental impacts of and alternatives to the [action taken] constitute violations of NEPA and of the APA and are therefore null and of no legal force and effect;

2. Issue a mandatory injunction requiring Defendants to rescind the [decision made] and prohibiting any activities to be conducted pursuant to [that decision] until such time as Defendants have complied with NEPA and have prepared an adequate environmental impact statement and have come to a decision in light of the statement;

3. Allow Plaintiffs to recover the costs of this action, including attorneys' fees;

4. Grant such other and further relief as the Court deems just and proper.

Dated: _____   (Signature block)

_____   _____